ATLAS
OF THE
WORLD

*A comprehensive record of the world,
with over 100 pages of reference maps.*

JOHN BARTHOLOMEW & SON LTD
EDINBURGH

ATLAS
OF THE
WORLD

A comprehensive record of the world,
with over 100 pages of reference maps.

JOHN BARTHOLOMEW & SON LTD
EDINBURGH

DIAMOND ◆ BOOKS

ISBN 0 583 31310 8

This edition published 1991 by Diamond
Books a division of HarperCollins *Publishers*

Printed in Spain by Graficomo

CONTENTS

INDEX TO MAP COVERAGE

VI

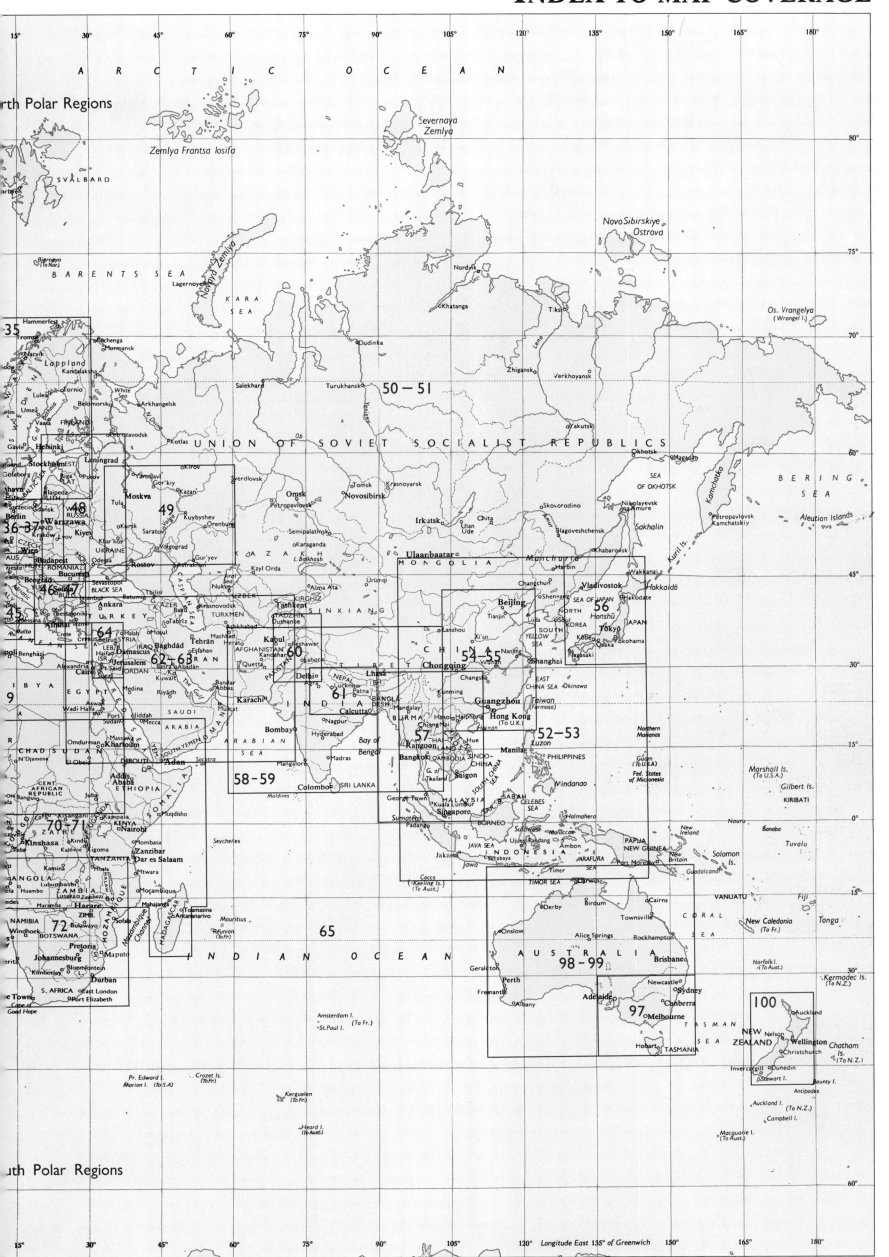

NATIONS AND POPULATIONS

Country	Capital	Area (sq km)	Population('000)
Afghanistan	Kabul	674 500	16 363
Albania	Tirane	28 752	2795
Algeria	Alger (El Djezair)	2 381 731	19 590
Andorra	Andorra la Vella	453	32
Angola	Luanda	1 246 694	7262
Antigua & Barbuda	St John's	442	77
Argentina	Buenos Aires	2 777 815	28 085
Australia	Canberra	7 682 300	14 927
Austria	Wien	83 848	7510
Bahamas, The	Nassau	13 864	248
Bahrain	Al Manamah	660	322
Bangladesh	Dhaka	14 020	90 626
Barbados	Bridgetown	430	266
Belgium	Bruxelles	30 512	9861
Belize	Belmopan	22 965	167
Benin	Porto Novo	112 622	3520
Bhutan	Thimphu	46 620	1325
Bolivia	La Paz	1 098 575	5755
Botswana	Gaborone	582 000	937
Brazil	Brasilia	8 511 968	121 547
Brunei	Bandar Seri Begawan	5765	192
Bulgaria	Sofiya	110 910	8890
Burma	Rangoon	678 031	36 166
Burundi	Bujumbura	27 834	4348
Cameroon	Yaounde	457 499	8650
Canada	Ottawa	9 976 147	24 231
Cape Verde	Praia	4033	329
Central African Republic	Bangui	622 996	2349
Chad	N'djamena	1 284 000	4547
Chile	Santiago	756 943	11 294
China	Beijing	9 561 000	1 007 755
Colombia	Bogotá	1 138 907	28 776
Comoros	Moroni	1862	369
Congo	Brazzaville	342 000	1578
Costa Rica	San José	50 899	2271
Cuba	Habana	114 524	9717
Cyprus	Nicosia	9251	637
Czechoslovakia	Praha	127 870	15 314
Denmark	Kobenhavn	43 030	5122
Djibouti	Djibouti	21 699	323
Dominica	Roseau	751	84
Dominican Republic	Santo Domingo	48 441	5581
Ecuador	Quito	455 502	8644
Egypt	Cairo	1 000 250	43 465
El Salvador	San Salvador	20 865	4938
Equatorial Guinea	Malabo	28 051	372
Ethiopia	Addis Ababa	1 221 918	32 158
Fiji	Suva	18 272	646
Finland	Helsinki	337 032	4801
France	Paris	551 000	53 963
Gabon	Libreville	267 667	555
Gambia, The	Banjul	10 688	619
Germany, East	Berlin	107 860	16 736
Germany, West	Bonn	248 528	61 666
Ghana	Accra	238 538	12 063
Greece	Athinai	131 955	9707
Grenada	St George's	344	112
Guatemala	Guatema	108 888	7007
Guinea	Conakry	245 855	5147
Guinea-Bissau	Bissau	36 125	810
Guyana	George Town	214 969	903
Haiti	Port au Prince	27 749	5009
Honduras	Tegucigalpa	112 087	3821
Hungary	Budapest	93 030	10 711
Iceland	Reykjavik	102 828	231
India	New Delhi	3 287 593	676 218
Indonesia	Jakarta	1 919 263	150 520
Iran	Tehrān	1 648 184	39 320
Iraq	Baghdād	434 924	13 527
Ireland, Republic of	Dublin	70 282	3440
Israel	Jerusalem	20 770	3954
Italy	Roma	301 345	57 197
Ivory Coast	Abidjan	322 463	8298
Jamaica	Kingston	11 425	2220
Japan	Tōkyō	371 000	117 645
Jordan	Amman	97 740	3364
Kampuchea (Cambodia)	Phnom Penh	181 035	6828
Kenya	Nairobi	582 644	17 348
Kiribati	Agaña	800	59
Korea, North	P'yŏngyang	121 248	18 317
Korea, South	Sŏul	98 447	38 723
Kuwait	Kuwait	24 300	1466
Laos	Vientiane	236 798	3811
Lebanon	Beirut	10 339	2685
Lesotho	Maseru	30 344	1374
Liberia	Monrovia	111 370	2038
Libya	Tripoli	1 759 530	3096
Liechtenstein	Vaduz	161	26
Luxembourg	Luxembourg	2587	364
Madagascar	Antananarivo	587 042	8955
Malawi	Lilongwe	94 100	6123
Malaysia	Kuala Lumpur	330 669	14 415
Maldives	Malé	298	157
Mali	Bamako	1 240 142	7160
Malta	Valletta	316	366
Mauretania	Nouakchott	1 030 700	1681
Mauritius	Port Louis	1865	971
Mexico	México	1 967 180	71 193
Monaco	Monaco	1.8	26
Mongolia	Ulaanbaatar	1 565 000	1710
Morocco	Rabat	459 000	20 646
Mozambique	Maputo	784 961	10 757
Nauru	Yaren (district rather than capital)	21	7
Nepal	Kathmandu	141 414	15 020
Netherlands	Amsterdam	33 940	14 246
New Zealand	Wellington	268 675	3125
Nicaragua	Managua	139 000	2824
Niger	Niamey	1 267 000	5479
Nigeria	Lagos	923 769	79 680
Norway	Oslo	324 218	4100
Oman	Masqat	212 379	919
Pakistan	Islamabad	803 941	84 579
Panama	Panama	75 648	1940
Papua New Guinea	Port Moresby	461 692	3061
Paraguay	Asuncion	406 705	3268
Peru	Lima	1 285 215	18 279
Philippines	Manila	299 565	49 530
Poland	Warszawa	312 683	35 902
Portugal	Lisboa	91 671	9931
Qatar	Doha	11 437	248
Romania	Bucuresti	237 500	22 457
Rwanda	Kigali	26 338	5109
São Tomé and Príncipe	São Tomé	964	86
St Kitts & Nevis	Basseterre	260	50
St Lucia	Castries	616	122
St Vincent	Kingstown	389	98
San Marino	San Marino	61	21
Saudi Arabia	Riyadh	2 400 930	9319
Senegal	Dakar	196 722	5811
Seychelles	Victoria	443	66
Sierra Leone	Freetown	71 740	3571
Singapore	Singapore	616	2443
Solomon Islands	Honiara	29 785	237
Somalia	Mogadishu	637 539	4895
South Africa	Pretoria	1 221 038	30 131
Spain	Madrid	504 745	37 654
Sri Lanka	Colombo	65 610	14 990
Sudan	Khartoum	2 505 792	18 901
Surinam	Paramaribo	163 820	397
Swaziland	Mbabane	17 366	566
Sweden	Stockholm	449 791	8324
Switzerland	Bern	41 287	6473
Syria	Damascus	185 179	9314
Taiwan	T'ai-pei	350 980	17 480
Tanzania	Dar-es-Salaam	942 000	18 510
Thailand	Bangkok	513 517	47 488
Togo	Lomé	56 785	2705
Tonga	Nuku'alofa	699	99
Trinidad & Tobago	Port of Spain	5128	1185
Tunisia	Tunis	164 148	6513
Turkey	Ankara	780 576	45 366
Tuvalu	Funafuti	25	7
Uganda	Kampala	236 036	13 620
United Arab Emirates	Abū Dhabi	83 600	762
United Kingdom	London	244 104	55 833
Union of Soviet Socialist Republics	Moskva	22 402 000	267 697
United States of America	Washington DC	9 363 130	228 959
Upper Volta	Ougadougou	274 122	6251
Uruguay	Montevideo	186 925	2927
Vanuatu	Vita	14 763	122
Vatican City	Vatican City	.4	1
Venezuela	Caracas	912 047	14 313
Vietnam	Hanoi	329 566	54 968
Western Samoa	Apia	2831	157
Yemen	San'ā'	195 000	5940
Yemen, South	Aden	333 038	2030
Yugoslavia	Beograd	255 803	22 516
Zaire	Kinshasa	2 344 885	29 270
Zambia	Lusaka	752 617	5961
Zimbabwe	Harare	390 308	7600

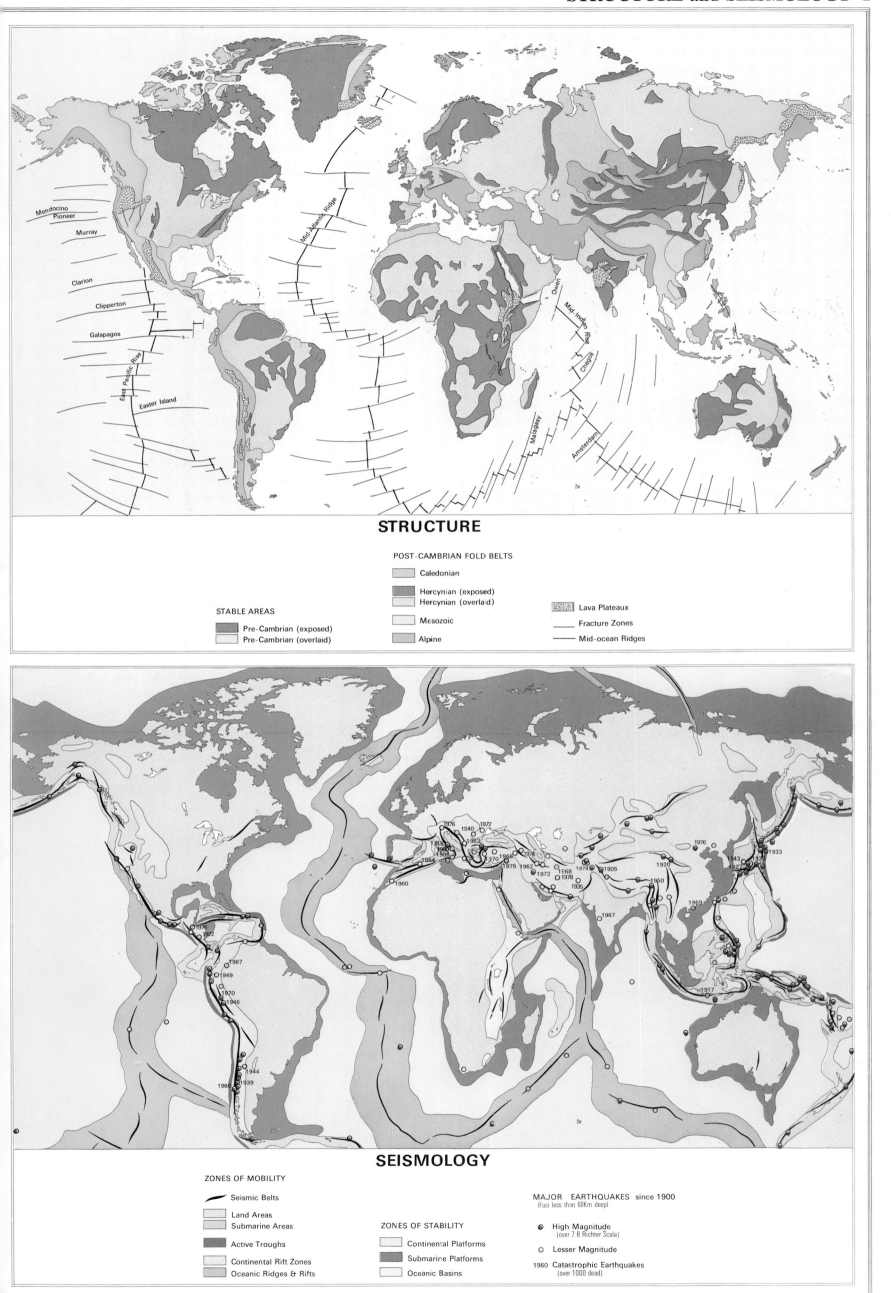

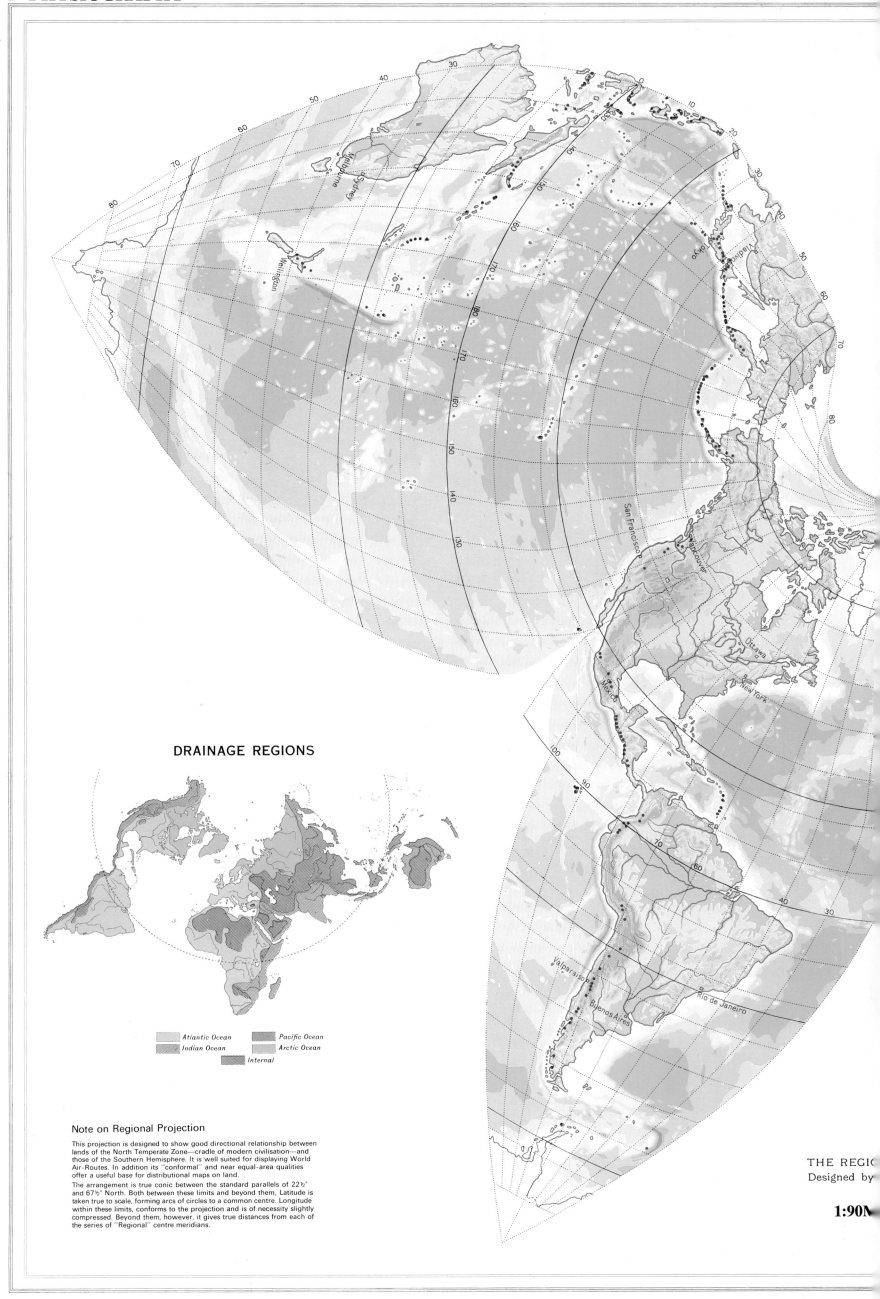

DRAINAGE REGIONS

Atlantic Ocean   Pacific Ocean

Indian Ocean   Arctic Ocean

Internal

Note on Regional Projection

This projection is designed to show good directional relationship between lands of the North Temperate Zone—cradle of modern civilisation—and those of the Southern Hemisphere. It is well suited for displaying World Air-Routes. In addition its "conformal" and near equal-area qualities offer a useful base for distributional maps on land.

The arrangement is true conic between the standard parallels of 22½° and 67½° North. Both between these limits and beyond them, Latitude is taken true to scale, forming arcs of circles to a common centre. Longitude within these limits, conforms to the projection and is of necessity slightly compressed. Beyond them, however, it gives true distances from each of the series of "Regional" centre meridians.

THE REGIO
Designed by

1:90M

Feet	22960	16400	13120	9840	3280	0
						Land Depression
Metres	7000	5000	4000	3000	1000	

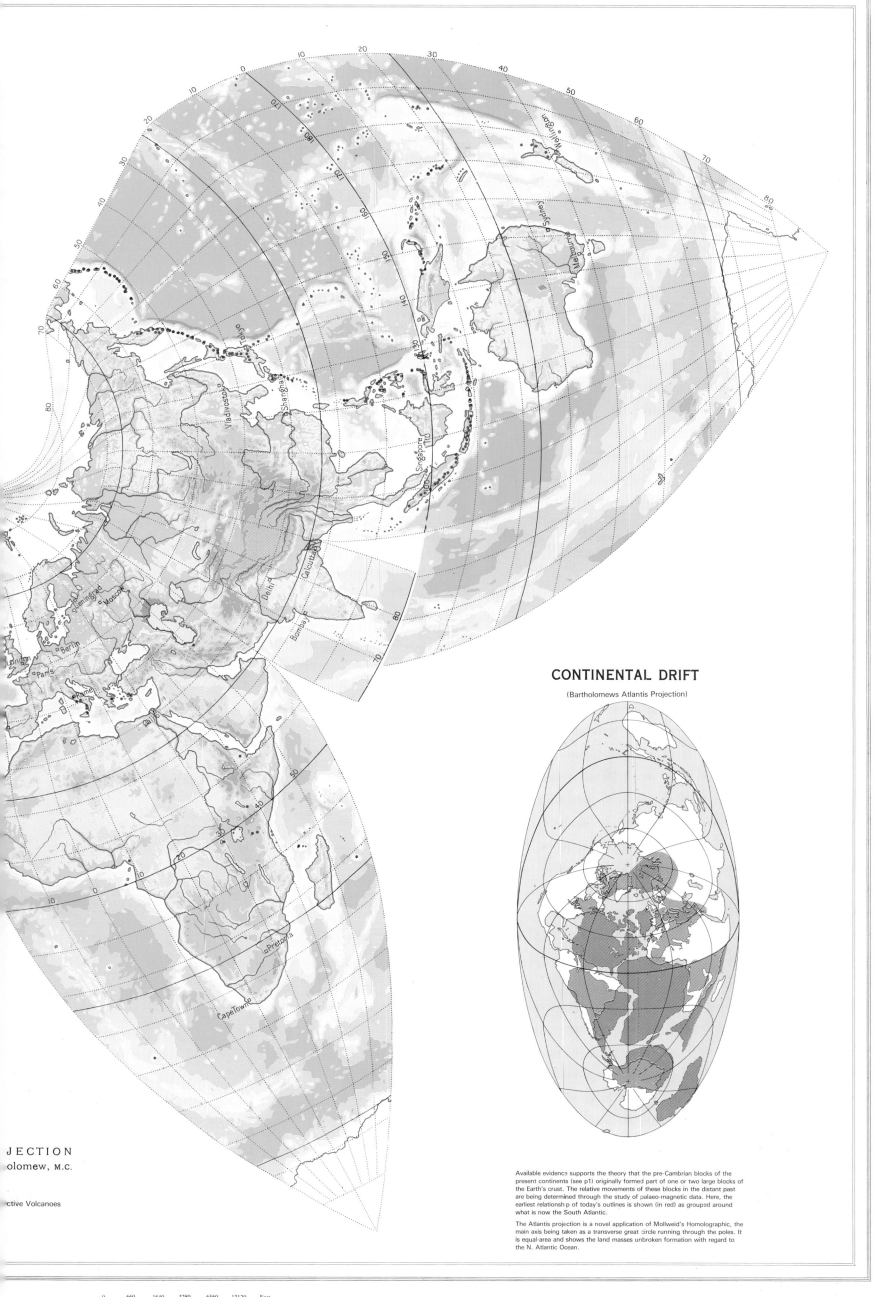

CONTINENTAL DRIFT

(Bartholomews Atlantis Projection)

Available evidence supports the theory that the pre-Cambrian blocks of the present continents (see p1) originally formed part of one or two large blocks of the Earth's crust. The relative movements of these blocks in the distant past are being determined through the study of palaeo-magnetic data. Here, the earliest relationship of today's outlines is shown (in red) as grouped around what is now the South Atlantic.

The Atlantis projection is a novel application of Mollweid's Homolographic, the main axis being taken as a transverse great circle running through the poles. It is equal-area and shows the land masses unbroken formation with regard to the N. Atlantic Ocean.

JECTION

olomew, M.C.

ctive Volcanoes

0	660	1640	3280	6560	13120	Feet
0	200	500	1000	2000	4000	Metres

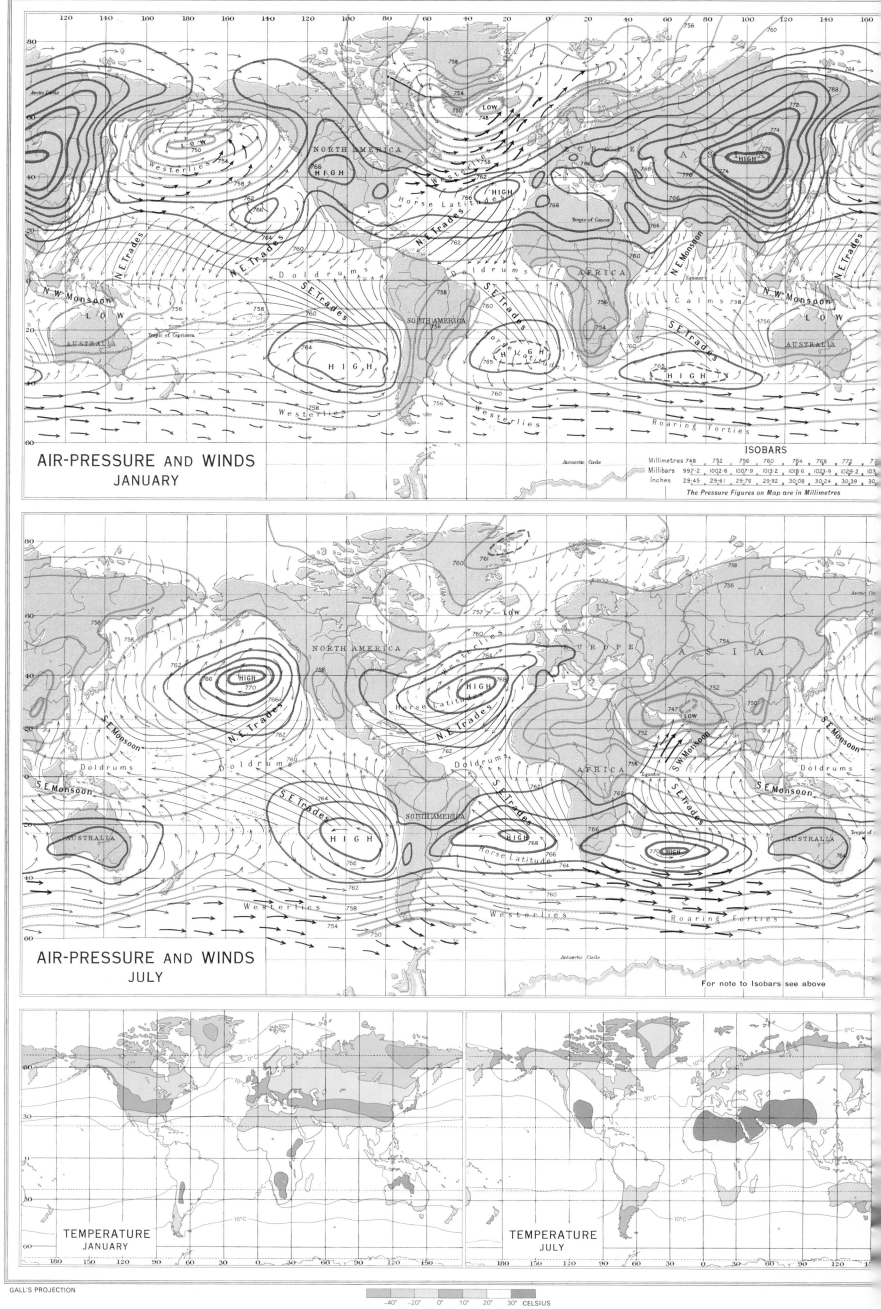

AIR-PRESSURE AND WINDS
JANUARY

ISOBARS
Millimetres	748	752	756	760	764	768	772	77
Millibars	997·2	1002·6	1007·9	1013·2	1018·6	1023·9	1029·2	103
Inches	29·45	29·61	29·76	29·92	30·08	30·24	30·39	30

The Pressure Figures on Map are in Millimetres

AIR-PRESSURE AND WINDS
JULY

For note to Isobars see above

TEMPERATURE
JANUARY

TEMPERATURE
JULY

GALL'S PROJECTION

−40° −20° 0° 10° 20° 30° CELSIUS

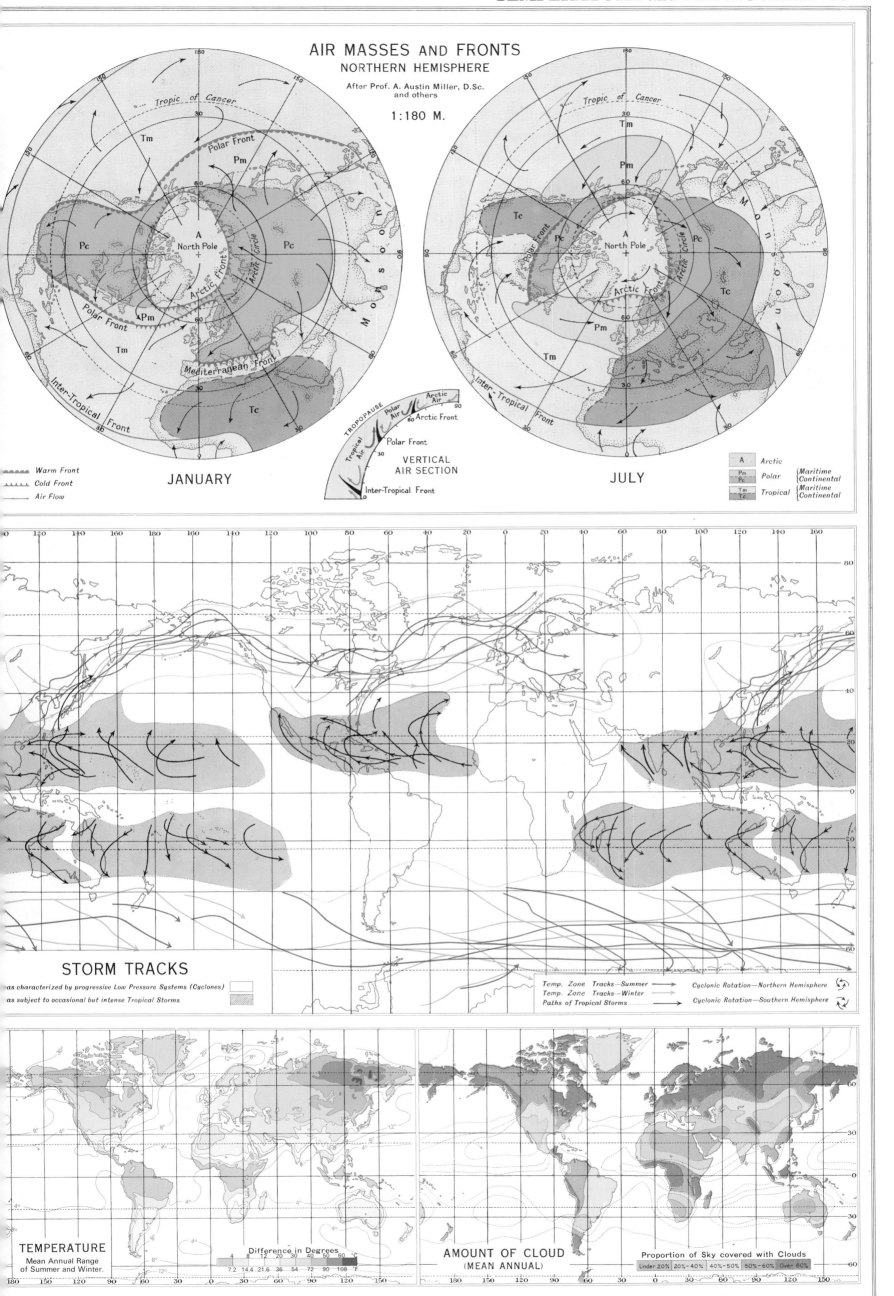

AIR MASSES AND FRONTS
NORTHERN HEMISPHERE
After Prof. A. Austin Miller, D.Sc.
and others
1:180 M.

JANUARY

VERTICAL AIR SECTION

JULY

Warm Front
Cold Front
Air Flow

A — Arctic
Pm / Pc — Polar {Maritime / Continental}
Tm / Tc — Tropical {Maritime / Continental}

STORM TRACKS

as characterized by progressive Low Pressure Systems (Cyclones)
as subject to occasional but intense Tropical Storms

Temp. Zone Tracks—Summer →
Temp. Zone Tracks—Winter →
Paths of Tropical Storms →

Cyclonic Rotation—Northern Hemisphere
Cyclonic Rotation—Southern Hemisphere

TEMPERATURE
Mean Annual Range
of Summer and Winter.

Difference in Degrees
7.2 14.4 21.6 36 54 72 90 108 °F

AMOUNT OF CLOUD
(MEAN ANNUAL)

Proportion of Sky covered with Clouds
Under 20% 20%–40% 40%–50% 50%–60% Over 60%

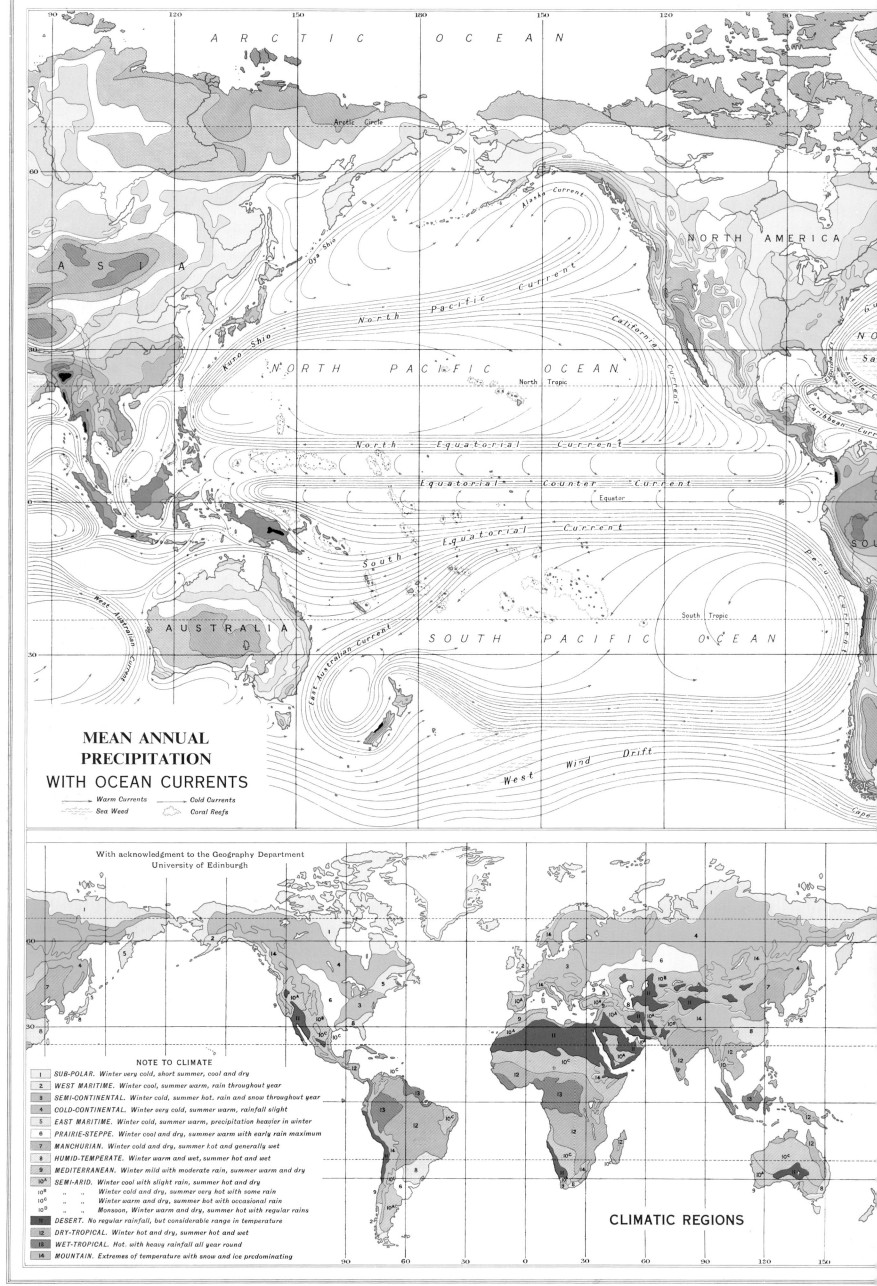

MEAN ANNUAL PRECIPITATION
WITH OCEAN CURRENTS

→ Warm Currents   → Cold Currents
Sea Weed   Coral Reefs

With acknowledgment to the Geography Department
University of Edinburgh

NOTE TO CLIMATE

1 SUB-POLAR. Winter very cold, short summer, cool and dry
2 WEST MARITIME. Winter cool, summer warm, rain throughout year
3 SEMI-CONTINENTAL. Winter cold, summer hot, rain and snow throughout year
4 COLD-CONTINENTAL. Winter very cold, summer warm, rainfall slight
5 EAST MARITIME. Winter cold, summer warm, precipitation heavier in winter
6 PRAIRIE-STEPPE. Winter cool and dry, summer warm with early rain maximum
7 MANCHURIAN. Winter cold and dry, summer hot and generally wet
8 HUMID-TEMPERATE. Winter warm and wet, summer hot and wet
9 MEDITERRANEAN. Winter mild with moderate rain, summer warm and dry
10A SEMI-ARID. Winter cool with slight rain, summer hot and dry
10B „ „ Winter cold and dry, summer very hot with some rain
10C „ „ Winter warm and dry, summer hot with occasional rain
10D „ „ Monsoon, Winter warm and dry, summer hot with regular rains
11 DESERT. No regular rainfall, but considerable range in temperature
12 DRY-TROPICAL. Winter hot and dry, summer hot and wet
13 WET-TROPICAL. Hot, with heavy rainfall all year round
14 MOUNTAIN. Extremes of temperature with snow and ice predominating

CLIMATIC REGIONS

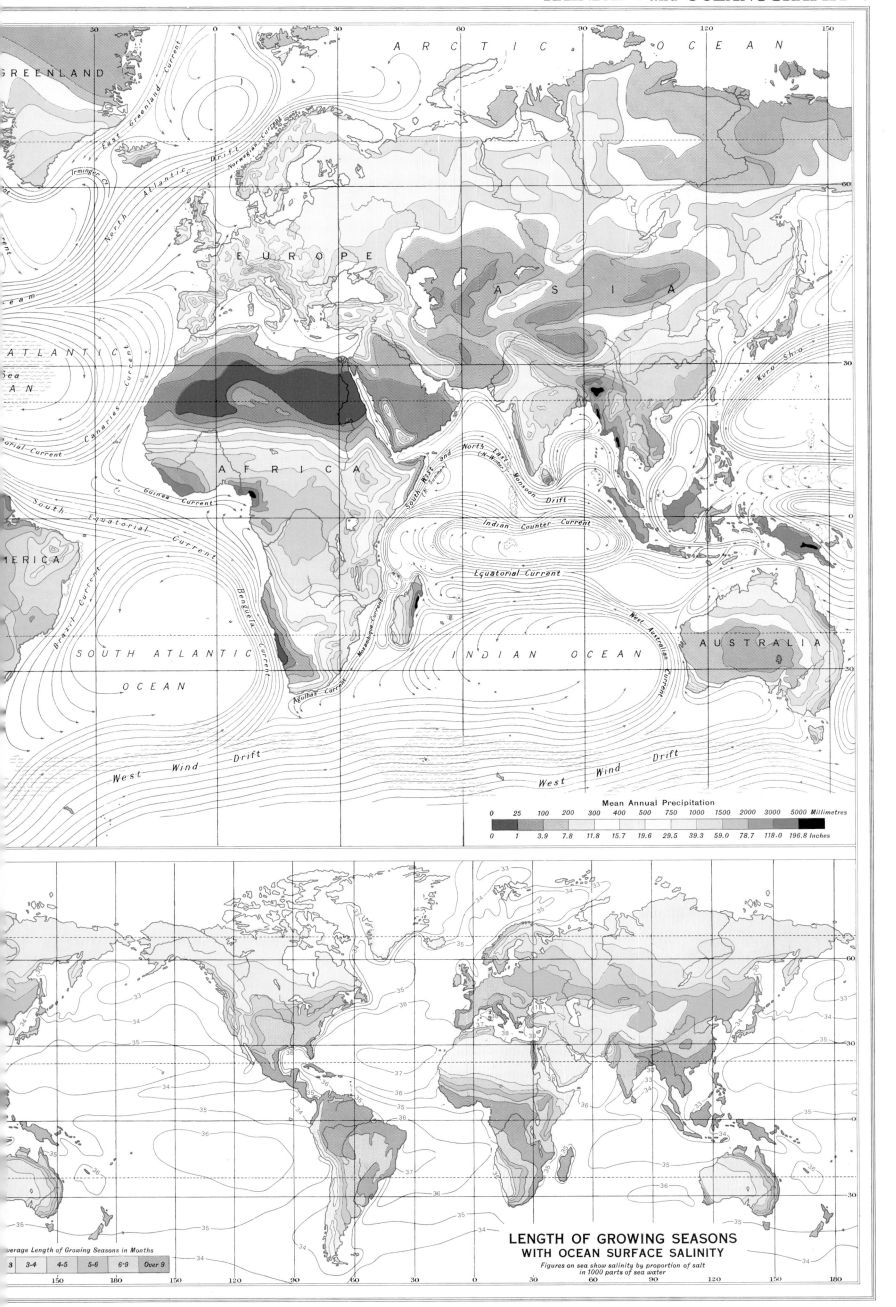

Mean Annual Precipitation

| 0 | 25 | 100 | 200 | 300 | 400 | 500 | 750 | 1000 | 1500 | 2000 | 3000 | 5000 Millimetres |
| 0 | 1 | 3.9 | 7.8 | 11.8 | 15.7 | 19.6 | 29.5 | 39.3 | 59.0 | 78.7 | 118.0 | 196.8 Inches |

LENGTH OF GROWING SEASONS
WITH OCEAN SURFACE SALINITY

*Figures on sea show salinity by proportion of salt
in 1000 parts of sea water*

Average Length of Growing Seasons in Months

| 3 | 3-4 | 4-5 | 5-6 | 6-9 | Over 9 |

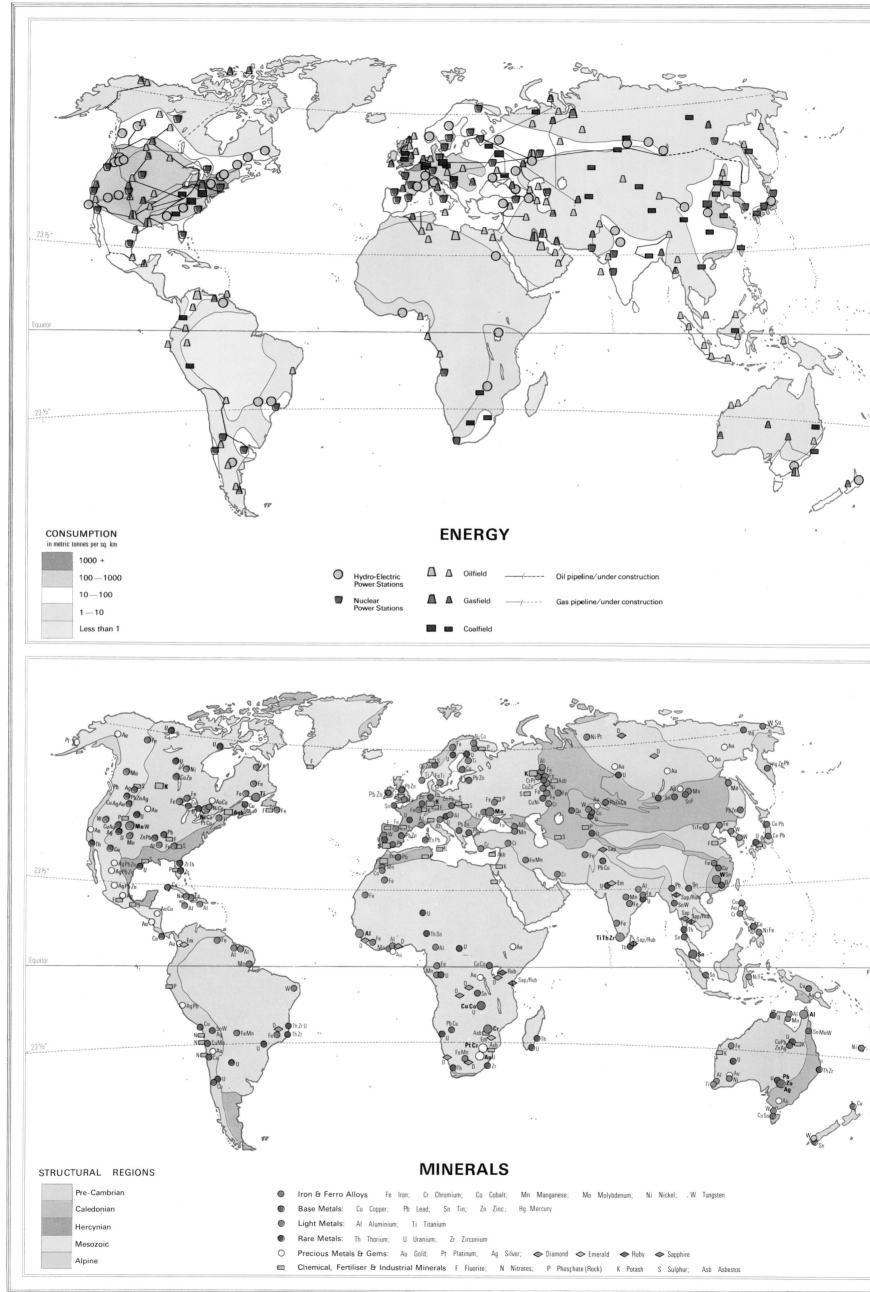

ENERGY

CONSUMPTION
in metric tonnes per sq. km

- 1000 +
- 100 — 1000
- 10 — 100
- 1 — 10
- Less than 1

- ◯ Hydro-Electric Power Stations
- ◗ Nuclear Power Stations
- △ Oilfield
- ◣ Gasfield
- ■ Coalfield
- —/----- Oil pipeline/under construction
- —/----- Gas pipeline/under construction

MINERALS

STRUCTURAL REGIONS

- Pre-Cambrian
- Caledonian
- Hercynian
- Mesozoic
- Alpine

- ● Iron & Ferro Alloys   Fe Iron;   Cr Chromium;   Co Cobalt;   Mn Manganese;   Mo Molybdenum;   Ni Nickel;   . W Tungsten
- ● Base Metals: Cu Copper;   Pb Lead;   Sn Tin;   Zn Zinc;   Hg Mercury
- ● Light Metals: Al Aluminium;   Ti Titanium
- ● Rare Metals: Th Thorium;   U Uranium;   Zr Zirconium
- ◯ Precious Metals & Gems: Au Gold;   Pt Platinum;   Ag Silver;   ◆ Diamond   ◆ Emerald   ◆ Ruby   ◆ Sapphire
- ▢ Chemical, Fertiliser & Industrial Minerals   F Fluorite;   N Nitrates;   P Phosphate (Rock)   K Potash   S Sulphur;   Asb Asbestos

WINKEL'S 'TRIPEL' PROJECTION

1:135M

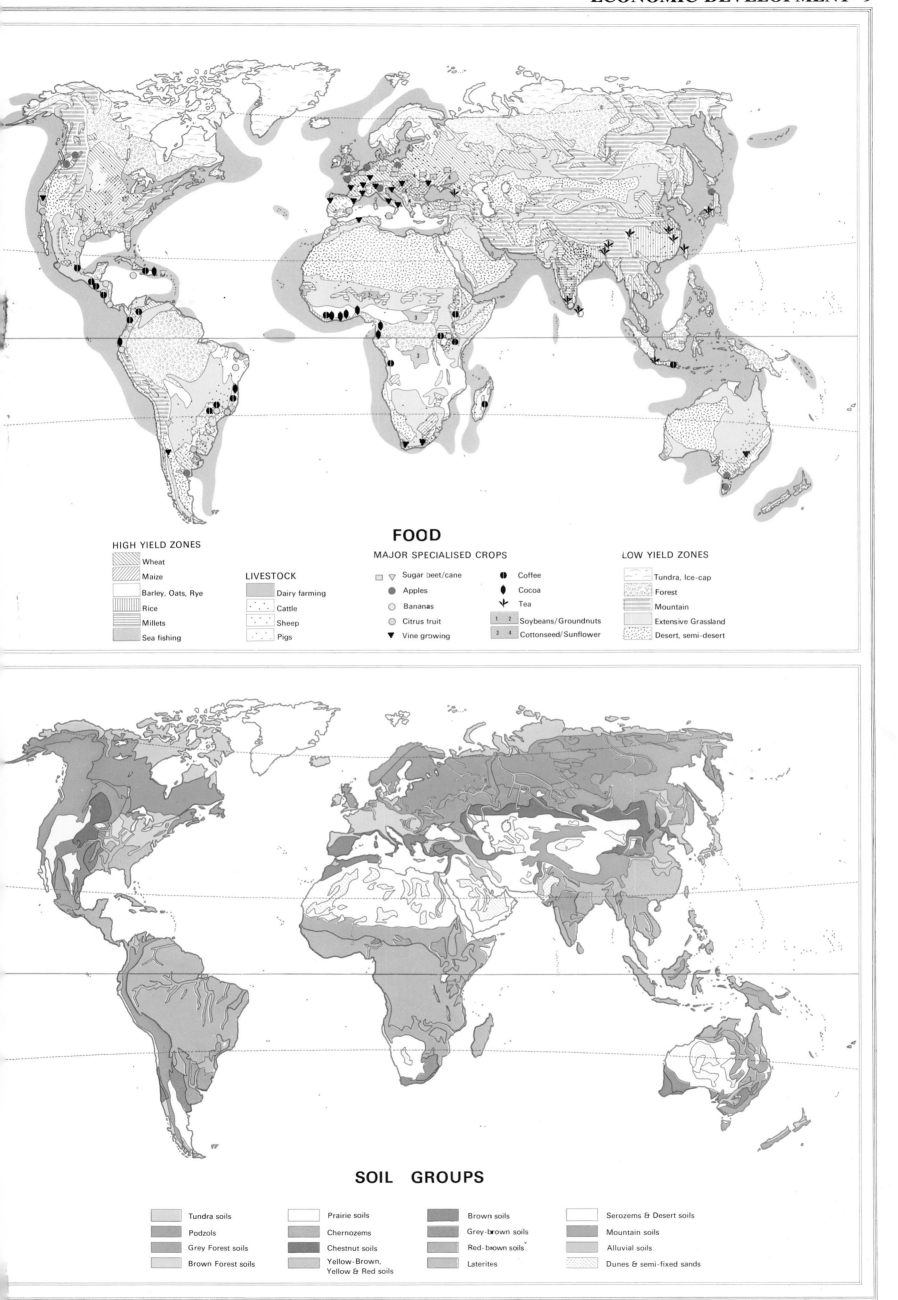

FOOD

HIGH YIELD ZONES

- Wheat
- Maize
- Barley, Oats, Rye
- Rice
- Millets
- Sea fishing

LIVESTOCK

- Dairy farming
- Cattle
- Sheep
- Pigs

MAJOR SPECIALISED CROPS

- Sugar beet/cane
- Apples
- Bananas
- Citrus fruit
- Vine growing
- Coffee
- Cocoa
- Tea
- 1 2 Soybeans/Groundnuts
- 3 4 Cottonseed/Sunflower

LOW YIELD ZONES

- Tundra, Ice-cap
- Forest
- Mountain
- Extensive Grassland
- Desert, semi-desert

SOIL GROUPS

- Tundra soils
- Podzols
- Grey Forest soils
- Brown Forest soils
- Prairie soils
- Chernozems
- Chestnut soils
- Yellow-Brown, Yellow & Red soils
- Brown soils
- Grey-brown soils
- Red-brown soils
- Laterites
- Serozems & Desert soils
- Mountain soils
- Alluvial soils
- Dunes & semi-fixed sands

1:135M

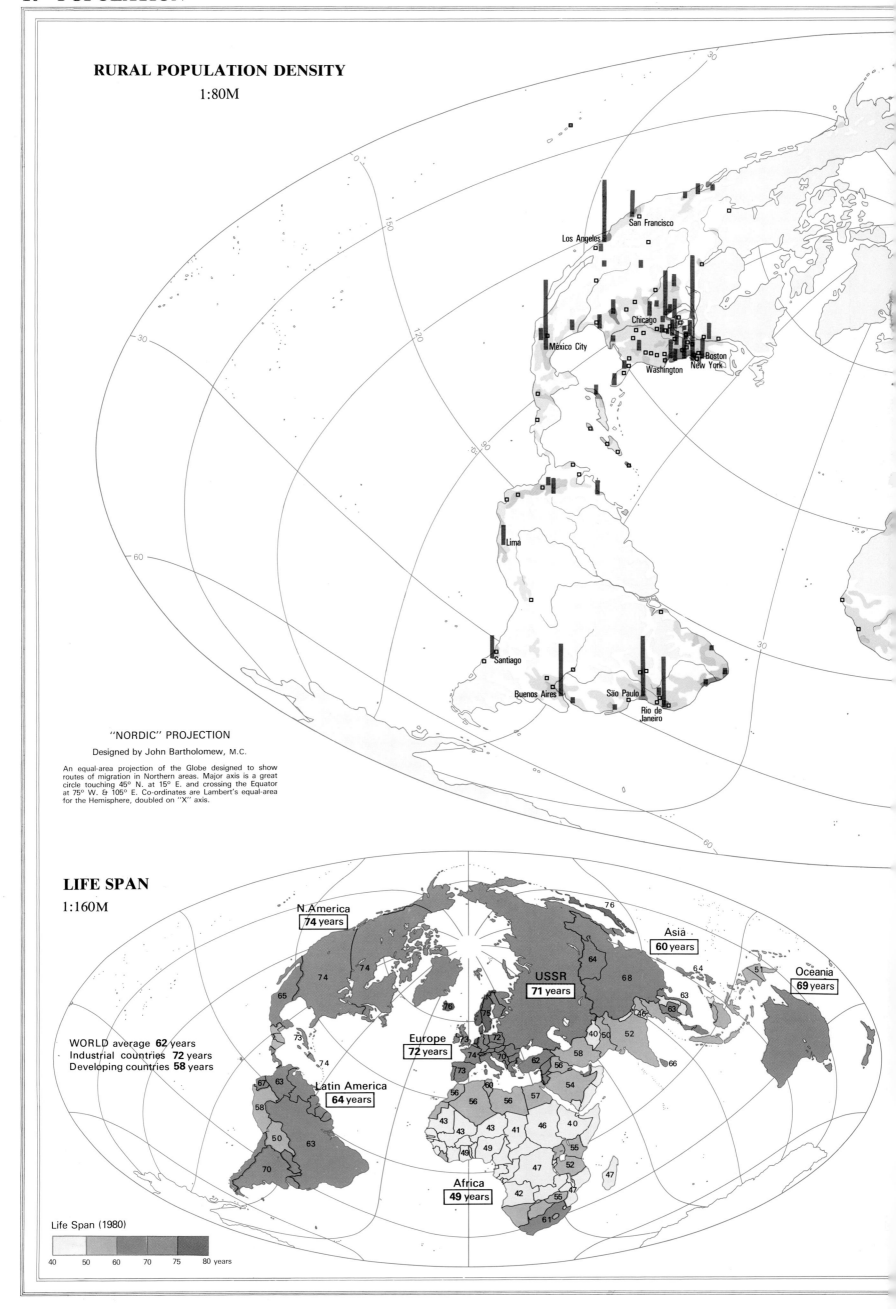

RURAL POPULATION DENSITY
1:80M

San Francisco
Los Angeles
Chicago
México City
Washington Boston New York
Lima
Santiago
Buenos Aires São Paulo
Rio de Janeiro

"NORDIC" PROJECTION

Designed by John Bartholomew, M.C.

An equal-area projection of the Globe designed to show routes of migration in Northern areas. Major axis is a great circle touching 45° N. at 15° E. and crossing the Equator at 75° W. & 105° E. Co-ordinates are Lambert's equal-area for the Hemisphere, doubled on "X" axis.

LIFE SPAN
1:160M

N.America
74 years

Asia
60 years

USSR
71 years

Oceania
69 years

Europe
72 years

WORLD average **62** years
Industrial countries **72** years
Developing countries **58** years

Latin America
64 years

Africa
49 years

Life Span (1980)

40   50   60   70   75   80 years

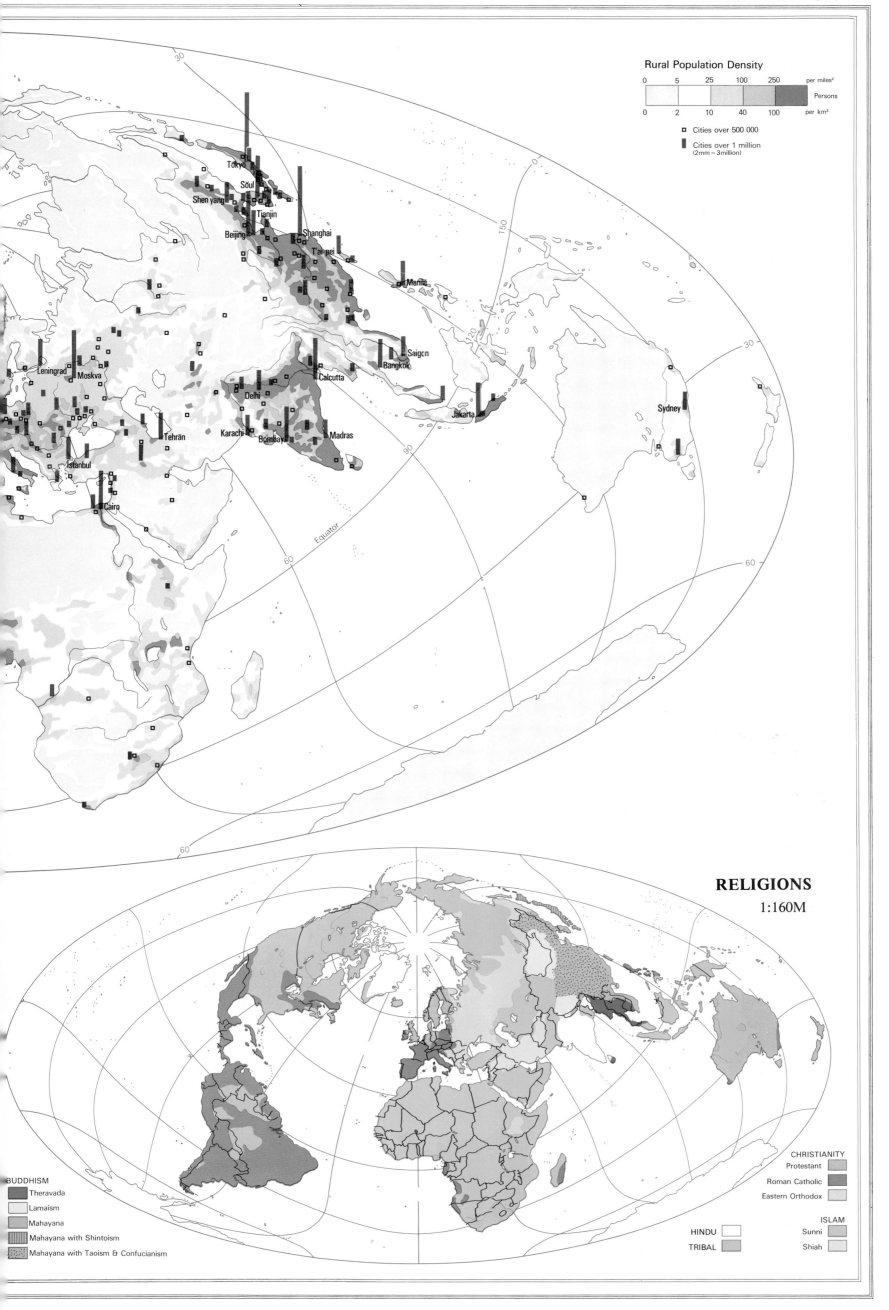

Rural Population Density

| 0 | 5 | 25 | 100 | 250 | per miles² |

Persons

| 0 | 2 | 10 | 40 | 100 | per km² |

□ Cities over 500 000

▮ Cities over 1 million
(2mm = 3million)

Tokyo

Sŏul

Shen yang

Tianjin

Beijing

Shanghai

T'ai-pei

Manila

Leningrad

Moskva

Saigon

Bangkok

Calcutta

Delhi

Tehrān

Karachi

Bombay

Madras

Jakarta

Sydney

Istanbul

Cairo

Equator

RELIGIONS

1:160M

BUDDHISM

■ Theravada

☐ Lamaism

▨ Mahayana

▦ Mahayana with Shintoism

▩ Mahayana with Taoism & Confucianism

HINDU

TRIBAL

CHRISTIANITY

Protestant

Roman Catholic

Eastern Orthodox

ISLAM

Sunni

Shiah

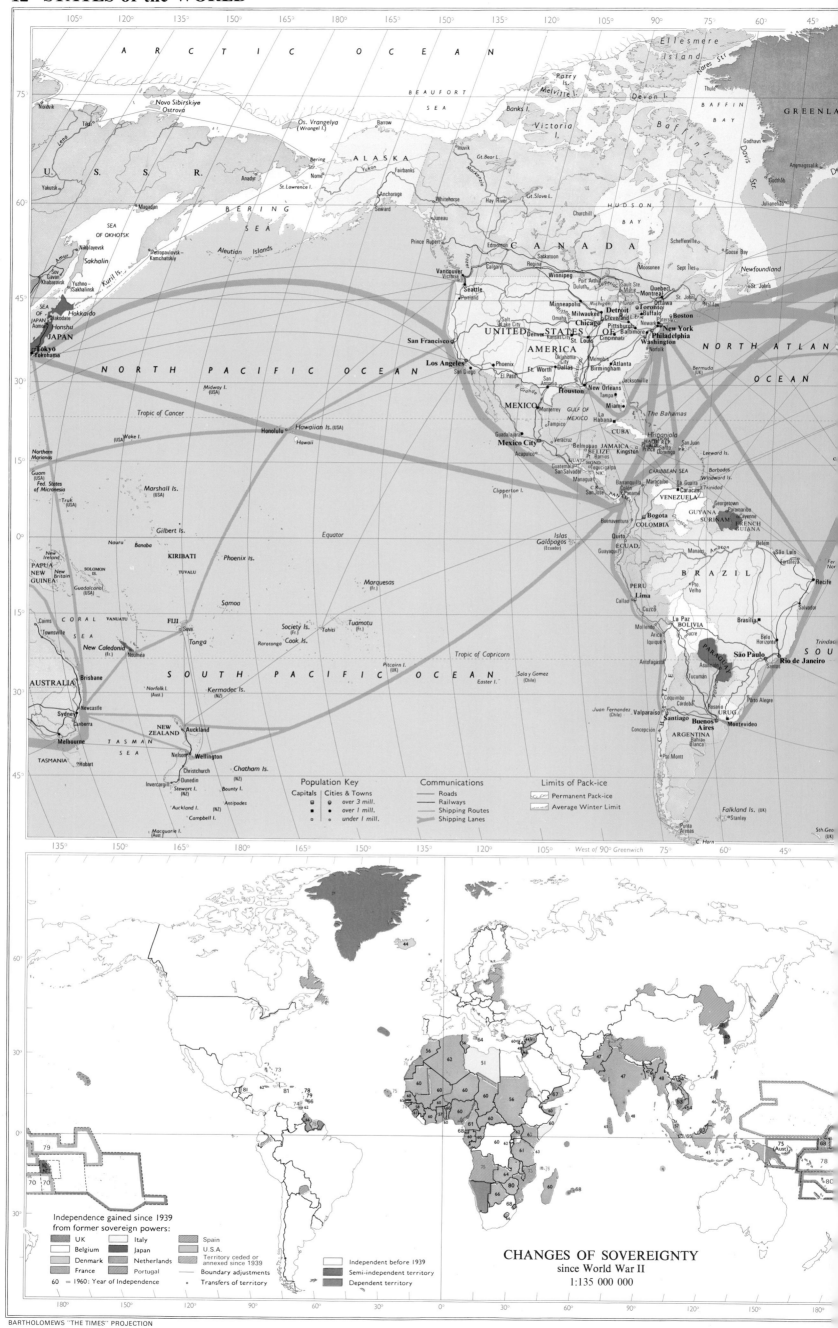

Population Key

Capitals | Cities & Towns
- □ ■ over 3 mill.
- ■ • over 1 mill.
- □ ○ under 1 mill.

Communications
- Roads
- Railways
- Shipping Routes
- Shipping Lanes

Limits of Pack-ice
- Permanent Pack-ice
- Average Winter Limit

Independence gained since 1939 from former sovereign powers:

- UK
- Belgium
- Denmark
- France
- Italy
- Japan
- Netherlands
- Portugal
- Spain
- U.S.A.
- Territory ceded or annexed since 1939
- Boundary adjustments
- Transfers of territory
- 60 = 1960: Year of Independence

- Independent before 1939
- Semi-independent territory
- Dependent territory

CHANGES OF SOVEREIGNTY
since World War II
1:135 000 000

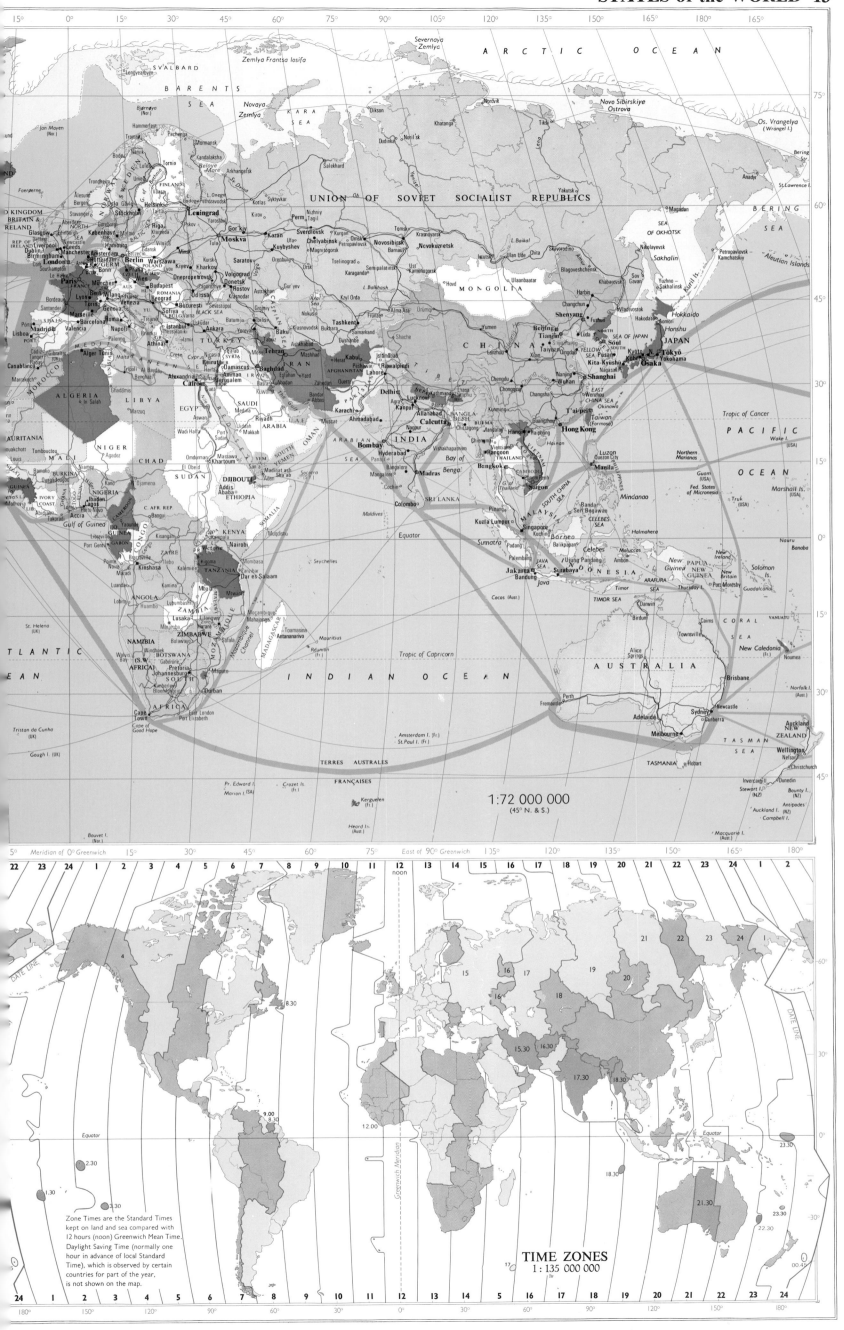

1:72 000 000
(45° N. & S.)

TIME ZONES
1 : 135 000 000

Zone Times are the Standard Times kept on land and sea compared with 12 hours (noon) Greenwich Mean Time. Daylight Saving Time (normally one hour in advance of local Standard Time), which is observed by certain countries for part of the year, is not shown on the map.

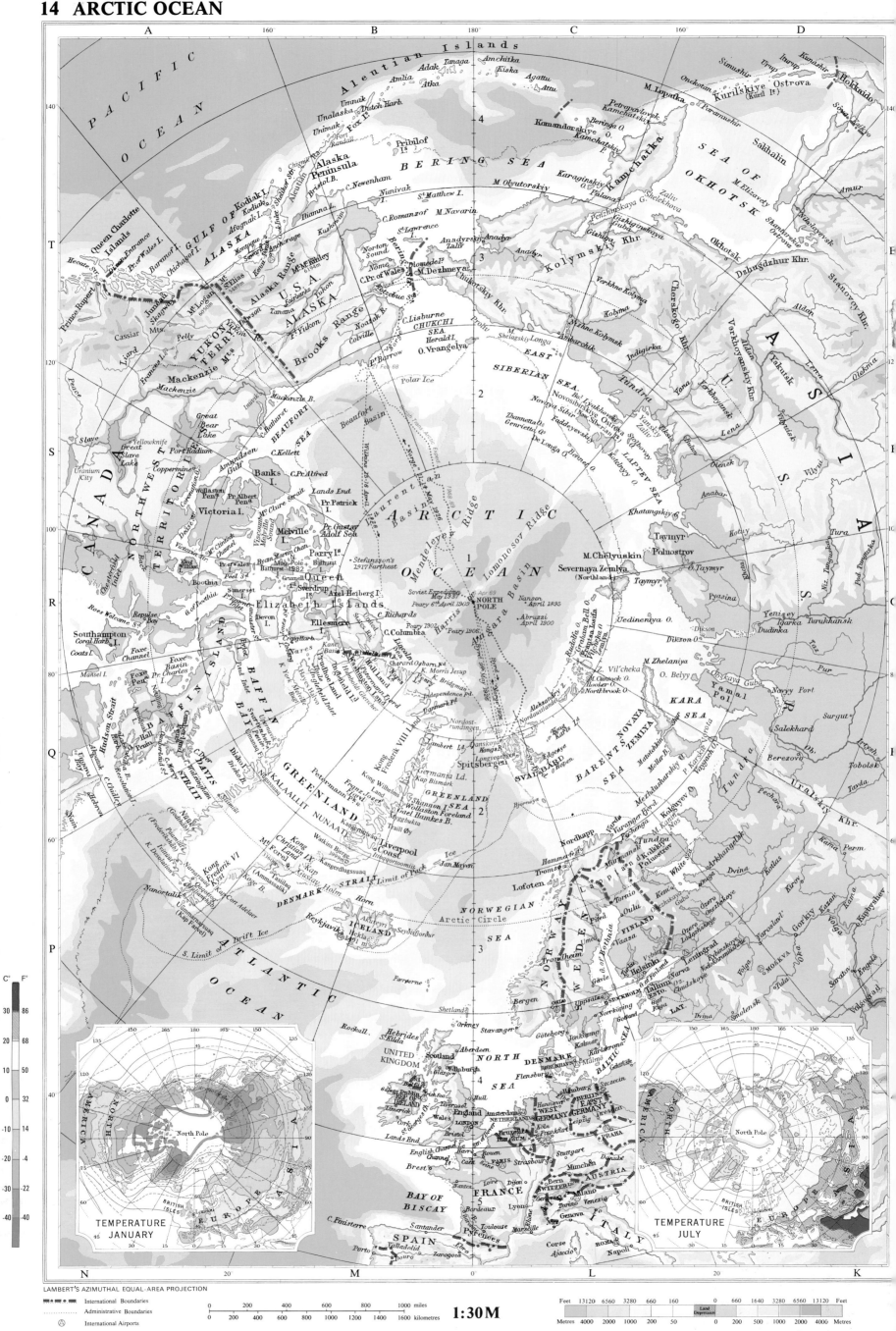

TEMPERATURE JANUARY

TEMPERATURE JULY

LAMBERT'S AZIMUTHAL EQUAL-AREA PROJECTION

1:30 M

International Boundaries
Administrative Boundaries
International Airports

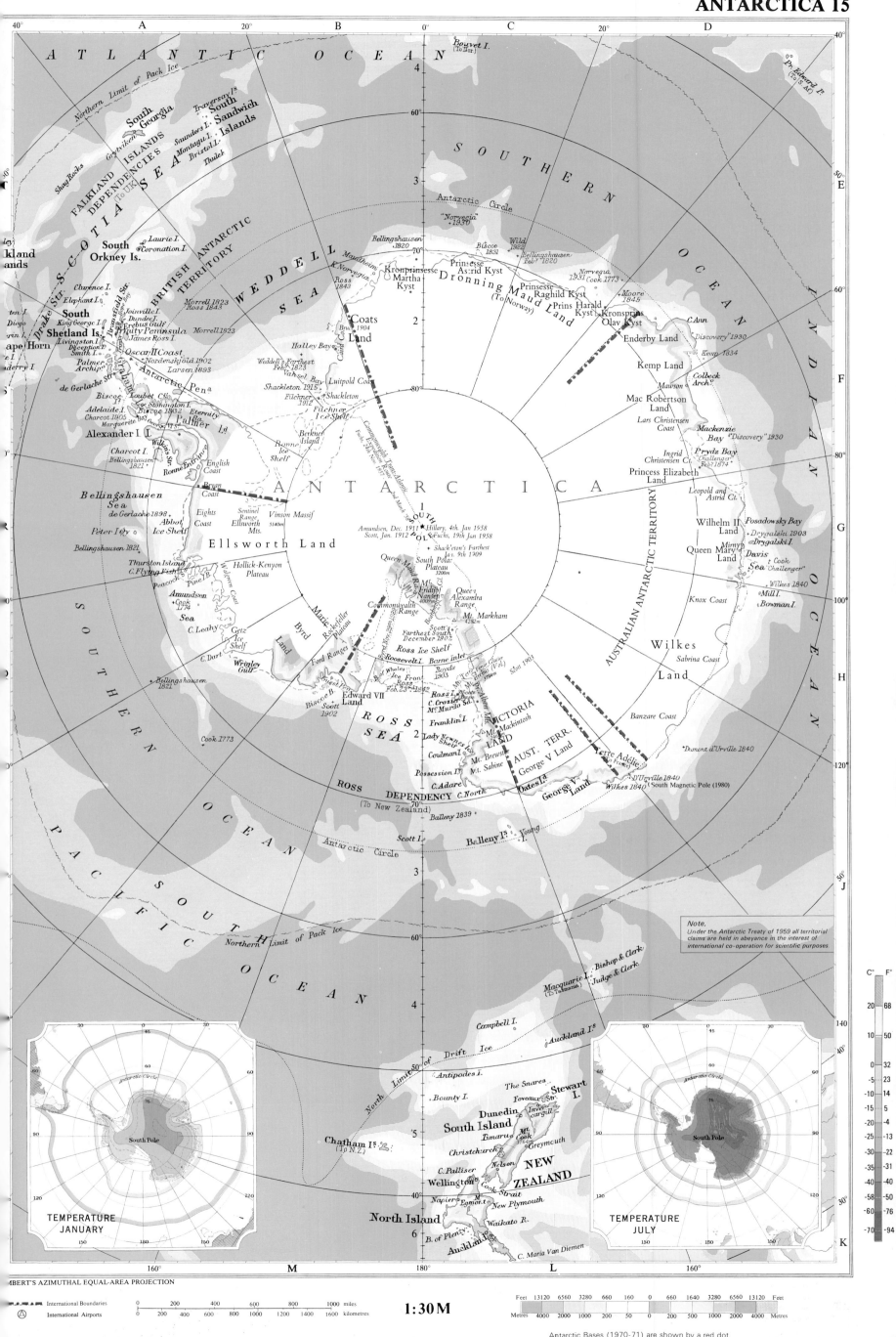

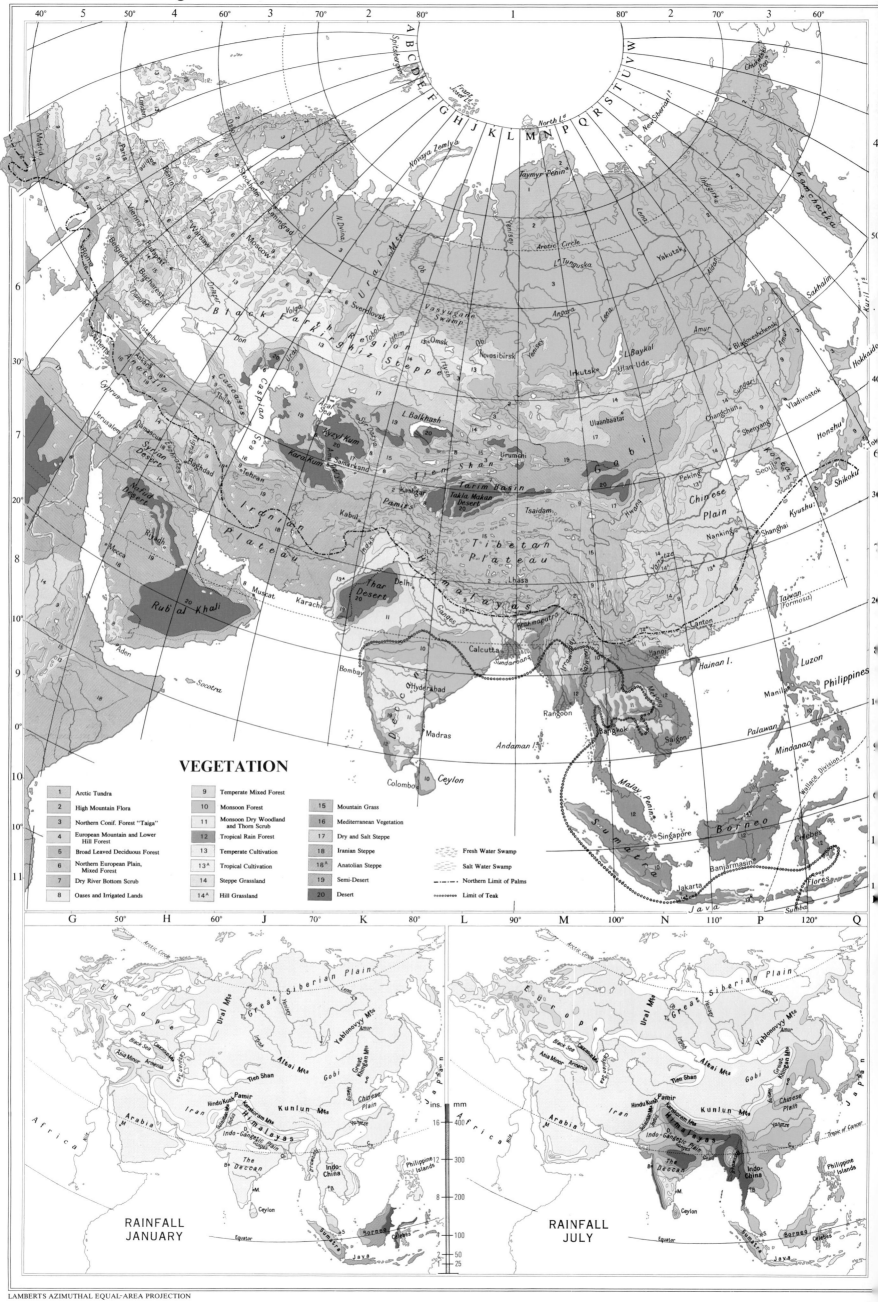

VEGETATION

1	Arctic Tundra	
2	High Mountain Flora	
3	Northern Conif. Forest "Taiga"	
4	European Mountain and Lower Hill Forest	
5	Broad Leaved Deciduous Forest	
6	Northern European Plain, Mixed Forest	
7	Dry River Bottom Scrub	
8	Oases and Irrigated Lands	

9	Temperate Mixed Forest
10	Monsoon Forest
11	Monsoon Dry Woodland and Thorn Scrub
12	Tropical Rain Forest
13	Temperate Cultivation
13ᴬ	Tropical Cultivation
14	Steppe Grassland
14ᴬ	Hill Grassland

15	Mountain Grass
16	Mediterranean Vegetation
17	Dry and Salt Steppe
18	Iranian Steppe
18ᴬ	Anatolian Steppe
19	Semi-Desert
20	Desert

- ≈≈≈ Fresh Water Swamp
- ≈≈≈ Salt Water Swamp
- —·—·— Northern Limit of Palms
- ○○○○○○ Limit of Teak

RAINFALL JANUARY

RAINFALL JULY

ins.	mm
16	400
12	300
8	200
4	100
2	50
1	25

LAMBERTS AZIMUTHAL EQUAL-AREA PROJECTION

0	200	400	600	800	1000 miles
0	400	800	1200	1600 kilometres	

1:45M

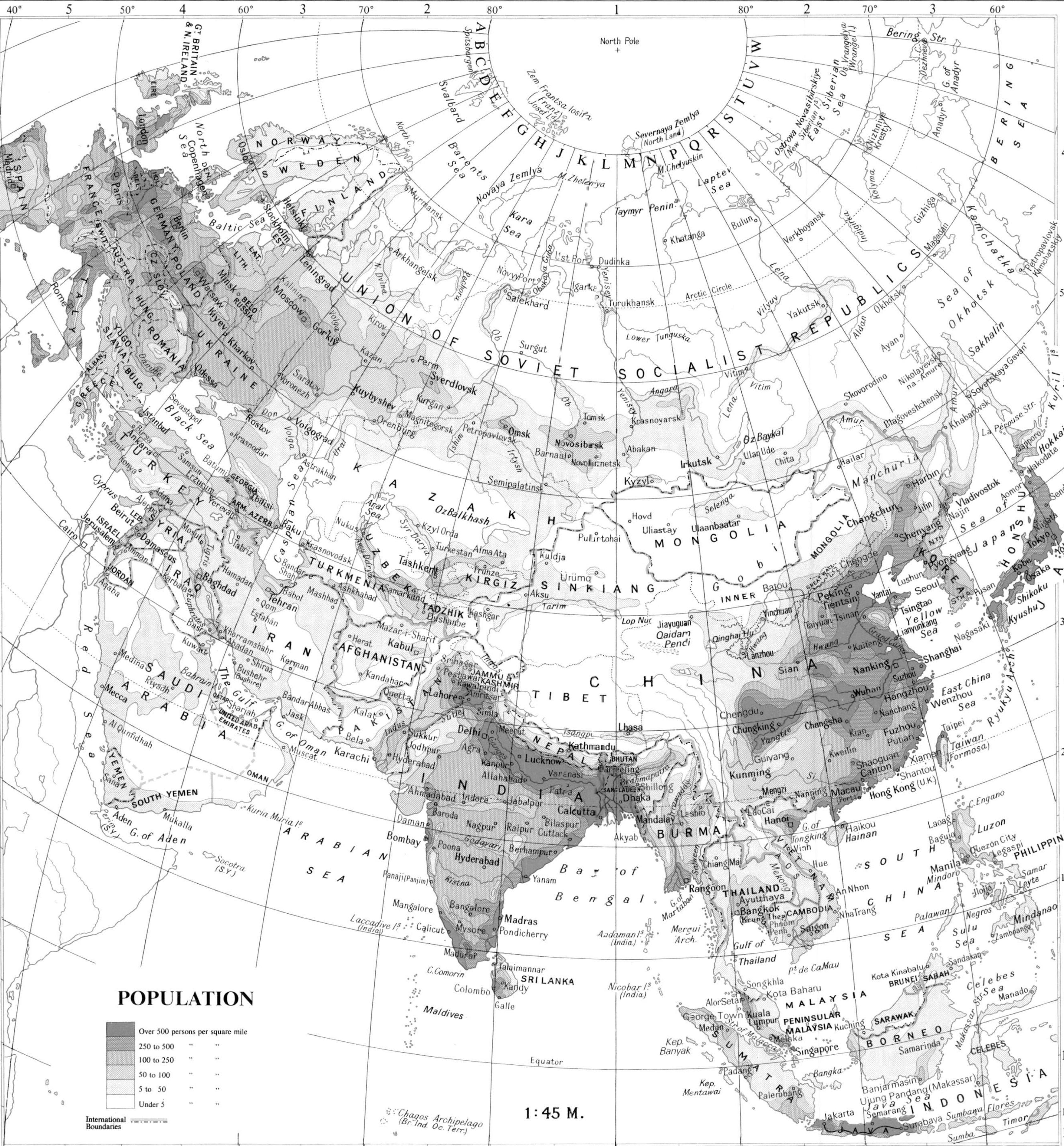

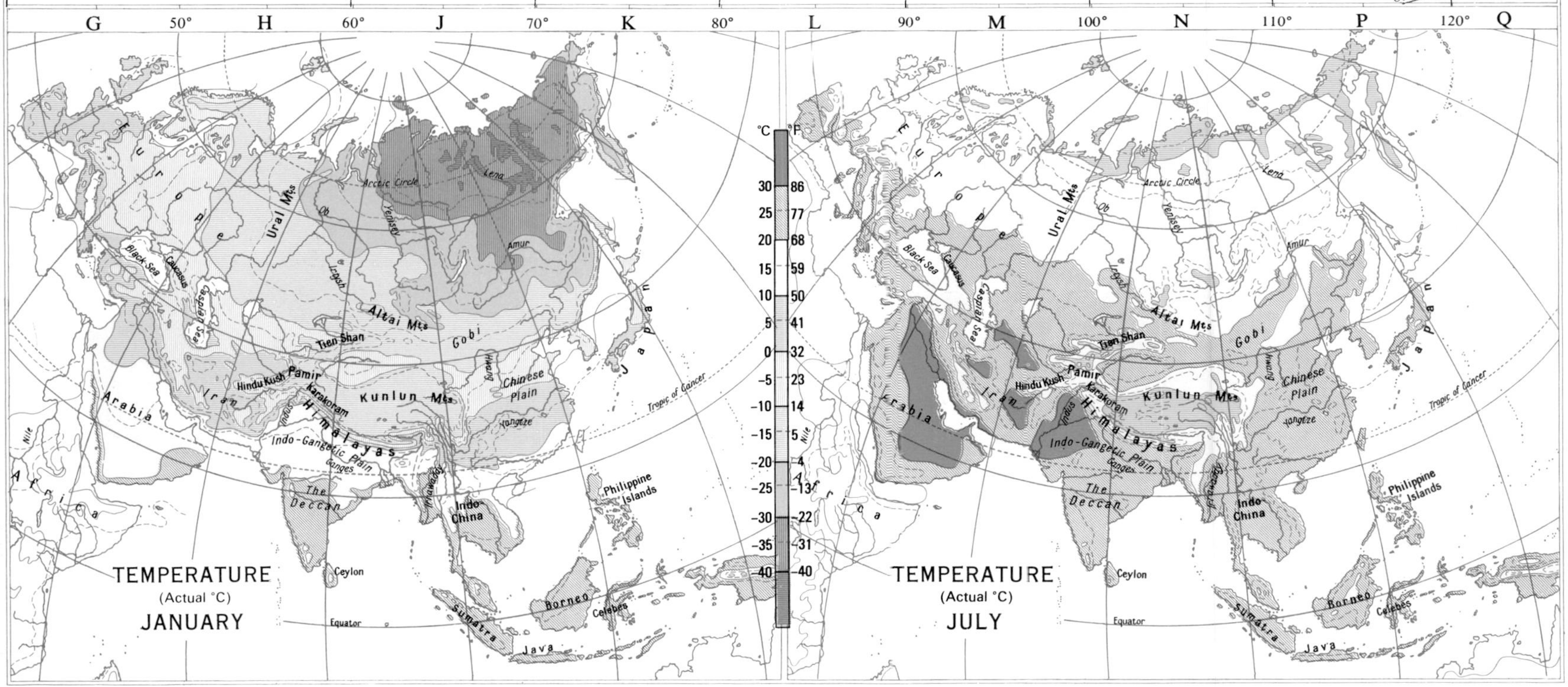

POPULATION
Over 500 persons per square mile
250 to 500
100 to 250
50 to 100
5 to 50
Under 5
International Boundaries
1:45 M.
North Pole
UNION OF SOVIET SOCIALIST REPUBLICS
MONGOLIA
SINKIANG
TIBET
CHINA
INDIA
IRAN
AFGHANISTAN
PAKISTAN
TURKEY
SAUDI ARABIA
BURMA
THAILAND
JAPAN
KOREA
INDONESIA
PHILIPPINES
MALAYSIA
ARABIAN SEA
Bay of Bengal
SOUTH CHINA SEA
Sea of Okhotsk
BERING SEA
Equator
Arctic Circle

TEMPERATURE
(Actual °C)
JANUARY
TEMPERATURE
(Actual °C)
JULY
°C
°F
30 86
25 77
20 68
15 59
10 50
5 41
0 32
-5 23
-10 14
-15 5
-20 -4
-25 -13
-30 -22
-35 -31
-40 -40

ᴍBERTS AZIMUTHAL EQUAL-AREA PROJECTION

0 200 400 600 800 1000 miles
0 400 800 1200 1600 kilometres

1:45M

LAMBERT'S AZIMUTHAL EQUAL-AREA PROJECTION

1:30M

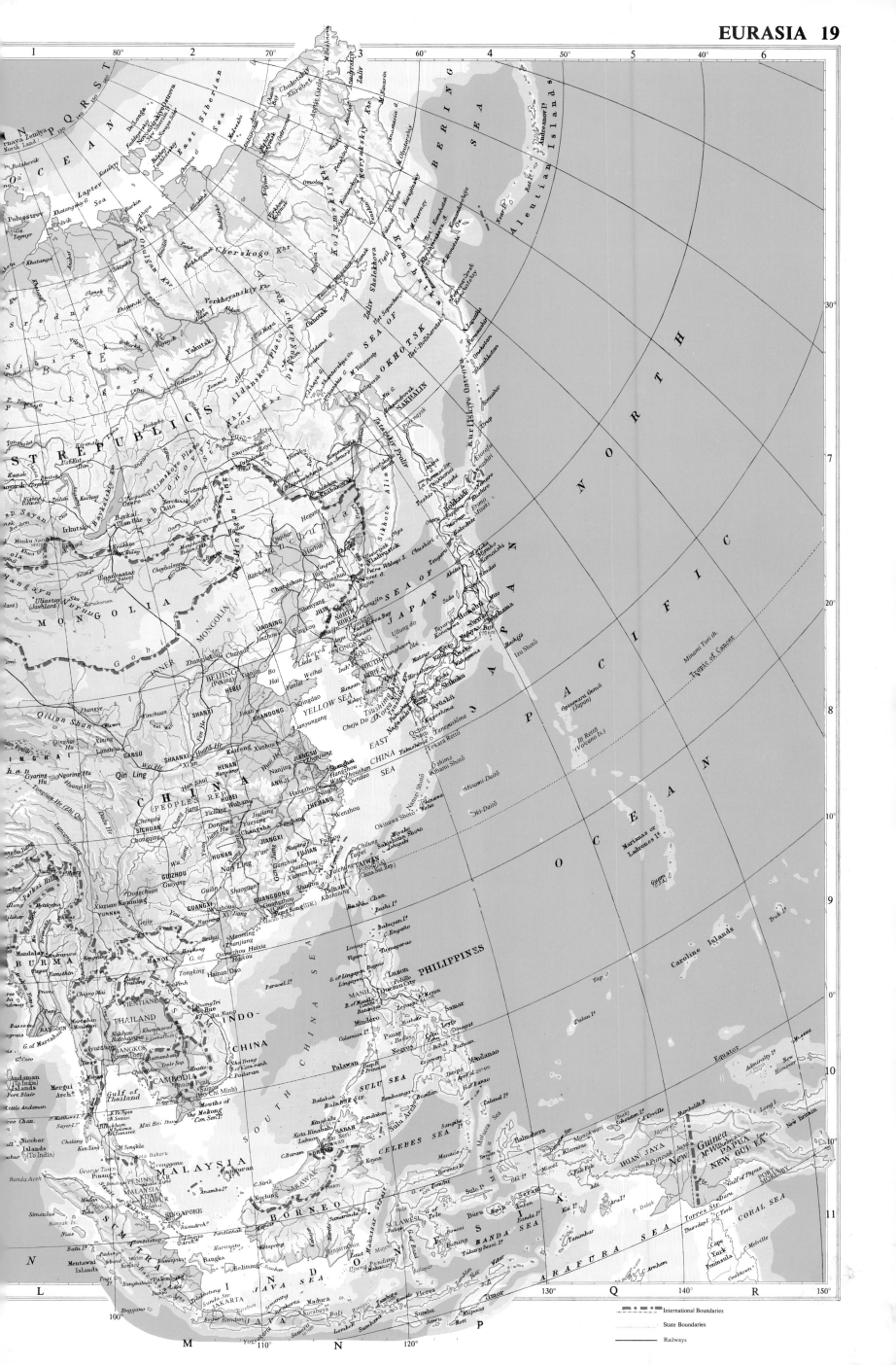

International Boundaries

State Boundaries

Railways

1:15M

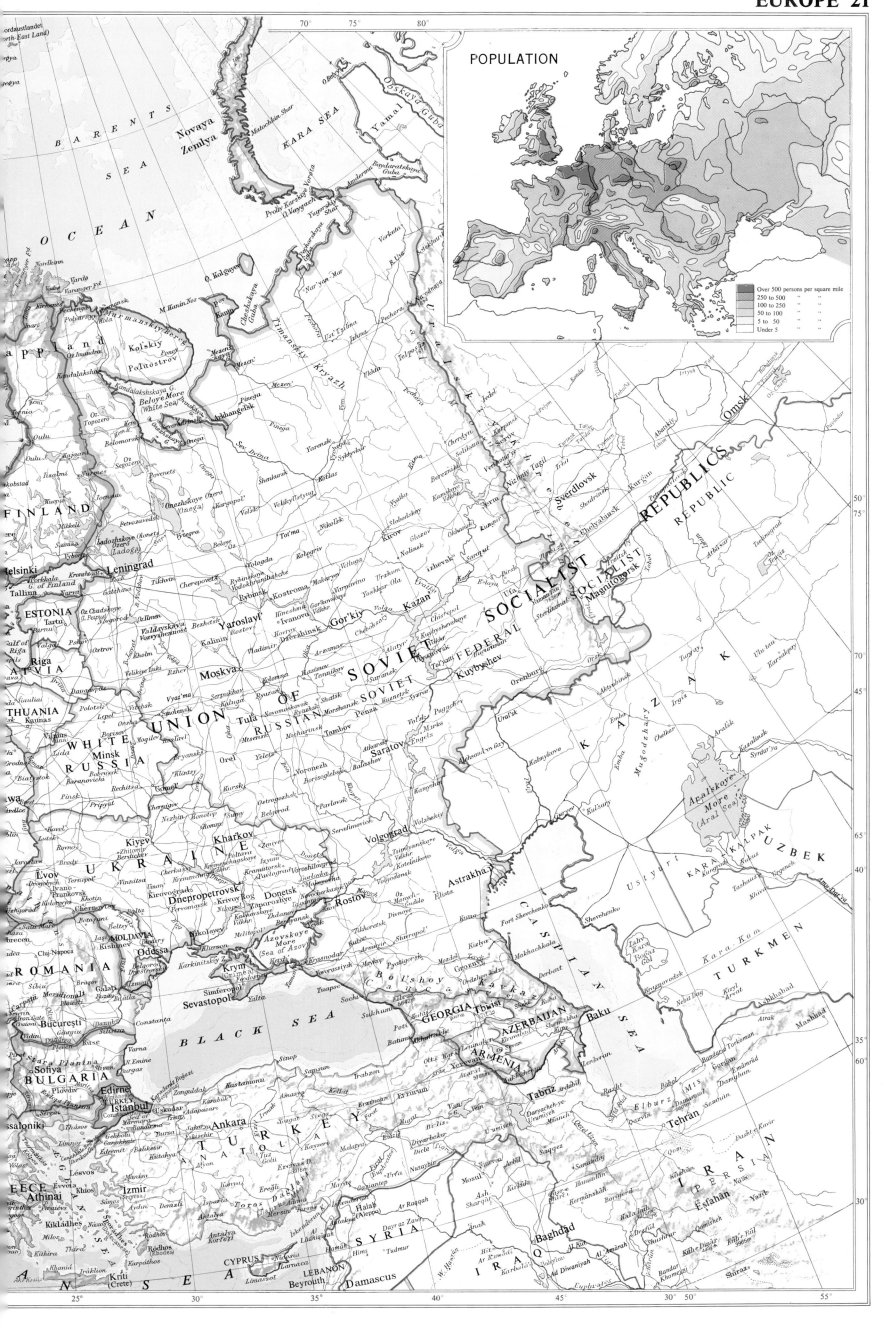

Over 500 persons per square mile
250 to 500 " " " "
100 to 250 " " " "
50 to 100 " " " "
5 to 50 " " " "
Under 5

UNION OF SOVIET SOCIALIST

RUSSIAN SOVIET FEDERAL SOCIALIST REPUBLICS

REPUBLIC

BARENTS SEA

KARA SEA

Novaya Zemlya

OCEAN

LAPLAND

FINLAND

Leningrad

Helsinki

Tallinn

ESTONIA

LITHUANIA

LATVIA

Riga

WHITE RUSSIA

Minsk

Moskva

UKRAINE

Kiyev

Kharkov

Dnepropetrovsk

Donetsk

Rostov

ROMANIA

MOLDAVIA

Kishinev

Odessa

București

Sofiya

BULGARIA

Edirne

İstanbul

Sevastopol

Krym

Simferopol

BLACK SEA

TURKEY

Ankara

GREECE

Athínai

GEORGIA

Tbilisi

ARMENIA

AZERBAIJAN

Baku

CASPIAN SEA

TURKMEN

Ashkhabad

Volgograd

Astrakhan

Saratov

Kuybyshev

Gor'kiy

Kazan'

KAZAK

Aral'skoye More (Aral Sea)

KARA KALPAK

UZBEK

Sverdlovsk

Chelyabinsk

Magnitogorsk

Omsk

SYRIA

Baghdad

IRAQ

Damascus

Beyrouth

LEBANON

CYPRUS

Tehrān

IRAN

PERSIA

Eṣfahān

Tabrīz

Mashhad

İzmir

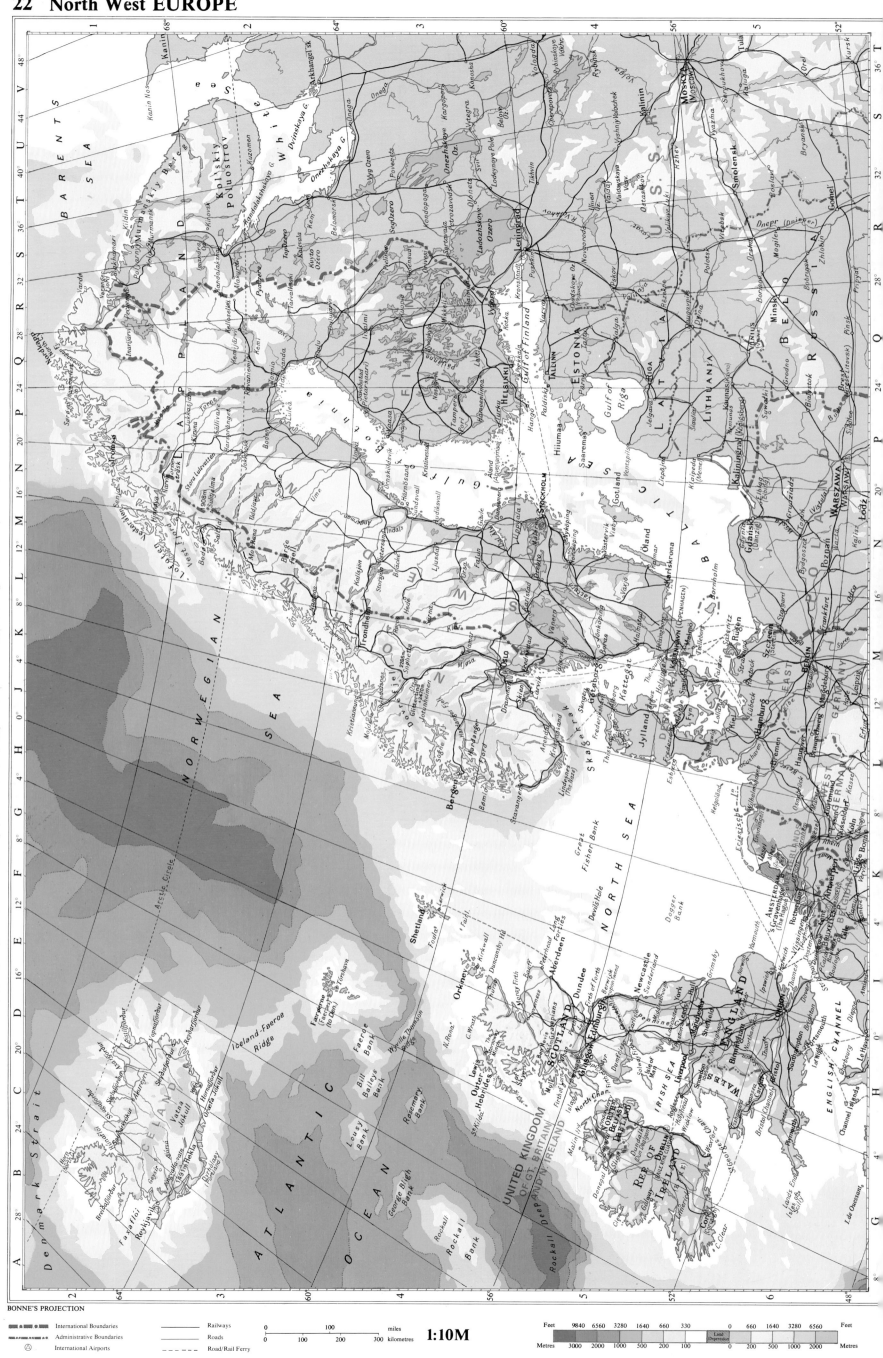

BONNE'S PROJECTION

International Boundaries	Railways		
Administrative Boundaries	Roads		
International Airports	Road/Rail Ferry		

0 100 miles
0 100 200 300 kilometres

1:10M

Feet	9840	6560	3280	1640	660	330		0	660	1640	3280	6560	Feet
Metres	3000	2000	1000	500	200	100		0	200	500	1000	2000	Metres

STRUCTURE 1:6M

AGE and ROCK TYPE

Sedimentary
ERA/PERIOD

CAINOZOIC–
Quaternary &
Tertiary
- clay
- sands
- clay and sands

MESOZOIC
(including
Permian)
- clay
- sandstone
- clay and sandstone
- chalk
- limestone

UPPER
PALAEOZOIC
- clay
- shale
- slate
- shale and sandstone
- shale and limestone
- sandstone
- limestone

LOWER
PALAEOZOIC
(including
Precambrian)
- slate
- shale and slate
- sandstone

Metamorphic

Igneous
- Intrusive
- Extrusive

- Anticline
- Syncline
- Cretaceous scarp
- Jurassic scarp
- Normal fault, with tick on downthrow side
- Wrench fault, with direction of lateral movement
- Thrust fault, with direction of overthrust
- Corries
- Maximum extent of ice

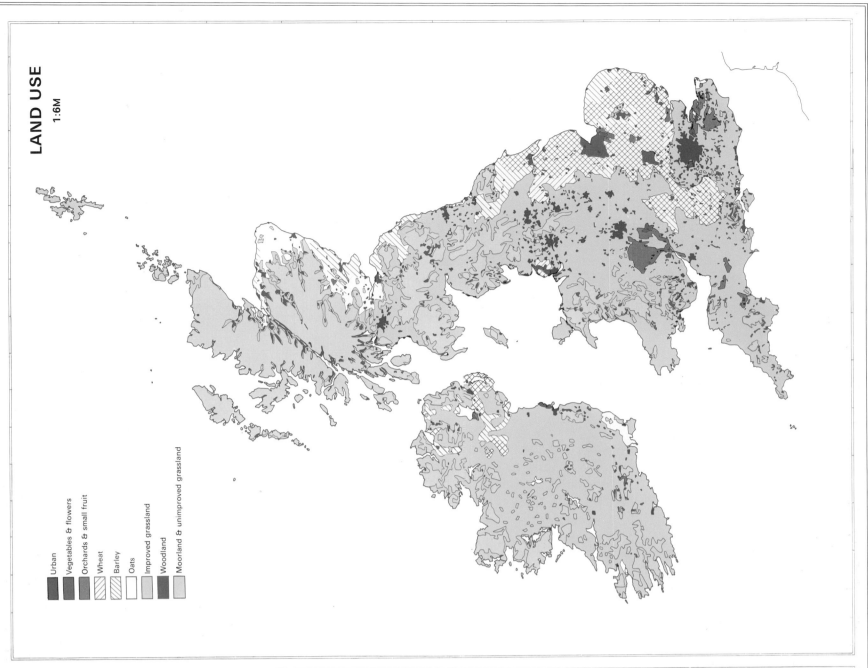

LAND USE 1:6M

- Urban
- Vegetables & flowers
- Orchards & small fruit
- Wheat
- Barley
- Oats
- Improved grassland
- Woodland
- Moorland & unimproved grassland

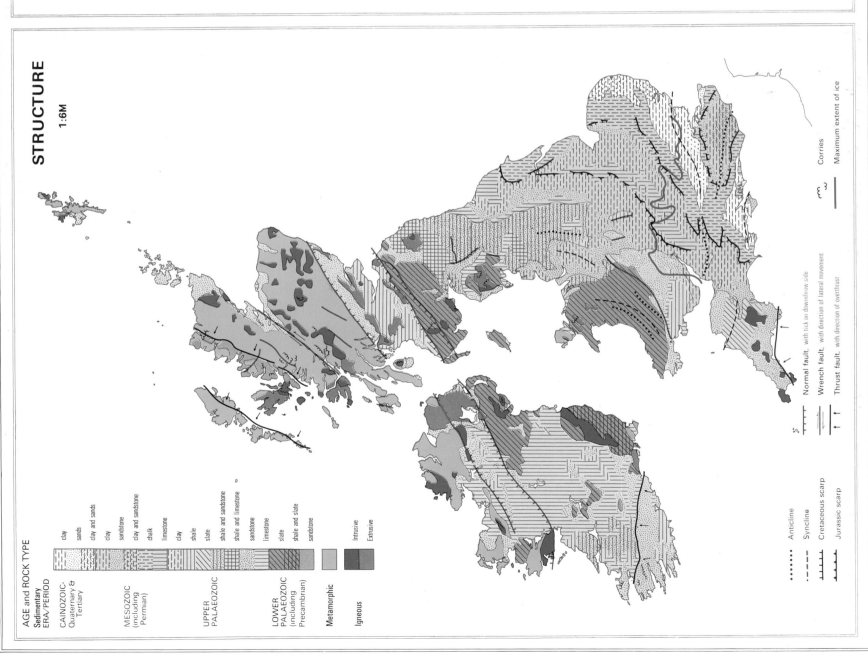

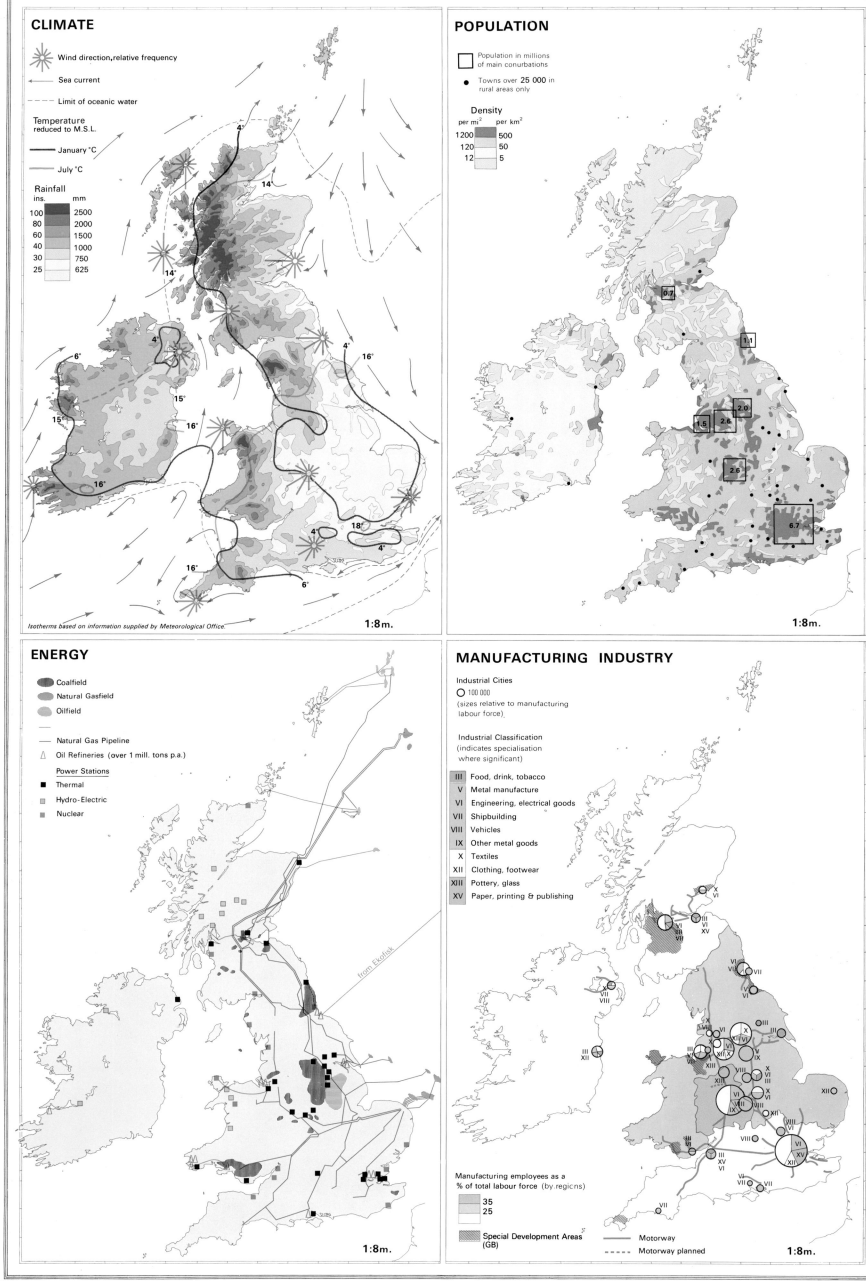

CLIMATE

Wind direction, relative frequency

→ Sea current

--- Limit of oceanic water

Temperature
reduced to M.S.L.

━━ January °C

━━ July °C

Rainfall
ins.	mm
100	2500
80	2000
60	1500
40	1000
30	750
25	625

Isotherms based on information supplied by Meteorological Office.

1:8m.

POPULATION

☐ Population in millions of main conurbations

● Towns over 25 000 in rural areas only

Density
per mi²		per km²
1200		500
120		50
12		5

1:8m.

ENERGY

▨ Coalfield

▨ Natural Gasfield

▨ Oilfield

━━ Natural Gas Pipeline

△ Oil Refineries (over 1 mill. tons p.a.)

Power Stations

■ Thermal

▪ Hydro-Electric

▪ Nuclear

from Ekofisk.

1:8m.

MANUFACTURING INDUSTRY

Industrial Cities

◯ 100 000

(sizes relative to manufacturing labour force)

Industrial Classification
(indicates specialisation where significant)

III	Food, drink, tobacco
V	Metal manufacture
VI	Engineering, electrical goods
VII	Shipbuilding
VIII	Vehicles
IX	Other metal goods
X	Textiles
XII	Clothing, footwear
XIII	Pottery, glass
XV	Paper, printing & publishing

Manufacturing employees as a
% of total labour force (by regions)

35
25

▨ Special Development Areas (GB)

━━ Motorway

--- Motorway planned

1:8m.

1:8M

© John Bartholomew & Son Ltd , Edinburgh

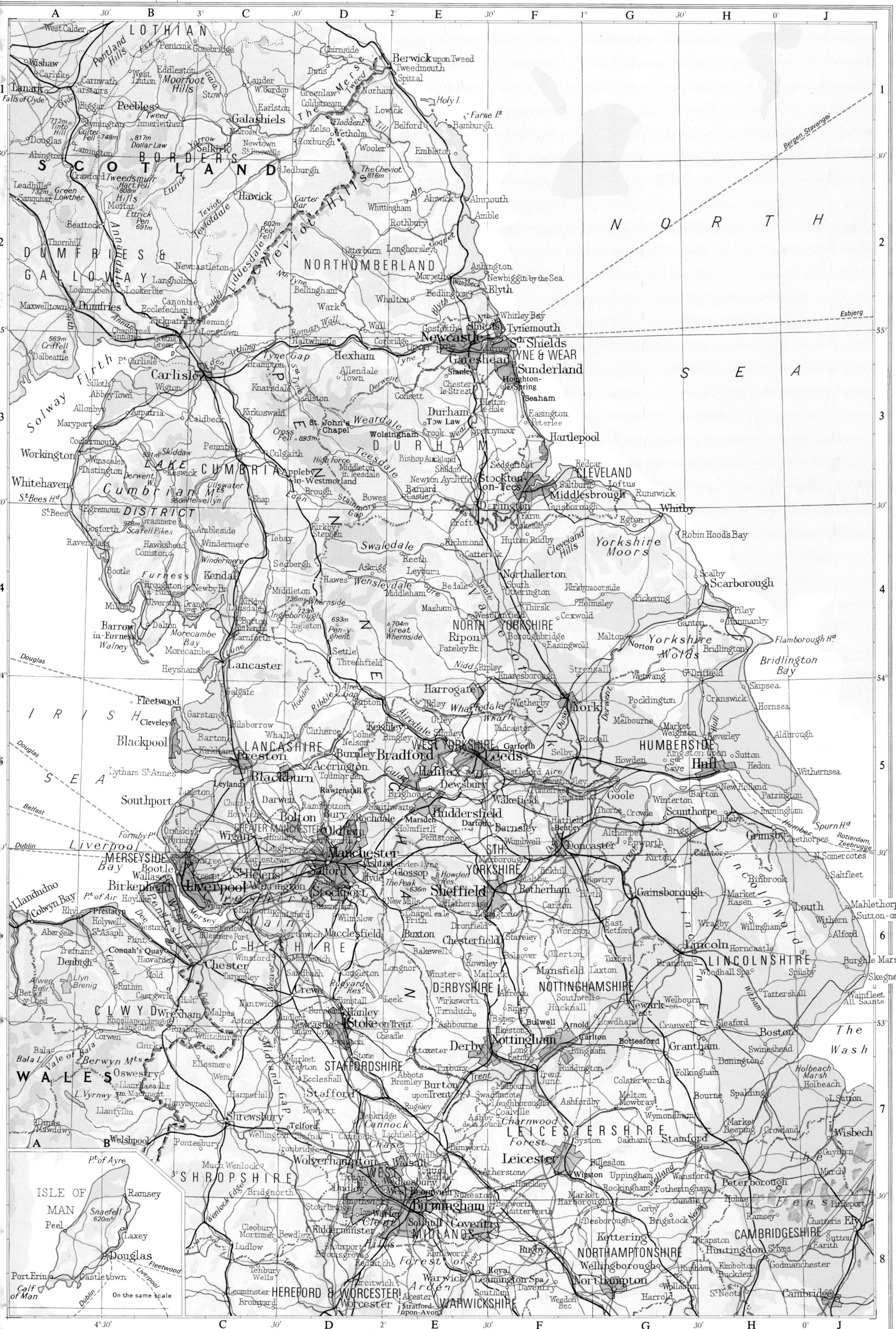

A 30' B 3° C 30' D 2° E 30' F 1° G 30' H 0° J

SCOTLAND

LOTHIAN
West Calder
Wishaw
Carluke
Lanark
Falls of Clyde
Carnwath
Carstairs
Biggar
Symington
Coulter Fell 748m
817m
Peebles
Innerleithen
Moorfoot Hills
Pentland Hills
Esk
Penicuik
Gorebridge
Eddleston
W. Gordon
Lauder
Stow
Earlston
Galashiels
Selkirk
BORDERS
Melrose
Newtown St Boswells
Jedburgh
Hawick
Carter Bar
The Cheviot 816m
Chirnside
Duns
Greenlaw
Coldstream
Kelso
Roxburgh
Yetholm
Wooler
Berwick upon Tweed
Tweedmouth
Spittal
Norham
Lowick
Holy I.
Farne Is
Belford
Bamburgh
Embleton

DUMFRIES & GALLOWAY
Thornhill
Sanquhar 732m
Green Lowther
Leadhills
Moffat
Ettrick Pen 691m
Peel Fell
602m
Tweedsmuir Hills
Hart Fell 808m
Beattock
Lockerbie
Langholm
Newcastleton
Bellingham
Wark
Whalton
NORTHUMBERLAND
Otterburn
Longhorsley
Rothbury
Whittingham
Alnwick
Alnmouth
Amble
Ashington
Morpeth
Wansbeck
Bedlington
Blyth
Newbiggin by the Sea

NORTH SEA

Dumfries
Maxwelltown
Annan
Gretna Green
Longtown
Brampton
Haltwhistle
Tyne Gap
Roman Wall
Hexham
Wall
Corbridge
Allendale Town
Bellingham
Gosforth
Whitley Bay
Tynemouth
South Shields
Newcastle upon Tyne
Gateshead
TYNE & WEAR
Sunderland
Seaham
Houghton le Spring
Hetton le Hole

Carlisle
Silloth
Abbey Town
Wigton
Caldbeck
Kirkoswald
Penrith
Alston
Cross Fell 893m
St. John's Chapel
Weardale
Tow Law
Consett
Stanley
Chester le Street
Durham
Crook
Spennymoor
Peterlee
Easington
Hartlepool
Sedgefield

Maryport
Cockermouth
Workington
Whitehaven
St Bees Hd
St Bees
Egremont
Wastwater
Skiddaw 931m
Keswick
Derwent W.
Ullswater
Helvellyn 950m
Shap
Appleby in-Westmorland
Brough
High Force
Middleton in Teesdale
Bowes
Barnard Castle
Teesdale
Bishop Auckland
Shildon
Newton Aycliffe
Stockton on Tees
Darlington
Redcar
Saltburn
CLEVELAND
Loftus
Middlesbrough
Guisborough
Runswick
Egton
Whitby

LAKE DISTRICT
CUMBRIA
Cumbrian Mts
978m Scafell Pikes
Grasmere
Ambleside
Windermere
Hawkshead
Coniston
Kendal
Sedbergh
Tebay
Kirkby Stephen
Stainmore Gap
Croft
Yarm
Stokesley
Great Ayton
Cleveland Hills
Hutton Rudby
Robin Hood's Bay
Yorkshire Moors

Ravenglass
Furness
Broughton
Ulverston
Dalton
Barrow in-Furness
Walney
Morecambe Bay
Grange
Milnthorpe
Kirkby Lonsdale
Ingleton
Ingleborough 723m
Pen-y-ghent 693m
Whernside 736m
Hawes
Askrigg
Reeth
Wensleydale
Swaledale
Leyburn
Middleham
Bedale
Richmond
Catterick
Northallerton
South Kilvington
Thirsk
Helmsley
Kirkbymoorside
Pickering
Scarborough
Filey
Ganton

Morecambe
Heysham
Lancaster
Carnforth
Settle
Threshfield
Malham
Wharfedale
Masham
Ripon
Pateley Br.
West Tanfield
NORTH YORKSHIRE
Boroughbridge
Easingwold
Malton
Norton
Coxwold
Yorkshire Wolds
Bridlington
Flamborough Hd
Bridlington Bay
Skipsea

Fleetwood
Cleveleys
Garstang
Bilsborrow
Blackpool
Lytham St Annes
Preston
Southport
Formby Pt
Ormskirk
Skelmersdale
LANCASHIRE
Clitheroe
Colne
Nelson
Burnley
Accrington
Blackburn
Darwen
Leyland
Chorley
Ribble
Aire Gap
Keighley
Bingley
Bradford
Halifax
Dewsbury
WEST YORKSHIRE
Leeds
Wetherby
Harrogate
Otley
Ilkley
Wharfe
Tadcaster
Knaresborough
Nidd
Ripley
York
Selby
Riccall
Howden
Pocklington
Market Weighton
Beverley
Cranswick
Hornsea
Great Driffield
Wetwang

IRISH SEA

Liverpool
Bootle
Wallasey
MERSEYSIDE
Birkenhead
Hoylake
Liverpool Bay
St Helens
Warrington
Widnes
Manchester
Salford
GREATER MANCHESTER
Bolton
Bury
Rochdale
Oldham
Wigan
Leigh
Ashton under Lyne
Hyde
Stockport
Glossop
The Peak 636m
Huddersfield
Marsden
Holmfirth
Penistone
Barnsley
Wombwell
Mexborough
Rotherham
SOUTH YORKSHIRE
Sheffield
Doncaster
Thorne
Goole
Scunthorpe
Brigg
Barton
Grimsby
Cleethorpes
Immingham
Humber
Spurn Hd
Hull
Kingston upon Hull
HUMBERSIDE
Hedon
Withernsea
Patrington

Llandudno
Colwyn Bay
Rhyl
Prestatyn
Holywell
St Asaph
Abergele
Denbigh
Ruthin
CLWYD
Mold
Flint
Connah's Quay
Hawarden
Chester
Ellesmere Port
Northwich
Winsford
Nantwich
Crewe
CHESHIRE
Macclesfield
Knutsford
Wilmslow
Congleton
Buxton
Leek
Chapel en le Frith
New Mills
Hathersage
Chesterfield
Dronfield
Bolsover
Staveley
Worksop
East Retford
Gainsborough
Lincoln
LINCOLNSHIRE
Market Rasen
Louth
Mablethorpe
Sutton-on-Sea
Alford
Horncastle
Woodhall Spa
Spilsby
Skegness
Wainfleet All Saints
Tattershall
Boston
The Wash

WALES
Wrexham
Llangollen
Chirk
Oswestry
Ellesmere
Whitchurch
Market Drayton
Newcastle under Lyme
Stoke on Trent
Stone
Uttoxeter
Ashbourne
Matlock
Wirksworth
Belper
Ripley
Alfreton
Mansfield
Hucknall
Southwell
Newark on Trent
Grantham
Sleaford
Cranwell
Bottesford
Melton Mowbray

Berwyn Mts
Bala
Bala L.
Corwen
Vale of Llangollen
Shrewsbury
Shropshire
Telford
Wellington
Newport
Stafford
STAFFORDSHIRE
Rugeley
Cannock
Cannock Chase
Burton upon Trent
Swadlincote
Coalville
Ashby de la Zouch
Charnwood Forest
LEICESTERSHIRE
Loughborough
Syston
Melton Mowbray
Oakham
Stamford
DERBYSHIRE
Derby
Long Eaton
NOTTINGHAMSHIRE
Nottingham
Carlton
Arnold
Bulwell

ISLE OF MAN
Pt of Ayre
Ramsey
Snaefell 620m
Laxey
Peel
Douglas
Port Erin
Castletown
Calf of Man
On the same scale

Welshpool
Pontesbury
Much Wenlock
Bridgnorth
Wenlock Edge
Kidderminster
Stourport
Bewdley
Bromsgrove
Redditch
HEREFORD & WORCESTER
Worcester
Droitwich
Leominster
Tenbury Wells
Ludlow
Cleobury Mortimer

Wolverhampton
Walsall
West Bromwich
WEST MIDLANDS
Birmingham
Dudley
Solihull
Coventry
Sutton Coldfield
Tamworth
Atherstone
Nuneaton
Hinckley
Market Bosworth
Leicester
Wigston
Uppingham
Rockingham
Corby
Kettering
NORTHAMPTONSHIRE
Wellingborough
Northampton
Market Harborough
Desborough
Rothwell
Peterborough
March
Wisbech
Guyhirn
The Fens
CAMBRIDGESHIRE
Ramsey
St Ives
Huntingdon
Godmanchester
St Neots
Cambridge

WARWICKSHIRE
Stratford upon Avon
Alcester
Warwick
Leamington Spa
Kenilworth
Rugby
Daventry
Royal Leamington
Weedon Bec
Harrold
Bozeat
Olney
Kimbolton
Buckden

Forest of Arden

1:1¼M

CONIC PROJECTION
— — — International Boundaries
— · — · County/Region Boundaries
━━━ Roads
━━━ Railways
- - - Road Ferry

0 10 20 30 miles
0 5 10 20 30 40 50 kilometres

Feet 330 160 0 160 330 660 1640 3280 Feet
Metres 100 50 0 50 100 200 500 1000 Metres

CONIC PROJECTION

0 5 10   20   30   40   50 miles

0 5 10 20 30 40 50 60 70 80 kilometres

1:1¼M

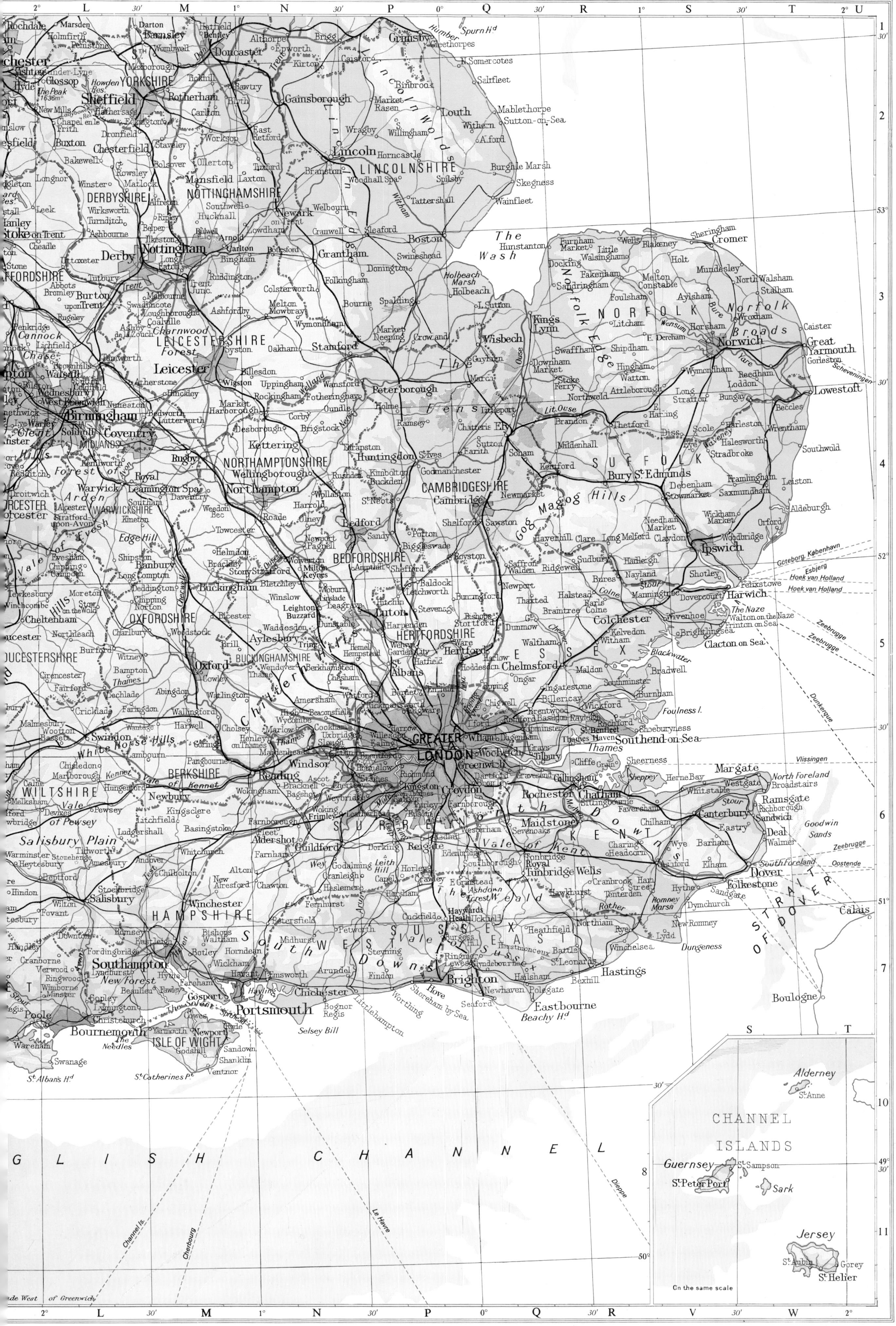

25

GREATER LONDON

YORKSHIRE
Sheffield
Rotherham
Doncaster
Barnsley
Chesterfield
DERBYSHIRE
NOTTINGHAMSHIRE
Nottingham
Derby
Mansfield
Lincoln
LINCOLNSHIRE
Gainsborough
Grimsby
Louth
Skegness
Boston
The Wash
Grantham
Newark
Stamford
Peterborough
LEICESTERSHIRE
Leicester
Loughborough
NORTHAMPTONSHIRE
Northampton
Wellingborough
Kettering
Corby
Rugby
Coventry
Birmingham
WARWICKSHIRE
Leamington Spa
Warwick
Stratford-upon-Avon
Banbury
OXFORDSHIRE
Oxford
BUCKINGHAMSHIRE
Buckingham
Aylesbury
Milton Keynes
Bedford
BEDFORDSHIRE
Luton
CAMBRIDGESHIRE
Cambridge
Huntingdon
St Ives
Newmarket
NORFOLK
King's Lynn
Norwich
Great Yarmouth
Lowestoft
Norfolk Broads
Cromer
Thetford
SUFFOLK
Bury St Edmunds
Ipswich
Harwich
Felixstowe
Colchester
ESSEX
Chelmsford
Southend-on-Sea
HERTFORDSHIRE
St Albans
Hertford
Watford
GREATER LONDON
Croydon
Kingston
Greenwich
Woolwich
BERKSHIRE
Reading
Newbury
Windsor
SURREY
Guildford
Dorking
Reigate
KENT
Maidstone
Rochester
Chatham
Canterbury
Margate
Ramsgate
Dover
Folkestone
Calais
Tunbridge Wells
Royal Tunbridge Wells
Ashford
SUSSEX
Brighton
Hove
Worthing
Eastbourne
Hastings
Bexhill
SUSSEX EAST
SUSSEX WEST
South Downs
Chichester
Arundel
HAMPSHIRE
Southampton
Portsmouth
Winchester
Basingstoke
Aldershot
Gosport
Fareham
ISLE OF WIGHT
Newport
Sandown
Shanklin
Ventnor
Cowes
WILTSHIRE
Salisbury
Salisbury Plain
Swindon
Marlborough
Devizes
Bournemouth
Poole
Christchurch
New Forest
GLOUCESTERSHIRE
Cheltenham
Cirencester
Gloucester
WORCESTER
STAFFORDSHIRE
Stoke on Trent
Burton upon Trent
Tamworth
Walsall
Wolverhampton
Cannock
Lichfield
Sheffield
The Peak
Buxton
Chesterfield
Bakewell
Matlock
Worksop
Mansfield
Spurn Head
Humber
ENGLISH CHANNEL

CHANNEL ISLANDS
Alderney
St Anne
Guernsey
St Peter Port
St Sampson
Sark
Jersey
St Helier
St Aubin
Gorey
On the same scale

STRAIT OF DOVER
Boulogne
Dungeness
Romney Marsh

Gog Magog Hills
The Fens
The Naze
Foulness I.
Selsey Bill
The Needles
St Catherine's Pt
Beachy Head

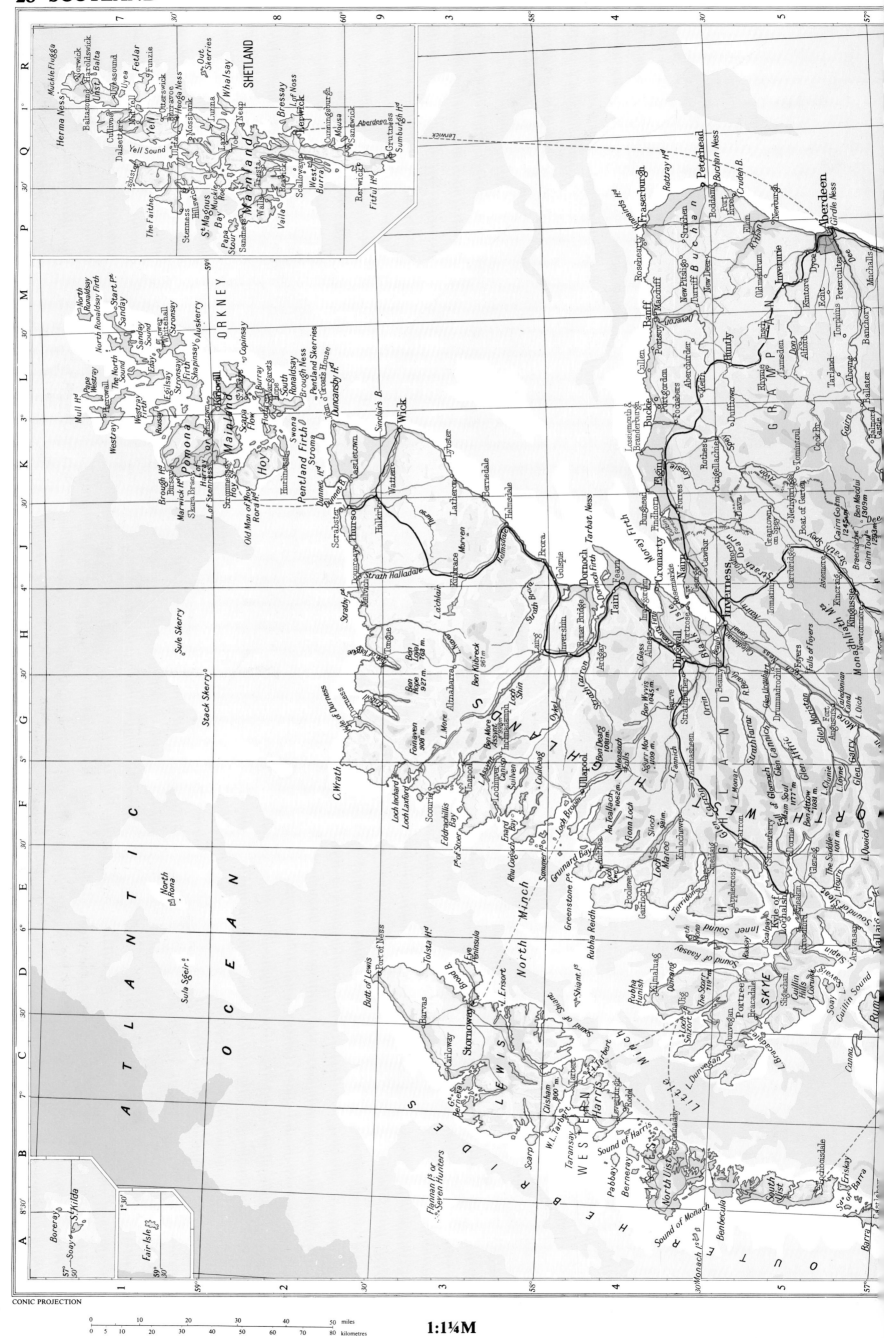

CONIC PROJECTION

0   10   20   30   40   50 miles
0 5 10 20 30 40 50 60 70 80 kilometres

1:1¼M

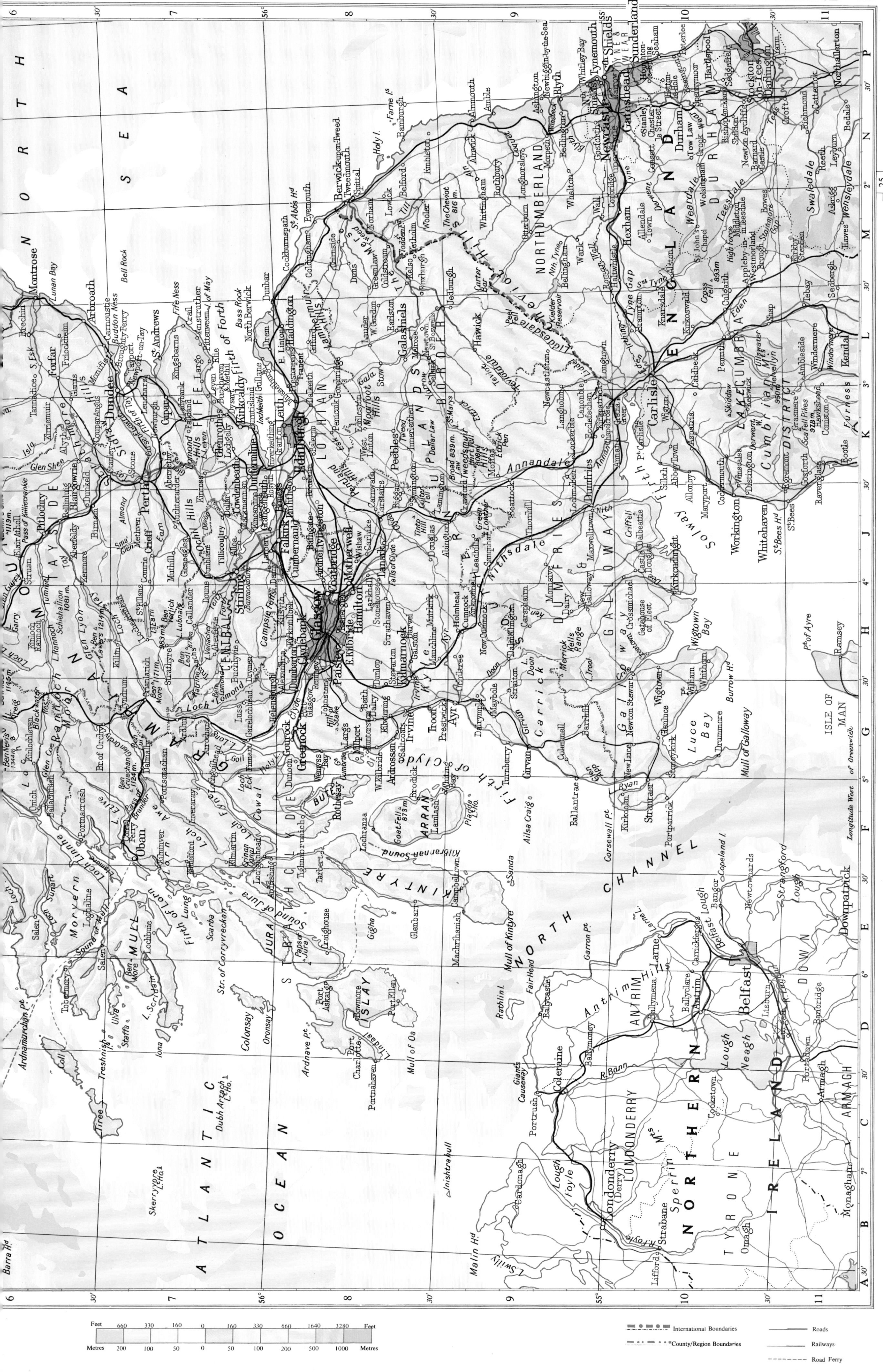

NORTH SEA

ATLANTIC OCEAN

NORTH CHANNEL

Major regions/labels:
GRAMPIAN MOUNTAINS · MOUNTAINS · CENTRAL LOWLANDS · SOUTHERN UPLANDS · BORDERS · LOTHIAN · FIFE · TAYSIDE · STRATHCLYDE · DUMFRIES & GALLOWAY · AYRSHIRE · KINTYRE · ARRAN · BUTE · MULL · ISLAY · JURA · MORVERN

NORTHUMBERLAND · DURHAM · CUMBRIA · LAKE DISTRICT · ENGLAND

NORTHERN IRELAND · ANTRIM · DOWN · LONDONDERRY (Derry) · TYRONE · ARMAGH

ISLE OF MAN

Selected place names:
Montrose · Arbroath · Forfar · Brechin · Dundee · Perth · St Andrews · Crail · Anstruther · Leven · Kirkcaldy · Dunfermline · Stirling · Edinburgh · Leith · Musselburgh · Haddington · Dunbar · North Berwick · Berwick-upon-Tweed · Eyemouth · Galashiels · Peebles · Hawick · Jedburgh · Kelso · Melrose · Selkirk · Lanark · Motherwell · Hamilton · Coatbridge · Airdrie · Cumbernauld · Falkirk · Glasgow · Paisley · Greenock · Gourock · Dunoon · Rothesay · Helensburgh · E. Kilbride · Kilmarnock · Ayr · Prestwick · Troon · Irvine · Ardrossan · Girvan · Stranraer · Newton Stewart · Wigtown · Dumfries · Lockerbie · Moffat · Thornhill · Sanquhar · Cumnock · Oban · Inveraray · Lochgilphead · Tarbert · Campbeltown · Port Ellen · Port Askaig · Bowmore · Tobermory · Iona · Colonsay

Carlisle · Penrith · Keswick · Windermere · Kendal · Workington · Whitehaven · St Bees · Maryport · Cockermouth · Newcastle · Gateshead · Sunderland · Durham · Hexham · Alnwick · Morpeth · Blyth · Berwick · Darlington · Stockton · Hartlepool · Bishop Auckland · Barnard Castle · Richmond · Appleby · Kirkby Stephen

Belfast · Lisburn · Bangor · Larne · Carrickfergus · Ballymena · Coleraine · Portrush · Londonderry (Derry) · Strabane · Omagh · Armagh · Newtownards · Downpatrick · Antrim · Ballymoney

Water features:
Firth of Forth · Firth of Tay · Firth of Clyde · Solway Firth · Luce Bay · Wigtown Bay · Loch Lomond · Loch Awe · Loch Fyne · Loch Linnhe · Loch Ness · Sound of Jura · Kilbrannan Sound · R. Tweed · R. Clyde · R. Tyne · R. Tees · Lough Neagh · Lough Foyle · Belfast Lough · Strangford Lough

Peaks:
Ben Nevis 1344 m · The Cheviot 816 m · Merrick 843 m · Goatfell 875 m · Scafell Pikes 978 m · Skiddaw 931 m · Cross Fell 893 m · Broad Law 839 m · Dollar Law 817 m

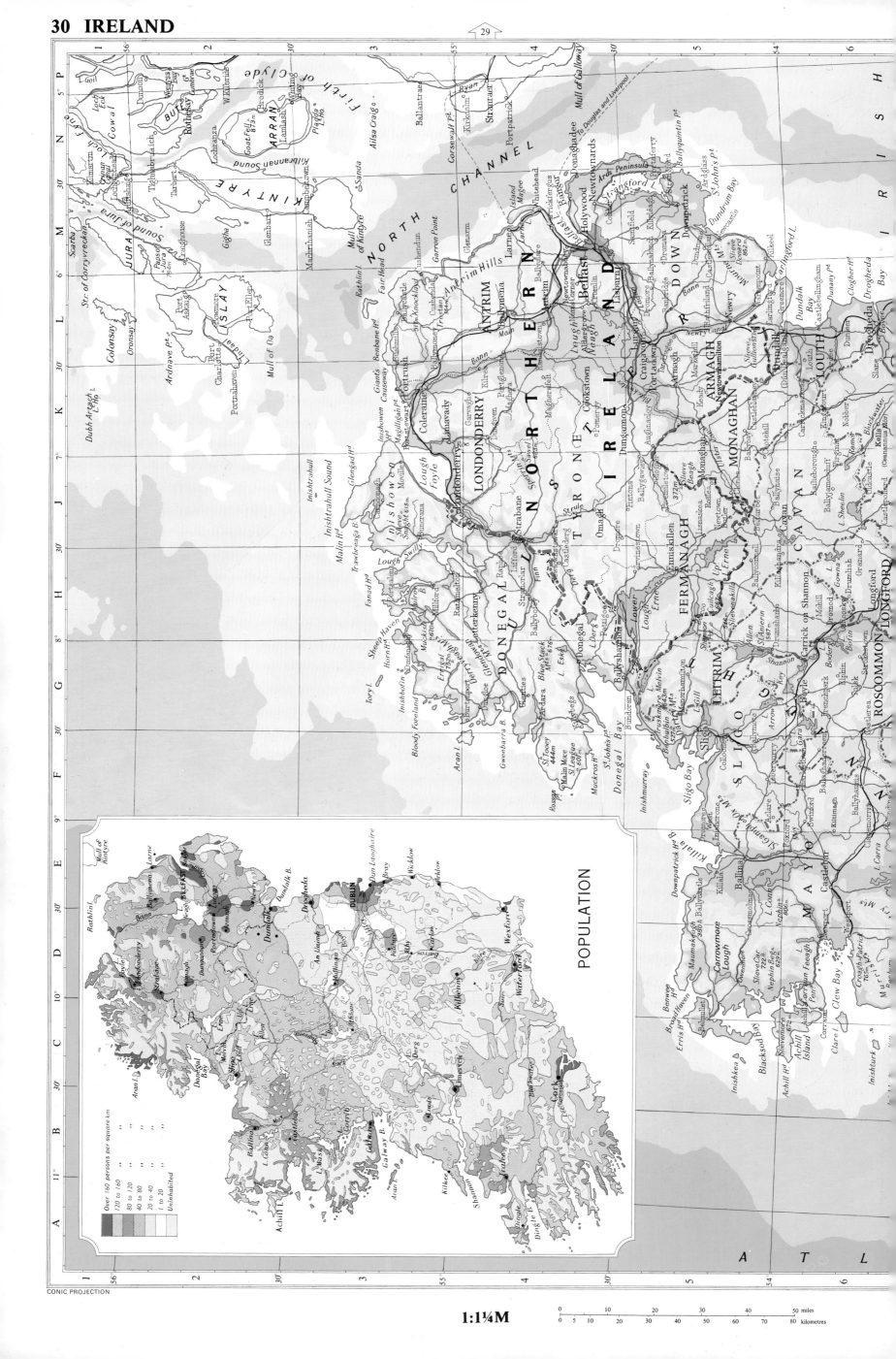

CONIC PROJECTION

1:1¼M

Feet 660 330 160 0 160 330 660 1640 3280 Feet

Metres 200 100 50 0 50 100 200 500 1000 Metres

International Boundaries   Roads

Administrative Boundaries   Railways

International Airports   Road Ferries

NORTH SEA

NETHERLANDS

BELGIUM

FRANCE

LUXEMBOURG (LUXEMBOURG)

CONIC PROJECTION

1:1¼M

	miles
0 10 20 30 miles	
0 5 10 20 30 40 50 kilometres	

International Boundaries — Roads
State — Railways
International Airports — Road/Rail Ferry

Feet 80 0 65 330 660
Metres 25 0 20 100

NIC PROJECTION

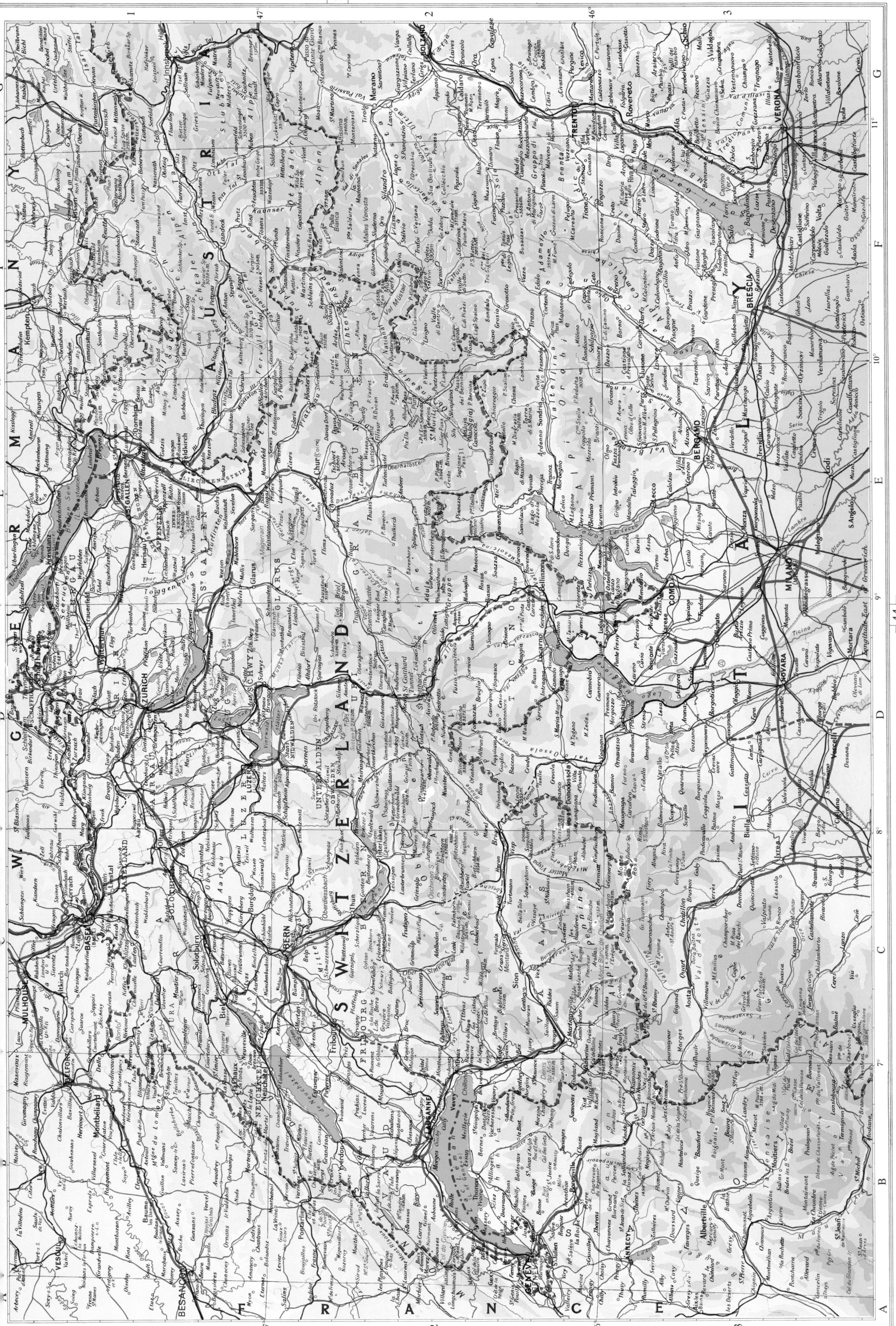

1:1¼M

0	10	20	30	40	50 miles
0	5 10	20	30	40	50	60	70	80 kilometres

Feet 0 330 660 1640 3280 6560 9840 13120 Feet

Metres 0 100 200 500 1000 2000 3000 4000 Metres

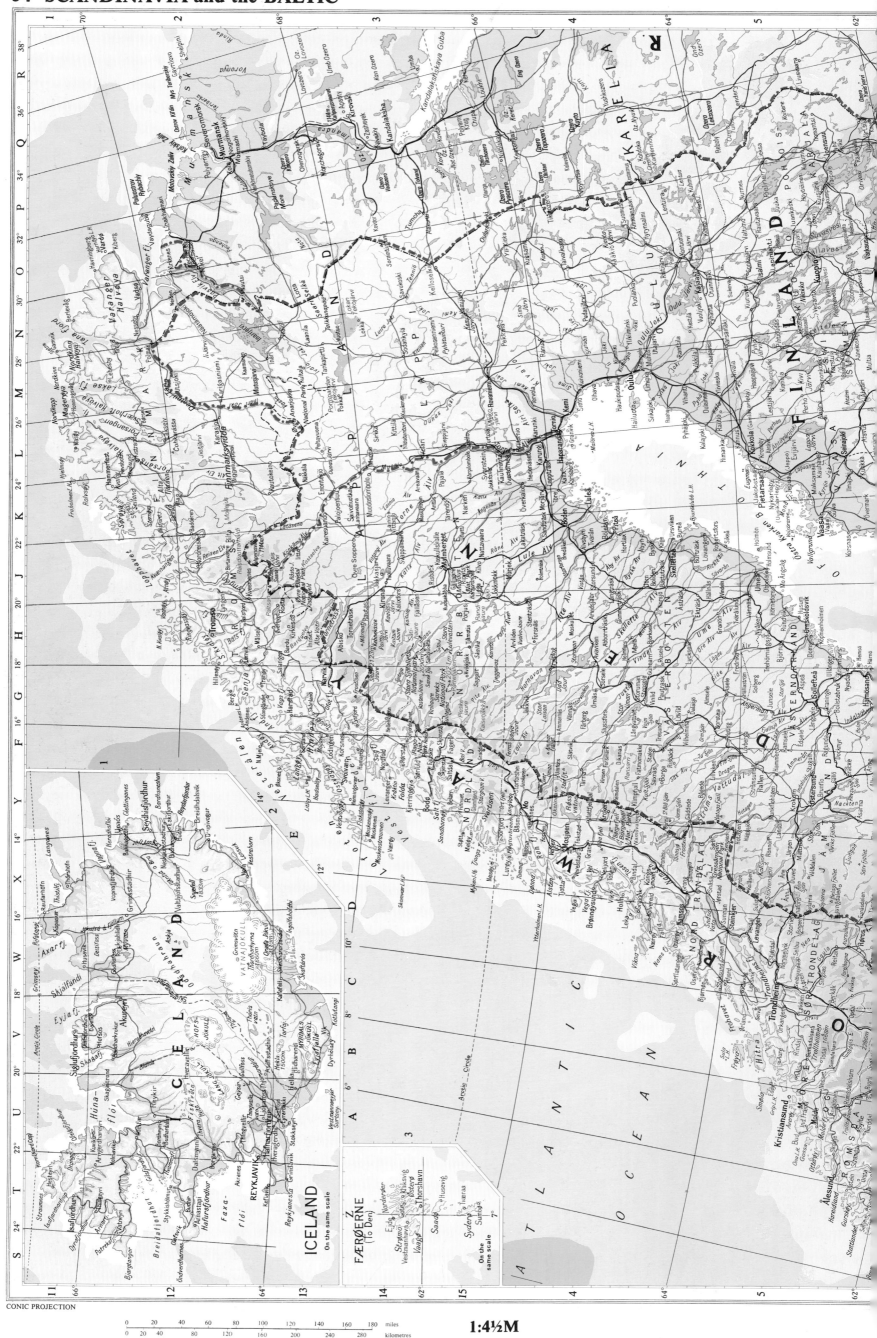

CONIC PROJECTION

1:4½M

ICELAND
On the same scale

FÆRØERNE
(To Den)

On the
same scale

| 0 | 20 | 40 | 60 | 80 | 100 | 120 | 140 | 160 | 180 miles |
| 0 | 20 | 40 | 80 | 120 | 160 | 200 | 240 | 280 | kilometres |

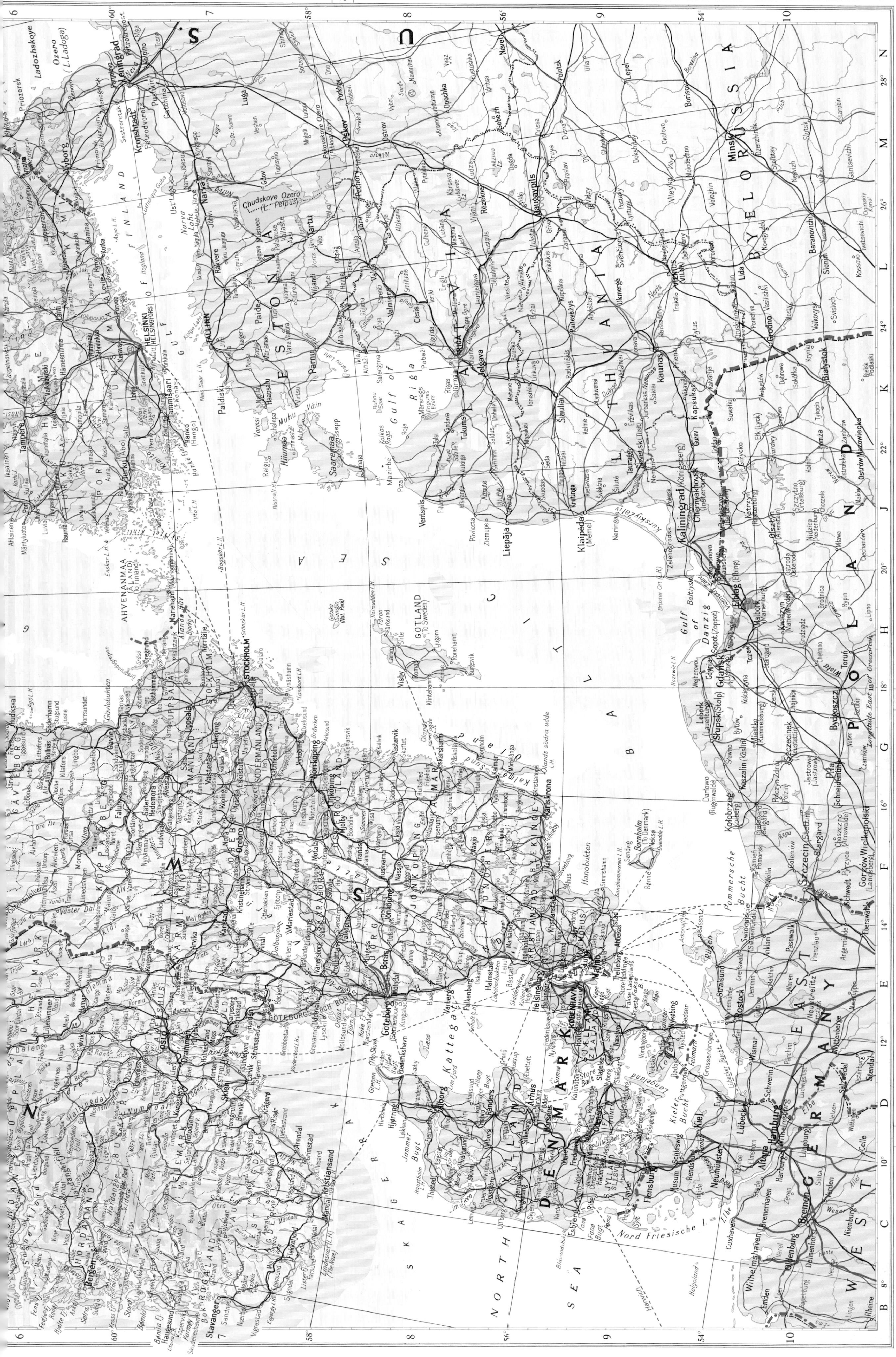

37

36

Feet 6560 660 160 0 330 660 1640 3280 6560 Feet

Metres 2000 200 50 0 100 200 500 1000 2000 Metres

International Boundaries — Roads

State Boundaries — Railways

International Airports ----- Road/Rail Ferry

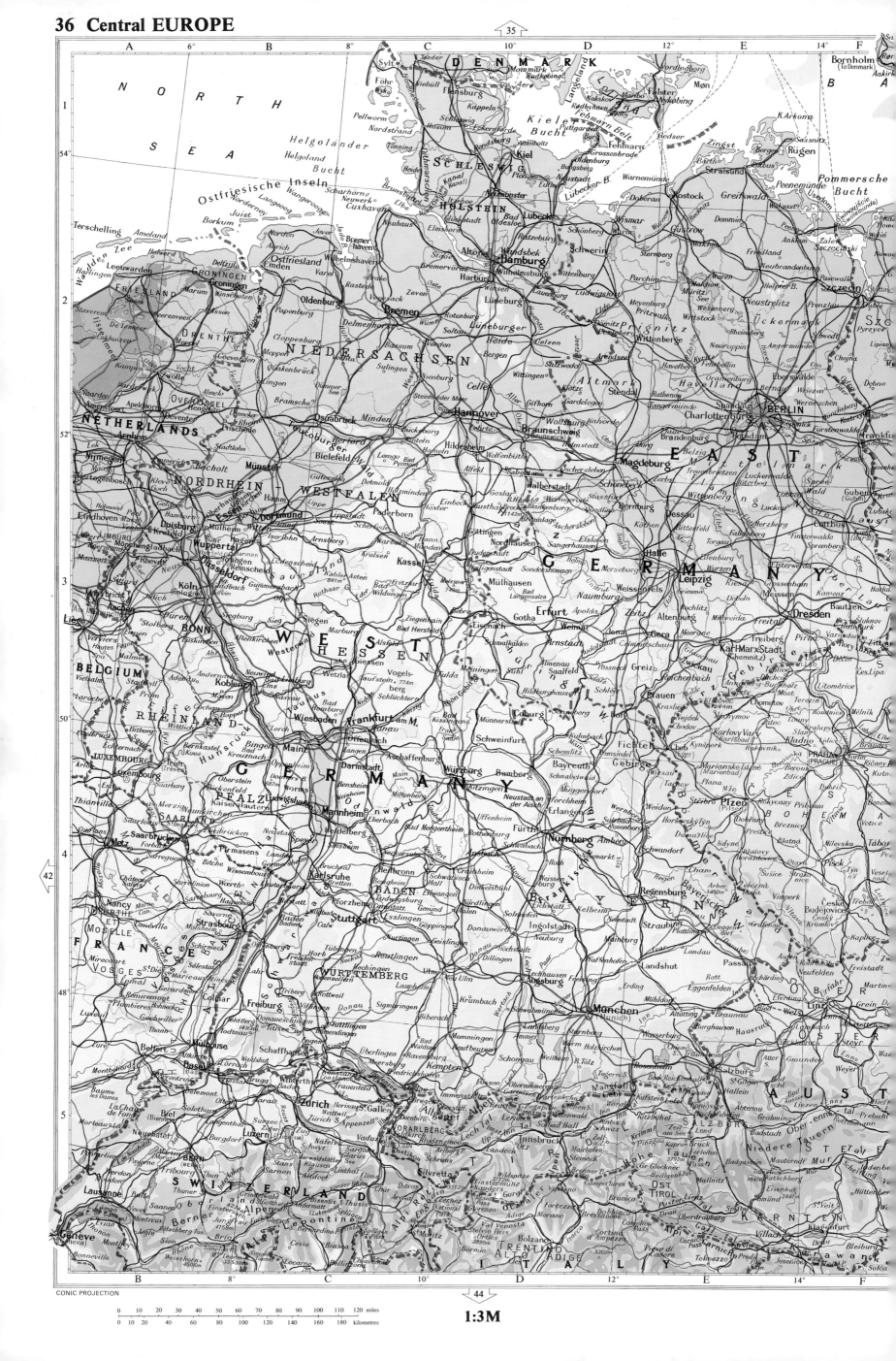

CONIC PROJECTION

0 10 20 30 40 50 60 70 80 90 100 110 120 miles
0 10 20   40   60   80   100 120 140 160 180 kilometres

Central Europe

Countries and regions: POLAND, U.S.S.R., CZECHOSLOVAKIA, HUNGARY, ROMANIA, BELO-RUSSKAYA S.S.R., UKRAINSKAYA S.S.R.

Selected places (north to south, approximate):

Gulf of Danzig, Gdynia, Gdańsk (Danzig), Elbląg, Słupsk (Stolp), Koszalin (Köslin), Białogard, Kaliningrad (Königsberg), Braniewo, Olsztyn, Suwałki, Grodno, Bydgoszcz, Toruń (Thorn), Grudziądz, Białystok (Belostok), Poznań (Posen), Gniezno, Włocławek, Płock, Warszawa (Warsaw), Siedlce, Brest (Brest-Litovsk), BELO-RUSSKAYA S.S.R., Leszno, Kalisz, Łódź, Łowicz, Radom, Lublin, Kovel', Wrocław (Breslau), Świdnica (Schweidnitz), Opole (Oppeln), Częstochowa, Kielce, Tarnobrzeg, Zamość, Vladimir Volynskiy, Lvov (Lemberg), KATOWICE, Kraków (Cracow), Tarnów, Rzeszów, Przemyśl, UKRAINSKAYA S.S.R., Ostrava, Olomouc, Brno (Brünn), Bielsko-Biała, Nowy Sącz, Sanok, Drogobych, Zilina, Tatry, Poprad, Prešov, Košice, Uzhgorod, Mukachevo, WIEN (VIENNA), Bratislava, Nitra, Lučenec, Miskolc, Satu Mare, MARAMURES, Sopron, Szombathely, BUDAPEST, Kecskemét, Szolnok, Debrecen, Oradea (Grosswardein), ROMANIA, HUNGARY, Balaton, Szeged, Békéscsaba, Hódmezővásárhely, Cluj (Klausenburg)

Scale bar:

Feet	100	0	330	660	1640	3280	6560	9840	13120	Feet
Metres	50	0	100	200	500	1000	2000	3000	4000	Metres

Legend:

International Boundaries ——— Railways

Administrative Boundaries ——— Roads

International Airports - - - - Road/Rail Ferry

Lublin Regional Capitals

BONNE'S PROJECTION

| 0 | | 100 | | miles |
| 0 | 100 | 200 | 300 | kilometres |

1:10M

CONIC PROJECTION

0 10 20 30 40 50 60 70 80 90 100 110 120 miles

0 10 20 40 60 80 100 120 140 160 180 kilometres

1:3M

Golfe du Lion
(Gulf of Lions)

Golfo de Valencia

ISLAS BALEARES
(BALEARIC ISLANDS)

Mallorca (Majorca)

Menorca (Minorca)

Ibiza (Iviza)

Formentera

MEDITERRANEAN SEA

FRANCE

PYRENEES

ANDORRA

Barcelona

Valencia

Zaragoza

Murcia

Cartagena

Alicante

ALGERIA

MOROCCO

Str. of Gibraltar

Gibraltar (UK)

Ceuta (Sp)

Melilla (Sp)

Er-Rif

On the same scale

Feet	6560	660	160	0	330	660	1640	3280	6560	9840	Feet
Metres	2000	200	50	0	100	200	500	1000	2000	3000	Metres

International Boundaries
State Boundaries
International Airports
Roads
Railways
Road

CONIC PROJECTION

1:3M

| 0 | 10 | 20 | 30 | 40 | 50 | 60 | 70 | 80 | 90 | 100 | 110 | 120 miles |

| 0 | 10 | 20 | 40 | 60 | 80 | 100 | 120 | 140 | 160 | 180 kilometres |

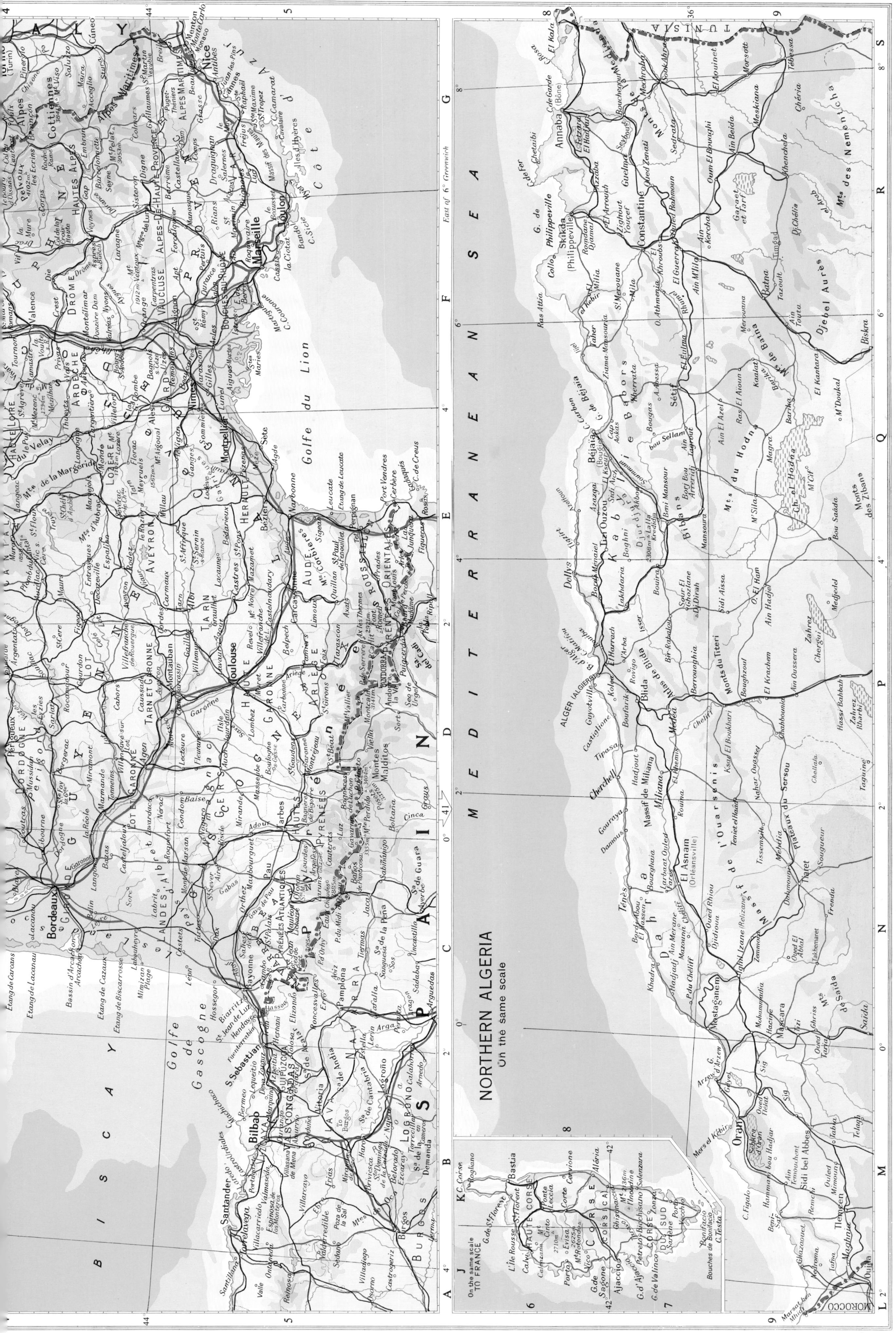

NORTHERN ALGERIA
On the same scale

MEDITERRANEAN SEA

Golfe du Lion

Golfe de Gascogne

BISCAY

FRANCE

SPAIN

ITALY

MOROCCO

TUNISIA

East of 6° Greenwich

Major places (France):
Nice · Antibes · Cannes · Marseille · Toulon · Montpellier · Nîmes · Béziers · Narbonne · Perpignan · Carcassonne · Toulouse · Montauban · Bordeaux · Agen · Valence · Pau · Tarbes · Bayonne · Biarritz

Regions/Departments: ALPES MARITIMES · HAUTE-PROVENCE · VAUCLUSE · DROME · ARDECHE · AVEYRON · TARN · HAUTE GARONNE · GERS · LOT ET GARONNE · LANDES · DORDOGNE · GIRONDE · PYRENEES ATLANTIQUES · HAUTES PYRENEES · ARIEGE · AUDE · HERAULT · GARD · LOT

Spain: Bilbao · S. Sebastian · Santander · Burgos · Pamplona · Logroño · GUIPUZCOA · NAVARRA · ALAVA

Algeria (Northern): ALGER (ALGIERS) · Oran · Constantine · Annaba (Bône) · Skikda (Philippeville) · Bejaia (Bougie) · Philippeville · Blida · Sétif · Batna · Biskra · Guelma · Tizi Ouzou · Médéa · Mostaganem · Mascara · Tlemcen · Tébessa

MEDITERRANEAN SEA

CORSE (Corsica) · Bastia · Ajaccio · Calvi · Corte · Bonifacio

ANDORRA

Scale

Feet	6560	660	160	0	330	660	1640	3280	6560	9840	13120	Feet
Metres	2000	200	50	0	100	200	500	1000	2000	3000	4000	Metres

Land Depression

Legend

International Boundaries
Administrative Boundaries
International Airports
Roads
Railways
Road/Rail Ferry

CONIC PROJECTION

1:3M

| 0 | 10 | 20 | 30 | 40 | 50 | 60 | 70 | 80 | 90 | 100 | 110 | 120 miles |
| 0 | 10 | 20 | 40 | 60 | 80 | 100 | 120 | 140 | 160 | 180 | kilometres |

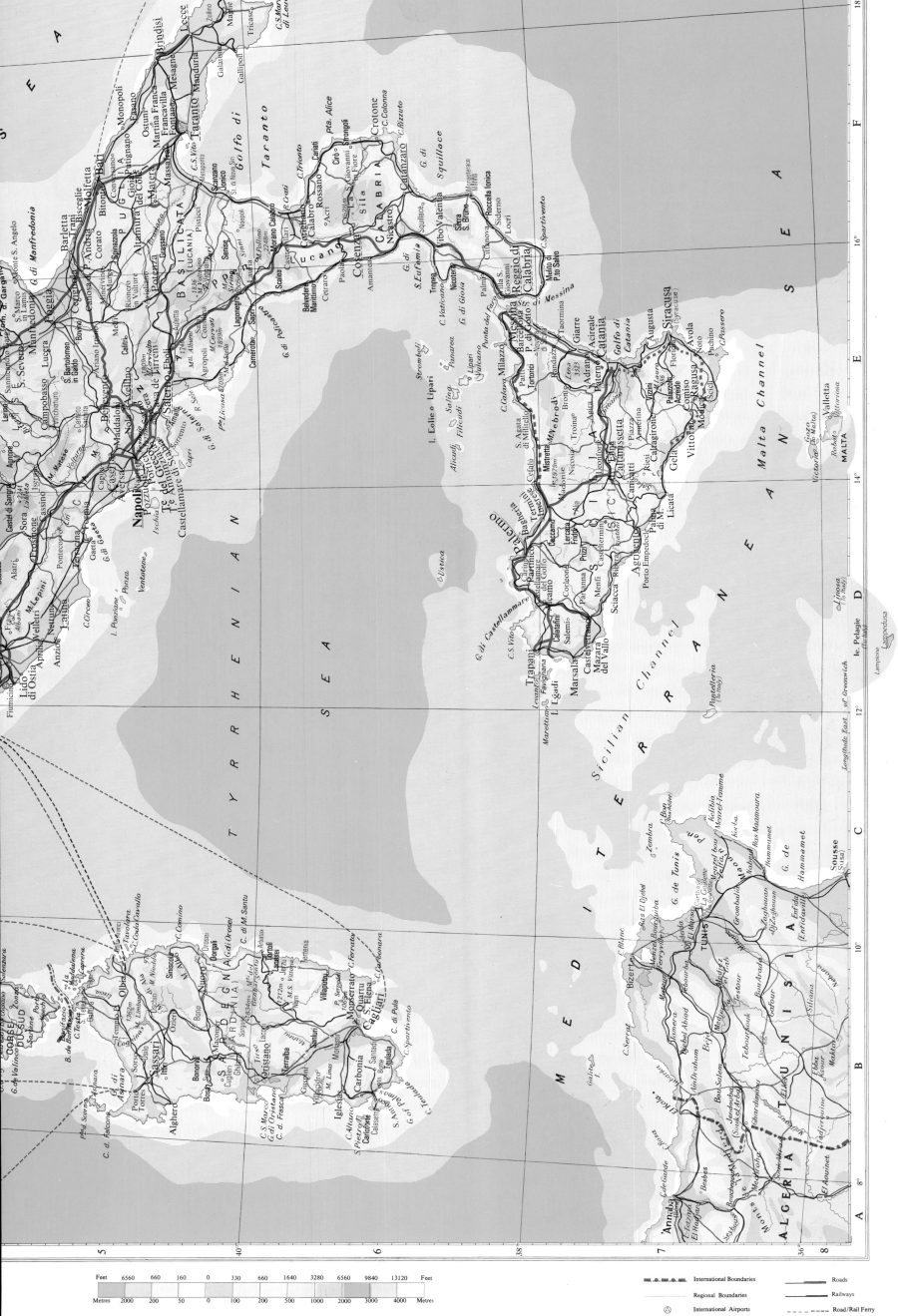

Feet	6560	660	160	0	330	660	1640	3280	6560	9840	13120	Feet
Metres	2000	200	50	0	100	200	500	1000	2000	3000	4000	Metres

International Boundaries — Roads
Regional Boundaries — Railways
International Airports — Road/Rail Ferry

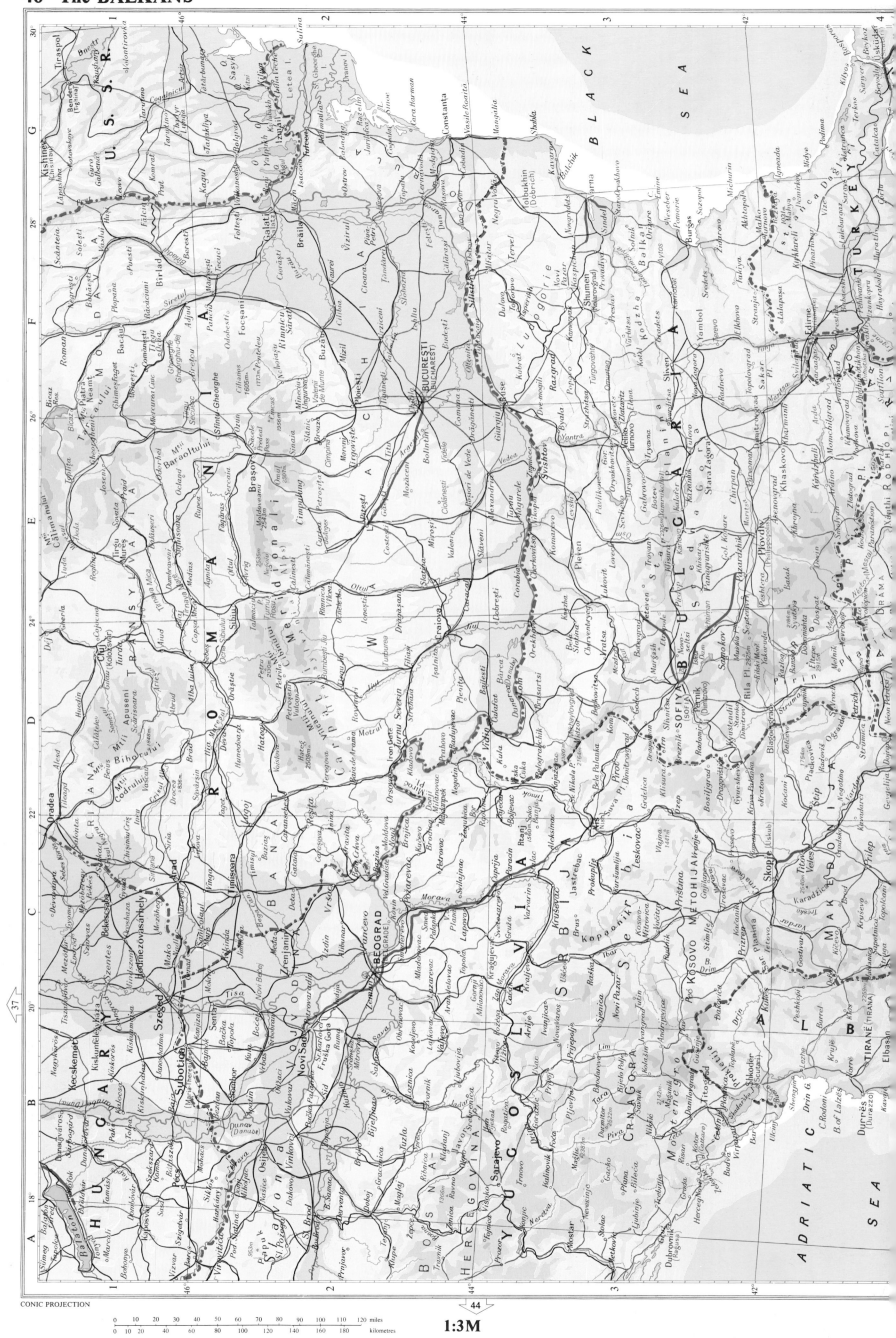

CONIC PROJECTION

| 0 | 10 | 20 | 30 | 40 | 50 | 60 | 70 | 80 | 90 | 100 | 110 | 120 miles |

| 0 | 10 | 20 | 40 | 60 | 80 | 100 | 120 | 140 | 160 | 180 kilometres |

1:3M

Feet	6560	660	160	0	100	660	1640	3280	6560	Feet
Metres	2000	200	50	0	330	200	500	1000	2000	Metres

International Boundaries ----------
Provincial Boundaries ----------
International Airports ⊕
Railways ————
Roads ————
Road/Rail Ferry ----------

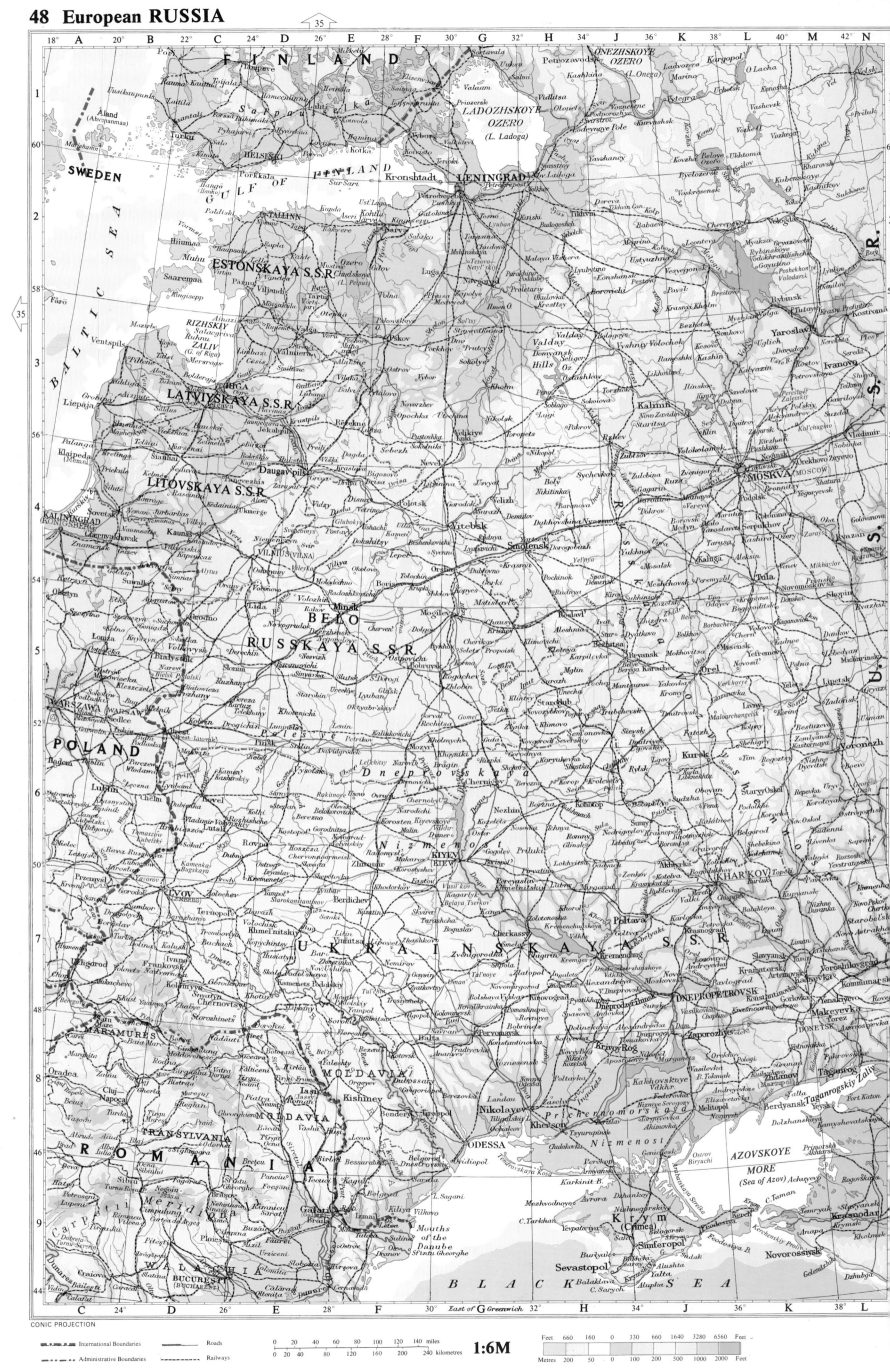

International Boundaries　　　　Roads

Administrative Boundaries　　　Railways

International Airports

0　20　40　60　80　100　120　140 miles
0　20　40　60　80　100　120　160　200　240 kilometres

1:6M

Feet　660　160　0　330　660　1640　3280　6560　Feet
Metres　200　50　0　100　200　500　1000　2000　Feet

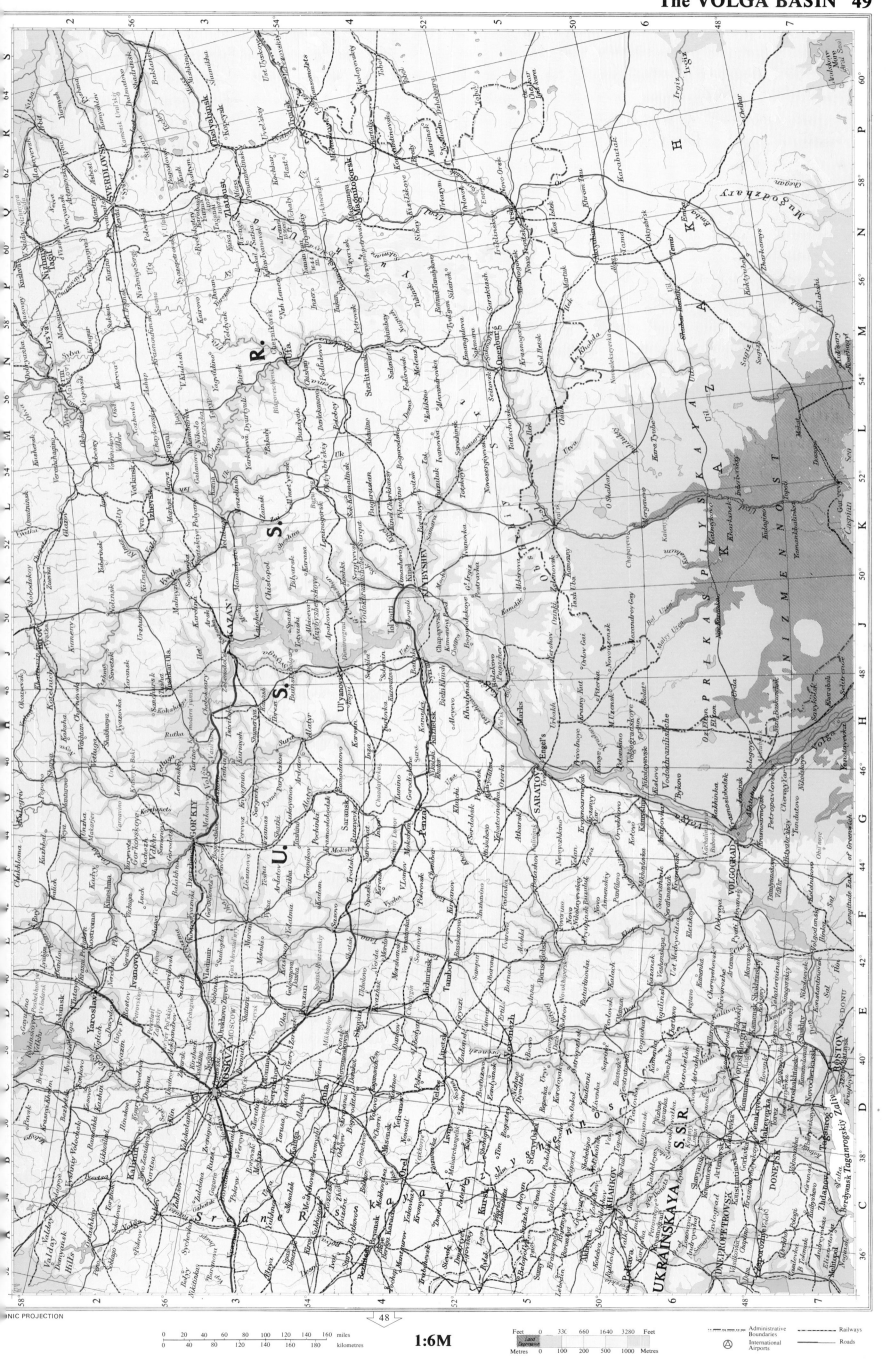

1:6M

0	20	40	60	80	100	120	140	160 miles
0	40	80	120	160	180 kilometres

| Feet | 0 | 330 | 660 | 1640 | 3280 | Feet |
| Metres | 0 | 100 | 200 | 500 | 1000 | Metres |

Administrative Boundaries ---

International Airports

Railways ----

Roads —

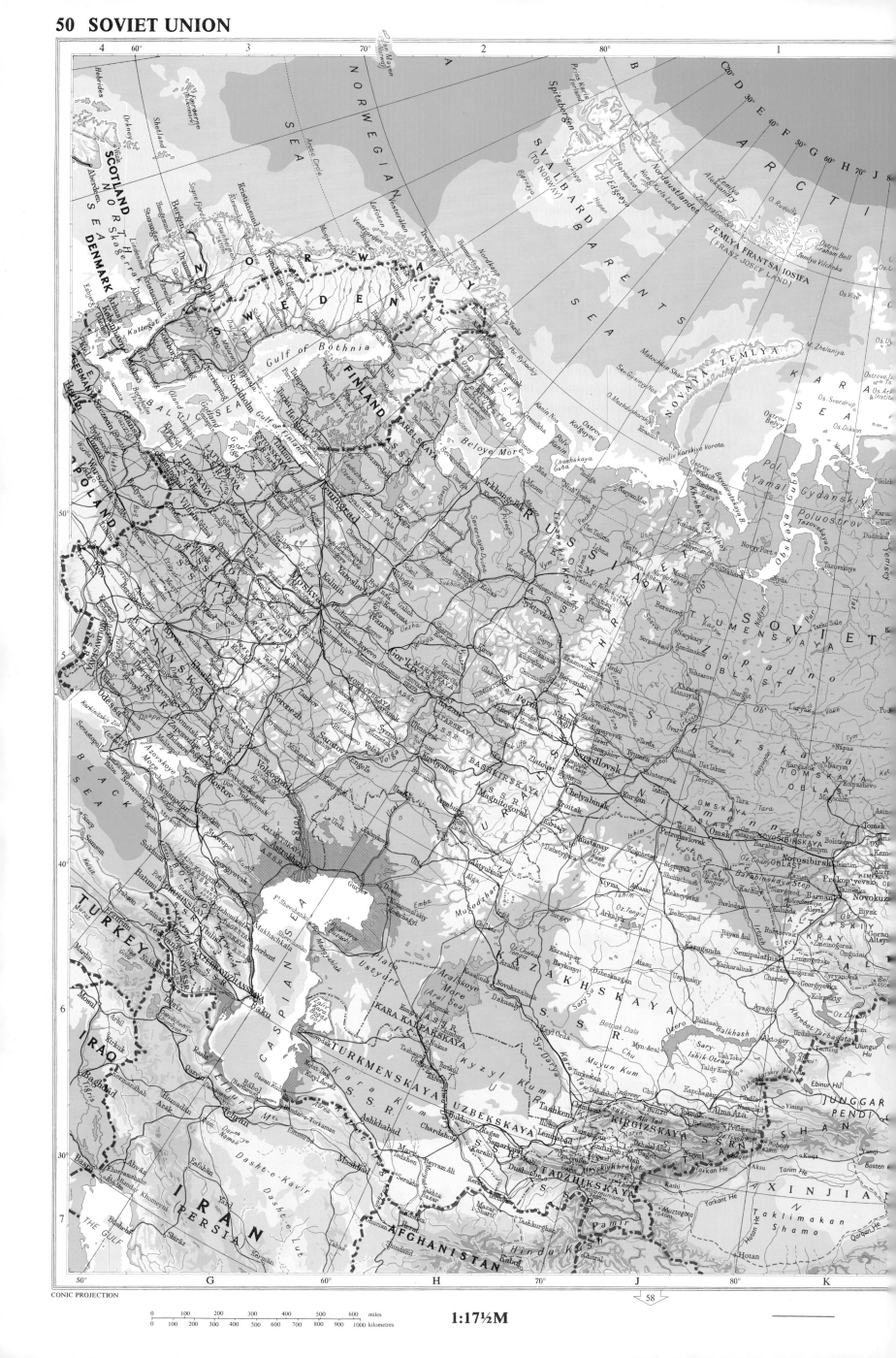

CONIC PROJECTION

1:17½M

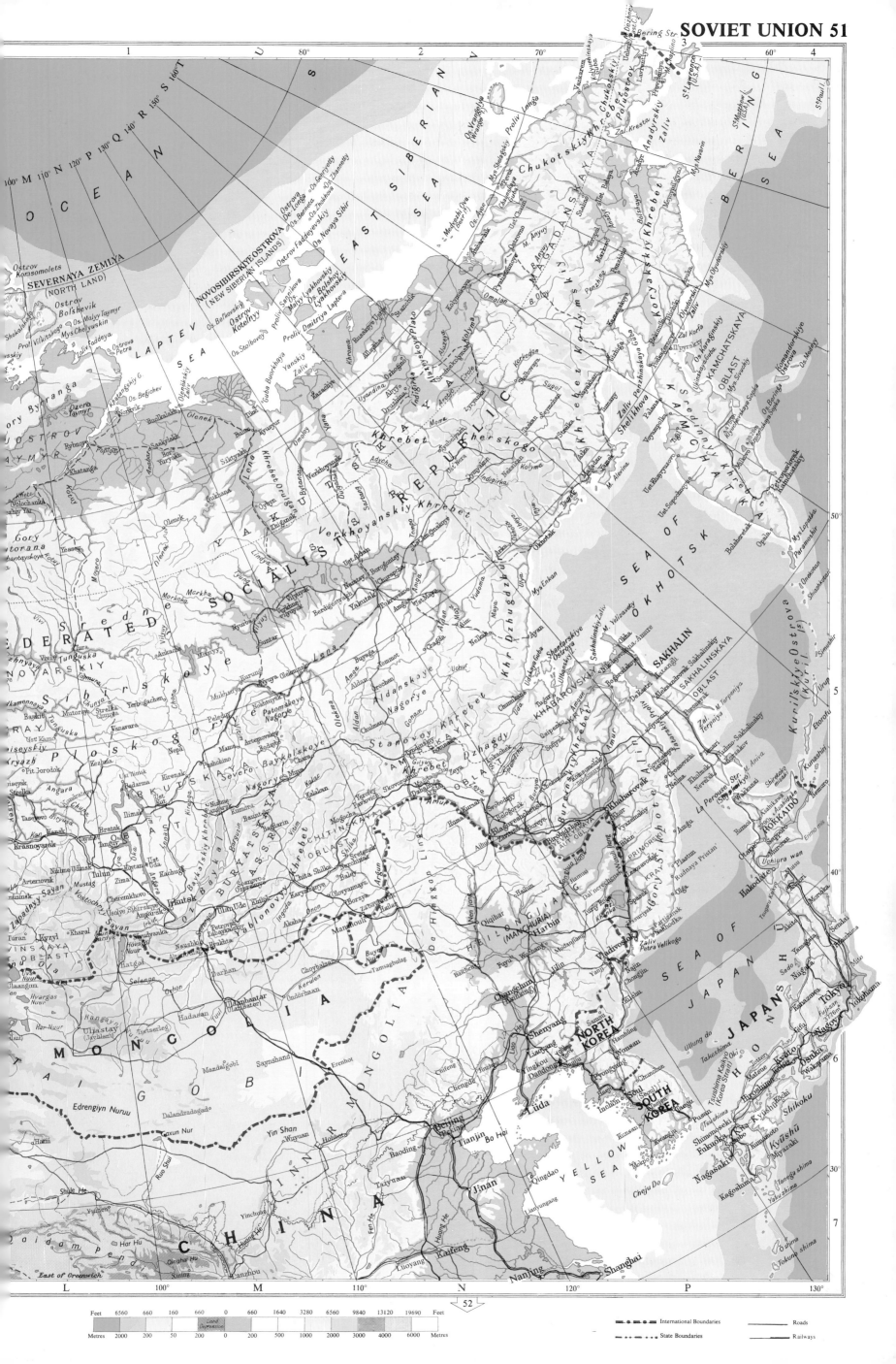

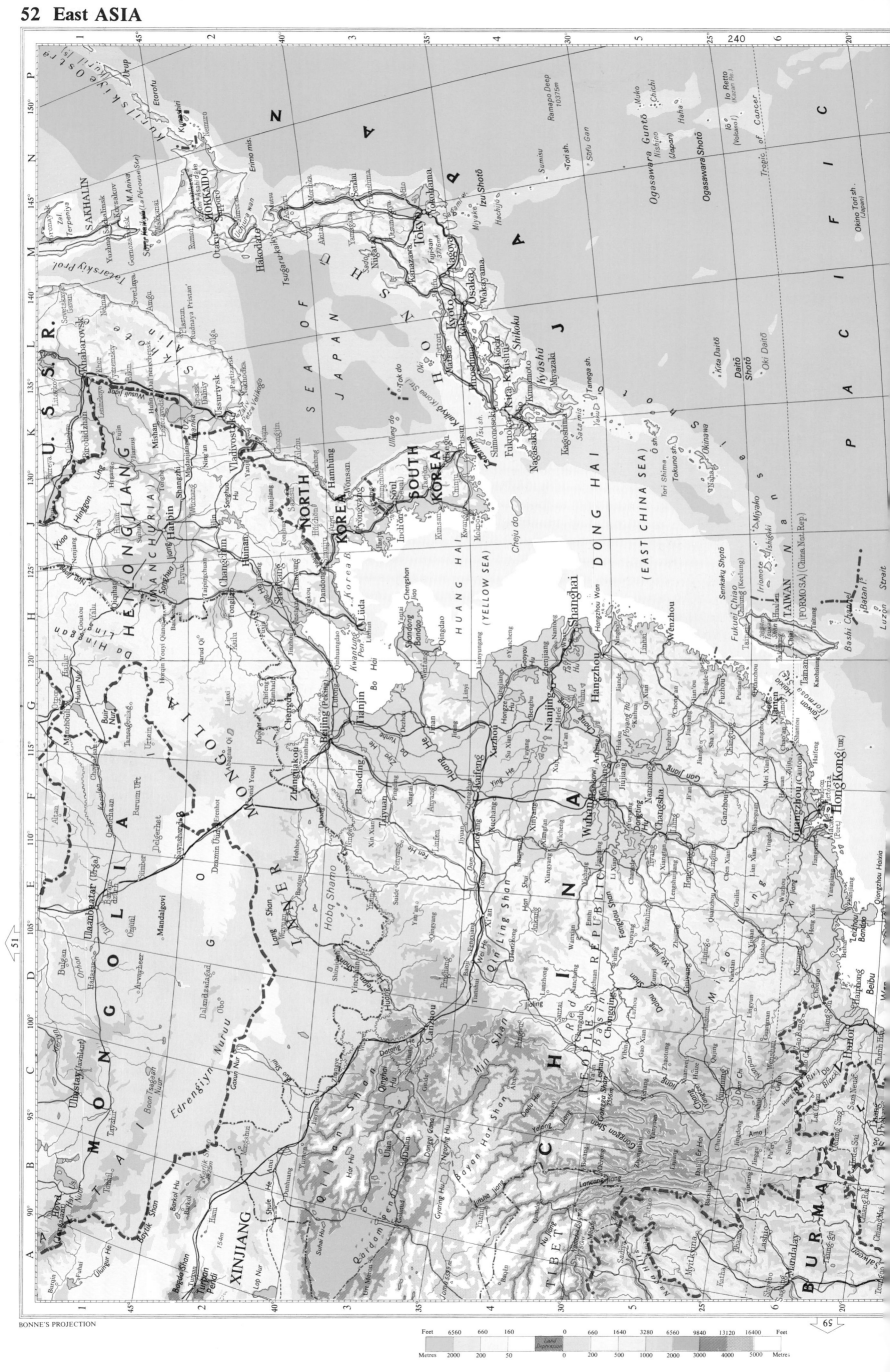

Feet 6560 660 160 0 660 1640 3280 6560 9840 13120 16400 Feet

Metres 2000 200 50 0 200 500 1000 2000 3000 4000 5000 Metres

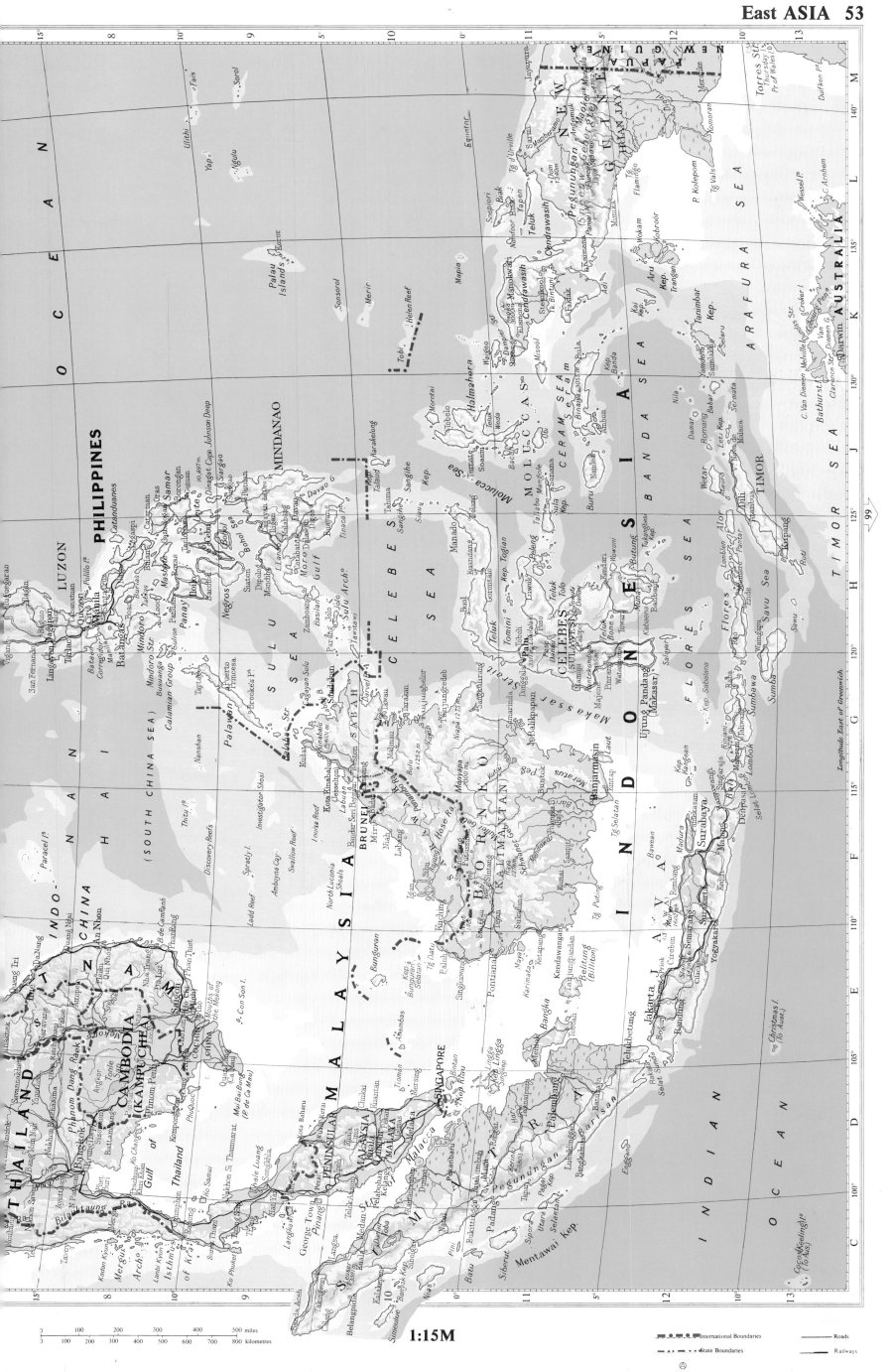

PHILIPPINES

THAILAND

CAMBODIA (KAMPUCHEA)

VIETNAM

INDO-CHINA

MALAYSIA

PENINSULAR MALAYSIA (MALAYA)

SINGAPORE

BRUNEI

SABAH

SARAWAK

KALIMANTAN

BORNEO

SUMATRA

JAVA

INDONESIA

LUZON

MINDANAO

PAPUA NEW GUINEA

IRIAN JAYA

AUSTRALIA

SOUTH CHINA SEA

SULU SEA

CELEBES SEA

CELEBES (SULAWESI)

MOLUCCAS

Molucca Sea

CERAM SEA

BANDA SEA

FLORES SEA

Savu Sea

TIMOR SEA

ARAFURA SEA

INDIAN OCEAN

PACIFIC OCEAN

Palau Islands

Hai Nan

NGUYEN (SOUTH CHINA SEA)

1:15M

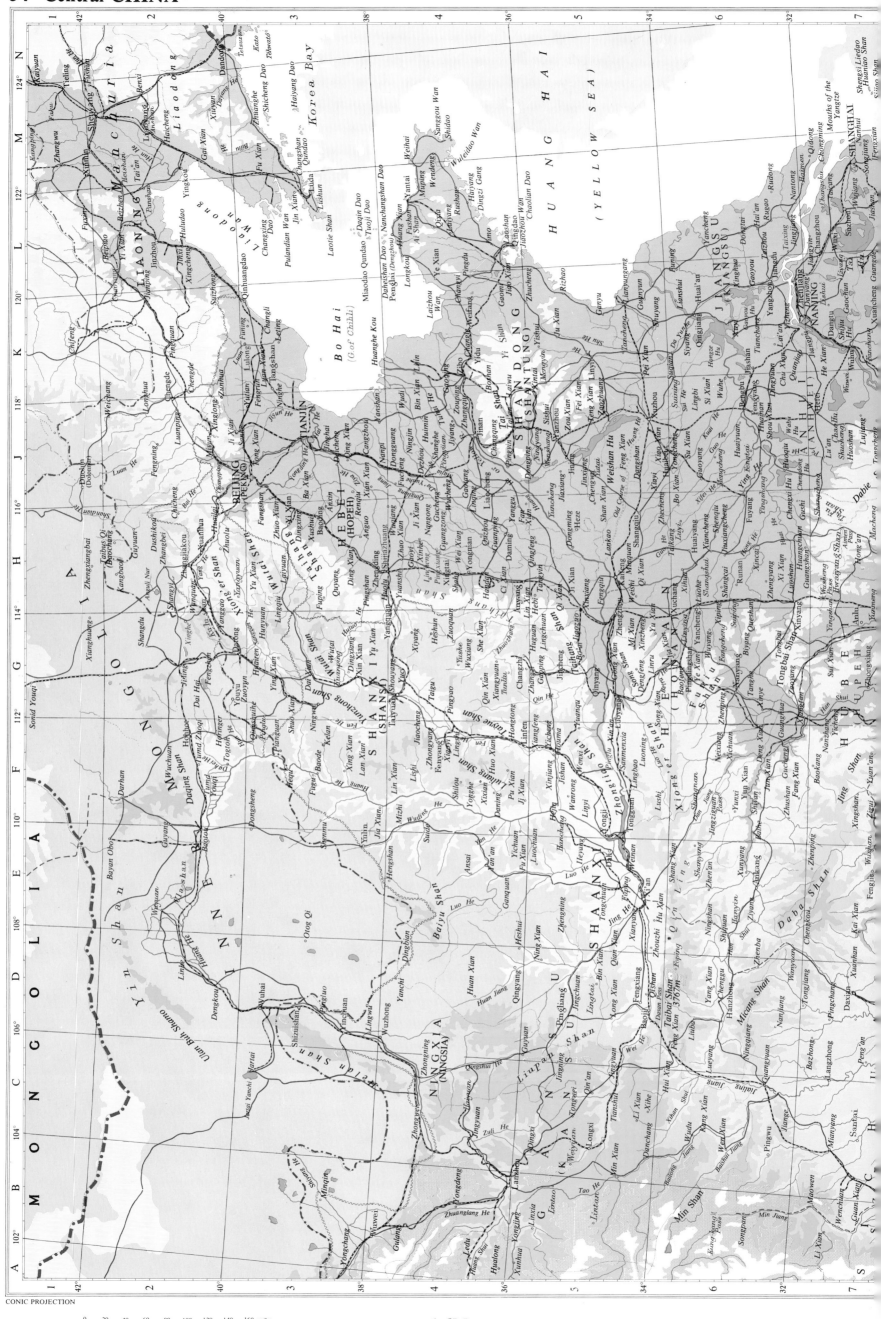

CONIC PROJECTION

0	20	40	60	80	100	120	140	160	miles
0	40	80	120	160	200	240			kilometres

1:6M

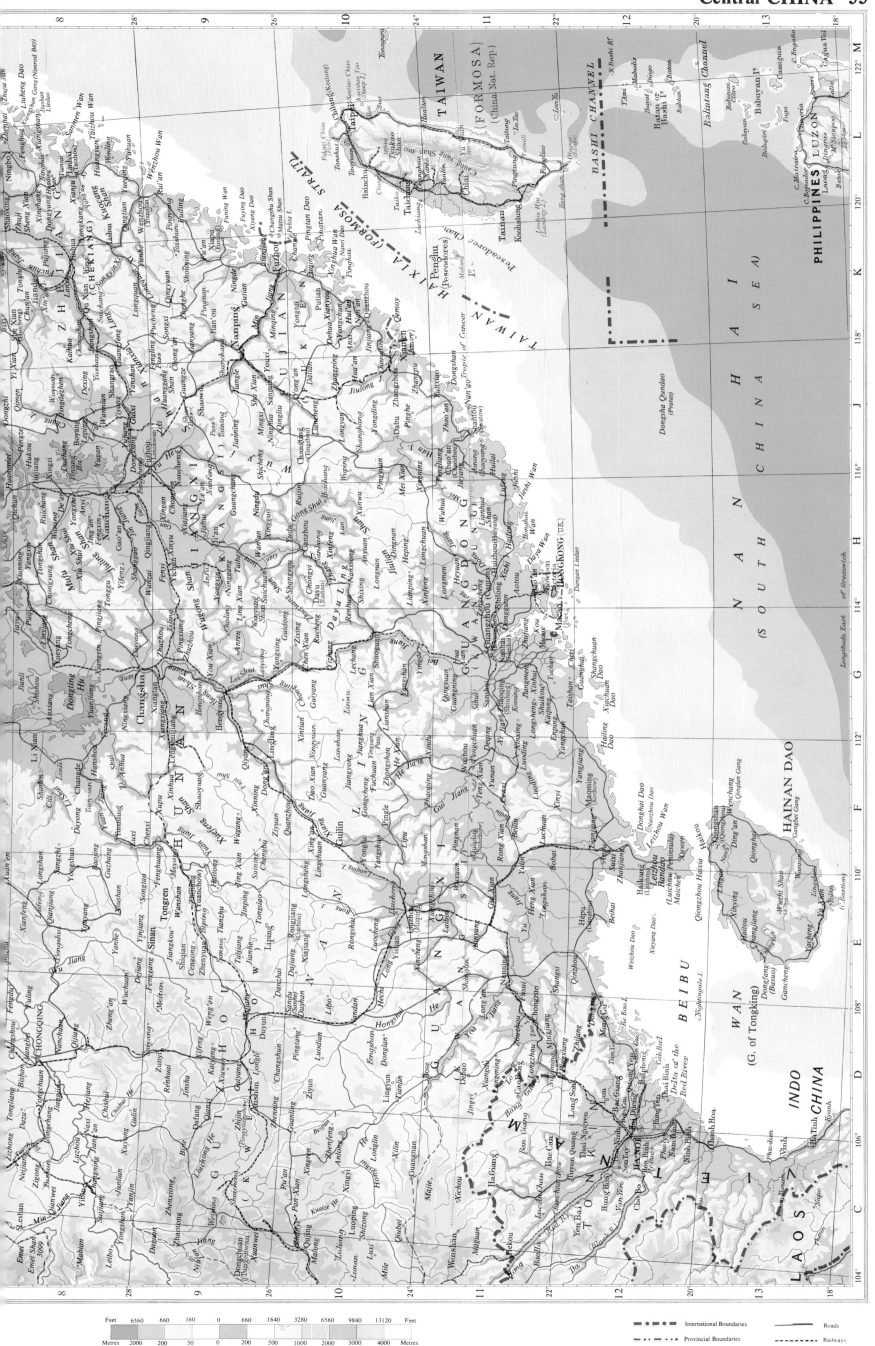

CONIC PROJECTION

		International Boundaries		Roads
		Provincial Boundaries		Railways

⊕ International Airports

0 20 40 60 80 100 120 miles
0 40 80 120 140 180 kilometres

1:6M

Feet 6560 660 16C 0 660 1640 3280 6560 9840 Feet
Metres 2000 200 50 0 200 500 1000 2000 3000 Metres

1:10M

IRAN

AFGHANISTAN

Hindu Kush

Karakoram

N.W. FRONTIER PROVINCE

JAMMU & KASHMIR

Ladakh

HIMACHAL PRADESH

PAKISTAN

BALUCHISTAN

PUNJAB

PUNJAB

HARYANA

DELHI

UTTAR PRADESH

SIND

RAJASTHAN

Thar or Indian Desert

GUJARAT

MADHYA PRADESH

Kathiawar

Satpura Range

Vindhya Ra.

Tropic of Cancer

Mouths of the Indus

Gulf of Kachchh

Gulf of Khambhat

DAMAN (G.D. & D.)

DIU (G.D. & D.)

BOMBAY

MAHARASHTRA

Berar

ARABIAN SEA

ANDHRA PRADESH

Hyderabad

GOA DAMAN & DIU

KARNATAKA

Bangalore

Mysore

Western Ghats

MADRAS

TAMIL NADU

Cherbaniani Reef

Byramgore Reef

Amindivi Islands

Bitra Par

Laccadive Islands

LAKSHADWEEP (to India)

Nine Degree Channel

Minicoy

Eight Degree Channel

KERALA

Cochin

Quilon / Kollam

Trivandrum

Cape Comorin

Gulf of Mannar

SRI LANKA (CEYLON)

Colombo

Galle

CONIC PROJECTION

0   100   200   300   400 miles

0   100   200   300   400   500   600 kilometres

1:10M

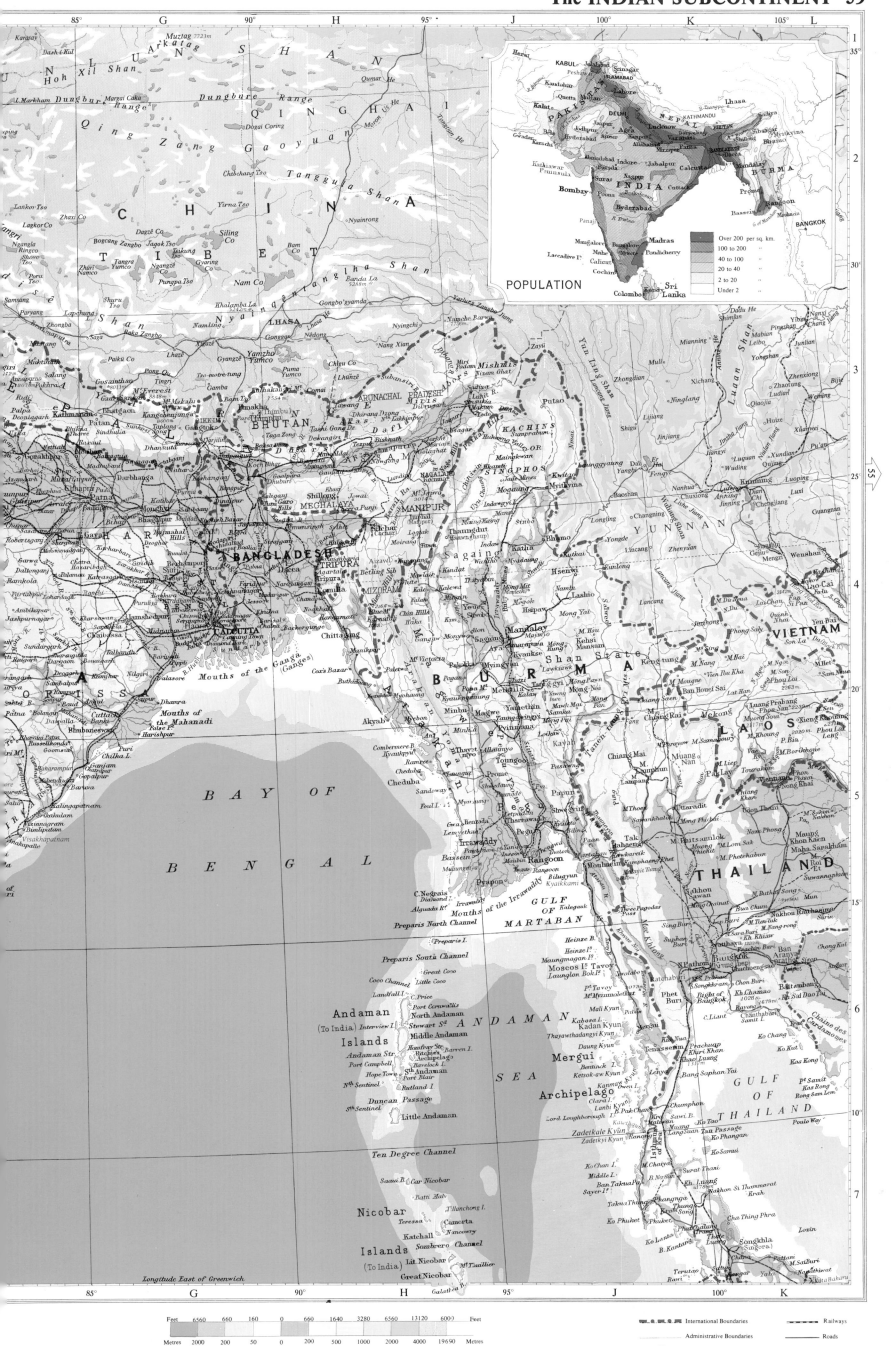

POPULATION

	Over 200 per sq. km.
	100 to 200 "
	40 to 100 "
	20 to 40 "
	2 to 20 "
	Under 2 "

BAY OF BENGAL

Mouths of the Ganga (Ganges)

Mouths of the Mahanadi

CHINA

TIBET

QINGHAI

Qing Zang Gaoyuan

KUN LUN SHAN

Tanggula Shan

LHASA

NEPAL

BHUTAN

BANGLADESH

CALCUTTA

ORISSA

BURMA

THAILAND

LAOS

VIETNAM

YUNNAN

Irrawaddy

Mandalay

Rangoon

GULF OF MARTABAN

Andaman Islands
(To India)

ANDAMAN SEA

Mergui Archipelago

Nicobar Islands
(To India)

Ten Degree Channel

Preparis North Channel

Preparis South Channel

Coco Channel

Duncan Passage

Sombrero Channel

GULF OF THAILAND

Chaîne des Cardamomes

BANGKOK

Feet 6560 660 160 0 660 1640 3280 6560 13120 600J Feet
Metres 2000 200 50 0 200 500 1000 2000 4000 19690 Metres

International Boundaries
Administrative Boundaries
International Airports
Railways
Roads

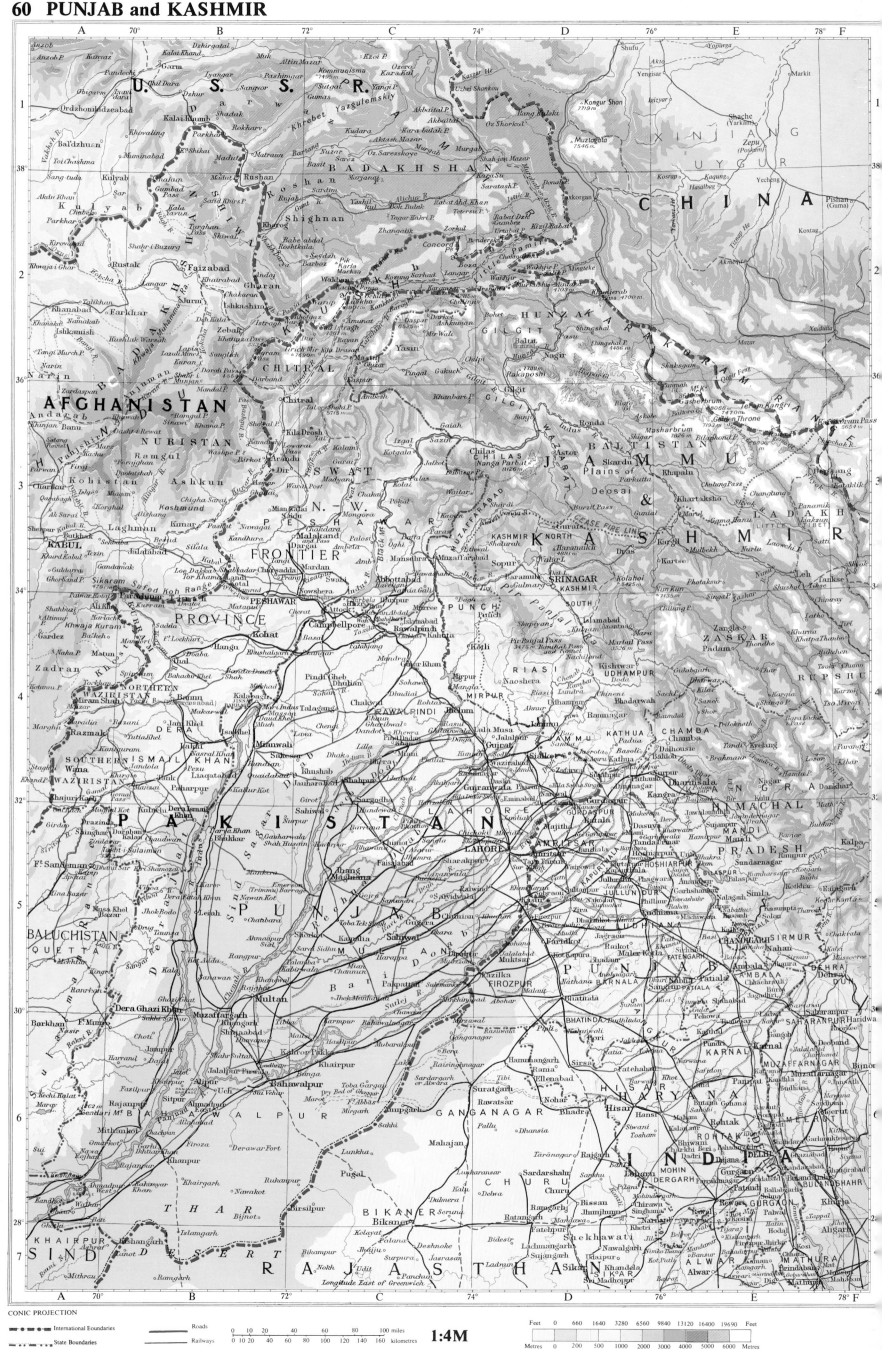

CONIC PROJECTION

International Boundaries

State Boundaries

International Airports

Roads

Railways

1:4M

| 0 | 10 | 20 | 40 | 60 | 80 | 100 miles |

| 0 10 20 | 40 | 60 | 80 | 100 | 120 | 140 | 160 kilometres |

Feet 0 660 1640 3280 6560 9840 13120 16400 19690 Feet

Metres 0 200 500 1000 2000 3000 4000 5000 6000 Metres

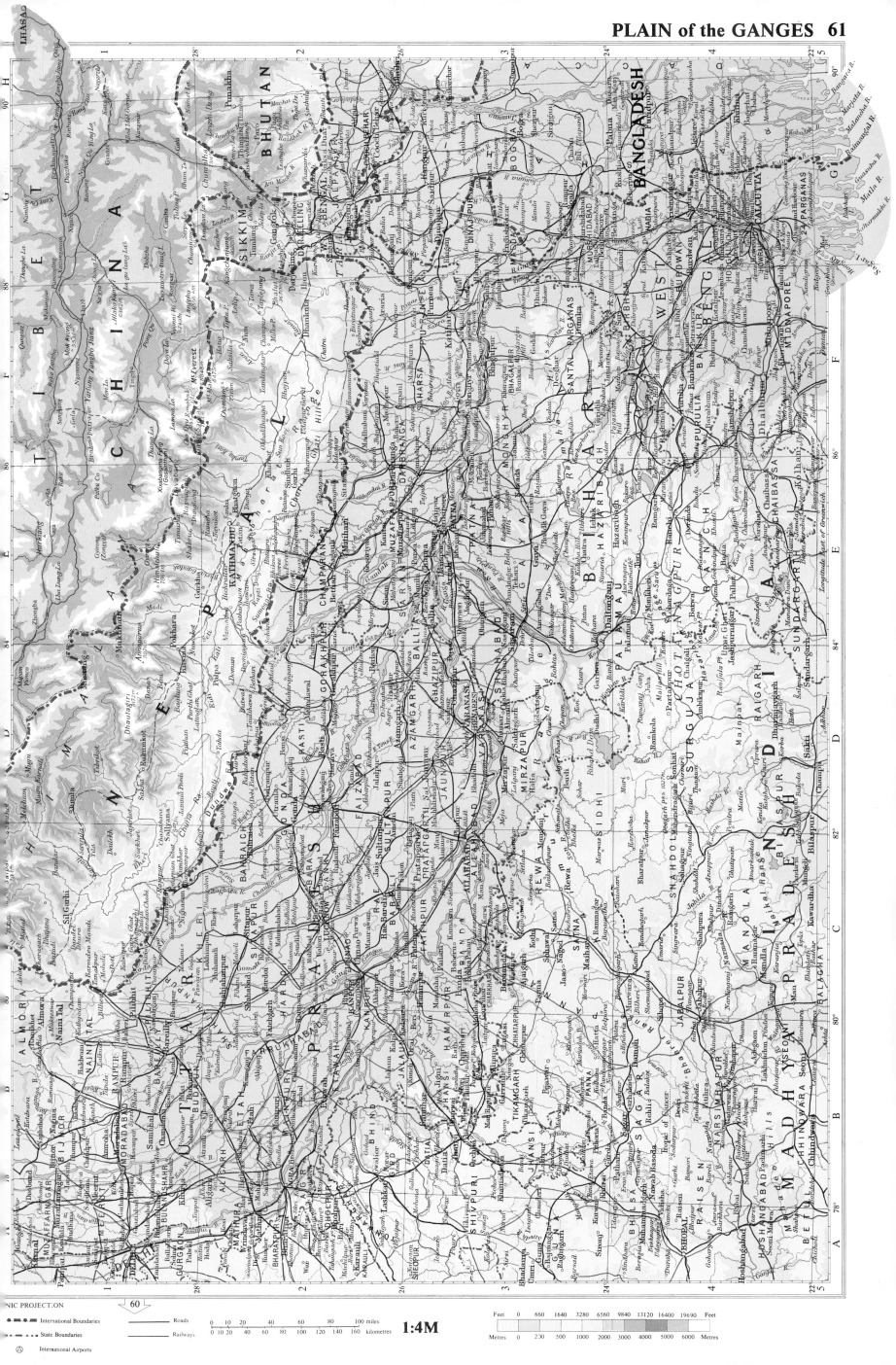

NIC PROJECTION

▬▬●▬▬ International Boundaries

─ ─ ─ ─ State Boundaries

Ⓐ International Airports

Roads

Railways

0 10 20   40   60   80   100 miles
0 20 40 60 80 100 120 140 160 kilometres

1:4M

Feet 0 660 1640 3280 6560 9840 13120 16400 19690 Feet

Metres 0 200 500 1000 2000 3000 4000 5000 6000 Metres

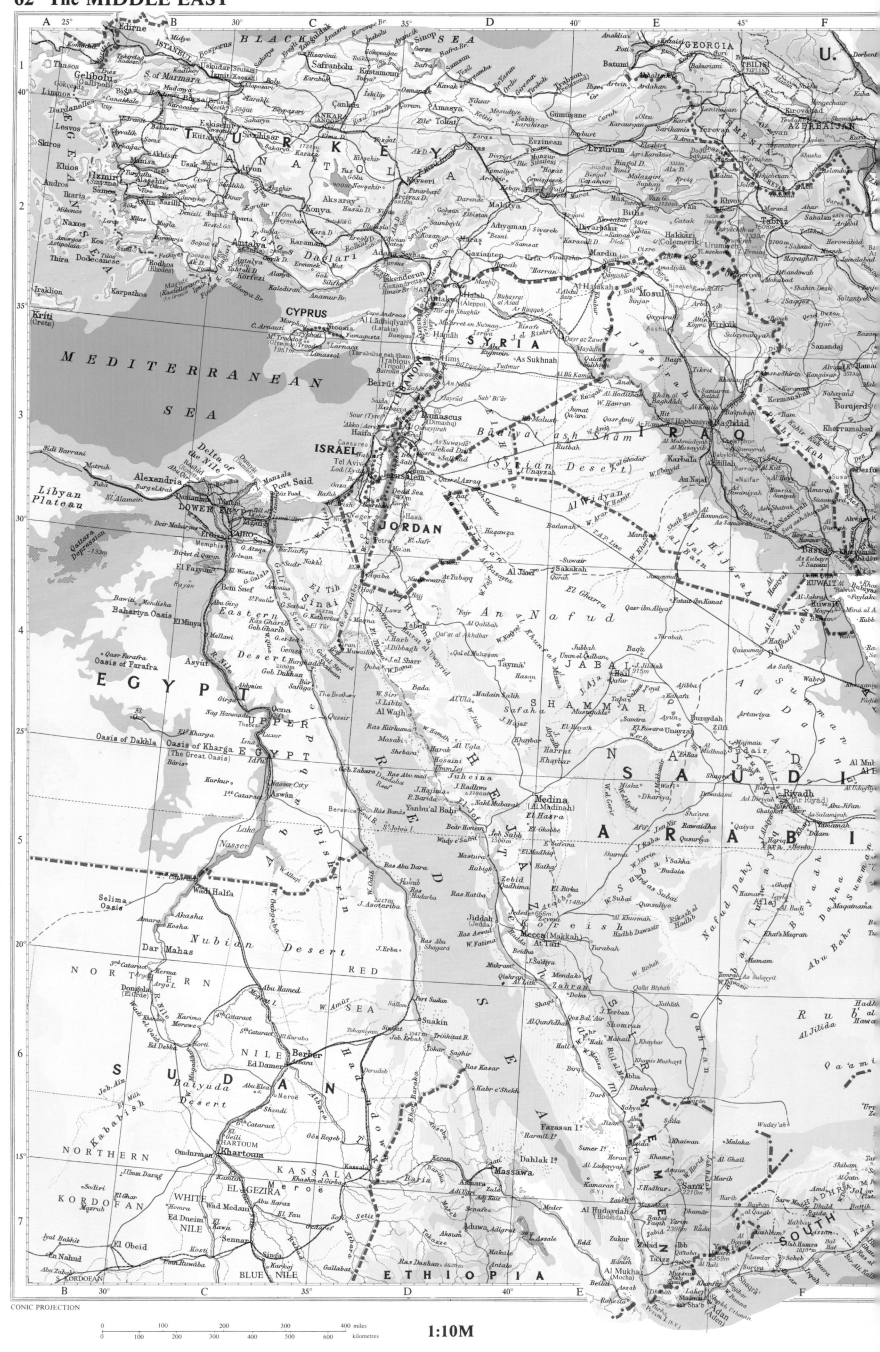

CONIC PROJECTION

1:10M

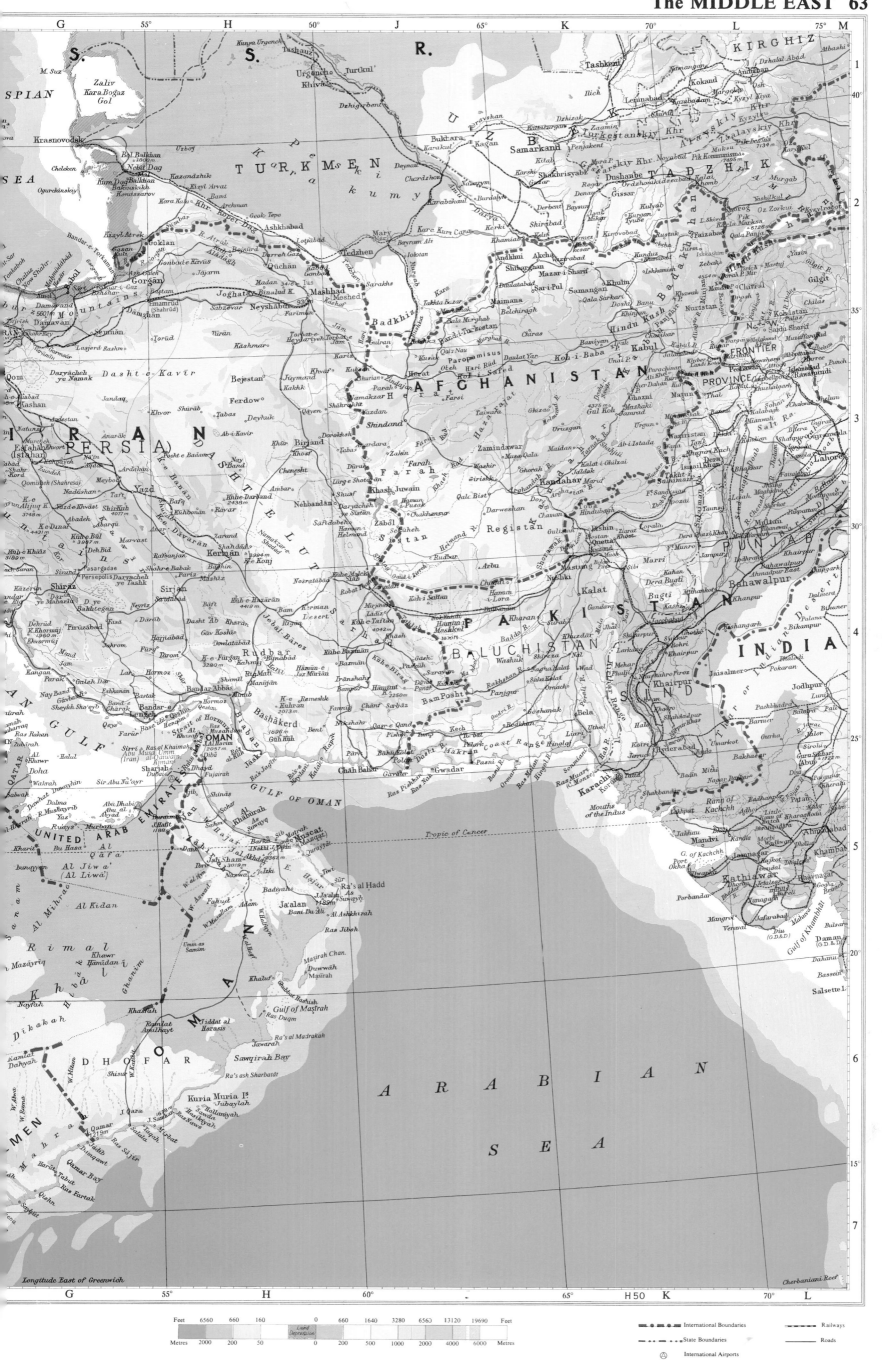

The MIDDLE EAST

ARABIAN SEA

GULF OF OMAN

IRAN

PERSIA

AFGHANISTAN

PAKISTAN

BALUCHISTAN

INDIA

OMAN

UNITED ARAB EMIRATES

YEMEN

DHOFAR

SIND

PUNJAB

TURKMEN

TADZHIK

KIRGHIZ

U Z B E K

S. S. R.

Tropic of Cancer

Longitude East of Greenwich

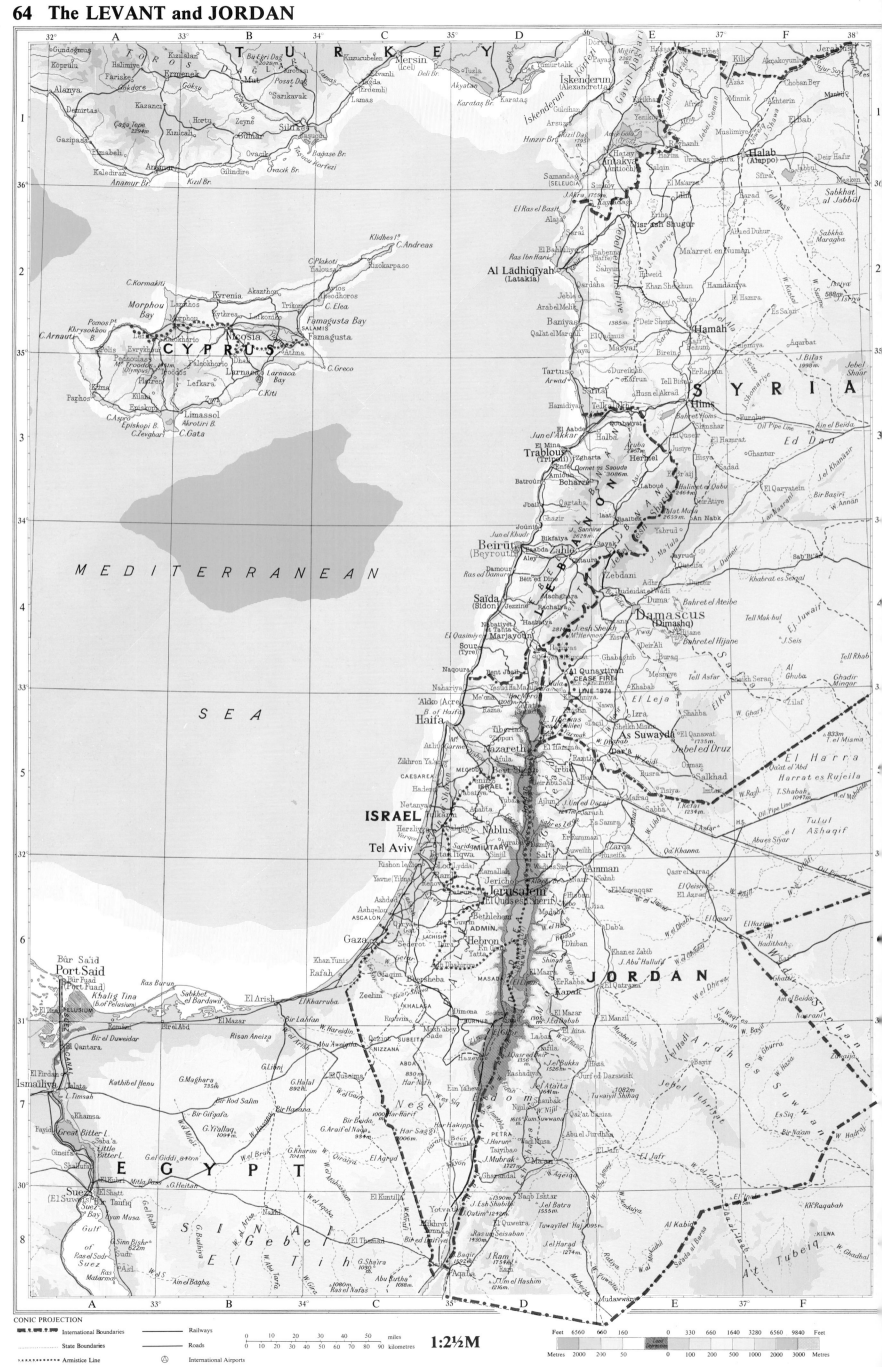

International Boundaries
State Boundaries
Armistice Line

Railways
Roads
International Airports

1:2½M

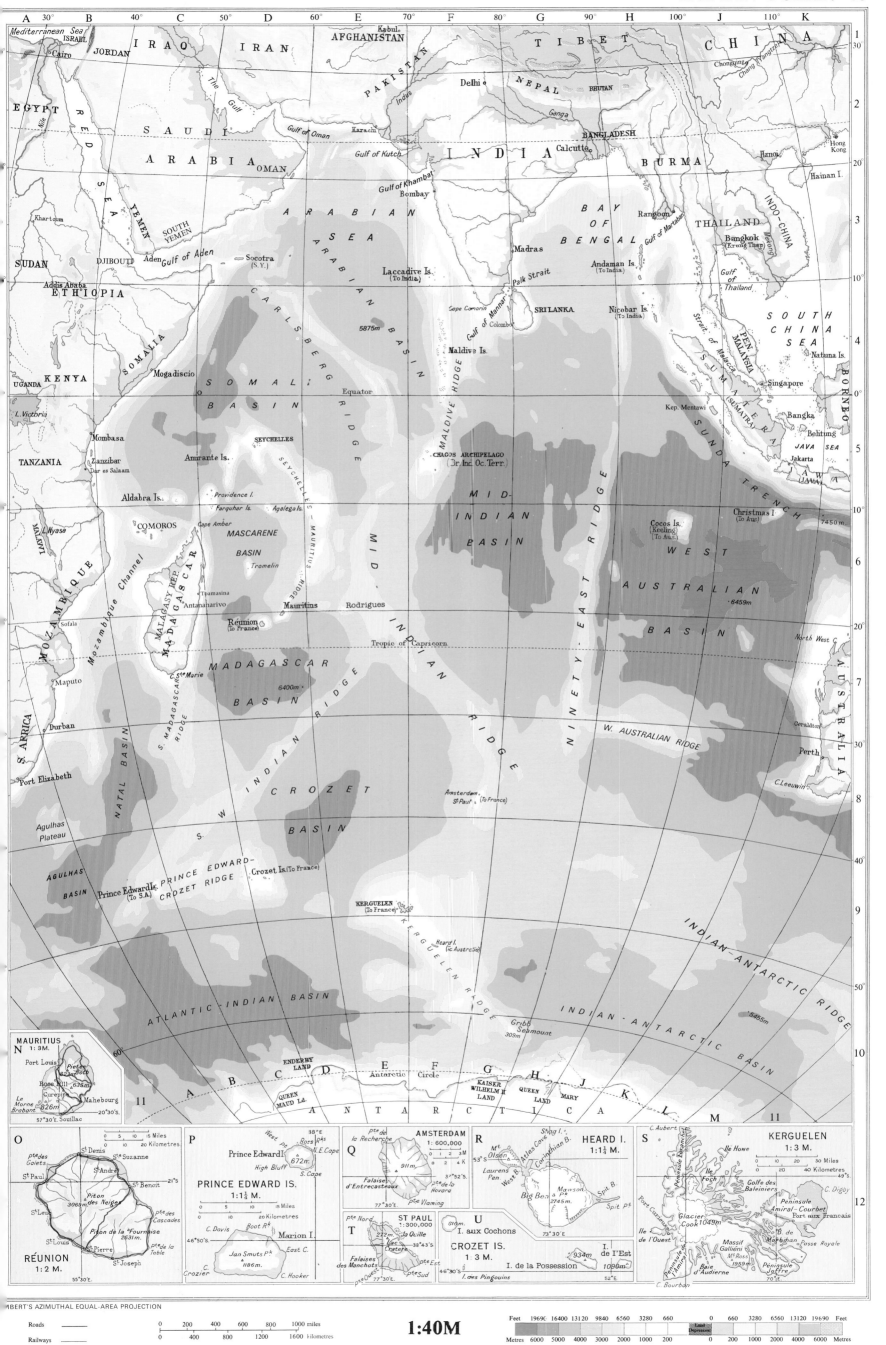

Mediterranean Sea
ISRAEL
Cairo
JORDAN
EGYPT
IRAQ
IRAN
AFGHANISTAN
Kabul
PAKISTAN
Delhi
NEPAL
BHUTAN
TIBET
CHINA
Chongqing
Hong
Chang Yangtze
Karachi
INDIA
Ganga
BANGLADESH
Calcutta
BURMA
Hanoi
Hong Kong
Hainan I.
SAUDI
ARABIA
OMAN
Gulf of Oman
Gulf of Kutch
Gulf of Khambat
Bombay
ARABIAN
SEA
Madras
BAY
OF
BENGAL
Rangoon
Gulf of Martaban
INDO-CHINA
THAILAND
Bangkok
(Krung Thep)
Mekong
RED SEA
YEMEN
SOUTH
YEMEN
Aden
Gulf of Aden
Socotra
(S.Y.)
ARABIAN BASIN
Laccadive Is.
(To India)
5875m
Palk Strait
Andaman Is.
(To India)
Gulf of
Thailand
Khartoum
SUDAN
DJIBOUTI
Addis Ababa
ETHIOPIA
SOMALIA
Cape Comorin
Gulf of Mannar
Gulf of Colombo
SRI LANKA
Nicobar Is.
(To India)
SOUTH
CHINA
SEA
Natuna Is.
CARLSBERG RIDGE
Maldive Is.
UGANDA
KENYA
Mogadiscio
SOMALI
BASIN
Equator
MALDIVE RIDGE
CHAGOS ARCHIPELAGO
(Br.Ind.Oc.Terr.)
Kep. Mentawi
SUMATRA
Singapore
BORNEO
L.Victoria
SEYCHELLES
SEYCHELLES — MAURITIUS RIDGE
Bangka
Belitung
JAVA SEA
Jakarta
TANZANIA
Mombasa
Zanzibar
Dar es Salaam
Amirante Is.
Providence I.
Aldabra Is.
Farquhar Is.
Agalega Is.
MID-
INDIAN
BASIN
WEST
AUSTRALIAN
BASIN
6459m
Cocos Is.
(Keeling)
(To Aus.)
Christmas I.
(To Aus.)
7450m
JAVA
SUNDA TRENCH
MALAWI
L. Nyasa
COMOROS
Cape Amber
MASCARENE
BASIN
Tromelin
MADAGASY REP.
MADAGASCAR
Toamasina
Antananarivo
Mauritius
Rodrigues
MID INDIAN RIDGE
NINETY-EAST RIDGE
MOZAMBIQUE
Mozambique Channel
Réunion
(To France)
Tropic of Capricorn
W. AUSTRALIAN RIDGE
North West C.
AUSTRALIA
MOZAMBIQUE
Sofala
C.Ste Marie
MADAGASCAR
BASIN
6400m
S. MADAGASCAR RIDGE
W. INDIAN RIDGE
Geraldton
Maputo
Perth
S. AFRICA
Durban
NATAL BASIN
CROZET
BASIN
Amsterdam
St.Paul (To France)
C.Leeuwin
Port Elizabeth
Agulhas
Plateau
AGULHAS
BASIN
PRINCE EDWARD–CROZET RIDGE
Prince Edward Is.
(To S.A.)
Crozet Is.(To France)
INDIAN–ANTARCTIC RIDGE
KERGUELEN
(To France)
KERGUELEN RIDGE
Heard I.
(To Australia)
ATLANTIC-INDIAN BASIN
INDIAN–ANTARCTIC BASIN
5455m
Gribb
Seamount
309m
MAURITIUS
1:3 M.
Port Louis
Pieter
623m Both
Rose Hill 633m
Curepipe
Le Morne
Brabant 826m
Mahebourg
57°30'E Souillac
20°30'S
ENDERBY
LAND
Antarctic Circle
QUEEN
MAUD Ld.
KAISER
WILHELM II
LAND
QUEEN
MARY
LAND
ANTARCTICA
A B C D E F G H J K L M

RÉUNION
1:2 M.
Pte des
Galets
St Denis
Ste Suzanne
St Paul
St André
Piton
des Neiges
3069m
St Benoit
Pte des
Cascades
St Leu
Piton de la Fournaise
2631m
St Louis
St Pierre
Pte de la
Table
St Joseph
55°30'E

PRINCE EDWARD IS.
1:1¼ M.
Prince Edward I.
West Pt.
Ross Rks.
38°E
N.E.Cape
High Bluff
672m
S.Cape
C. Davis
Boot Rk.
46°50'S
Marion I.
Jan Smuts Pk.
1186m
East C.
C.
Crozier
C. Hooker

AMSTERDAM
1:600,000
Pte de
la Recherche
911m
53° S
Falaises
d'Entrecasteaux
77°30'E
Pte de la
Novara
Pte Vlaming
37°52'S

ST PAUL
1:300,000
Pte Nord
212m
la Quille
Vac.
Cratère
Falaises
des Manchots
Pte Est
33°43'S
Pte Ouest
77°30'E
Pte Sud
38°E

CROZET IS.
1:3 M.
I. aux Cochons
U
73°30'E
934m
I. de l'Est
1090m
I. des Pingouins
46°30'S
52°E

HEARD I.
1:1¼ M.
Shag I.
Atlas Cove
C. Aubert
Mt Olsen
Corinthian B.
Laurens
Pen.
West Pt.
Big Ben
2745m
Mawson
Spit B.
Spit Pt.

KERGUELEN
1:3 M.
Péninsule Loranchet
Ile Howe
C. Digoy
Golfe des
Baleiniers
Péninsule
Amiral–Courbet
Port aux Francais
Glacier
Cook 1049m
Massif
Gallieni
1959m
B. de
Morbihan
Bale
d'Audierne
Péninsule
Jeanne
d'Arc
Passe Royale
C. Bourbon
70°E

Roads
Railways

0 200 400 600 800 1000 miles
0 400 800 1200 1600 kilometres

Feet 19690 16400 13120 9840 6560 3280 660   0   660 3280 6560 13120 19690 Feet
Land Depression
Metres 6000 5000 4000 3000 2000 1000 200   0   200 1000 2000 4000 6000 Metres

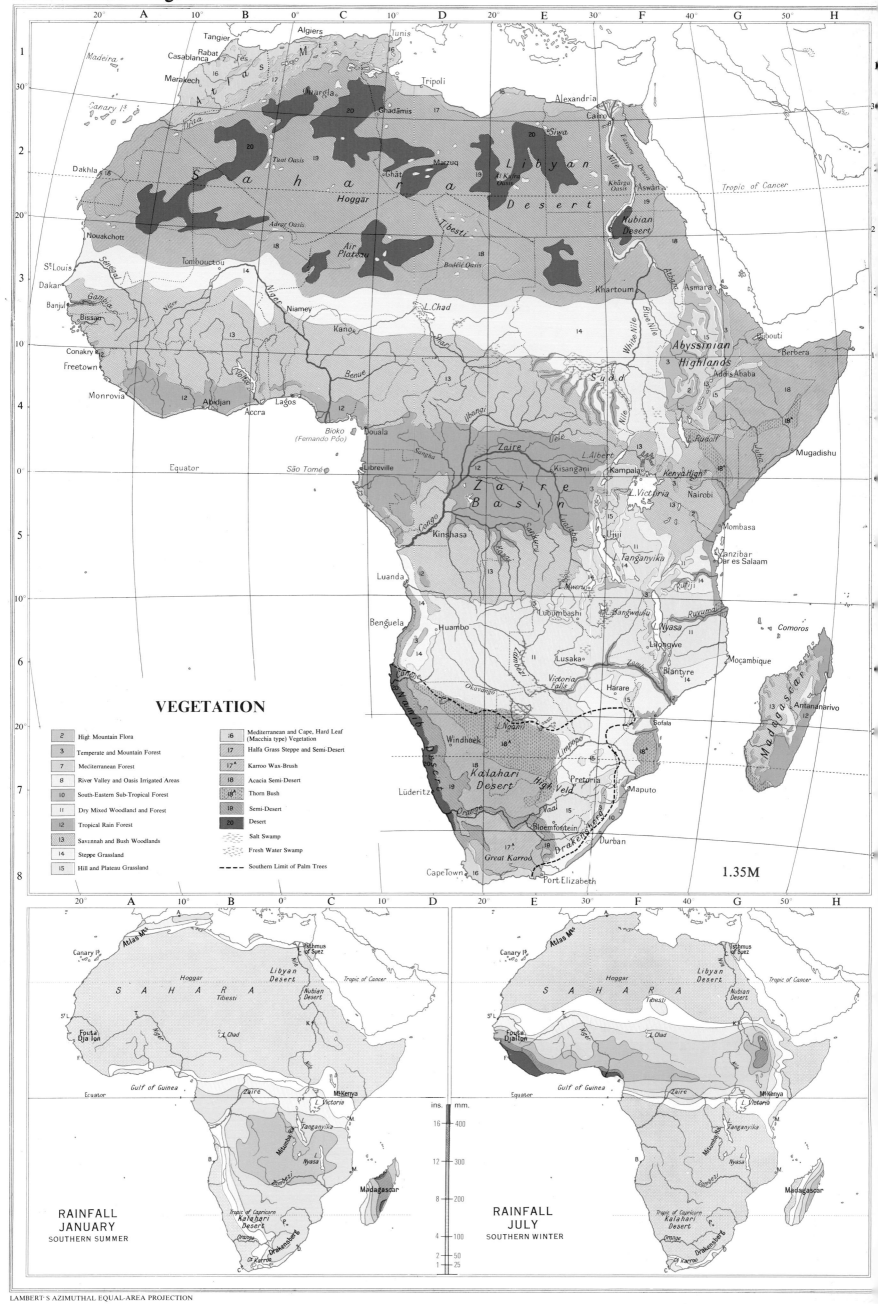

VEGETATION

2	High Mountain Flora
3	Temperate and Mountain Forest
7	Mediterranean Forest
8	River Valley and Oasis Irrigated Areas
10	South-Eastern Sub-Tropical Forest
11	Dry Mixed Woodland and Forest
12	Tropical Rain Forest
13	Savannah and Bush Woodlands
14	Steppe Grassland
15	Hill and Plateau Grassland
16	Mediterranean and Cape, Hard Leaf (Macchia type) Vegetation
17	Halfa Grass Steppe and Semi-Desert
17^	Karroo Wax-Brush
18	Acacia Semi-Desert
18^	Thorn Bush
19	Semi-Desert
20	Desert
	Salt Swamp
	Fresh Water Swamp
- - -	Southern Limit of Palm Trees

1.35M

RAINFALL
JANUARY
SOUTHERN SUMMER

RAINFALL
JULY
SOUTHERN WINTER

ins.	mm.
16	400
12	300
8	200
4	100
2	50
1	25

LAMBERT'S AZIMUTHAL EQUAL-AREA PROJECTION

| 0 | 200 | 400 | 600 | 800 | 1000 miles |

| 0 | 200 | 400 | 600 | 800 | 1000 | 1200 | 1400 | 1600 kilometres |

1:35M

Main Map (Population)

MEDITERRANEAN SEA

MOROCCO — Funchal, Madeira Is (Port), Casablanca, Rabat, Tangier, Gibraltar, Ceuta (Sp), Fes (Fez), Marrakech, Sidi Ifni, Canary Is, Las Palmas, La'youn, Dakhla

ALGERIA — Oran, Algiers, Constantine, Annaba, Tunis, Oued, Béchar, Ouargla, Touggourt, Ghardäïa, Reggane, Ghät

TUNISIA — G. of Gabès, Tripoli, Benghazi, G. of Sirte

LIBYA — Marzuq, Al Kufrah, Libyan Desert

EGYPT — Alexandria, Port Said, Suez, Cairo, Asyût, Khârga Oasis, Aswân, L. Nasser, Wadi Halfa

MAURITANIA — C. Blanco, Nouakchott, St Louis, C. Verde, Dakar

SAHARA, Desert, Bilma, Tropic of Cancer, Red Sea

MALI — Tombouctou, Bamako, Niger

SENEGAL — THE GAMBIA, Banjul

GUINEA BISSAU — Bissau

GUINEA — Conakry

SIERRA LEONE — Freetown

LIBERIA — Monrovia

IVORY COAST — Abidjan

BURKINA — Ouagadougou

NIGER — Niamey, L. Chad

GHANA — Accra, Takoradi, L. Volta, TOGO, BENIN, Lomé

NIGERIA — Kano, Kaduna, Ibadan, Lagos, Benue, N'Djamena, Chari

CHAD —

SUDAN — Nyala, El Obeid, Omdurman, Khartoum, Atbara, Berber, Port Sudan, White Nile, Blue Nile, Massawa, Asmara

CAMEROON — Douala, Yaoundé, Pt Harcourt

CENTRAL AFRICAN REPUBLIC — Bangui, Uele

DJIBOUTI — Djibouti, Berbera, G. of Aden

ETHIOPIA — Addis Ababa, Harar, L. Rudolf, Juba

SOMALIA — Mugadishu

Bioko (Fernando Póo), EQUAT. GUINEA, Bight of Biafra, Principe, São Tomé, Gulf of Guinea, Annobon, C. Lopez, Equator

GABON — Libreville

CONGO — Brazzaville, Pte Noire, CABINDA, Boma, Matadi

ZAIRE — Mbandaka, Kisangani, Kindu, Kananga, Kalemie, Ujiji, Kigoma, Zaire, Kasai, Lualaba

UGANDA — Entebbe, Kampala

KENYA — Kisumu, Nairobi, Mombasa, L. Victoria

RWANDA — **BURUNDI**

TANZANIA — Mwanza, Tanga, Zanzibar, Dar es Salaam, Kilosa, L. Tanganyika, Mbeya, Rufiji, Aldabra Is

ANGOLA — Luanda, Malange, Huambo, Lobito, Benguela, Moçâmedes, Cunene, Okavango, L. Mweru, L. Bengweulu

ZAMBIA — Lubumbashi, Kabwe, Lusaka, Kariba, Zambezi

MALAWI — Lilongwe, L. Nyasa, Blantyre

MOZAMBIQUE — Nampula, Moçambique, Mahajanga, Quelimane, Sofala, Beira, Inhambane, Maputo, Rovuma, Mozambique Channel

ZIMBABWE — Maramba, Wankie, Harare, Mutare, Bulawayo, Victoria Falls, Limpopo

NAMIBIA (S.W. AFRICA) — Swakopmund, Walvis Bay, Windhoek, Lüderitz

BOTSWANA — Grootfontein, Kalahari Desert

SOUTH AFRICA — Mafeking, Johannesburg, Pretoria, SWAZI, Kimberley, Bloemfontein, Vaal, Orange, Cape Town, C. of Good Hope, Worcester, Mossel Bay, Port Elizabeth, East London, Durban, Pietermaritzburg, Drakensberg, Beitbridge

MADAGASCAR — C. d'Ambre, Antseranana, Antananarivo, Toamasina, Antananarivo, C. Ste Marie, Comoros

SOUTH ATLANTIC OCEAN, Ascension (U.K.), St Helena (U.K.)

INDIAN OCEAN

Tropic of Capricorn

POPULATION

- Over 200 persons per square kilometre
- 100 to 200 " " "
- 40 to 100 " " "
- 20 to 40 " " "
- 1 to 20 " " "
- Under 1 " " "
- International Boundaries

1:35 M

Lower Maps

TEMPERATURE (Actual °C) JANUARY SOUTHERN SUMMER

Canary Is, Atlas Mts, Libyan Desert, Tropic of Cancer, SAHARA, Hoggar, Tibesti, Nubian Desert, Fouta Djallon, L. Chad, Niger, Zaire, Equator, L. Victoria, Tanganyika, Zambezi, Nyasa, Madagascar, Tropic of Capricorn, Kalahari Desert, Orange, Drakensberg

Temperature scale: °C / °F — 35/95, 30/86, 25/77, 20/68, 15/59, 10/50, 0/32

TEMPERATURE (Actual °C) JULY SOUTHERN WINTER

Canary Is, Atlas Mts, Libyan Desert, Tropic of Cancer, SAHARA, Hoggar, Tibesti, Nubian Desert, Fouta Djallon, L. Chad, Niger, Zaire, Equator, L. Victoria, L. Nyasa, Zambezi, Madagascar, Tropic of Capricorn, Kalahari Desert, Orange, Gt Karroo, C.T.

LAMBERT'S AZIMUTHAL EQUAL-AREA PROJECTION

1:12½M

| 0 | 100 | 200 | 300 | 400 miles |
| 0 | 100 | 200 | 300 | 400 | 500 | 600 kilometres |

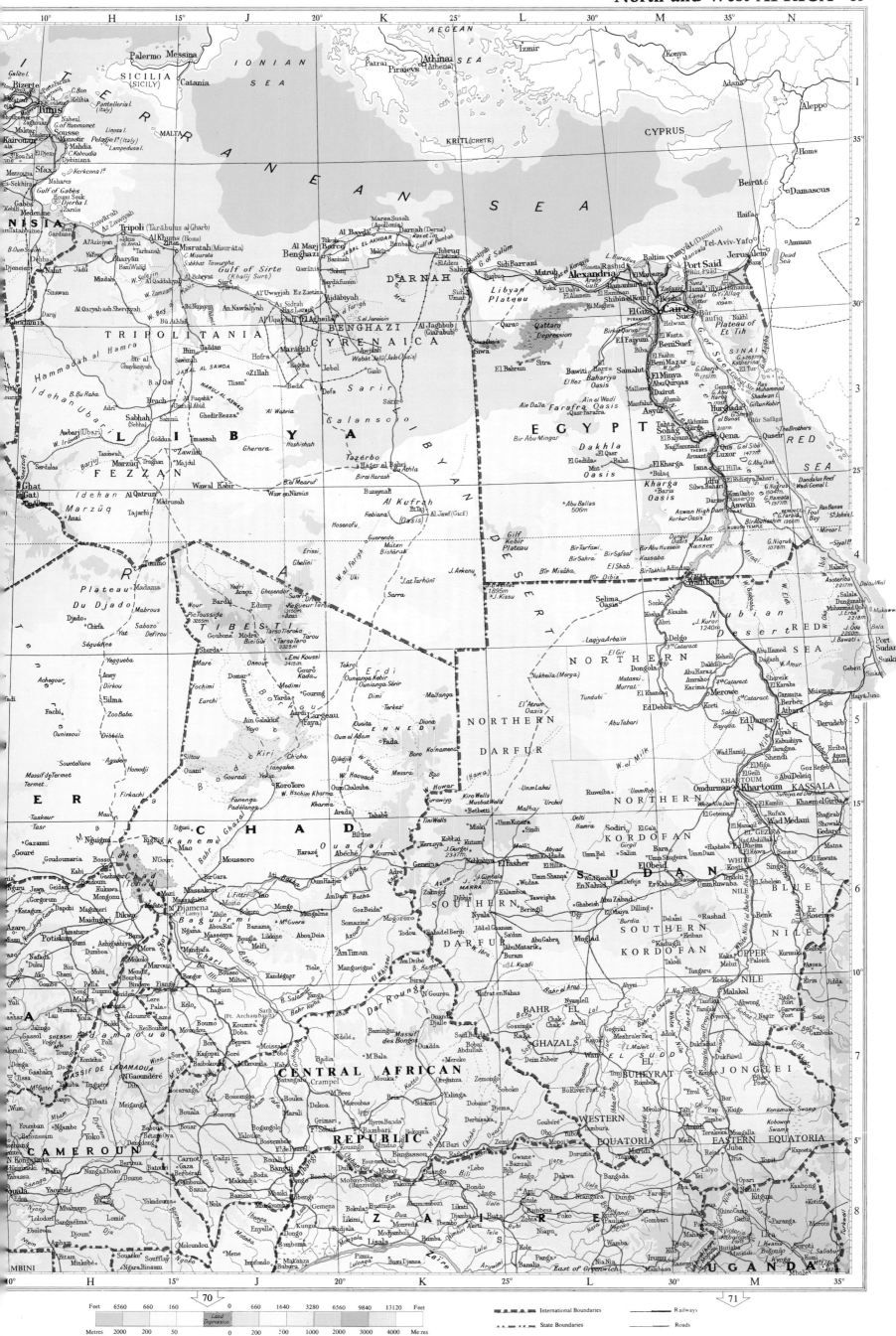

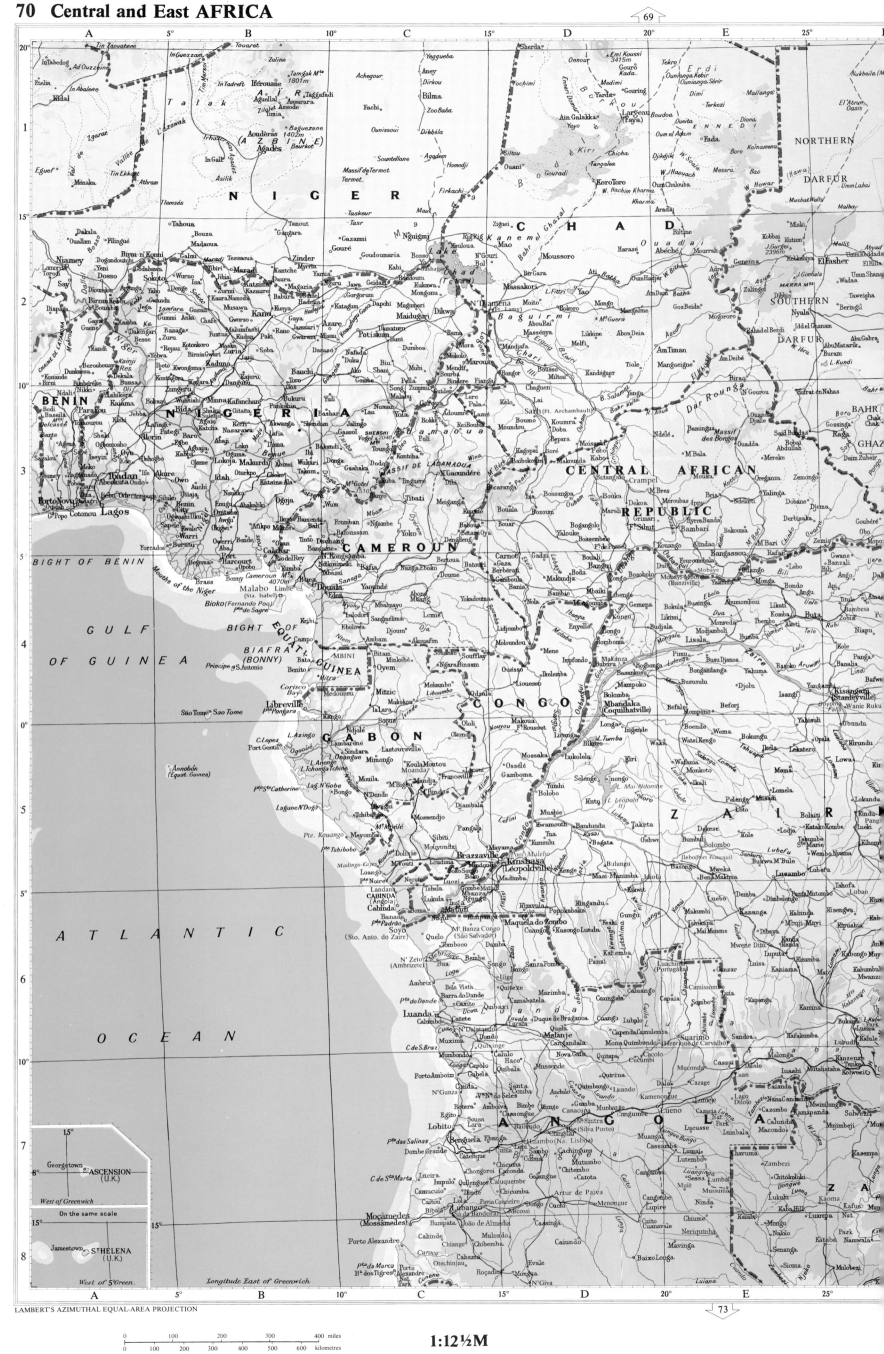

LAMBERT'S AZIMUTHAL EQUAL-AREA PROJECTION

1:12½M

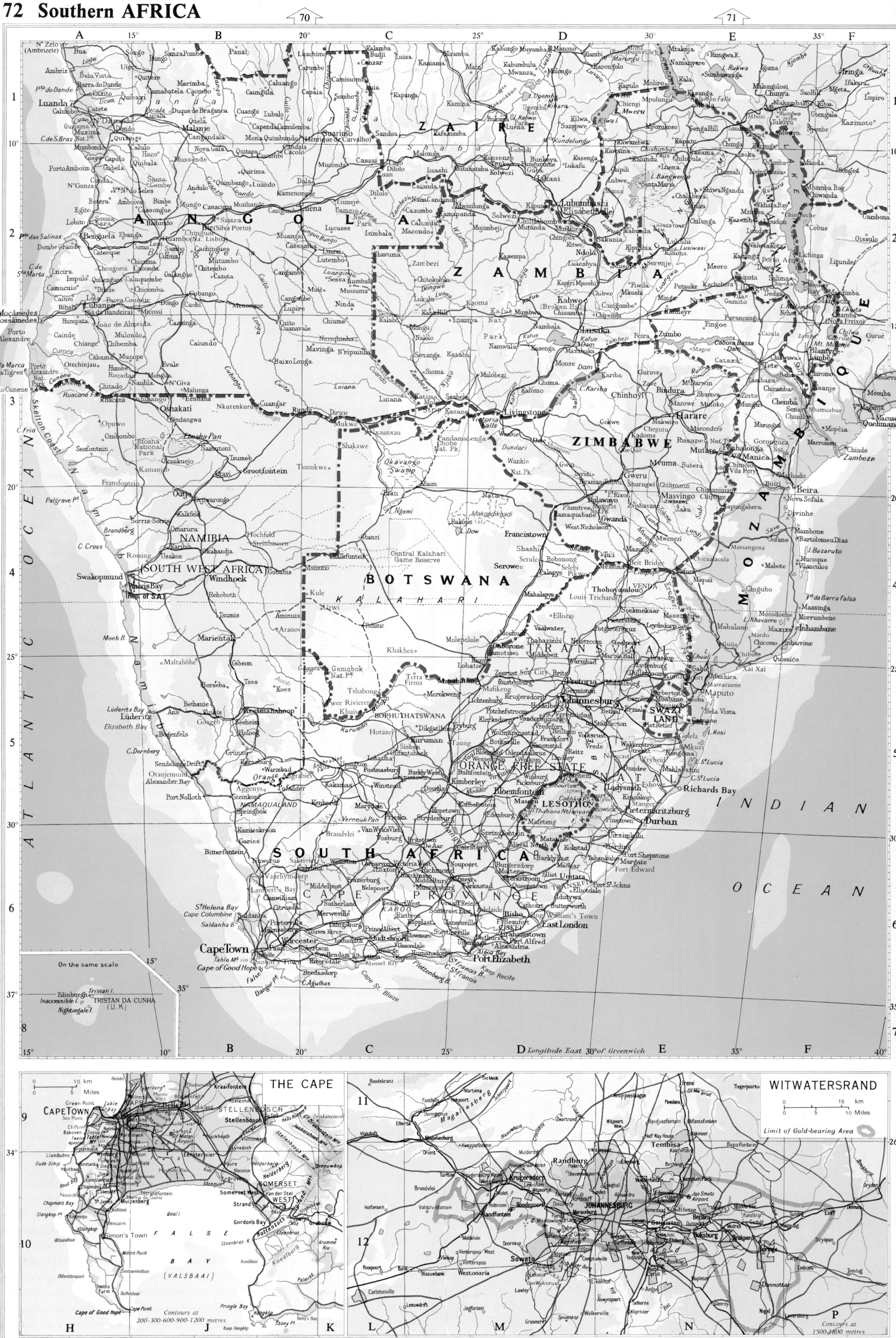

ZAIRE

ANGOLA

ZAMBIA

NAMIBIA

SOUTH WEST AFRICA

BOTSWANA

KALAHARI

Central Kalahari Game Reserve

ZIMBABWE

MOZAMBIQUE

TRANSVAL

ORANGE FREE STATE

NATAL

LESOTHO

SWAZILAND

BOPHUTHATSWANA

SOUTH AFRICA

CAPE PROVINCE

KAROO

NAMAQUALAND

ATLANTIC OCEAN

INDIAN OCEAN

Skeleton Coast

Cape of Good Hope

CapeTown

Port Elizabeth

East London

Durban

Johannesburg

Pretoria

Bloemfontein

Kimberley

Windhoek

Luanda

Benguela

Lubumbashi (Elisabethville)

Lusaka

Harare

Bulawayo

Beira

Maputo

Victoria Falls

Okavango Swamp

Etosha Pan

Etosha National Park

Gemsbok Nat. Pk.

False Bay

Maseru

Richards Bay

On the same scale

Tristan I.
Edinburgh
Inaccessible I.
Nightingale I.
TRISTAN DA CUNHA (U.K.)

THE CAPE

CapeTown
Green Point
Sea Point
STELLENBOSCH
Stellenbosch
SOMERSET WEST
Somerset West
Strand
Gordon's Bay
Simon's Town
FALSE BAY (VALSBAAI)
Cape Point
Cape of Good Hope

Contours at 200·300·600·900·1200 metres

WITWATERSRAND

Limit of Gold-bearing Area

Randburg
Krugersdorp
Randfontein
JOHANNESBURG
Soweto
Germiston
Benoni
Boksburg
Springs
Tembisa
Jan Smuts Airport
Carletonville
Nigel

Contours at 1500·1800 metres

LAMBERT'S AZIMUTHAL EQUAL-AREA PROJECTION

International Boundaries
State Boundaries
Railways
Roads

Miles 0   100   200   300 miles
Kilometres 0 100 200 300 400 500 kilometres

1:12½M

Feet 6560 660 160 0 660 1640 3280 6560 9840 Feet
Metres 2000 200 50 0 200 500 1000 2000 3000 Metres

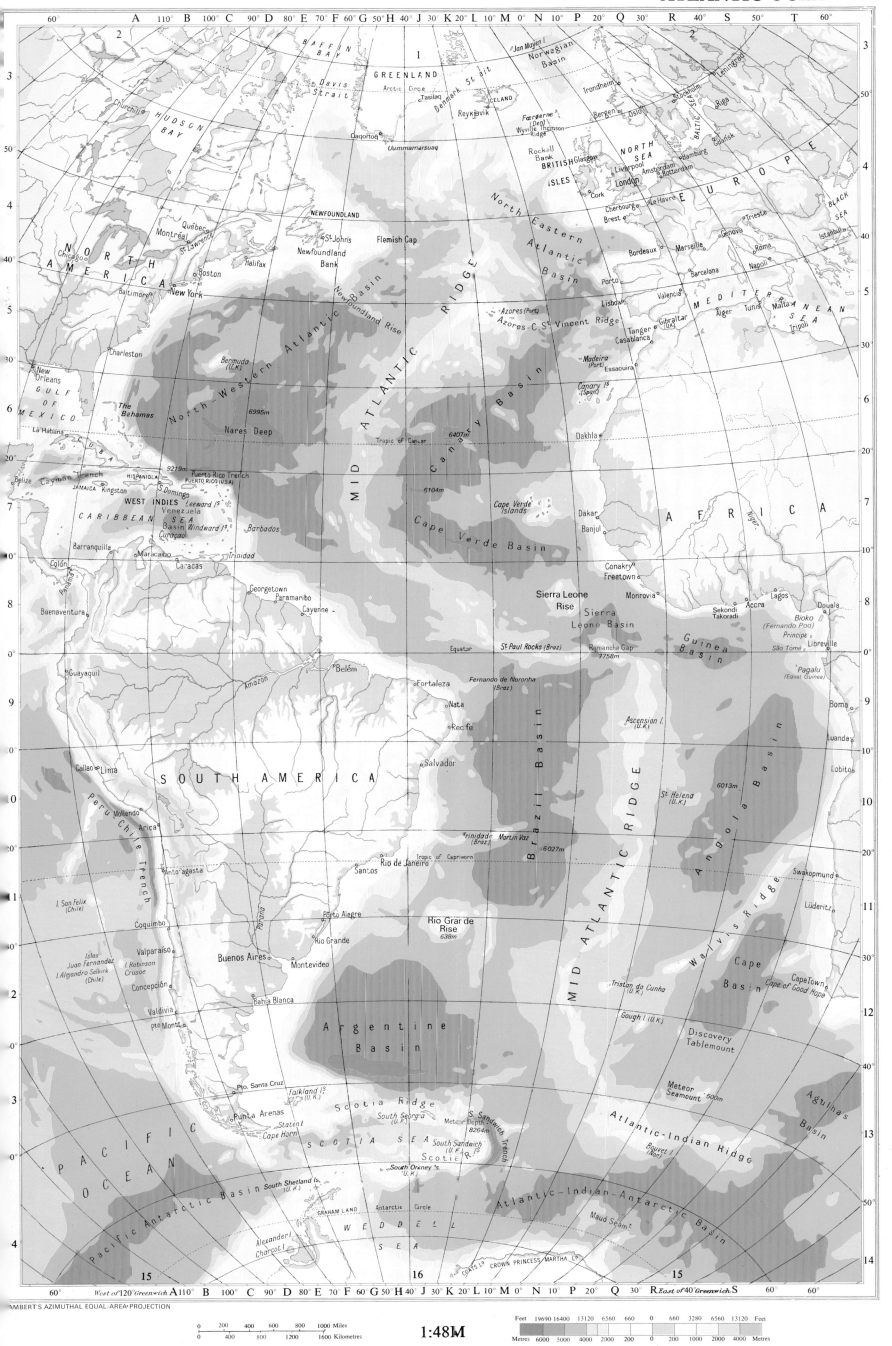

1:48M

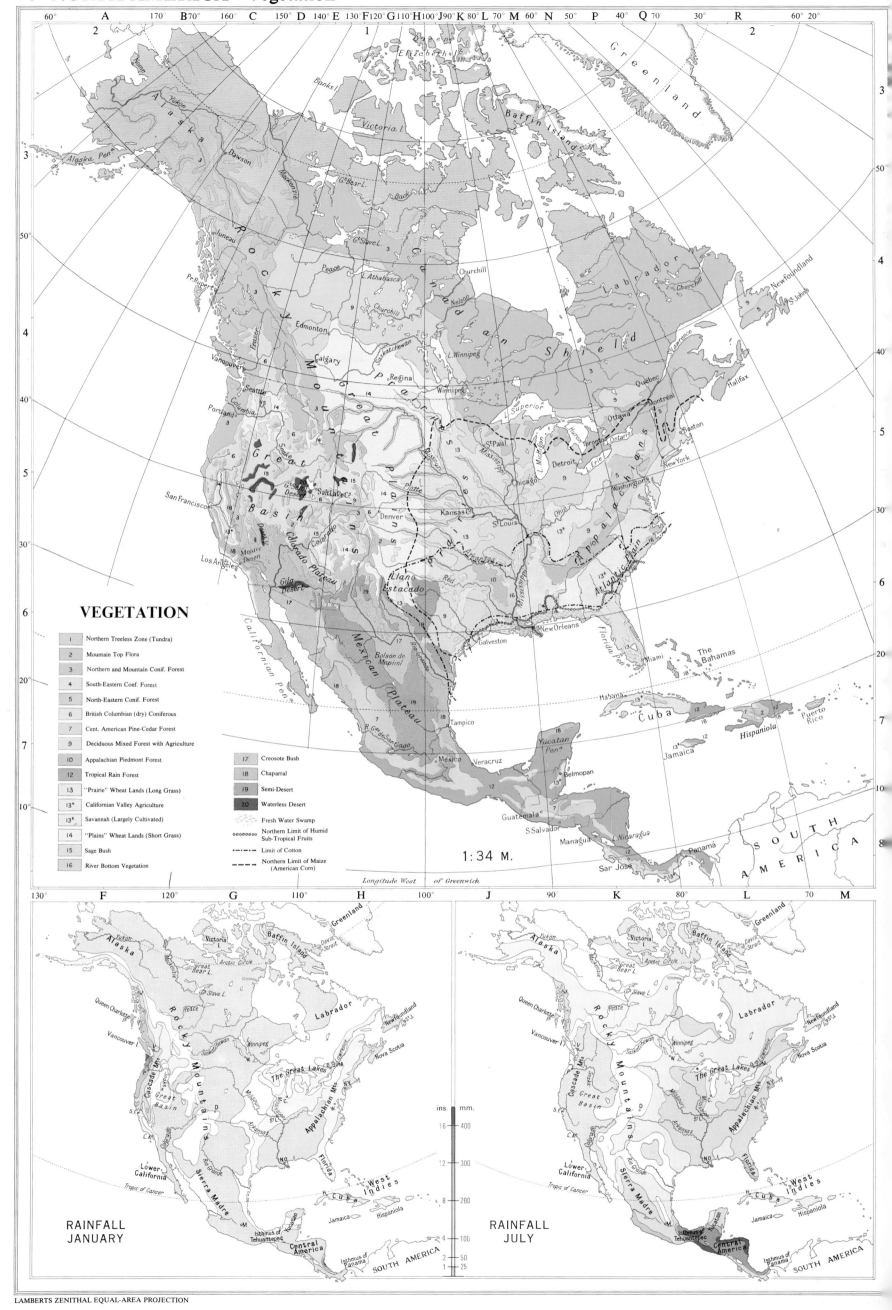

VEGETATION

1	Northern Treeless Zone (Tundra)
2	Mountain Top Flora
3	Northern and Mountain Conif. Forest
4	South-Eastern Conif. Forest
5	North-Eastern Conif. Forest
6	British Columbian (dry) Coniferous
7	Cent. American Pine-Cedar Forest
9	Deciduous Mixed Forest with Agriculture
10	Appalachian Piedmont Forest
12	Tropical Rain Forest
13	"Prairie" Wheat Lands (Long Grass)
13ᴬ	Californian Valley Agriculture
13ᴮ	Savannah (Largely Cultivated)
14	"Plains" Wheat Lands (Short Grass)
15	Sage Bush
16	River Bottom Vegetation

17	Creosote Bush
18	Chaparral
19	Semi-Desert
20	Waterless Desert

- Fresh Water Swamp
- Northern Limit of Humid Sub-Tropical Fruits
- Limit of Cotton
- Northern Limit of Maize (American Corn)

1:34 M.

Longitude West of Greenwich

RAINFALL
JANUARY

RAINFALL
JULY

ins.	mm.
16	400
12	300
8	200
4	100
2	50
1	25

LAMBERTS ZENITHAL EQUAL-AREA PROJECTION

1:34M

0	200	400	600	800 miles
0	200	400	600	800	1000	1200 kilometres

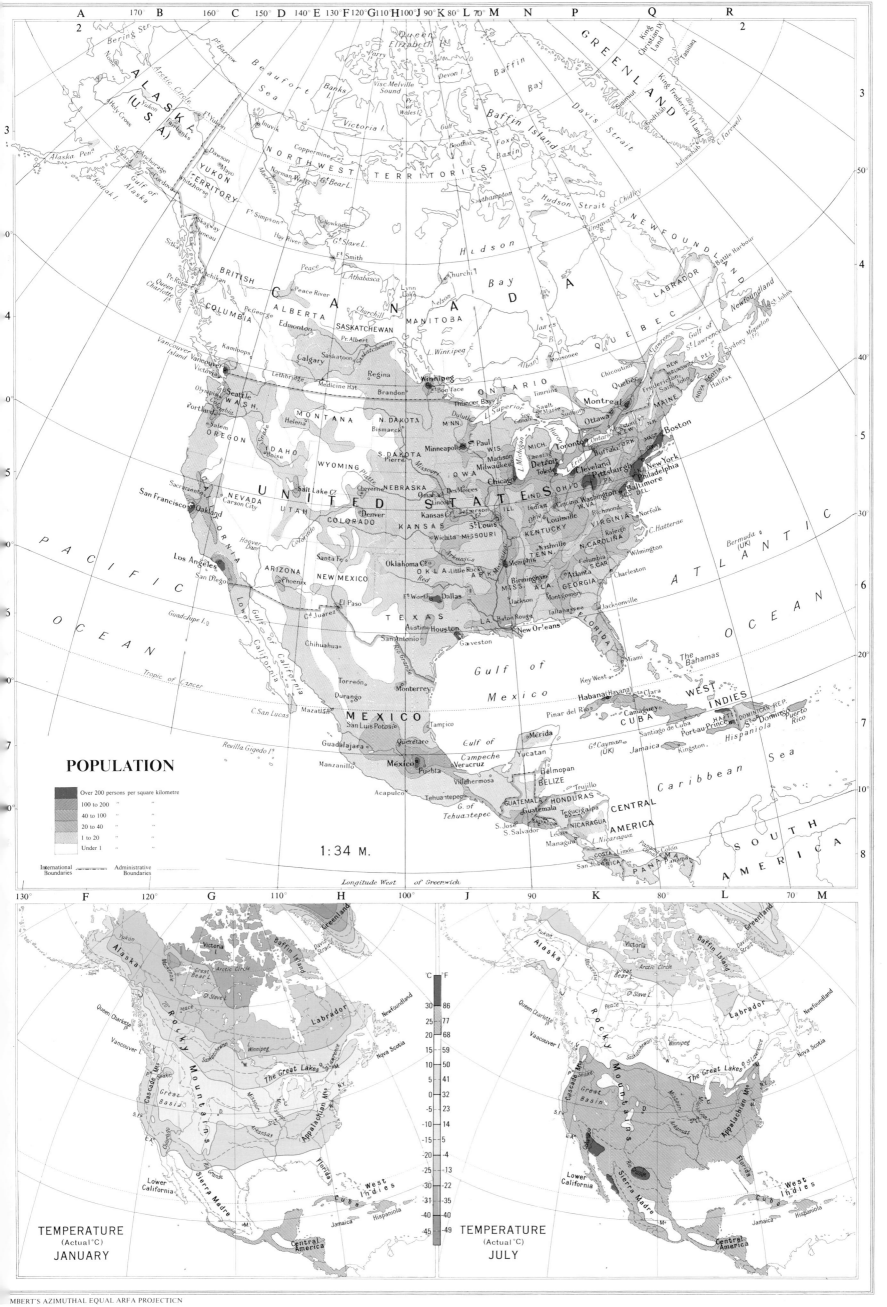

POPULATION

	Over 200 persons per square kilometre
	100 to 200 "
	40 to 100 "
	20 to 40 "
	1 to 20 "
	Under 1 "

International Boundaries

Administrative Boundaries

1:34 M.

Longitude West of Greenwich

TEMPERATURE
(Actual °C)
JANUARY

°C °F

TEMPERATURE
(Actual °C)
JULY

LAMBERT'S AZIMUTHAL EQUAL AREA PROJECTION

0   200   400   600   800 miles
0   200   400   600   800 1000 1200 kilometres

1:34M

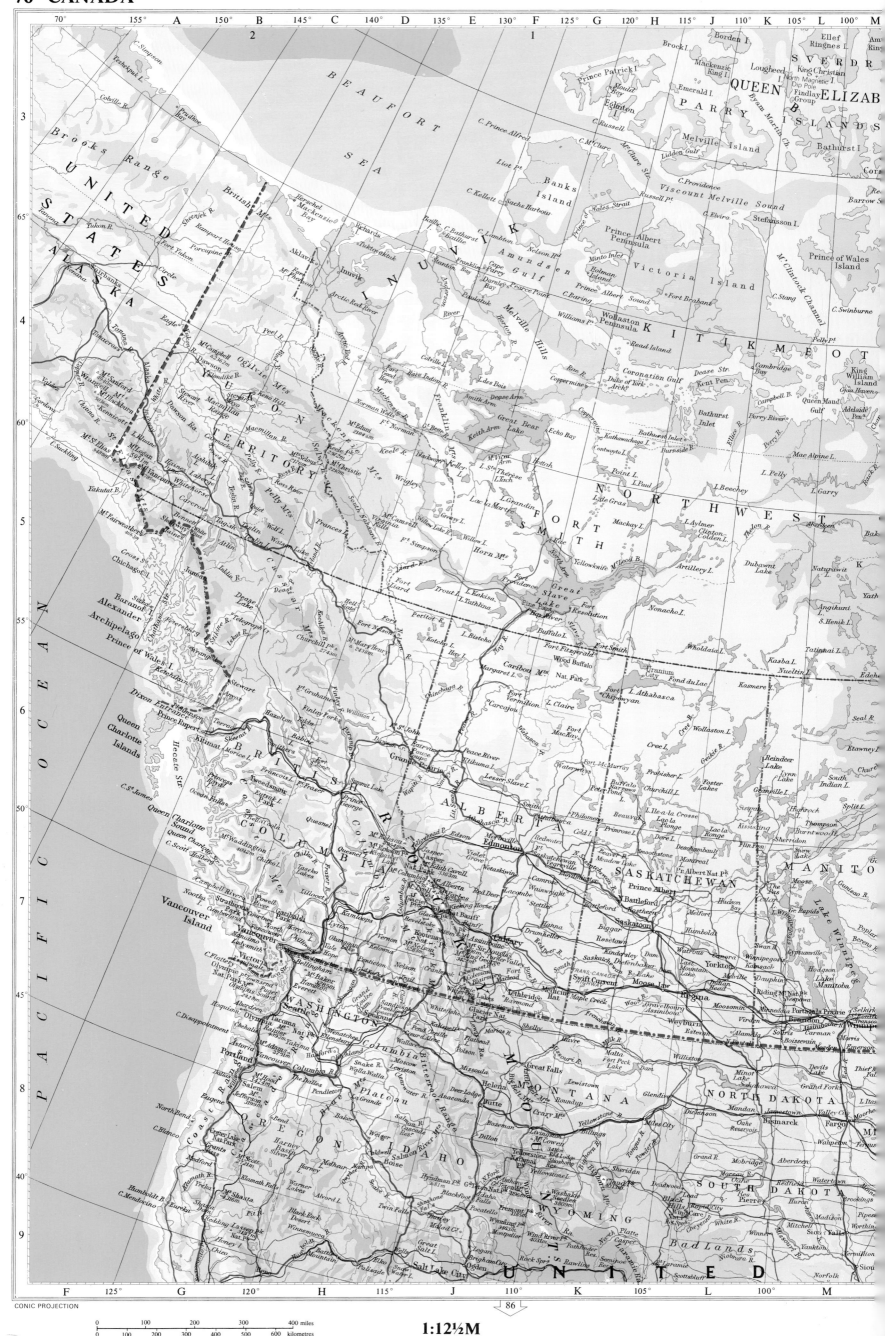

CONIC PROJECTION

1:12½M

| 0 | 100 | 200 | 300 | 400 miles |

| 0 | 100 | 200 | 300 | 400 | 500 | 600 kilometres |

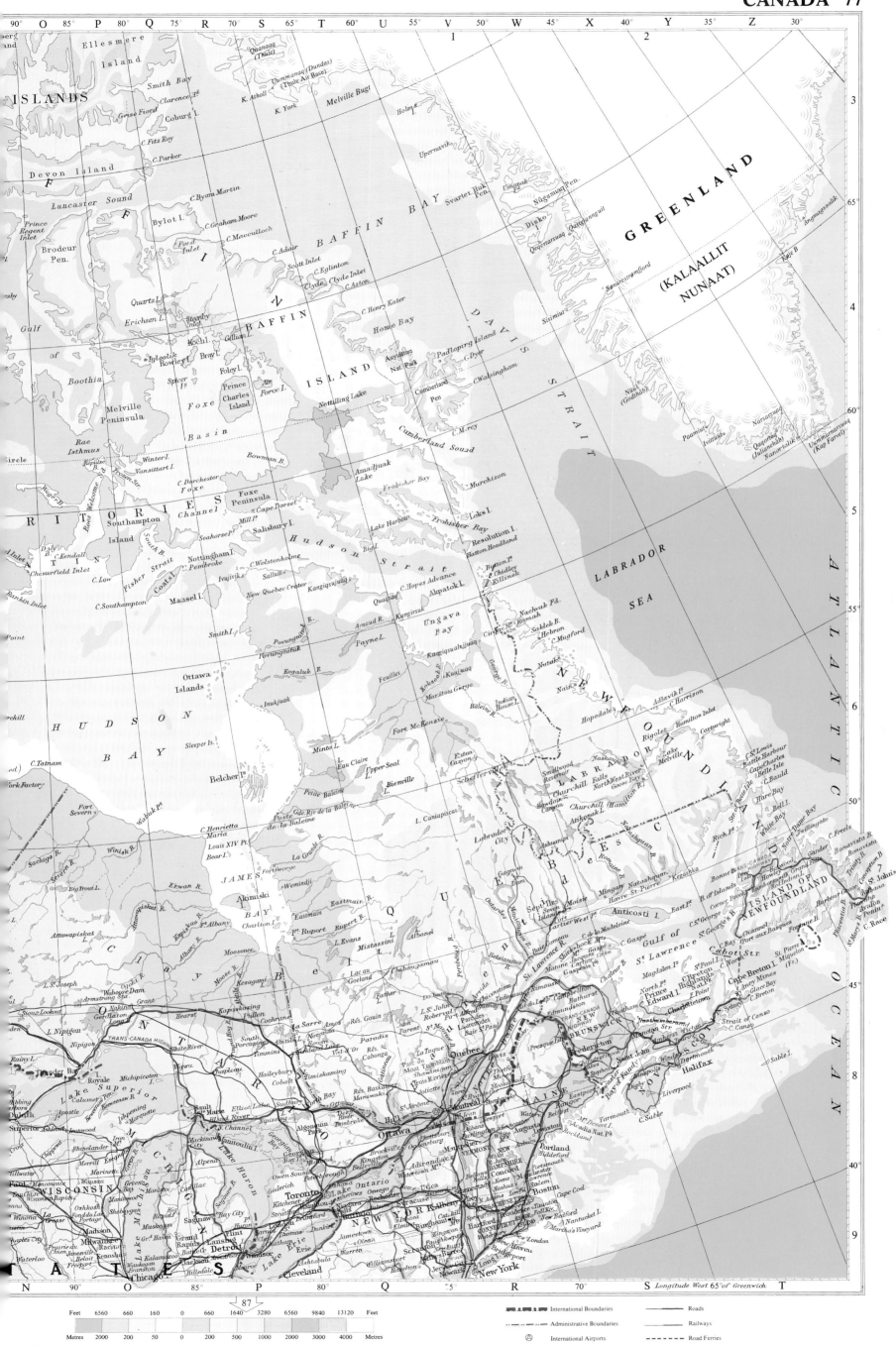

Feet 6560 660 160 0 660 1640 3280 6560 9840 13120 Feet
Metres 2000 200 50 0 200 500 1000 2000 3000 4000 Metres

International Boundaries .... Roads
------ Administrative Boundaries .... Railways
Ⓐ International Airports - - - - - Road Ferries

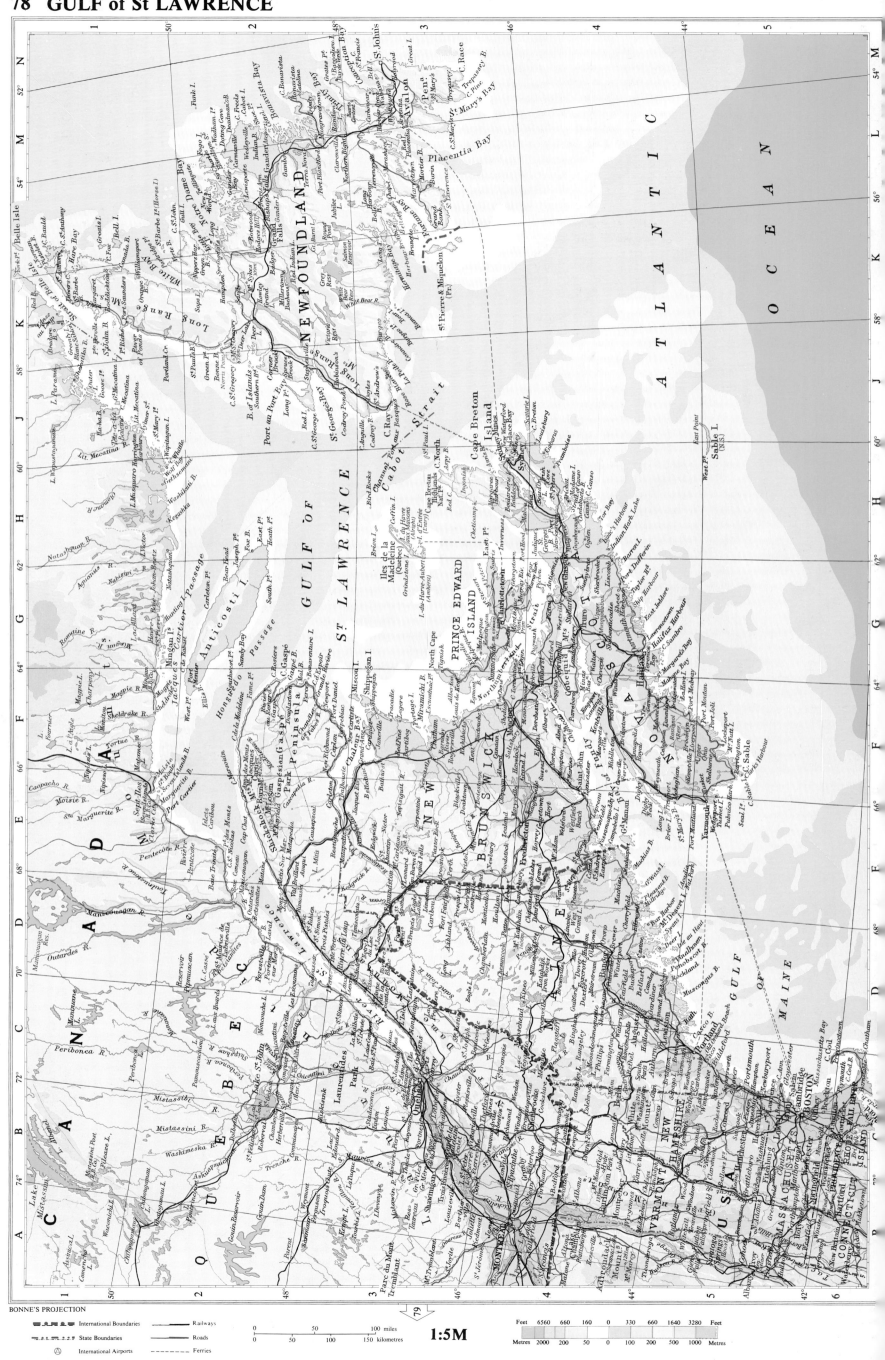

International Boundaries — Railways
State Boundaries — Roads
International Airports - - - - Ferries

0   50   100 miles
0   50   100   150 kilometres

1:5M

Feet 6560 660 160 0 330 660 1640 3280 Feet
Metres 2000 200 50 0 100 200 500 1000 Metres

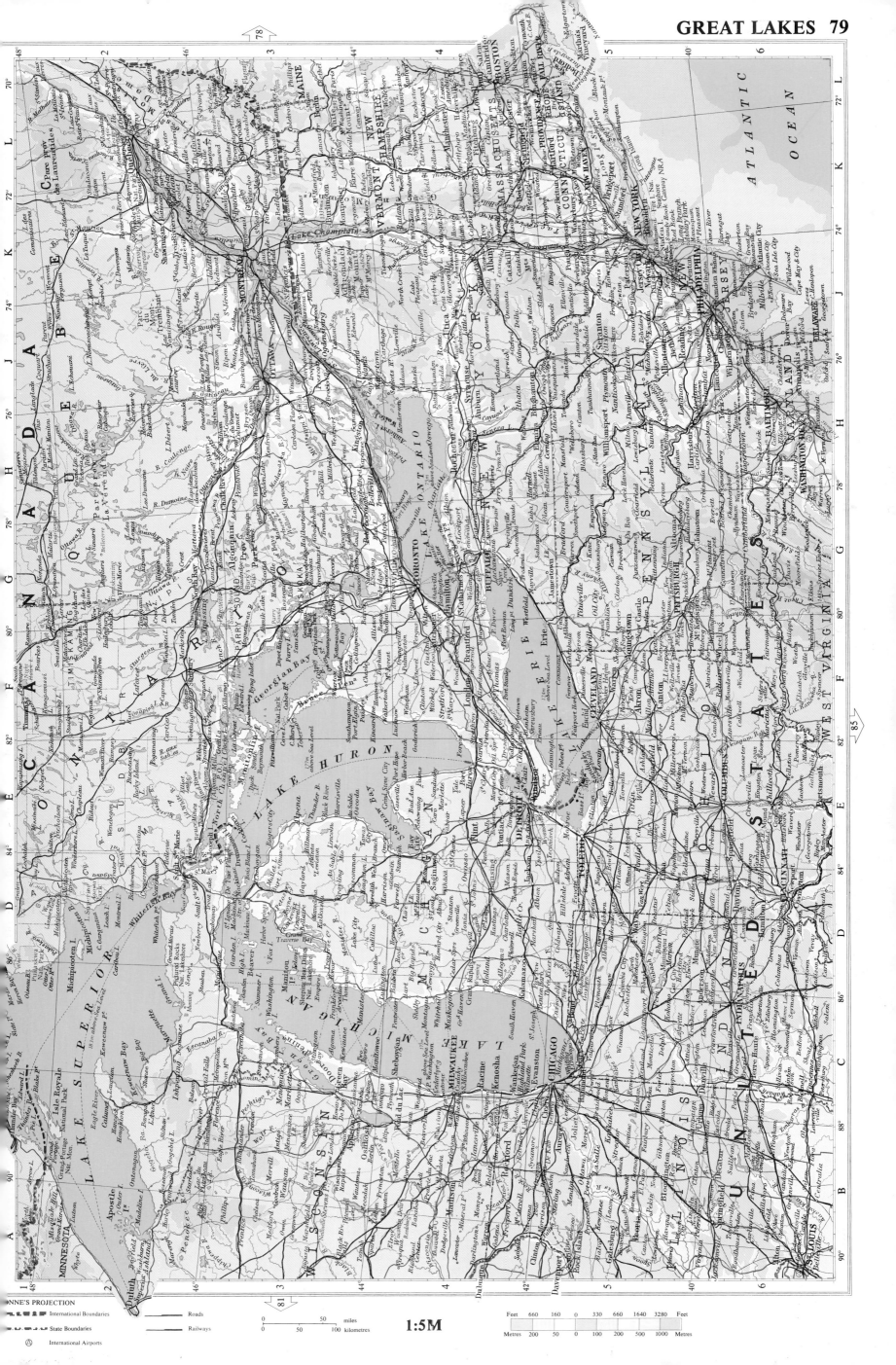

BONNE'S PROJECTION

International Boundaries

State Boundaries

Roads

Railways

International Airports

0   50 miles
0   50   100 kilometres

1:5M

Feet 660 160 0 330 660 1640 3280 Feet
Metres 200 50 0 100 200 500 1000 Metres

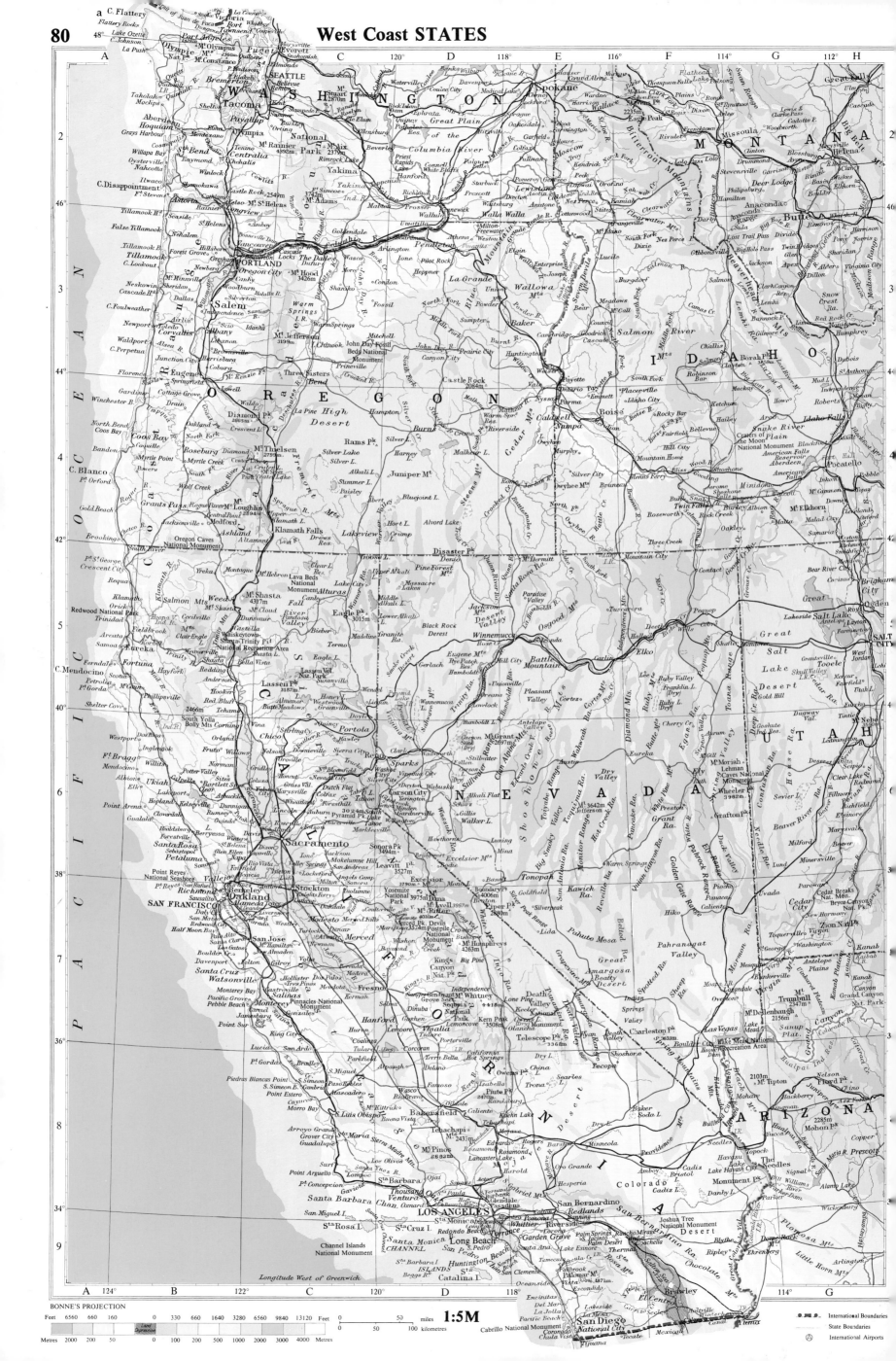

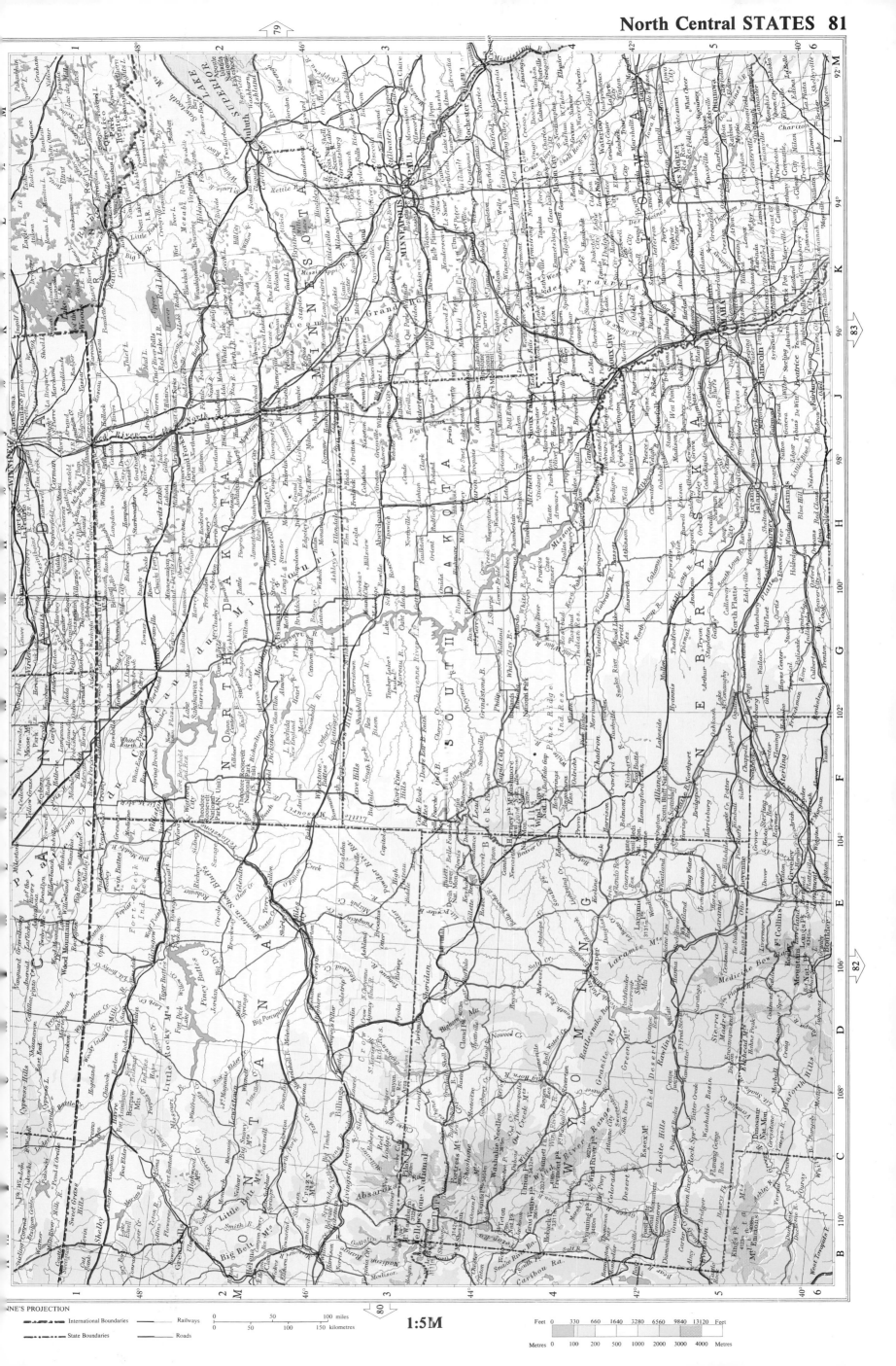

1:5M

International Boundaries — Railways

State Boundaries — Roads

0   50   100 miles
0   50   100   150 kilometres

Feet 0 330 660 1640 3280 6560 9840 13120 Feet

Metres 0 100 200 500 1000 2000 3000 4000 Metres

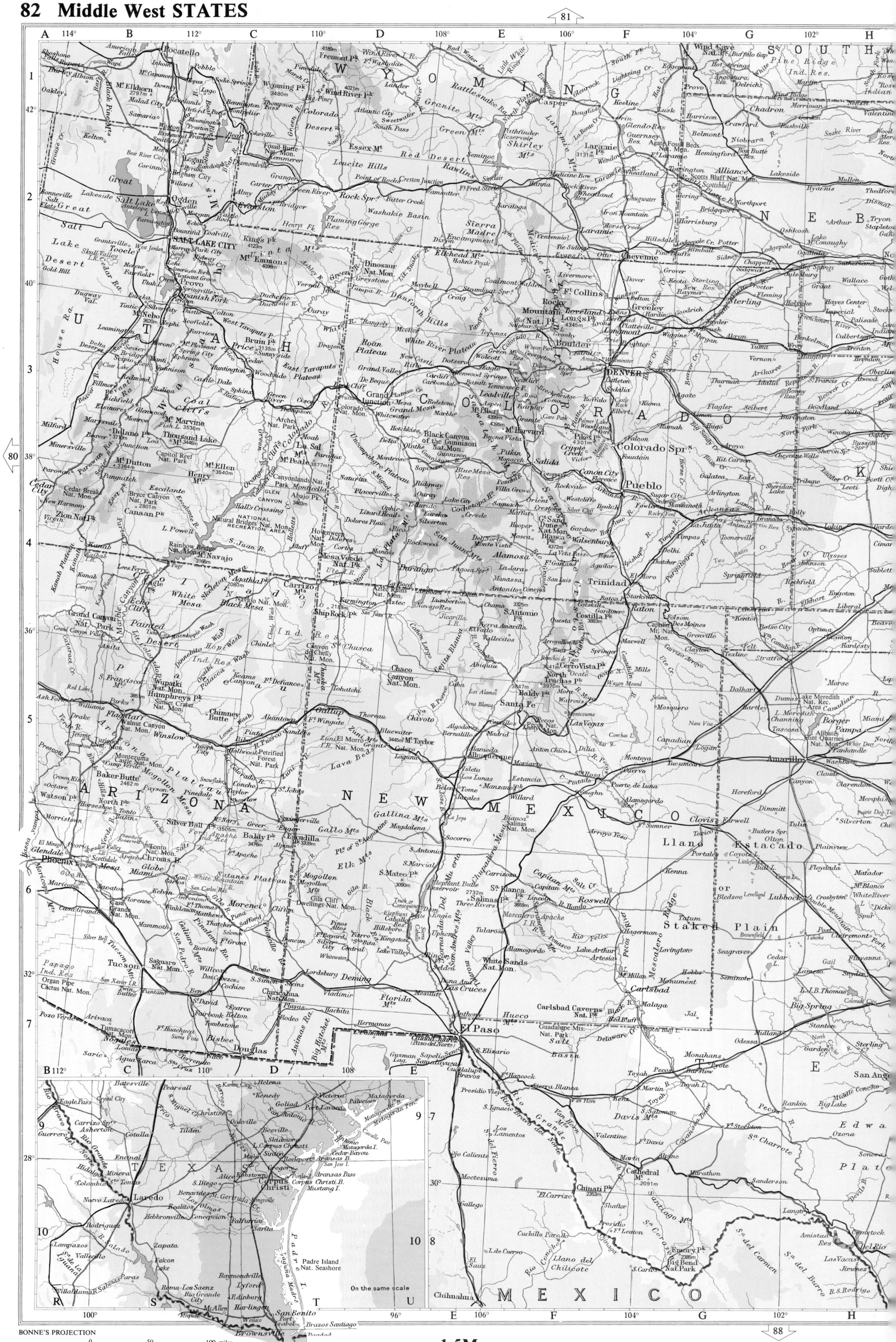

81

A 114° B 112° C 110° D 108° E 106° F 104° G 102° H

1

WYOMING

2

42°

UTAH

40°

NEBRASKA

COLORADO

3

80°

38°

Denver

4

36°

ARIZONA NEW MEXICO

5

6

Phoenix

32°

Tucson

7

El Paso

B 112° C 110° D 108° E

TEXAS

8

9

28°

On the same scale

10

MEXICO

R 100° S 96° T U E 106° F 104° G 102° H

BONNE'S PROJECTION

0   50   100 miles
0   50   100   150 kilometres

1:5M

88

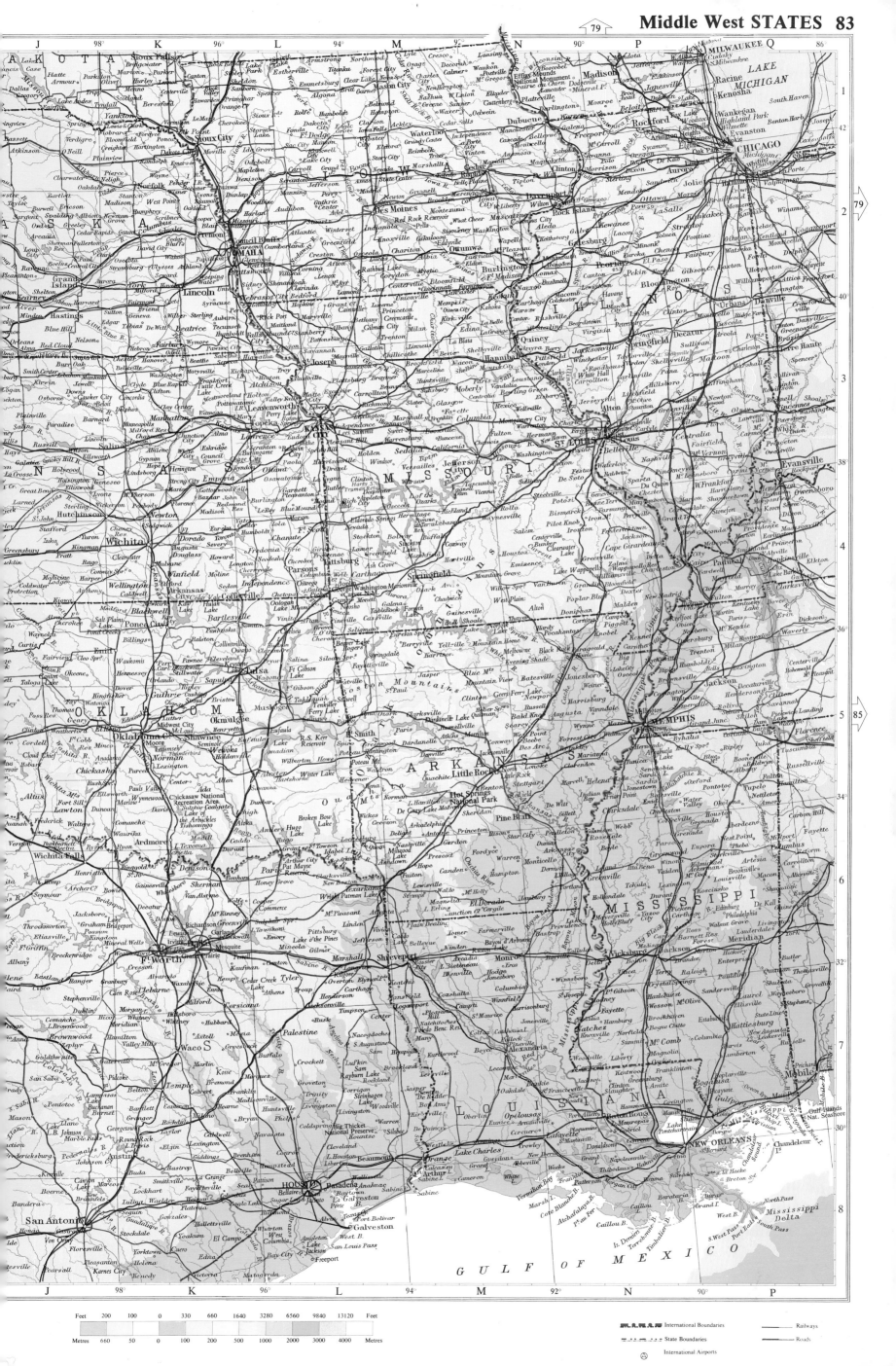

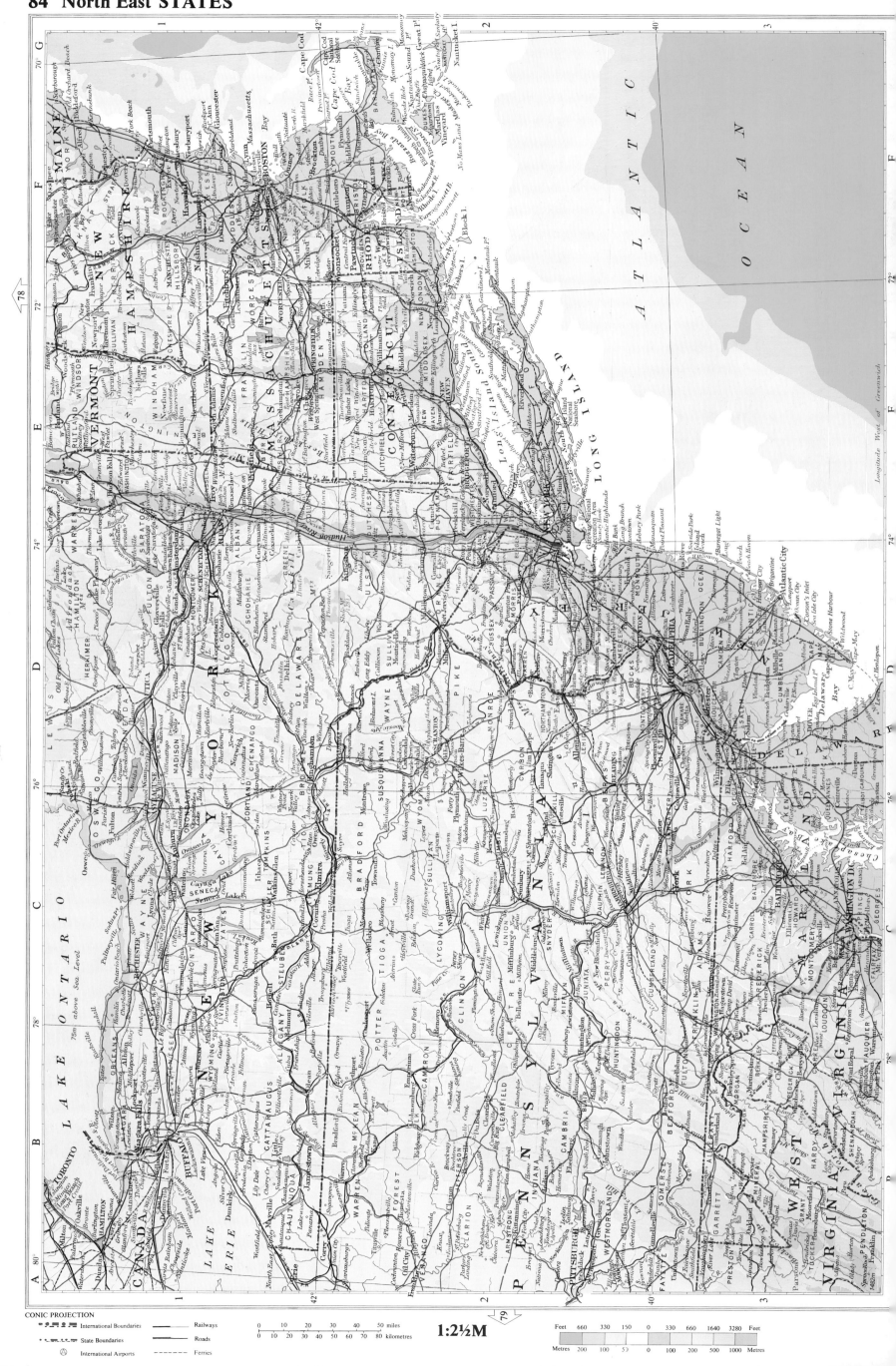

CONIC PROJECTION

International Boundaries   ——— Railways

—— State Boundaries   —— Roads

International Airports   - - - Ferries

0 10 20 30 40 50 miles
0 10 20 30 40 50 60 70 80 kilometres

1:2½M

Feet 660 330 150 0 330 660 1640 3280 Feet

Metres 200 100 50 0 100 200 500 1000 Metres

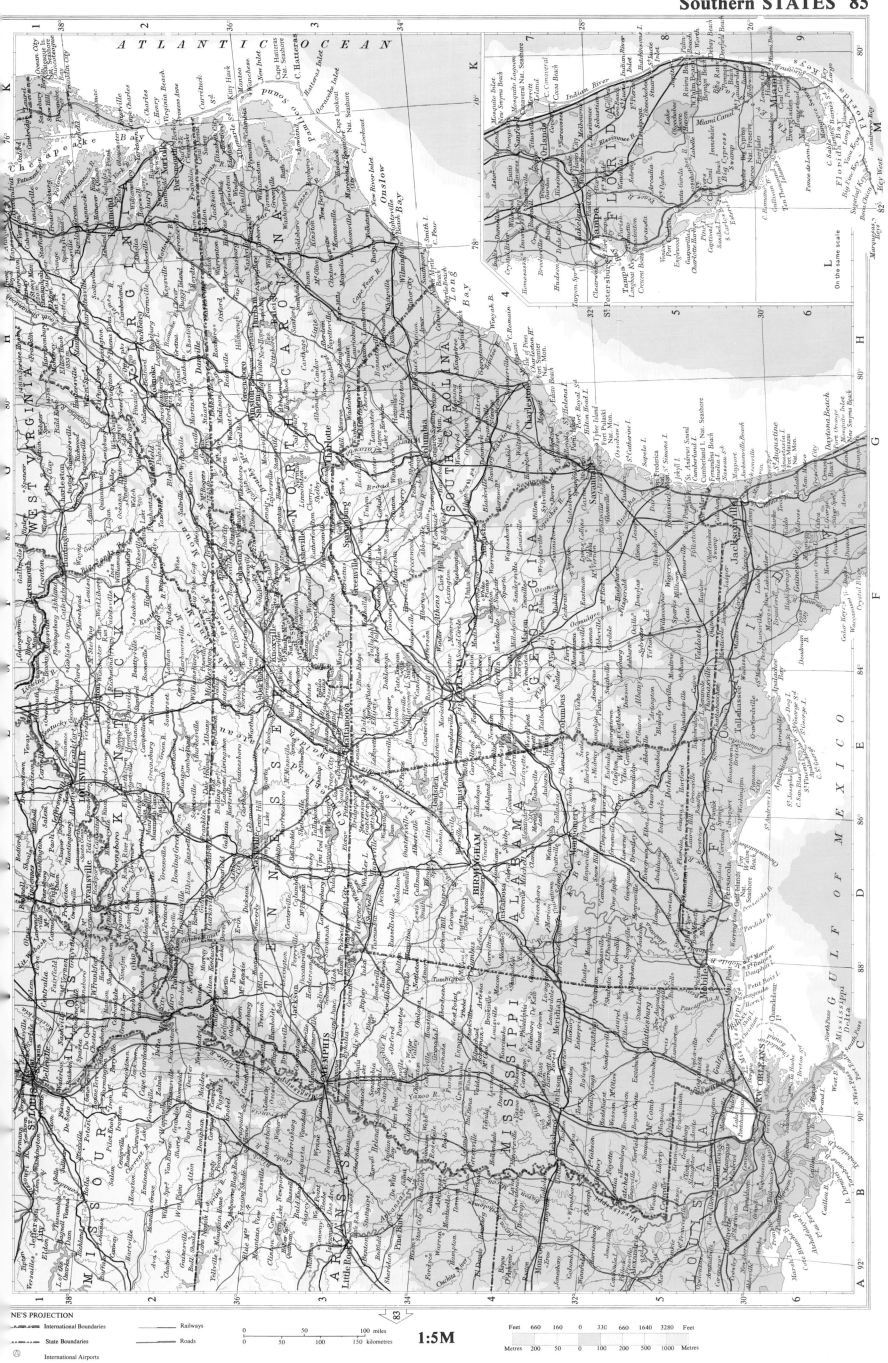

NE'S PROJECTION

International Boundaries   Railways

State Boundaries   Roads

International Airports

1:5M

0   50   100 miles

0   50   100   150 kilometres

Feet 660 160 0 330 660 1640 3280 Feet

Metres 200 50 0 100 200 500 1000 Metres

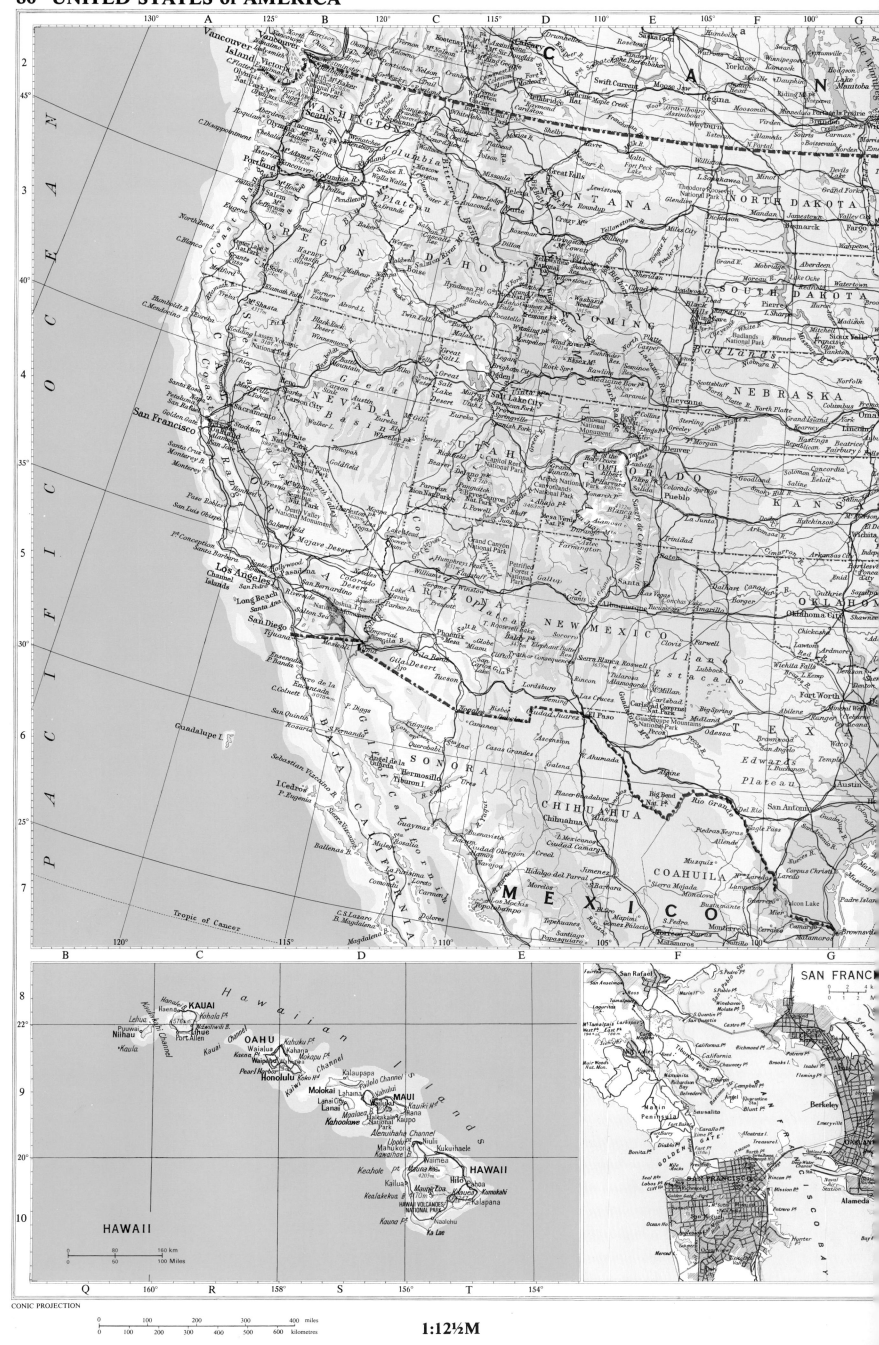

CONIC PROJECTION

1:12½M

Main Map — Eastern United States and Canada

Labels and features (selected, as printed on the map):

Canada / Great Lakes region: ONTARIO, Thunder Bay, Lake Superior, Duluth, Sault Ste Marie, Sudbury, North Bay, Ottawa, Toronto, Lake Huron, Lake Michigan, Lake Erie, Lake Ontario, Georgian Bay, Manitoulin I., QUÉBEC, Montréal, Québec, Trois-Rivières, Sherbrooke, St Lawrence R., Gulf of St Lawrence, Gaspé, Anticosti I., NEW BRUNSWICK, Fredericton, Edmundston, NOVA SCOTIA, Halifax, Cape Breton I., Sydney, Prince Edward I., Charlottetown, Sable I.

United States: WISCONSIN, Madison, Milwaukee, MICHIGAN, Detroit, Grand Rapids, Lansing, Flint, ILLINOIS, Chicago, Springfield, INDIANA, Indianapolis, OHIO, Cleveland, Columbus, Cincinnati, Toledo, Akron, MISSOURI, St Louis, KENTUCKY, Louisville, Frankfort, Lexington, TENNESSEE, Nashville, Memphis, Knoxville, Chattanooga, ARKANSAS, Little Rock, MISSISSIPPI, Jackson, Vicksburg, ALABAMA, Birmingham, Montgomery, Mobile, LOUISIANA, Baton Rouge, New Orleans, GEORGIA, Atlanta, Savannah, Columbus, Macon, Augusta, SOUTH CAROLINA, Columbia, Charleston, NORTH CAROLINA, Raleigh, Charlotte, Greensboro, Winston Salem, Wilmington, C. Hatteras, C. Fear, VIRGINIA, Richmond, Norfolk, Roanoke, Lynchburg, WEST VIRGINIA, Charleston, Huntington, MARYLAND, Baltimore, Annapolis, PENNSYLVANIA, Pittsburgh, Philadelphia, Harrisburg, Scranton, NEW JERSEY, Trenton, Atlantic City, C. May, NEW YORK, New York, Buffalo, Rochester, Syracuse, Albany, Utica, CONNECTICUT, Hartford, New Haven, RHODE ISLAND, MASSACHUSETTS, Boston, Cape Cod, Nantucket I., Martha's Vineyard, New Bedford, VERMONT, Montpelier, NEW HAMPSHIRE, Concord, MAINE, Augusta, Portland, Bangor, Bath.

FLORIDA: Tallahassee, Jacksonville, Orlando, Tampa, St Petersburg, Miami, Key West, Lake Okeechobee, C. Canaveral, Daytona Beach, West Palm Beach, Everglades Nat. Pk., Cedar Key, Panama City, Pensacola, St Augustine, Ten Thousand Is., C. Sable.

Water bodies: ATLANTIC OCEAN, GULF OF MEXICO, Delta of the Mississippi, Long Bay, Raleigh Bay, Pamlico Sound, Chesapeake Bay.

THE BAHAMAS: Nassau, Grand Bahama, Great Abaco, Eleuthera I., Andros I., San Salvador or Watling I., Cat I., Exuma Is., Bimini Is., Berry Is., Providence. Bermudas. Tropic of Cancer.

Longitude West 90° of Greenwich

Inset Map — New York

NEW YORK. 0 5 km / 0 2 Miles. BRONX, MANHATTAN, BROOKLYN, QUEENS, LONG ISLAND, Hudson River, East River, Jersey City, Newark, Upper Bay, Lower Bay, Jamaica Bay, Staten Island, Coney I., Rockaway Inlet, The Narrows, Statue of Liberty, Governors I., Ellis I., La Guardia Airport, Newark Airport, International Airport.

Inset Map — Alaska

ALASKA. UNITED STATES, CANADA, U.S.S.R., Siberia, Chukchi Sea, Bering Sea, Bering Strait, Gulf of Alaska, Arctic Circle, Barrow, Cape Halkett, Prudhoe Bay, Point Hope, Kotzebue, Nome, Fairbanks, Anchorage, Juneau, Mt McKinley, Mt Logan, Mt St Elias, Yukon R., Brooks Range, Alaska Range, Mackenzie Bay, Great Bear Lake, Aleutian Is., Kodiak I., Bristol Bay, Cook Inlet, Seward Pen., Nunivak I., St Lawrence I., Pribilof Is., Prince of Wales I., Queen Charlotte Is., Rocky Mts., Mackenzie Mts.

Scale: 0 100 200 300 Miles / 0 200 400 km

Legend

Feet: 6560 660 160 0 660 1640 3280 6560 9840 13120 Feet
Metres: 2000 200 50 0 200 500 1000 2000 3000 <6000 Metres
Land Depression

— · — · International Boundaries
········· State Boundaries
——— Railways
——— Roads

MEXICO

UNITED STATES

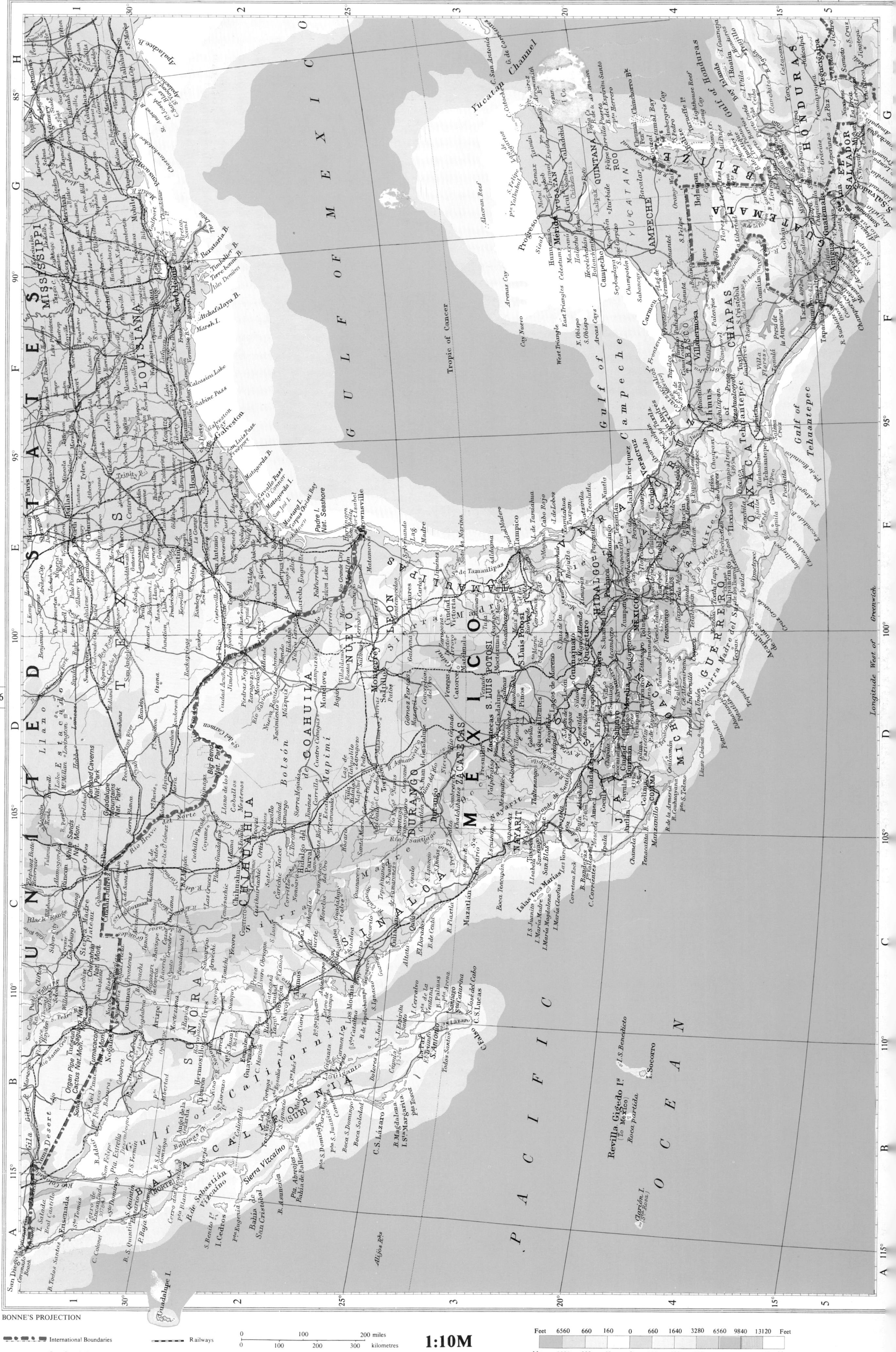

TEXAS

LOUISIANA

MISSISSIPPI

GULF OF MEXICO

Tropic of Cancer

SONORA

CHIHUAHUA

COAHUILA

NUEVO LEON

DURANGO

SINALOA

ZACATECAS

S. LUIS POTOSI

TAMAULIPAS

M E X I C O

NAYARIT

JALISCO

GUANAJUATO

QUERETARO

HIDALGO

VERA CRUZ

MICHOACAN

GUERRERO

OAXACA

MEXICO

MORELOS

PUEBLA

TLAXCALA

TABASCO

CHIAPAS

CAMPECHE

YUCATAN

QUINTANA ROO

Gulf of Campeche

Yucatan Channel

Gulf of Tehuantepec

BELIZE

GUATEMALA

HONDURAS

EL SALVADOR

Gulf of Honduras

BAJA CALIFORNIA NORTE

BAJA CALIFORNIA SUR

Gulf of California

P A C I F I C   O C E A N

Revilla Gigedo Is. (to Mexico)

Longitude West of Greenwich

BONNE'S PROJECTION

1:10M

International Boundaries	Railways
State Boundaries	Roads

0   100   200 miles

0   100   200   300 kilometres

Feet	6560	660	160	0	660	1640	3280	6560	9840	13120	Feet
Metres	2000	200	50	0	200	500	1000	2000	3000	4000	Metres

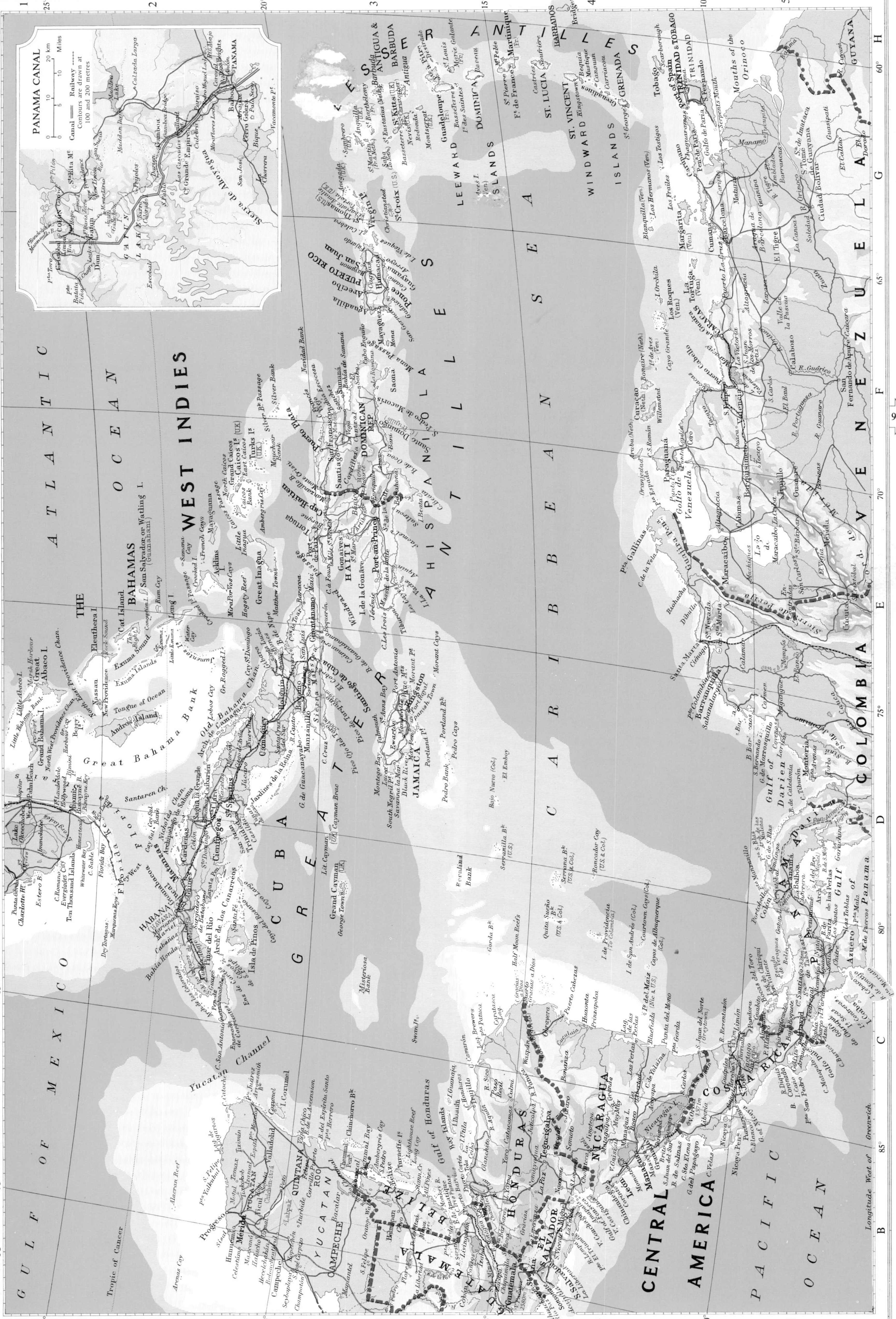

PANAMA CANAL

Canal ——— Railway ——
Contours are drawn at
100 and 200 metres

0 5 10 Miles
0 5 10 20 km

WEST INDIES

THE BAHAMAS

ATLANTIC OCEAN

GULF OF MEXICO

Tropic of Cancer

CUBA

JAMAICA

HAITI

DOMINICAN REP.

PUERTO RICO

GREATER ANTILLES

LESSER ANTILLES

LEEWARD ISLANDS

WINDWARD ISLANDS

ANTIGUA & BARBUDA

GUADELOUPE

DOMINICA

MARTINIQUE

ST. LUCIA

ST. VINCENT

BARBADOS

GRENADA

TRINIDAD & TOBAGO

CARIBBEAN SEA

CENTRAL AMERICA

BELIZE

GUATEMALA

HONDURAS

EL SALVADOR

NICARAGUA

COSTA RICA

PANAMA

COLOMBIA

VENEZUELA

GUYANA

Mouths of the Orinoco

PACIFIC OCEAN

YUCATAN

QUINTANA ROO

CAMPECHE

Grand Cayman

HABANA
(HAVANA)

Kingston

Port-au-Prince

Santo Domingo

San Juan

Caracas

Panama

ANNE'S PROJECTION

■■■■■ International Boundaries   ----- Railways
        State Boundaries   ——— Roads

0   100   150 miles
0   100   200 kilometres

Feet 6560 660 160 0 660 1640 3280 6560 9840 13120 Feet
Metres 2000 200 50 0 200 500 1000 2000 3000 4000 Metres

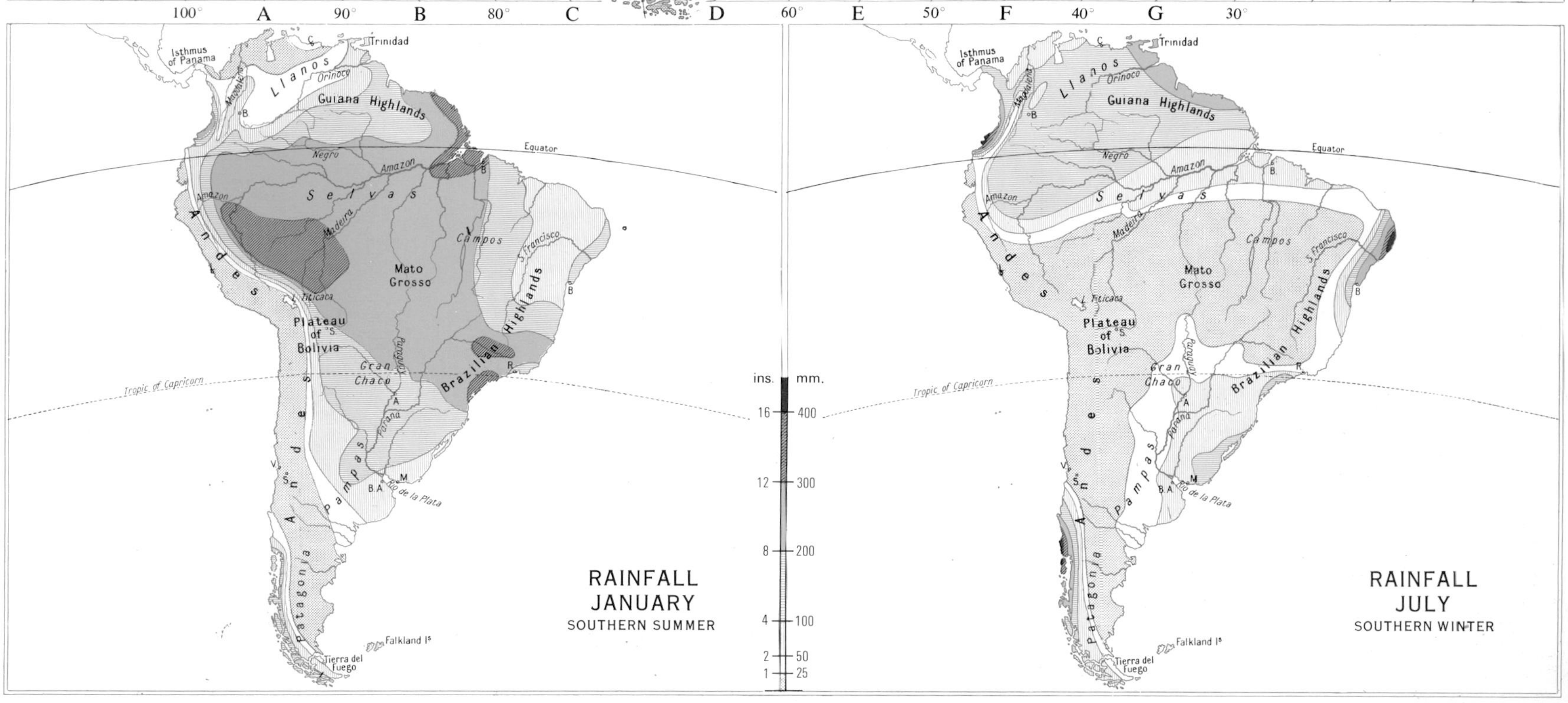

VEGETATION

1	Antarctic Tundra	
2A	Andean Mountain Zone, Paramos (wet)	
2B	" " " Punas (dry)	
2C	" " " Tola (arid)	
3	Hill Tropical Forest	
5	Catingas	
6	Chaco	
7	Inter-Andean Basin Cultivation	
9	Park Land	
10	Temperate Forest	
11	Mixed Tropical Forest	
12	Tropical Rain Forest	

13	Pampas (Rich Grass)
14	Llanos (Plateau Grass)
15	Campos Cerrados and Savannah
16	Mediterranean Type Vegetation
17	"Monte," Xerophil Bush
17A	Salt Swamp
18	Patagonian Steppe
19	Semi-Desert
20	Waterless Desert

Fresh Water Swamp

Southern Limit of Hevea (Wild Rubber)

Southern Limit of Quebracho

Extent of Yerba Maté

1 : 32 M.

Longitude West of Greenwich

Map labels (main map)

Barranquilla · Caracas · Trinidad · Cauca · Apure · Orinoco · Llanos · Georgetown · Paramaribo · Cayenne · Magdalena · Bogota · Guaviare · Guiana Highlands · Branco · Amazon · Equator · Quito · Putumayo · Japurá · Negro · Belém · Guayaquil · Marañón · Selvas · Juruá · Purus · Tapajós · Xingu · Tocantins · Parnaíba · Recife · Madeira · Catingas · São Francisco · Lima · Ucayali · Beni · Guaporé · Mato Grosso · Cerrados · Salvador · L. Titicaca · La Paz · Campos · Brasília · Arica · Bolivian Plateau · L. Poopó · Sucre · Pilcomayo · Gran Chaco · Paraguay · Paraná · São Paulo · Atacama Desert · Antofagasta · Tropic of Capricorn · Asunción · Uruguay · Rio de Janeiro · Valparaíso · Santiago · Paraná · Rosario · Buenos Aires · Montevideo · Pampas · Concepción · Colorado · Bahía Blanca · Andes · Patagonian Desert · Falkland Is · Punta Arenas

RAINFALL JANUARY
SOUTHERN SUMMER

Isthmus of Panama · Trinidad · Llanos · Orinoco · Guiana Highlands · Negro · Amazon · Equator · Selvas · Madeira · Campos · S. Francisco · Brazilian Highlands · Mato Grosso · Plateau of Bolivia · Gran Chaco · Paraná · Tropic of Capricorn · Andes · Pampas · de la Plata · Patagonia · Falkland Is · Tierra del Fuego

ins.	mm.
16	400
12	300
8	200
4	100
2	50
1	25

RAINFALL JULY
SOUTHERN WINTER

Isthmus of Panama · Trinidad · Llanos · Orinoco · Guiana Highlands · Negro · Amazon · Equator · Selvas · Madeira · Campos · S. Francisco · Brazilian Highlands · Mato Grosso · Plateau of Bolivia · Gran Chaco · Tropic of Capricorn · Andes · Pampas · de la Plata · Patagonia · Falkland Is · Tierra del Fuego

LAMBERTS AZIMUTHAL EQUAL AREA PROJECTION

0	100	200	300	400	500 miles
0	200	400		600	800 kilometres

1:32M

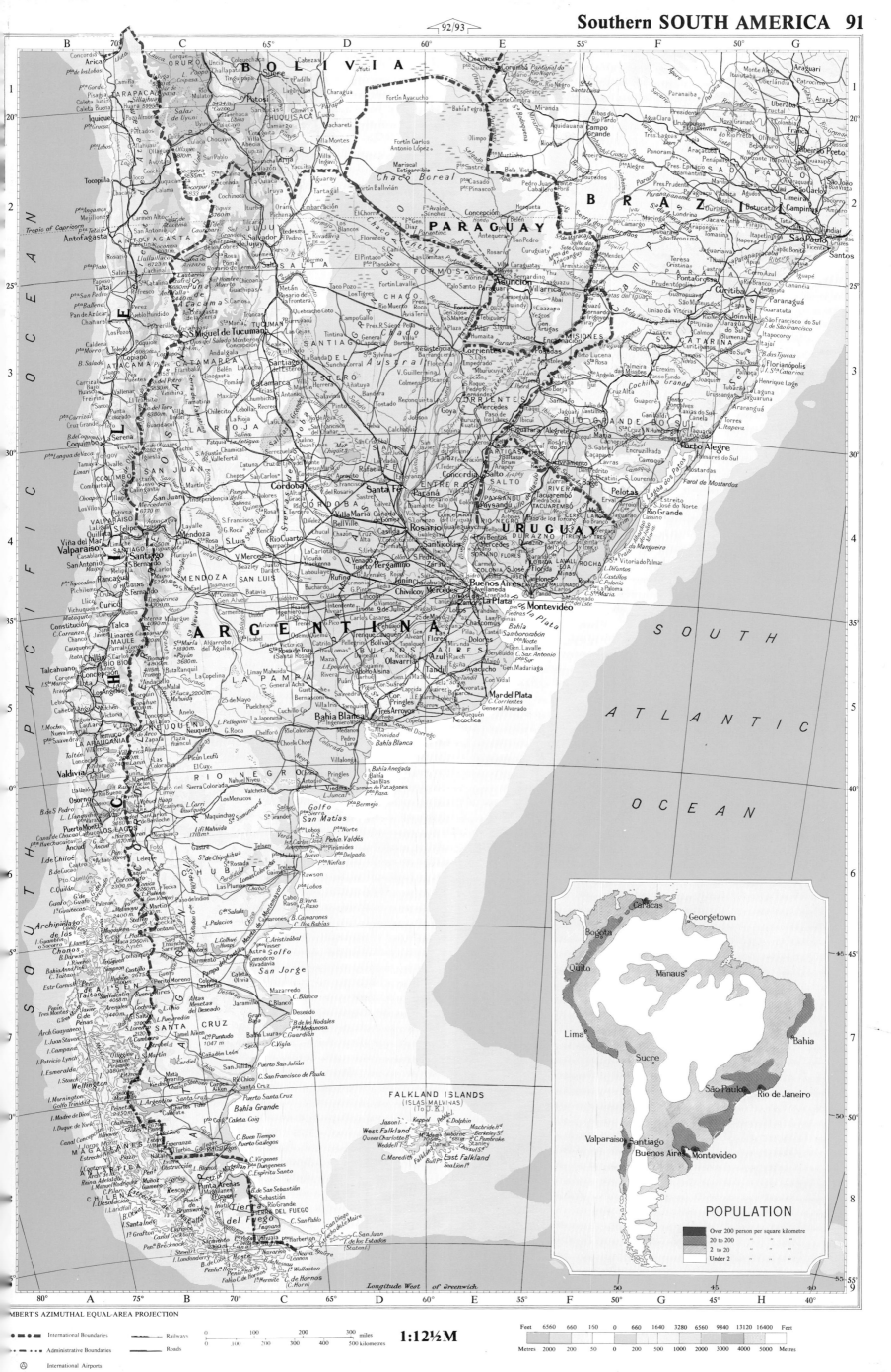

POPULATION

	Over 200 person per square kilometre
	20 to 200 " " " "
	2 to 20 " " " "
	Under 2 " " " "

LAMBERT'S AZIMUTHAL EQUAL-AREA PROJECTION

- - - - International Boundaries
- · - · - Administrative Boundaries
       International Airports

       Railways
       Roads

| 0 | 100 | 200 | 300 miles |
| 0 | 100 200 300 | 400 | 500 kilometres |

1:12½ M

| Feet | 6560 | 660 | 160 | 0 | 660 | 1640 | 3280 | 6560 | 9840 | 13120 | 16400 | Feet |
| Metres | 2000 | 200 | 50 | 0 | 200 | 500 | 1000 | 2000 | 3000 | 4000 | 5000 | Metres |

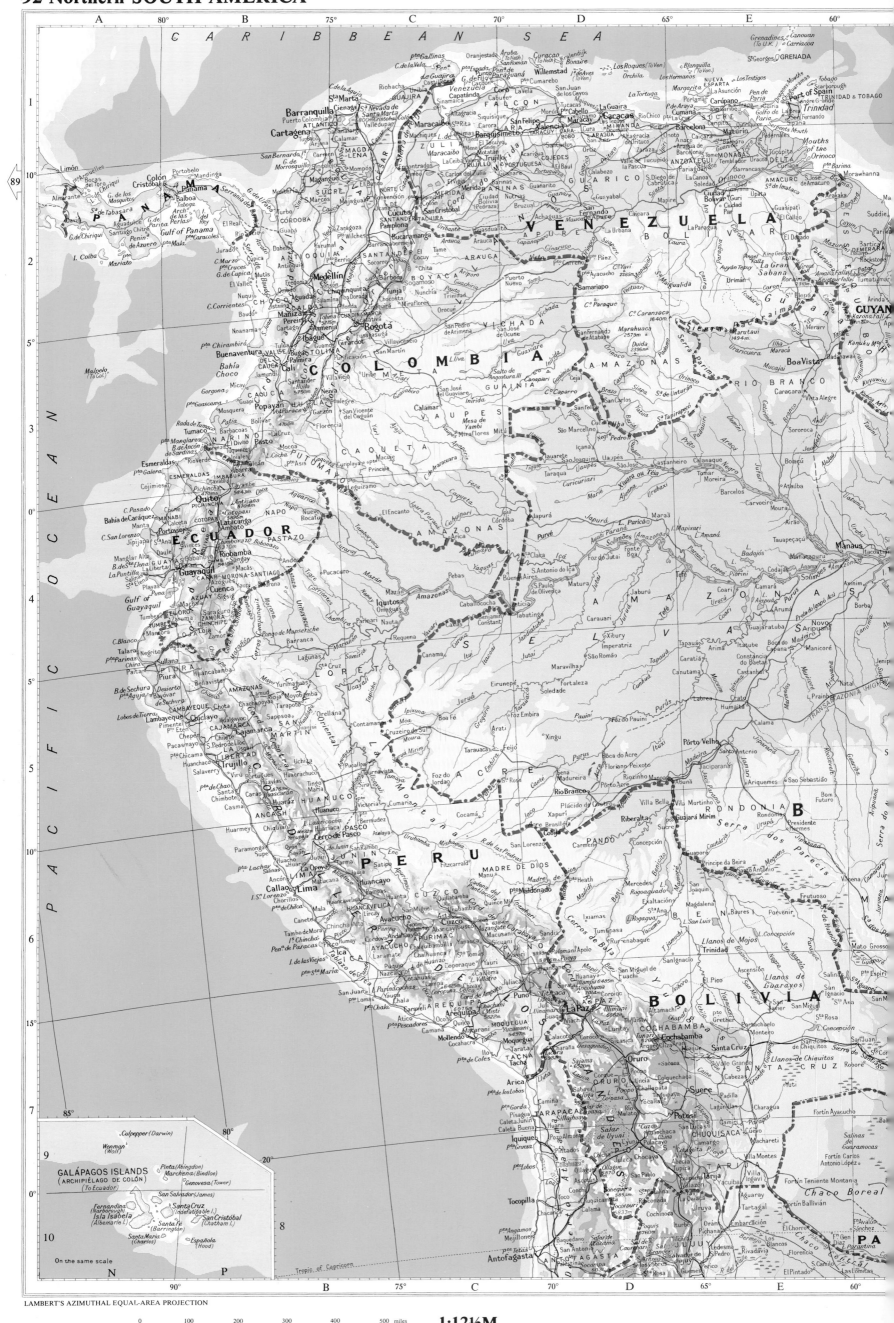

LAMBERT'S AZIMUTHAL EQUAL-AREA PROJECTION

1:12½M

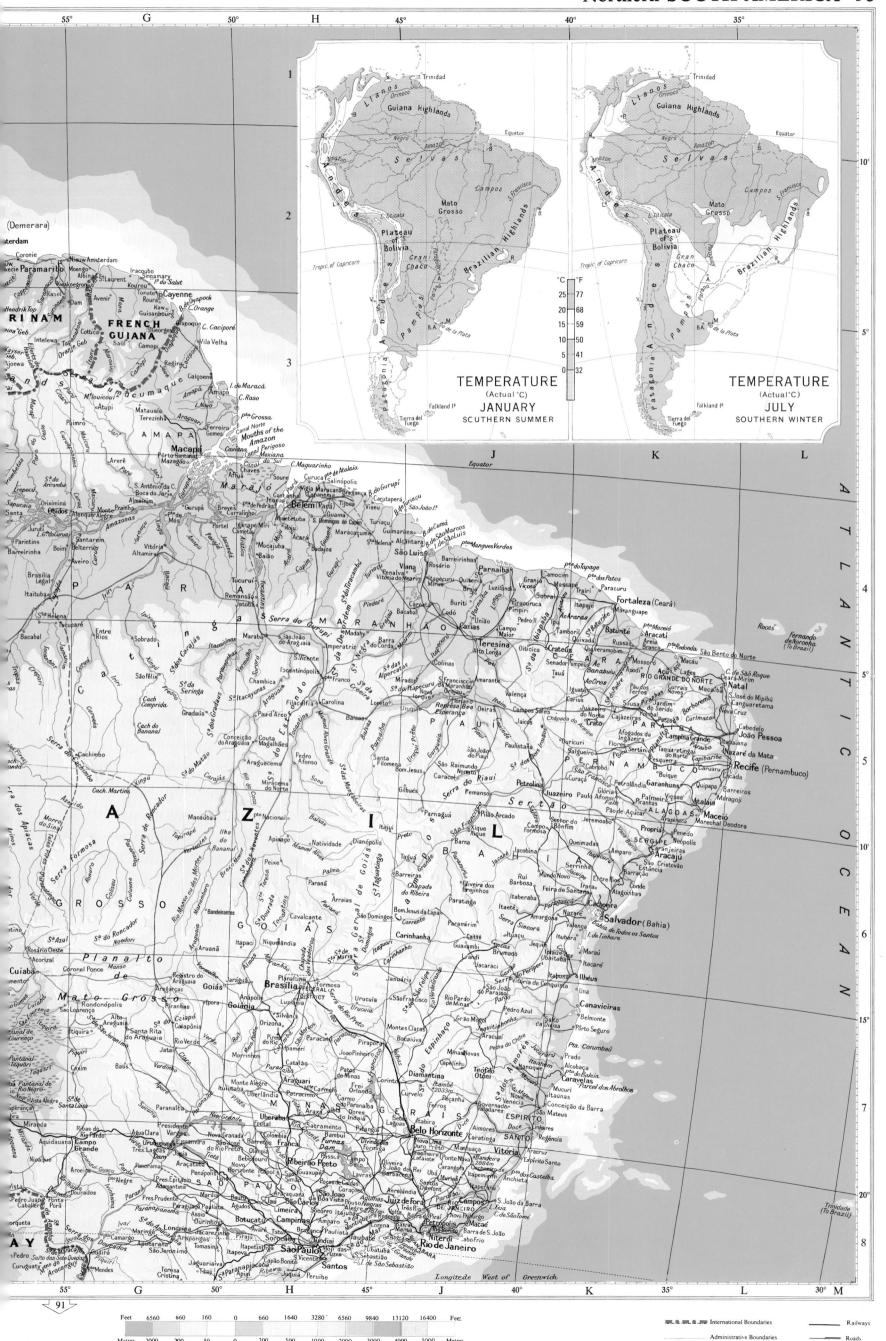

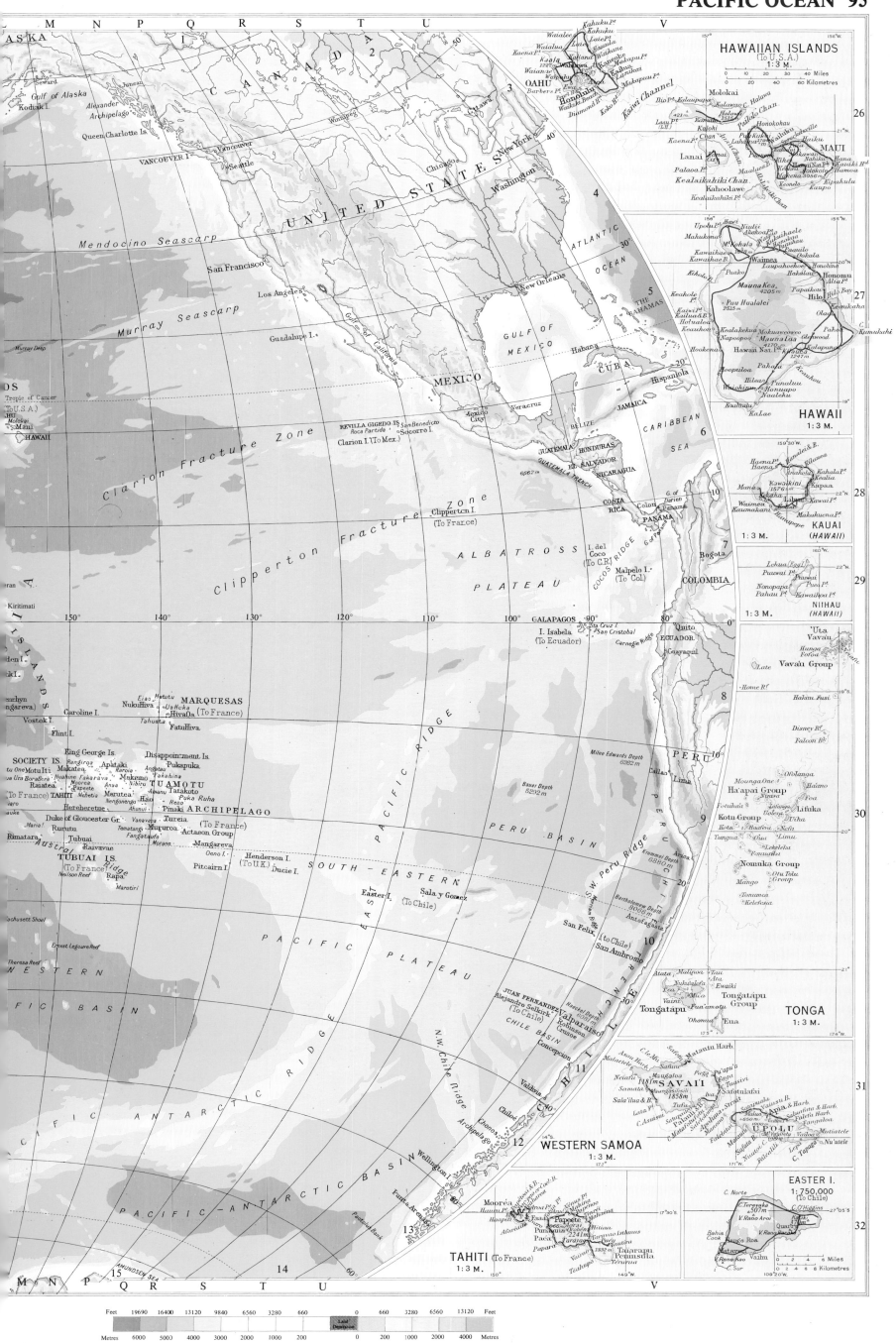

HAWAIIAN ISLANDS
(To U.S.A.)
1:3 M.
0   10   20   30   40 Miles
0   20   40   60 Kilometres

MAUI

HAWAII
1:3 M.

KAUAI
(HAWAII)
1:3 M.

NIIHAU
(HAWAII)
1:3 M.

'Uta Vavaù
Vavaù Group

Ha'apai Group

Kotu Group

Nomuka Group
Otu Tolu Group

Tongatapu Group

TONGA
1:3 M.

WESTERN SAMOA
1:3 M.

SAVAI'I

UPOLU

EASTER I.
1:750,000
(To Chile)
0   2   4   6 Miles
0   2   4   6   8 Kilometres

TAHITI (To France)
1:3 M.

Feet 19690 16400 13120 9840 6560 3280 660   0   660 3280 6560 13120 Feet
Metres 6000 5000 4000 3000 2000 1000 200   0   200 1000 2000 4000 Metres
Land Depression

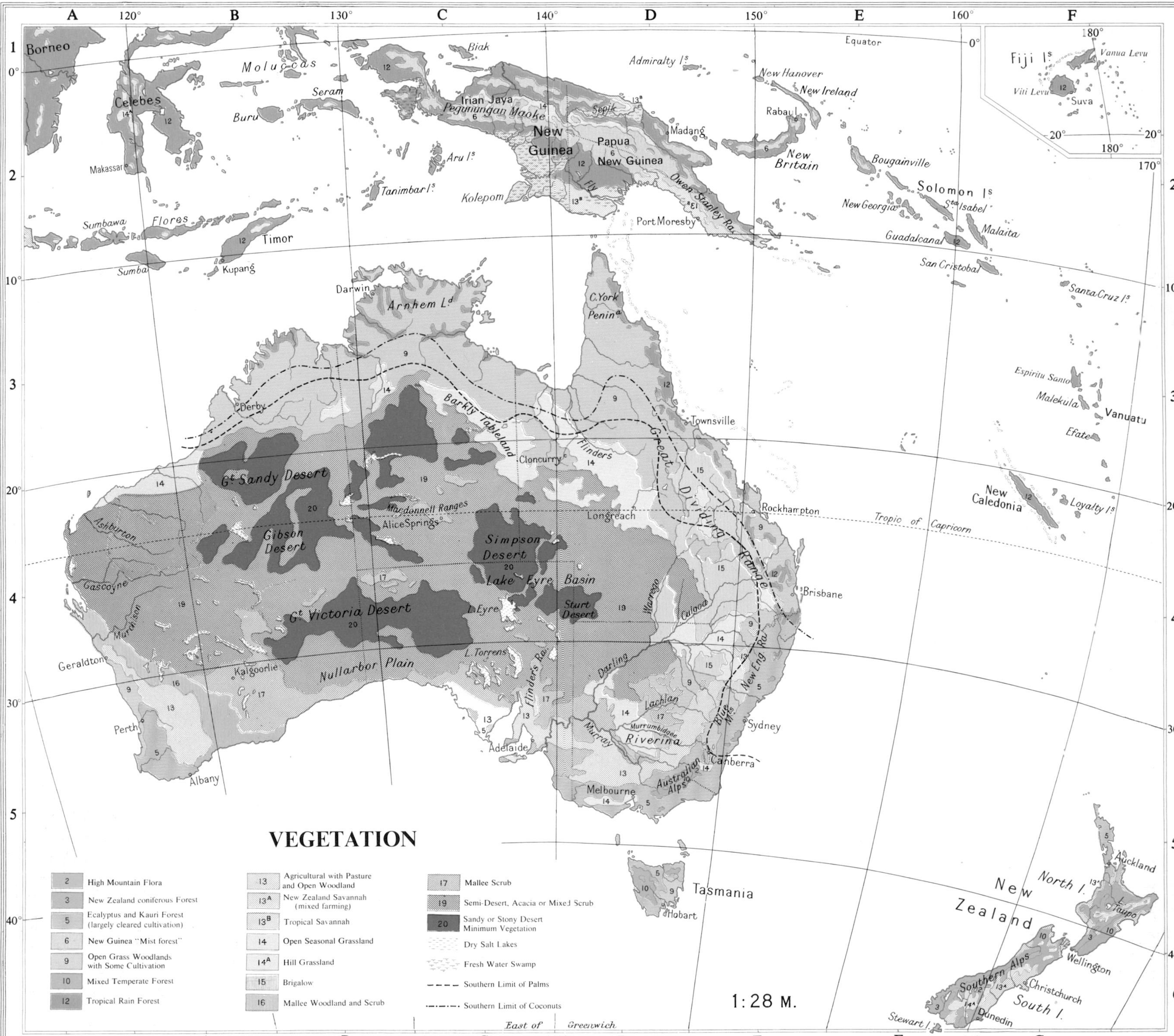

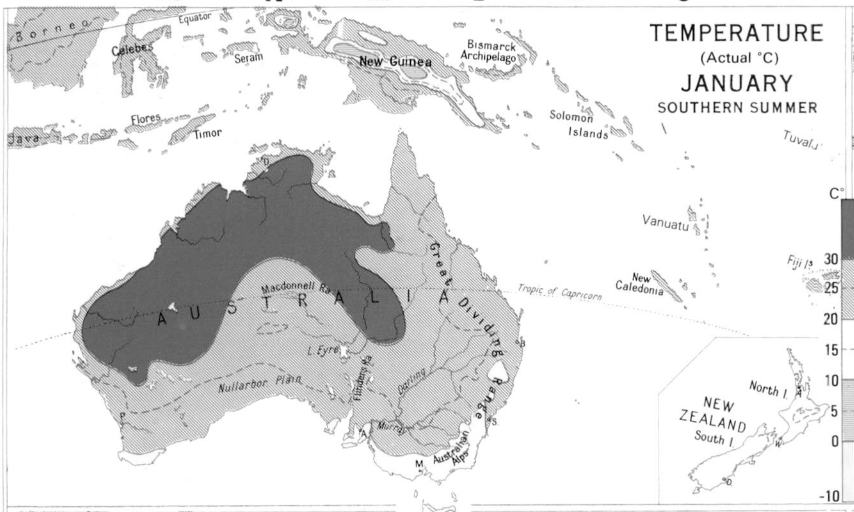

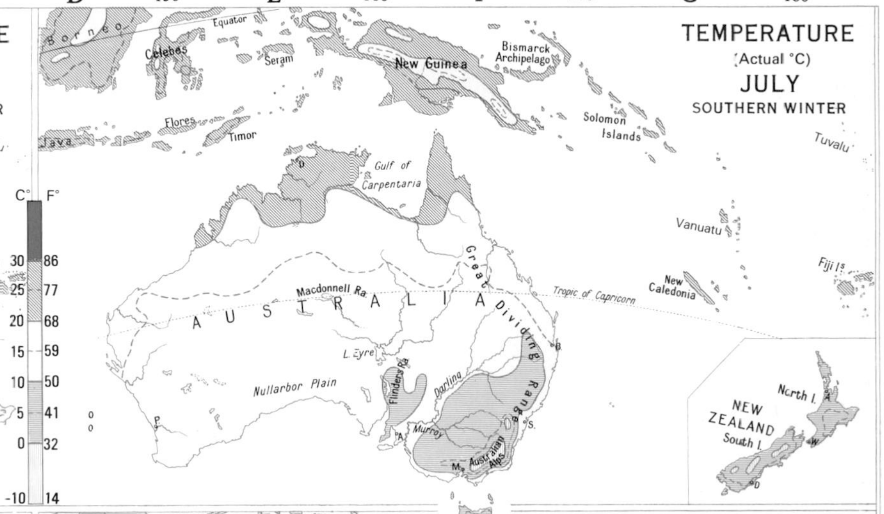

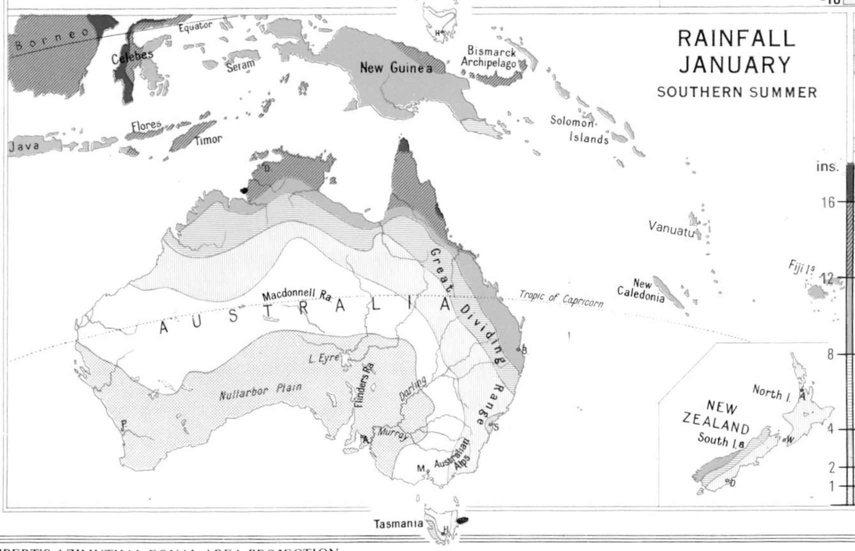

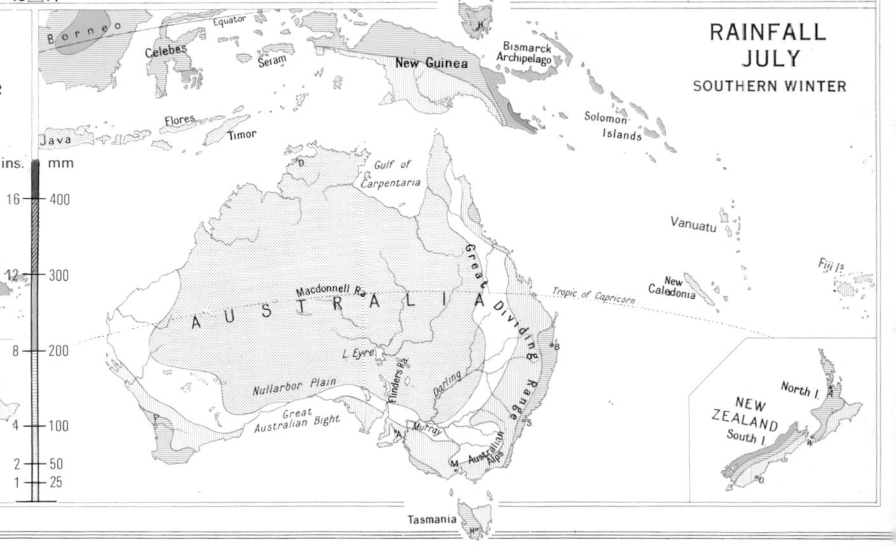

Borneo
Celebes
Makassar
Sumbawa
Flores
Sumba
Kupang
Timor
Tanimbar Is
Aru Is
Moluccas
Seram
Buru
Biak
Irian Jaya
Pegunungan Maoke
New Guinea
Sepik
Papua New Guinea
Port Moresby
Kolepom
Admiralty Is
New Hanover
New Ireland
Rabaul
New Britain
Madang
Owen Stanley Ra.
Bougainville
New Georgia
Solomon Is
St. Isabel
Guadalcanal
Malaita
San Cristobal
Santa Cruz Is
Espiritu Santo
Malakula
Vanuatu
Efate
New Caledonia
Loyalty Is
Equator

Fiji Is
Viti Levu
Vanua Levu
Suva

Darwin
Arnhem Ld
C. York Penin.
Derby
Barkly Tableland
Townsville
Gt. Sandy Desert
Macdonnell Ranges
Alice Springs
Cloncurry
Flinders
Longreach
Rockhampton
Tropic of Capricorn
Gibson Desert
Simpson Desert
Lake Eyre Basin
Brisbane
Ashburton
Gascoyne
Murchison
Gt. Victoria Desert
L. Eyre
Sturt Desert
Warrego
Culgoa
New Eng. Ra.
Geraldton
Nullarbor Plain
L. Torrens
Flinders Ra.
Darling
Lachlan
Murrumbidgee
Blue Mts.
Sydney
Riverina
Perth
Kalgoorlie
Adelaide
Murray
Canberra
Albany
Melbourne
Australian Alps

Tasmania
Hobart

New Zealand
North I.
South I.
Auckland
Taupo
Wellington
Southern Alps
Christchurch
Dunedin
Stewart I.

VEGETATION

2	High Mountain Flora	
3	New Zealand coniferous Forest	
5	Eucalyptus and Kauri Forest (largely cleared cultivation)	
6	New Guinea "Mist forest"	
9	Open Grass Woodlands with Some Cultivation	
10	Mixed Temperate Forest	
12	Tropical Rain Forest	
13	Agricultural with Pasture and Open Woodland	
13A	New Zealand Savannah (mixed farming)	
13B	Tropical Savannah	
14	Open Seasonal Grassland	
14A	Hill Grassland	
15	Brigalow	
16	Mallee Woodland and Scrub	
17	Mallee Scrub	
19	Semi-Desert, Acacia or Mixed Scrub	
20	Sandy or Stony Desert Minimum Vegetation	

Dry Salt Lakes
Fresh Water Swamp
-- Southern Limit of Palms
-·- Southern Limit of Coconuts

1 : 28 M.

East of Greenwich

TEMPERATURE
(Actual °C)
JANUARY
SOUTHERN SUMMER

Borneo
Celebes
New Guinea
Bismarck Archipelago
Seram
Java
Flores
Timor
Solomon Islands
Tuvalu
Vanuatu
Fiji Is
New Caledonia
AUSTRALIA
Macdonnell Ra.
Great Dividing Range
Tropic of Capricorn
L. Eyre
Nullarbor Plain
Darling
Murray
Australian Alps
NEW ZEALAND
North I.
South I.
Tasmania

C°	F°
30	86
25	77
20	68
15	59
10	50
5	41
0	32
-10	14

TEMPERATURE
(Actual °C)
JULY
SOUTHERN WINTER

Borneo
Celebes
New Guinea
Bismarck Archipelago
Seram
Java
Flores
Timor
Gulf of Carpentaria
Solomon Islands
Tuvalu
Vanuatu
Fiji Is
New Caledonia
AUSTRALIA
Macdonnell Ra.
Great Dividing Range
Tropic of Capricorn
L. Eyre
Nullarbor Plain
Darling
Murray
NEW ZEALAND
North I.
South I.

RAINFALL
JANUARY
SOUTHERN SUMMER

Borneo
Celebes
New Guinea
Bismarck Archipelago
Seram
Java
Flores
Timor
Solomon Islands
Vanuatu
Fiji Is
New Caledonia
AUSTRALIA
Macdonnell Ra.
Great Dividing Range
Tropic of Capricorn
L. Eyre
Nullarbor Plain
Darling
Murray
Australian Alps
NEW ZEALAND
North I.
South I.

ins.	mm
16	400
12	300
8	200
4	100
2	50
1	25

RAINFALL
JULY
SOUTHERN WINTER

Borneo
Celebes
New Guinea
Bismarck Archipelago
Seram
Java
Flores
Timor
Gulf of Carpentaria
Solomon Islands
Vanuatu
Fiji Is
New Caledonia
AUSTRALIA
Macdonnell Ra.
Great Dividing Range
Tropic of Capricorn
L. Eyre
Nullarbor Plain
Great Australian Bight
Darling
Murray
NEW ZEALAND
North I.
South I.
Tasmania

0 200 400 600 800 miles
0 200 400 600 800 1000 1200 kilometres

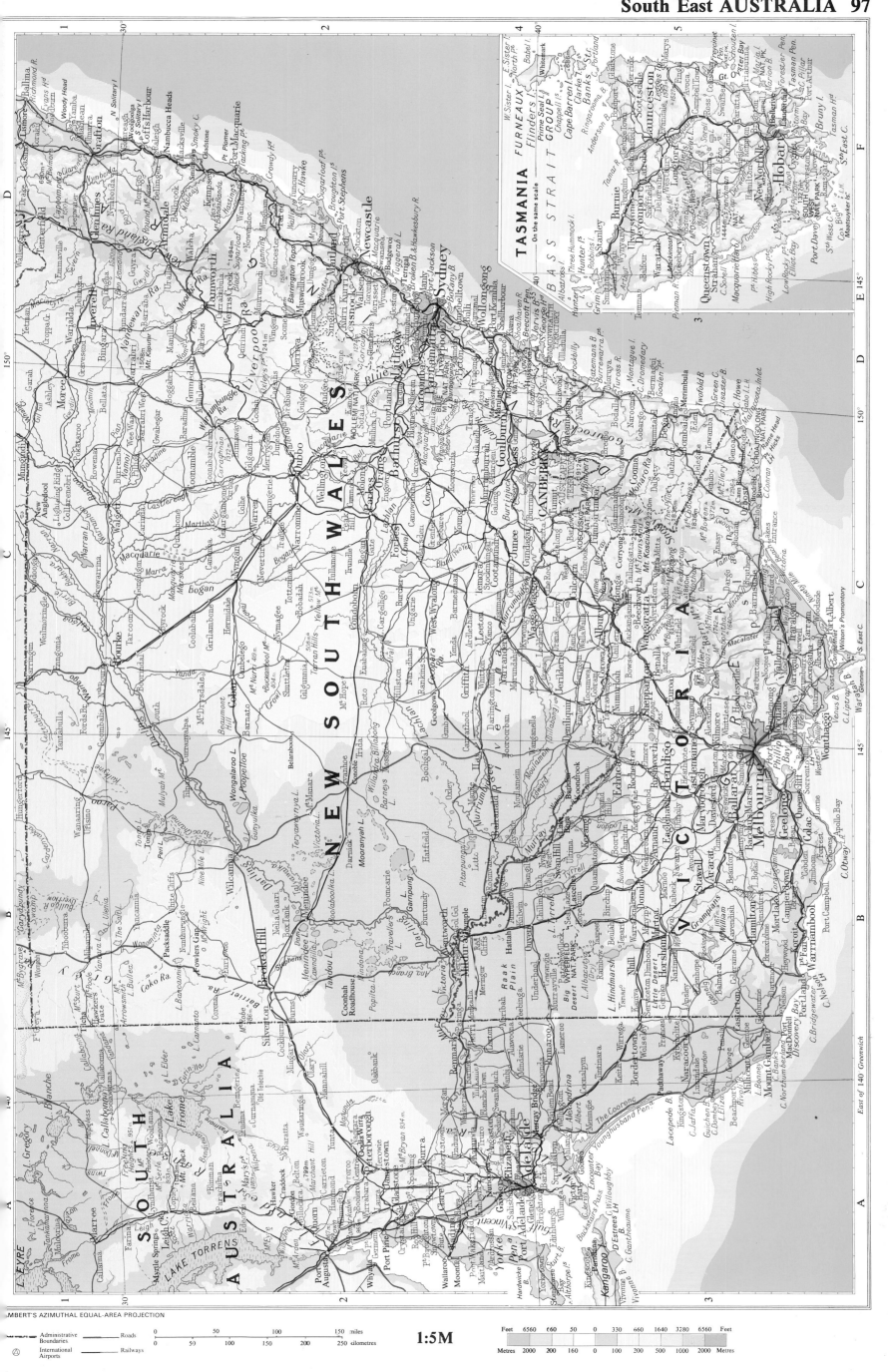

Administrative Boundaries _____ Roads
International Airports _____ Railways

| 0 | 50 | 100 | 150 miles |
| 0 | 50 | 100 | 150 | 200 | 250 kilometres |

| Feet | 6560 | 660 | 50 | 0 | 330 | 660 | 1640 | 3280 | 6560 | Feet |
| Metres | 2000 | 200 | 160 | 0 | 100 | 200 | 500 | 1000 | 2000 | Metres |

BONNE'S PROJECTION

1:12½M

International Boundaries   Roads

Administrative Boundaries   Railways

International Airports   Artesian Basins

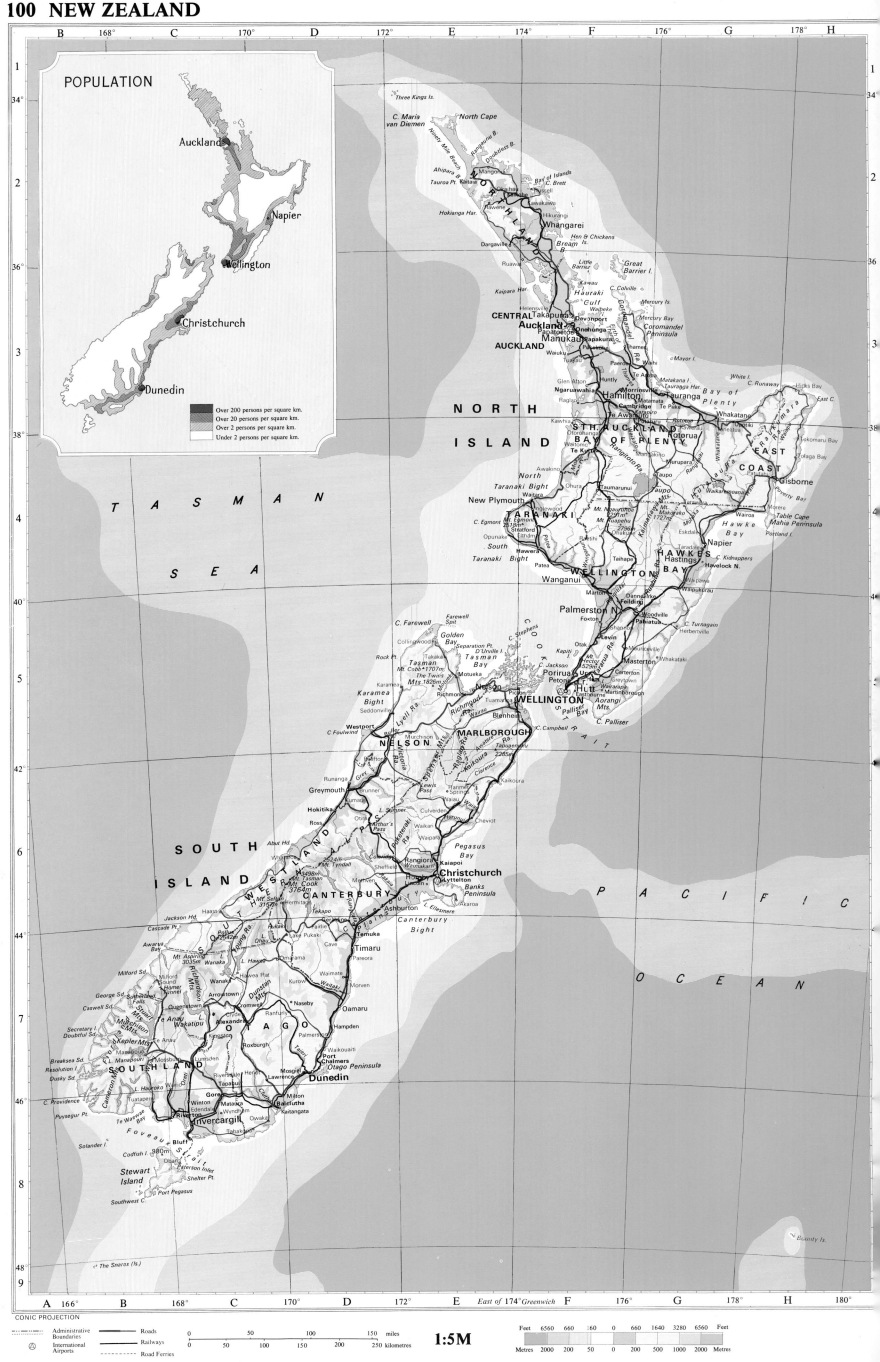

POPULATION

Over 200 persons per square km.
Over 20 persons per square km.
Over 2 persons per square km.
Under 2 persons per square km.

Auckland
Napier
Wellington
Christchurch
Dunedin

T A S M A N
S E A

P A C I F I C

O C E A N

NORTH
ISLAND

SOUTH
ISLAND

CONIC PROJECTION

Administrative
Boundaries
International
Airports

Roads
Railways
Road Ferries

0   50   100   150 miles
0   50   100   150   200   250 kilometres

1:5M

Feet 6560 660 160 0 660 1640 3280 6560 Feet
Metres 2000 200 50 0 200 500 1000 2000 Metres

INDEX

In the index, the first number refers to the page and the
following letter and number to the section of the map in
which the entry can be found. For example, Madrid 40E2
means that Madrid can be found where column E and row 2 meet.

Abbreviations used in the index

Ala.	Alabama	Kazakh.	Kazakhskaya	Pk	peak
Alta	Alberta	Kirgiz.	Kirgizskaya	Plat.	plateau
Arch.	archipelago	Ky	Kentucky	Pr.Ed.I.	Prince Edward Island
Ariz.	Arizona	L(s)	lake(s)	Prom.	promintory
Ark.	Arkansas	La	Louisiana	Pt	point, port
Armyan.	Armyanskaya	Latviy.	Latviyskaya	Que.	Quebec
Aust. Cap.		Litov.	Litovskaya	Queens.	Queensland
Terr.	Australian Capital Territory	Man.	Manitoba	R	river
Azerbay.	Azerbaydzhanskaya	Mass.	Massachussets	Ra.	range
B.	bay	Md	Maryland	Res.	reservoir
BC	British Columbia	Mich.	Michigan	RI	Rhode Island
Belorus.	Beloruskaya	Minn.	Minnesota	Rk	rock
C.	Cape	Miss.	Mississippi	Rossiy.	Rossiyskaya
Calif.	California	Mo.	Missouri	Sask.	Saskatchewan
Chan.	channel	Moldav.	Moldavskaya	S Aus.	South Australia
Col.	Colorado	Mont.	Montana	S Car.	South Carolina
Conn.	Connecticut	Mt(s)	mountain(s)	Sd	sound
Cr.	creek	N Car.	North Carolina	S Dak.	South Dakota
DC	District of Columbia	N Dak.	North Dakota	Str(s)	strait(s)
Del.	Delaware	Nebr.	Nebraska	Tadzhik.	Tadzhikskaya
Des.	desert	Nev.	Nevada	Tas.	Tasmania
Eston.	Estonskaya	New Br.	New Brunswick	Tenn.	Tennessee
Fla	Florida	Newf.	Newfoundland	Turkmen.	Turkmenskaya
Fj.	fjord	New H.	New Hampshire	Ukrain.	Ukrainskaya
Fk	fork	New J.	New Jersey	Uzbek.	Uzbekskaya
Ft	fort	New Mex.	New Mexico	V	valley
G	gulf	No. Sc.	Nova Scotia	Va	Virginia
Ga	Georgia	NSW	New South Wales	Vic.	Victoria
Gl.	glacier	N Terr.	Northern Territory	Vir. Is	Virgin Islands
Grp	group	NW Terr.	Northwest Territory	Vol.	volcano
Gruzin.	Gruzinskaya	NY	New York	Vt	Vermont
Hd	head	Okla.	Oklahoma	Wash.	Washington
Heilong.	Heilongjiang	Ont.	Ontario	W Aus.	Western Australia
I(s)	island(s)	Oreg.	Oregon	Wis.	Wisconsin
Ill.	Illinois	P.	pass	W Va	West Virginia
Ind.	Indiana	Pa	Pennsylvania	Wyo.	Wyoming
Inl.	inlet	Pass.	passage	Yukon.	Yukon
Kans.	Kansas	Pen.	peninsula		

Aachen   **Ahtari**

A

Aachen W Germany 36B3
Aalen W Germany 36D4
Aalsmeer Netherlands 32C2
Aalst Belgium 32C4
Aalten Netherlands 32E3
Aalter Belgium 32B3
Aarau Switzerland 33C1
Aarberg Switzerland 33C1
Aarburg Switzerland 33C1
Aardenburg Netherlands 32B3
Aare,R Switzerland 33C1
Aargau canton Switzerland 33D1
Aarlen = Arlon
Aarschot Belgium 32C4
Aba Nigeria 68G7
Aba Zaire 71G4
Abacaxis,R Brazil 92F4
Abādān Iran 62F3
Abadeh Iran 63G3
Abaetetuba Brazil 93H4
Abagnar Qi China 52G1
Abai Paraguay 91E3
Abajo Pk Utah USA 82D4
Abakan USSR 51L4
Abancay Peru 92C6
Abarqū Iran 63G3
Abashiri Japan 56J2
Abashiri wan bay Japan 56J2
Abau Papua New Guinea 99K2
Abaya,L Ethiopia 71H3
Abbekas Sweden 35E9
Abbeville France 42D1
Abbeville Ga USA 85F4
Abbeville La USA 83M8
Abbeyfeale Ireland, Rep. of 31E9
Abbeyleix Ireland, Rep. of 31J8
Abborträsk Sweden 34H4
Abbot Ice Shelf Antarctica 15R2
Abbots Bromley England UK 25E7
Abbotsbury England UK 26J7
Abbottabad Pakistan 60C3
Abdal Kuri island Indian Ocean 71L2
Abdulino USSR 49L4
Abéché Chad 69K6
Abele Belgium 32A4
Abelessa Algeria 68F4
Abengourou Ivory Coast 68E7
Abenra Denmark 35C9
Abeokuta Nigeria 68F7
Aberaeron Wales UK 26F4
Abercrombie,R NSW Australia 97C2
Aberdare Wales UK 26H5

Aberdeen Idaho USA 80G4
Aberdeen Miss. USA 85C4
Aberdeen Scotland UK 28M5
Aberdeen S Dak. USA 81H3
Aberdeen Wash. USA 80B2
Aberdeen L NW Terr. Canada 76M4
Aberdyfi Wales UK 26F3
Aberfeldy Scotland UK 29J6
Aberfoyle Scotland UK 29H7
Abergavenny Wales UK 26H5
Abergele Wales UK 26G2
Abernethy Scotland UK 29K7
Aberystwyth Wales UK 26F4
Abetone P Italy 44C3
Abha Saudi Arabia 62E6
Abidjan Benin 68E7
Ab-i-Istada lake Afghanistan 63K3
Abilene Kans. USA 83K3
Abilene Texas USA 83J6
Abingdon England UK 27M5
Abingdon Va USA 85F2
Abington Mass. USA 84F1
Abington Scotland UK 29J8
Abisko Sweden 34H2
Abitibi L Ont. Canada 77Q7
Abitibi,R Ont. Canada 77P6
Abo = Turku
Abomey Benin 68F7
Abong Mbang Cameroun 69H8
Abou Deia Chad 69J6
Aboyne Scotland UK 28L5
Abqaiq Saudi Arabia 62F4
Abrantes Portugal 40B3
Abri Sudan 69M4
Abrud Romania 46D1
Abruzzi region Italy 44D4
Abtenau Austria 36E5
Abu India 58D4
Abu al Abyad island UAE 63G5
Abū 'Arish Saudi Arabia 62E6
Abu Deleiq Sudan 69M5
Abu Dhabi UAE 63G5
Abu ed Duhur Syria 64F2
Abū el Jurdhān Jordan 64D7
Abu Hamed Sudan 69M5
Abu Jifan Saudi Arabia 62F5
Abumombozi Zaire 70E4
Abunã Brazil 92D5
Abu Qurqas Egypt 69M3
Abut Hd New Zealand 100D6
Abuya Myeda,Mt Ethiopia 71H2
Abu Zabad Sudan 69L6
Abwong Sudan 69M7
Åby Alv river Sweden 34J4
Abyei Sudan 69L7
Åbyn Sweden 34J4
Abyssinia = Ethiopia
Abyy USSR 51R3

Acadia Nat. Pk = Mt Desert I
Acajutla El Salvador 89B4
Acambaro Mexico 88D3
Acaponeta Mexico 88C3
Acapulco de Juárez Mexico 88E4
Acará Brazil 93H4
Acarigua Venezuela 92D2
Acatlan Mexico 88E4
Accomac Va USA 85K2
Accra Ghana 68E7
Accrington England UK 25D5
Achaguas Venezuela 92D2
Achalpur India 58E4
Achao Chile 91B6
Achill Ireland, Rep. of 30D6
Achill I Ireland,Rep. of 30C6
Achinsk USSR 51L4
Achnasheen Scotland UK 28F4
Achray Ont. Canada 79H3
Acklins I The Bahamas 89E2
Aclare Ireland,Rep. of 30F5
Aconcagua,Mt Argentina 91C4
Acores,Is Atlantic Ocean 88E4
Acoyapa Nicaragua 89B4
Acquarossa Switzerland 33D2
Acre = 'Akko
Actaeon Group,Is Tuamotu Arch. 95N10
Acton Calif. USA 80D8
Acton Vale Que. Canada 79K3
Açu Brazil 93K5
Ada Minn. USA 81J2
Ada Okla. USA 83K5
Adair,C NW Terr. Canada 77R2
Adairville Ky USA 85D2
Adak island Aleutian Is USA 87V13
Adalia = Antalya
Adam Oman 63H5
Adamello mt Italy 44C2
Adamimaby NSW Australia 97C3
Adams NY USA 79H4
Adam's Bridge India/Sri Lanka 58E7
Adams,Mt Wash. USA 80C2
Adams Pk Sri Lanka 58E7
Adan South Yemen 62E7
Adana Turkey 62D2
Adapazari Turkey 62C1
Adare Ireland, Rep. of 31F8
Adare,C Antarctica 15L2
Adavale Queens. Australia 99J5
Ad Dahna' region Saudi Arabia 62F4
Ad Dammam Saudi Arabia 63G4
Ad Diriyah Saudi Arabia 62F5
Addis Ababa Ethiopia 71H3
Addis Derra Ethiopia 71H2

Addison NY USA 84C1
Ad Diwaniyah Iraq 62E3
Adegaon India 61B4
Adelaide S Aus. Australia 97A2
Adelaide South Africa 72D6
Adelaide I Antarctica 15S3
Adelaide Pen. NW Terr. Canada 76M3
Adelaide River N Terr. Australia 98G2
Adelboden Switzerland 33C2
Adelong NSW Australia 97C3
Ademuz Spain 41F2
Aden = Adan
Aden, G. of Africa/Arabia 18F8
Adh Dhahiriya Jordan 64C6
Adhoi India 58D4
Adhra Syria 64E4
Adi island New Guinea Indon. 53K11
Adige,R Italy 44C3
Adi Kaie Ethiopia 71H2
Adilabad India 58E5
Adirondack Mts NY USA 79J3
Adi Ugri Ethiopia 71H2
Admiralty G W Aus. Australia 98E2
Admiralty,Is Pacific Ocean 94E8
Adolfo Alsina = Carhué
Adoni India 58E5
Adoumre Cameroun 69H7
Adour,R France 43C5
Adra Spain 40E4
Adrano Sicily Italy 45E7
Adrar Algeria 68E3
Adrar des Iforas plat. Algeria/Mali 68F4
Adri Libya 69H3
Adria Italy 44D3
Adrian Mich. USA 79D5
Adriatic Sea Italy 44E4
Adula Gruppe mts Switzerland 33E2
Aduwa Ethiopia 71H2
Aegean Sea Greece 47E5
Aeolian Is = Lipari Is
Ærøskøbing Denmark 35D9
Aesch Switzerland 33C1
Afferden Netherlands 32E3
Affoltern Switzerland 33D1
Affuá Brazil 93G4
Afghanistan country SW Asia 18H6
Afif Saudi Arabia 62E5
Afogados de Ingazeira Brazil 93K5
Afognak I Alaska USA 87X13
Afrin Syria 64E1
Afula Israel 64D5
Afyon Turkey 62C2

Agab Workei Ethiopia 71H2
Agadès Niger 68G5
Agadir Morocco 68D2
Agalega Is Indian Ocean 65D6
Agartala India 59H4
Agathla Pk Ariz. USA 82C4
Agatti island Amindivi Is India 58D6
Agattu island Aleutian Is USA 87U13
Agawa Ont. Canada 79D2
Agboville Ivory Coast 68E7
'Agda Iran 63G3
Agde France 43E5
Agder,Aust county Norway 35B7
Agder,Vest county Norway 35B7
Agen France 43D4
Ägeri See lake Switzerland 33D1
Agh Galeh Iran 63G2
Agiabampo Mexico 88C2
Agira Sicily Italy 45E7
Agizyar China 60E1
Agno Switzerland 33D3
Agon France 42C2
Agordat Ethiopia 71H1
Agra India 61B2
Agram = Zagreb
Agram PAfghan./Pakistan 60B2
Agrigento Sicily Italy 45D7
Agrihan,I Mariana Is 94E6
Agri Karakose Turkey 62E2
Agrínion Greece 47C5
Agropoli Italy 45E5
Agua Clara Brazil 93G8
Aguadas Colombia 92B2
Aguadilla Puerto Rico 89F3
Aguadulce Panama 89C5
Aguan,R Honduras 89B3
Agua Prieta Mexico 88C1
Aguaray Argentina 91D2
Aguarico,R Ecuador 92B4
Aguascalientes Mexico 88D3
Agudo Spain 40D3
Agudos Brazil 93H8
Aguilar Spain 40D4
Aguilar de Campó Spain 40D1
Aguilas Spain 41F4
Aguirre,B Argentina 91C8
Agulhas,C South Africa 72C6
Ahar Iran 62F2
Ahipara B New Zealand 100E2
Ahlainen Finland 35J6
Ahmadabad India 58D4
Ahmadnagar India 58D5
Ahmadpur East Pakistan 60B6
Ahmik Lake Ont. Canada 79G3
Ahraura India 61D3
Ahtari Finland 34L5

1

Ähtärin Järvi Amatique,B de

Ähtärin Järvi *lake* Finland 34L5
Ahtävä Finland 34K5
Ähtäyänjoki,R Finland 34K5
Ahuachapán El Salvador 89B4
Ahualulco *Jalisco* Mexico 88D3
Ahus Sweden 35F9
Ahväz Iran 62F3
Ahvenanmaa,I Finland 35H6
Ahwar South Yemen 62F7
Aiapuá,L Brazil 92E4
Aichi *prefecture* Japan 56E7
Aiea *Hawaii* USA 95V26
Aigle Switzerland 33B2
Aigoual,Mt France 43E4
Aiguilles Rouges *mt* Switzerland 33C2
Aihui China 52J1
Aikawa Japan 56F5
Ailsa Craig,I *Scotland* UK 29F9
Aim USSR 51Q4
Aimen Pass China 54H7
Aimores Brazil 93J7
Ain *dep.* France 42F3
Ainaži *Latvia* USSR 35L8
Ain Galakka Chad 69J5
Ain Safra Mauritania 68C5
Ain Sefra Algeria 68E2
Ainsworth *Nebr.* USA 83J1
Aintree *England* UK 25C6
Airdrie *Scotland* UK 29J8
Aire France 43C5
Airedale *England* UK 25E5
Aire Gap *England* UK 25D5
Aire,R *England* UK 25F5
Airlie *Oreg.* USA 80B3
Airolo Switzerland 33D2
Aisen *prov.* Chile 91B7
Ai Shan China 54L4
Aishihik L *Yukon* Canada 76D4
Aisne *dep.* France 42E2
Aitkin *Minn.* USA 81L2
Aiviekste,R *Latviy* USSR 35M8
Aix France 43F5
Aix-la-Chapelle = Aachen
Aix les Bains France 42G4
Aix,Mt *Wash.* USA 80C2
Aiyina *island* Greece 47D6
Aiyion Greece 47C5
Aizawl India 59H4
Aizpute *Latvia* USSR 35J8
Aizuwakamatsu Japan 56F6
Ajaccio *Corsica* France 43J7
Ajaigarh India 61C3
Ajanta India 58E4
Ajanta Ra. = Sahiadriparvat Ra
Ajdabiyah Libya 69K2
Ajibba Saudi Arabia 62E4
Ajigasawa Japan 56G4
Ajlun Jordan 64D5
Ajman UAE 63H4
Ajmer India 58D3
Ajoewa Surinam 93F3
Ajuana,R Brazil 92D4
Akalkot India 58E5
Akan Nat. Pk Japan 56H3
Akanthou Cyprus 64B2
Akaoka Japan 56C8
Akarnania & Aitolia *dist.* Greece 47C5
Akaroa New Zealand 100E6
Akashi Japan 56D7
Akbarpur India 61C2
Akcha Afghanistan 63K2
Akershus *county* Norway 35D6
Akhaia *dist.* Greece 47C5
Akhisar Turkey 62B2
Akhterin Syria 64F1
Akhtopol Bulgaria 46F3
Akhtubinsk USSR 49H6
Akhtyrka *Ukrain.* USSR 48J6
Akimiski I *NW Terr.* Canada 77P6
Akita Japan 56G5
Akita *prefecture* Japan 56G5
Akitras,C Greece 47C6
Akjoujt Mauritania 68C5
'Akko Israel 64D5
Akkrum Netherlands 32D1
Aklavik *NW Terr.* Canada 76D3
Ako Nigeria 70C2
Akobo,R Sudan 69M7
Akola India 58E4
Akpatok I *NW Terr.* Canada 77S4
Akranes Iceland 34T12
Akron *Col.* USA 82G2
Akron *Ohio* USA 79F5
Akrotiri Pen. *Kríti* Greece 47E7
Aksaray Turkey 62C2
Aksehir Turkey 62C2
Aksha USSR 51N4
Aksi *Eston.* USSR 35M7
Aksu *Xinjiang* China 50J5
Aksum Ethiopia 71H2
Akti *pen.* Greece 47E4
Aktogay USSR 50J5
Aktyubinsk *Kazakh.* USSR 50G4
Akure Nigeria 68G7
Akureyri Iceland 34V12
Akyab Burma 59H4
Alabama *state* USA 87J5
Alabama,R *Ala.* USA 85D5
Alaejos Spain 40D2
Alagoas *state* Brazil 93K5
Alagoinhas Brazil 93K6
Alagon Spain 41F2
Alaja Syria 64D2
Alajuela Costa Rica 89C4
Al'Amarah Iraq 62F3
Alameda *Calif.* USA 80B7
Alameda *Sask.* Canada 76L7
Alamogordo *New Mex.* USA 82F6
Alamogordo Res. *New Mex.* USA 82F5
Alamo L *Ariz.* USA 80G8
Alamos Mexico 88C2
Alamosa *Col.* USA 82F4
Åland = Ahvenanmaa
Ålands Hav *bay* Finland/Sweden 35H7
Alapayevsk USSR 49Q2
Alasehir Turkey 62B2
Al Ashkhirah Oman 63H5
Alaska *state* USA 87X12
Alaska,G of *Alaska* USA 87Y13
Alaska Highway Canada/USA 76C4
Alaska Pen. *Alaska* USA 87X13
Alaska Ra *mts* *Alaska* USA 87X12
Alatyr USSR 49H3
Alava *region* Spain 41E1
Alavus Finland 34K5
Alawoona *S Aus.* Australia 97B2
Alayor *Menorca* Spain 41J3
Alaysky Khrebet *Kirgiz.* USSR 50J6
Alazeyskoye Plat. USSR 51R3
Albacete Spain 41F3
Albacete *prov.* Spain 41E3
Albacutya,L *Vic.* Australia 97B3
Alba de Tormes Spain 40D2
Albaek Bugt *bay* Denmark 35D8
Albaida Spain 41F3
Alba Iulia Romania 46D1
Albanel,L *Que.* Canada 78B1
Albania *country* Europe 39L5
Albany *Ga* USA 85E5
Albany *Ky* USA 85E2
Albany *Mo* USA 83L2
Albany *NY* USA 84E1
Albany *Oreg.* USA 80B3
Albany *W Aus.* Australia 98D6
Albany,R *Ont.* Canada 77P6
Albarracin Spain 41F2
Al Bayda' Libya 69K2
Al Baydā Yemen 62F7
Albemarle Sd *N Car.* USA 85J2
Albergaria a-Velha Portugal 40B2
Alberique Spain 41F3
Albert *New Br.* Canada 78F4
Alberta *prov.* Canada 76H6
Alberta, Mt *Alta* Canada 76H6
Albert Edward,Mt Papua New Guinea 99K1
Albert,L *Oreg.* USA 80C4
Albert,L Zaire 71G4
Albert Lea *Minn.* USA 81L4
Alberton *Pr. Ed. I.* Canada 78F3
Alberton *Vic.* Australia 97C3
Albertville = Kalemie
Albertville France 42G4
Albi France 43E5
Albia *Iowa* USA 83M2
Albina Surinam 93G2
Albion *Calif.* USA 80B6
Albion *Idaho* USA 80G4
Albion *Mich.* USA 79D4
Albion *NY* USA 84B1
Albocácer Spain 41F2
Alborg Denmark 35C8
Alborg Bugt *bay* Denmark 35D8
Al Buaryat Libya 69J2
Albufeira Portugal 40B4
Al Bū Kamāl Syria 62E3
Albula P Switzerland 33E2
Albula Tun. Switzerland 33E2
Albuñol Spain 40E4
Albuquerque *New Mex.* USA 82E5
Alburquerque Spain 40C3
Albury *NSW* Australia 97C3
Alcacer do Sal Portugal 40B3
Alcala de Henares Spain 40E2
Alcamo *Sicily* Italy 45D6
Alcañices Spain 40C2
Alcañiz Spain 41F2
Alcântara Brazil 93J4
Alcantára Spain 40C3
Alcantarilla Spain 41F4
Alcaraz Spain 41E3
Alcázar de San Juan Spain 40E3
Alcobaça Portugal 40B3
Alcolea del Pinar Spain 41E2
Alcoutim Portugal 40C4
Alcoy Spain 41F3
Aldabra,Is Indian Ocean 65C5
Aldama *Chihuahua* Mexico 88C2
Aldama *Tamaulipas* Mexico 88E3
Aldan USSR 51P4
Aldan,R USSR 51P4
Aldanskoye Nagorye *region* USSR 51P4
Aldbrough *England* UK 25H5
Aldeburgh *England* UK 27T4
Aldergrove *N Ireland* UK 30L4
Alderney,I *Channel Is* UK 42B2
Aldershot *England* UK 27N6
Aledo *Ill.* USA 83N2
Aleg Mauritania 68C5
Alegrete Brazil 91E3
Alejandro Selkirk,I Juan Fernandez Is 95T11
Aleksandrov USSR 48L3
Aleksandrovsk Sakhalinskiy USSR 51R4
Alekseyeka *Kazakh.* USSR 50J4
Alencia *region* Spain 41F3
Alençon France 42D2
Alenquer Brazil 93G4
Alenquer Portugal 40B3
Alentejo *region* Portugal 40C3
Aleppo = Halab
Aléria *Corsica* France 43K6
Ales France 43F4
Aleshki USSR 49E5
Alessandria Italy 44B3
Alestrup Denmark 35C8
Ålesund Norway 34B5
Aletschhorn *mt* Switzerland 33C2
Aleutian Is USA 87U13
Alexander Arch. *Alaska* USA 87Z13
Alexander Bay South Africa 72B5
Alexander I Island Antarctica 15S3
Alexandra New Zealand 100C7
Alexandra *Vic.* Australia 97C3
Alexandretta = İskenderun
Alexandria Egypt 69L2
Alexandria *La* USA 83M7
Alexandria *Minn.* USA 81K3
Alexandria *Ont.* Canada 79J3
Alexandria Romania 46E3
Alexandria *Scotland* UK 29H8
Alexandria *Va* USA 84C3
Alexandrina,L *S Aus.* Australia 97A3
Alexandroúpolis Greece 47E4
Alexyeevka USSR 49H4
Aley Lebanon 64D4
Aleysk USSR 50K4
Alfaro Spain 41F1
Al Faw Iraq 62F3
Alford *England* UK 25J6
Alfred *Maine* USA 84F1
Alga *Kazakh.* USSR 50G5
Ålgård Norway 35A7
Algarroba del Aguila Argentina 91C5
Algarve *region* Portugal 40B4
Algauer Alpen Austria/W Ger. 36D5
Algeciras Spain 40D4
Alger Algeria 68G1
Algeria *country* Africa 68F1
Al Ghail Yemen 62F6
Alghero *Sardinia* Italy 45B5
Algiers = Alger
Algoa,B South Africa 72D6
Algoma *Ont.* Canada 79E2
Algoma *Wis.* USA 79C3
Algona *Iowa* USA 83L1
Algonquin Park *Ont.* Canada 79G3
Alguada Reef Burma 59H5
Al Hadīthah Iraq 62E3
Alhama de Granada Spain 40E4
Alhambra *Calif.* USA 80D8
Al Hammām Iraq 62E3
Al Hasakah Syria 62E2
Al Hijārah *des.* Iraq 62E3
Al Hillah Iraq 62E3
Al Hoceima Morocco 68E1
Al Ḥudaydah Yemen 62E7
Al Hufūf Saudi Arabia 62F4
Alia *Sicily* Italy 45D7
Aliaga Spain 41F2
Alibag India 58D5
Alicante Spain 41F3
Alicante *prov.* Spain 41F3
Alice *Texas* USA 82S10
Alice Springs *N Terr.* Australia 99G4
Aliceville *Ala.* USA 85C4
Alicudi *island* Italy 45E6
Aligarh India 61B2
Ali Khel Afghanistan 63K3
Alimnia *island* Greece 47F6
Aling Kangri,Mt *Tibet* China 58F2
Alingsås Sweden 35E8
Alipur India 61G2
Alipur Pakistan 60B6
Alipura India 61B3
Alirajpur India 58D4
Alivérion Greece 47D5
Al Jaghbub Libya 69K3
Al Jahrah Kuwait 62F4
Al Jawf Saudi Arabia 62D4
Al Jazirah *des.* Iraq/Syria 62E2
Al Jubayl Saudi Arabia 62F4
Aljustrel Portugal 40B4
Alken Belgium 32D4
Al Khasab UAE 63H4
Al Khawr Qatar 63G4
Al Khums Libya 69H2
Al Khurmah Saudi Arabia 62E5
Al Kidan *region* Saudi Arabia 63G5
Alkmaar Netherlands 32C2
Al Kut Iraq 62F3
Al Lādiqīyah Syria 64D2
Allahabad India 61C3
Allanmyo Burma 59J5
Allariz Spain 40C1
Allaykha USSR 51R2
Alle Belgium 32C5
Allegan *Mich.* USA 79D4
Allegheny Mts USA 87K4
Allegheny,R *NY/Pa* USA 84B1
Allen, Bog of Ireland, Rep. of 31J7
Allenby Bridge Jordan 64D6
Allendale Town *England* UK 25D2
Allende Mexico 88C2
Allen,L Ireland, Rep. of 30G5
Allentown *Pa* USA 84D2
Alleppey India 58E7
Alliance *Nebr.* USA 82G1
Alliance *Ohio* USA 79F5
Allier *dep.* France 42E3
Allier,R France 42E3
Allier,R France 42E4
Alliston *Ont.* Canada 79G3
Al Lith Saudi Arabia 62E5
Alloa *Scotland* UK 29J7
Allonby *England* UK 25B3
All Pines Belize 89B3
Al Luḥayyah Yemen 62E6
Allumettes,I des *Que.* Canada 79H3
Alma *Mich.* USA 79D4
Alma *New Br.* Canada 78F4
Alma Ata *Kazakh.* USSR 50J5
Almadén Spain 40D3
Al Madinah = Medina
Almagro Spain 40E3
Almanor,L *Calif.* USA 80C5
Almansa Spain 41F3
Al Marj Libya 69K2
Almazán Spain 41E2
Almefrim Brazil 93G4
Almeirim Portugal 40B3
Almelo Netherlands 32E2
Almere-Haven Netherlands 32D2
Almere-Stad Netherlands 32D2
Almeria Spain 41F4
Almeria *prov.* Spain 41E4
Almeria,G de Spain 41E4
Al Midhnab Saudi Arabia 62E4
Almirante Panama 89C5
Almiropótamos Greece 47E5
Almirós Greece 47D5
Almodôvar Portugal 40B4
Almodóvar Spain 40D3
Almond,R *Scotland* UK 29J7
Almont *N Dak.* USA 81G2
Almonte *Ont.* Canada 79H3
Almora India 61B1
Almorox Spain 40D2
Al Mubarraz Saudi Arabia 62F4
Almudébar Spain 41F1
Al Mukallā South Yemen 62F7
Al Mukha Yemen 62E7
Al Musayyib Iraq 62E3
Al Muwailih Saudi Arabia 62D4
Alness *Scotland* UK 28H4
Alnmouth *England* UK 25E2
Aln,R *England* UK 25E2
Alnwick *England* UK 25E2
Alocén Spain 41E2
Aloja *Latvia* USSR 35L8
Alón = Iliodhrómia
Alon Burma 59J4
Alor *island* Indonesia 53H12
Alora Spain 40D4
Alor Setar Malaysia 57C5
Alost = Aalst
Aloysius,Mt *W Aus.* Australia 98F5
Alpaugh *Calif.* USA 80D8
Alpena *Mich.* USA 79E3
Alpes Cottiennes *mts* France 43G4
Alpes-de-Haute-Provence *dep.* France 43F4
Alpes-Maritimes *dep.* France 43G5
Alphen aan den Rijn Netherlands 32C2
Alphubel *mt* Switzerland 33C2
Alpi Dolomitiche *mts* Italy 44C2
Alpi Graie *mts* France/Italy 44A3
Alpi Lepontine *mt* Italy/Switz. 33D2
Alpi Marittime *mts* France/Italy 44A3
Alpine *Texas* USA 82G7
Alpi Pennine Switzerland 33C3
Alpi Venezi *mts* Italy 44D2
Alpnach Switzerland 33D2
Alps *mts* Europe 38G4
Al Qalibah Saudi Arabia 62D4
Al Qāmishlī Syria 62E2
Al Qatīf Saudi Arabia 62F4
Al Qatrun Libya 69H4
Al Qayyarh Iraq 62E2
Al Qunayṭirah Syria 64D4
Al Qunfidhah Saudi Arabia 62E6
Al Qurnah Iraq 62F3
Alsace France 42G2
Alsea,R *Oreg.* USA 80B3
Alsfeld W Germany 36C3
Als,I Denmark 35C9
Alstätten Switzerland 33E1
Alsten,I Norway 34E4
Alston *England* UK 25D3
Alsvanga *Latvia* USSR 35J8
Alta Fjorden Norway 34K1
Alta Gracia Argentina 91D4
Altagracia Venezuela 92C1
Altagracia de Orituco Venezuela 92D2
Altai *mts* USSR 50K4
Altamachi Bolivia 92D7
Altamaha,R *Ga* USA 85G5
Altamira Brazil 93G4
Altamont *Oreg.* USA 80C4
Altamura Italy 45F5
Altanbulag Mongolia 51M4
Altar Mexico 88B1
Altata Mexico 88C3
Altdorf Switzerland 33D2
Altea Spain 41F3
Alt Elv *river* Norway 34K2
Altenburg E Germany 36E3
Alte Vatn *lake* Norway 34H2
Althorpe *England* UK 25G5
Altin Köprü Iraq 62E2
Altmark *region* E Germany 36D2
Alto Longa Brazil 93J5
Alto Molocue Mozambique 71H8
Alton *England* UK 27N6
Alton *Ill.* USA 83N3
Alton *Mo* USA 83N4
Altona *NY* USA 79K3
Altona W Germany 36C2
Altoona *Pa* USA 84B2
Altrincham *England* UK 25D6
Altun Shan *mts.* China 18K6
Alturas *Calif.* USA 80C5
Altus *Okla.* USA 83J5
Al Ugla Saudi Arabia 62D4
Al 'Uj Saudi Arabia 62F5
Alūksne *Latvia* USSR 35M8
Al'Ulā Saudi Arabia 62D4
Aluminé Argentina 91B5
Alupka USSR 48J9
Al'Uqaylah Libya 69J2
Alushta USSR 48J9
Alva *Okla.* USA 83J4
Alvarado *Calif.* USA 80B7
Alvarado Mexico 88E4
Älvdalen Sweden 35F6
Älvesta Sweden 35F8
Alvho Sweden 35F6
Alvin *Texas* USA 83L8
Alvito Portugal 40B3
Alvord,L *Oreg.* USA 80D4
Älvsbyff Sweden 34J4
Al Wajh Saudi Arabia 62D4
Alwar India 60E7
Alward *New Br.* Canada 78F3
Al Widyan *des.* Iraq/S Arabia 62E3
Alyab Sudan 69M5
Alyth *Scotland* UK 29K6
Alytus *Lith.* USSR 35L9
Alzira Spain 41F3
Amadeus,L *N Terr.* Australia 98G4
Amadi Sudan 69M7
Amadiyah Iraq 62E2
Amadjuak L *NW Terr.* Canada 77R4
Amaila Falls Guyana 92F2
Amakusa nada *bay* Japan 56A8
Åmål Sweden 35E7
Amalfi Italy 45E5
Amaliás Greece 47C6
Amami Shotō *islands* Japan 56N12
Amaná,L Brazil 92E4
Amanalco Mexico 88D4
Amandola Italy 44D4
Amantea Italy 45E6
Amapá Brazil 93G3
Amapala Honduras 89B4
Amarante Brazil 93J5
Amarapura Burma 59J4
Amargosa Brazil 93K6
Amarillo *Texas* USA 82H5
Amasra Turkey 62C1
Amasya Turkey 62D1
Amatique,B de Guatemala 88G4

Amazonas,R Brazil 93G4
Amazonas,R Peru 92C4
Amazon,Mouths of the Brazil 93H3
Amb Pakistan 60C3
Ambala India 60E5
Ambam Cameroun 69H8
Ambar Iran 63H3
Ambarchik USSR 51T3
Ambato Ecuador 92B4
Ambato-Boéni Madagascar 71N10
Amberg W Germany 36D4
Ambergris Cay Belize 89B3
Ambergris Cay The Bahamas 89E2
Ambérieu France 42F3
Ambert France 42E4
Ambesh Pakistan 60C3
Ambikapur India 61D4
Ambilobe Madagascar 71N9
Amble England UK 25E2
Ambleside England UK 25C4
Amblève = Amel
Ambohimahasoa Madagascar 71N11
Amboise France 42C3
Ambon,I Indonesia 53J11
Amboseli,L Kenya 71H5
Ambositra Madagascar 71N11
Amboy Calif. USA 80F8
Amboy Oreg. USA 80B3
Ambrim,I Vanuatu 94G9
Ambriz Angola 70C6
Amchitka island Aleutian Is USA 87U13
Amd South Yemen 62F6
Am Dam Chad 69K6
Amderma USSR 50H3
Ameca Mexico 88D3
Amedamit Ethiopia 71H2
Amel Belgium 32E4
Ameland island Netherlands 32D1
Amelia Va USA 85J2
American Falls Idaho USA 80G4
American Falls Res. Idaho USA 80G4
American Fork Utah USA 82C2
Americus Ga USA 85E4
Amerongen Netherlands 32D2
Amersfoort Netherlands 32D2
Amersham England UK 27N5
Ames Iowa USA 83M1
Amesbury England UK 27L6
Amesbury Mass. USA 84F1
Amethi India 61C2
Amfíklia Greece 47D5
Amfilokhía Greece 47C5
Amga USSR 51Q3
Amga,R USSR 51Q3
Amgu USSR 51Q5
Amherst Mass. USA 84E1
Amherst No. Sc. Canada 78F4
Amherstburg Ont. Canada 79E4
Amherst I Ont. Canada 79H4
Amiens France 42E2
Amindivi,Is Lakshadweep India 58D6
Amingnon India 59H3
Amini island Amindivi Is India 58D6
Aminuis Namibia 72B4
Amioune Lebanon 64D3
Amiral-Courbet,Pen. Kerguelen 65S12
Amirante,Is Indian Ocean 65D5
Amlwch Wales UK 26F2
Amm Adam Sudan 69N5
Amman Jordan 64D6
Ammanford Wales UK 26G5
Ammassalik = Tasiilaq
Ammerån,R Sweden 34F5
Amöl Iran 63G2
Amorgós island Greece 47E6
Amos Que. Canada 77Q7
Amoy = Xiamen
Amparo Brazil 93H8
Ampato,Cord. de mts Peru 92C7
Amqui Que. Canada 78E2
Amraho Sudan 69M5
Amran Yemen 62E6
Amravati India 58E4
Amreli India 58D4
Amriswil Switzerland 33E1
Amritsar India 60D5
Amroha India 61D4
Amsteg Switzerland 33D2
Amstelveen Netherlands 32C2
Amsterdam Netherlands 32C2
Amsterdam NY USA 84D1
Amsterdam,I Indian Ocean 65F8
Am Timan Chad 69K6
Amu Darya,R Turkmen./Uzbek. USSR 50H5
Amund Ringnes I NW Terr. Canada 76M1
Amundsen G NW Terr. Canada 76G2

Amundsen Sea Antarctica 15Q2
Amur,R China/USSR 51P4
Amurskaya Oblast region USSR 51P4
Amyun = Amioune
An Burma 59H5
Anabar Nauru 94A22
Anabta Jordan 64D5
Anaconda Mont. USA 80G2
Anadarko Okla. USA 83J5
Anadyr USSR 51U3
Anadyr,R USSR 51U3
Anadyrskiy Zaliv gulf USSR 51V3
Anáfi island Greece 47E6
Anah Iraq 62E3
Anai Libya 69H4
Anaimalai Hills India 58E6
Anakapalle India 59F5
Analalava Madagascar 71N9
Anama Brazil 92E4
Anambas islands Indonesia 53E10
Anamizu Japan 56E6
Anamosa Iowa USA 83N1
Anandpur India 60E5
Anantapur India 58E6
Anantnag = Islamabad, Kashmir
Anápolis Brazil 93H7
Anar Iran 63H3
Anarak Iran 63G3
Anardara Afghanistan 63J3
Anatolia region Turkey 62C2
Anatuya Argentina 91D3
Ancenis France 42C3
Anchorage Alaska USA 87X12
Anchuras Spain 40D3
Ancohuma,Mt Bolivia 92D7
Ancón Peru 92B6
Ancona Italy 44D4
Ancud Chile 91B6
Andacollo Argentina 91B5
Andalgala Argentina 91C3
Andalsnes Norway 34B5
Andalucía region Spain 40D4
Andaman,Is Bay of Bengal 59H6
Andaman,Middle Andaman Is India 59H6
Andaman,North Andaman Is India 59H6
Andaman Sea Indian Ocean 59J6
Andaman,South Andaman Is India 59H6
Andeer Switzerland 33E2
Andelfingen Switzerland 33D1
Andenne Belgium 32D4
Andermatt Switzerland 33D2
Andernach W Germany 36B3
Anderson Calif. USA 80B5
Anderson Ind. USA 79D5
Anderson S Car. USA 85F3
Anderson B Tas. Australia 97F5
Anderson,R NW Terr. Canada 76F3
Andes,Cordillera de los S America 91B6
Andevoranto Madagascar 71N10
And,Fj. Norway 34G2
Andhra Pradesh state India 58E5
Andikithira island Greece 47D7
Andímilos island Greece 47E6
Andíparos island Greece 47E6
Andiyaman Turkey 62D2
Andizhan Uzbek. USSR 50J5
Andkhui Afghanistan 63K2
Andoas Ecuador 92B4
Andorra country Europe 41G1
Andorra la Vella Andorra 41G1
Andover England UK 27M6
Andover Mass. USA 84F1
Andover S Dak. USA 81J3
Andøy,I Norway 34F2
Andreanof Is Aleutian Is USA 87V13
Andreas,C Cyprus 64C2
Andreyevka Ukrain. USSR 48J7
Andria Italy 45F5
Andriba Madagascar 71N10
Andritsaina Greece 47C6
Ándros island Greece 47E6
Androscoggin R Maine USA 78C4
Andros I The Bahamas 89D2
Androth islands Amindivi Is India 58D6
Anegada island Virgin Is 89G3
Anegada,B Argentina 91D6
Anelo Argentina 91C5
Aneta N Dak. USA 81H2
Aney Niger 69H5
Anfu China 55H9
Angangueo Mexico 88D4
Angaston S Aus. Australia 97A2
Angel de la Guarda island Mexico 88B2
Angel Falls Venezuela 92E2

Ängelholm Sweden 35E8
Angels Camp Calif. USA 80C6
Angemuk mt New Guinea Indon. 53L11
Angerman Alv river Sweden 34G5
Angermunde E Germany 36E2
Angers France 42C3
Angesan,R Sweden 34K3
Angikuni L NW Terr. Canada 76M4
Angkor Cambodia 57C4
Anglesey,I Wales UK 26F2
Angliers Que. Canada 79G2
Angoche Mozambique 71H8
Angol Chile 91B5
Angola NY USA 84B1
Angola country Africa 70D7
Angora = Ankara
Angoulême France 42D4
Angoumois prov. France 42D4
Angra Brazil 93J8
Anguilla island Leeward Is 89G3
Angul India 59G4
Anguli Nur lake China 54H2
Anguo China 54H3
An Hoa Vietnam 57D3
Anholt,I Denmark 35D8
Anhua China 55F8
Anhui province China 54J6
Anhwei = Anhui
Anibare B Nauru 94A22
Animas Ra New Mex. USA 82D7
Anina Romania 46C2
Anjalankoski Finland 35M6
Anjengo India 58E7
Anji China 54K7
Anjou prov. France 42C3
Anjouan,I Comoros 71J7
Anjozorobe Madagascar 71N10
Ankabamby,C Madagascar 71N9
Ankacho USSR 51M3
Ankang China 54E6
Ankara Turkey 62C2
Anklam E Germany 36E2
Ankober Ethiop a 71H3
Anlier Belgium 32D5
Anlo Netherlands 32E1
Anlong China 55C10
Anna Ill. USA 83P4
Annan,R Scotland UK 29K9
Annapolis Md USA 84C3
Annapolis Royal No. Sc. Canada 78F4
Annapurna,Mt Nepal 61D1
Ann Arbor Mich. USA 79E4
An Nasiriyah Iraq 62F3
Ann,C Antarctica 15E3
Ann,C Mass. USA 84F1
Annecy France 42G4
An Nhon Vietnam 57D4
Anniston Ala. USA 85E4
Annobón,I G. of Guinea 70B5
Annonay France 43F4
Annuello Vic. Australia 97B2
Anole Somalia 71J5
Ano Viannos Kríti Greece 47E7
Anpu China 55F12
Anqing China 55J7
Anren China 55G9
Ansai China 54E4
Ansbach W Germany 36D4
Anseremme Belgium 32C4
Anshan China 54M2
Anshun China 55D9
Anson B N Terr. Australia 96F3
Ansongo Mali 68F5
Ansonia Conn. USA 84E2
Anstruther Scotland UK 29L7
Anta Peru 92C6
Antakya Turkey 64E1
Antalo Ethiop a 71H2
Antalya Turkey 62C2
Antalya Körfezi gulf Turkey 62C2
Antananarivo Madagascar 71N10
Antarctic Pen. Antarctica 15S3
An Teallach mt Scotland UK 28F4
Antelope I Utah USA 82B2
Antelope Plains Ariz. USA 80G7
Antelope V Nev. USA 80E6
Antequera Paraguay 91E2
Antequera Spain 40D4
Anthony Kans. USA 83J4
Anthony Lagoon N Terr. Austral a 99H3
Anti Atlas mts Morocco 68D3
Antibes France 43G5
Anticosti I Que. Canada 78G2
Antigo Wis. USA 79B3
Antigonish No. Sc. Canada 78G4

Antigua & Barbuda country Leeward s 89G3
Antigua,I Leeward s 89G3
Antilhue Chi e 91B5
Antilla Cuba 89D2
Antilles, Greater West Indies 89
Antilles ,Lesser West Indies 89
Antioch = Antakya
Antioch Calif. USA 80C7
Antioquia Colomb a 92B2
Antipodes,Is Pacific Ocean 94H12
Antlers Okla. USA 83L5
Antofagasta Chi e 91B2
Antofagasta prov. Chi e 91C2
Antofagasta de la Sierra Argentina 91C3
Antofalla,Mt Argentina 91C3
Antoing Belgium 32B4
Antongil,B d' Madagascar 71N10
Antonito Col. USA 82E4
Antrain France 42C2
Antrim N Ireland 30L4
Antrim county N Ireland UK 30L4
Antrim Hills N Ireland 30L3
Antsirabe Madagascar 71N10
Antsiranana Madagascar 71N9
Antsla Eston. USSR 35M8
Antwerp = Antwerpen
Antwerpen Belgium 32C3
Antwerpen prov. Belgium 32C3
Anupgarh Ind a 60C6
Anupshahr Ind a 61B1
Anuradhapura Sri Lanka 58F7
Anvers = Antwerpen
Anxi Fujian China 55K10
Anxi Gansu China 52C2
Anxiang China 55G8
Anxin China 54H3
Anyang China 54H4
Anyi China 55H8
Anyksciai Lith. USSR 35L9
Anyuan China 55H10
Anzhero Sudzhensh USSR 50K4
Anzio Ita y 45D5
Aomori Japan 56G4
Aomori prefecture Japan 56G4
Aonla Ind a 61B1
Aorai Orohen mt Tahiti 95V32
Aorangi Mts New Zealand 100F5
Aosta Ita y 44A3
Aotou China 55H11
Aoudèras Niger 68G5
Aoulef el Arab Algeria 68F3
Aozou Chad 69J4
Apakova USSR 49J3
Apalachee B Fla USA 85E6
Apalachicola Fla USA 85E6
Apalachicola B Fla USA 85E6
Apaporis,R Columb a 92C3
Aparri Philippines 53H7
Apataki,I Tuamotu Arch. 95M9
Apatin Yugoslav a 46B2
Ape Latvia USSR 35M8
Apeldoorn Netherlands 32D2
Apennines mts Ita y 38H4
Apex Mont. USA 80G3
Apia Western Samoa 95V31
Apiacas,Serra dos mts Brazil 93F6
Apiai Brazil 91G3
Api,Mt Nepal 61C1
Apodi Brazil 93K5
Apolima Str. Western Samoa 95V31
Apollo Bay Vic. Austral a 97B3
Apollonia = Marsah Susah
Apolo Bolivia 92D6
Apore,R Brazil 93G7
Apostle Is Wis. USA 79A2
Apostoles Argentina 91E3
Apoteri Guyana 92F3
Apozai Pakistan 60A5
Appalachian Mts USA 87K5
Appennino Ligure mts Italy 44B3
Appennino Lucano mts Italy 45E5
Appennino Marchigiano mts Ita y 44D4
Appennino Tosco-Emiliano mts Ita y 44C3
Appenzell Switzerland 33E1
Appenzell Ausser-Rhoden canton Switzerland 33E1
Appenzell Inner-Rhoden canton Switzerland 33E1
Appingedam Netherlands 32E1
Appleby-in-Westmorland England UK 25D3
Applecross Scotland UK 28E5
Appleton Wis. USA 79B3
Appleton City Mo USA 83L3
Aprilia Ita y 45D5
Apsley Tas. Australia 97F5
Apsley Vic. Austral a 97B3
Apt France 43F5
Apucarama,Serra do mts Brazil 93G8

Apuka USSR 51T3
Apure,R Venezuela 92D2
Apuseni,Mtii mts Romania 46D1
Aqaba Jordan 64D8
Aqaba,G of Red Sea 69M3
Aqarbat Syria 64F2
Aqiq Sudan 71H1
Aqraba Jordan 64D5
Aquidauana Brazil 93F8
Aquin Haiti 89E3
Arabatskaya Strelka pen USSR 48J9
Arabian Sea S Asia 18H8
Arabs G Egypt 69L2
Aracajú Brazil 93K6
Araça,R Brazil 92E3
Aracatí Brazil 93K4
Araçatuoa Brazil 93G8
Aracuai Brazil 93J7
Arad Romania 46C1
Arada Chad 69K5
Arafura Sea Austral./Indon. 53K12
Aragon region Spain 41F2
Aragua de Barcelona Venezuela 92E2
Araguaia,R Brazil 93H5
Araguari Brazil 93H7
Arak Iran 62F3
Arakaka Guyana 92E2
Arakan state Burma 59H4
Arakan Yoma,Mts Burma 59H4
Arak Bdj. Algeria 68F3
Araks,R Iran/USSR 50F6
Aral Sea = Aral'skoye Mora
Aralsk Kazakh. USSR 50H5
Aralskoye More sea Kazakh/Uzbek. USSR 50G5
Aramac Queens. Australia 99K4
Arambagh India 61F4
Aranda de Deuro Spain 40E2
Arandu Pakistan 60B3
Arani Bolivia 92D7
Aran I Ireland, Rep. of 30F3
Aran Is Ireland, Rep. of 31D7
Aranjuez Spain 40E2
Aran Mawddwy Wales UK 26G3
Aransas B Texas USA 82T9
Araouane Mali 68E5
Arapey Uruguay 91E4
Arapiraca Brazil 93K5
Arapkir Turkey 62D2
Araranguá Brazil 91G3
Ararat Vic. Australia 97B3
Ararat mt Turkey 62E2
Araria India 61F2
Aras,R Turkey 62E1
Arati Brazil 92C5
Arauca Colombia 92C2
Arauca,R Columb./Venez. 92C2
Arauco Chile 91B5
Aravalli Ra mts India 58D3
Araxá Brazil 93H7
Araya,Pen. de Venezuela 92E1
Arba Mench Ethiopia 71H3
Arbatax Sardinia Italy 45B6
Arbil Iraq 62E2
Arboga Sweden 35F7
Arbois France 42F3
Arbon Switzerland 33E1
Arbroath Scotland UK 29L6
Arbuckle Calif. USA 80B6
Arcachon France 43C4
Arcade NY USA 84B1
Arcadia Mich. USA 79C3
Arcadia Wis. USA 81M3
Arcata Calif. USA 80A5
Arcen Netherlands 32E3
Archbald Pa USA 84D2
Archidona Spain 40D4
Arco Idaho USA 80G4
Arcot India 58E6
Arctic Red,R NW Terr. Canada 76E3
Arctic Red River NW Terr. Canada 76E3
Ardabil Iran 62F2
Ardahan Turkey 62E1
Ardakán Iran 63G3
Ardal Iran 63G3
Årdal Norway 35B6
Ardara Ireland, Rep. of 30G4
Ardatov USSR 49F3
Ardèche dep. France 43F4
Ardee Ireland, Rep. of 30K6
Arden, Forest of England UK 27L4
Ardennes dep. France 42F2
Ardennes mts Belgium 32C5
Arderin mt Ireland, Rep. of 31H7
Ardestan Iran 63G3
Ardez Switzerland 33F2
Ardgay Scotland UK 28H4
Ardglass N Ireland 30M5
Ardino Bulgaria 46E4
Ardlethan NSW Australia 97C2
Ardmore Okla. USA 83K5
Ardmore B Ireland, Rep. of 31H10

3

Ardnamurchan Point Azov, Sea of

Ardnamurchan Point Scotland UK 29D6
Ardrishaig Scotland UK 29F7
Ardrossan S Aus. Australia 97A2
Ardrossan Scotland UK 29G8
Ards Pen. N Ireland UK 30M4
Ardud Romania 37K5
Arecibo Puerto Rico 89F3
Areia Branca Brazil 93K4
Arekalong Pen. Palau Is 94A20
Arenales,Mt Chile 91B7
Arenas de San Pedro Spain 40D2
Arendal Norway 35C7
Arenys de Mar Spain 41H2
Arequipa Peru 92C7
Arèvalo Spain 40D2
Arezzo Italy 44C4
Argentan France 42C2
Argentat France 43D4
Argenteuil France 42E2
Argentina country S America 91C5
Argentino,L Argentina 91B8
Argenton France 42C3
Argent-sur-Sauldre France 42E3
Arghandab,R Afghanistan 63K3
Argo Sudan 69M5
Argolís,G of Greece 47D6
Argonne region France 42F2
Árgos Greece 47D6
Arguari,R Brazil 93G3
Arguedas Spain 41F1
Arguello,Point Calif. USA 80C8
Argungu Nigeria 68F6
Argun,R China/USSR 51N4
Argyle,L W Aus. Australia 98F2
Århus Denmark 35D8
Ariano Irpino Italy 45E5
Arica Chile 91B1
Arica Colombia 92C4
Ariège dep. France 43D5
Arijejen Nauru 94A22
Arilje Yugoslavia 46C3
Arima Brazil 92E5
Arinda Guyana 92F3
Ario Mexico 88D4
Ariporo,R Columbia 92C2
Aripuana,R Brazil 92E5
Ariquemes Brazil 92E5
Arisaig Scotland UK 29E6
Arisaig,Sd of Scotland UK 29E6
Arivechi Mexico 88C2
Ariza Spain 41E2
Arizona Argentina 91C5
Arizona state USA 86D5
Arizona Plat. Ariz. USA 82C5
Arizpe Mexico 88B1
Arjona Columbia 92B1
Arka USSR 51R3
Arkabutla L Miss. USA 85B3
Arkadelphia Ark. USA 83M5
Arkadhía Greece 47D6
Arkaig,L Scotland UK 28F6
Arkansas state USA 87H5
Arkansas City Ark. USA 83N6
Arkansas City Kans. USA 83K4
Arkansas,R Ark./Okla. USA 83N5
Arkhangel'sk USSR 50F3
Arkhipelag Nordenshelda USSR 51L2
Arklow Ireland, Rep. of 31L8
Arkoi island Greece 47F6
Arkona,K cape E Germany 36E1
Arleo Mont. USA 80F2
Arles France 43F5
Arlesheim Switzerland 33C1
Arlington Ariz. USA 80G9
Arlington Oreg. USA 80C3
Arlington Heights Ill. USA 83P1
Arlon Belgium 32D5
Arltunga N Terr. Australia 99G4
Armagh N Ireland UK 30K5
Armagh county N Ireland UK 30K5
Armagnac region France 43D5
Armagosa Ra. Calif. USA 80E7
Armenia = Armyanskaya
Armenia Colombia 92B3
Armentiéres France 42E1
Armidale NSW Australia 97D2
Armirós,B of Kríti Greece 47E7
Armisticio Paraguay 91F2
Armori India 58F4
Armstrong Sta. Ont. Canada 77O6
Armyanskaya SSR rep. USSR 50F5
Arnastapi Iceland 34T12
Arnaud,R Que. Canada 77R4
Arnaudville La USA 83M7
Arnauti,C Cyprus 64A2
Arnhem Netherlands 32D2
Arnhem,C N Terr. Australia 99H2
Arnhem Land N Terr. Australia 98G2
Arnissa Greece 47C4
Arno,R Italy 44C4
Arnöy,I Norway 34J1
Arnprior Ont. Canada 79H3
Arnsberg W Germany 36C3
Arnstadt E Germany 36D3
Arolla Switzerland 33C2
Aroostook New Br. Canada 78E3
Arorae,I Kiribati 94H8
Arosa Switzerland 33E2
Aroser Rothorn mt Switzerland 33E2
Aroya Col. USA 82G3
Arrah India 61E3
Arraias Brazil 93H6
Ar Ramadi Iraq 62E3
Arra Mts Ireland,Rep. of 31G8
Arran,I Scotland UK 29F8
Ar Raqqah Syria 62D2
Arras France 42E1
Ar Riyād = Riyadh
Arroba Spain 40D3
Arromanches France 42C2
Arronches Portugal 40C3
Arrow,L Ireland, Rep. of 30G5
Arrowsmith,Mt NSW Australia 97B2
Arrowtown New Zealand 100C7
Arroyo Puerto Rico 89F3
Arroyo Grande Calif. USA 80C8
Ar Rutba Iraq 62E3
Ars Denmark 35C8
Arsk USSR 49J2
Árta Greece 47C5
Arta Mallorca Spain 41H3
Árta dist. Greece 47C5
Artawiya Saudi Arabia 62F4
Artemovsk Ukrain. USSR 48K7
Artemovsk USSR 51L4
Artemovski USSR 49Q2
Artemovskiy USSR 51N4
Artenay France 42D2
Artesia New Mex. USA 82F6
Arth Switzerland 33D1
Arthur's P New Zealand 100D6
Artibonite,R Haiti 89E3
Artigas Uruguay 91E4
Artigas dep. Uruguay 91E4
Artillery L NW Terr. Canada 76K4
Artois prov. France 42E1
Artvin Turkey 62E1
Aru Zaire 71G4
Arua Uganda 71G4
Aruanà Brazil 93G6
Aruba island Caribbean Sea 92D1
Aru Kep. archipelago Indonesia 53K12
Arum Netherlands 32D1
Arumá Brazil 92E4
Aruma Trinidad 89G4
Arunachal Pradesh territory India 59H3
Arundel England UK 27N7
Arundel Que. Canada 79J3
Arun,R England UK 27P6
Aruppukkottai India 58E7
Arusha Tanzania 71H5
Aru Tso lake Tibet China 59F2
Aruwimi,R Zaire 70E4
Arvada Wyo. USA 81D3
Arvida Que. Canada 78C2
Arvika Sweden 35E7
Arvilla N Dak. USA 81J2
Arzamas USSR 49F3
Arzew Algeria 68E1
Arzúa Spain 40B1
As Belgium 32D3
Aš Czech. 36E3
Asahikawa Japan 56H3
Asansol India 61F4
Åsarna Sweden 34F5
Asbestos Que. Canada 78C4
Asbury Park New J USA 84D2
Ascensión Bolivia 92E7
Ascension,B de la Mexico 88G4
Ascension,I Atlantic Ocean 73L9
Aschaffenburg W Germany 36C4
Aschersleben E Germany 36D3
Ascoli Piceno Italy 44D4
Ascona Switzerland 33D2
Ascot England UK 27N6
Ascotán Chile 91C2
Aseda Sweden 35F8
Åsele Sweden 34G4
Åsen Sweden 35E6
Asenovgrad Bulgaria 46E3
Ashanti region Ghana 68E7
Ashbourne England UK 25E6
Ashburton England UK 26G7
Ashburton New Zealand 100D6
Ashburton,R W Aus. Australia 98D4
Ashby de la Zouch England UK 25E7
Ashdod Israel 64C6
Ashdown Forest England UK 27Q6
Asheboro N Car. USA 85H3
Asheville N Car. USA 85F3
Ashford England UK 27R6
Ashfordby England UK 25G7
Ash Fork Ariz. USA 80G8
Ashington England UK 25E2
Ashkhabad Turkmen. USSR 50G6
Ashland Kans. USA 83J4
Ashland Ky USA 85F1
Ashland Maine USA 78D3
Ashland Mont. USA 81D3
Ashland Ohio USA 79E5
Ashland Oreg. USA 80B4
Ashland Pa USA 84C2
Ashland Va USA 85J2
Ashland Wis. USA 81M2
Ashland City Tenn. USA 85D2
Ashley N Dak. USA 81H2
Ashley NSW Australia 97C1
Ashqelon Israel 64C6
Ash Shatrah Iraq 62F3
Ash Shihr South Yemen 62F7
Ashtabula Ohio USA 79F5
Ashton-under-Lyne England UK 25D6
Ashuanipi L Newf. Canada 77S6
Ashville Ala. USA 85D4
Asinara island Sardinia Italy 45B5
Asinara,G di Sardinia Italy 45B5
Asino USSR 50K4
Āsi,R Syria 62D2
Asir region Saudi Arabia 62E5
Askeaton Ireland, Rep. of 31F8
Askersund Sweden 35F7
Askot India 61C1
Askøy island Norway 35A6
Askvoll Norway 35A6
Aslandus Iran 62F2
Asmara Ethiopia 71H1
Asotin Wash. USA 80E2
Aspeå Sweden 34G5
Aspern Austria 37G4
Aspiring,Mt New Zealand 100C7
Aspres-sur-Buech France 43F4
Assab Ethiopia 71J2
As Safa Saudi Arabia 62F4
As Salamiya Saudi Arabia 62F5
Assale,L Ethiopia 71H2
Assam state India 59H3
As Samāwah Iraq 62F3
Assaye India 58E4
Asse Belgium 32C4
Assen Netherlands 32E2
Asshur Iraq 62E2
Assiniboia Sask. Canada 76K7
Assiniboine,Mt Alta Canada 76H6
Assiniboine,R Man. Canada 76M7
Assinica L Que. Canada 78A1
Assisi Italy 44D4
As Sukhnah Syria 62D3
As Sulayyil Saudi Arabia 62F5
Assumption island Indian Ocean 71L1
As Suwaydā Syria 64E5
As Suwayḩ Oman 63H5
As Suwayq Oman 63H5
Assynt,L Scotland UK 28F3
Asten Netherlands 32D3
Asti Italy 44B3
Astipálaia island Greece 47F6
Aston England UK 25C6
Aston,C NW Terr. Canada 77S2
Astor Kashmir India 60D3
Astorga Spain 40C1
Astoria Oreg. USA 80B2
Astrakhan USSR 50F5
Åsträsk Sweden 34H4
Ástros Greece 47D6
Astudillo Spain 40D1
Asuncion Paraguay 91E3
Aswân Egypt 69M4
Aswan High Dam Egypt 69M4
Asyût Egypt 69M3
Atacama prov. Chile 91B3
Atacama,Des. Chile 91C2
Atafu island Tokelau 94J8
Atakpame Togo 68F7
Atalaia Brazil 93K5
Atalándi Greece 47D5
Atambua Timor Indonesia 53H12
Atar Mauritania 68C4
Ataran,R Burma 59J5
Atascadero Calif. USA 80C8
Atbara Sudan 69M5
Atbasar Kazakh. USSR 50H4
Atchafalaya B La USA 83N8
Atchison Kans. USA 83L3
Ateca Spain 41F2
Ath Belgium 32B4
Athabasca Alta Canada 76J6
Athabasca,L Alta/Sask. Canada 76K5
Athabasca,R Alta Canada 76H6
Athboy Ireland, Rep. of 30K6
Athena Oreg. USA 80D3
Athenry Ireland, Rep. of 31F7
Athens = Athínai
Athens Ga USA 85F4
Athens Tenn. USA 85E3
Atherton Queens. Australia 99K3
Atherton Plat. Queens. Australia 99J3
Athínai Greece 47D5
Athleague Ireland, Rep. of 31G6
Athlone Ireland, Rep. of 31H7
Athna Cyprus 64B2
Athol Mass. USA 84E1
Atholl,Forest of Scotland UK 29H6
Athos mt Greece 47E4
Athos,Mt = Áyion Óros
Athy Ireland, Rep. of 31K8
Ati Chad 69J6
Atico Peru 92C7
Atienza Spain 40E2
Atikonak L Newf. Canada 77T6
Atka USSR 51S3
Atka island Aleutian Is USA 87V13
Atkarsk USSR 49G5
Atlanta Ga USA 85E4
Atlanta Mich. USA 79D3
Atlantic Iowa USA 83L2
Atlantic City New J USA 84D3
Atlin BC Canada 76E5
Atlit Israel 64C5
Atoka Okla. USA 83K5
Atotonilco Mexico 88D3
Atrato,R Columbia 92B2
Atrauli India 61B1
At Ta'if Saudi Arabia 62E5
Attalla Ala. USA 85D3
Attape Laos 57D4
Attawapiskat,L Ont. Canada 77O6
Attawapiskat,R Ont. Canada 77O6
Attayskiy Kray region USSR 50K4
Attica Ind. USA 79C5
Attica NY USA 84B1
Attiki dist. Greece 47D5
Attleboro Mass. USA 84F2
Attleborough England UK 27S3
Attock Pakistan 60C4
Attu island Aleutian Is USA 87U13
At Tubayq Saudi Arabia 62F8
At Tubayq upland Saudi Arabia 62D4
Atukesi Japan 56J3
Atupi Brazil 93G3
Atwater Calif. USA 80C7
Aube dep. France 42F2
Aubel Belgium 32D4
Aubenas France 43F4
Aubonne Switzerland 33B2
Auburn Ala. USA 85E4
Auburn Calif. USA 80C6
Auburn Ind. USA 79D5
Auburn Maine USA 78C4
Auburn Nebr. USA 83L2
Auburn NY USA 84C1
Aubusson France 42E4
Auce Latvia USSR 35K8
Auch France 43D5
Auchterarder Scotland UK 29J7
Auckland New Zealand 100F3
Auckland,Is Pacific Ocean 94G13
Aude dep. France 43E5
Audeghle Somalia 71J4
Audenarde = Oudenaarde
Audubon Iowa USA 83L2
Augathella Queens. Australia 99K5
Aughnacloy N Ireland 30K5
Aughrim Ireland, Rep. of 31L8
Augsburg W Germany 36D4
Augusta Ark. USA 85B3
Augusta Ga USA 85F4
Augusta Kans. USA 83K4
Augusta Ky USA 85F1
Augusta Maine USA 78D4
Augusta Sicily Italy 45E7
Augusta W Aus. Australia 98D6
Augusta Wis. USA 79A3
Augustów Poland 37K2
Augustus,Mt W Aus. Australia 98D4
Auletta Italy 45E5
Aulu China 54G7
Aunis prov. France 42C3
Aur island Malaysia 57C6
Aura Finland 35K6
Auraiya India 61B2
Aurangabad India 58E5
Aurangabad India 61E3
Auray France 42B3
Aurillac France 43E4
Aurora Ill. USA 83P2
Aurora Ont. Canada 79G3
Aurum Nev. USA 80F6
Aus Namibia 72B5
Au Sable Mich. USA 79E3
Au Sable Forks NY USA 79K3
Auskerry island Orkney Scotland 28L1
Austerlitz = Slavkov
Austin Minn. USA 81L4
Austin Nev. USA 80E6
Austin Texas USA 83K7
Austin,L W Aus. Australia 98D5
Australia country Australajia 94D10
Australian Antarctic Terr. Antarctica 15H2
Australian Cap. Terr. Australia 97C3
Austria country Europe 36E5
Autlan Mexico 88D4
Autun France 42F3
Auvergne prov. France 43E4
Auxerre France 42E3
Auxonne France 42F3
Aux Sources,Mt Lesotho 72D5
Avallon France 42E3
Avalon Pen. Newf. Canada 78M3
Avaré Brazil 93H8
Avaviken Sweden 34H4
Aveiro Brazil 93F4
Aveiro Portugal 40B2
Avelgem Belgium 32B4
Avellaneda Argentina 91E4
Avellino Italy 45E5
Avenches Switzerland 33C2
Avenir Fr. Guiana 93G3
Averøy,I Norway 34B5
Aversa Italy 45E5
Aves,Is de Venezuela 92D1
Avesnes France 42E1
Avesta Sweden 35G6
Aveyron dep. France 43E4
Avezzano Italy 45D5
Avia Teria Argentina 91D3
Aviemore Scotland UK 28J5
Avigliano Italy 45E5
Avignon France 43F5
Avila Spain 40D2
Avila prov. Spain 40D2
Aviz Portugal 40C3
Avoca Iowa USA 83L2
Avoca Ireland,Rep. of 31L8
Avoca Tas. Australia 97F5
Avoca Vic. Australia 97B3
Avola Sicily Italy 45E7
Avon Mont. USA 80G2
Avon county England UK 26J5
Avonmouth England UK 26J5
Avon,R England UK 27L4
Avon,R Scotland UK 28K5
Avranches France 42C2
Awaji shima island Japan 56D7
Awakino New Zealand 100F4
Awbari Libya 69H3
Awe,Loch Scotland UK 29F7
Awjilah Libya 69K3
Awusa,L Ethiopia 71H3
Axar Fj. Iceland 34W11
Axat France 43E5
Axel Netherlands 32B3
Axel Heiberg I NW Terr. Canada 77N1
Axim Ghana 68E7
Axminster England UK 26J7
Aya Burma 59J4
Ayabaca Peru 92B4
Ayacucho Argentina 91E5
Ayacucho Peru 92C6
Ayaguz Kazakh. USSR 50K5
Ayamonte Spain 40C4
Ayan USSR 51Q4
Ayancik Turkey 62C1
Ayaviri Peru 92C6
Aydin Turkey 62B2
Ayer Switzerland 33C2
Ayerbe Spain 41F1
Ayia Greece 47D5
Áyion Óros pen Greece 47E4
Áyios Evstratios Greece 47E5
Aylesbury England UK 27N5
Aylmer Ont. Canada 79F4
Aylmer,L NW Terr. Canada 76K4
Aylsham England UK 27S3
Aylwin Que. Canada 79H2
Ayodhya India 61D2
Ayora Spain 41F3
Ayr Queens. Australia 99K3
Ayr Scotland UK 29G9
Ayr,R Scotland UK 29H8
Ayun Saudi Arabia 62E4
Ayutla Guatemala 88F5
Ayutla Mexico 88E4
Ayutthaya Thailand 57C4
Ayvalik Turkey 62B2
Aywaille Belgium 32D4
Azaila Spain 41F2
Azamgarh India 61D2
Azare Nigeria 69H6
Azaz Syria 64F1
Azerbaydzhanskaya SSR rep USSR 50F5
Azingo,L Gabon 70B5
Azogues Ecuador 92B4
Azores islands Atlantic Ocean 73K5
Azores,Is = Açores,Is
Azoum,R Chad 69K6
Azov, Sea of = Azovskoye More

Azovskoye More Barcelona

Azovskoye More *sea* USSR 48K9
Azpeitia Spain 41E1
Aztec *New Mex.* USA 82D4
Azua Dom. Rep. 89E3
Azuaga Spain 40D3
Azuero *pen.* Panama 89C5
Azul Argentina 91E5
Azum,R Sudan 69K6
Azzan South Yemen 62F7
Az Zawiyah Libya 69H2
Az Zubayr Iraq 62F3

B

Ba *Viti Levu* Fiji 94A25
Baabda Lebanon 64D4
Baalbek Lebanon 64E3
Baar Switzerland 33D1
Baargaal Somalia 71L2
Baarle-Hertog Belgium 32C3
Baarle Nassau Netherlands 32C3
Baarn Netherlands 32D2
Bababar Hills India 61E3
Babadag Romania 46G2
Babaeski Turkey 46F4
Babahoyo Ecuador 92B4
Babai India 61A4
Bab al Mandab *strait* Djibouti/S Yemen 18F8
Babar *island* Indonesia 53J12
Babati Tanzania 71H5
Babel I *Tas.* Australia 97F4
Babelthuap,I Palau Is 94A20
Babenna Syria 64E2
Baberu India 61C3
Babine L *BC* Canada 76F5
Babol Iran 63G2
Babonazo,R Ecuador 92B4
Babura Nigeria 70B2
Babuyan Is Philippines 52H7
Babylon Iraq 62E3
Bacabal Brazil 93F5
Bacabal Brazil 93J4
Bacadehuachi Mexico 88C2
Bacalar Mexico 88G4
Bacan *island* Indonesia 53J11
Bacău Romania 46F1
Bacchus Marsh *Vic.* Australia 97B3
Bacerac Mexico 88C1
Backbone Mts *Md/W Va* USA 84B3
Bäckefors Sweden 35E7
Backergunge Bangladesh 59H4
Back,R *NW Terr.* Canada 76M3
Backstairs Pass. *S Aus.* Australia 97A3
Bac Ninh Vietnam 57D2
Bacoachi Mexico 88C1
Bacolod Philippines 53H8
Bada Saudi Arabia 62D4
Badajos,L Brazil 92E4
Badajoz Brazil 93H4
Badajoz Spain 40C3
Badajoz *prov.* Spain 40C3
Badalona Spain 41H2
Badarma USSR 51M4
Badas Brunei 53F10
Bad Axe *Mich.* USA 79E4
Baddeck *No. Sc.* Canada 78H3
Bad Ems W Germany 36B3
Baden Switzerland 33D1
Baden-Baden W Germany 36C4
Badgastein Austria 36E5
Badger *Newf.* Canada 78K2
Badin Pakistan 58C4
Badiyah Oman 63H5
Bādiyat ash Shām *des.* Iraq/Jordan 62D3
Bad Kissingen W Germany 36D3
Bad Kreuznach W Germany 36B4
Bad Lands *Nebr./S Dak.* USA 86F3
Badlands Nat. Pk *S Dak.* USA 81G4
Bad Langensalza E Germany 36D3
Bad Mergentheim W Germany 36C4
Badon Senegal 68C6
Badong China 54F7
Bado,R Pakistan 58B3
Bad Ragaz Switzerland 33E1
Badrinath India 58E2
Bad Tölz W Germany 36D5
Baduen Somalia 71K3
Badulla Sri Lanka 58F7
Baena Spain 40D4
Baerle-Duc = Baarle-Hertog
Baffin B *NW Terr.* Canada 77S2
Baffin I *NW Terr.* Canada 77R3
Bafia Cameroun 69H8
Bafoulabé Mali 68C6
Baf'q Iran 63H3
Bafra Turkey 62D1
Bafra Burun *cape* Turkey 62D1
Bāft Iran 63H4
Bagata Zaire 70D5
Bagdarin USSR 51N4
Bagé Brazil 91F4
Baghdād Iraq 62E3
Bagherhat Bangladesh 61G4
Baghin Iran 63H3
Baghpat India 60E6
Baginbun Hd Ireland, Rep. of 31K9
Bagley *Minn.* USA 81K2
Bagnell Dam *Mo* USA 83M3
Bagnères de Luchon France 43D5
Bagniati,R Nepal 61E2
Bagnols-sur-Céze France 43F4
Bagoe,R Mali 68D6
Bagotville *Que.* Canada 78C2
Bagshot *England* UK 27N6
Baguio Philippines 53H7
Bahaar-i-Gaz Iran 63G2
Bahadurgarh India 60E6
Bahamas,The *country* G. of Mexico 60E6
Baharampur India 59F5
Bahawalpur Pakistan 60B6
Bahera India 61F2
Baheri India 61B1
Bahia = Salvador (Brazil)
Bahia Blanca Argentina 91D5
Bahía de Caráquez Ecuador 92A4
Bahia Laura Argentina 91C7
Bahía Negra Paraguay 91E2
Bahraich India 61C2
Bahrain *country* Middle East 63G4
Bahr El Ghazal *region* Sudan 69L7
Bahret el Ateibe Syria 64E4
Bahret el Hijane Syria 64E4
Bahret Homs Syria 64E3
Bahret Lut = Dead Sea
Bāhū Kālāt Iran 63J4
Baiao Brazil 93H4
Baibokoum Chad 69J7
Baicheng China 52H1
Baie d'Audierne *bay* France 42A3
Baie St Paul *Que.* Canada 79L2
Baihe China 54F6
Bai He *river* China 54J2
Baiji Iraq 62E2
Bai Jiang *river* China 55G10
Baile Átha Cliath = Dublin, Rep. of Ireland
Bailen Spain 40E3
Bailesti Romania 46D2
Bailieborough Ireland,Rep. of 30K6
Baillie I *NW Terr.* Canada 76F2
Bailong Jiang *river* China 54C6
Baimak Tanalykovo USSR 49N4
Bainbridge *Ga* USA 85E5
Bairnsdale *Vic.* Australia 97C3
Baishui Jiang China 54C6
Baital Faqih Yemen 62E7
Baixo Longa Angola 72B3
Baiyu Shan *mts* China 54E4
Baja Hungary 46B1
Baja California *state* Mexico 88A1
Baján Mexico 88D2
Baja Neuvo,I Colombia 89D2
Bajmok Yugoslavia 46B2
Bajo Boquete Panama 89C5
Bajranggarh India 61A3
Bakaly USSR 49L3
Bakel Senegal 68C6
Baker *Calif.* USA 80E8
Baker *Mont.* USA 81E2
Baker *Oreg.* USA 80E3
Baker Butte *Ariz.* USA 82C5
Baker,I Pacific Ocean 94J7
Baker L *NW Terr.* Canada 76M4
Baker,Mt *Wash.* USA 86B2
Bakersfield *Calif.* USA 80D8
Bakewell *England* UK 25E6
Bakhasar India 58D4
Bakkagerdhi Iceland 34Y12
Baklansk USSR 49S3
Bakloh India 60D4
Bako Ethiopia 71H3
Bakonyerdo *region* Hungary 37G5
Bakoven South Africa 72H9
Bakoy,R Mali 68D6
Baku *Azerbay.* USSR 50F5
Bala *Wales* UK 26G3
Balabac Str. Malay./Philippines 53G9
Balabat Yap Is 94A19
Balagnat India 58F4
Balakhta USSR 51L4
Balaklava *S Aus.* Australia 97A2
Balaklava USSR 48H9
Bala L *Wales* UK 26G3
Bala Murghab Afghanistan 63J2
Balancán Mexico 88F4
Balaquer Spain 41G2
Balashov USSR 49F5
Balasore India 59G4
Balat Egypt 69L3
Balaton,L Hungary 37G5
Bala,Vale of *Wales* UK 26G3
Balazote Spain 41E3
Balboa Panama 89D5
Balbriggan Ireland, Rep. of 30L6
Balcanoona *S Aus.* Australia 97A2
Balcarce Argentina 91E5
Balchari I India 61G5
Balchik Bulgaria 46G3
Balclutha New Zealand 100C8
Baldegg See *lake* Switzerland 33D1
Bald Knob *Ark.* USA 83N5
Bald Knob *mt W Va* USA 85G1
Baldock *England* UK 27P5
Baldwin *Ill.* USA 83P3
Baldwin *Mich.* USA 79D4
Baldwinsville *NY* USA 84C1
Baldy Pk *Ariz.* USA 82C6
Baldy Pk *New Mex.* USA 82F5
Baleares,Is Medit. Sea 41H3
Balearic Is = Islas Baleares
Baleine,Gde R de la *river Que.* Canada 77Q5
Baleine,Petite *river Que.* Canada 77Q5
Baleine,R *Que.* Canada 77S5
Baleiniers,G des Kerguelen 65S12
Balen Belgium 32D3
Baler Philippines 53H7
Balerno *Scotland* UK 29K8
Balestrand Norway 35B6
Baley USSR 51N4
Balfour *N Dak.* USA 81G2
Balfour *Tas.* Australia 97E5
Bali *island* Indonesia 53F12
Balikesir Turkey 62B2
Balikpapan *Borneo* Indon. 53G11
Balk Netherlands 32D2
Balkhash *Kazakh.* USSR 50J5
Ballabgarh India 60E6
Ballachulish *Scotland* UK 29F6
Ballaghaderreen Ireland, Rep. of 30F6
Ballantrae *Scotland* UK 29F9
Ballarat *Vic.* Australia 97B3
Ballater *Scotland* UK 28K5
Ballé Mali 68D5
Ballenas,B de Mexico 88B2
Ballenas Chan. Mexico 88B2
Balleny Is Antarctica 15L3
Ballia India 61E3
Ballina Ireland, Rep. of 30E5
Ballina *NSW* Australia 97D1
Ballinasloe Ireland, Rep. of 31G7
Ballindine Ireland, Rep. of 30F6
Ballingarry Ireland, Rep. of 31F9
Ballinluig *Scotland* UK 29J6
Ballinrobe Ireland, Rep. of 30E6
Ballinskelligs B Ireland, Rep. of 31C10
Ballston Spa *NY* USA 84E1
Ballybay Ireland, Rep. of 30K5
Ballybofey Ireland, Rep. of 30H4
Ballybunion Ireland, Rep. of 31D8
Ballycastle Ireland, Rep. of 30E5
Ballycastle N Ireland 30L3
Ballyclare N Ireland 30M4
Ballyconnell Ireland, Rep. of 30H5
Ballycotton B Ireland, Rep. of 31H10
Ballyduff Ireland, Rep. of 31G9
Ballygar Ireland, Rep. of 31G6
Ballygawley N Ireland 30J5
Ballyhaise Ireland, Rep of 30J5
Ballyhaunis Ireland, Rep. of 30F6
Ballyhoura Hills Ireland, Rep. of 31F9
Ballyjamesduff Ireland, Rep. of 30J6
Ballymahon Ireland, Rep. of 31H6
Ballymena N Ireland 30L4
Ballymoney N Ireland 30K3
Ballymote Ireland, Rep. of 30F5
Ballynahinch N Ireland 30M5
Ballyquintin Point N Ireland 30M5
Ballyragget Ireland, Rep. of 31J8
Ballyshannon Ireland, Rep. of 30G4
Ballytore Ireland,Rep of 31K7
Ballyvaghan Ireland, Rep. of 31E7
Balmhorn *mt* Switzerland 33C2
Balmoral *Vic.* Australia 97B3
Balmoral Castle *Scotland* UK 28K5
Balotra India 58D3
Balpahari Res. India 61F3
Balrampur India 61D2
Balranald *NSW* Australia 97B2
Balsas Brazil 93H5
Balsas,R Mexico 88D4
Bals Fj. Norway 34H2
Balsthal Switzerland 33C1
Balta *Ukrain.* USSR 48F8
Balta *island Shetland* Scotland 28R7
Baltanás Spain 40D2
Baltat *Kashmir* India 60D2
Baltic Sea Europe 35G9
Baltim Egypt 69M2
Baltimore Ireland, Rep. of 31E11
Baltimore *Md* USA 84C3
Baltinglass Ireland, Rep. of 31K8
Baltistan *district Kashmir* India 60D3
Baltiysk *Lith.* USSR 35H9
Baluchistan *region* Pakistan 58B3
Balurghat India 61G3
Balzers Liechtenstein 33E1
Bam Iran 63H4
Bama Nigeria 69H6
Bamako Mali 68D6
Bamba Mali 68E5
Bambari CAR 69K7
Bamberg W Germany 36D4
Bambui Brazil 93H8
Bamburgh *England* UK 25E1
Bamenda Cameroun 69H7
Bamiyan Afghanistan 63K3
Bampton *England* UK 26H7
Bampur Iran 63J4
Bam Tso *lake Tibet* China 59G3
Banaba,I Pacific Ocean 94G8
Banagher Ireland,Rep. of 31H7
Banalia Zaire 70F4
Banamba Mali 68D6
Ban Aranyaprathet Thailand 57C4
Banat *region* Romania 46C2
Banbridge N Ireland 30L5
Banbury *England* UK 27M4
Baň Bystrica Czech. 37H4
Banchory *Scotland* UK 28L5
Ban Co *lake Tibet* China 59H2
Bancroft *Ont.* Canada 79H3
Banda India 61B3
Banda India 61C3
Banda Aceh *Sumatra* Indon. 53C9
Banda Banda,Mt *NSW* Australia 97D2
Banda La *mt Tibet* China 59H2
Bandar = Machilipatnam
Bandar Nepal 61C1
Bandar 'Abbās Iran 63H4
Bandar Anzali Iran 62F2
Bandarawela Sri Lanka 58F7
Bandar e Deylam Iran 63G3
Bandar-e Lengeh Iran 63G4
Bandar-e Rig Iran 63G4
Bandar-e-Torkaman Iran 63G2
Bandar Khomeyni Iran 62F3
Banda Sea Indonesia 53J12
Bande Belgium 32D4
Bandera Argentina 91D3
Banderas,B Mexico 88C3
Bandiagara Mali 68E6
Bandikui India 58E3
Bandirma Turkey 62B1
Band-i-Turkestan *mts* Afghanistan 63J2
Bandol France 43F5
Bandon Ireland, Rep. of 31F10
Bandon *Oreg.* USA 80A4
Bandon,R Ireland,Rep. of 31F10
Band Qir Iran 62F3
Bandundu Zaire 70D5
Bandung *Java* Indon. 53E12
Banes Cuba 89D2
Banff *Alta* Canada 76H6
Banff *Scotland* UK 28L4
Banff Nat. Pk *Alta* Canada 76H6
Banfora Upper Volta 68E6
Bangada Congo 71F4
Bangalore India 58E6
Banganga,R India/Nepal 61D2
Bangara,R Bangladesh 61G4
Bangassou CAR 69K8
Bang Giang China 55D11
Bangka *island* Indonesia 53E11
Bangkok Thailand 57C4
Bangkok, Bight of *bay* Thailand 57C4
Bangladesh *country* S Asia 59G4
Bangong Co *lake* China/India 58E2
Bangor *Maine* USA 78D4
Bangor N Ireland 30M4
Bangor *Pa* USA 84D2
Bangor *Wales* UK 26F2
Bang Saphan Yai Thailand 57B4
Bangui CAR 69J8
Bangweulu L Zambia 72D2
Ban Houei Sai Laos 57C2
Baní Dom. Rep. 89E3
Bania CAR 70D4
Bani Bu'Ali Oman 63H5
Banica Dom. Rep. 89E3
Banifina,R Mali 68D6
Baniyas Syria 64D2
Baniyas Syria 64D4
Banja Luka Yugoslavia 44F3
Banjarmasin *Borneo* Indon. 53F11
Ban Jaruga Yugoslavia 44F3
Banjul The Gambia 68B6
Banka India 61F3
Banka Pahari India 61C3
Banki India 59G4
Bankipore India 61E3
Banks I *NW Terr.* Canada 76G2
Banks I *Queens.* Australia 99J2
Banks,Is Pacific Ocean 94G9
Banks,L *Wash.* USA 80D2
Banks Pen. New Zealand 100E6
Banks Str. *Tas.* Australia 97F5
Bankura India 61F4
Ban Me Thuot *mt* Cambodia 57D4
Banning *Calif.* USA 80E8
Banningville = Bandundu
Bannockburn *Scotland* UK 29J7
Bannock P *Idaho* USA 80G3
Bann,R Ireland, Rep. of 31L8
Bann,R *N Ireland* UK 30K4
Bannu Pakistan 60B4
Baños de Montemayor Spain 40D2
Bansda India 58D4
Bansi India 61D2
Bansloi,R India 61F3
Banswara India 58D4
Ban Takua Pa Thailand 57B5
Bantalor *New Br.* Canada 78E3
Ban Tha Uthen Thailand 57C3
Bantry Ireland, Rep. of 31E10
Bantry B Ireland,Rep. of 31D10
Banu Afghanistan 63K2
Banur India 60E5
Banyak Kep. *island* Indon 53C10
Banyo Cameroun 69H7
Banyoles Spain 41H1
Banyuwangi *Java* Indon. 53F12
Banzare Coast Antarctica 15J3
Banzyville = Yasanyama
Banzyville = Mobayi-Mbongo
Bao'an China 55H11
Baochang = Taibus Qi
Baode China 54F3
Baoding China 54H3
Baofeng China 54G6
Baoji China 54D5
Baojing China 55E8
Baokang China 54F7
Baoshan China 52C5
Baotou China 54E2
Baoulé,R Mali 68D6
Bapaume France 42E1
Bapsfontein South Africa 72N12
Ba'qubah Iraq 62E3
Baquezane *mt* Niger 69G5
Ba,R *Viti Levu* Fiji 94A25
Bar Yugoslavia 46B3
Bara Sudan 69M6
Baraawe Somalia 71J4
Bara Banki India 61C2
Barabhum India 61F4
Barabinsk USSR 50J4
Baraboo *Wis.* USA 79B4
Baracoa Cuba 89E2
Barād Syria 64E4
Baradine *NSW* Australia 97C2
Baradine,R *NSW* Australia 97C2
Barahona Dom. Rep. 89E3
Barahona Spain 41E2
Barail Ra *mts* India 59H3
Barak,R India 59H3
Bara Lacha P India 60E4
Barama,R Guyana 92F2
Baramula *Kashmir* India 60D3
Baranagar India 61G4
Baranof I *Alaska* USA 87Z13
Baranovichi USSR 48E5
Baranów Poland 37J3
Baraque Michel Belgium 32E4
Barataria B *La* USA 83N8
Baratta *S Aus.* Australia 97A2
Baraunda India 61C3
Baraut India 60E6
Barbacena Brazil 93J8
Barbacoas Colombia 92B3
Barbadillo del Mercado Spain 40E1
Barbados *country* Lesser Antilles 89H4
Barbas,C Morocco 68B4
Barbastro Spain 41G1
Barbezieux France 42C4
Barbigha India 61E3
Barbuda,I Leeward Is 89G3
Barcaldine *Queens.* Australia 99K4
Barcarrota Spain 40C3
Barce = Al Marj
Barcellona Pozza di Gotto *Sicily* Italy 45E6
Barcelona Spain 41H2

Barcelona, Beltana

Barcelona Venezuela **92E1**
Barcelona prov. Spain **41H2**
Barcelonnette France **43G4**
Barcelos Brazil **92E4**
Barcelos Portugal **40B2**
Barcoo,R Queens. Australia **99J4**
Bardai Chad **69J4**
Bardejov Czech. **37J4**
Bardheere Somalia **71J4**
Bardi India **61D3**
Bardiyah Libya **69L2**
Bardsey,I Wales UK **26E3**
Bardstown Ky USA **85E2**
Bardu Norway **34H2**
Barduelva,R Norway **34H2**
Bareilly India **61B1**
Bärenhorn mt Switzerland **33E2**
Barentsøya,I Arctic Ocean **50D2**
Barents Sea Arctic Ocean **50E2**
Barentu Ethiopia **71H1**
Barfurush = **Bābol**
Bargen Switzerland **33D1**
Bargoed Wales UK **26H5**
Barh India **61E3**
Barhaj India **61D2**
Bar Harbor Maine USA **78D4**
Bari India **61A2**
Bari Italy **45F5**
Bari Doab region Pakistan **60C5**
Barika Algeria **68G1**
Barima,R Guyana/Venez. **92E2**
Barinas Venezuela **92C2**
Baring,C NW Terr. Canada **76H2**
Barisal Bangladesh **59H4**
Barito,R Borneo Indon. **53F11**
Barkā Oman **63H5**
Barkald Norway **35D6**
Barkhan Pakistan **60A6**
Barkley,L Ky USA **85D2**
Barkly Tableland plateau N Terr. Australia **99H3**
Bar le Duc France **42F2**
Barlee,L W Aus. Australia **98D5**
Barlee Ra mts W Aus. Australia **98D4**
Barletta Italy **45F5**
Barmdeo Mandi Nepal **61C1**
Barmedman NSW Australia **97C2**
Barmer India **58D3**
Barmera S Aus. Australia **97B2**
Barmouth Wales UK **26F3**
Barnaby River New Br. Canada **78F3**
Barnard Castle England UK **25E3**
Barnato NSW Australia **97B2**
Barnaul USSR **50K4**
Barn Bluff mt Tas. Australia **97F5**
Barnegat B New J USA **84D3**
Barne Inlet Antarctica **15L1**
Barnesville Minn. USA **81J2**
Barnet England UK **27P5**
Barneveld Netherlands **32D2**
Barneys L NSW Australia **97B2**
Barnihal Pass & Tunnel India **60D4**
Barnsley England UK **25F5**
Barnstable Mass. USA **84F2**
Barnstaple England UK **26F6**
Baroda = **Vadodara**
Baro,R Sudan **69M7**
Barpeta India **59H3**
Barquisimeto Venezuela **92D1**
Barra Brazil **93J6**
Barra Saudi Arabia **62F5**
Barraba NSW Australia **97D2**
Barrackpore India **61G4**
Barra do Bugres Brazil **92F6**
Barra do Corda Brazil **93H5**
Barra do Piraí Brazil **93J8**
Barra Hd Scotland UK **29A6**
Barra,I Scotland UK **28A5**
Barra Mansa Brazil **93J8**
Barran Somalia **71K2**
Barranca Peru **92B4**
Barrancabermeja Colombia **92C2**
Barrancas Venezuela **92E2**
Barrancos Portugal **40C3**
Barranqueras Argentina **91E3**
Barranquilla Colombia **92C1**
Barra,Sd of Scotland UK **28B5**
Barre Vt USA **79K3**
Barreiras Brazil **93J6**
Barreirinha Brazil **93F4**
Barreirinhas Brazil **93J4**
Barreiro Portugal **40B3**
Barreiros Brazil **93K5**
Barrême France **43G5**
Barren I Andaman Is India **59H6**
Barretos Brazil **93H8**
Barrhill Scotland UK **29G9**
Barrie Ont. Canada **79G3**
Barrington No. Sc. Canada **78F5**
Barrington Tops mt NSW Australia **97D2**
Barringun NSW Australia **97C1**
Barron Wis. USA **81M3**
Barrow Argentina **91D5**
Barrow Creek N Terr. Australia **99G4**
Barrow I W Aus. Australia **98D4**
Barrow-in-Furness England UK **25B4**
Barrow,R Ireland, Rep. of **31K9**
Barrow Str NW Terr. Canada **76M2**
Barry Wales UK **26H6**
Barry Mts Vic. Australia **97C3**
Barsi India **58E5**
Barstow Calif. USA **80E8**
Bar-sur-Aube France **42F2**
Bar-sur-Seine France **42F2**
Bartibog New Br. Canada **78F3**
Bartica Guyana **92F2**
Bartle Frere,Mt Queens. Australia **99J3**
Bartlesville Okla. USA **83K4**
Bartlett Springs Calif. USA **80B6**
Barton Humb.,England UK **25H5**
Barton Lancs,England UK **25C5**
Bartoszyce Poland **37J1**
Baruva India **59F5**
Barvaux Belgium **32D4**
Barwa India **61E4**
Barwani India **58D4**
Barwon,R NSW Australia **97C1**
Basal Pakistan **60C4**
Basalt Idaho USA **80G4**
Basalt Nev. USA **80D6**
Basankusu Zaire **70D4**
Basel Switzerland **33C1**
Baselland canton Switzerland **33C1**
Bashākerd region Iran **63H4**
Bashkirskaya ASSR rep. USSR **50G4**
Basia India **61E4**
Basilan island Philippines **53H9**
Basildon England UK **27Q5**
Basilicata region Italy **45F5**
Basingstoke England UK **27M6**
Basirhat India **61G4**
Baskatong,Res. Que. Canada **79H2**
Basle = **Basel**
Båsmo Norway **34E3**
Basodino mt Italy/Switz. **33D2**
Basoko Zaire **70E4**
Basongo Zaire **70E5**
Basra Iraq **62F3**
Bas-Rhin dep. France **42G2**
Bassein Burma **59H5**
Bassein India **58D5**
Basses-Alpes = **Alpes-de-Haute Provence**
Basses,Great,I Sri Lanka **58F7**
Basses,Little island Sri Lanka **58F7**
Basses-Pyrénées = **Pyrénées Atlantiques**
Basse Terre Guadeloupe **89G3**
Basseterre St Kitts **89G3**
Bassevelde Belgium **32B3**
Bassikounou Mauritania **68D5**
Bass Rk Scotland UK **29L7**
Bass Str. Tas./Vic. Australia **99J7**
Båstad Sweden **35E8**
Bastak Iran **63G4**
Bastenaken = **Bastogne**
Basti India **61D2**
Bastia Corsica France **43K6**
Bastion,C China **55E13**
Bastogne Belgium **32D4**
Bastrop La USA **83N6**
Bastuträsk Sweden **34J4**
Basul,R Pakistan **58B3**
Basuo = **Dongfang**
Basura Mexico **88B1**
Basutoland = **Lesotho**
Bata Eq. Guinea **70B4**
Bataan Philippines **53H8**
Batacosa Mexico **88C2**
Batala India **60D5**
Batalha Portugal **40B3**
Batang China **52C5**
Batangafo CAR **69J7**
Batangas Philippines **53H8**
Batan Is Philippines **52H6**
Batavia Argentina **91C4**
Batavia NY USA **84B1**
Bataysk USSR **49D7**
Batchawana Ont. Canada **79D2**
Batchelor N Terr. Australia **98G2**
Batemans B NSW Australia **97D3**
Batenburg Netherlands **32D3**
Batesburg S Car. USA **85G4**
Batesville Ark. USA **83N5**
Batesville Miss. USA **85B3**
Bath England UK **26K6**
Bath Maine USA **78D5**
Bath NY USA **84C1**
Batha,R Chad **69J6**
Bathgate Scotland UK **29J8**
Bathurst = **Banjul**
Bathurst New Br. Canada **78F3**
Bathurst NSW Australia **97C2**
Bathurst I N Terr. Australia **98F2**
Bathurst I NW Terr. Canada **76L1**
Bathurst Inl. NW Terr. Canada **76K3**
Bathurst,L NSW Australia **97C3**
Batie Upper Volta **68E7**
Batiscan Que. Canada **79K2**
Batley England UK **25E5**
Batlow NSW Australia **97C3**
Batna Algeria **68G1**
Baton Rouge La USA **83N7**
Batopilas Mexico **88C2**
Batraki USSR **49J4**
Batroun Lebanon **64D3**
Battambang Cambodia **57C4**
Bätterkinden Switzerland **33C1**
Batticaloa Sri Lanka **58F7**
Battice Belgium **32D4**
Battih South Yemen **62F6**
Batti Malv island Nicobar Is India **59H7**
Battle England UK **27Q7**
Battle Creek Mich. USA **79D4**
Battleford Sask. Canada **76K6**
Battle Harbour Newf. Canada **77U6**
Battle Mountain Nev. USA **80E5**
Batu island Indonesia **53C11**
Batumi Gruzin. USSR **50F5**
Baturaja Sumatra Indon. **53D11**
Baturi Mexico **88C2**
Baturité Brazil **93K4**
Baubau Celebes Indon. **53H12**
Bauchi Nigeria **69G6**
Baud India **59F4**
Baudette Minn. USA **81K1**
Baudó Colombia **92B2**
Baudó,Sierra de mts Columbia **92B2**
Baudouinville = **Moba**
Bauge France **42C3**
Bauma Switzerland **33D1**
Baunt USSR **51N4**
Baures Bolivia **92E6**
Bauru Brazil **93H8**
Baús Brazil **93G7**
Bauska Latvia USSR **35L8**
Bautzen E Germany **36F3**
Bavispe Mexico **88C1**
Bawal India **60E6**
Bawean island Indonesia **53F12**
Bawiti Egypt **69L3**
Bawku Ghana **68E6**
Bawtry England UK **25F6**
Ba Xian China **54J3**
Bayamo Cuba **89D2**
Bayana India **61A2**
Bayan Aul Kazakh. USSR **50J4**
Bayandzurh Mongolia **52E1**
Bayan Har Shan mts China **52C4**
Bayan Obo China **54E2**
Bayburt Turkey **62E1**
Bay City Mich. USA **79E4**
Bay City Texas USA **83L8**
Baydaratskaya B USSR **50H2**
Baydhabo Somalia **71J4**
Bayerischer Wald W Germany **36E4**
Bayern state W Germany **36D4**
Bayeux France **42C2**
Bayhān al Qasāb South Yemen **62F7**
Bayir Jordan **64E7**
Bay Is Honduras **89B3**
Baykit USSR **51L3**
Baykonur Kazakh. USSR **50H5**
Bay Minette Ala. USA **85D5**
Bayona Spain **40B1**
Bayonne France **43C5**
Bayóvar Peru **92A5**
Bayram Ali Turkmen. USSR **50H6**
Bayreuth W Germany **36D4**
Bays,L of Ont. Canada **79G3**
Baytik Shan mts China **52B1**
Bazaruto,I Mozambique **72F4**
Bazas France **43C4**
Bazhong China **54D7**
Bazias Romania **46C2**
Bazmān Iran **63H4**
Bcharre Lebanon **64D3**
Beach N Dak. USA **81F2**
Beachport S Aus. Australia **97A3**
Beachy Hd England UK **27Q7**
Beacon NY USA **84E2**
Beaconsfield England UK **27N5**
Beaconsfield Tas. Australia **97F5**
Beagle,Ca Argentina **91C8**
Beal Ra mts Queens. Australia **99J4**
Beaminster England UK **26J7**
Beardmore Gl. Antarctica **15L1**
Bear I Ireland,Rep. of **31D10**
Bear Is = **Medvezhi Ova**
Bear L Idaho/Utah USA **82C1**
Bearn prov. France **43C5**
Bear Paw Mts Mont. USA **81C1**
Bear,R Idaho/Utah USA **82C1**
Beata,I Dom. Rep. **89E3**
Beatenberg Switzerland **33C2**
Beatrice Nebr. USA **83K2**
Beattock Scotland UK **29K9**
Beatty Nev. USA **80E7**
Beattyville Ky USA **85F2**
Beauceville Que. Canada **79L2**
Beaufort S Car. USA **85G4**
Beaufort Vic. Australia **97B3**
Beaufort West South Africa **72C6**
Beaugency France **42D3**
Beaulieu England UK **27M7**
Beauly Scotland UK **28H5**
Beauly Firth Scotland UK **28H4**
Beaumaris Wales UK **26F2**
Beaumont Belgium **32C4**
Beaumont France **42E2**
Beaumont Texas USA **83L7**
Beaune France **42F3**
Beauport Que. Canada **79L2**
Beauraing Belgium **32C4**
Beauvais France **42E2**
Beauval Sask. Canada **76K5**
Beauvoir-sur-Mer France **42B3**
Beaver Okla. USA **82H4**
Beaver Utah USA **82B3**
Beaver Dam Wis. USA **79B4**
Beaver Falls Pa USA **79F5**
Beaverhead Mts Idaho USA **80G3**
Beaverhead,R Mont. USA **80G3**
Beaver I Mich. USA **79D3**
Beaver L Ark. USA **83L4**
Beaver,R Sask. Canada **76K6**
Beaver,R Utah USA **82B3**
Beaver River Ra. Utah USA **80G6**
Beaverton Oreg. USA **80B3**
Beawar India **58D3**
Beazley Argentina **91C4**
Bebedouro Brazil **93H8**
Beccles England UK **27T4**
Bečej Yugoslavia **46B2**
Becerrea Spain **40C1**
Béchar Algeria **68E2**
Bechuanaland = **Botswana**
Becleau Romania **37L5**
Bédar Spain **41E4**
Bédarieux France **43E5**
Beddgelert Wales UK **26F2**
Bedford England UK **27P4**
Bedford Pa USA **84B2**
Bedford Que. Canada **79K3**
Bedford Va USA **85H2**
Bedfordshire county England UK **27P4**
Bedlington England UK **25E2**
Bedouri Queens. Australia **99H4**
Bedretto Switzerland **33D2**
Bedr Honein Saudi Arabia **62D5**
Bedworth England UK **27M4**
Bedzin Poland **37H3**
Beeac Vic. Australia **97B3**
Beebe Ark. USA **83N5**
Beechey,L NW Terr. Canada **76K3**
Beechworth Vic. Australia **97C3**
Beecroft Pen. NSW Australia **97D2**
Beek Netherlands **32D3**
Beek Netherlands **32D4**
Beekbergen Netherlands **32D2**
Beenoskee mt Ireland, Rep. of **31C9**
Beerlegem Belgium **32B4**
Beer Menuha Israel **64D7**
Beernem Belgium **32B3**
Beers Netherlands **32D3**
Beersheba Israel **64C6**
Beeville Texas USA **82T9**
Befale Zaire **70E4**
Befandriana Madagascar **71N10**
Bega NSW Australia **97C3**
Begnins Switzerland **33B2**
Behbehan Iran **63G3**
Beho Belgium **32E4**
Bei'an China **52J1**
Beibu Wan SE Asia **57D2**
Beidha Saudi Arabia **62D5**
Beihai China **55E12**
Beijing China **54J2**
Beilen Netherlands **32E2**
Beiliu China **55F11**
Beiliu Jiang river China **55F11**
Beilul Ethiopia **71J2**
Beinn à Ghlò mt Scotland UK **29J6**
Beinwil Switzerland **33D1**
Beipan Jiang river China **55C10**
Beipiao China **54L2**
Beira Mozambique **72E3**
Beira region Portugal **40B3**
Beirūt Lebanon **64D4**
Beit Bridge Zimbabwe **72E4**
Bëit ed Dine Lebanon **64D4**
Beius Romania **46D1**
Beizhen China **54L2**
Beja Portugal **40C3**
Bejaïa Algeria **68F1**
Béjaïa,G de Algeria **68G1**
Béjar Spain **40D2**
Bejestan Iran **63H3**
Bejucal Cuba **89C2**
Békéscsaba Hungary **37J5**
Bela Pakistan **58C3**
Belagunj India **61D3**
Belang Celebes Indon. **53H10**
Belangpidie Sumatra Indon. **53C10**
Belaraboon NSW Australia **97B2**
Belaya Tserkov' Ukrain. USSR **48G7**
Belcher Is NW Terr. Canada **77Q5**
Belchiragh Afghanistan **63K2**
Belchite Spain **41F2**
Belcoo Ireland, Rep. of **30H5**
Beldanga India **61G4**
Belebey USSR **49M3**
Belém Brazil **93H4**
Belén Argentina **91C3**
Belen New Mex. USA **82E5**
Belen Panama **89C5**
Belfast Maine USA **78D4**
Belfast N Ireland **30M4**
Belfast Lough N Ireland UK **30M4**
Belfeld Netherlands **32E3**
Belfield N Dak. USA **81F2**
Belford England UK **25E1**
Belfort France **42G3**
Belgaum India **58D5**
Belgium country Europe **32B4**
Belgorod USSR **48K6**
Belgorod Dnestrovskiy Ukrain. USSR **48G8**
Belgrade = **Beograd**
Belin France **43C4**
Belitung island Indonesia **53E11**
Belize Belize **89B3**
Belize country Central America **89B3**
Bellac France **42D3**
Bella Coola BC Canada **76F6**
Bellaire Mich. USA **79D3**
Bellaire Ohio USA **79F5**
Bellary India **58E5**
Bellata NSW Australia **97C1**
Bella Tola mt Switzerland **33C2**
Bella Vista Calif. USA **80B5**
Bellavista Peru **92B5**
Bellbrook NSW Australia **97D2**
Belledune New Br. Canada **78F3**
Bellefontaine Ohio USA **79E5**
Bellefonte Pa USA **84C2**
Belle Fourche S Dak. USA **81F3**
Belle Ile island France **42B3**
Belle Isle Newf. Canada **78L1**
Belle Isle,Str of Newf. Canada **78K1**
Belleme France **42D2**
Belle Plain Iowa USA **83M2**
Bellerive Tas. Australia **97F5**
Belleville France **42F3**
Belleville Ill. USA **83N3**
Belleville Kans. USA **83K3**
Belleville Ont. Canada **79H3**
Bellevue Idaho USA **80F4**
Bellevue Iowa USA **83N1**
Bellevue Ont. Canada **79D2**
Bellevue Wash. USA **80B2**
Belley France **42F4**
Belle Yella Liberia **68C7**
Bell I Newf. Canada **78L1**
Bellingen NSW Australia **97D2**
Bellingham England UK **25D2**
Bellingham Wash. USA **86B2**
Bellingshausen Sea Antarctica **15R3**
Bellinzona Switzerland **33E2**
Bellmullet Ireland, Rep. of **30C5**
Bellows Falls Vt USA **84E1**
Belluno Italy **44D2**
Bell Ville Argentina **91D4**
Bellville South Africa **72J9**
Bélmez Spain **40D3**
Belmond Iowa USA **83M1**
Belmont NY USA **84B1**
Belmonte Brazil **93K7**
Belmonte Portugal **40C2**
Belmont L Pa USA **84D2**
Belmopan Belize **89B3**
Belo Horizonte Brazil **93J7**
Beloit Kans. USA **83J3**
Beloit Wis. USA **79B4**
Belomorsk Karel. USSR **50E3**
Belopolye Ukrain. USSR **48J6**
Belorado Spain **40E1**
Beloretsk USSR **49P4**
Belorusskaya S.S.R = **Byelorussia**
Belo Russkaya SSR rep. USSR **50D4**
Belostok = **Białystok**
Belo-Tsiribihina Madagascar **71M10**
Beloye Ozero lake USSR **48K1**
Beloyo More gulf USSR **50E3**
Belp Switzerland **33C2**
Beltana S Aus. Australia **97A2**

Belted Ra. Blacksod B

Belted Ra. Nev. USA 80E7
Belterra Brazil 93G4
Beltigen Switzerland 33C2
Belton S Aus. Australia 97A2
Belturbet Ireland, Rep. of 30J5
Belukha mt USSR 50K4
Belvedere Marittimo Italy 45E6
Belver Portugal 40C3
Belvidere Ill. USA 83P1
Belvidere New J USA 84D2
Bemidji Minn. USA 81K2
Benagerie S Aus. Australia 97B2
Ben Alder mt Scotland UK 29H6
Benalla Vic. Australia 97C3
Benapol India 61G4
Benaras = Varanasi
Benares = Varanasi
Ben Attow mt Scotland UK 28F5
Benavente Spain 40D2
Benbecula,I Scotland UK 28B5
Benbury mt Ireland, Rep. of 30D6
Ben Cruachan mt Scotland UK 29F7
Bencubbin W Aus. Australia 98D6
Bend Oreg. USA 80C3
Ben Dearg Scotland UK 28G4
Bender Beyla Somalia 71L3
Bendery Moldav. USSR 48F8
Bendigo Vic. Australia 97B3
Bendoc Vic. Australia 97C3
Benešov Czech. 36F4
Benevento Italy 45E5
Bengal,B of India 59G5
Bengal, West state India 61F4
Ben Gardane Tunisia 69H2
Bengbu China 54J6
Benghazi Libya 69K2
Benghazi Libya 69K3
Benguela Angola 70C7
Benguela region Angola 70D7
Benha Egypt 69M2
Ben Hope mt Scotland UK 28G3
Beni Abbès Algeria 68E2
Benicarlo Spain 41G2
Benicia Calif. USA 80B6
Beni Mazar Egypt 69M3
Beni Mellal Morocco 68D2
Benin country Africa 68F7
Benin, Bight of bay Africa 68F8
Benin City Nigeria 68G7
Beni,R Bolivia 92D6
Beni Saf Algeria 68E1
Beni Suef Egypt 69M3
Benito Eq. Guinea 70B4
Benjamin Constant Brazil 92C4
Benkelman Nebr. USA 82H2
Ben Klibreck mt Scotland UK 28H3
Benkovac Yugoslavia 44E3
Ben Lawers mt Scotland UK 29H6
Ben Ledi mt Scotland UK 29H7
Ben Lomond mt NSW Australia 97D2
Ben Lomond mt Scotland UK 29G7
Ben Macdhui mt Scotland UK 28J5
Ben More mt Scotland UK 29D7
Ben More mt Scotland UK 29G7
Ben More Assynt mt Scotland UK 28G3
Bennett BC Canada 76D5
Bennettsville S Car. USA 85H3
Ben Nevis mt Scotland UK 29G6
Bennington Vt USA 84E1
Benoni South Africa 72N12
Benson Ariz. USA 82C6
Benson Minn. USA 81K3
Bent Iran 63H4
Bentinck,I Burma 59J6
Benton Ark. USA 83M5
Benton Harbor Mich. USA 79C4
Benton,Mt Malaysia 57C6
Benue,R Nigeria 68G7
Ben Vorlich mt Scotland UK 29H7
Benwee Hd Ireland, Rep. of 30D5
Ben Wyvis mt Scotland UK 28G4
Benxi China 54M2
Beograd Yugoslavia 46C2
Beppu Japan 56B8
Berar prov. India 58E4
Berat Albania 47B4
Berber Sudan 69M5
Berbera Somalia 71K2
Berbérati CAR 69J8
Berbice,R Guyana 92F2
Bercher Switzerland 33B2
Berdichev Ukrain. USSR 48F7
Berdigyastyakh USSR 51P3
Berdyansk Ukrain. USSR 48K8
Berenda Calif. USA 80C7
Bere Regis England UK 27K7
Beresford S Dak. USA 81J4
Beresti Romania 46F1
Berezniki USSR 50G4
Berezovo USSR 50H3
Berg Norway 34G2
Berga Spain 41G1
Bergamo Italy 44B3
Bergeijk Netherlands 32D3
Bergen E Germany 36E1
Bergen Norway 35A6
Bergen W Germany 36C2
Bergen op Zoom Netherlands 32C3
Bergerac France 43D4
Bergisch Gladbach W Germany 36B3
Bergün Switzerland 33E2
Berhampore India 61G3
Beri India 60E6
Beri India 61B3
Beringen Belgium 32D3
Beringil Sudhan 69L6
Bering Str. America/Asia 87V12
Berislav Ukrain. USSR 48H8
Berkåk Norway 34D5
Berkeley Calif. USA 80B7
Berkeley England UK 26K5
Berkhamsted England UK 27N5
Berkley Va USA 85J2
Berkner I Antarctica 15T2
Berkovitsa Bulgaria 46D3
Berkshire county England UK 27M6
Berkshire Hills Mass. USA 84E1
Berlikum Netherlands 32D1
Berlin Germany 36E2
Berlin New H USA 79L3
Berlin Wis. USA 79B4
Bermagui NSW Australia 97D3
Bermillo de Savago Spain 40C2
Bermio Italy 44C2
Bermuda island Atlantic Ocean 73F5
Bern Switzerland 33C2
Bern canton Switzerland 33C2
Bernalillo New Mex. USA 82E5
Bernasconi Argentina 91D5
Bernay France 42D2
Bernburg E Germany 36D3
Berne = Bern
Berneau Belgium 32D4
Berneck Switzerland 33E1
Berner Alpen mts Switzerland 33C2
Berneray island Scotland UK 28B4
Berner Oberland mts Switzerland 33C2
Beromünster Switzerland 33D1
Berra mt Switzerland 33C2
Berrechid Morocco 68D2
Berri S Aus. Australia 97B2
Berri prov. France 42E3
Berriedale Scotland UK 28J3
Berrigan NSW Australia 97C3
Berry NSW Australia 97D2
Berryessa,L Calif. USA 80B6
Berry Is The Bahamas 89D1
Berryville Va USA 84B3
Bersillies Belgium 32C4
Berthierville Que. Canada 79K2
Berthold N Dak. USA 81G1
Bertogne Belgium 32D4
Bertoua Cameroun 69H8
Bertraghboy B Ireland, Rep. of 31D7
Bertrix Belgium 32D5
Beru,I Kiribati 94H8
Berwick Pa USA 84C2
Berwick upon Tweed England UK 25D1
Berwyn Mts Wales UK 26H3
Berzee Belgium 32C4
Besançon France 42G3
Beskidy Zachodnie mts Europe 37H4
Besni Turkey 62D2
Bessemer Ala. USA 85D4
Best Netherlands 32D3
Betanzos Spain 40B1
Betaré Oya Cameroun 69H7
Betbetti Sudan 69K5
Bet Guvrin Israel 64C6
Bethanie Namibia 72B5
Bethany Mo USA 83L2
Bethel Maine USA 78C4
Bethesda Wales UK 26F2
Bethlehem Israel 64D6
Bethlehem Pa USA 84D2
Bethlehem South Africa 72D5
Béthune France 42E1
Betling Sib,Mt India 59H4
Betru He river China 54G5
Betsiamites Que. Canada 78D2
Betsiamites,R Que. Canada 78D2
Bettiah India 61E2
Betwa,R India 61B3
Betws-y-coed Wales UK 26G2
Beugen Netherlands 32D3
Beulah Vic. Australia 97B3
Beurnevésin Switzerland 33C1
Beveland, Noord island Netherlands 32B3
Beveland, Zuid island Netherlands 32B3
Beveren Belgium 32C3
Beverley England UK 25H5
Beverley Wash. USA 80D2
Beverlo Belgium 32D3
Beverly Mass. USA 84F1
Beverly Hills Calif. USA 80D8
Beverst Belgium 32D4
Beverwijk Netherlands 32C2
Bewdley England UK 26K4
Bex Switzerland 33C2
Bexhill England UK 27Q7
Beyla Guinea 68D7
Beypazari Turkey 62C1
Beypore India 58E6
Beyrouth = Beirūt
Beysehir Turkey 62C2
Beyt Shean Israel 64D5
Bezdan Yugoslavia 46B2
Bezhitsa USSR 48J5
Béziers France 43E5
Bhabua India 61D3
Bhadarwah Kashmir India 60D4
Bhadaur India 60D5
Bhadaura India 58E4
Bhadaura India 61A3
Bhadohi India 61D3
Bhadra India 60D6
Bhadra,R India 58E6
Bhadreswar India 61G4
Bhagalpur India 61F3
Bhakkar Pakistan 60B5
Bhamo Burma 59J4
Bhandara India 58E4
Bhanrer Ra mts India 61B4
Bharatpur India 61A2
Bharatpur India 61C4
Bhatgaon Nepal 61E2
Bhatinda India 60D5
Bhatpara India 61G4
Bhāvnagar India 58D4
Bhawani Patna India 59F5
Bhera Pakistan 60C4
Bheri,R Nepal 61C1
Bhilara India 58D3
Bhilwara India 58D3
Bhima,R India 58E5
Bhimlath India 61C4
Bhind India 61B2
Bhiwani India 60E6
Bhojpur India 61A4
Bhojpur Nepal 61F2
Bhopal India 61A4
Bhubaneswan India 59G4
Bhudar,R India 58C4
Bhuj India 58C4
Bhusawal India 58E4
Bhutan country S Asia 59H3
Biaban region Iran 63H4
Biafra, Bight of bay Africa 70B4
Biak island New Guinea Indon. 53L11
Biala Podlaska Poland 37K2
Białogard Poland 37F1
Białowieza Poland 37K2
Białystok Poland 37K2
Bialystok voivodship Poland 37K2
Biarritz France 43C5
Biasca Switzerland 33D2
Biberach W Germany 36C4
Bic Que. Canada 78D2
Bicester England UK 27M5
Bicknell Ind. USA 79C6
Bida Nigeria 68G7
Bidar India 58E5
Biddeford Maine USA 78C5
Bideford England UK 26F6
Bideford B England UK 26F6
Bie Angola 70D7
Bieber Calif. USA 80C5
Biel Switzerland 33C1
Bielawa Poland 37G3
Bielefeld W Germany 36C2
Bieler See lake Switzerland 33C1
Biella Italy 44B3
Bielsko Biała Poland 37H4
Bielsk Podlaski Poland 37K2
Bien Hoa Vietnam 57D4
Bienne = Biel
Bière Switzerland 33B2
Bietschhorn mt Switzerland 33C2
Biga Turkey 62B1
Big Bell W Aus. Australia 98D5
Big Belt Mts Mont. USA 81B2
Big Ben mt Heard I 65R12
Big Bend Nat. Pk Texas USA 82G8
Big Blue,R Kans./Nebr. USA 83K2
Bigbury B England UK 26G8
Big Creek Calif. USA 80D7
Big Desert Vic. Australia 97B3
Bigeji,I Kwajalein Is 94A17
Biggar Sask. Canada 76K6
Biggar Scotland UK 29J8
Biggleswade England UK 27P4
Big Hatchet Mts New Mex. USA 82D7
Big Hole,R Mont. USA 80G3
Bighorn Mts Wyo. USA 81D3
Bighorn,R Mont./Wyo. USA 81D3
Big I NW Terr. Canada 77R4
Big I Kwajalein Is 94A17
Big L Ark. USA 83N5
Bignasco Switzerland 33D2
Bignona Senegal 68B6
Big Pine Calif. USA 80D7
Big Rapids Mich. USA 79D4
Big Salmon,R Yukon Canada 76E4
Big Sandy,R Ariz. USA 80G8
Big Sandy R Ky/W Va USA 85F2
Big Smoky V Nev. USA 80E6
Big Spring Texas USA 82H6
Big Sur Calif. USA 80C7
Big Timber Mont. USA 81C3
Big Trout L Ont. Canada 77O6
Bihac Yugoslavia 44E3
Bihar India 61E3
Bihar state India 59F4
Biharamulo Tanzania 71G5
Bihorului,Mtii. mts Romania 46D1
Bijagos,Arquipelago Dos Guinea-Bissau 68B6
Bijapur India 58E5
Bijar Iran 62F2
Bijawar India 61B3
Bijeljina Yugoslavia 46B2
Bijie China 55C9
Bijnābād Iran 63H4
Bijni India 61B3
Bijnor India 60F6
Bikaner India 60C6
Bikin USSR 51Q5
Bikini,I Marshall Is 94G6
Bilaphond P Kashmir India 60E3
Bilaspur India 60E5
Bilaspur India 61D4
Bilauktaung Ra mts Burma/Thailand 53C8
Bilbao Spain 40E1
Bileća Yugoslavia 46B3
Bilecik Turkey 62B1
Bilé Karpaty region Czech. 37G4
Bilimbaevski USSR 49P2
Bilin Burma 59J5
Bilisht Albania 47C4
Biliu He China 54M3
Billabong,R = Moulamein,R
Billericay England UK 27Q5
Billings Mont. USA 81C3
Billiton,I = Belitung,I
Bilma Niger 69H5
Biloela Queens. Australia 99L4
Bilo Goro upland Yugoslavia 44F3
Biloxi Miss. USA 85C5
Bilsborrow England UK 25C5
Bilsi India 61B1
Bilta Norway 34J2
Bilthoven Netherlands 32D2
Biltine Chad 69K6
Bilugyun,I Burma 59J5
Bilyarsk USSR 49K3
Bilzen Belgium 32D4
Bimbe Angola 70D7
Bimbéréke Benin 68F6
Bimberi,Mt NSW Australia 97C3
Bimlipatam India 59F5
Binaiya mt Seram Indon. 53J11
Binbrook England UK 25H6
Binche Belgium 32C4
Bindki India 61C2
Bindura Zimbabwe 72E3
Binéfar Spain 41G2
Bingara NSW Australia 97D1
Bingen W Germany 36B4
Bingerville Ivory Coast 68E7
Bingham England UK 25F7
Bingham Maine USA 78D4
Binghamton NY USA 84D1
Bingley England UK 25E5
Bingol Turkey 62E2
Binn Switzerland 33D2
Binnaway NSW Australia 97C2
Bintan island Indon 53D10
Bin Xian China 54D5
Bin Xion China 54J4
Binyang China 55E11
Bio Bio prov. Chile 91B5
Bioko,I G. of Guinea 68G8
Bir India 58E5
Bir Ali South Yemen 62F7
Birchip Vic. Australia 97B3
Birdsboro Pa USA 84D2
Birdsville Queens. Australia 99H5
Birdum N Terr. Australia 98G3
Birecik Turkey 62D2
Birein Syria 64E2
Bir Fadhil well Saudi Arabia 62F5
Bir Gara Chad 69J6
Birhan,Mt Ethiopia 71H2
Birjand Iran 63H3
Birkenhead England UK 25B6
Birlad Romania 46F1
Bir Malusi Iraq 62D3
Bir Maqran well Saudi Arabia 62F5
Birmingham Ala. USA 85D4
Birmingham England UK 27E7
Birmingham Mich. USA 79E4
Birnam Scotland UK 29J6
Birney Mont. USA 81D3
Birnie I Phoenix Is 94J8
Birnin Kebbi Nigeria 68F6
Birni-n'Konni Niger 68G6
Birobidzhan USSR 51Q5
Birq Saudi Arabia 62E6
Birr Ireland, Rep. of 31H7
Birrie,R NSW Australia 97C1
Birsilpur India 60C6
Birsk USSR 49M3
Birzai Lith. USSR 35L8
Bisalpur India 61B1
Bisauli India 61B1
Bisbee Ariz. USA 82D7
Bisbee N Dak. USA 81H1
Biscay,B of France/Spain 38D4
Bisceglie Italy 45F5
Bischofszell Switzerland 33E1
Biscoe B Antarctica 15N2
Biscoe Is Antarctica 15S3
Biscotasing Ont. Canada 79E2
Bishan China 55D8
Bishnath India 59H3
Bishnupur India 61F4
Bisho South Africa 72D6
Bishop Calif. USA 80D7
Bishop Auckland England UK 25E3
Bishops Castle England UK 26J4
Bishop's Falls Newf. Canada 78L2
Bishops Stortford England UK 27Q5
Bishops Waltham England UK 27M7
Bisina,L Uganda 71G4
Bisisthal Switzerland 33D2
Biskia Ethiopia 71H1
Bismarck N Dak. USA 81G2
Bismarck Arch. Pacific Ocean 94E8
Bison S Dak. USA 81F3
Bissau Guinea-Bissau 68B6
Bissau India 60D6
Bistcho,L Alta Canada 76H5
Bitam Gabon 70C4
Bitburg W Germany 36B4
Bithur India 61C2
Bitlis Turkey 62E2
Bitola Yugoslavia 46C4
Bitonto Italy 45F5
Bitra Par islands Amindivi Is India 58D6
Bitterfeld E Germany 36E3
Bitterfontein South Africa 72B6
Bitterroot Mts Idaho USA 80F2
Bitterroot,R Mont. USA 80F2
Biu Nigeria 69H6
Bivio Switzerland 33E2
Biwa ko lake Japan 56D7
Biyadh region Saudi Arabia 62F5
Biyang China 54G6
Biysk USSR 50K4
Bizerte Tunisia 69G1
Bjargtangar peninsula Iceland 34S12
Bjelóvar Yugoslavia 44F3
Björkö,I Sweden 35H7
Bjorli Norway 34C5
Björna Sweden 34H5
Bjørnør Norway 34D4
Bjørnøya,I Barents Sea 50C2
Blaauwbank,R South Africa 72M11
Blackall Queens. Australia 99K4
Blackburn England UK 25C5
Blackdown Hills England UK 26H7
Blackfoot Idaho USA 80G4
Blackfoot Mts Idaho USA 80G3
Black Hd Ireland, Rep. of 31E7
Black Hills S Dak. USA 81E3
Black Isle Scotland UK 28H4
Blackmoor England UK 26K7
Black,Mt Pakistan 60C3
Black Mt Wales UK 26G5
Black Mts Ariz. USA 80F8
Black Mts Wales UK 26H5
Blackpool England UK 25B5
Black,R = Da,R
Black,R Ark. USA 83N5
Black Ra New Mex. USA 82E6
Black River Jamaica 89D2
Black River Mich. USA 79E3
Black River Falls Wis. USA 79A3
Black Rock Ark. USA 83N4
Black Rock Des. Nev. USA 80D5
Black Sea Asia/Europe 39N5
Blacksod B Ireland, Rep. of 30C5

Blackstairs Mts Brasilia

Blackstairs Mts Ireland,Rep. of 31K8
Black Sugar Loaf mt NSW Australia 97D2
Blackville New Br. Canada 78F3
Blackville S Car. USA 85G4
Black Volta,R Ghana 68E7
Blackwater Ireland, Rep. of 31L9
Blackwater B England UK 27R5
Blackwater L NW Terr. Canada 76G4
Blackwater,R Cork N Ireland 30K5
Blackwater,R Ireland, Rep. of 31F9
Blackwater,R Meath Ireland, Rep. of 30K6
Blackwater Res. Scotland UK 29G6
Blackwell Okla. USA 83K4
Blaenavon Wales UK 26H5
Blagdon England UK 26J6
Blagoevgrad Bulgaria 46D3
Blagoveschensk USSR 49M3
Blagoveshchensk USSR 51P4
Blair Nebr. USA 83K2
Blair Atholl Scotland UK 29J6
Blairgowrie Scotland UK 29K6
Blairmore Alta Canada 76J7
Blaj Romania 46D1
Blakeney Gloucs., England UK 26K5
Blakeney Nflk.,England UK 27S3
Blanca,B Argentina 91D5
Blanca,L Chile 91B8
Blanca Pk Col. USA 82F4
Blanca,Sa New Mex. USA 82F6
Blanc,C Mauritania 68B4
Blanche,L S Aus. Australia 97A1
Blanche Town S Aus. Australia 97A2
Blanco,C Argentina 91C7
Blanco,C Oreg. USA 80A4
Bland Va USA 85G2
Blanda,R Iceland 34V12
Blandford England UK 27K7
Bland,R NSW Australia 97C2
Blanes Spain 41H2
Blangy France 42D2
Blankenberge Belgium 32B3
Blanquilla island Venezuela 92E1
Blantyre Malawi 71H8
Blaregnies Belgium 32B4
Blarney Ireland,Rep. of 31F10
Blasket Sd Ireland, Rep. of 31B9
Blaton Belgium 32B4
Blavet,R France 42B3
Blaye France 43C4
Blayney NSW Australia 97C2
Błazowa Poland 37K4
Blekinge county Sweden 35F8
Blenheim New Zealand 100E5
Blenheim Ont. Canada 79F4
Blesbok,R South Africa 72N12
Blessington Ireland, Rep. of 31L7
Bletchley England UK 27M5
Blida Algeria 68F1
Blinden Horn mt Italy/Switz. 33D2
Blind River Ont. Canada 79E2
Blinman S Aus. Australia 97A2
Bliss Idaho USA 80F4
Blitta Togo 68F7
Block I RI USA 84F2
Bloemfontein South Africa 72D5
Blois France 42D3
Blokzijl Netherlands 32D2
Bloody Foreland cape Ireland, Rep. of 30G3
Bloomfield Iowa USA 83M2
Bloomington Ill. USA 83P2
Bloomington Ind. USA 79C6
Bloomsburg Pa USA 84C2
Blossburg Mont. USA 80G2
Blossburg Pa USA 84C2
Blount Springs Ala. USA 85D3
Blue Earth Minn. USA 81K4
Bluefield W Va USA 85G2
Bluefields Nicaragua 89C4
Blue,Mt India 59H4
Blue Mts Jamaica 89D3
Blue Mts NSW Australia 97D2
Blue Mts Oreg. USA 80D3
Blue Mts Pa USA 84D2
Blue Mts Nat. Pk NSW Australia 97D2
Blue Nile,R Sudan 69M6
Blue Ridge mts USA 87K4
Blue Stack Mts Ireland, Rep. of 30G4
Bluff New Zealand 100C8
Bluff Utah USA 86E4
Bluff Knoll mt W Aus. Australia 98D6
Blumenau Brazil 91G3
Blümlisalp mt Switzerland 33C2
Blyth Northumb.,England UK 25E2
Blyth Notts.,England UK 25F6
Blythe Calif. USA 80F9
Blytheville Ark. USA 83P5
Blyth,R England UK 25E2
Bo Norway 35C7
Bo Sierra Leone 68C7
Boac Philippines 53H8
Boaco Nicaragua 89B4
Boa Fé Brazil 92C5
Bo'ai China 54G5
Boardman N Car. USA 85H3
Boardman Oreg. USA 80D3
Boat of Garten Scotland UK 28J5
Boa Vista Brazil 92E3
Boa Vista island Cape Verde 68T10
Bobadah NSW Australia 97C2
Bobai China 55F11
Bobbio Italy 44B3
Bobo Dioulasso Upper Volta 68E6
Bobolice Poland 37G2
Bobrov USSR 49E5
Bobruysk Belorus. USSR 48F5
Bôca do Acre Brazil 92D5
Boca do Capana Brazil 92E5
Bocaiúva Brazil 93J7
Bocanda Ivory Coast 68E7
Bocaranga CAR 69J7
Bocas del Toro Panama 89C5
Bochnia Poland 37J4
Bocholt Belgium 32D3
Bocholt W Germany 36B3
Bochum W Germany 36B3
Bodalla NSW Australia 97C3
Bodaybo USSR 51N4
Boden Sweden 34J4
Boden See lake Switz./W Ger. 33E1
Boderg,L Ireland, Rep. of 30G6
Bodie Calif. USA 80D6
Bodinayakkanur India 58E6
Bodmin England UK 26E8
Bodmin Moor England UK 26E7
Bodø Norway 34F3
Boende Zaire 70E5
Boffa Guinea 68C6
Bofin,L Ireland, Rep. of 30H6
Bogalusa La USA 83P7
Bogandé Upper Volta 68E6
Bogan Gate NSW Australia 97C2
Bogan,R NSW Australia 97C2
Bogbonga Zaire 70D4
Bogda Shan mts China 52A2
Bogenfels Namibia 72B5
Boggabri NSW Australia 97C2
Boggeragh Mts Ireland, Rep. of 31E9
Boggeriki I Kwajalein Is 94A17
Boghari = Ksar El Boukhari
Boghe Mauritania 68C5
Bognor Regis England UK 27N7
Bogong,Mt Vic. Australia 97C3
Bogor Java Indon. 53E12
Bogorodskoye USSR 49J4
Bogorodskoye USSR 51R4
Bogotá Colombia 92C3
Bogotol USSR 50K4
Bogra Bangladesh 61G3
Bo Hai gulf China 54K3
Bohemia region Czech. 36E4
Böhmer Wald region Czech./Germany 36E4
Bohol island Philippines 53H9
Boiacú Brazil 92E4
Boiestown New Br. Canada 78E3
Boigu island Papua New Guinea 99J1
Boim Brazil 93F4
Bois Blanc I Mich. USA 79D3
Boisé Idaho USA 80E4
Boise City Okla. USA 82G4
Boise,R Idaho USA 80F4
Bois,L des NW Terr. Canada 76G3
Bois-le-Duc = 'sHertogenbosch
Boissevain Man. Canada 76L7
Bojador,C Morocco 68C3
Bojeador,C Philippines 53H7
Bokaro India 61E4
Boké Guinea 68C6
Bokhara,R NSW Australia 97C1
Bokki Cameroun 69H7
Bokn Fj Norway 35A7
Bokoro Chad 69J6
Boksburg South Africa 72N12
Bolac,L Vic. Australia 97B3
Bolan Pakistan 58C3
Bolangir India 59F4
Bolan Pass Pakistan 58C3
Bolbee France 42D2
Bole Ghana 68E7
Bölebyn Sweden 34J4
Bolesławiec Poland 37F3
Bolgrad Ukrain. USSR 48F9
Boliden Sweden 34J4
Bolintin Romania 46E2
Bolivar Argentina 91C5
Bolivar Colombia 92B3
Bolivar Mo USA 83M4
Bolivia country S America 92D7
Bollnäs Sweden 35G6
Bollstabruk Sweden 34G5
Bolmen,L Sweden 35E8
Bolobo Zaire 70D5
Bologna Italy 44C3
Bologoye USSR 48J3
Bolomba Zaire 70D4
Bolombo Zaire 70E5
Bolotnoye USSR 50K4
Boloven Plat. Laos 57D3
Bolsena,L di Italy 44C4
Bolsheretsk USSR 51S4
Bol'shoy Kavkas mts USSR 50F5
Bolson de Mapimi des. Mexico 88D2
Bolsover England UK 25F6
Boltaña Spain 41G1
Bolton England UK 25D5
Bolu Turkey 62C1
Bolus Hd Ireland, Rep. of 31C10
Bolzano Italy 44C2
Bomal Belgium 32D4
Bombala NSW Australia 97C3
Bombarral Portugal 40B3
Bombay India 58D5
Bomboma Zaire 70D4
Bomi Hills Liberia 68C7
Bom Jesus Brazil 93J5
Bom Jesus da Lapa Brazil 93J6
Bømla Fj. Norway 35A7
Bømlo,I Norway 35A7
Bomnak USSR 51P4
Bomoseen,L Vt USA 84E1
Bonaduz Switzerland 33E2
Bonaire island Caribbean Sea 92D1
Bonaire,I Neth. Antilles 89F4
Bonanza Nicaragua 89C4
Bonar Bridge Scotland UK 28H4
Bonaventure I Que. Canada 78F2
Bonavista Newf. Canada 78M2
Bonavista B Newf. Canada 78M2
Bon,C Tunisia 69H1
Boncourt Switzerland 33C1
Bondo Zaire 70E4
Bondoukou Ivory Coast 68E7
Bo'ness Scotland UK 29J7
Bonfol Switzerland 33C1
Bongor Chad 69J6
Bonham Texas USA 83K6
Bonifacio Corsica France 43K7
Bönigen Switzerland 33C2
Boni,R Mali 68D6
Bonn W Germany 36B3
Bonne B Newf. Canada 78J2
Bonnétable France 42D2
Bonne Terre Mo USA 85B2
Bonneval France 42D2
Bonneville Salt Flats Utah USA 82B2
Bonney,L S Aus. Australia 97B3
Bonnie Rock W Aus. Australia 98D6
Bonny France 42E3
Bonny Nigeria 68G8
Bonthe Sierra Leone 68C7
Boolaboolka L NSW Australia 97B2
Booleroo Centre S Aus. Australia 97A2
Booligal NSW Australia 97B2
Boom Belgium 32C3
Boone Iowa USA 83M1
Boone N Car. USA 85G2
Booneville Miss. USA 85C3
Boon Tsagaan Nur lake Mongolia 52C1
Boonville Mo USA 83M3
Boonville NY USA 84D1
Boorama Somalia 71J3
Boorindal NSW Australia 97C2
Booroorban NSW Australia 97B2
Boorowa NSW Australia 97C2
Boort Vic. Australia 97B3
Boothia,G of NW Terr. Canada 77O2
Boothia Pen. NW Terr. Canada 76M2
Bootle Cumbria,England UK 25B4
Bootle Mersey.,England UK 25B6
Booue Gabon 70C5
Booysens South Africa 72N12
Bophuthatswana district South Africa 72C5
Boquerón Cuba 89D3
Bor Sudan 69M7
Borah Pk Idaho USA 80G3
Borås Sweden 35E8
Borāzjān Iran 63G4
Borba Brazil 92F4
Borculo Netherlands 32E2
Bordeaux France 43C4
Borden Pr. Ed. I. Canada 78G3
Borders region Scotland UK 29L8
Bordertown S Aus. Australia 97B3
Bordj Omar Driss Algeria 68G3
Boreray island Scotland UK 28A1
Borga Sweden 34F4
Borgarnes Iceland 34U12
Børgefjell,Mt Norway 34E4
Börgefjell Nat. Pk Norway 34E4
Borger Netherlands 32E2
Borger Texas USA 82H5
Borgholm Sweden 35G8
Borgne Haiti 89E3
Borgne,R Switzerland 33C2
Borikhone Laos 57C3
Borisoglebsk USSR 49F5
Borisov Belorus. USSR 48F4
Borispol' USSR 48G6
Bo River Post Sudan 69L7
Borja Spain 41F2
Borkum island W Germany 36B2
Borlänge Sweden 35F6
Borneo state Indonesia 53F10
Bornholm,I Denmark 35F9
Borodino USSR 48J4
Borogontsy USSR 51Q3
Boromo Upper Volta 68E6
Borongan Philippines 53J8
Boroughbridge England UK 25F4
Borovichi USSR 48H2
Borris Ireland, Rep. of 31K8
Borrisoleigh Ireland, Rep. of 31H8
Borroloola N Terr. Australia 99H3
Borskoye USSR 49K4
Borūjerd Iran 62F3
Borzya USSR 51N4
Bosa Sardinia Italy 45B5
Bosco Switzerland 33D2
Boscobel Wis. USA 79A4
Bose China 55D11
Boshan China 54J4
Bosiljgrad Yugoslavia 46D3
Boskoop Netherlands 32C2
Bosna-Hercegovina rep. Yugoslavia 46A2
Bosnia & Herzegovina = Bosna-Hercegovina
Bosobolo Zaire 70D4
Bōsō Hantō peninsula Japan 56G7
Bosporus strait Turkey 62B1
Bossier City La USA 83M6
Bosso Niger 69H6
Bostan Pakistan 58C2
Boston England UK 25H7
Boston Mass. USA 84F1
Boston Mts Ark. USA 83L5
Botany B NSW Australia 97D2
Botera Angola 70C7
Bothaville South Africa 72D5
Bothnia,G of Finland/Sweden 34K4
Botswana country Africa 72C4
Botucatu Brazil 93H8
Bouaké Ivory Coast 68D7
Bouar CAR 69J7
Bouârfa Morocco 68E2
Bouches-du-Rhône dep. France 43F5
Bou Djébéha Mali 68E5
Boudry Switzerland 33B1
Bougainville,I Solomon Is 94F8
Bougaroun,C Algeria 68G1
Bougouni Mali 68D6
Bouillon Belgium 32D5
Bou Izakan Morocco 68D3
Bouka CAR 69J7
Boularderie I No. Sc. Canada 78H3
Boulder Col. USA 82F2
Boulder Mont. USA 80G2
Boulder W Aus. Australia 98E6
Boulder City Nev. USA 80F8
Boulia Queens. Australia 99H4
Boulogne France 42D1
Bouna Ivory Coast 68E7
Boundary Pk Nev. USA 80D6
Boundiali Ivory Coast 68D7
Bountiful Utah USA 82C2
Bounty,Is Pacific Ocean 94H12
Bourbon,C Kerguelen 65S12
Bourbonnais prov. France 42E3
Bourem Mali 68E5
Bourg France 42F3
Bourganeau France 42C4
Bourg Argental France 43F4
Bourges France 42E3
Bourget,L du France 42F4
Bourgogne prov. France 42F3
Bourg St Pierre Switzerland 33C2
Bourke NSW Australia 97C2
Bourkes Ont. Canada 79F1
Bourne England UK 25H6
Bournemouth England UK 27L7
Bourtange Netherlands 32E1
Bousso Chad 69J6
Boutilimit Mauritania 68C5
Bouveret Switzerland 33B2
Bouvet I Atlantic Ocean 73N14
Bovey Tracey England UK 26G7
Bovigny Belgium 32D4
Bovino Italy 45E5
Bowbells N Dakota USA 81F1
Bowen Queens. Australia 99K3
Bowen,Mt Vic. Australia 97C3
Bowie Texas USA 83K6
Bowling Green Ky USA 85D2
Bowling Green Mo USA 83N3
Bowling Green Ohio USA 79E5
Bowling Green Va USA 85J1
Bowman N Dak. USA 81F2
Bowman B NW Terr. Canada 77Q3
Bowman I Antarctica 15H3
Bowmanville Ont. Canada 79G4
Bow,R Alta Canada 76J6
Bowral NSW Australia 97D2
Bowser Vic. Australia 97C3
Box Elder Mont. USA 81B1
Boxholm Sweden 35F7
Bo Xian China 54H6
Boxmeer Netherlands 32D3
Box Tank NSW Australia 97B2
Boxtel Netherlands 32D3
Boyang China 55J8
Boydton Va USA 85H2
Boyle Ireland, Rep. of 30G6
Boyne City Mich. USA 79D3
Boyne,R Ireland, Rep. of 30L6
Boynton Beach Fla USA 85M8
Boyoma Falls Zaire 70F4
Bozeman Mont. USA 81B3
Bozoum CAR 69J7
Bra Italy 44A3
Brabant prov. Belgium 32C4
Brač island Yugoslavia 44F4
Bracadale Scotland UK 28D5
Bracadale,L Scotland UK 28C5
Bracebridge Ont. Canada 79G3
Brach Libya 69H3
Bräcke Sweden 34F5
Brackley England UK 27M4
Bracknell England UK 27N6
Brád Romania 46D1
Braddock N Dak. USA 81G2
Braddock Pa USA 79A2
Bradford England UK 25E5
Bradford Pa USA 84B2
Bradford on Avon England UK 27K6
Bradley Calif. USA 80C8
Bradore Bay Que. Canada 78K1
Bradwell England UK 27R5
Braemar Scotland UK 28K5
Braeriach Scotland UK 28J5
Braga Portugal 40B2
Bragado Argentina 91D5
Braganca Brazil 93H4
Braganca Portugal 40C2
Braganca Paulista Brazil 93H8
Brahmanbaria Bangladesh 59H4
Brahmaputra,R S Asia 59H3
Brahmaur India 60E4
Braidwood Ill. USA 83P2
Braidwood NSW Australia 97C3
Brail Switzerland 33F2
Brăila Romania 46F2
Braine l'Alleud Belgium 32C4
Braine-le-Comte Belgium 32C4
Brainerd Minn. USA 81K2
Braintree England UK 27R5
Brakpan South Africa 72N12
Brampton England UK 25C3
Brampton Ont. Canada 79G4
Bran Buri Thailand 57B4
Branchville S Car. USA 85G4
Branco,R Brazil 92E3
Brandberg mt Namibia 72A4
Brande Denmark 35C9
Brandenburg E Germany 36E2
Branderburgh Scotland UK 28K4
Brandon England UK 27R4
Brandon Man. Canada 76M7
Brandon B Ireland, Rep. of 31C9
Brandon,Mt Kerry Ireland,Rep. of 31C9
Brandon Mt Kilkenny Ireland, Rep. of 31K9
Brandsen Argentina 91E5
Brandvlei Cape Province South Africa 72C6
Brandvlei Transvaal South Africa 72M12
Branford Fla USA 85F6
Braniewa Poland 37H1
Bransfield Str. Antarctica 15T3
Bransk Poland 37K2
Branston England UK 25H6
Brantford Ont. Canada 79F4
Brantôme France 43D4
Branxholme Vic. Australia 97B3
Bras d'Or L No. Sc. Canada 78H4
Braşgov Romania 46E2
Brasilia district Brazil 93H7

Bratislava, Buttes

Bratislava Czech. 37G4
Bratsk USSR 51M4
Brattleboro Vt USA 84E1
Braunau Austria 36E4
Braunschweig W Germany 36D2
Braunton England UK 26F6
Braunwald Switzerland 33D2
Brawley Calif. USA 80F9
Bray Ireland, Rep. of 31L7
Bray Hd Ireland, Rep. of 31C10
Brazil Ind. USA 79C6
Brazil country S America 92E6
Brazos,R Texas USA 83L8
Brazos Santiago Texas USA 82T10
Brazzaville Congo 70D5
Brčko Yugoslavia 46B2
Breaksea Sd New Zealand 100B7
Bream B New Zealand 100F2
Breaza Romania 46E2
Brechin Scotland UK 29L6
Brecknock,Pen. Chile 91B8
Břeclav Czech. 37G4
Brecon Wales UK 26H5
Brecon Beacons mts Wales UK 26H5
Breda Netherlands 32C3
Bredasdorp South Africa 72C6
Bredbo NSW Australia 97C3
Bredene Belgium 32A3
Bredy USSR 49Q4
Bree Belgium 32D3
Breidhafjördhur Iceland 34S12
Breil France 43G5
Breitenbach Switzerland 33C1
Breithorn mt Switzerland 33C2
Brejo Brazil 93J4
Brekenridge Minn. USA 81J2
Bremanger Norway 34A6
Bremangerland Norway 34A6
Bremen W Germany 36C2
Bremerhaven W Germany 36C2
Bremerton Wash. USA 80B2
Bremgarten Switzerland 33D1
Brendon Hills England UK 26H6
Brenham Texas USA 83K7
Brenner P Austria/Italy 36D5
Brenner,P del Austria/Italy 44C2
Breno Italy 44C3
Brent Ont. Canada 79G2
Brenta,R Italy 44D3
Brentford England UK 27P6
Brentwood England UK 27Q5
Brescia Italy 44C3
Breskens Netherlands 32B3
Breslau = Wrocław
Bressay,I Scotland UK 28Q8
Bressuire France 42C3
Brest Belorus. USSR 48C5
Brest France 42A2
Brest-litovsk = Brest (USSR)
Bretagne prov. France 42B2
Bretaye Switzerland 33C2
Breţcu Romania 46F1
Breton Sd La USA 83Q8
Brett,C New Zealand 100F2
Breugel Netherlands 32D3
Brevard N Car. USA 85F3
Brevik Norway 35C7
Brewarrina NSW Australia 97C1
Brewer Maine USA 78D4
Brewster,Mt Antarctica 15L2
Brewton Ala. USA 85D5
Brežic Yugoslavia 44E3
Brézina Algeria 68F2
Breznice Czech. 36E4
Březová Czech. 37G4
Bria CAR 69K7
Briancon France 43G4
Briare France 42E3
Bribbaree NSW Australia 97C2
Bride,R Ireland,Rep. of 31G9
Bridgehampton NY USA 84E2
Bridgend Wales UK 26G6
Bridge of Orchy Scotland UK 29G6
Bridgeport Calif. USA 80D6
Bridgeport Conn. USA 84E2
Bridgeport Nebr. USA 82G2
Bridgeport,L Texas USA 83J6
Bridgeton New J USA 84D3
Bridgetown Barbados 89H4
Bridgetown No. Sc. Canada 78F4
Bridgnorth England UK 25D7
Bridgton Maine USA 78C4
Bridgwater England UK 26J6
Bridgwater B England UK 26H6
Bridlington England UK 25H4
Bridlington B England UK 25H4
Bridport England UK 26J7
Bridport Tas. Australia 97F5
Briel/Brigels Switzerland 33E2
Brielle Netherlands 32C3
Brienz Switzerland 33C2
Brienzer See lake Switzerland 33C2
Brier I No. Sc. Canada 78E4
Brig Switzerland 33C2
Brigg England UK 25H5
Brigham City Utah USA 82B2
Brighouse England UK 25E5
Bright Vic. Australia 97C3
Brightlingsea England UK 27S5
Brighton Col. USA 82F2
Brighton England UK 27P7
Brighton S Aus. Australia 97A3
Brighton Tas. Australia 97F5
Brignoles France 43G5
Brill England UK 27M5
Brindaban India 60E7
Brindisi Italy 45F5
Brinkley Ark. USA 83N5
Brinkworth S Aus. Australia 97A2
Brintbodarne Sweden 35F6
Brione Switzerland 33D2
Brioude France 43E4
Brisbane Queens. Australia 99L5
Brissago Switzerland 33D2
Bristenstock mt Switzerland 33D2
Bristol England UK 26J6
Bristol New Br. Canada 78E3
Bristol Pa USA 84D2
Bristol RI USA 84F2
Bristol Tenn. USA 85F2
Bristol B Alaska USA 87W13
Bristol Chan England UK 26F6
Bristol I S Sandwich Is Antarctica 15A4
British Antarctic Terr. Antarctica 15T3
British Columbia prov. Canada 76F6
British Guiana = Guyana
British Honduras = Belize
British Isles Europe 22H5
Brito Nicaragua 89B4
Britstown South Africa 72C6
Brive-la-Gaillarde France 43D4
Briviesca Spain 40E1
Brixham England UK 26G8
Brno Czech. 37G4
Broadalbin NY USA 84D1
Broad B Scotland UK 28D3
Broadford Scotland UK 28E5
Broadhaven bay Ireland, Rep. of 30C5
Broad Law mt Scotland UK 29K9
Broadstairs England UK 27S6
Broadus Mont. USA 81E3
Broc Switzerland 33C2
Brock I NW Terr. Canada 76J1
Brockton Mass. USA 84F1
Brockville Ont. Canada 79J3
Brod Yugoslavia 46C4
Brodeur Pen. NW Terr. Canada 77O2
Brodhead Wis. USA 79B4
Brodick Scotland UK 29F8
Brodribb River Vic. Australia 97C3
Broek-in-Waterland Netherlands 32C2
Broglio Switzerland 33D2
Broken B NSW Australia 97D2
Broken Bow Nebr. USA 83J2
Broken Bow L Okla. USA 83L5
Broken Hill = Kabwe
Broken Hill NSW Australia 97B2
Bromberg = Bydgoszcz
Bromley England UK 27Q6
Bromptonville Que. Canada 79L3
Bromsgrove England UK 27K4
Bromyard England UK 26J4
Bronderslev Denmark 35C8
Brønnøysund Norway 34E4
Bronte Sicily Italy 45E7
Brooke's Point Philippines 53G9
Brookfield Mo USA 83M3
Brookhaven Miss. USA 85B5
Brookings Oreg. USA 80A4
Brookings S Dak. USA 81J3
Brooklyn Iowa USA 83M2
Brooklyn No. Sc. Canada 78F4
Brooklyn NY USA 84D2
Brooks Ra mts Alaska USA 87X12
Brookville Pa USA 84B2
Broome W Aus. Australia 98E3
Broom, Loch Scotland UK 28F4
Brora Scotland UK 28J3
Brorup Denmark 35C9
Brosna,R Ireland, Rep. of 31H7
Brough Hd Orkney Scotland 28K1
Broughton-in-Furness England UK 25B4
Broughton Is NSW Australia 97D2
Broughty Ferry Scotland UK 29L7
Broumov Czech. 37G3
Brouwershaven Netherlands 32B3
Brown,Mt S Aus. Australia 97A2
Browns Valley Minn. USA 81J3
Brownsville Oreg. USA 80B3
Brownsville Tenn. USA 85C3
Brownsville Texas USA 82T10
Brownville Maine USA 78D4
Brownwood Texas USA 83J7
Brownwood,L Texas USA 83J7
Broxburn Scotland UK 29K8
Broye,R Switzerland 33B2
Brozas Spain 40C3
Bruce Mines Ont. Canada 79E2
Bruce,Mt W Aus. Australia 98D4
Bruck Austria 36E5
Bruff Ireland, Rep. of 31F9
Bruges = Brugge
Brugg Switzerland 33D1
Brugge Belgium 32B3
Bruin Pk Utah USA 82C3
Bruly Belgium 32C5
Brummen Netherlands 32E2
Bruneau Idaho USA 80F4
Brunei country SE Asia 53F10
Brunette Downs N Terr. Australia 99H3
Brunette I Newf. Canada 78L3
Brunflo Sweden 34F5
Brünig P Switzerland 33D2
Brunlage W Germany 36D3
Brunn = Brno
Brunner New Zealand 100D6
Brunssum Netherlands 32D4
Brunswick = Braunschweig
Brunswick Ga USA 85G5
Brunswick Maine USA 78C5
Brunswick Md USA 84C3
Brunswick Mo USA 83M3
Brunswick B W Aus Australia 98E3
Brunswick, Pen. de Chile 91B8
Bruny I Tas. Australia 97F5
Brusa = Bursa
Brusartsi Bulgaria 46D3
Brush Col. USA 82G2
Brúsio Switzerland 33F2
Brussel = Bruxelles
Bruthen Vic. Australia 97C3
Bruxelles Belgium 32C4
Bruzual Venezuela 92D2
Bryan Coast Antarctica 15S2
Bryan,Mt S Aus. Australia 97A2
Bryansk USSR 48J5
Bryce Canyon Nat. Pk Utah USA 82C4
Brynmawr Wales UK 26H5
Bryson Que. Canada 79H3
Bryson City N Car. USA 85F3
Brzeg Poland 37G3
Brzesko Poland 37J4
B Salamai,R Chad 69J7
Bsharri = Bcharre
Bua Angola 70C6
Buakonikai Banaba I 94A18
Buayan Philippines 53J9
Bubasa Ethiopia 71J3
Bubiyan island Kuwait 62F4
Bubulu Uganda 71G4
Bucaramanga Colombia 92C2
Buchach Ukrain. USSR 48D7
Buchan Vic. Australia 97C3
Buchanan Liberia 68C7
Buchanan,L Queens. Australia 99K4
Buchanan,L Texas USA 83J7
Buchan Ness cape Scotland UK 28N5
Buchardo Argentina 91D4
Bucharest = București
Buchlyvie Scotland UK 29H7
Buchs Switzerland 33E1
Buckden England UK 27P4
Buckhannon W Va USA 79F6
Buckhaven Scotland UK 29K7
Buckie Scotland UK 28L4
Buckingham England UK 27N4
Buckingham Que. Canada 79J3
Buckinghamshire county England UK 27N5
Buckley Wash. USA 80B2
Bucksport Maine USA 78D4
Buctouche New Br. Canada 78F3
București Romania 46F2
Bud Norway 34B5
Buda Texas USA 83K7
Budaia Saudi Arabia 62E5
Budapest Hungary 37H5
Budaun India 61B1
Bud Bud India 61F4
Buddh Gaya India 61E3
Bude England UK 26E7
Budeşti Romania 46F2
Budgewoi NSW Australia 97D2
Budhana India 60E6
Budjala Zaire 70D4
Budleigh Salterton England UK 26H7
Budva Yugoslavia 46B3
Buea Cameroun 69G8
Buenaventura Colombia 92B3
Buenaventura Mexico 88C2
Buena Vista Ga USA 85E4
Buena Vista Va USA 85H2
Buena Vista L Calif. USA 80D8
Buenos Aires Argentina 91E4
Buenos Aires Colombia 92C4
Buenos Aires prov. Argentina 91D5
Buenos Aires,L Argentina/Chile 91B7
Bufa Mexico 88D3
Buffalo Minn. USA 81L3
Buffalo Mo USA 83M4
Buffalo NY USA 84B1
Buffalo S Dak. USA 81F3
Buffalo Wyo. USA 81D3
Buffalo L NW Terr. Canada 76H4
Buff City Tenn. USA 85F2
Buga Colombia 92B3
Bug,R Poland 37J2
Bug,R USSR 48G7
Bugul'ma USSR 49L3
Buguruslan USSR 49L4
Buhl Idaho USA 80F4
Builth Wells Wales UK 26H4
Buinsk USSR 49J3
Buique Brazil 93K5
Buir Nur lake China 52G1
Buitenpost Netherlands 32E1
Bujumbura Burundi 71F5
Buka,I Solomon Is 94F8
Bukama Zaire 70F6
Bukavu Zaire 71F5
Bukene Tanzania 71G5
Bukhara Uzbek. USSR 50H6
Bukoba Tanzania 71G5
Buksa Duar India 61G2
Bukwimba Tanzania 71G5
Bula Ceram Indon. 53K11
Bülach Switzerland 33D1
Bulan Philippines 53H8
Bulandshahr India 60E6
Bulawayo Zimbabwe 72D4
Bulgan Mongolia 52D1
Bulgaria country Europe 46D3
Bullange Belgium 32E4
Bulle Switzerland 33C2
Buller,Mt Vic. Australia 97C3
Buller,R New Zealand 100D5
Bullhead City Ariz. USA 80F8
Bulli NSW Australia 97D2
Bulloo Cr. Queens. Australia 99J5
Bull Shoals L Ark. USA 83M4
Bulnes Chile 91B5
Buloke,L Vic. Australia 97B3
Bulsar India 58D4
Bulu mt Borneo Indon. 53G10
Bulun USSR 51P2
Bumba Zaire 70E4
Bümpliz Switzerland 33C2
Buna Kenya 71H4
Buna Papua New Guinea 99K1
Bunayyan Saudi Arabia 63G5
Bunbah,G of Libya 69K2
Bunbury W Aus. Australia 98D6
Bunclody Ireland, Rep. of 31K8
Buncrana Ireland, Rep. of 30H3
Bundaberg Queens. Australia 99L4
Bundarra NSW Australia 97D2
Bundi India 58E3
Bundoran Ireland, Rep. of 30G5
Bungay England UK 27S4
Bungo Angola 70D6
Bungo suidō strait Japan 56C8
Bunguran island Malaysia 53E10
Buninyong Vic. Australia 97B3
Bunker Mo USA 83N4
Bunkie La USA 83M7
Buntok Borneo Indon. 53F11
Buochs Switzerland 33D2
Buol Celebes Indon. 53H10
Buolkalakh USSR 51N2
Buqbuq Egypt 69L2
Bura Kenya 71H5
Buraimi UAE 63H5
Buram Sudan 69L6
Buraq Syria 64E4
Burayda Saudi Arabia 62E4
Burbank Calif. USA 80D8
Burcher NSW Australia 97C2
Burco Somalia 71K3
Burdekin,R Queens. Australia 99K3
Burdur Turkey 62C2
Burdwan India 61F4
Bureå Sweden 34J4
Bureinskiy Khrebet mts USSR 51Q4
Buren Netherlands 32D3
Büren Switzerland 33C1
Bure,R England UK 27S3
Bureya USSR 51P5
Burford England UK 27L5
Burg E Germany 36D2
Burgas Bulgaria 46F3
Bur Gavo Somalia 71J5
Burgaw N Car. USA 85J3
Burgdorf Idaho USA 80F3
Burgdorf Switzerland 33C1
Burgenland state Austria 37G5
Burgersdorp South Africa 72D6
Burgess Hill England UK 27P7
Burgh le Marsh England UK 25J6
Bürglen Switzerland 33E1
Burgos Spain 40E1
Burgos prov. Spain 40E1
Burgsvik Sweden 35H8
Burhanpur India 58E4
Buria India 60E5
Buriti Brazil 93J4
Burkesville Ky USA 85E2
Burketown Queens. Australia 99H3
Burkeville Va USA 85H2
Burkina = Upper Volta
Burks Falls Ont. Canada 79G3
Burley Idaho USA 82B1
Burlington Col. USA 82G3
Burlington Iowa USA 83N2
Burlington New J USA 84D2
Burlington Ont. Canada 79G4
Burlington Vt USA 79K3
Burlington Wis. USA 79B4
Burma country SE Asia 59H4
Burnak USSR 49E5
Burnham Essex,England UK 27R5
Burnham Somerset,England UK 26H6
Burnham Market England UK 27R3
Burnie Tas. Australia 97F5
Burnley England UK 25D5
Burns NSW Australia 97B2
Burns Oreg. USA 80D4
Burnside,R NW Terr. Canada 76K3
Burntisland Scotland UK 29K7
Burqin China 52A1
Burra S Aus. Australia 97A2
Burragorang,L NSW Australia 97C2
Burren Junction NSW Australia 97C2
Burrewarra Point NSW Australia 97D3
Burriana Spain 41F3
Burrinjuck NSW Australia 97C2
Burrinjuck Res. NSW Australia 97C2
Burrow Hd Scotland UK 29H10
Burrundie N Terr. Australia 98G2
Burruyacú Argentina 91D3
Burry Port Wales UK 26F5
Bursa Turkey 62B1
Bûr Safâga Egypt 69M3
Burslem England UK 25D6
Bûr Taufiq Egypt 69M3
Burt L Mich. USA 79D3
Burton-in-Kendal England UK 25C4
Burtonport Ireland, Rep. of 30G4
Burton upon Trent England UK 25E7
Burträsk Sweden 34J4
Burtundy NSW Australia 97B2
Buru island Indonesia 53J11
Burullus,L Egypt 69M2
Burum South Yemen 62F7
Burundi country Africa 71G5
Burun Urt Mongolia 52F1
Buruta Nigeria 68G7
Bury England UK 25D5
Buryatskaya ASSR rep. USSR 51M4
Bury St Edmunds England UK 27R4
Burzil P Kashmir India 60D3
Busembatia Uganda 71G4
Büshehr Iran 63G4
Bushire = Büshehr
Bushmills N Ireland 30K3
Bushnell Fla USA 85L7
Businga Zaire 70E4
Buskerud county Norway 35C6
Buskozdroj Poland 37J3
Busra Syria 64E5
Bussa Nigeria 68F6
Busselton W Aus. Australia 98D6
Bussigny Switzerland 33B2
Bussum Netherlands 32D2
Busswil Switzerland 33C1
Busto Arsizio Italy 44B3
Busuanga island Philippines 53G8
Busu Djanoa Zaire 70E4
Buta Zaire 70E4
Butana India 60E6
Buta Ranquil Argentina 91C5
Butaritari,I Kiribati 94H7
Bute S Aus. Australia 97A2
Bute,I Scotland UK 29F8
Bütgenbach Belgium 32E4
Buthidaung Burma 59H4
Butler Mo USA 83L3
Butler Pa USA 79G5
Bütschwil Switzerland 33E1
Butte Mont. USA 80G2
Butte Meadows Calif. USA 80C5
Buttes Switzerland 33B2

Buttevant, Carlos Casares

Buttevant Ireland, Rep. of 31F9
Button Is *Que.* Canada 77T4
Butuan Philippines 53J9
Butung I Indonesia 53H11
Buturlinovka USSR 49E5
Buuhoodle Somalia 71K3
Buulo Barde Somalia 71K4
Buur Hakaba Somalia 71J4
Buxar India 61E3
Buxton *England* UK 25E6
Buy USSR 48M2
Buyaga USSR 51P4
Buyr Nuur *lake,* Mongolia 51N5
Buzançais France 42D3
Buzău Romania 46F2
Buzdyak USSR 49M3
Buzuluk USSR 49L4
Buzzards B *Mass.* USA 84F2
Byam Martin Chan. *NW Terr.* Canada 76K1
Bydgoszcz Poland 37G2
Bydgoszcz *voivodship* Poland 37H2
Byelaya,R USSR 49L3
Byelokatay USSR 49P3
Byelozersk USSR 48K2
Bygland Norway 35B7
Byglandsfjord Norway 35B7
Bylot I *NW Terr.* Canada 77Q2
Byng Inl. *Ont.* Canada 79F3
Byrock *NSW* Australia 97C2
Byron,C *NSW* Australia 99L5
Byske Sweden 34J4
Byske Alv *river* Sweden 34J4
Bytom Poland 37H3
Bytów Poland 37G1

C

Caaguazu Paraguay 91E3
Caballococha Peru 92C4
Caballo Res. *New Mex.* USA 82E6
Caballo,Sa *mts New Mex.* USA 82E6
Cabañas Cuba 89C2
Cabanatuan Philippines 53H7
Cabar Yugoslavia 44E3
Cabedelo Brazil 93L5
Cabezas Bolivia 92E7
Cabezo del Buey Spain 40D3
Cabinda Angola 70C6
Cabinda *region* Angola 70C6
Cabo Blanco Argentina 91C7
Cabo Frio Brazil 93J8
Cabonga,Res. *Que.* Canada 79H2
Cabora Bassa Dam Mozambique 72E3
Cabo Raso Argentina 91C6
Cabot Hd *Ont.* Canada 79F3
Cabot Str. *Newf./No. Sc.* Canada 78H3
Cabra Spain 40D4
Cabrera,I *Balearic Is* Spain 41H3
Cabrillo Nat. Mon. *Calif.* USA 80E9
Cabrobó Brazil 93K5
Cabuérniga Spain 40D1
Cabure Venezuela 92D1
Čačak Yugoslavia 46C3
Cacapon,R *W Va* USA 84B3
Cacequi Brazil 91F3
Cáceres Spain 40C3
Cáceres *prov.* Spain 40C3
Cachar = Silchar
Cachimbo,Serra do *mts* Brazil 93F5
Cachinal Chile 91C2
Cachoeira Brazil 93K6
Cachoeira do Sul Brazil 91F4
Cachoeiro de Itapemirim Brazil 93J8
Cacipore,R Brazil 93G3
Caconda Angola 70D7
Cadaqués Spain 41H1
Caddo L *La* USA 83M6
Cadereyta Mexico 88E2
Cader Idris *mt Wales* UK 26G3
Cadillac *Mich.* USA 79D3
Cadiz *Calif.* USA 80F8
Cadiz Spain 40C4
Cádiz *prov.* Spain 40D4
Cadotts P *Mont.* USA 80G2
Cadzand Netherlands 32B3
Caen France 42C2
Caergwrle *Wales* UK 26H2
Caerleon *Wales* UK 26J5
Caernarfon *Wales* UK 26F2
Caernarfon B *Wales* UK 26E2
Caerphilly *Wales* UK 26H5
Caersws *Wales* UK 26H3
Caesarea *hist. site* Israel 64C5
Cagayan de Oro Philippines 53H9
Cagayan Sulu *island* Philippines 53G9
Cagliari *Sardinia* Italy 45B6
Caguas Puerto Rico 89F3
Caha Ireland, Rep. of 31D10
Cahama Angola 72A3
Caha Mts Ireland, Rep. of 31D10
Caher Ireland, Rep. of 31H9
Cahirsiveen Ireland, Rep. of 31C10
Cahore Point Ireland, Rep. of 31L8
Cahors France 43D4
Caibarién Cuba 89D2
Caicara Venezuela 92D2
Caicara Venezuela 92E2
Caicos Is West Indies 89E2
Cailloma Peru 92C7
Caillou B *La* USA 83N8
Caimanera Cuba 89D3
Caipó,Serra do *mts* Brazil 93G7
Caird Coast Antarctica 15A2
Cairn Gorm *mt Scotland* UK 28J5
Cairns *Queens.* Australia 99K3
Cairn Toul *mt Scotland* UK 28J5
Cairo Egypt 69M2
Cairo *Ga* USA 85E5
Cairo *Ill.* USA 83P4
Caister *England* UK 27T3
Caistor *England* UK 25H5
Caitité Brazil 93J6
Caiundo Angola 72B3
Caizi Hu *lake* China 54J7
Cajamarca Peru 92B5
Cajàzeiras Brazil 93K5
Čakovec Yugoslavia 44F2
Cala Spain 40C4
Calabar Nigeria 68G7
Calabozo Venezuela 92D2
Calabria *region* Italy 45F6
Calacoto Bolivia 92D7
Calafat Romania 46D3
Calafate Argentina 91B8
Calais France 42D1
Calais *Maine* USA 78E4
Calama Brazil 92E5
Calama Chile 91C2
Calamar Colombia 92C1
Calamar Colombia 92C3
Calamian Group *islands* Philippines 53G8
Calamocha Spain 41F2
Calanda *upland* Switzerland 33E2
Calang *Sumatra* Indon. 53C10
Calatayud Spain 41F2
Calava,C *Sicily* Italy 45E6
Calbuco Chile 91B6
Calcasieu L *La* USA 83M8
Calceta Ecuador 92A4
Calchaqui Argentina 91D3
Calcutta India 61G4
Caldas da Rainha Portugal 40B3
Caldera Chile 91B3
Calder,R *England* UK 25E5
Caldwell *Idaho* USA 80E4
Caldwell *Texas* USA 83K7
Caledonia *Minn.* USA 81M4
Caledonian Ca. *Scotland* UK 28H5
Calella Spain 41H2
Calenzana *Corsica* France 43J6
Caleta Buena Chile 91B1
Caleta Junin Chile 91B1
Caleta Olivia Argentina 91C7
Calexico *Calif.* USA 80F9
Calgary *Alta* Canada 76J6
Cali Colombia 92B3
Calicut India 58E6
Caliente *Calif.* USA 80D8
Caliente *Nev.* USA 80F7
California *state* USA 86B3
California,G of Mexico 88B2
California Hot Springs *Calif.* USA 80D8
Calimali Mexico 88B2
Calimanului,Mtii *mts* Romania 46E1
Calitri Italy 45E5
Calla Spain 41F2
Callabonna *S Aus.* Australia 97B1
Callabonna,L *S Aus.* Australia 97B1
Callan Ireland, Rep. of 31J8
Callander *Ont.* Canada 79G2
Callander *Scotland* UK 29H7
Callanna *S Aus.* Australia 97A1
Callantsoog Netherlands 32C2
Callao Peru 92B6
Callington *England* UK 26F8
Calmon Brazil 91F3
Calmpthout = Kalmthout
Calne *England* UK 27K6
Calpella *Calif.* USA 80B6
Caltagirone *Sicily* Italy 45E7
Caltanissetta *Sicily* Italy 45E7
Caluango Angola 70D6
Calulo Angola 70C7
Calunda Angola 70E7
Caluula Somalia 71L2
Calvados *dep.* France 42C2
Calverton *Va* USA 85J1
Calvi *Corsica* France 43J6
Calvillo Mexico 88D3
Calvinia South Africa 72B6
Camabatela Angola 70D6
Camaguey Cuba 89D2
Camaguey,Arch. de Cuba 89D2
Camana Peru 92C7
Camaquã Brazil 91F4
Camaquã,R Brazil 91F4
Camará Brazil 92E4
Camarat,C France 43G5
Camargo Bolivia 92D8
Camargo Mexico 88E2
Camarones Argentina 91C6
Camas *Oreg.* USA 80B3
Camas Cr. *Idaho* USA 80F3
Ca-Mau,Pt = Mui Bai Bung
Cambados Spain 40B1
Cambay,G of = Khambhat,G of
Cambermere,B Burma 59H5
Cambodia *country* SE Asia 57C4
Camborne *England* UK 26D8
Cambrai France 42E1
Cambria *Calif.* USA 80C8
Cambrian Mts *Wales* UK 26G3
Cambridge *England* UK 24Q4
Cambridge *Idaho* USA 80E3
Cambridge *Mass.* USA 84F1
Cambridge New Zealand 100F3
Cambridgeshire *county England* UK 27Q4
Camcia Nat. Pk Angola 70E7
Camden *Ark.* USA 83M6
Camden *Maine* USA 78D4
Camden *New J* USA 84D3
Camden *NSW* Australia 97D2
Camden *NY* USA 84D1
Camden *S Car.* USA 85G3
Camedo Switzerland 33D2
Camerino Italy 44D4
Cameron *Mo* USA 83L3
Cameron *Texas* USA 83K7
Cameron Mts New Zealand 100B7
Cameroon = Cameroun
Camerota Italy 45E5
Cameroun *country* Africa 69H7
Cameta Brazil 93H4
Camilla *Ga* USA 85E5
Camiña Chile 91C1
Caminha Portugal 40B2
Caminreal Spain 41F2
Camoa Mexico 88C2
Camocim Brazil 93J4
Camoghe *mt* Switzerland 33E2
Camooweal *Queens.* Australia 99H3
Camorta,I *Nicobar Is* India 59H7
Campana Argentina 91E4
Campana,I Chile 91A7
Campania *region* Italy 45E5
Campas Mexico 88C1
Campbell *Mo* USA 83N4
Campbell B *NW Terr.* Canada 76L3
Campbell,C New Zealand 100F5
Campbellford *Ont.* Canada 79H3
Campbell,I Pacific Ocean 94G13
Campbell,Mt *Yukon* Canada 76D4
Campbellpore Pakistan 60C4
Campbell River *BC* Canada 76F6
Campbellton *New Br.* Canada 78E2
Campbelltown *NSW* Australia 97D2
Campbell Town *Tas.* Australia 97F5
Campbeltown *Scotland* UK 29E9
Campeche Mexico 88F4
Campeche *state* Mexico 88F4
Campeche,G of Mexico 88F3
Camperdown *Vic.* Australia 97B3
Campiglia Marittima Italy 44C4
Campillos Spain 40D4
Campina Grande Brazil 93K5
Campinas Brazil 93H8
Campobasso Italy 45E5
Campobello I *New Br.* Canada 78E4
Campo Belo Brazil 93H8
Campo Formosa Brazil 93J6
Campo Gallo Argentina 91D3
Campo Grande Brazil 93G8
Campo Maior Brazil 93J4
Campo Maior Portugal 40C3
Campos Brazil 93J8
Campos Novos Brazil 91F3
Campos Sales Brazil 93J5
Campo Tencia *mt* Switzerland 33D2
Campsie Fells *mts Scotland* UK 29H7
Camrose *Alta* Canada 76J6
Camsell Mt *NW Terr.* Canada 76G4
Canaan *New Br.* Canada 78F3
Canaan *New H* USA 84F1
Canada *country* N America 88
Cañada de Gómez Argentina 91D4
Canadian *Texas* USA 82H5
Canadian,R *Okla./Texas* USA 82H5
Canakkale Turkey 62B1
Canama Brazil 92C5
Canandaigua *NY* USA 84C1
Canandaigua L *NY* USA 84C1
Cananea Mexico 88B1
Cananéia Brazil 91G3
Canarias,Islas Atlantic Ocean 68B3
Canarreos, Arch. de los Cuba 89C2
Canary Is = Canarias,Islas
Canas Portugal 40C2
Canaseraga *NY* USA 84C1
Canatlán Mexico 88D3
Cañaveral Spain 40C3
Canaveral,C *Fla* USA 85M7
Cañaveras Spain 41E2
Canavieiras Brazil 93K7
Canbelego *NSW* Australia 97C2
Canberra *Aust. Cap. Terr.* Australia 97C3
Canby *Calif.* USA 80C5
Canby *Minn.* USA 81J3
Canby *Oreg.* USA 80B3
Candasnos Spain 41G2
Candelo *NSW* Australia 97C3
Candia = Iráklion
Canea = Khania
Canela Brazil 91F3
Canelones Uruguay 91E4
Cañete Chile 91B5
Canete Peru 92B6
Cañete Spain 41F2
Cangamba Angola 70D7
Cangandala Angola 70D6
Cangas Spain 40C1
Canguaretama Brazil 93K5
Cangzhou China 54J3
Canicatti *Sicily* Italy 45D7
Çankiri Turkey 62C1
Canna, I *Scotland* UK 28C5
Cannanore India 58E6
Cannelton *Ind.* USA 85D2
Cannes France 43G5
Canning Town India 61G4
Cannock *England* UK 25D7
Cannock Chase *England* UK 25D7
Cannon Ball *N Dak.* USA 81G2
Cann River *Vic.* Australia 97C3
Canôas,R Brazil 91F3
Canonba *NSW* Australia 97C2
Canon City *Col.* USA 82F3
Canora *Sask.* Canada 76L6
Canosa di Puglia Italy 45E5
Canowindra *NSW* Australia 97C2
Canso *No. Sc.* Canada 78H4
Canso,C *No. Sc.* Canada 78H4
Canso,Str of *No. Sc.* Canada 78H4
Cantabria *region* Spain 40D1
Cantal *dep.* France 43E4
Cantanhede Portugal 40B2
Canterbury *England* UK 27S6
Canterbury *New Br.* Canada 78E4
Canterbury *stat. area* New Zealand 100D6
Canterbury Bight *bay* New Zealand 100E6
Canterbury Plains New Zealand 100D7
Can Tho Vietnam 57D4
Canton = Guangzhou
Canton *Miss.* USA 85C4
Canton *NY* USA 79J3
Canton *Ohio* USA 79F5
Canton *S Dak.* USA 81J4
Canton,I Phoenix Is 94J8
Canton L *Okla.* USA 83J4
Canuelas Argentina 91E5
Canutama Brazil 92E5
Canyon City *Oreg.* USA 80D3
Canyon de Chelly Nat. Mon. *Ariz.* USA 82D4
Cao Bang Vietnam 57D2
Capaia Angola 70E6
Capakçur = Bingol
Capanaparo,R Venezuela 92D2
Capão Bonito Brazil 91G2
Capatánda Venezuela 92C1
Cap de la Hague *cape* France 42C2
Cap-de-la-Madeleine *Que.* Canada 79K2
Cape Barren I *Tas.* Australia 97F5
Cape Breton Highlands Nat. Pk *No. Sc.* Canada 78H3
Cape Breton I *No. Sc.* Canada 78H3
Cape Charles *Va* USA 85J2
Cape Coast Ghana 68E7
Cape Cod B *Mass.* USA 84F2
Cape Fear,R *N Car.* USA 85H3
Cape Girardeau *Mo* USA 83P4
Capelle Netherlands 32C3
Cape May *New J* USA 84D3
Cape May Court House *New J* USA 84D3
Cape Province *prov.* South Africa 72C6
Cape Tormentine *New Br.* Canada 78G3
Cape Town South Africa 72B6
Cape Verde *islands* Atlantic Ocean 73K7
Cape York Pen. *Queens.* Australia 99J2
Cap-Haïtien Haiti 89E3
Capilla Argentina 91E4
Capilla del Monte Argentina 91D4
Capitan Mts *New Mex.* USA 82F6
Caplan *Que.* Canada 78F2
Capoompeta *mt NSW* Australia 97D1
Cappoquin Ireland, Rep. of 31H9
Capraia *island* Italy 44B4
Capreol *Ont.* Canada 79F2
Caprera *island Sardinia* Italy 45B5
Capri *island* Italy 45E5
Capricorn Chan. *Queens.* Australia 99L4
Caprivi Strip Namibia 72C3
Carabaya, Cord. de Peru 92C6
Caracal Romania 46E2
Caracarai Brazil 92E3
Caracas Venezuela 92D1
Caracol Brazil 93J5
Caragh,L Ireland, Rep. of 31D9
Caraghnan Mt *NSW* Australia 97C2
Caraguatay Paraguay 91E2
Carajas,Serra da *mts* Brazil 93G5
Carangola Brazil 93J8
Caransebes Romania 46D2
Carapegua Paraguay 91E3
Caraquet *New Br.* Canada 78F3
Caras Peru 92B5
Carasso Switzerland 33E2
Caratasca Laguna *lagoon* Honduras 89C3
Caratiá Brazil 92E5
Caratinga Brazil 93J7
Carauari Brazil 92D4
Caravaca Spain 41F3
Caravelas Brazil 93K7
Caraveli Peru 92C7
Carballiño Spain 40B1
Carballo Spain 40B1
Carbonara,C *Sardinia* Italy 45B6
Carbon,C Algeria 68G1
Carbondale *Ill.* USA 83P4
Carbondale *Pa* USA 84D2
Carbonear *Newf.* Canada 78M3
Carbon Hill *Ala.* USA 85D4
Carbonia *Sardinia* Italy 45B6
Carcajou *Alta* Canada 76H5
Carcassone France 43E5
Carcoar *NSW* Australia 97C2
Carcross *Yukon* Canada 76E4
Cardamom Hills India 58E6
Cardenas Cuba 89C2
Cardenas Mexico 88E3
Cardiel,L Argentina 91B7
Cardiff *Wales* UK 26H6
Cardigan *Wales* UK 26E4
Cardigan B *Wales* UK 26E3
Cardwell *Queens.* Australia 99K3
Carey,L *W Aus.* Australia 98E5
Careysburg Liberia 68C7
Cargelligo,L *NSW* Australia 97C2
Carhaix France 42B2
Caribbean Sea Central America 89
Caribou *Maine* USA 78D3
Caribou Mts *Alta* Canada 76H5
Caribrod = Dimitrovgrad
Carichic Mexico 88C2
Carillo Mexico 88F2
Carinda *NSW* Australia 97C2
Cariñena Spain 41F2
Carinhanha Brazil 93J6
Caripito Venezuela 92E1
Carius Brazil 93K5
Carlet Spain 41F3
Carleton *Que.* Canada 78E2
Carleton,Mt *New Br.* Canada 78E3
Carleton Place *Ont.* Canada 79H3
Carletonville South Africa 72L12
Carlin *Nev.* USA 80E5
Carlingford Ireland, Rep. of 30L5
Carlinville *Ill.* USA 83P3
Carlisle *England* UK 25C3
Carlisle *Ky* USA 85E1
Carlisle *Pa* USA 84C2
Carlisle *S Car.* USA 85G3
Carl,L *Okla.* USA 83K4
Carlos Casares Argentina 91D5

Carlow Changzhou

Carlow Ireland, Rep. of **31K8**
Carlow *county* Ireland,Rep. of **31K8**
Carlsbad *New Mex.* USA **82F6**
Carlsbad Caverns Nat. Pk *New Mex.* USA **82F6**
Carlton *Minn.* USA **81L2**
Carluke *Scotland* UK **29J8**
Carmacks *Yukon* Canada **76D4**
Carmagnola Italy **44A3**
Carman *Man.* Canada **76M7**
Carmarthen *Wales* UK **26F5**
Carmarthen B *Wales* UK **26E5**
Carmaux France **43E4**
Carmel *Calif.* USA **80C7**
Carmel *NY* USA **84E2**
Carmel,Mt Israel **64C5**
Carmelo Uruguay **91E4**
Carmen Bolivia **92D6**
Carmen Colombia **92B2**
Carmen Mexico **88F4**
Carmen de Patagones Argentina **91D6**
Carmen I Mexico **88B2**
Carmensa Argentina **91C5**
Carmi *Ill.* USA **83P3**
Carmona Spain **40D4**
Carnarvon South Africa **72C6**
Carnarvon *W Aus.* Australia **98C4**
Carndonagh Ireland, Rep. of **30J3**
Carnegie,L *W Aus.* Australia **98E5**
Carnforth *England* UK **25C4**
Car Nicobar *island* Nicobar Is India **59H7**
Carno *Wales* UK **26G3**
Carnot CAR **69J8**
Carnoustie *Scotland* UK **29L6**
Carnsore Point Ireland, Rep. of **31L9**
Carnwath *Scotland* UK **29J8**
Caro *Mich.* USA **79E4**
Carolina Brazil **93H5**
Carolina South Africa **72E5**
Caroline,I Pacific Ocean **95L8**
Caroline,Is Pacific Ocean **94E7**
Caroni,R Venezuela **92E2**
Carora Venezuela **92C1**
Carouge Switzerland **33B2**
Carpathian Mts Europe **37K4**
Carpatii Meridionali Romania **46D2**
Carpentaria,G of Australia **99H2**
Carpentras France **43F4**
Carpi Italy **44C3**
Carra,L Ireland,Rep. of **30E6**
Carrara Italy **44C3**
Carrathool *NSW* Australia **97C2**
Carrauntoohill Ireland, Rep. of **31D10**
Carrbridge *Scotland* UK **28J5**
Carreño Spain **40D1**
Carrickfergus N Ireland **30M4**
Carrickmacross Ireland, Rep. of **30K6**
Carrick on Shannon Ireland, Rep. of **30G6**
Carrick-on-Suir Ireland, Rep. of **31J9**
Carrieton *S Aus.* Australia **97A2**
Carri Laufquén,L Argentina **91C6**
Carrington *N Dak.* USA **81H2**
Carrión-de-los-Condes Spain **40D1**
Carrizal Bajo Chile **91B3**
Carrizo Mts *Ariz.* USA **82D4**
Carrizo Springs *Texas* USA **82S9**
Carrizozo *New Mex.* USA **82F6**
Carroll *Iowa* USA **83L1**
Carrollton *Ala.* USA **85C4**
Carrollton *Ky* USA **85E1**
Carrollton *Mo* USA **83M3**
Carrowmore L Ireland, Rep. of **30D5**
Carşamba Turkey **62D1**
Carse of Gowrie *valley Scotland* UK **29K7**
Carson City *Nev.* USA **80D6**
Carson Sink *lake Nev.* USA **80D6**
Carstairs *Scotland* UK **29J8**
Cartagena Colombia **92B1**
Cartagena Spain **41F4**
Cartago Colombia **92B3**
Cartago Costa Rica **89C5**
Cartaxo Portugal **40B3**
Cartaya Spain **40C4**
Carter *Wyo.* USA **81B5**
Carter Bar *pass Eng./Scot.* UK **29M9**
Carteret France **42C2**
Cartersville *Ga* USA **85E3**
Carterton New Zealand **100F5**
Carthage *Ill.* USA **83N2**
Carthage *Mo* USA **83L4**
Carthage *N Car.* USA **85H3**
Carthage *NY* USA **79J4**
Carthage *Tenn.* USA **85E2**
Cartier *Ont.* Canada **79F2**
Cartwright *Newf.* Canada **77U6**
Caruaru Brazil **93K5**
Carúpano Venezuela **92E1**
Carutaperá Brazil **93H4**
Caruthersville *Mo* USA **83P4**
Carvoeiro Brazil **92E4**
Carvoeiro,C Portugal **40B3**
Caryapundy Swamp *NSW/Queens.* Australia **97B1**
Casablanca Chile **91B4**
Casablanca Morocco **68D2**
Casaccia Switzerland **33E2**
Casa Grande *Ariz.* USA **82B6**
Casale Monferrato Italy **44B3**
Casas Grandes Mexico **88C1**
Casas Ibañez Spain **41F3**
Casas,R de Mexico **88C1**
Cascade *Idaho* USA **80E3**
Cascade *Mont.* USA **81B2**
Cascade Hd *Oreg.* USA **80A3**
Cascade Locks *Oreg.* USA **80C3**
Cascade Point New Zealand **100C7**
Cascade Ra *mts* USA **86B3**
Cascais Portugal **40B3**
Cascapedia,R *New Br.* Canada **78E2**
Cascina Italy **44C4**
Casco B *Maine* USA **78C5**
Caserta Italy **45E5**
Caseville *Mich.* USA **79E4**
Cashel Ireland, Rep. of **31H8**
Casilda Argentina **91D4**
Casilda Cuba **89D2**
Casino *NSW* Australia **97D1**
Casiquare,R Venezuela **92D3**
Casma Peru **92B5**
Caspe Spain **41F2**
Casper *Wyo.* USA **81D4**
Caspian Sea Asia/Europe **18F5**
Cassai Angola **70E7**
Cassamba Angola **70E7**
Cassel France **42E1**
Casselton *N Dak.* USA **81J2**
Cassiar Mts *BC* Canada **76F5**
Cassilis *NSW* Australia **97C2**
Cassinga Angola **72B3**
Cassino Brazil **91F4**
Cassino Italy **45D5**
Cassis France **43F5**
Cassopolis *Mich.* USA **79C5**
Cassville *Mo* USA **83M4**
Castanhal Brazil **92E5**
Castanheiro Brazil **92D4**
Castaño Argentina **91C4**
Castasegna Switzerland **33E2**
Casteljaloux France **43C4**
Castella *Calif.* USA **80B5**
Castella la Vieja *region* Spain **40D2**
Castellamare del Golfo *Sicily* Italy **45D6**
Castellammare di Stabia Italy **45E5**
Castellammare,G di *Sicily* Italy **45D6**
Castellane France **43G5**
Castellar de Santiago Spain **40E3**
Castelli Argentina **91E5**
Castellón *prov.* Spain **41F2**
Castellón de la Plana Spain **41F3**
Castellote Spain **41F2**
Castelnaudary France **43D5**
Castelo Branco Portugal **40C3**
Castelo de Vide Portugal **40C3**
Castelsarrasin France **43D4**
Castelvetrano *Sicily* Italy **45D7**
Casterton *Vic.* Australia **97B3**
Castets France **43C5**
Castillina la Neuva *region* Spain **40C3**
Castillo,Mt Chile **91B7**
Castillos,L Uruguay **91F4**
Castine *Maine* USA **78D4**
Castione Switzerland **33E2**
Castlebar Ireland, Rep. of **30E6**
Castlebay *Scotland* UK **28A6**
Castlebellingham Ireland, Rep. of **30L6**
Castleblayney Ireland, Rep. of **30K5**
Castlecomer Ireland, Rep. of **31J8**
Castlederg N Ireland **30H4**
Castledermot Ireland, Rep. of **31K8**
Castle Douglas *Scotland* UK **29J10**
Castleford *England* UK **25F5**
Castleisland Ireland, Rep. of **31E9**
Castlemaine Ireland, Rep. of **31D9**
Castlemaine *Vic.* Australia **97B3**
Castlemartyr Ireland, Rep. of **31G10**
Castlepollard Ireland, Rep. of **30J6**
Castlerea Ireland, Rep. of **30G6**
Castlereagh,R *NSW* Australia **97C2**
Castle Rock *Oreg.* USA **80D3**
Castle Rock *Utah* USA **82C2**
Castle Rock *Wash.* USA **80B2**
Castle Rock Buttes *S Dak.* USA **81F3**
Castletown *Isle of Man* UK **25K9**
Castletown *Scotland* UK **28K2**
Castletown Bere Ireland, Rep. of **31D10**
Castlewellan N Ireland **30M5**
Castres France **43E5**
Castricum Netherlands **32C2**
Castries St Lucia **89G4**
Castro Brazil **91F2**
Castro Chile **91B6**
Castro Marim Portugal **40C4**
Castropol Spain **40C1**
Castrovillari Italy **45F6**
Castroville *Calif.* USA **80C7**
Castuera Spain **40D3**
Caswell Sd New Zealand **100B7**
Catabalogan Philippines **53H8**
Catacamas Honduras **89B4**
Catahoula L *La* USA **83M7**
Catak Turkey **62E2**
Catalão Brazil **93H7**
Cataluña *region* Spain **41G2**
Catamarca Argentina **91C3**
Catamarca *prov.* Argentina **91C3**
Catanduanes *island* Philippines **53H8**
Catania *Sicily* Italy **45E7**
Catania,G di *Sicily* Italy **45E7**
Catanzaro Italy **45F6**
Cataract Cr. *Ariz.* USA **80G8**
Catarina *state* Brazil **91F3**
Catarman Philippines **53H8**
Catastrophe,C *S Aus.* Australia **99H6**
Catatumbo,R Columb./Venez. **92C2**
Cathcart *NSW* Australia **97C3**
Cathedral Mt *Texas* USA **82G7**
Cathlamet *Wash.* USA **80B2**
Cat I The Bahamas **89D2**
Catirimani,R Brazil **92E3**
Catlettsburg *Ky* USA **85F1**
Catoche,C Mexico **88G3**
Catonsville *Md* USA **84C3**
Catorce Mexico **88D3**
Catrilo Argentina **91D5**
Catskill *NY* USA **84E1**
Catskill Mts *NY* USA **84D1**
Cattaraugus *NY* USA **84B1**
Catterick *England* UK **25E4**
Cauca,R Columbia **92B2**
Caudebec France **42D2**
Caungula Angola **70D6**
Cauquenes Chile **91B5**
Caura,R Venezuela **92E2**
Causapscal *Que.* Canada **78E2**
Cauto,R Cuba **89D2**
Cauvery,R India **58E6**
Cava dé Tirreni Italy **45E5**
Cavalcante Brazil **93H6**
Cavallo Pass *Texas* USA **82T9**
Cavally,R Ivory Coast/Liberia **68D7**
Cavan Ireland, Rep. of **30J6**
Cavan *county* Ireland,Rep. of **30H6**
Cave New Zealand **100D7**
Cavendish *Vic.* Australia **97B3**
Cavergno Switzerland **33D2**
Caviana,I Brazil **93G3**
Cawdor *Scotland* UK **28J4**
Cawnpore = **Kanpur**
Caxias Brazil **92C4**
Caxias Brazil **93J4**
Caxias do Sul Brazil **91F3**
Caxito Angola **70C6**
Cayambe Ecuador **92B3**
Cayenne Fr. Guiana **93G3**
Cayes, Les Haiti **89E3**
Cayman Brac *island* West Indies **89C3**
Cayman Is West Indies **89C3**
Cayncos *Calif.* USA **80C8**
Cayo Belize **89B3**
Cayo Largo *island* Cuba **89C2**
Cayuga *Ont.* Canada **79G4**
Cayuga,L *NY* USA **84C1**
Cazage Angola **70E7**
Cazalla de la Sierra Spain **40D4**
Cazenovia *NY* USA **84D1**
Cazin Yugoslavia **44E3**
Cazorla Spain **40E4**
Ceanannus Mór = **Kells**
Ceará = **Fortaleza**
Ceará-Mirim Brazil **93K5**
Cebaco,I Panama **89C5**
Cebollar Argentina **91C3**
Cebollera,Sa *mts* Spain **41E2**
Cebu Philippines **53H8**
Cecil *Ga* USA **85F5**
Cecilville *Calif.* USA **80B5**
Ceclavin Spain **40C3**
Cedar *Utah* USA **82C3**
Cedar Breaks Nat. Mon. *Utah* USA **80G7**
Cedarburg *Wis.* USA **79C4**
Cedar City *Utah* USA **80G7**
Cedar Falls *Iowa* USA **83M1**
Cedar Key *Fla* USA **85F6**
Cedar L *Texas* USA **82G6**
Cedar Mts *Oreg.* USA **80E4**
Cedar Ra *Utah* USA **82B2**
Cedar Rapids *Iowa* USA **83N2**
Cedar Springs *Mich.* USA **79D4**
Cedral Mexico **88D3**
Cedros,I Mexico **88A2**
Ceduna *S Aus.* Australia **99G6**
Ceerigaabo Somalia **71K2**
Cefalu *Sicily* Italy **45E6**
Cegled Hungary **37H5**
Cehegín Spain **41F3**
Cejal Colombia **92D3**
Cejita Blanca *New Mex.* USA **82E4**
Celanova Spain **40C1**
Celaya Mexico **88D3**
Celebes *island* Indonesia **53G11**
Celebes Sea Indonesia/Philippines **53G10**
Celerina Switzerland **33E2**
Celje Yugoslavia **44E2**
Celle W Germany **36C2**
Celles Belgium **32B4**
Çemisgezek Turkey **62D2**
Cengong China **55E9**
Cenis,Col de Mt France **43G4**
Center *Texas* USA **83L7**
Centerville *Ala.* USA **85D4**
Centerville *Iowa* USA **83M2**
Centerville *Mo* USA **83N4**
Centerville *Tenn.* USA **85D3**
Cento Italy **44C3**
Central *region Scotland* UK **29H7**
Central African Republic *country* Africa **69J7**
Central America *region* **89B4**
Central Auckland *stat. area* New Zealand **100E3**
Central City *Nebr.* USA **83J2**
Central, Cord. *mts* Peru **92B5**
Centralia *Ill.* USA **83P3**
Centralia *Wash.* USA **80B2**
Central Kalahari Game Reserve Botswana **72C4**
Central Lake *Mich.* USA **79D3**
Central Point *Oreg.* USA **80B4**
Centreville *New Br.* Canada **78E3**
Cenxi China **55F11**
Cephalonia,I = **Kefallinía,I**
Ceram Sea Indonesia **53J11**
Cerignola Italy **45E5**
Cerigo = **Kithira**
Cerigo,I = **Kíthira,I**
Cerigotto = **Andikithira**
Cerigotto,I = **Andikíthira,I**
Cerknica Yugoslavia **44E3**
Cerne Abbas *England* UK **26K7**
Cerralvo Mexico **88E2**
Cerralvo,I Mexico **88C3**
Cerreto P Italy **44C3**
Cerreto Sannita Italy **45E5**
Cerro de la Encantada *mt* Mexico **88A1**
Cerro de Pasco Peru **92B6**
Cerro Santiago *mt* Panama **89C5**
Cerros de Bala *plat.* Bolivia **92D6**
Cervera de Pisuerga Spain **40D1**
Cesar,R Columbia **92C1**
Cesena Italy **44D3**
Cēsis *Latvia* USSR **35L8**
Ceská Lipa Czech. **36F3**
České Budějovice Czech. **36F4**
Cesky Krumlov Czech. **36F4**
Cessnock *NSW* Australia **97D2**
Cetinje Yugoslavia **46B3**
Cetraro Italy **45E6**
Ceuta Africa **68D1**
Ceuta,B de Mexico **88C3**
Cevennes *region* France **43E4**
Cevio Switzerland **33D2**
Ceylon = **Sri Lanka**
Chablis France **42E3**
Chacabuco Argentina **91D4**
Chacance Chile **91C2**
Chacani *mt* Peru **92C7**
Chachapoyas Peru **92B5**
Chachoengsao Thailand **57C4**
Chaco *prov.* Argentina **91D3**
Chaco Canyon Nat. Mon. *New Mex.* USA **82E4**
Chaco,R *New Mex.* USA **82D4**
Chad *country* Africa **69J6**
Chadileo,R Argentina **91C5**
Chadron *Nebr.* USA **82G1**
Chadwick *Mo* USA **83M4**
Chagai Pakistan **58B3**
Chagda USSR **51Q4**
Chaghara,R India **61C2**
Chagny France **42F3**
Chagos,Arch. Indian Ocean **65F5**
Chaguaramas Trinidad **89G4**
Chāh Bahār Iran **63J4**
Chaibassa India **61E4**
Chaîne des Cardamomes *mts* Cambodia **57C4**
Chaise Dieu France **43E4**
Chakai Pakistan **60C3**
Chak Chak Sudan **69L7**
Chakhansur Afghanistan **63J3**
Chakia India **61D3**
Chakwal Pakistan **60C4**
Chala Peru **92C7**
Chalan Bil India **61G3**
Chalchihuites Mexico **88D3**
Chalcis = **Khalkís**
Chaleur B *New Br./Que.* Canada **78F3**
Chalham,I Chile **91B8**
Chalhuanca Peru **92C6**
Chaling China **55G9**
Chalisgaon India **58E4**
Chalk River *Ont.* Canada **79H2**
Challans France **42C3**
Challapata Bolivia **92D7**
Challis *Idaho* USA **80F3**
Chalna Bangladesh **61G4**
Châlons-sur-Marne France **42F2**
Chalon-sur-Saône France **42F3**
Châlus France **42D4**
Cham Switzerland **33D1**
Cham W Germany **36E4**
Chama *New Mex.* USA **82E4**
Chaman Pakistan **58C2**
Chamba India **60E4**
Chamba *district* India **60D4**
Chambal,R India **58E3**
Chamberlain *S Dak.* USA **81H4**
Chamberlain L *Maine* USA **78D3**
Chambersburg *Pa* USA **84C3**
Chambéry France **42F4**
Chambica Brazil **93H5**
Chambord *Que.* Canada **78B2**
Chambrelien Switzerland **33B2**
Chamela Mexico **88C4**
Chamical Argentina **91C4**
Chamlang *mt* Nepal **61F2**
Chamo,L Ethiopia **71H3**
Chamonix France **42G4**
Champa India **61D4**
Champagne *prov.* France **42F2**
Champaign *Ill.* USA **83P2**
Champerico Guatemala **88F5**
Champéry Switzerland **33B2**
Champlain L *NY/Vt* USA **79K3**
Champlitte France **42F3**
Champlon Belgium **32D4**
Champotón Mexico **88F4**
Chamusca Portugal **40B3**
Chana Thailand **57C5**
Chanab,R India **60D4**
Chañaral Chile **91B3**
Chanco Chile **91B5**
Chancy Switzerland **33A2**
Chandarnagar India **61G4**
Chandausi India **61B1**
Chandeleur Is *La* USA **83P8**
Chandeleur Sd *La* USA **83P8**
Chanderi India **61B3**
Chandigarh India **60E5**
Chandod India **58D4**
Chandpur Bangladesh **59H4**
Chandpur India **61B1**
Chandrakona India **61F4**
Chandrapur India **58E5**
Chandra,R India **60E4**
Chanduria Bangladesh **61G4**
Chānf Iran **63J4**
Changchun China **52J2**
Changde China **55F8**
Changhua Taiwan **55L10**
Changhua Jiang *river* China **55E13**
Changjiang China **55E13**
Chang Jiang *river* China **54F7**
Chang Jiang *river* China **55J8**
Changle China **54K4**
Changle China **55K10**
Changli China **54K3**
Changlung *Kashmir* India **60E3**
Changming China **55G9**
Changning China **55C8**
Changping China **54J2**
Changqinq China **54J4**
Changsha China **55G8**
Changshan China **55K8**
Changshan Qundao *islands* China **54M3**
Changshou China **55D8**
Changshu China **54L7**
Changshun China **55D9**
Changshu Shan *island* China **55L9**
Changtai China **55J10**
Changting China **55J10**
Changxing Dao *island* China **54L3**
Changyi China **54K4**
Changzhi China **54G4**
Changzhou China **54K7**

Chanje Cirebon

Chanje Angola 72A3
Channel Is Calif. USA 80D9
Channel Is UK 42B2
Channel Islands Nat. Mon. Calif. USA 80C9
Channel Port aux Basques Newf. Canada 78J3
Chantada Spain 40C1
Chanthaburi Thailand 57C4
Chantilly France 42E2
Chanute Kans. USA 83L4
Chanyang China 55F7
Chao'an China 55J11
Chao Hu lake China 54J7
Chaolian Dao island China 54L5
Chaoyang China 54L2
Chaoyang China 55J11
Chaozhou = Chao'an
Chapala,L Mexico 88D3
Chapayevsk USSR 49J4
Chapleau Ont. Canada 79E2
Chaplino USSR 48K7
Chapmans B South Africa 72H10
Chappell Is Tas. Australia 97F5
Chapra India 61E3
Char India 60E4
Char Mauritania 68C4
Chara USSR 51N4
Charagua Bolivia 92E7
Charaña Bolivia 92D7
Charco Azul,B Panama 89C5
Charcot I Antarctica 15S3
Chard England UK 26J7
Chardzhou Turkmen. USSR 50H6
Charente dep. France 42D4
Charente-Maritime dep. France 42C4
Charente,R France 42C4
Charikar Afghanistan 63K2
Chari,R Chad 69J6
Chariton Iowa USA 83M2
Charkhari India 61B3
Charleroi Belgium 32C4
Charles City Iowa USA 83M1
Charles,R Mass. USA 84F1
Charleston Ill. USA 83P3
Charleston Miss. USA 85B3
Charleston Mo USA 83P4
Charleston S Car. USA 85G4
Charleston W Va USA 85G1
Charleston Pk mt Nev. USA 80F7
Charlestown Ireland, Rep. of 30F6
Charles Town W Va USA 84C3
Charleville France 42F2
Charleville Queens. Australia 99K5
Charlevoix Mich. USA 79D3
Charlotte Mich. USA 79D4
Charlotte N Car. USA 85G3
Charlotte NY USA 84C1
Charlotte Amalie Virgin Is 89G3
Charlotte Harbor Fla USA 85L8
Charlottenburg Berlin Germany 36E2
Charlottesville Va USA 85H1
Charlottetown Pr. Ed. I. Canada 78G3
Charlton Vic. Australia 97B3
Charlton I NW Terr. Canada 77P6
Charmey Switzerland 33C2
Charmoille Switzerland 33C1
Charnwood Forest England UK 25F7
Charolles France 42F3
Charrote,Sa USA 82G7
Charsadda Pakistan 60B3
Charters Towers Queens. Australia 99K4
Chartres France 42D2
Chascomus Argentina 91E5
Chaska Minn. USA 81L3
Chasseneuil France 42D4
Chasseral mt Switzerland 33C1
Chat,C Que. Canada 78E2
Châteaubriant France 42C3
Château Chinon France 42E3
Château-du-Loir France 42D3
Châteaudun France 42D2
Château Gontier France 42C3
Château-la-Valliere France 42D3
Chateaulin France 42A2
Châteauneuf-en-Thymerais France 42D2
Château Renault France 42D3
Châteauroux France 42D3
Château Salins France 42G2
Château Thierry France 42E2
Châteauvillain France 42F2
Châteaux d'Oex Switzerland 33C2
Châtelet Belgium 32C4
Châtellerault France 42D3
Châtel-St Denis Switzerland 33B2
Chatfield Minn. USA 81L4
Chatham England UK 27R6
Chatham New Br. Canada 78F3
Chatham NY USA 84E1
Chatham Ont. Canada 79E4
Chatham Va USA 85H2
Chatham,Is Pacific Ocean 94J12
Châtillon Italy 44A3
Chatillon-sur-Seine France 42F3
Chatonnay France 42C3
Chatra India 61E3
Chatra Nepal 61F2
Chatrapur India 59G5
Chattahoochee,R Ga USA 87K5
Chattanooga Tenn. USA 85E3
Chattarpur India 61E3
Chaudière,R de la Que. Canada 79L2
Chauka,R India 61C2
Chaumont France 42F2
Chaumont mt Switzerland 33B1
Chaunskaya Guba bay USSR 51T3
Chauny France 42E2
Chau Phu Cambodia 57C4
Chausa India 61D3
Chautauqua,L NY USA 84B1
Chaves Brazil 93H4
Chaves Portugal 40C2
Chavornay Switzerland 33B2
Chaykovskiy USSR 49M2
Chazón Argentina 91D4
Cheadle England UK 25E7
Cheb Czech. 36E3
Cheboksary USSR 49H2
Cheboygan Mich. USA 79D3
Cheddar England UK 26J6
Cheduba,I Burma 59H5
Chef-Boutonne France 42C3
Che foo = Yantai
Chehalis Wash. USA 80B2
Chehalis,R Wash. USA 80B2
Chekiang = Zhejiang
Chekunda USSR 51Q4
Chelforó Argentina 91C5
Chelkar Kazakh. USSR 50G5
Chełm Poland 37K3
Chelmer,R England UK 27Q5
Chełmno Poland 37H2
Chelmsford England UK 27Q5
Chelsea Vt USA 79K3
Chelsea Wis. USA 79A3
Cheltenham England UK 27K5
Chelva Spain 41F3
Chelyabinsk USSR 49Q3
Chemba Mozambique 72E3
Chembar USSR 49F4
Chemnitz = Karl Marx Stadt
Chenab,R Pakistan 60B5
Chenesht Iran 63H3
Cheney Wash. USA 80E2
Chengbu China 55F9
Chengde China 54J2
Chengde China 54K2
Chengdong Hu lake China 54J6
Chengdu river China 54C7
Chenggu China 54D6
Chengkou China 54E7
Chengwu China 54H5
Chengxi Hu lake China 54J6
Chenoa Ill. USA 83P2
Chenxi China 55F8
Chen Xian China 55G10
Chepen Peru 92B5
Chepes Argentina 91C4
Chepstow Wales UK 26J5
Cher dep. France 42E3
Cherain Belgium 32D4
Cherbourg France 42C2
Cherchell Algeria 68F1
Cheremkhovo USSR 51M4
Cherepovets USSR 48L2
Cheriyam island Laccadive Is India 58D6
Cherkassy Ukrain. USSR 48G7
Chermoz USSR 50G4
Chernigov Ukrain. USSR 48G6
Chernikovsk USSR 49N3
Chernovsk USSR 49J1
Chernovtsy Ukrain. USSR 48D7
Chernyakhovsk Lith. USSR 35J9
Cherokee Iowa USA 83L1
Cherokees,L o'the Okla. USA 83L4
Cher,R France 42D3
Cherra Punji India 59H3
Cherry Creek Nev. USA 80F6
Cherryfield Maine USA 78E4
Chertkovo Ukrain. USSR 48M7
Chertsey England UK 27N6
Chervenbryeg Bulgaria 46E3
Cherwell,R England UK 27M5
Chesapeake Va USA 85J2
Chesapeake B Md USA 87L4
Cheseaux Switzerland 33B2
Chesham England UK 27N5
Cheshire county England UK 25C6
Cheshire Plain England UK 25C6
Cheshskaya Guba bay USSR 50F3
Chesières Switzerland 33C2
Chesil Bank England UK 26J7
Chesley Ont. Canada 79F3
Chester England UK 25C6
Chester Ill. USA 83P4
Chester Pa USA 84D3
Chester S Car. USA 85G3
Chesterfield England UK 25F6
Chesterfield S Car. USA 85G3
Chesterfield Inl. NW Terr. Canada 77N4
Chesterfield,Is Pacific Ocean 94F9
Chester-le-Street England UK 25E3
Chestertown Md USA 84C3
Chesuncook L Maine USA 78D3
Chetco,R Oreg. USA 80A4
Chetlat island Amindivi Is India 58D6
Chetumal Mexico 88G4
Chetumal B Mexico 88G4
Chetumal Pen. Mexico 88G4
Cheverie No. Sc. Canada 78F4
Cheviot New Zealand 100E6
Cheviot Hills Eng./Scot. UK 25C2
Chew Valley Res. England UK 26J6
Chexbres Switzerland 33B2
Cheyenne Wyo. USA 81E5
Cheyenne,R S Dak. USA 81G3
Chhachrauli India 60E5
Chhata India 60E7
Chhata India 61A2
Chhatarpur India 61B3
Chhibramau India 61B2
Chhindwara India 61B4
Chiai Taiwan 55L11
Chiang Khan Thailand 57C3
Chiang Mai Thailand 57B3
Chiang Rai Thailand 57B3
Chiang Saen Thailand 57C2
Chiapa Mexico 88F4
Chiapas state Mexico 88F4
Chiasso Switzerland 33E3
Chiavari Italy 44B3
Chiba Japan 56G7
Chiba prefecture Japan 56G7
Chibchange Tso lake Tibet China 59G2
Chibemba Angola 72A3
Chibougamau L Que. Canada 78A2
Chicago Ill. USA 83Q2
Chichagof I Alaska USA 87Z13
Chicheng China 54H2
Chichen-itza Mexico 88G3
Chichester England UK 27N7
Chickasha Okla. USA 83J5
Chiclayo Peru 92B5
Chico Calif. USA 80C6
Chicoana Argentina 91C3
Chicoli India 61A5
Chicopee Mass. USA 84E1
Chicopee,R Mass. USA 84E1
Chico,R Argentina 91C6
Chicoutimi Que. Canada 78C2
Chidambaram India 58E6
Chidley,C Que. Canada 77T4
Chiem See lake W Germany 36E5
Chieri Italy 44A3
Chieti Italy 44E4
Chièvres Belgium 32B4
Chifeng China 54K1
Chignecto B New Br./No. Sc. Canada 78F4
Chigubo Mozambique 72E4
Chigwell England UK 27Q5
Chihli,G of = Bo Hai
Chihuahua Mexico 88C2
Chihuahua state Mexico 88C2
Chik-Ballapur India 58E6
Chikmagalur India 58E6
Chikwawa Malawi 71G8
Chilas Kashmir India 60D3
Childress Texas USA 82H5
Chile country S America 91B3
Chilecito Argentina 91C3
Chilete Peru 92B5
Chilia Veche Romania 46G2
Chilka,L India 59G5
Chilko L BC Canada 76G6
Chilko,R BC Canada 76G6
Chillán Chile 91B5
Chillicothe Mo USA 83M3
Chillicothe Ohio USA 79E6
Chillingollah Vic. Australia 97B3
Chilliwack BC Canada 76G7
Chillon Switzerland 33B2
Chiloé,I de Chile 91B6
Chilonga Zambia 72E2
Chilpancingo Mexico 88E4
Chilpi Kashmir India 60C2
Chiltern Vic. Australia 97C3
Chiltern Hills England UK 27N5
Chilton Wis. USA 79B3
Chilubula Zambia 72E2
Chilung Taiwan 55L10
Chilwa,L Malawi 71H8
Chimay Belgium 32C4
Chimbay Uzbek. USSR 50G5
Chimbote Peru 92B5
Chimkent Kazakh. USSR 50H5
Chimoio Mozambique 72E3
China country Asia 19M6
Chinandega Nicaragua 89B4
Chincha Alta Peru 92B6
Chinchaga,R Alta Canada 76H5
Chinchon Spain 40E2
Chindwin,R Burma 59H4
Chingleput India 58F6
Chinguetta Mauritania 68C4
Chin Hills Burma 59H4
Chinhoyi Zimbabwe 72E3
Chiniot Pakistan 60C5
Chinju S Korea 52J3
Chinko,R CAR 69K7
Chino Ariz. USA 80G8
Chinook Mont. USA 81C1
Chinook,L Oreg. USA 80C3
Chinsura India 61G4
Chioggia Italy 44D3
Chios,I = Khíos,I
Chipata Zambia 72E2
Chipili Zambia 72D2
Chipman New Br. Canada 78F3
Chippenham England UK 27K6
Chippewa Falls Wis. USA 81M3
Chippewa,R Wis. USA 79A3
Chipping Campden England UK 27L4
Chipping Norton England UK 27L5
Chipping Sodbury England UK 26K5
Chiputneticook Ls Canada/USA 78E4
Chiquian Peru 92B6
Chiquimula Guatemala 88G5
Chiquinquira Colombia 92C2
Chiramba Mozambique 72E3
Chiras Afghanistan 63K2
Chirawa India 60D6
Chirfa Niger 69H4
Chiricahua Nat. Mon. Ariz. USA 82D6
Chiriqui,G de Panama 89C5
Chiriqui Grande Panama 89C5
Chiriqui,Laguna de lagoon Panama 89C5
Chirk Wales UK 26H3
Chirpan Bulgaria 46E3
Chirripo Grande mt Costa Rica 89C5
Chisamba Falls Zambia 72E2
Chishui China 55C8
Chishui He river China 55C8
Chisinau = Kishinev
Chismy USSR 49M3
Chistopol USSR 49K3
Chita USSR 51N4
Chitembo Angola 70D7
Chitinskaya Oblast region USSR 51N4
Chitipa Malawi 71G6
Chitradurga India 58E6
Chitral Pakistan 60B3
Chitral district Kashmir India 60B2
Chitral,R Pakistan 60B2
Chitre Panama 89C5
Chittagong Bangladesh 59H4
Chittaurgarh India 58D4
Chittoor India 58E6
Chiusi Italy 44C4
Chiuta,L Malawi 71H7
Chiva Spain 41F3
Chivasso Italy 44A3
Chivay Peru 92C7
Chivilcoy Argentina 91D4
Chivota,Sa mts New Mex. USA 82E5
Chiwanda Tanzania 71G7
Chixi China 55G11
Chmielnik Poland 37J3
Choapam Mexico 88E4
Choban Bey Syria 64F1
Chobe Nat. Pk Botswana 72C3
Chocaya Bolivia 92D8
Chocen Czech. 37G3
Choco region Colombia 92B2
Choco,B Columbia 92B3
Chocolate Mts Calif. USA 80F9
Choconta Colombia 92C2
Choele Choel Argentina 91C5
Choinice Poland 37G2
Choiseul,I Solomon Is 94F8
Choix Mexico 88C2
Chojna Poland 36F2
Choke,Mts Ethiopia 71H2
Cholet France 42C3
Cholon Vietnam 57D4
Choluteca Honduras 89B4
Choma Zambia 72D3
Chomutov Czech. 36E3
Chone Ecuador 92A4
Chong'an China 55J9
Chongjin Korea 52J2
Chong Kal Cambodia 57C4
Chongling Shui river China 55G9
Chongming China 54L7
Chongqing China 54B7
Chongqing China 55D8
Chongren China 55H9
Chongyang China 55H8
Chongyi China 55H10
Chongzuo China 55D11
Chonos, Arch. de los Chile 91A6
Chorillos Peru 92B6
Chorley England UK 25C5
Chorzele Poland 37J2
Chorzow Poland 37H3
Chōshi Japan 56G7
Chos Malal Argentina 91B5
Choszczno Poland 37F2
Chota Peru 92B5
Chota Nagpur plateau India 61D4
Choybalsan Mongolia 52F1
Christchurch England UK 27L7
Christchurch New Zealand 100E6
Christiansburg Va USA 85G2
Christiansted St Croix Leeward Is 89G3
Christie,Mt Yukon Canada 76F4
Christmas I Indian Ocean 53E13
Chrudim Czech. 37F4
Chrzanów Poland 37H3
Chtaura Lebanon 64D4
Chuale,L Mozambique 72E4
Chubut prov. Argentina 91C6
Chubut,R Argentina 91C6
Chucul Argentina 91D4
Chudleigh England UK 26G7
Chudovo USSR 48G2
Chudskoye,Ozero lake Eston. USSR 35M7
Chukai Malaysia 53D10
Chukhloma USSR 49F1
Chukotskiy Khrebet mts USSR 51U3
Chukotskiy Poluostrov peninsula USSR 51V3
Chulman USSR 51P4
Chulmleigh England UK 26G7
Chulung P Kashmir India 60E3
Chulym USSR 50K4
Chumbicha Argentina 91C3
Chumikan USSR 51Q4
Chumphon Thailand 57B4
Chun'an China 55K8
Chunar India 61D3
Chuna,R USSR 51L4
Chunchŏn S Korea 52J3
Chung Yang mts Taiwan 55L11
Chunian Pakistan 60D5
Chunya Tanzania 71G6
Chuquibambilla Peru 92C6
Chuquicamata Chile 91C2
Chur Switzerland 33E2
Churapcha USSR 51Q3
Churches Ferry N Dak. USA 81H1
Churchill Man. Canada 76N5
Churchill,C Man. Canada 77N5
Churchill Falls Newf. Canada 77T6
Churchill L Sask. Canada 76K5
Churchill,R Man. Canada 76M5
Churchill,R Newf. Canada 77T6
Churfirsten mts Switzerland 33E1
Churia Ghati Hills Nepal 61E2
Churia Ra mts Nepal 61C1
Churu India 60D6
Chusca,Sa mts New Mex. USA 82D4
Chusovoi USSR 50G4
Chuvashskaya ASSR rep. USSR 50F4
Chu Xian China 54K6
Cicero Ill. USA 83Q2
Cidones Spain 41E2
Ciechanów Poland 37J2
Ciego de Avila Cuba 89D2
Cienaga Colombia 92C1
Cienfuegos Cuba 89C2
Cierfs Switzerland 33F2
Cieszyn Poland 37H4
Cieza Spain 41F3
Cifuentes Spain 41E2
Cilacap Java Indon. 53E12
Cili China 55F8
Cimaltepec Mexico 88E4
Cimarron,R Kans./Okla. USA 82J4
Cimone,Mt Italy 44C3
Cîmpina Romania 46E2
Cîmpulung Romania 46E2
Cincinnati Ohio USA 79D6
Cinto,Mt Corsica France 43J6
Cintra,G de Morocco 68B4
Cioara Romania 46F2
Circeo,C Italy 45D5
Circle Alaska USA 87Y12
Circle Mont. USA 81E2
Circleville Ohio USA 79E6
Cirebon Java Indon. 53E12

Cirencester, Coporaque

Cirencester England UK **27L5**
Ciro Italy **45F6**
Cirque Mt Newf. Canada **77T5**
Citaltépetl mt Mexico **88E4**
Citrusdal South Africa **72B6**
Citta del Vaticano Italy **45D5**
Cittanova Italy **45F6**
Ciudad Acuña Mexico **88D2**
Ciudad Bolivar Venezuela **92E2**
Ciudad Camargo Mexico **88C2**
Ciudad de Valles Mexico **88E3**
Ciudad Guzman Mexico **88D4**
Ciudad Juárez Mexico **88C1**
Ciudad Madero Mexico **88E3**
Ciudad Obregón Mexico **88C2**
Ciudad Real Spain **40E3**
Ciudad Real prov. Spain **40D3**
Ciudad Rodrigo Spain **40C2**
Ciudad Victoria Mexico **88E3**
Civitanova Marche Italy **44D4**
Civitavecchia Italy **44C4**
Civray France **42D3**
Civril Turkey **62B2**
Ci Xian China **54H4**
Cizre Turkey **62E2**
Clackmannan Scotland UK **29J7**
Clacton on Sea England UK **27S5**
Claire,L Alta Canada **76J5**
Clair Engle L Calif. USA **80B5**
Clamecy France **42E3**
Clan Alpine Mts Nev. USA **80E6**
Clara Ireland, Rep. of **31H7**
Clara,I Burma **59J6**
Clare Mich. USA **79D4**
Clare S Aus. Australia **97A2**
Clare county Ireland, Rep. of **31E8**
Clarecastle Ireland, Rep. of **31F8**
Clare I Ireland, Rep. Of **30C6**
Claremont New H USA **84E1**
Claremont South Africa **72H9**
Claremore Okla. USA **83L4**
Claremorris Ireland, Rep. of **30F6**
Clarence Hd NW Terr. Canada **77Q1**
Clarence I Antarctica **15T3**
Clarence,I Chile **91B8**
Clarence,R New Zealand **100E6**
Clarence,R NSW Australia **97D1**
Clarence Str. N Terr. Australia **98G2**
Clarendon Ark. USA **83N5**
Clarenville Newf. Canada **78L2**
Clare,R Ireland,Rep. of **31F7**
Clarinda Iowa USA **83L2**
Clarion Iowa USA **83M1**
Clarion Pa USA **84B2**
Clarion,R Pa USA **84B2**
Clark Nev. USA **80D6**
Clark S Dak. USA **81J3**
Clark Canyon Res. Mont. USA **80G3**
Clarke I Tas. Australia **97F5**
Clarkesville Texas USA **83L6**
Clark Fork,R Mont. USA **80F2**
Clarksburg W Va USA **79F6**
Clarksdale Miss. USA **85B3**
Clarksville Tenn. USA **85D2**
Claro Switzerland **33E2**
Claro,R Brazil **93G7**
Clausthal W Germany **36D3**
Clay Center Kans. USA **83K3**
Claydon England UK **27S4**
Clayton Ala. USA **85E5**
Clayton Idaho USA **80F3**
Clayton New J USA **84D3**
Clayton New Mex. USA **82G4**
Clear,C Ireland, Rep. of **31D11**
Clearfield Pa USA **84B2**
Clear I Ireland, Rep. of **31E11**
Clear,L Calif. USA **80B6**
Clear Lake Iowa USA **83M1**
Clearmont Wyo. USA **81D3**
Clearwater Fla USA **85L8**
Clearwater Mts Idaho USA **80F2**
Clearwater,R Idaho USA **80F2**
Cleburne Texas USA **83K6**
Cleddau,R Wales UK **26E5**
Cle Elum Wash. USA **80C2**
Cleethorpes England UK **25H5**
Clent Hills England UK **27K4**
Cleobury Mortimer England UK **26J4**
Clermont Queens. Australia **99K4**
Clermont-Ferrand France **42E4**
Clevedon England UK **26J6**
Cleveland Idaho USA **80G3**
Cleveland Ohio USA **79F5**
Cleveland Tenn. USA **85E3**
Cleveland Texas USA **83L7**
Cleveland county England UK **25F3**
Cleveland Hills England UK **25F4**
Clew B Ireland, Rep. of **30D6**
Clifden Ireland, Rep. of **31C7**
Clifton Ariz. USA **82D6**
Clifton South Africa **72H9**
Clifton Tenn. USA **85C3**
Clifton Forge Va USA **85H2**
Clifton Hills S Aus. Australia **99H5**
Clinch Mts Tenn./Va USA **85F2**
Clinton Ark. USA **83M5**
Clinton Ill. USA **83P2**
Clinton Iowa USA **83N2**
Clinton Mass. USA **84F1**
Clinton Mo USA **83M3**
Clinton Mont. USA **80G2**
Clinton Okla. USA **83J5**
Clinton Ont. Canada **79F4**
Clinton Colden L NW Terr. Canada **76K4**
Clintonville Wis. USA **79B3**
Clipperton,I Pacific Ocean **95R6**
Clisson France **42C3**
Clitheroe England UK **25D5**
Cloghan Ireland, Rep. of **31H7**
Clogher N Ireland **30J5**
Clonakilty Ireland, Rep. of **31F10**
Cloncurry Queens. Australia **99J4**
Clondalkin Ireland,Rep. of **31L7**
Clonegal Ireland, Rep. of **31K8**
Clones Ireland, Rep. of **30J5**
Clonmel Ireland, Rep. of **31H9**
Cloquet Minn. USA **81L2**
Clorinda Argentina **91E3**
Cloud Pk Wyo. USA **81D3**
Clover Va USA **85H2**
Cloverdale Calif. USA **80B6**
Clovis New Mex. USA **82G5**
Cloyne Ireland, Rep. of **31G10**
Cluj Romania **46D1**
Clun England UK **26H4**
Clunes Vic. Australia **97B3**
Clun Forest Wales UK **26H4**
Clunie,L Scotland UK **28F5**
Clusone Italy **44B3**
Clwyd county Wales UK **26H2**
Clwyd,R Wales UK **26H2**
Clyde New Zealand **100C7**
Clydebank Scotland UK **29H8**
Clyde, Firth of Scotland UK **29F9**
Clyde Inl. NW Terr. Canada **77S2**
Clyde,R Scotland UK **29G8**
Clyde,R Scotland UK **29J8**
Coachella Calif. USA **80E9**
Coahuila state Mexico **88D2**
Coalcomán Mexico **88D4**
Coalinga Calif. USA **80C7**
Coamo Puerto Rico **89F3**
Coarga,R Pakistan **58B3**
Coari Brazil **92E4**
Coast Mts BC Canada **76F6**
Coast Ra. USA **80B5**
Coatbridge Scotland UK **29H8**
Coatepeque Guatemala **88F5**
Coatesville Pa USA **84D3**
Coaticook Que. Canada **79L3**
Coats I NW Terr. Canada **77P4**
Coats Land Antarctica **15B2**
Coatzacoalcos Mexico **88F4**
Coatzintla Mexico **88E3**
Cobalt Ont. Canada **79G2**
Cobán Guatemala **88F4**
Cobar NSW Australia **97C2**
Cobargo NSW Australia **97C3**
Cobb,Mt New Zealand **100E5**
Cobden Vic. Australia **97B3**
Cobequid Mts No. Sc. Canada **78F4**
Cóbh Ireland, Rep. of **31G10**
Cobija Bolivia **92D6**
Cobleskill NY USA **84D1**
Coboconk Ont. Canada **79G3**
Cobooras,Mt Vic. Australia **97C3**
Cobourg Ont. Canada **79G3**
Cobourg Pen. N Terr. Australia **98G2**
Cobram Vic. Australia **97C3**
Cobre Nev. USA **80F5**
Coburg Oreg. USA **80B3**
Coburg W Germany **36D3**
Coburg I NW Terr. Canada **77Q1**
Cocahacra Peru **92C7**
Cocamá Peru **92C6**
Coca,R Ecuador **92B4**
Cochabamba Bolivia **92D7**
Cocha,L Columbia **92B3**
Cochin India **58E7**
Cochin China region Vietnam **57D4**
Cochinoca Argentina **91C2**
Cochons,I aux Crozet Is **65U12**
Cochran Ga USA **85F4**
Cochrane Ont. Canada **77P7**
Cochrane,L Argentina/Chile **91B7**
Cock Bridge Scotland UK **28K5**
Cockburn S Aus. Australia **97B2**
Cockburn,Ca. Chile **91B8**
Cockburn I Ont. Canada **79E3**
Cockburnspath Scotland UK **29M8**
Cockermouth England UK **25B3**
Coco Chan. Bay of Bengal **59H6**
Coco,I del Pacific Ocean **95T7**
Cocopara Ra. mts NSW Australia **97C2**
Coco,R Nicaragua **89C4**
Cocos,Is Indian Ocean **65H6**
Cocula Mexico **88D3**
Cocuy Colombia **92C2**
Codajas Brazil **92E4**
Cod,C Mass. USA **84F1**
Codfish I New Zealand **100B8**
Codó Brazil **93J4**
Cod's Hd Ireland, Rep. of **31C10**
Cody Wyo. USA **81C3**
Coe Hill Ont. Canada **79H3**
Coen Queens. Australia **99J2**
Coeur d'Alene Idaho USA **80E2**
Coevorden Netherlands **32E2**
Coeymans NY USA **84E1**
Coffeyville Kans. USA **83L4**
Coffs Harbour NSW Australia **97D2**
Cognac France **42C4**
Cogolludo Spain **40E2**
Cohoes NY USA **84E1**
Cohuna Vic. Australia **97B3**
Coiba,I Panama **89C5**
Coihaique Chile **91B7**
Coimbatore India **58E6**
Coimbra Portugal **40B2**
Coin Spain **40D4**
Coire = **Chur**
Cojimies Ecuador **92A3**
Coko Ra mts NSW Australia **97B2**
Colac Vic. Australia **97B3**
Colachel India **58E7**
Colair,L India **58F5**
Colbeck Arch. Antarctica **15F3**
Colby Kans. USA **82H3**
Colcha Bolivia **92D8**
Colchester England UK **27R5**
Col de Balme Switzerland **33B2**
Col de la Givrine pass Switzerland **33B2**
Col de Pillon pass Switzerland **33C2**
Col des Roches pass Switzerland **33B1**
Coldingham Scotland UK **29M8**
Coldstream Scotland UK **29M8**
Col du Grand St Bernard pass Italy/Switz. **33C3**
Colebrook New H USA **79L3**
Coleman Alta Canada **76J7**
Coleman Texas USA **83J7**
Colemerik = **Hakkâri**
Coleraine N Ireland **30K3**
Coleraine Vic. Australia **97B3**
Coleridge,L New Zealand **100D6**
Coles Bay Tas. Australia **97F5**
Colfax Calif. USA **80C6**
Colfax Wash. USA **80E2**
Col Ferret pass Italy/Switz. **33C3**
Colgong India **61F3**
Colhué Huapi,L Argentina **91C7**
Colima Mexico **88D4**
Colima state Mexico **88D4**
Collahuasi Chile **91C2**
Collarenebri NSW Australia **97C1**
Coll,I Scotland UK **29C6**
Collie NSW Australia **97C2**
Collie W Aus. Australia **98D6**
Collier B W Aus. Australia **98E3**
Collines de Normandie region France **42C2**
Collingwood New Zealand **100E5**
Collingwood Ont. Canada **79F3**
Collingwood Queens. Australia **99J4**
Collinstown Ireland,Rep. of **31L7**
Collinsville Queens. Australia **99K4**
Collo Algeria **68G1**
Collooney Ireland, Rep. of **30G5**
Colmar France **42G2**
Colmars France **43G4**
Colmena Argentina **91D3**
Colmenar de Oreja Spain **40E2**
Colmenar Viejo Spain **40E2**
Colmi Honduras **89B3**
Colmonell Scotland UK **29G9**
Colne England UK **25D5**
Colne,R England UK **27R5**
Cologne = **Köln**
Colombia Brazil **93H8**
Colombia country S America **92C3**
Colombier Switzerland **33B2**
Colombo Sri Lanka **58E7**
Colón Argentina **91D4**
Colon Argentina **91E4**
Colón Cuba **89C2**
Colón Panama **89D5**
Colón Venezuela **92C2**
Colonia Uruguay **91E4**
Colonia Las Heras Argentina **91C7**
Colonna,C Italy **45F6**
Colonsay,I Scotland UK **29D7**
Colorado Texas USA **82H6**
Colorado state USA **86E4**
Colorado Des. Calif. USA **80E8**
Colorado Des. Wyo. USA **81C4**
Colorado Plat. Ariz. USA **82C4**
Colorado,R Argentina **91C5**
Colorado,R Argentina **91D5**
Colorado,R Texas USA **83K8**
Colorado,R USA **86D4**
Colorados, Arch. de los Cuba **89C2**
Colorado Springs Col. USA **82F3**
Colotlán Mexico **88D3**
Colpoy B Ont. Canada **79F3**
Colquechaca Bolivia **92D7**
Colsterworth England UK **25G7**
Colton Calif. USA **80E8**
Columbia Ala. USA **85E5**
Columbia Ky USA **85E2**
Columbia La USA **83M6**
Columbia Miss. USA **85C5**
Columbia Mo USA **83M3**
Columbia Pa USA **84C2**
Columbia S Car. USA **85G3**
Columbia Tenn. USA **85D3**
Columbia City Ind. USA **79D5**
Columbia, Dist. of USA **79H6**
Columbia,Mt Alta Canada **76H6**
Columbiana Ala. USA **85D4**
Columbia Plat. USA **86C2**
Columbia,R Canada/USA **80C3**
Columbine,C South Africa **72B6**
Columbretes,Is Medit. Sea **41G3**
Columbus Ga USA **85E4**
Columbus Ind. USA **79D6**
Columbus Kans. USA **83L4**
Columbus Miss. USA **85C4**
Columbus Mont. USA **81C3**
Columbus Nebr. USA **83K2**
Columbus Ohio USA **79E6**
Columbus Texas USA **83K8**
Colusa Calif. USA **80C6**
Colville,C New Zealand **100F3**
Colville L NW Terr. Canada **76F3**
Colwyn Bay Wales UK **26G2**
Colyton England UK **26H7**
Comacchio Italy **44D3**
Comacchio,Valli di Italy **44C3**
Comalcalco Mexico **88F4**
Comana Romania **46F2**
Comayagua Honduras **89B4**
Combarbalá Chile **91B4**
Comber N Ireland **30M4**
Comblain Belgium **32D4**
Combolo mt Italy/Switz. **33F2**
Combourg France **42C2**
Comeragh Mts Ireland, Rep. of **31H9**
Comilla Bangladesh **59H4**
Comino,C Sardinia Italy **45B5**
Comiso Sicily Italy **45E7**
Comitán Mexico **88F4**
Commentry France **42E3**
Commissaires L Que. Canada **78B2**
Commissioners L = **Commissaires L**
Commodoro Rivadavia Argentina **91C7**
Commonwealth Ra. Antarctica **15N2**
Commonwealth Terr. NSW Australia **97D3**
Como Italy **44B3**
Comoe,R Ivory Coast **68E7**
Como,L di Italy **44B3**
Comorin,C India **58E7**
Comoros,Is Indian Ocean **71J7**
Compiègne France **42E2**
Comporta Portugal **40B3**
Compostela Mexico **88D3**
Compton Calif. USA **80D9**
Comrie Scotland UK **29J7**
Conakry Guinea **68C7**
Concarneau France **42B3**
Conceicao do Araguaia Brazil **93H5**
Concepción Argentina **91E3**
Concepcion Argentina **91E4**
Concepcion Bolivia **92D6**
Concepción Chile **91B5**
Concepción Paraguay **91E2**
Concepcion del Oro Mexico **88D3**
Concepcion del Uruguay Argentina **91E4**
Concepción,L Bolivia **92E6**
Concepción,L Bolivia **92E7**
Conception B Newf. Canada **78M3**
Conception,Ca. Chile **91A8**
Conception I The Bahamas **89D2**
Conception,Point Calif. USA **80C8**
Conchas L New Mex. USA **82F5**
Conches France **42D2**
Conchi Chile **91C2**
Conchos,R Mexico **88C2**
Concise Switzerland **33B2**
Concord Mass. USA **84F1**
Concord N Car. USA **85G3**
Concord New H USA **84F1**
Concordia Argentina **91E4**
Concordia Kans. USA **83K3**
Concordia Mexico **88C3**
Condobolin NSW Australia **97C2**
Condole NSW Australia **97B2**
Condom France **43D5**
Condon Oreg. USA **80C3**
Conegliano Italy **44D3**
Conemaugh Pa USA **84B2**
Conesa Argentina **91D6**
Confolens France **42D3**
Confusion Ra. Utah USA **80G6**
Confuso,R Paraguay **91E2**
Congleton England UK **25D6**
Congo country Africa **70D4**
Congo,R (Zaire) Africa **70D5**
Conida Angola **70C7**
Coniston England UK **25B4**
Connah's Quay Wales UK **26H2**
Connaught prov. Ireland, Rep. of **30E6**
Connecticut state USA **87M3**
Connecticut,R Vt USA **84E1**
Connell Wash. USA **80D2**
Connellsville Pa USA **84B2**
Connemara Ireland, Rep. of **31C6**
Conn L Ireland, Rep. of **30E5**
Conrad Mont. USA **81B1**
Conroe Texas USA **83L7**
Conselheiro Lafaiete Brazil **93J8**
Consett England UK **25E3**
Conshohocken New J USA **84D2**
Con Son Is Vietnam **57D5**
Constance = **Konstanz**
Constance,L = **Boden See**
Constance,Mt Wash. USA **80B1**
Constancia do Baetas Brazil **92E5**
Constanta Romania **46G2**
Constantine Algeria **68G1**
Constitución Chile **91B5**
Consuegra Spain **40E3**
Contact Nev. USA **80F5**
Contamana Peru **92C5**
Conthey Switzerland **33C2**
Contreras,I Chile **91A8**
Contwoyto L NW Terr. Canada **76J3**
Conway Ark. USA **83M5**
Conway Mo USA **83M4**
Conway New H USA **79L3**
Conway S Car. USA **85H4**
Conwy Wales UK **26G2**
Coober Pedy S Aus. Australia **99G5**
Cooch Behar India **61G2**
Cook,B de Chile **91B9**
Cook Inl. Alaska USA **87X13**
Cook,Is Pacific Ocean **94K9**
Cook,Mt New Zealand **100D6**
Cookshire Que. Canada **79L3**
Cook's Pass. Queens. Australia **99K2**
Cookstown N Ireland **30K4**
Cook Str. New Zealand **100F5**
Cooktown Queens. Australia **99K3**
Coolabah NSW Australia **97C2**
Coolah NSW Australia **97C2**
Coolamon NSW Australia **97C2**
Coolgardie W Aus. Australia **98E6**
Cooma NSW Australia **97C3**
Coomacarrea mt Ireland, Rep. of **31C10**
Coonabarabran NSW Australia **97C2**
Coonalpyn S Aus. Australia **97A3**
Coonamble NSW Australia **97C2**
Coonoor India **58E6**
Cooper Cr. S Aus. Australia **99H5**
Cooperstown N Dak. USA **81H2**
Cooperstown NY USA **84D1**
Coorong, The S Aus. Australia **97A3**
Cooroy Queens. Australia **99L5**
Coos Bay Oreg. USA **80A4**
Cootamundra NSW Australia **97C2**
Cootehill Ireland, Rep. of **30J5**
Copenhagen = **København**
Copetonas Argentina **91D5**
Copiapo Chile **91B3**
Copinsay island Orkney Scotland **28L2**
Copley S Aus. Australia **97A2**
Coporaque Peru **92C6**

Copper Cliff, Daedalus Reef

Copper Cliff *Ont.* Canada 79F2
Coppermine *NW Terr.* Canada 76H3
Coppermine,R *NW Terr.* Canada 76H3
Coppet Switzerland 33B2
Coquar *Que.* Canada 79J1
Coqueta,R Columbia 92C4
Coquet,R *England* UK 25E2
Coquilhatville = Mbandaka
Coquille *Oreg.* USA 80A4
Coquimbo Chile 91B3
Coquimbo *prov.* Chile 91B4
Corabia Romania 46E3
Coraçoes Brazil 93H8
Coraki *NSW* Australia 97D1
Corangamite,L *Vic.* Australia 97B3
Corato Italy 45F5
Corazon,Sa *Texas* USA 82G8
Corby *England* UK 27N4
Corcaigh = Cork
Corcovado,G del Chile 91B6
Corcovado,Mt Chile 91B6
Corcubión Spain 40B1
Cordell *Okla.* USA 83J5
Cordillera Cantabrica Spain 40D1
Cordillera Central *mts* Columbia 92B3
Cordillera Central *mts* Dom. Rep. 89E3
Cordillera de Ollita *mts* Chile 91B4
Córdoba Argentina 91D4
Córdoba Mexico 88E4
Córdoba Spain 40D4
Cordoba *prov.* Argentina 91D4
Córdoba *prov.* Spain 40D4
Cordoba,Sierra de *mts* Argentina 91D4
Cordova *Alaska* USA 87Y12
Cordova Peru 92B6
Coreca,R Angola 72A3
Corfu,I = Kérkira,I
Corfu, Str. of Greece 47B5
Coria Spain 40C2
Coricudgy *mt* *NSW* Australia 97D2
Corigliano Calabro Italy 45F6
Coringa India 59F5
Corinne *Utah* USA 82B2
Corinth = Kórinthos
Corinth *Miss.* USA 85C3
Corinthian B Heard I 65R12
Corinto Brazil 93J7
Corinto Nicaragua 89B4
Corisco B Eq. Guinea 70B4
Cork Ireland, Rep. of 31G10
Cork *county* Ireland,Rep. of 31F10
Cork Harb. Ireland, Rep. of 31G10
Corleone *Sicily* Italy 45D7
Çorlu Turkey 46F4
Corna di Campo *mt* Italy/Switz. 33F2
Corner Brook *Newf.* Canada 78J2
Corner Inlet *Vic.* Australia 97C3
Corning *Calif.* USA 80B6
Corning *Iowa* USA 83L2
Corning *NY* USA 84C1
Cornwall *NY* USA 84D2
Cornwall *Ont.* Canada 79J3
Cornwall *county* *England* UK 26E8
Cornwall,C *England* UK 26C8
Coro Venezuela 92D1
Coroata Brazil 93J4
Corocan *Calif.* USA 80D7
Corocoro Bolivia 92D7
Coroico Bolivia 92D7
Coromandel Coast India 58F6
Coromandel Pen. New Zealand 100F3
Coromandel Ra. *mts* New Zealand 100F3
Corona *Calif.* USA 80E9
Corona *NSW* Australia 97B2
Coronada,B Costa Rica 89C5
Coronado *Calif.* USA 80E9
Coronation G *NW Terr.* Canada 76J3
Coronation I *S Orkneys* Antartica 15T3
Coronel Chile 91B5
Coronel Dorrego Argentina 91D5
Coronel Pringles Argentina 91D5
Coronel Suárez Argentina 91D5
Coronie Surinam 93F2
Coropuna,Mt Peru 92C7
Corowa *NSW* Australia 97C3
Corozal Belize 89B3
Corpen Aiken Argentina 91C7
Corps France 43F4
Corpus Christi *Texas* USA 82T10
Corpus Christi B *Texas* USA 82T10
Corpus Christi,L *Texas* USA 82T9
Corque Bolivia 92D7
Corrales Uruguay 91E4
Corralitos Mexico 88C1
Corraun Ireland,Rep. of 30D6
Corraun Pen. Ireland, Rep. of 30D6
Corregidor *island* Philippines 53H8
Correze *dep.* France 43D4
Correze *dep.* France 43D4
Corrib,L Ireland, Rep. of 31E7
Corrientes Argentina 91E3
Corrientes *prov.* Argentina 91E3
Corrientes,C Columbia 92B2
Corrientes,C Mexico 88C3
Corrientes,R Peru 92B4
Corrigin *W Aus.* Australia 98D6
Corrimal *NSW* Australia 97D2
Corrlentes,C Argentina 91E5
Corrofin Ireland, Rep. of 31E8
Corry *Pa* USA 84B2
Corryong *Vic.* Australia 97C3
Corryvreckan,Str. of *Scotland* UK 29E7
Corse,I Mediteranean Sea 43J6
Corsewall Point *Scotland* UK 29F9
Corsham *England* UK 27K6
Corsica,I = Corse,I
Corsicana *Texas* USA 83K6
Corsier Switzerland 33B2
Cortez Mts *Nev.* USA 80E5
Cortina d'Ampezzo Italy 44D2
Cortland *NY* USA 84C1
Cortona Italy 44C4
Coruche Portugal 40B3
Coruh,R Turkey 62E1
Çorum Turkey 62C1
Corumbá Brazil 93F7
Corunna = La Coruña
Corvallis *Oreg.* USA 80B3
Corvo *island* Açores 68P9
Corwen *Wales* UK 26H3
Corwin *Alaska* USA 87W12
Corydon *Iowa* USA 83M2
Cosalo Mexico 88C3
Coscurita Spain 41E2
Coseguina *vol.* Nicaragua 89B4
Cosenza Italy 45F6
Cosmoledo Is Indian Ocean 71L1
Cosmopolis *Wash.* USA 80B2
Cosne France 42E3
Cosquin Argentina 91D4
Cossonay Switzerland 33B2
Costa Blanca *region* Spain 41F3
Costa Brava *region* Spain 41H2
Costa del Azahar *region* Spain 41G3
Costa del Sol *region* Spain 40D4
Costa Dorado *region* Spain 41G2
Costa Rica *country* Central America 89C4
Costermansville = Bukavu
Costillo Pk *New Mex.* USA 82F4
Cotabato Philippines 53H9
Cotagaita Bolivia 92D8
Cotahuasi Peru 92C7
Côte Blanche B *La* USA 83N8
Côte d'Or *dep.* France 42F3
Côtes du Nord *dep.* France 42B2
Cotonou Benin 68F7
Cotswold Hills *England* UK 27K5
Cottage Grove *Oreg.* USA 80B4
Cottbus E Germany 36F3
Cottel I *Newf.* Canada 78M2
Cottica Surinam 93G3
Cottonwood *Idaho* USA 80E2
Cotulla *Texas* USA 82S9
Coudersport *Pa* USA 84B2
Coudres,I aux *Que.* Canada 79L2
Coulagh B Ireland, Rep. of 31C10
Coulee City *Wash.* USA 80D2
Coulman I Antarctica 15L2
Council *Idaho* USA 80E3
Council Bluffs *Iowa* USA 83L2
Council Grove *Kans.* USA 83K3
Coupar Angus *Scotland* UK 29K6
Coupeville *Wash.* USA 80B1
Courantyne,R Guyana/Surinam 92F3
Courgenay Switzerland 33C1
Couronne C France 43F5
Courrendlin Switzerland 33C1
Courtelary Switzerland 33C1
Courtenay *N Dak.* USA 81H2
Courtmacsherry Ireland, Rep. of 31F10
Courtrai = Kortrijk
Court St Etienne Belgium 32C4
Coutances France 42C2
Couterne France 42C2
Couthuin Belgium 32D4
Couvin Belgium 32C4
Coventry *England* UK 27L4
Covilhã Portugal 40C2
Covington *Ky* USA 79D6
Covington *Tenn.* USA 85C3
Covington *Va* USA 85H2
Cowal,L *NSW* Australia 97C2
Cowangie *Vic.* Australia 97B3
Cowan,L *W Aus.* Australia 98E6
Cowbridge *Wales* UK 26H6
Cowdenbeath *Scotland* UK 29K7
Cowell *S Aus.* Australia 99H6
Cowes *I of Wight* England 27M7
Cowley *England* UK 27M5
Cowlitz,R *Wash.* USA 80B2
Cowra *NSW* Australia 97C2
Cox Bight *Tas.* Australia 97F5
Coxsackie *NY* USA 84E1
Cox's Bazar Bangladesh 59H4
Coxwold *England* UK 25F4
Coyame Mexico 88C2
Coyle,R Argentina 91B8
Coyuca Mexico 88D4
Cozumel Mexico 88F4
Cozumel,I Mexico 88G3
Crab Cr. *Wash.* USA 80D2
Craboon *NSW* Australia 97C2
Cracow = Kraków
Cradle Mt *Tas.* Australia 97F5
Craig *Col.* USA 82E2
Craigavon N Ireland 30L5
Craigue Ireland, Rep. of 31K8
Craigville *Minn.* USA 81L2
Crail *Scotland* UK 29L7
Crailsheim W Germany 36D4
Craiova Romania 46D2
Crampel CAR 69J7
Cranborne *England* UK 27L7
Cranbrook *BC* Canada 76H7
Crandon *Wis.* USA 79B3
Crane *Oreg.* USA 80D4
Crane I = Grues,I aux
Cranleigh *England* UK 27P6
Crans Switzerland 33C2
Cranswick *England* UK 25H5
Cranwell *England* UK 25H6
Crassier Switzerland 33B2
Crater L *Oreg.* USA 80B4
Crater Lake *Oreg.* USA 80B4
Crater Lake Nat. Pk *Oreg.* USA 80B4
Craters of the Moon Nat. Mon. *Idaho* USA 80G4
Crateús Brazil 93J5
Crato Brazil 92E5
Crato Brazil 93K5
Craven Arms *England* UK 26J4
Crawford *Nebr.* USA 82G1
Crawford *Scotland* UK 29J9
Crawley *England* UK 27P6
Crazy Mts *Mont.* USA 81B2
Creag Meagaidh *mt* *Scotland* UK 28G6
Crediton *England* UK 26G7
Cree L *Sask.* Canada 76K5
Cree,R *Sask.* Canada 76K5
Cree,R *Scotland* UK 29H10
Creil Netherlands 32D2
Crema Italy 44B3
Cremona Italy 44B3
Cres *island* Yugoslavia 44E3
Crescent City *Calif.* USA 80A5
Crescent L *Oreg.* USA 80B4
Cresco *Iowa* USA 83M1
Cressy *Vic.* Australia 97B3
Crest *Que.* Canada 79G2
Cresta Switzerland 33E2
Creston *Iowa* USA 83L2
Creswell B *NW Terr.* Canada 77N2
Creswick *Vic.* Australia 97B3
Crete = Kríti
Crete *Nebr.* USA 83K2
Crete, Sea of Greece 47E7
Creuse *dep.* France 42D3
Creuse,R France 42C3
Crewe *England* UK 25D6
Crewkerne *England* UK 26J7
Crianlarich *Scotland* UK 29G7
Criccieth *Wales* UK 26F3
Crickhowell *Wales* UK 26H5
Cricklade *England* UK 27L5
Crieff *Scotland* UK 29J7
Crimea = Krym
Crimmitschau E Germany 36E3
Crinan Ca. *Scotland* UK 29F7
Cripple Creek *Col.* USA 82F3
Crisana *region* Romania 46C1
Cristóbal Panama 89D5
Crna Gora *rep.* Yugoslavia 46B3
Croagh Patrick *mt* Ireland, Rep. Of 30D6
Croajingolong Nat. Pk *Vic.* Australia 97C3
Crockett *Texas* USA 83L7
Crocodile,R South Africa 72M11
Croeira,Serra da *mts* Brazil 93H5
Croker I *N Terr.* Australia 98G2
Cromarty *Scotland* UK 28H4
Cromarty Firth *Scotland* UK 28H4
Cromer *England* UK 27S3
Cromwell New Zealand 100C7
Crook *England* UK 25E3
Crooked I The Bahamas 89E2
Crookhaven Ireland,Rep. of 31D11
Crookston *Minn.* USA 81J2
Crookwell *NSW* Australia 97C2
Croom Ireland, Rep. of 31F8
Croppa Creek *NSW* Australia 97D1
Crosby *England* UK 25B6
Cross Fell *England* UK 25D3
Crosshaven Ireland, Rep. of 31G10
Crossmichael *Scotland* UK 29J10
Crossmolina Ireland, Rep. of 30E5
Crotone Italy 45F6
Crow Agency *Mont.* USA 81D3
Crowdy Hd *NSW* Australia 97D2
Crowes *Vic.* Australia 97B3
Crow Ind. Resn *Mont.* USA 81D3
Crowland *England* UK 25H6
Crowle *England* UK 25G5
Crowley *La* USA 83M7
Crowley,L *Calif.* USA 80D7
Crowsnest P *Alta* Canada 76J7
Croydon *England* UK 27P6
Croydon *Queens.* Australia 99J3
Crozet,Is Indian Ocean 65D9
Crozier,C Antarctica 15L2
Crozier,C *Prince Edward Is* Indian Ocean 65P12
Cruden B *Scotland* UK 28N5
Crumlin N Ireland 30L4
Crump L *Oreg.* USA 80D4
Cruz Alta Argentina 91D4
Cruz Alta Brazil 91F3
Cruz de Eje Argentina 91D4
Cruzeiro do Sul Brazil 92C5
Cruz Grande Chile 91B3
Cruz Grande Mexico 88E4
Crymych *Wales* UK 26E5
Crystal Brook *S Aus.* Australia 97A2
Crystal Falls *Mich.* USA 79B2
Crystal Springs *Miss.* USA 85B5
Cte d'Azur *region* France 43G5
Cuamba Mozambique 71H7
Cuangar Angola 72B3
Cuango Angola 70D6
Cuango,R Angola 70D6
Cuanza,R Angola 70C6
Cuarto,R Argentina 91D4
Cuatro Cienegas Mexico 88D2
Cuba *New Mex.* USA 82E5
Cuba *NY* USA 84B1
Cuba Portugal 40C3
Cuba *country* West Indies 89C2
Cubango,R Angola 72B3
Cuchi Angola 70D7
Cuchillo-Co Argentina 91D5
Cuchillo de Haedo,R Uruguay 91E4
Cuchillo Parado Mexico 88D2
Cuckfield *England* UK 27P6
Cucumbi Angola 70D7
Cúcuta Columbia 92C2
Cudahy *Wis.* USA 79C4
Cuddalore India 58E6
Cuddapah India 58E6
Cuéllar Spain 40D2
Cuenca Ecuador 92B4
Cuenca Spain 41E2
Cuenca *prov.* Spain 41E3
Cuencame Mexico 88D3
Cuernavaca Mexico 88E4
Cuero *Texas* USA 83K8
Cuevo Bolivia 92E8
Cuglieri *Sardinia* Italy 45B5
Cuiabá Brazil 92F5
Cuiaba Brazil 93F7
Cuilcagh *mt* Ireland 30H5
Cuillin Hills *Scotland* UK 28D5
Cuillin Sd *Scotland* UK 28D5
Cuiña,P de *mt* Spain 40C1
Cuita,R Angola 72B3
Cuito Cuanavale Angola 72B3
Cu Lao *island* Vietnam 57D4
Culcairn *NSW* Australia 97C3
Culdesac *Idaho* USA 80E2
Culebra,I Puerto Rico 89F3
Culemborg Netherlands 32D3
Culgaith *England* UK 25C3
Culgoa,R *NSW* Australia 97C1
Culgoa,R Queensland 99K5
Culiacan Mexico 88C3
Cullarin Ra *mts* *NSW* Australia 97C2
Cullaun *mt* Ireland,Rep. of 31G8
Cullen *Scotland* UK 28L4
Cullera Spain 41F3
Cullompton *England* UK 26H7
Cully Switzerland 33B2
Culpeper *Va* USA 85H1
Culverden New Zealand 100E6
Cumaná Venezuela 92E1
Cumaria Peru 92C5
Cumberland *BC* Canada 76F7
Cumberland *Md* USA 84B3
Cumberland *Va* USA 85H2
Cumberland *Wis.* USA 81L3
Cumberland I *Ga* USA 85G5
Cumberland,L *Ky* USA 85E2
Cumberland Mts *Ky/Tenn.* USA 85F2
Cumberland Plat. *Tenn.* USA 85D3
Cumberland,R *Ky* USA 85C2
Cumberland Sd *NW Terr.* Canada 77S3
Cumbernauld *Scotland* UK 29J8
Cumbrae,Great,I *Scotland* UK 29G8
Cumbria *county* *England* UK 25C3
Cumbrian Mts *England* UK 25B3
Cumbum India 58E5
Cumnock *NSW* Australia 97C2
Cumnock *Scotland* UK 29H9
Cunene,R Angola/Namibia 72A3
Cuneo Italy 44A3
Cunnamulla *Queens.* Australia 99K5
Cupar *Scotland* UK 29K7
Cupica,G of Colombia 92B2
Cuprija Yugoslavia 46C2
Cura Venezuela 92D1
Curaçá Brazil 93K5
Curaçoa,I Caribbean Sea 92D1
Curaglia Switzerland 33D2
Curaray,R Peru 92C4
Curban *NSW* Australia 97C2
Curepipe Mauritius 65N12
Curiapo Venezuela 92E2
Curicó Chile 91B4
Curiplaya Colombia 92C3
Curitiba Brazil 91G3
Curitibanos Brazil 91F3
Curlewis *NSW* Australia 97D2
Curnamona *S Aus.* Australia 97A2
Currabubula *NSW* Australia 97D2
Currais Novos Brazil 93K5
Curralinho Brazil 93H4
Currane,L Ireland, Rep. of 31C10
Curranyalpa *NSW* Australia 97B2
Currituck Sd *N Car.* USA 85K2
Currockbilly,Mt *NSW* Australia 97D3
Curtis,I Pacific Ocean 94J11
Curuai,Gde do,L Brazil 93F4
Curua,R Brazil 93G4
Curuca Brazil 93H4
Curuguaty Paraguay 91E2
Curuzú Cuatiá Argentina 91E3
Curvelo Brazil 93J7
Curwensville *Pa* USA 84B2
Cushendall N Ireland 30L3
Cushendun N Ireland 30L3
Cushing *Okla.* USA 83K5
Cusihuiriachic Mexico 88C2
Custer *S Dak.* USA 81F4
Cut Bank *Mont.* USA 81A1
Cuthbert *Ga* USA 85E5
Cutra,L Ireland, Rep. of 31F7
Cuttack India 59G4
Cuxhaven W Germany 36C2
Cuzco Peru 92C6
Cwmbran *Wales* UK 26H5
Cyclådes,Is = Kikládhes,Is
Cygnet *Tas.* Australia 97F5
Cynthiana *Ky* USA 85E1
Cynwyl Elfed *Wales* UK 26F5
Cyprus *country* Medit. Sea 64A2
Cyrenaica *region* Libya 69K3
Czechoslovakia *country* Europe 37F4
Czersk Poland 37H2
Czestochowa Poland 37H3

D

Dab'a Jordan 64E6
Dabakala Ivory Coast 68E7
Dabaro Somalia 71K3
Daba Shan *mts* China 54E6
Dabeiba Colombia 92B2
Dąbie Poland 36F2
Dabie Shan *mts* China 54H7
Dabola Guinea 68C6
Dabrowa Górnicza Poland 37H3
Dabu China 55J10
Dacca Bangladesh 59H4
Dachangtu Shan *island* China 55M7
Dadanawa Guyana 92F3
Dade City *Fla* USA 85L7
Dadri India 60E6
Dadu He *river* China 52D4
Daedalus Reef Red Sea 69N4

Dafang Devli

Dafang China 55C9
Dagana Senegal 68B5
Dagash Sudan 69M5
Dagda Latvia USSR 35M8
Dagenham England UK 27Q5
Daguan China 55B9
Dagupan Philippines 53H7
Dagzê Co lake Tibet China 59G2
Dahei He river China 54F2
Da Hinggan Ling mts China 52H1
Dahlak Arch. Ethiopia 71J1
Daicheng China 54J3
Dai Hai lake China 54G2
Dailekh Nepal 61C1
Daimiel Spain 40E3
Daireaux Argentina 91D5
Dairen = Lüda
Dairut Egypt 69M3
Dai Shan China 55L7
Dai Xian China 54G3
Dajarra Queens. Australia 99H4
Dakar Senegal 68B6
Dakhla Western Sahara 68B4
Dakovica Yugoslavia 46C3
Dal Norway 35D6
Dala Angola 70E7
Dal Alv river Sweden 35G6
Dalandzadagad Mongolia 52D2
Dalaro Sweden 35H7
Dalat Vietnam 57D4
Dalbandin Pakistan 58B3
Dalbeattie Scotland UK 29J10
Dalbosjön,Pen. Sweden 35E7
Dalby Queens. Australia 99L5
Dalby Sweden 35E6
Dalen Netherlands 32E2
Dalen Norway 35B7
Dalgety NSW Australia 97C3
Dalhart Texas USA 82G4
Dalhousie India 60E4
Dalhousie New Br. Canada 78E2
Dali China 52D5
Dali China 54E5
Dalkeith Scotland UK 29K8
Dalkey Ireland, Rep. of 31L7
Dallas Oreg. USA 80B3
Dallas Texas USA 83K6
Dalles, The Oreg. USA 80C3
Dalmacio Velez Argentina 91D4
Dalmally Scotland UK 29G7
Dalmatia region Yugoslavia 44F4
Dalmatovo USSR 49R2
Dalmau India 61C2
Dalmellington Scotland UK 29H9
Daloa Ivory Coast 68D7
Dalry Scotland UK 29G8
Dalry Scotland UK 29H9
Dalrymple Scotland UK 29G9
Dalrymple,Mt Queens. Australia 99K4
Dals Fj. Norway 35A6
Dalsmynni Iceland 34U12
Dalton England UK 25B4
Dalton Ont. Canada 79D1
Daltonganj India 61E3
Dal Verme Falls Ethiopia 71J3
Dalvik Iceland 34V12
Dalwhinnie Scotland UK 28H6
Daly,R N Terr. Australia 98G2
Daly Waters N Terr. Australia 98G2
Dam Surinam 93F3
Daman India 58D4
Damanhur Egypt 69M2
Damar island Indonesia 53J12
Damascus Syria 62D3
Damävand mt Iran 63G2
Damba Angola 70D6
Dämghan Iran 63G2
Daming China 54H4
Damiya Jordan 64D5
Dammastock mt Switzerland 33D2
Damodar,R India 61F4
Damoh India 61B4
Damour Lebanon 64D4
Dampier W Aus. Australia 98D4
Dampier Arch. W Aus. Australia 98D4
Dampier Land W Aus. Australia 98E3
Dampier Str. Indonesia 53K11
Damqawt South Yemen 63G6
Damvant Switzerland 33C1
Dana,Mt Calif. USA 80D7
Da Nang Vietnam 57D3
Danapur India 61E3
Danau Toba lake Sumatra Indon. 53C10
Danbury Conn. USA 84E2
Danby Calif. USA 80F8
Danchang China 54C5
Dandenong Vic. Australia 97C3
Dandong China 54N2
Danforth Maine USA 78E4
Dangan Liedao China 55G12
Danger Point South Africa 72B6
Dangouadougou Ivory Coast 68E6
Dangshan China 54J5
Dangtu China 54K7
Dangyang China 54F7
Danilov USSR 48M2
Daning China 54F4
Dan Jiang river China 54F6
Dank Oman 63H5
Dankaz Ethiopia 71H2
Dankhar India 60F4
Danmark Fj. Greenland 14N1
Dannevirke New Zealand 100G4
Dansville NY USA 84C1
Danube,R Europe 39K4
Danville Ill. USA 83Q2
Danville Ky USA 85E2
Danville Pa USA 84C2
Danville Va USA 85H2
Danyang China 54K7
Danzhai China 55D9
Danzig = Gdańsk
Danzig,G of Poland 37H1
Dao Xian China 55F10
Daqin Dao island China 54L3
Daqu Shan China 54M7
Da,R Vietnam 57C2
Da'ra Syria 64E5
Daraban Kalan Pakistan 60B5
Darān Iran 63G3
Daraw Egypt 69M4
Darb Saudi Arabia 62E6
Darbhanga India 61E2
Darby Mont. USA 80F2
Dardanelles str. Turkey 62B1
Darende Turkey 62D2
Dar-es-Salaam Tanzania 71H6
Darfur,Northern region Sudan 69L5
Darfur,Southern region Sudan 69K6
Dargai Pakistan 60B3
Dargaon India 59F4
Dargaville New Zealand 100E2
Dargo Vic. Australia 97C3
Darhan China 54F2
Darien = Lüda
Darien Ga USA 85G5
Darien region Panama 89D5
Darjeeling India 61G2
Darling Downs upland Queens. Australia 99K5
Darling,R NSW Australia 97B2
Darling Ra mts W Aus. Australia 98D6
Darlington England UK 25E3
Darlington S Car. USA 85H3
Darlington Wis. USA 79A4
Darlington Point NSW Australia 97C2
Darłowo Poland 37G1
Darmstadt W Germany 36C4
Darnah Libya 69K2
Darnah prov. Libya 69K2
Darnick NSW Australia 97B2
Darnley B NW Terr. Canada 76G3
Daroca Spain 41F2
Dart,C Antarctica 15P2
Dartford England UK 27Q6
Dartmoor Vic. Australia 97B3
Dartmoor upland England UK 26G7
Dartmouth England UK 26G8
Dartmouth Harb. No. Sc. Canada 78G4
Dart,R England UK 26G7
Darty Mts Ireland,Rep. of 30G5
Daru island Papua New Guinea 99J1
Daruvar Yugoslavia 44F3
Darwen England UK 25D5
Darweshan Afghanistan 63J3
Darwin N Terr. Australia 98G2
Darwin,B Chile 91A7
Daryabad India 61C2
Daryācheh-ue Urumīyeh lake Iran 62F2
Daryācheh-ye Bakhtegān lake Iran 63G4
Daryacheh ye Maharlu lake Iran 63G4
Daryācheh ye Namak salt flat Iran 63G3
Daryacheh ye Tashk lake Iran 63G4
Dasan Pass China 54D5
Dasara Bangladesh 61H4
Dash-i-Kul lake Tibet China 59F1
Dash,R Pakistan 58B3
Dasht Āb Iran 63H4
Dasht-e-Kavīr salt desert Iran 63G3
Dasht-e Lut salt desert Iran 63H3
Daska Pakistan 60D4
Daspalla India 59F4
Daspar mt Kashmir India 60C2
Dasuya India 60D5
Dataganj India 61B1
Datia India 61B3
Datian China 55J10
Datong China 54G2
Datong He river China 52D3
Dauben See lake Switzerland 33C2
d'Audierne,B Kerguelen 65S12
Daudnagar India 61E3
Daugava,R Latvia USSR 35L8
Daugavpils Latvia USSR 35M9
Daulatabad Afghanistan 63J2
Daulatabad India 58E5
Daulat Yar Afghanistan 63K3
Daule Ecuador 92B4
Daund India 58D5
Daung Kyun island Burma 59J6
Dauphin Man. Canada 76L6
Dauphine prov. France 43F4
Davao Phillipines 53J9
Davao G Philippines 53J9
Dave China 55H7
Davenport Calif. USA 80B7
Davenport Iowa USA 83N2
Davenport Wash. USA 80D2
Davenport Ra mts N Terr. Australia 99G4
Daventry England UK 27M4
David Panama 89C5
David City Nebr. USA 83K2
Davis Calif. USA 80C6
Davis,C Prince Edward Is Indian Ocean 65P12
Davis Mts Texas USA 82F7
Davis Sea Antarctica 15G3
Davis Str. Can./Greenland 14P3
Davos valley Switzerland 33E2
Davos Dorf Switzerland 33E2
Davos Platz Switzerland 33E2
Davr az Zawr Syria 62E2
Dawhat Salwah inlet Qatar/S Arabia 63G4
Dawlish England UK 26H7
Dawna Ra mts Burma 59J5
Dawson Ga USA 85E5
Dawson Minn. USA 81J3
Dawson N Dak. USA 81H2
Dawson Yukon Canada 76D4
Dawson Creek BC Canada 76G5
Dawson,R Queens. Australia 99K5
Dawson Ra mts Yukon Canada 76D4
Dawsonville Ga USA 85E3
Dax France 43C5
Daxian China 54D7
Dayana,R India 59H3
Dayang He river China 54M2
Daya Wan bay China 55H11
Daylesford Vic. Australia 97B3
Dayong China 55F8
Dayton Ohio USA 79D6
Dayton Tenn. USA 85E3
Dayton Wash. USA 80E2
Daytona Beach Fla USA 85G6
Dayu China 55H10
Dayu Ling mts China 55H10
Da'Yunhe river China 54J4
Da Yunhe river China 54K6
Dazhu China 54D7
Dazu China 55C8
De Aar South Africa 72C6
Dead Sea salt lake Israel/Jordan 64D6
Deadwood S Dak. USA 81F3
Deal England UK 27S6
De'an China 55H8
Dean, Forest of England UK 26J5
Dean Funes Argentina 91D4
Dease Arm bay NW Terr. Canada 76G3
Dease Lake BC Canada 76E5
Dease,R BC Canada 76F5
Dease Str. NW Terr. Canada 76K3
Death V Calif. USA 80E7
Deatnul Tana,R Norway 34M2
Deauville France 42C2
Debao China 55D11
Debar Yugoslavia 46C4
Debec New Br. Canada 78E3
Debenham England UK 27S4
Debessy USSR 49L2
Debica Poland 37J3
Deblin Poland 37J3
Debno Poland 36F2
Debo,L Mali 68E5
Debra Markos Ethiopia 71H2
Debrecen Hungary 37J5
Decatur Ala. USA 85D3
Decatur Ga USA 85E4
Decatur Ill. USA 83P3
Decaturville Tenn. USA 85C3
Decazville France 43E4
Deccan upland India 58E6
Deception I Antarctica 15S3
Děčín Czech. 36F3
Decize France 42E3
Decorah Iowa USA 83N1
Deddington England UK 27M5
Dedegach = Alexandroúpolis
Dedemsvaart Netherlands 32E2
Dedham Mass. USA 84F1
Dédougou Upper Volta 68E6
Dedza Malawi 71G7
Deel,R Ireland, Rep. of 31E8
Deep Creek L Md USA 84B3
Deepwater NSW Australia 97D1
Dee,R Scotland UK 28M5
Dee,R Wales UK 26H2
Deer I Maine USA 78D4
Deer Lake Newf. Canada 78K2
Deerlijk Belgium 32B4
Deer Lodge Mont. USA 80G3
Deer River Minn. USA 81L2
Deeth Nev. USA 80F5
Defferrari Argentina 91E5
De Funiak Springs Fla USA 85D5
Degana India 58D3
de Gerlache Str. Antarctica 15S3
Degh,R India 60D4
De Grey,R W Aus. Australia 98D4
De Haan Belgium 32B3
Deh Bid Iran 63G3
Dehdez Iran 63G3
Dehra India 60F5
Dehrūd Iran 63G4
Dehua China 55K10
Deim Zubeir Sudan 69L7
Deinze Belgium 32B4
Deir Abu Said Jordan 64D5
Deir 'Ali Syria 64E4
Deir Atiye Syria 64E3
Deir Hafir Syria 64F1
Deir Shemil Syria 64E2
Dej Romania 37K5
Dejiang China 55E8
De Kalb Ill. USA 83P2
De Kalb Miss. USA 85C4
De Kastri USSR 51R4
De Koven Ky USA 85C2
Delano Calif. USA 80D8
Delano Pk Utah USA 82B3
Delavan Wis. USA 79B4
Delaware Ohio USA 79E5
Delaware state USA 87L4
Delaware B Del./New J USA 84D3
Delaware City Del. USA 84D3
Delaware,R USA 84D2
Delden Netherlands 32E2
Delegate NSW Australia 97C3
Deleitosa Spain 40D3
De Lemmer Netherlands 32D2
Delémont Switzerland 33C1
Delft Netherlands 32C2
Delfzijl Netherlands 32E1
Delgado,C Mozambique 71J7
Delgerhet Mongolia 52F1
Delgo Sudan 69M4
Delhi India 60E6
Delhi NY USA 84D1
Dellenbaugh,Mt Ariz. USA 80G7
Dellys Algeria 68F1
Del Mar Calif. USA 80E9
Delmas South Africa 72P12
Delmenhorst W Germany 36C2
Del Norte Col. USA 82E4
Deloraine Tas. Australia 97F5
Del Rio Texas USA 82H8
Delta Col. USA 82D3
Delta La USA 83N6
Delta Mo USA 83P4
Delta Pa USA 84C3
Delta Utah USA 82B3
Delungra NSW Australia 97D1
Demanda,Sa de la mts Spain 40E1
Demba Zaire 70E6
Demerara = Georgetown
Demerara,R Guyana 92F2
Demgog Tibet China 58E2
Deming New Mex. USA 82E6
Demini,R Brazil 92E3
Demirköy Turkey 46F4
Demmin E Germany 36E2
Demopolis Ala. USA 85D4
Denar Calif. USA 80C7
Dena,R USSR 49M3
Denbigh Wales UK 26H2
Den Burg Netherlands 32C1
Denderleeuw Belgium 32C4
Dendermonde Belgium 32C3
Dendi,Mt Ethiopia 71H3
Denekamp Netherlands 32E2
Dengfeng China 54G5
Dengkou China 54D2
Deng Xian China 54F6
Dengzhou = Penglai
Den Haag = s'Gravenhage
Den Helder Netherlands 32C2
Den Hoorn Netherlands 32C1
Denia Spain 41G3
Deniliquin NSW Australia 97B3
Denio Nev. USA 80D5
Denison Iowa USA 83L1
Denison Texas USA 83K6
Denizli Turkey 62B2
Denman NSW Australia 97D2
Denmark S Car. USA 85G4
Denmark country Europe 35C9
Denmark Str. Greenld/Iceland 14N3
Denny Scotland UK 29J7
Den Oever Netherlands 32C2
Denpasar Bali Indon. 53F12
Dent Blanche mt Switzerland 33C2
Denton Md USA 84D3
Denton Texas USA 83K6
D'Entrecasteaux Is Papua New Guinea 99L1
D'Entrecasteaux,Point W Aus. Australia 98D6
Dents du Midi mts Switzerland 33B2
Denver Col. USA 82F3
Deoband India 60E6
Deobhog India 59F5
Deogarh India 59F4
Deogarh Pk India 61D4
Deoghar India 61F3
Deori India 61B4
Deoria India 61D2
Deosai,Plains of Kashmir India 60D3
De Panne Belgium 32A3
De Pere Wis. USA 79B3
Deposit NY USA 84D1
Depot Harbour Ont. Canada 79F3
Deptford England UK 27L6
Deqing China 55F11
Dera Bugti Pakistan 58C3
Dera Ghazi Khan Pakistan 60B5
Dera Ismail Khan Pakistan 60B5
Dera Nanak India 60D4
Derbent USSR 50F5
Derby England UK 25E7
Derby W Aus. Australia 98E3
Derbyshire county England UK 25E6
Derecske Hungary 37J5
Derg,L Donegal Ireland, Rep. of 30H4
Derg,L Tipperary Ireland, Rep. of 31G7
Derg,R N Ireland 30H4
De Ridder La USA 83M7
De Rijp Netherlands 32C2
Dermott Ark. USA 83N6
Dernberg,C Namibia 72B5
Derravaragh,L Ireland, Rep. of 30J6
Derryveagh Mts Ireland, Rep. of 30G4
Derudeb Sudan 69N5
De Ruyter NY USA 84D1
Derventa Yugoslavia 44F3
Derwent,R Durham,England UK 25D3
Derwent,R Tas. Australia 97F5
Derwent,R Yorks.,England UK 25G5
Derwent Water lake England UK 25B3
Des Arc Ark. USA 83N5
Descalvados Brazil 93F7
Descartes France 42D3
Deschaillons-sur-St Laurent Que. Canada 79K2
Deschutes,R Oreg. USA 80C3
Deseado Argentina 91C7
Deseado,R Argentina 91C7
Desembopue Mexico 88B1
Deseret Utah USA 82B3
Desert V Nev. USA 80D5
Deshambault L Sask. Canada 76K6
Des Moines Iowa USA 83M2
Des Moines,R Iowa USA 83M2
Desna,R Ukrain. USSR 48G6
Desolacion,I Chile 91B8
De Soto Mo USA 83N3
Dessau E Germany 36E3
Dessye Ethiopia 71H2
D'Estrees B S Aus. Australia 97A3
Deta Romania 46C2
Dete Zimbabwe 72D3
Detroit Mich. USA 79E4
Detroit Lakes Minn. USA 81K2
Deurne Netherlands 32D3
Deux Montagnes,L des Que. Canada 79J3
Deux Rivières Ont. Canada 79G2
Deux Sèvres dep. France 42C3
Déva Romania 46D2
Dévávanya Hungary 37J5
Deventer Netherlands 32E2
Deveron R Scotland UK 28L4
Devilsbit Mt Ireland,Rep. of 31H8
Devil's Bridge Wales UK 26G4
Devil's Elbow Scotland UK 28K6
Devils Lake N Dak. USA 81H1
Devils Postpile Nat. Mon. Calif. USA 80D6
Devin Bulgaria 46E4
Devizes England UK 27L6
Devli India 58E3

Devon, Dunblane

Devon county England UK 26G7
Devon I NW Terr. Canada 77O1
Devonport England UK 26F8
Devonport New Zealand 100F3
Devonport Tas. Australia 97F5
De Witt Ark. USA 83N5
Dewsbury England UK 25E5
Dexing China 55J8
Dexter Maine USA 78D4
Dexter Mo USA 83P4
Deyhuk Iran 63H3
Dezful Iran 62F3
Dezhou China 54J4
Dhahran Saudi Arabia 63G4
Dhak Pakistan 60C4
Dhamār Yemen 62E7
Dhampur India 61B1
Dhamra India 59G4
Dhamtari India 58F4
Dhangain India 61E3
Dhankuta Nepal 61F2
Dharampur India 58D4
Dhariya Saudi Arabia 62E5
Dharmjaygarh India 61D4
Dharmkot India 60D5
Dharmsala India 60E4
Dharwar India 58E5
Dharwas India 60E4
Dhasan,R India 61B3
Dhaulagiri,Mt Nepal 61D1
Dhayd UAE 63H4
Dhebar L India 58D4
Dhiban Jordan 64D6
Dhidhimótikhon Greece 46F4
Dhikti Óri mt Kríti Greece 47E7
Dhionisiadhes,Is = Yianisadhes,Is
Dhirang Dzong India 59H3
Dhofar region Oman 63G6
Dholera India 58D4
Dholpur India 61A2
Dhubri India 61H2
Dhuld South Yemen 62F6
Dhule India 58D4
Dhulian India 61F3
Dhulian Pakistan 60C4
Dhurwai India 61B3
Diablerets mt Switzerland 33C2
Día I Kríti Greece 47E7
Diamante Argentina 91D4
Diamantina Brazil 93F6
Diamantina Brazil 93J7
Diamantina Queens. Australia 99J4
Diamond Harbour India 61G4
Diamond,I Burma 59H5
Diamond L Oreg. USA 80B4
Diamond Mts Nev. USA 80F6
Diamond Pk Oreg. USA 80B4
Diba UAE 63H4
Dibbéla Niger 69H5
Dibdibah region Saudi Arabia 62F4
Dibrugarh India 59H3
Dickinson N Dak. USA 81F2
Dickson Tenn. USA 85D2
Die France 43F4
Diebougou Upper Volta 68E6
Diefenbaker L Sask. Canada 76K6
Diego Suarez = Antsiranana
Dielsdorf Switzerland 33D1
Dien Bien Phu Vietnam 57C2
Diepoldsau Switzerland 33E1
Dieppe France 42D2
Diessenhofen Switzerland 33D1
Diest Belgium 32D4
Dietikon Switzerland 33D1
Diever Netherlands 32E2
Difuntos,L Uruguay 91F4
Dig India 60E7
Digby No. Sc. Canada 78F4
Digby,C Kerguelen 65S12
Digby Neck island No. Sc. Canada 78E4
Digne France 43G4
Digoin France 42E3
Diguel,R Irian Jaya Indon. 53L12
Dijon France 42F3
Dikakah region Saudi Arabia 63G6
Dikgatlhong South Africa 72C5
Diksmuide Belgium 32A3
Dikwa Nigeria 69H6
Dilam Saudi Arabia 62F5
Dili Timor Indon. 53J12
Di Linh Vietnam 57D4
Dilling Sudan 69L6
Dillon Mont. USA 80G3
Dilolo Zaire 70E7
Dilsen Belgium 32D3
Dimashq = Damascus
Dimbelenge Zaire 70E6
Dimbokro Ivory Coast 68E7
Dimboola Vic. Australia 97B3
Dimitrovgrad Bulgaria 46E3
Dimitrovgrad Yugoslavia 46D3
Dimitrovo = Pernik
Dimla Bangladesh 61G2
Dimona Israel 64D6
Dimotika = Dhidhimótikhon
Dinagat island Philippines 53J8
Dinajpur Bangladesh 61G3
Dinan France 42B2
Dinanagar India 60D4
Dinant Belgium 32C4
Dinar Turkey 62C2
Dinard France 42B2
Dinarske Planina mts Yugoslavia 44F3
Dinas Mawddwy Wales UK 26G3
Dindigul India 58E6
Dindori India 61C4
Ding'an China 55E13
Dingbian China 54D4
Dinghai China 55M7
Dingle Ireland, Rep. of 31C9
Dingle B Ireland,Rep. of 31C9
Dingnan China 55H10
Dinguiraye Guinea 68C6
Dingwall Scotland UK 28H4
Dingxi China 54C5
Ding Xian China 54H3
Dingxiang China 54G3
Dingxing China 54H3
Dingyuan China 54J6
Dingzi Gang China 54L4
Dino Switzerland 33D2
Dinosaur Nat. Mon. Col. USA 82D2
Dinteloord Netherlands 32C3
Diourbel Senegal 68B6
Dipalpur Pakistan 60C5
Dir Pakistan 60B3
Direction,C Queens. Australia 99J2
Diredawe Ethiopia 71J3
Diriamba Nicaragua 89B4
Dirico Angola 72C3
Dirk Hartogs I W Aus. Australia 98C5
Dirksland Netherlands 32C3
Dirranbandi Queens. Australia 99K5
Disa India 58D4
Disappointment,C Wash. USA 80A2
Disappointment,Is Tuamotu Arch. 95M9
Disappointment,L W Aus. Australia 98E4
Disaster B NSW Australia 97C3
Disaster Pk Nev. USA 80D4
Discovery B Vic. Australia 97B3
Discovery Reef Paracel Is China 57E3
Disentis/Mustér Switzerland 33D2
Disko B Greenland 14P3
Disko I Greenland 14P3
Disna Belorus. USSR 48F4
Dison Belgium 32D4
Distington England UK 25A3
Diu India 58D4
Diver Ont. Canada 79G2
Divide Mont. USA 80G3
Divrigi Turkey 62D2
Diwangiri India 59H3
Dix Que. Canada 79H1
Dixmude = Diksmuide
Dixon Calif. USA 80C6
Dixon Ill. USA 83P2
Dixon Ky USA 85D2
Dixon Mont. USA 80F2
Dixon Entrance sd BC Canada 76E6
Diyarbakir Turkey 62E2
Djado Niger 69H4
Djado,Plat. de Niger 69H4
Djambala Congo 70C5
Djelfa Algeria 68F2
Djeneien Tunisia 69H2
Djerba,I Tunisia 69H2
Djibo Upper Volta 68E6
Djibouti Djibouti 71J2
Djibouti country Africa 71J2
Djidjelh Algeria 68G1
Djolu Zaire 70E4
Djougou Benin 68F7
Djursholm Sweden 35H7
Dneprodzerzhinsk Ukrain. USSR 48J7
Dnepropetrovsk Ukrain. USSR 48J7
Dnepr,R Ukrain. USSR 48G6
Dnester,R Ukrain. USSR 48D7
Doaba Pakistan 60B4
Doaktown New Br. Canada 78E3
Dobbyn Queens. Australia 99H3
Dobele Latvia USSR 35K8
Doberan E Germany 36D1
Dobra Czech. 37J4
Dobřany Czech. 36E4
Dobrich = Tolbukhin.
Dobruja Romania 46G2
Dobryanka USSR 49N1
Dobrzyń Poland 37H2
Doce,Rio river Brazil 93J7
Doctor Arroyo Mexico 88D3
Dodecanese = Sporadhes
Dodge City Kans. USA 83H4
Dodgeville Wis. USA 79A4
Dodman Pt England UK 26E8
Dodoma Tanzania 71H6
Dodson Mont. USA 81C1
Doegal Point Ireland, Rep. of 31D8
Doel Belgium 32C3
Doesburg Netherlands 32E2
Doetinchem Netherlands 32E3
Dogai Coring lake Tibet China 59G2
Dogger Bank North Sea 22J5
Dogwbayazit Turkey 62E2
Doha Qatar 63G4
Dohad India 58D4
Doka Saudi Arabia 62E6
Dokkum Netherlands 32E1
Dol France 42C2
Do,L Mali 68E5
Dolbeau Que. Canada 78B2
Dôle France 42F3
Dolent,Mt Switzerland 33B3
Dolgellau Wales UK 26G3
Dolinskoya USSR 48H7
Dollar Scotland UK 29J7
Dolo Ethiopia 71J4
Dolonnur = Duolun
Dolores Argentina 91E5
Dolores Mexico 88B2
Dolores Spain 41F3
Dolphin,C Falkland Is 91E8
Dom mt Irian Jaya Indon. 53L11
Dom mt Switzerland 33C2
Domariaganj India 61D2
Dombås Norway 34C5
Dombresson Switzerland 33B1
Domburg Netherlands 32B3
Dome Rock Mts Ariz. USA 80F9
Domfront France 42C2
Dominica country Windward Is 89G3
Dominican Republic country West Indies 89E3
Dömitz E Germany 36D2
Domleschg valley Switzerland 33E2
Domodossola Italy 44B2
Dom Pedrito Brazil 91F4
Domuyo,Mt Argentina 91B5
Domvraina Greece 47D5
Dona di Piave Italy 44D3
Donaghadee N Ireland 30M4
Donald Vic. Australia 97B3
Donaldson La USA 83N7
Donard Ireland,Rep. of 31K7
Donau = Danube
Donaueschingen W Germany 36C5
Donau,R Europe 36E4
Donauwörth W Germany 36D4
Don Benito Spain 40D3
Doncaster England UK 25F5
Dondo Angola 70C6
Dondra Hd Sri Lanka 58F7
Donegal Ireland, Rep. of 30G4
Donegal county Ireland,Rep. of 30G4
Donegal B Ireland, Rep. of 30F4
Done,R Laos 57D3
Doneraile Ireland,Rep. of 31F9
Donetsk Ukrain. USSR 48K8
Donets,R USSR 49E6
Donga Nigeria 69H7
Dong'an China 55F9
Dongara W Aus. Australia 98C5
Dongchuan China 55B9
Dongfang China 55E13
Donggala Celebes Indon. 53G11
Dongguan China 55G11
Dongguang China 54J4
Donghai Dao island China 55F12
Dong Hoi Vietnam 57D3
Dong Jiang river China 55H11
Donglan China 55D10
Dongming China 54H5
Dongo Angola 70D7
Dongola Sudan 69M5
Dongping China 54J5
Dongshan China 55J11
Dongsha Qundao island China 55J12
Dongsheng China 54E3
Dongtai China 54L6
Dongting Hu lake China 55G8
Dongxiang China 55J8
Dongxing China 55D12
Dongyang China 55L8
Dongzhi China 55J7
Donington England UK 25H6
Doniphan Mo USA 83N4
Donji Miholjac Yugoslavia 44G3
Dønna Norway 34E3
Don,R England UK 25F5
Don,R Scotland UK 28L5
Don,R USSR 50F5
Doon,L Scotland UK 29H9
Doon,R Scotland UK 29H9
Doorn Netherlands 32D2
Doornik = Tournai
Dora,L W Aus. Australia 98E4
Doranda India 61E4
Dorchester England UK 26K7
Dorchester New Br. Canada 78F4
Dorchester,C NW Terr. Canada 77Q3
Dordogne dep. France 43D4
Dordogne,R France 43C4
Dordrecht Netherlands 32C3
Dore L Sask. Canada 76K6
Dore,Mt France 42E4
Dores de Indaia Brazil 93H7
Dori Upper Volta 68E6
Dorking England UK 27P6
Dorking Gap England UK 27P6
Dornie Scotland UK 28F5
Dornoch Scotland UK 28H4
Dornoch Firth Scotland UK 28H4
Dorokhsh Iran 63H3
Dorotea Sweden 34G4
Dorrigo NSW Australia 97D2
Dorset county England UK 26K7
Dortmund W Germany 36B3
Doruma Zaire 70F4
Dos Bahias,C Argentina 91C6
Doshi Afghanistan 63K2
Dospat Bulgaria 46E4
Dos Rios Calif. USA 80B6
Dosso Cameroun 68F6
Dossor Kazakh. USSR 50G5
Dothan Ala. USA 85E5
Doti India 61C2
Douai France 42E1
Douala Cameroun 69G8
Douarnenez France 42A2
Doubs dep. France 42G3
Doubs,R France/Switz. 33C1
Doubtless B New Zealand 100E2
Doucados,Serra dos mts Brazil 93G8
Douglas Ariz. USA 82D7
Douglas Ga USA 85F5
Douglas Isle of Man UK 25L9
Douglas Scotland UK 29J8
Douglas South Africa 72C5
Douglas Wyo. USA 81E4
Douglastown Que. Canada 78F2
Douglasville Ga USA 85E4
Doullens France 42E1
Doulun China 54J1
Doulus Hd Ireland, Rep. of 31C9
Doume Cameroun 69H8
Doune Scotland UK 29H7
Dounreay Scotland UK 28J2
Dountza Mali 68E6
Douobé Liberia 68D7
Douro Port./Spain 40B2
Douro Litoral region Portugal 40B2
Douro,R Port./Spain 40B2
Dover Del. USA 84D3
Dover England UK 27S6
Dover New H USA 84F1
Dover New J USA 84D2
Dover Ohio USA 79F5
Dover Tas. Australia 97F5
Dover Tenn. USA 85D2
Dover Foxcroft Maine USA 78D4
Dover,Str. of England/France 42D1
Dovrefjell mts Norway 34C5
Dowa Malawi 71G7
Dow,L Botswana 72C4
Down county N Ireland 30L5
Downey Idaho USA 80G4
Downham Market England UK 27Q3
Downieville Calif. USA 80C6
Downpatrick N Ireland 30M5
Downpatrick Hd Ireland, Rep. of 30E5
Doyle Calif. USA 80C5
Doyles Newf. Canada 78J3
Doylestown Pa USA 84D2
Drachten Netherlands 32E1
Drăgășani Romania 46E2
Draguignan France 43G5
Drain Oreg. USA 80B4
Drake NSW Australia 97D1
Drakensberg,Mts South Africa 72D5
Drake Str. Antarctica 15S4
Dráma Greece 46E4
Drammen Norway 35D7
Drance,R Switzerland 33C2
Dranov I Romania 46G2
Dras Kashmir India 60D3
Drawsko Poland 37F2
Drayton N Dak. USA 81J1
Drazinda Pakistan 60A5
Drem Scotland UK 29L7
Drenthe prov. Netherlands 32E2
Dresden E Germany 36E3
Dresden Ont. Canada 79E4
Dreux France 42D2
Drews Res. Oreg. USA 80C4
Drimoleague Ireland, Rep. of 31E10
Drina,R Yugoslavia 46B3
Drin G Albania 46B4
Drøbak Norway 35D7
Drogheda Ireland, Rep. of 30L6
Drogheda B Ireland,Rep. of 30L6
Droitwich England UK 27K4
Dromara N Ireland UK 30M5
Drôme dep. France 43F4
Drôme,R France 43F4
Dromod Ireland, Rep. of 30H6
Dromore Down N Ireland 30L5
Dromore Tyrone N Ireland 30J4
Dromore West Ireland, Rep. of 30F5
Drongen Belgium 32B3
Dronning Maud Land Antarctica 15C2
Drua Vanua Levu Fiji 94A24
Drumheller Alta Canada 76J6
Drum Hills upland Ireland, Rep. of 31H9
Drumlish Ireland,Rep. of 30H6
Drummond Mont. USA 80G2
Drummond I Mich. USA 79D3
Drummondville Que. Canada 79K3
Drummore Scotland UK 29G10
Drumnadrochit Scotland UK 28H5
Drumochter P Scotland UK 29H6
Drumshanbo Ireland, Rep. of 30G5
Drunen Netherlands 32D3
Druten Netherlands 32D3
Dryden Ont. Canada 77N7
Drygalski I Antarctica 15G3
Drymen Scotland UK 29H7
Dschang Cameroun 69H7
Dtangdj glacier Iceland 34T11
Ḑuba Saudi Arabia 62D4
Ḑubai UAE 63H4
Dubawnt L NW Terr. Canada 76L4
Dubbo NSW Australia 97C2
Dublin Ga USA 85F4
Dublin Ireland, Rep. of 31L7
Dublin Texas USA 83J6
Dublin county Ireland,Rep. of 31L7
Dublon island Truk Is 94A16
Dubno Ukrain. USSR 48D6
Dubois Idaho USA 80G3
Du Bois Pa USA 84B2
Dubossary USSR 48F8
Dubreka Guinea 68C7
Dubrovnik Yugoslavia 46B3
Dubuque Iowa USA 83N1
Dubyasa,R Litov USSR 35K9
Duc Co Vietnam 57D4
Duchcov Czech. 36E3
Duchesne Utah USA 82C2
Ducie,I Pacific Ocean 95P10
Duck Is Ont. Canada 79E3
Duck V Nev. USA 80F6
Duck Valley Ind. Resn Idaho USA 80E4
Dudhi India 61D3
Dudinka USSR 50K3
Dudley England UK 25D7
Dudna,R India 58E5
Duehang China 55J8
Duero,R Spain 40D2
Duffel Belgium 32C3
Dufftown Scotland UK 28K5
Dufour Spitze mt Italy/Switz. 33C3
Dufur Oreg. USA 80C3
Dugi Otok island Yugoslavia 44E3
Dugway V Utah USA 82B3
Duifken Point Queens. Australia 99J2
Duisburg W Germany 36B3
Dujana India 60E6
Dujiang China 55D10
Dukambia Ethiopia 71H2
Duke of Gloucester Group,Is Tuamotu Arch. 95M10
Duke of York Arch NW Terr. Canada 76J3
Duk Faiwil Sudan 69M7
Dulan China 52C3
Dulce,G Costa Rica 89C5
Duluth Minn. USA 81L2
Dulverton England UK 26G6
Duma Syria 64E4
Dumas Ark. USA 83N6
Dumas Texas USA 82H5
Dumbarton Scotland UK 29G8
Dumbier mt Czech. 37H4
Dum-Dum India 61G4
Dumeir Syria 64E4
Dumfries Scotland UK 29J9
Dumfries & Galloway region Scotland UK 29H9
Dumka India 61F3
Dumoine,L Que. Canada 79H2
Dumraon India 61E3
Dumyât Egypt 69M2
Duna = Danube
Dunărea = Danube
Dunaújváros Hungary 37H5
Dunbar Scotland UK 29L7
Dunblane Scotland UK 29J7

Dunboyne, Emangulova

Dunboyne Ireland, Rep. of 31L7
Duncan Okla. USA 83J5
Duncan I Paracel Is China 57E3
Duncannon Ireland, Rep. of 31K9
Duncan Pass Andaman Is India 59H6
Duncansby Hd Scotland UK 28K2
Dundalk Ireland, Rep. of 30L5
Dundalk B Ireland,Rep. of 30L6
Dundas Ont. Canada 79G4
Dundas Str. N Terr. Australia 98G2
Dún Dealgan = Dundalk
Dundee Scotland UK 29L7
Dundee South Africa 72E5
Dundee I Antarctica 15T3
Dundrum N Ireland 30M5
Dundrum B N Ireland UK 30M5
Dundwa Ra mts Nepal 61D2
Dunedin New Zealand 100D7
Dunedoo NSW Australia 97C2
Dunfanaghy Ireland, Rep. of 30G3
Dunfermline Scotland UK 29K7
Dungannon N Ireland 30K4
Dungarvan Ireland, Rep. of 31H9
Dungbure Ra mts Tibet China 59F1
Dungeness cape England UK 27R7
Dungiven N Ireland 30K4
Dungloe Ireland, Rep. of 30G4
Dungog NSW Australia 97D2
Dungu Zaire 71F4
Dunhuang China 52B2
Dunkeld Scotland UK 29J6
Dunkerque France 42E1
Dunkery Beacon upland England UK 26G6
Dunkirk = Dunkerque
Dunkirk NY USA 84B1
Dunkur Ethiopia 71H2
Dunkwa Ghana 68E7
Dún Laoghaire Ireland, Rep. of 31L7
Dunlap Iowa USA 83L2
Dunlavin Ireland, Rep. of 31K7
Dunleer Ireland, Rep. of 30L6
Dunlop Scotland UK 29G8
Dunmanus B Ireland, Rep. of 31D10
Dunmanway Ireland, Rep. of 31E10
Dunmara N Terr. Australia 99G3
Dunmore Ireland, Rep. of 30F6
Dunn N Car. USA 85H3
Dunnet B Scotland UK 28K2
Dunnet Hd Scotland UK 28K2
Dunnottar South Africa 72N12
Dunolly Vic. Australia 97B3
Dunoon Scotland UK 29G8
Duns Scotland UK 29M8
Dunsmuir Calif. USA 80B5
Dunstable England UK 27N5
Dunstan Mts New Zealand 100C7
Dunvegan Scotland UK 28C5
Dunvegan,L Scotland UK 28C4
Duque de York,I Chile 91A8
Du Quoin Ill. USA 83P3
Dura Jordan 64D6
Durance France 43F5
Durango Col. USA 82E4
Durango Mexico 88D3
Durango state Mexico 88D3
Durant Miss. USA 85C4
Durant Okla. USA 83K6
Durazno Uruguay 91E4
Durazzo = Durrës
Durban South Africa 72E5
Durbe Latvia USSR 35J8
Durbuy Belgium 32D4
Durdevac Yugoslavia 44F2
Durdureh Somalia 71K2
Dureikish Syria 64E3
Düren W Germany 36B3
Durgapur India 61F4
Durham England UK 25E3
Durham N Car. USA 85H2
Durham Ont. Canada 79F3
Durham county England UK 25E3
Durness Scotland UK 28G2
Durness,Kyle of inlet Scotland UK 28G2
Durrës Albania 46B4
Durrow Ireland, Rep. of 31J8
Dursey I Ireland, Rep. of 31C10
Dursley England UK 26K5
Duruh Iran 63J3
D'Urville I New Zealand 100E5
Dushan China 55D10
Dushanbe Tadzhik. USSR 50H6
Dushikou China 54H2
Dushore Pa USA 84C2
Dusky Sd New Zealand 100B7
Düsseldorf W Germany 36B3
Dussen Netherlands 32C3
Düssi mt Switzerland 33D2
Duszniki Zdrój Poland 37G3
Dutch Flat Calif. USA 80C6
Dutch Guiana = Suriname
Dutch Harb. Aleutian Is USA 87W13
Dutton,Mt Utah USA 82B3
Duvan USSR 49N3
Duwadami Saudi Arabia 62E5
Duwwâh Oman 63H5
Duyun China 55D9
Dwingelo Netherlands 32E2
Dyatkovo USSR 48J5
Dyce Scotland UK 28M5
Dyer,C NW Terr. Canada 77T3
Dyersburg Tenn. USA 85C2
Dyfed county Wales UK 26F5
Dyfi,R Wales UK 26G3
Dyle,R Belgium 32C4
Dymer USSR 48G6
Dyurtyuli USSR 49M3
Dzamin Üüd Mongolia 52F2
Dzep Yugoslavia 46D3
Dzerzhinsk Belorus. USSR 48E5
Dzerzhinsk USSR 49F2
Dzhalal Abad Kirgiz. USSR 50J5
Dzhalinda USSR 51P4
Dzhambul Kazakh. USSR 50J5
Dzhetygara Kazakh. USSR 50H4
Dzhezkazgan Kazakh. USSR 50H5
Dzhungarskiy Ala-Tau mt Kazakh. USSR 50J5
Dzialdowo Poland 37J2
Dzierzoniow Poland 37G3
Dzioua Algeria 68G2

E

Eagle Alaska USA 87Y12
Eagle Col. USA 82E3
Eagle Grove Iowa USA 83M1
Eaglehawk Vic. Australia 97B3
Eagle L Calif. USA 80C5
Eagle L Maine USA 78D3
Eagle Lake Maine USA 78D3
Eagle Pass Texas USA 82R9
Eagle Pk Calif. USA 80C5
Eagle Pk Idaho/Mont. USA 80F2
Eagle River Wis. USA 79B3
Ealing England UK 27P5
Eardisley England UK 26J4
Earith England UK 27Q4
Earlston Scotland UK 29L8
Earlville NY USA 84D1
Earn,L Scotland UK 29H7
Earn,R Scotland UK 29J7
Easington England UK 25F3
Easingwold England UK 25F4
East Aurora NY USA 84B1
Eastbourne England UK 27Q7
Eastbourne New Zealand 100F5
East Coast stat. area. New Zealand 100G4
East Dereham England UK 27R3
Easter,I Pacific Ocean 95R10
Eastern B Md USA 84C3
East Germany country Europe 36E2
East Grand Forks Minn. USA 81J2
East Helena Mont. USA 80H2
East Kilbride Scotland UK 29H8
Eastland Texas USA 83J6
East Linton Scotland UK 29L8
East Liverpool Ohio USA 79F5
East London South Africa 72D6
Eastmain,R Que. Canada 77Q6
Eastman Ga USA 85F4
Easton Md USA 84C3
Easton Pa USA 84D2
Eastport Maine USA 78E4
East Retford England UK 25G6
East St Louis Ill. USA 83N3
East Siberian Sea USSR 51T2
East Sioux Falls S Dak. USA 81J4
East Sussex county England UK 27Q7
Eastville Va USA 85J2
Eaton Rapids Mich. USA 79D4
Eau Claire Wis. USA 81M3
Eau Claire,L Que. Canada 77R5
Ebadon I Kwajalein Is 94A17
Ebbw Vale Wales UK 26H5
Ebensburg Pa USA 84B2
Eberswalde E Germany 36E2
Ebeye I Kwajalein Is 94A17
Ebnat Switzerland 33E1
Eboli Italy 45E5
Ebolowa Cameroun 69H8
Ebro,R Spain 41F1
Ecaussines Belgium 32C4
Ecclefechan Scotland UK 29K9
Eccles England UK 25D6
Echallens Switzerland 33B2
Echo Bay NW Terr. Canada 76H3
Echo Cliffs Ariz. USA 82C4
Echo,L Tas. Australia 97F5
Echt Netherlands 32D3
Echten Netherlands 32E2
Echternach Luxembourg 36B4
Echuca Vic. Australia 97B3
Eck,Loch Scotland UK 29F7
Eclépens Switzerland 33B2
Ecuador country S America 92B4
Edam Netherlands 32D2
Eday,I Orkney Scotland 28L1
Ed Damer Sudan 69M5
Ed Debba Sudan 69M5
Eddrachillis B Scotland UK 28F3
Ed Dueim Sudan 69M6
Ede Netherlands 32D2
Edebäck Sweden 35E6
Eden NSW Australia 97C3
Eden NY USA 84B1
Edenburg South Africa 72D5
Edendale New Zealand 100C8
Edenderry Ireland, Rep. of 31J7
Edenhope Vic. Australia 97B3
Eden,R England UK 25C3
Edenton N Car. USA 85J2
Edeowie S Aus. Australia 97A2
Edge Hill England UK 27L4
Edgeley N Dak. USA 81H2
Edgemont S Dak. USA 81F4
Edgeøya,I Arctic Ocean 50D2
Edgerton Wis. USA 79B4
Edgeworthstown Ireland, Rep. of 30H6
Edhessa Greece 47D4
Edina Mo USA 83M2
Edinburg Texas USA 82S10
Edinburgh Scotland UK 29K8
Edirne Turkey 62B1
Edithburgh S Aus. Australia 97A3
Edith Cavell,Mt Alta Canada 76H6
Edmonds Wash. USA 80B1
Edmonton Alta Canada 76J6
Edmundston New Br. Canada 78D3
Edom region Jordan 64D7
Edremit Turkey 62B2
Edrengiyn Nuruu region Mongolia 52C2
Edsele Sweden 34G5
Edson Alta Canada 76H6
Eduni,Mt NW Terr. Canada 76F4
Edwardesabad = Bannu
Edward,L Zaire/Uganda 71F5
Edward,R NSW Australia 97B3
Edwards Calif. USA 80E8
Edwards NY USA 79J3
Edwards Creek V Nev. USA 80E6
Edwards Plat. Texas USA 82H7
Edwardsville Ill. USA 83P3
Edward VII Land Antarctica 15N2
Eeklo Belgium 32B3
Eelde Netherlands 32E1
Eel,R Calif. USA 80B5
Eernegem Belgium 32B3
Efate,I Vanuatu 94G9
Eferding Austria 36E4
Effingham Ill. USA 83P3
Effretikon Switzerland 33D1
Egadi,Is Sicily Italy 45D7
Egan S Dak. USA 81J3
Egaña Argentina 91E5
Egan Ra. Nev. USA 80F6
Eganville Ont. Canada 79H3
Eger = Cheb
Eger Hungary 37J5
Egersund Norway 35B7
Eggenfelden W Germany 36E4
Egg,I = Lehua,I
Eggiwil Switzerland 33C2
Eghezée Belgium 32C4
Egilsay island Orkney Scotland 28L1
Eglinton,C NW Terr. Canada 77S2
Eglisau Switzerland 33D1
Egmont B Pr. Ed. I. Canada 78F3
Egmont,C New Zealand 100E4
Egmont,Mt New Zealand 100F4
Egremont England UK 25A4
Egridir Turkey 62C2
Egton England UK 25G3
Egypt country Africa 69L3
Ehime prefecture Japan 56C8
Ehrenberg Calif. USA 80F9
Eibergen Netherlands 32E2
Eichstätt W Germany 36D4
Eidsvoll Norway 35D6
Eifel region W Germany 36B3
Eiger mt Switzerland 33C2
Eigg,I Scotland UK 29D6
Eight Degree Chan. Arabian Sea 58D7
Eights Coast Antarctica 15R2
Eighty Mile Beach W Aus. Australia 98D3
Eildon,L Vic. Australia 97C3
Eiling China 55G9
Eil,L Scotland UK 29F6
Einbeck W Germany 36C3
Eindhoven Netherlands 32D3
Einsiedeln Switzerland 33D1
Eire = Ireland,Rep. of
Eisden Netherlands 32D4
Eisenach E Germany 36D3
Eisenerz Austria 36F5
Eisleben E Germany 36D3
Eivissa Ibiza Spain 41G3
Ejde Faerøerne 34Z14
Ejutla Mexico 88E4
Eke Belgium 32B4
Ekenäs = Tammisaari
Ekeren Belgium 32C3
Ekhinádhes Is Greece 47C5
Eksjö Sweden 35F8
Ekträsk Sweden 34H4
Ekwan,R Ont. Canada 77P6
El Aabde Lebanon 64D3
Elafónisi Chan. Greece 47D6
Élafos island Greece 47D6
El Aina Jordan 64D7
El Alamein Egypt 69L2
El Aricha Algeria 68E2
El Arish Egypt 69M2
El Asnam Algeria 68F1
Elasson Greece 47D5
Elat Israel 64C8
Elâzig Turkey 62D2
Elba island Italy 44C4
El Bab Syria 64F1
El Bahluliye Syria 64D2
El Banco Colombia 92C2
El Barco de Avila Spain 40D2
Elbasan Albania 46C4
El Baul Venezuela 92D2
El Bayadh Algeria 68F2
Elbe,R Germany 36D2
Elbert,Mt Col. USA 82E3
Elbeuf France 42D2
Elbing = Elblag
El-Birka Saudi Arabia 62E5
Elbistan Turkey 62D2
Elblag Poland 37H1
El Br'aij Syria 64E3
Elbrus mt USSR 50F5
El Buheyrat region Sudan 69L7
Elburg Netherlands 32D2
Elburz Mts Iran 63G2
El Callao Venezuela 92E2
El Centro Calif. USA 80F9
Elche Spain 41F3
El Chorro Argentina 91D2
El Cobre Cuba 89D2
El Cuy Argentina 91C5
El Dab Somalia 71K3
El Diviso Colombia 92B3
El Donfar Somalia 71K2
Eldora Iowa USA 83M1
El Dorado Ark. USA 83M6
El Dorado Kans. USA 83K4
El Dorado Mexico 88C3
El Dorado Venezuela 92E2
Eldorado Mts Nev. USA 80F8
Eldoret Kenya 71H4
El Encanto Colombia 92C4
Elephant Butte Res. New Mex. USA 82E6
Elephant I Antarctica 15T4
Eleşkirt Turkey 62E2
Eleuthera I The Bahamas 89D1
Elewijt Belgium 32C4
El Faiyum Egypt 69M3
El Fasher Sudan 69L6
El Ferrol Spain 40B1
El Fuerte Mexico 88C2
El Fuwara Saudi Arabia 62E4
El Geteina Sudan 69M6
El Gezra Sudan 69M6
Elgg Switzerland 33D1
Elghena Ethiopia 71H1
El Ghobbe Saudi Arabia 62D5
Elgin Ill. USA 83P1
Elgin New Br. Canada 78F4
Elgin Oreg. USA 80E3
Elgin Scotland UK 28K4
El Giof = Al Jawf
El Giza Egypt 69M2
El Golea Algeria 68F2
Elgon,Mt Uganda 71G4
El Hadjiri Algeria 68G2
El Hamad des. Jordan/S Arabia 62D3
El Hamra Syria 64F2
El Hamrat Syria 64E3
El Hanurre Somalia 71K3
El Harrach Algeria 68F1
El-Hayath Saudi Arabia 62E4
El Hijane Syria 64E4
El Hilla Egypt 69M3
El Hilla Sudan 69L6
Elie Scotland UK 29L7
Elisabethville = Lubumbashi
Elizabeth New J USA 84D2
Elizabeth S Aus. Australia 97A2
Elizabeth W Va USA 79F6
Elizabeth B Namibia 72B5
Elizabeth City N Car. USA 85J2
Elizabeth Is Mass. USA 84F2
Elizabethtown Ky USA 85E2
Elizondo Spain 41F1
El Jadida Morocco 68D2
El Jafr Jordan 64E7
El Jawf Libya 69K4
Elk Calif. USA 80B6
Elk Poland 37K2
Elk City Okla. USA 83J5
El Kef Tunisia 69G1
El Khandaq Sudan 69M5
El Kharga Egypt 69M3
Elkhart Ind. USA 79D5
Elkhead Mts Col. USA 82E2
Elkhorn,Mt Idaho USA 82B1
Elkins W Va USA 79G6
Elk Mts New Mex. USA 82D6
Elko Nev. USA 80F5
Elk Point S Dak. USA 81J4
Elk River Minn. USA 81L3
Elkton Md USA 84D3
El Lādhiqīya = Latakia
Ellas region Greece 47D5
Ellef Ringnes I NW Terr. Canada 76L1
Ellenabad India 60D6
Ellendale N Dak. USA 81H2
Ellen,Mt Utah USA 82C3
Ellensburg Wash. USA 80C2
Eller I Kwajalein Is 94A17
Ellerslie Pr. Ed. I. Canada 78G3
Ellery,Mt Vic. Australia 97C3
Ellesmere England UK 25C7
Ellesmere I NW Terr. Canada 77P1
Ellesmere,L New Zealand 100E6
Ellesmere Port England UK 25C6
Ellezelles Belgium 32B4
Ellice,Is = Tuvalu
Ellice,R NW Terr. Canada 76K3
Ellicott City Md USA 84C3
Elliot N Terr. Australia 99G3
Elliot South Africa 72D6
Elliston Mont. USA 80G2
Ellon Scotland UK 28M5
Ellora India 58E4
Ellsworth Maine USA 78D4
Ellsworth Land Antarctica 15R2
Ellsworth Mts Antarctica 15R2
Elm Switzerland 33E2
Elma Wash. USA 80B2
El Ma'arra Syria 64E1
Elma Dagh mt Turkey 62C2
El Madhiq Saudi Arabia 62D5
El Mansura Egypt 69M2
El Manzil Jordan 64E6
El Mazar Jordan 64D6
El Mazra Jordan 64D6
El Mina Lebanon 64D3
El Minya Egypt 69M3
Elmira NY USA 84C1
El Molar Spain 40E2
Elmore Vic. Australia 97B3
Elmshorn W Germany 36C2
El Muwaqqar Jordan 64E6
El Obeid Sudan 69M6
El Odaiya Sudan 69L6
Eloff South Africa 72P12
Elora Kenn. USA 85D3
El Oued Algeria 68G2
El Pardo Spain 40E2
El Paso Ill. USA 83P2
El Paso Texas USA 82E7
Elphin Ireland, Rep. of 30G6
El Pico Bolivia 92E7
El Pintado Argentina 91D2
El Puente del Arzobispo Spain 40D3
El Puerto de Santa Maria Spain 40C4
El Qadmus Syria 64E2
El Qanawat Syria 64E5
El Qaryatein Syria 64F3
El Qatrana Jordan 64E6
El Quds esh Sherif = Jerusalem
El Quseir Syria 64E3
El Quweira Jordan 64D8
El Reno Okla. USA 83J5
Elroy Wis. USA 79A4
El Sadi = Wajir
El Salto Mexico 88C3
El Salvador country Central America 89B4
Elsenborn Belgium 32E4
Elsinore Utah USA 82B3
Elslo Netherlands 32D4
Elspeet Netherlands 32D2
Elst Netherlands 32D3
Elsterwerda E Germany 36E3
Eltham New Zealand 100F4
El Tigre Venezuela 92E2
El Tih,Plat. of Egypt 69M3
El Toro Spain 41F2
El Transito Chile 91B3
El Triunfo Mexico 88B3
Eluru India 58F5
El Valle Colombia 92B2
Elvas Portugal 40C3
Elverum Norway 35D6
El Vigia Venezuela 92C2
Elvira,C NW Terr. Canada 76K2
El Wak Kenya 71J4
Ely England UK 27Q4
Ely Minn. USA 81M2
Ely Nev. USA 80F6
Emajõg,R Eston. USSR 35M7
Emamrūd Iran 63G2
Emangulova USSR 49M4

Embalse de Alcantara Fatehgarh

Embalse de Alcantara *res.* Spain **40C3**
Embalse de Almendra *res.* Spain **40C2**
Embalse de Valdecanas *res.* Spain **40D3**
Embalse Gabriel y Galan *res.* Spain **40C2**
Emba,R *Kazakh.* USSR **50G5**
Embarcación Argentina **91D2**
Embóna *Ródhos* Greece **47F6**
Embrun France **43G4**
Embu Kenya **71H5**
Emden W Germany **36B2**
Emei China **55B8**
Emei Shan China **55B8**
Emerald *Queens.* Australia **99K4**
Emerald I *NW Terr.* Canada **76J1**
Emerson *Man.* Canada **76M7**
Emilia-Romagna *region* Italy **44C3**
Eminabad Pakistan **60D4**
Eminence *Mo* USA **83N4**
Emmaste *Eston.* USSR **35K7**
Emmaville *NSW* Australia **97D1**
Emmeloord Netherlands **32D2**
Emmen Netherlands **32E2**
Emmen Tal *valley* Switzerland **33C2**
Emme,R Switzerland **33C2**
Emmetsburg *Iowa* USA **83L1**
Emmons,Mt *Utah* USA **82C2**
Emory Pk *Texas* USA **82G8**
Empalme Mexico **88B2**
Empedrado Argentina **91E3**
Empire *Mich.* USA **79C3**
Empoli Italy **44C4**
Emporia *Kans.* USA **83K3**
Emporia *Va* USA **85J2**
Emporium *Pa* USA **84B2**
Emptinne Belgium **32D4**
Emsworth *England* UK **27N7**
Enard B *Scotland* UK **28F3**
Encarnación Paraguay **91E3**
Encinitas *Calif.* USA **80E9**
Encontrados Venezuela **92C2**
Encounter B *S Aus.* Australia **97A3**
Encruzilhada Brazil **91F4**
Ende *Flores* Indon. **53H12**
Enderbury,I Phoenix Is **94J8**
Enderby Land Antarctica **15E3**
Enderlin *N Dak.* USA **81J2**
Endicott *NY* USA **84C1**
Endicott Mts *Alaska* USA **87X12**
Enez Turkey **62B1**
Enez,G of Greece **47E4**
Enfe Lebanon **64D3**
Enfield *England* UK **27P5**
Engaño,C Philippines **53H7**
En Gedi Israel **64D6**
Engelberg Switzerland **33D2**
Engels USSR **49H5**
Enggano *island* Indonesia **53D12**
Enghien Belgium **32C4**
England *country* Great Britain **22H5**
Englehart *Ont.* Canada **79G2**
Englewood *New J* USA **84D2**
English Bazar India **61G3**
English Chan. Eng./France **42B1**
English Coast Antarctica **15S2**
English,R *Ont.* Canada **76N6**
Engures Ezers *lake Latviy* USSR **35K8**
Enid *Okla.* USA **83J4**
Enkhuizen Netherlands **32D2**
Enköping Sweden **35G7**
Enna *Sicily* Italy **45E7**
En Nahud Sudan **69L6**
Ennedi *plat.* Chad **69K5**
Ennell,L Ireland, Rep. of **31J7**
Enngonia *NSW* Australia **97C1**
Ennis Ireland, Rep. of **31F8**
Enniscorthy Ireland, Rep. of **31K8**
Enniskillen N Ireland **30H5**
Ennistimon Ireland, Rep. of **31E8**
Enns Austria **36F4**
Enns,R Austria **36F5**
Ennylabegan,I Kwajalein,Is **94A17**
Enontekiö Finland **34K2**
Enping China **55G11**
Enriquillo,L Dom. Rep. **89E3**
Ens Netherlands **32D2**
Ensanche Sarmiento Argentina **91B7**
Ensay *Vic.* Australia **97C3**
Enschede Netherlands **32E2**
Enseñada Argentina **91E4**
Ensenada Mexico **88A1**
Ensenada de Cortes *bay* Cuba **89C2**
Enshi China **54E7**
Enshi China **55E7**
Entebbe Uganda **71G5**
Enterprise *Ala.* USA **85E5**
Enterprise *Miss.* USA **85C4**
Enterprise *Oreg.* USA **80E3**
Entlebuch Switzerland **33D2**
Entraygues France **43E4**
Entre Rios Brazil **93K6**
Entre Rios *prov.* Argentina **91E4**
Eolie Is = **Lipari Is**
Epe Netherlands **32D2**
Epequén,L Argentina **91D5**
Épernay France **42E2**
Ephraim *Utah* USA **82C3**
Ephrata *Wash.* USA **80D2**
Épinal France **42F2**
Episkopi Cyprus **64A3**
Episkopi B Cyprus **64A3**
Epping *England* UK **27Q5**
Epping Forest *England* UK **27Q5**
Epsom *England* UK **27P6**
Epworth *England* UK **25G5**
Equatoria,Eastern *region* Sudan **69M7**
Equatorial Guinea *country* Africa **70B4**
Equatoria,Western *region* Sudan **69L7**
Erciş Turkey **62E2**
Erd Hungary **37H5**
Erebus Gulf Antarctica **15T3**
Erebus,Mt Antarctica **15L2**
Eregli Turkey **62C1**
Ereğli Turkey **62C2**
Erenhot China **51N5**
Erepecú,L Brazil **93F4**
Eressós *Lésvos* Greece **47E5**
Erexim Brazil **91F3**
Erfurt E Germany **36D3**
Ergli *Latviy* USSR **35L8**
Erguig,R Chad **69J6**
Er Hai *lake* China **52D5**
Ericau *Ont.* Canada **79E4**
Erich,Loch *Scotland* UK **29H6**
Erie *Pa* USA **79F4**
Erie,L Canada/USA **79E5**
Eriha Syria **64E2**
Erimo Misaki *cape* Japan **56H4**
Eriskay *island Scotland* UK **28B5**
Erisort,L *Scotland* UK **28D3**
Eriswil Switzerland **33C1**
Erlach Switzerland **33C1**
Erlangen W Germany **36D4**
Erlenbach Switzerland **33C2**
Er Malk,I Palau Is **94A20**
Ermelo Netherlands **32D2**
Ermenek Turkey **62C2**
Ernakulam India **58E6**
Ernée France **42C2**
Erne,L N Ireland **30H5**
Eromanga,I Vanautu **94G9**
Erquelinnes Belgium **32C4**
Erquy France **42B2**
Er Rabba Jordan **64D6**
Er Rachida Morocco **68E2**
Er Rahad Sudan **69M6**
Er Rastan Syria **64E3**
Er Rif *mts* Morocco **68E2**
Errigal *mt* Ireland, Rep. of **30G3**
Erris Hd Ireland, Rep. of **30C5**
Er Roseires Sudan **69M6**
Er Rumman Jordan **64D5**
Ersterivier South Africa **72J10**
Erudina *S Aus.* Australia **97A2**
Erval Brazil **91F4**
Erz Gebirge *mts* E Germany **36E3**
Erzincan Turkey **62D2**
Erzurum Turkey **62E2**
Erživilkas *Lith.* USSR **35K9**
Esashi Japan **56H2**
Esbjerg Denmark **35C9**
Escada Brazil **93K5**
Escalante *Utah* USA **82C4**
Escalón Mexico **88D2**
Escanaba *Mich.* USA **79C3**
Escanaba,R *Mich.* USA **79C2**
Escaut,R Belgium **32C3**
Esch Luxembourg **36A4**
Escholzmatt Switzerland **33C2**
Escudilla Pk *Ariz.* USA **82D6**
Escudo de Veragua Panama **89C5**
Escuinapa Mexico **88C3**
Escuintla Guatemala **88F5**
Escuminac Point *New Br.* Canada **78F3**
Esfahān Iran **63G3**
Eshkanān Iran **63G4**
Eshowe South Africa **72E5**
Eskdale New Zealand **100G4**
Eske,L Ireland, Rep. of **30G4**
Eskifjordhur Iceland **34Y12**
Eskilstuna Sweden **35G7**
Eskimo,C *NW Terr.* Canada **77N4**
Eskisehir Turkey **62C2**
Esk,R *Scotland* UK **29K8**
Esla,R Spain **40D2**
Eslöv Sweden **35E9**
Esmeralda,I Chile **91A7**
Esmeraldas Ecuador **92B3**
Espalion France **43E4**
Espanola *Ont.* Canada **79F2**
Esperance *W Aus.* Australia **98E6**
Esperanza Argentina **91D4**
Espiel Spain **40D3**
Espinho Portugal **40B2**
Espinosa de los Monteros Spain **40E1**
Espírito Santo Brazil **93J8**
Espíritu Santo,C Argentina **91C8**
Espíritu Santo,I Mexico **88B3**
Espiritu Santo,I Vanuatu **94G9**
Espita Mexico **88F4**
Esquel Argentina **91B6**
Esquimalt *BC* Canada **76G7**
Esquina Argentina **91E3**
Es Sa'an Syria **64F2**
Es Samra Jordan **64E5**
Es Sanamein Syria **64E4**
Essaouria Morocco **68D2**
Essen Belgium **32C3**
Essen W Germany **36B3**
Essequibo,R Guyana **92F2**
Essequibo,R Guyana **92F3**
Essex *Ont.* Canada **79E4**
Essex *county England* UK **27Q5**
Essex Mt *Wyo.* USA **81C4**
Esslingen Switzerland **33D1**
Esslingen W Germany **36C4**
Estabuchie *Miss.* USA **85C5**
Estados,I de los Argentina **91D8**
Estavayer Switzerland **33B2**
Estcourt South Africa **72D5**
Esteli Nicaragua **89B4**
Esternay France **42E2**
Estero Point *Calif.* USA **80C8**
Esteros del Ibera *region* Argentina **91E3**
Estevan *Sask.* Canada **76L7**
Estherville *Iowa* USA **83L1**
Estonia = **Estonskaya SSR**
Estonskaya SSR *rep.* USSR **50D4**
Estreito Brazil **91F4**
Estremadura *region* Portugal **40B3**
Estremoz Portugal **40C3**
Estrondo,Sa do *mts* Brazil **93H5**
E'Sufeina Saudi Arabia **62E5**
Etadunna *S Aus.* Australia **99H5**
Etah India **61B2**
Étain France **42F2**
Etalle Belgium **32D5**
Étampes France **42E2**
Étaples France **42D1**
Etawah India **61B2**
Etawney L *Man.* Canada **76M5**
Etcharai I Kwajalein Is **94A17**
Etelia Mali **68F5**
Eternity Ra. Antarctica **15S2**
Ethe Belgium **32D5**
Ethiopia *country* Africa **71H3**
Etive,L *Scotland* UK **29F7**
Etna *vol. Sicily* Italy **45E7**
Eton *England* UK **27N6**
E Tons,R India **61D2**
Etosha Pan *lake* Namibia **72B3**
Etretat France **42D2**
Ettelbrück Luxembourg **36B4**
Etten-Leur Netherlands **32C3**
Ettrick,R *Scotland* UK **29K9**
Etzwilen Switzerland **33D1**
Eua *island* Tonga **95V30**
Euabalong *NSW* Australia **97C2**
Euboea,I = **Évvoia,I.**
Eucla *W Aus.* Australia **98F6**
Eucumbene,L *NSW* Australia **97C3**
Eudunda *S Aus.* Australia **97A2**
Eufaula *Ala.* USA **85E5**
Eufaula *Okla.* USA **83L5**
Eufaula L *Okla.* USA **83L5**
Eugene *Oreg.* USA **80B2**
Eugene Mts *Nev.* USA **80D5**
Eugm,I Finland **34K5**
Eugowra *NSW* Australia **97C2**
Eumungerie *NSW* Australia **97C2**
Eunice *La* USA **83M7**
Eupen Belgium **32D4**
Euphrates,R Iraq **62F3**
Eure *dep.* France **42D2**
Eure-et-Loir *dep.* France **42D2**
Eureka *Calif.* USA **80A5**
Eureka *Kans.* USA **83K4**
Eureka *Nev.* USA **80F6**
Eureka *Utah* USA **82B3**
Euriowie *NSW* Australia **97B2**
Euroa *Vic.* Australia **97C3**
Europoort Netherlands **32C3**
Eursinge Netherlands **32E2**
Euskirchen W Germany **36B3**
Euston *NSW* Australia **97B2**
Eutaw *Ala.* USA **85D4**
Eutin W Germany **36D1**
Eutsuk L *BC* Canada **76F6**
Evale Angola **72B3**
Evandale *Tas.* Australia **97F5**
Evans Hd *NSW* Australia **97D1**
Evans,L *Que.* Canada **77Q6**
Evanston *Ill.* USA **83Q1**
Evanston *Wyo.* USA **81B5**
Evansville *Ind.* USA **85D1**
Evansville *Minn.* USA **81K2**
Evansville *Wyo.* USA **81D4**
Évaux France **42E3**
Eveleth *Minn.* USA **81L2**
Everard,L *S Aus.* Australia **99G6**
Everest,Mt China/Nepal **59G3**
Everett *Wash.* USA **86B2**
Evergem Belgium **32B3**
Everglades Nat. Pk *Fla* USA **85M9**
Evergreen *Ala.* USA **85D5**
Evesham *England* UK **27L4**
Evesham,Vale of *England* UK **27K4**
Evijärvi Finland **34K5**
Evje Norway **35B7**
Evolène Switzerland **33C2**
Evora Portugal **40C3**
Evran France **42B2**
Evreux France **42D2**
Evros *dist.* Greece **46F4**
Evrykhou Cyprus **64A2**
Evrytania *dist.* Greece **47C5**
Évvoia *island* Greece **47D5**
Évvoia,G of Greece **47D5**
Ewarton Jamaica **89D3**
Ewe, Loch *Scotland* UK **28E4**
Exaltación Bolivia **92D6**
Excelsior Mt *Nev.* USA **80D6**
Exe,R. *England* UK **26G7**
Exeter *England* UK **26G7**
Exeter *New H* USA **84F1**
Exminster *England* UK **26H7**
Exmoor *upland England* UK **26G6**
Exmouth *England* UK **26H7**
Exmouth G *W Aus.* Australia **98C4**
Expedition Ra *mts Queens.* Australia **99K4**
Extremadura *region* Spain **40C3**
Exuma Is The Bahamas **89D2**
Exuma Sd The Bahamas **89D2**
Eyarbakki Iceland **34U13**
Eyasi,L Tanzania **71G5**
Eyemouth *Scotland* UK **29M8**
Eye Pen. *Scotland* UK **28D3**
Eyja Fj. Iceland **34V11**
Eyl Somalia **71K3**
Eymoutiers France **42D4**
Eyre *W Aus.* Australia **98F6**
Eyrecourt Ireland, Rep. of **31G7**
Eyre Cr. *S Aus.* Australia **99H5**
Eyre,L *S Aus.* Australia **99H5**
Eyre Pen. *S Aus.* Australia **99H6**
Ezcaray Spain **40E1**

F

Faaa Tahiti **95V32**
Fåberg Norway **35D6**
Fåborg Denmark **35D9**
Facatativá Columbia **92C3**
Fachi Niger **69H5**
Fada Chad **69K5**
Fadan' Gourma Upper Volta **68F6**
Faenza Italy **44C3**
Faerøerne *islands* Atlantic Ocean **22F3**
Faeroes,Is = **Faerøerne,Is**
Fafa Mali **68F5**
Fafa,R CAR **69J7**
Făgăras Romania **46E2**
Fågelsja Sweden **35F6**
Fagerli Norway **34G3**
Fagernes Norway **35C6**
Fagnano,L Argentina **91C8**
Fahrwangen Switzerland **33D1**
Fahud Oman **63H5**
Fahy Switzerland **33C1**
Faial *island* Açores **68Q9**
Faido Switzerland **33D2**
Faifo = **Hoi An**
Fairbanks *Alaska* USA **87Y12**
Fairbury *Ill.* USA **83P2**
Fairbury *Nebr.* USA **83K2**
Fairfield *Calif.* USA **80B6**
Fairfield *Ill.* USA **83P3**
Fairfield *Iowa* USA **83N2**
Fairfield *Maine* USA **78D4**
Fairfield *Utah* USA **82B2**
Fairford *England* UK **27L5**
Fairhaven *Mass.* USA **84F2**
Fair Hd N Ireland **30L3**
Fair I *Scotland* UK **22H4**
Fair,I *Scotland* UK **28A1**
Fairlie New Zealand **100D7**
Fairmont *Minn.* USA **81K4**
Fairmont *W Va* USA **79F6**
Fairview *Alta* Canada **76H5**
Fairweather,Mt *Alaska* USA **87Z13**
Faisalabad Pakistan **60C5**
Faith *S Dak.* USA **81F3**
Faizabad Afghanistan **63L2**
Faizabad India **61D2**
Fajardo Puerto Rico **89F3**
Fajr Saudi Arabia **62D4**
Fakenham *England* UK **27R3**
Fakfak *Irian Jaya* Indon. **53K11**
Fakiya Bulgaria **46F3**
Fakse B Denmark **35E9**
Faku China **54M1**
Falaise d'Entrecasteaux *point* Amsterdam I **65Q12**
Falaises des Manchots St Paul I **65T12**
Falam Burma **59H4**
Falama Guinea **68D6**
Fălciu Romania **46G1**
Falcone,C di *Sardinia* Italy **45B5**
Falcon L Mexico/USA **82S10**
Falkenberg Sweden **35E8**
Falkirk *Scotland* UK **29J8**
Falkland *Scotland* UK **29K7**
Falkland Is S Atlantic Ocean **91D8**
Falköping Sweden **35E7**
Fallberg Sweden **35F6**
Fallon *Nev.* USA **80D6**
Fall River *Mass.* USA **84F2**
Falls City *Nebr.* USA **83L2**
Falmagne Belgium **32C4**
Falmouth *England* UK **26D8**
Falmouth Jamaica **89D3**
Falmouth *Ky* USA **85E1**
Falmouth B *England* UK **26D8**
False,B South Africa **72B6**
False Point India **59G4**
Falset Spain **41G2**
Falso,C Mexico **88B3**
Falster,I Denmark **35D9**
Falun Sweden **35F6**
Famagusta Cyprus **64B2**
Famagusta B Cyprus **64B2**
Famatina Argentina **91C3**
Famoso *Calif.* USA **80D8**
Fanad Hd Ireland, Rep. of **30H3**
Fanan *island* Truk Is **94A16**
Fanchang China **54K7**
Fang Thailand **57B3**
Fangak Sudan **69M7**
Fangcheng China **54G6**
Fangliao Taiwan **55L11**
Fangshan China **54J3**
Fang Xian China **54F6**
Fannich,L *Scotland* UK **28F4**
Fannūj Iran **63H4**
Fano Italy **44D4**
Fanø Bugt *bay* Denmark **35C9**
Fanø,I Denmark **35C9**
Fan Si Pan *mt* Vietnam **57C2**
Fan Xian China **54H5**
Faradje Congo **71F4**
Farafangana Madagascar **71N11**
Farah Afghanistan **63J3**
Farah Rud *river* Afghanistan **63J3**
Farajah Saudi Arabia **63G5**
Faranah Guinea **68C6**
Faranlep,I Caroline Is **94E7**
Farasan Is Red Sea **62E6**
Fårberg Sweden **34G4**
Fareham *England* UK **27M7**
Farewell,C = **Uummarnarsuaq**
Farewell,C New Zealand **100E5**
Fargo *N Dak.* USA **81J2**
Faribault *Minn.* USA **81L3**
Faridabad India **60E6**
Faridkot India **60D5**
Faridpur Bangladesh **61G4**
Faridpur India **61B1**
Farimān Iran **63H2**
Farina *S Aus.* Australia **97A2**
Farmington *Maine* USA **78C4**
Farmington *Mo* USA **83N4**
Farmington *New Mex.* USA **82D4**
Farmington *Utah* USA **82B2**
Farmville *Va* USA **85H2**
Farnborough *Gr. London, England* UK **27Q6**
Farnborough *Hamps.,England* UK **27N6**
Farne Is *England* UK **25E1**
Farnes Norway **35B6**
Farnham *England* UK **27N6**
Farnham *Que.* Canada **79K3**
Farnworth *England* UK **25D5**
Faro Brazil **93F4**
Faro Portugal **40C4**
Farol de Mostardos Brazil **91F4**
Fårön,I Sweden **35H8**
Farquhar Is Indian Ocean **71L1**
Farrukhabad India **61B2**
Farrukhnagar India **60E6**
Fársala Greece **47D5**
Farsi Afghanistan **63J3**
Farsund Norway **35B7**
Fartura,Serra da *mts* Brazil **91F3**
Farvagny Switzerland **33C2**
Farwell *Mich.* USA **79D4**
Farwell *Texas* USA **82G5**
Fasā Iran **63G4**
Fasano Italy **45F5**
Fastnet Rk *island* Ireland,Rep. of **31D11**
Fatait ibn Kanat Saudi Arabia **62E4**
Fatehabad India **60D6**
Fatehabad India **61B2**
Fatehgarh India **61B2**

Fatehpur, Frankfurt-an-der-Oder

Fatehpur India 60D7
Fatehpur India 61C3
Father L *Que.* Canada 77Q7
Fatmomakke Sweden 34F4
Fatu Hiva,I Marquesas Is 95N9
Faulhorn *mt* Switzerland 33C2
Faüske Norway 34F3
Faversham *England* UK 27R6
Fawley *England* UK 27M7
Faxaflói,B Iceland 34T12
Faxe Alv *river* Sweden 34G5
Fayd Saudi Arabia 62E4
Fayette *Ala.* USA 85D4
Fayette *Mo* USA 83M3
Fayetteville *Ark.* USA 83L4
Fayetteville *N Car.* USA 85H3
Fayetteville *Pa* USA 84C3
Fayetteville *W Va* USA 85G1
Faylakah *island* Kuwait 62F4
Fazilka India 60D5
Fdérik Mauritania 68C4
Feale,R Ireland, Rep. of 31D9
Fear,C *N Car.* USA 85J4
Fearn *Scotland* UK 28J4
Feather,R *Calif.* USA 80C6
Feathertop,Mt *Vic.* Australia 97C3
Fécamp France 42D2
Fedaración Argentina 91E4
Fedje Fj. Norway 35A6
Feeagh L Ireland, Rep. of 30D6
Fefan *island* Truk Is 94A16
Fehmarn *island* W Germany 36D1
Feilding New Zealand 100F5
Feira Zambia 72E3
Feira de Santana Brazil 93K6
Fei Xian China 54K5
Felanitx *Mallorca* Spain 41H3
Feldbach Austria 37F5
Feldkirch Austria 36C5
Felipe Carrillo Puerto Mexico 88G4
Felixstowe *England* UK 27S5
Felton *Calif.* USA 80B7
Femund,L Norway 34D5
Femundsmarka Nat. Pk Norway 34D5
Fengcheng China 55H8
Fengchuan China 55F11
Fengdu China 55D8
Fenggang China 55D9
Fenghua China 55L8
Fenghuang China 55E9
Fengjie China 54E7
Fengliang China 55J11
Fengling P China 55J9
Fengning China 54J2
Fengqiu China 54H5
Fengrun China 54K3
Fengshan China 55D10
Fengtai China 54J6
Fengxian China 54L7
Feng Xian *Shaanxi* China 54D6
Feng Xian *Shandong* China 54J5
Fengxiang China 54D5
Fengxin China 55H8
Fengyang China 54J6
Fengzhen China 54G2
Fen He *river* China 54F4
Fenit Ireland, Rep. of 31D9
Fens Fj. Norway 35A6
Fenton *Mich.* USA 79E4
Fenyang China 54F4
Fenyi China 55H9
Feodosiya USSR 48J9
Feodosiya B. USSR 48J9
Ferdow Iran 63H3
Fergus *Ont.* Canada 79F4
Fergus Falls *Minn.* USA 81J2
Ferguson *Mo* USA 83N3
Ferguson *Que.* Canada 79K2
Fergusson I Papua New Guinea 99L1
Fermanagh *county* N Ireland 30H5
Fermo Italy 44D4
Fermoy Ireland, Rep. of 31G9
Fernando de Noronha *island* Brazil 93L4
Fernando Poo,I = Bioko,I
Ferndale *Calif.* USA 80A5
Fernie *BC* Canada 76J7
Ferns Ireland, Rep. of 31L8
Ferrara Italy 44C3
Ferrar Gl. Antarctica 15K2
Ferrato,C *Sardinia* Italy 45B6
Ferreira do Zezere Portugal 40B3
Ferreira Gomes Brazil 93G3
Ferste,R South Africa 72J9
Fertile *Minn.* USA 81J2
Fertö tó = Neusiedler See
Fès Morocco 68D2
Feshi Zaire 70D6
Festus *Mo* USA 83N3
Fetesti Romania 46F2
Fethard Ireland, Rep. of 31H9
Fetlar,I. *Shetland* Scotland 28R7
Feuilles,R *Que.* Canada 77R5
Fez = Fès
Fezzan *prov.* Libya 69H3
Ffestiniog *Wales* UK 26G3
Fiambalá Argentina 91C3
Fichtel Gebirge *region* W Germany 36D3
Fideris Switzerland 33E2
Fieldbrook *Calif.* USA 80A5
Fier Albania 47B4
Fiesch Switzerland 33D2
Fife *region* *Scotland* UK 29K7
Fife Ness *cape* *Scotland* UK 29L7
Figeac France 43E4
Figline Vald Italy 44C4
Figueira de Castelo Rodrigo Portugal 40C2
Figueres Spain 41H1
Figuig Morocco 68E2
Fiji,Is Pacific Ocean 94H9
Filakovo Czech. 37H4
Filchner Ice Shelf Antarctica 15T2
Filey *England* UK 25H4
Filiaşi Romania 46D2
Filiátes Greece 47C5
Filicudi *island* Italy 45E6
Filingué Niger 68F6
Filipów Poland 37K1
Filipstad Sweden 35F7
Filisur Switzerland 33E2
Fillmore *Utah* USA 82B3
Fincastle *Va* USA 85H2
Findhorn *Scotland* UK 28J4
Findhorn,R
Findlay *Ohio* USA 79E5
Findlay Grp *islands* *NW Terr.* Canada 76K1
Fingal *N Dak.* USA 81J2
Fingal *Tas.* Australia 97F5
Finhaut Switzerland 33B2
Finistère *dep.* France 42A2
Finisterre,C Spain 40B1
Finke,R *N Terr.* Australia 99G5
Finland *country* Europe 22P3
Finland,G of Europe 35L7
Finlay Forks *BC* Canada 76G5
Finlay R *BC* Canada 76G5
Finley *NSW* Australia 97C3
Finnmark *county* Norway 34K1
Finnmarksvidda *region* Norway 34K2
Finn,R Ireland,Rep. of 30H4
Finschhafen Papua New Guinea 99K1
Finspång Sweden 35F7
Finsteraarhorn *mt* Switzerland 33D2
Finsterwalde E Germany 36E3
Fintona N Ireland 30J5
Fionnay Switzerland 33C2
Fionn,Loch *Scotland* UK 28F4
Fiq Syria 64D5
Firat,R Turkey 62D2
Firenze Italy 44C4
Firmat Argentina 91D4
Firozabad India 61B2
Firozpur India 60D5
Firozpur Jhirka India 60E7
Firūzābad Iran 63G4
Fishers I *NY* USA 84F2
Fisher Str. *NW Terr.* Canada 77P4
Fishguard *Wales* UK 26E5
Fishguard B *Wales* UK 26D4
Fitchburg *Mass.* USA 84F1
Fitful Hd *Shetland* Scotland 28Q9
Fittri,L Chad 69J6
Fitzcarrald Peru 92C6
Fitzpatrick *Ala.* USA 85E4
Fitzroy *W Aus.* Australia 98F3
Fitz Roy,C *NW Terr.* Canada 77P1
Fitzroy,R *Queens.* Australia 99K4
Fitzroy,R *W Aus.* Australia 98E3
Fitzwilliam I *Ont.* Canada 79F3
Fiume = Rijeka
Fivemiletown N Ireland 30J5
Fjällåsen Sweden 34J3
Fjallsjö Alv *river* Sweden 34G5
Flagstaff *Ariz.* USA 82C5
Flagstaff,L *Maine* USA 78C4
Flakstadøy *island* Norway 34E2
Flam Norway 35B6
Flamborough Hd *England* UK 25H4
Flaming *region* E Germany 36E3
Flamingo,Tg *point* *Irian Jaya* Indon. 53L12
Flannan Is *Scotland* UK 28B3
Flat *Alaska* USA 87X12
Flathead,L *Mont.* USA 80F2
Flattery,C *Queens.* Australia 99K2
Flattery,C *Wash.* USA 86B2
Fleet *England* UK 27N6
Fleetwood *England* UK 25B5
Flekkefjord Norway 35B7
Flemington *New J* USA 84D2
Flensburg W Germany 36C1
Flers France 42C2
Fleurance France 43D5
Fleurier Switzerland 33B2
Fleuru Belgium 32C4
Flevoland *region* Netherlands 32D2
Flims Switzerland 33E2
Flinders I *S Aus.* Australia 99G6
Flinders I *Tas.* Australia 97F4
Flinders Pass. *Queens.* Australia 99K3
Flinders,R *Queens.* Australia 99J3
Flinders Ra *mts* *S Aus.* Australia 97A2
Flin Flon *Man.* Canada 76L6
Flint *Mich.* USA 79E4
Flint *Wales* UK 26H2
Flint,I Pacific Ocean 95L9
Flint,R *Ga* USA 87K5
Flisa Norway 35E6
Flodden Field *hist. site* *England* UK 25D1
Flora *Ill.* USA 83P3
Florac France 43E4
Floreffe Belgium 32C4
Florence = Firenze
Florence *Ala.* USA 85D3
Florence *Ariz.* USA 82C6
Florence *Col.* USA 82F3
Florence *Oreg.* USA 80A4
Florence *S Car.* USA 85H3
Florence *Wis.* USA 79B3
Florence,L *S Aus.* Australia 97A1
Florencia Argentina 91D2
Florencia Argentina 91E3
Florencia Colombia 92B3
Florennes Belgium 32C4
Florenville Belgium 32D5
Flores Guatemala 88G4
Flores *island* Indonesia 53H12
Flores,I Açores Is 68P9
Flores Sea Indonesia 53H12
Floriano Brazil 93J5
Floriano Peixoto Brazil 92D5
Florianópolis Brazil 91G3
Florida *Sicily* Italy 45E7
Florida Uruguay 91E4
Florida *state* USA 87J5
Florida B *Fla* USA 85M9
Florida,C *Fla* USA 87K6
Florida City *Fla* USA 87K6
Florida Keys *islands* *Fla* USA 85M9
Florida Mts *New Mex.* USA 82E6
Florida Strs USA/The Bahamas 89C2
Flórina Greece 47C4
Flórina *dist.* Greece 47C4
Flöro Norway 34A6
Florø *island* Norway 34A6
Flo Sjön,R Sweden 34F4
Flotta, I *Orkney* Scotland 28K2
Floydada *Texas* USA 82H6
Floyd Pk *Ariz.* USA 80G8
Fluchthorn *mt* Austria/Switz. 33F2
Flüela P Switzerland 33E2
Flüelen Switzerland 33D2
Flüh Switzerland 33C1
Flushing = Vlissingen
Flushing *NY* USA 84E2
Flying Fish,C Antarctica 15Q2
Fly,R Papua New Guinea 99J1
Foća Yugoslavia 46B3
Foch,I Kerguelen 65S12
Focşani Romania 46F2
Fod *island* Tonga 95V30
Foggia Italy 45E5
Fogo *island* Cape Verde 68T10
Fogo I *Newf.* Canada 78L2
Föhr *island* W Germany 36C1
Foilclogh *mt* Ireland,Rep. of 31C10
Foinaven *mt* *Scotland* UK 28G3
Foix France 43D5
Fokis *dist.* Greece 47D5
Folda,Fj. Norway 34F3
Folégandros *island* Greece 47E6
Foleyet *Ont.* Canada 79E1
Folge Fomma *peninsula* Norway 35B6
Foligno Italy 44D4
Folkestone *England* UK 27S6
Folkston *Ga* USA 85F5
Folkstone *N Car.* USA 85J3
Folsom *Calif.* USA 80C6
Fonda *NY* USA 84D1
Fond du Lac *Sask.* Canada 76K5
Fond du Lac *Wis.* USA 79B4
Fonsagrada Spain 40C1
Fonseca,G of Honduras 89B4
Fontaine Belgium 32C4
Fontainebleau France 42E2
Fontanna,L Argentina 91B6
Fonte Boa Brazil 92D4
Fontenay le Comte France 42C3
Fonuaika Tonga 95V30
Foping China 54D6
Forbes *NSW* Australia 97C2
Forbes,Mt *Alta* Canada 76H6
Forcados Nigeria 68G7
Forcalquier France 43F5
Førde Norway 35A6
Ford Ras Antarctica 15N2
Fords Bridge *NSW* Australia 97C1
Fordyce *Ark.* USA 83M6
Forécariah Guinea 68C7
Foreland Point *England* UK 26G6
Forel,Mt Greenland 14P3
Forest *Ont.* Canada 79E4
Forest Grove *Oreg.* USA 80B3
Foresthill *Calif.* USA 80C6
Forestier Pen. *Tas.* Australia 97F5
Forestville *Calif.* USA 80B6
Forestville *Que.* Canada 78D2
Forfar *Scotland* UK 29L6
Forli Italy 44D3
Forlorn Point Ireland, Rep. of 31K9
Formby *England* UK 25B5
Formby Pt *region* *England* UK 25B5
Formentera,I *Balearic Is* Spain 41G3
Formia Italy 45D5
Formosa Argentina 91E3
Formosa Brazil 93H7
Formosa,Serra *mts* Brazil 93F6
Formosa Strait = Taiwan Haixia
Fornos d'Algôdres Portugal 40C2
Forres *Scotland* UK 28J4
Forrest *Vic.* Australia 97B3
Forrest *W Aus.* Australia 98F6
Forrest City *Ark.* USA 83N5
Fors Sweden 35G6
Forsayth *Queens.* Australia 99J3
Forsnäs Sweden 34H3
Forssa Finland 35K6
Forsyth *Mont.* USA 81D2
Fort Albany *Ont.* Canada 77P6
Fortaleza Brazil 92D5
Fortaleza Brazil 93K4
Fort Ann *NY* USA 84E1
Fort Archambault = Sarh
Fort Atkinson *Wis.* USA 79B4
Fort Augustus *Scotland* UK 28G5
Fort Beaufort South Africa 72D6
Fort Benton *Mont.* USA 81B2
Fort Brabant *NW Terr.* Canada 76J2
Fort Bragg *Calif.* USA 80B6
Fort Chipewyan *Alta* Canada 76J5
Fort Collins *Col.* USA 82F2
Fort Coulonge *Que.* Canada 79H3
Fort de France Martinique 89G4
Fort de Polignac = Illizi
Fort Dodge *Iowa* USA 83L1
Fort Edward *NY* USA 84E1
Fortescue,R *W Aus.* Australia 98D4
Fort Fairfield *Maine* USA 78E3
Fort Fitzgerald *Alta* Canada 76J5
Fort Flatters = Bordj Omar Driss
Fort Fraser *BC* Canada 76G6
Fort George *Scotland* UK 28H4
Fort Good Hope *NW Terr.* Canada 76F3
Fort Gourand = Fdérik
Fort Grahame *BC* Canada 76G5
Fort Grey *NSW* Australia 97B1
Forth, Firth of *Scotland* UK 29L7
Fort Hill = Chitipa
Forth,R *Scotland* UK 29H7
Fort Hunter *NY* USA 84D1
Fortin Carlos Antonio López Paraguay 91E2
Fort Kent *Maine* USA 78D3
Fort Lallemand Algeria 68G2
Fort Lamy = N'Djamena
Fort Laperrine = Tamanrasset
Fort Laramie *Wyo.* USA 81E4
Fort Lauderdale *Fla* USA 85M8
Fort Liard *NW Terr.* Canada 76G4
Fort Lockhart Pakistan 60B4
Fort Mackay *Alta* Canada 76J5
Fort Macleod *Alta* Canada 76J7
Fort McMurray *Alta* Canada 76J5
Fort McPherson *NW Terr.* Canada 76E3
Fort Madison *Iowa* USA 83N2
Fort Maginnis *Mont.* USA 81C2
Fort Morgan *Ala.* USA 85C5
Fort Morgan *Col.* USA 82G2
Fort Munro Pakistan 60B6
Fort Myers *Fla* USA 85M8
Fort Nelson *BC* Canada 76G5
Fort Nelson,R *BC* Canada 76G5
Fort Norman *NW Terr.* Canada 76F4
Fort Ogden *Fla* USA 85M8
Fort Peck Dam *Mont.* USA 81D2
Fort Peck Ind. Resn *Mont.* USA 81E1
Fort Peck L *Mont.* USA 81D2
Fort Pierre *S Dak.* USA 81G3
Fort Plain *NY* USA 84D1
Fort Portal Uganda 71G4
Fort Providence *NW Terr.* Canada 76H4
Fort Resolution *NW Terr.* Canada 76J4
Fortress Mt *Wyo.* USA 81B3
Fort Rice *N Dak.* USA 81G2
Fortrose *Scotland* UK 28H4
Fort St. George = Madras
Fort St John *BC* Canada 76G5
Fort Sandeman Pakistan 60A5
Fort Saskatchewan *Alta* Canada 76J6
Fort Scott *Kans.* USA 83L4
Fort Severn *Ont.* Canada 77O5
Fort Sibut CAR 69J7
Fort Sill *Okla.* USA 83J5
Fort Simcoe *Wash.* USA 80C2
Fort Simpson *NW Terr.* Canada 76G4
Fort Smith *Ark.* USA 83L5
Fort Smith *NW Terr.* Canada 76J4
Fort Stockton *Texas* USA 82G7
Fort Sumner *New Mex.* USA 82F5
Fortuna *Calif.* USA 80A5
Fortuna Spain 41F3
Fortune B *Newf.* Canada 78K3
Fort Valley *Ga* USA 85F4
Fort Vermilion *Alta* Canada 76H5
Fort Wayne *Ind.* USA 79D5
Fort White Burma 59H4
Fort William *Scotland* UK 29F6
Fort Worth *Texas* USA 83K6
Fort Yates *N Dak.* USA 81G2
Fort Yukon *Alaska* USA 87Y12
Forville Belgium 32C4
Fossano Italy 44A3
Fosse Belgium 32C4
Fossil *Oreg.* USA 80C3
Fossombrone Italy 44D4
Foster *Vic.* Australia 97C3
Foster Ls *Sask.* Canada 76K5
Fotheringhay *England* UK 25H7
Foto Argentina 91B6
Fotuhaa *island* Tonga 95V30
Fougères France 42C2
Foula *island* *Scotland* UK 22H3
Foul,B Egypt 69N4
Foul,I Burma 59H5
Foulness,I *England* UK 27R5
Foulweather,C *Oreg.* USA 80A3
Fournier,L *Que.* Canada 78F1
Foúrnoi *islands* Greece 47F6
Fouta Djallon *mts* Guinea 68C6
Foveaux Str. New Zealand 100B8
Fowler *Col.* USA 82F3
Fowlers B *S Aus.* Australia 98G6
Fowlers Gap *NSW* Australia 97B2
Foxe Basin *NW Terr.* Canada 77Q3
Foxe Chan. *NW Terr.* Canada 77P3
Foxe Pen. *NW Terr.* Canada 77Q4
Foxford Ireland, Rep. of 30E6
Fox Is *Aleutian Is* USA 87W13
Fox R *Man.* Canada 76N5
Fox River = Rivière au Renard
Foxton New Zealand 100F5
Foyle,R N Ireland 30J3
Foynes Ireland, Rep. of 31E8
Foz do Cunene Angola 72A3
Foz do Iguacú Argentina 91F3
Foz do Jordao Brazil 92C5
Foz do Jutai Brazil 92D4
Foz Embira Brazil 92C5
Fraire Belgium 32C4
Framboise *No. Sc.* Canada 78H4
Frameries Belgium 32B4
Framingham *Mass.* USA 84F1
Franca Brazil 93H8
Francavilla Fontana Italy 45F5
France *country* Europe 38F4
Frances *S Aus.* Australia 97B3
Frances L *Yukon* Canada 76F4
Franceville Gabon 70C5
Franche-Comte *prov.* France 42G3
Francistown Botswana 72D4
Francois L *BC* Canada 76F6
Franeker Netherlands 32D1
Frankfort *Kans.* USA 83K3
Frankfort *Ky* USA 85E1
Frankfort *Mich.* USA 79C3
Frankfurt-am-Main W Germany 36C3
Frankfurt-an-der-Oder E Germany 36F2

Fränkischer Jura, Genoa

Fränkischer Jura region W Germany 36D4
Franklin La USA 83N8
Franklin N Car. USA 85F3
Franklin New H USA 84F1
Franklin New J USA 84D2
Franklin Pa USA 84B2
Franklin Tenn. USA 85D3
Franklin Va USA 85J2
Franklin W Va USA 85H1
Franklin City Va USA 85K2
Franklin I Antarctica 15L2
Franklin Mts NW Terr. Canada 76G3
Franz Josef Fj. Greenland 14N2
Franz Josef Land,Is = Zemlya Frantsa Iosifa,Is
Fraserburg South Africa 72C6
Fraserburgh Scotland UK 28N4
Fraser I Queens. Australia 99L5
Fraser,R BC Canada 76G6
Frasnes Belgium 32B4
Frater Ont. Canada 79D2
Fraubrunnen Switzerland 33C1
Frauenfeld Switzerland 33D1
Fray Bentos Uruguay 91E4
Fredericia Denmark 35C9
Frederick Md USA 84C3
Frederick Okla. USA 83J5
Frederick S Dak. USA 81H3
Fredericksburg Va USA 85J1
Fredericktown Mo USA 83N4
Fredericton New Br. Canada 78E4
Frederikshåb = Paamiut
Frederikshavn Denmark 35D8
Fredonia Colombia 92B2
Fredonia Kans. USA 83L4
Fredonia NY USA 84B1
Fredrika Sweden 34H4
Fredrikstad Norway 35D7
Freehold New J USA 84D2
Freeling Heights mts S Aus. Australia 97A2
Freemont,Mt Oreg. USA 80C4
Freeport Ill. USA 83P1
Freeport Pa USA 84B2
Freeport The Bahamas 89D1
Freetown Sierra Leone 68C7
Fregenal de la Sierra Spain 40C3
Fréhel,C France 42B2
Freiberg E Germany 36E3
Freiberge mts Switzerland 33E2
Freiburg W Germany 36B4
Freirina Chile 91B3
Freistadt Austria 36F4
Freital E Germany 36E3
Freixiel Portugal 40C2
Freixo Portugal 40C2
Fremantle W Aus. Australia 98D6
Fremont Nebr. USA 83K2
Fremont Ohio USA 79E5
Fremont Pk Wyo. USA 81C4
French Guiana country S America 93G3
French I Vic. Australia 97C3
Frenchman Cap mt Tas. Australia 97F5
Frenchman,R Sask. Canada 76K7
Frenchpark Ireland, Rep. of 30G6
French,R Ont. Canada 79F2
Frenchtown Mont. USA 80F2
Fresco Ivory Coast 68D7
Freshford Ireland,Rep. of 31J8
Fresnillo Mexico 88D3
Fresno Calif. USA 80D7
Frewena N Terr. Australia 99H3
Freycinet Pen. Nat. Pk Tas. Australia 97F5
Fria,C Namibia 72A3
Frias Argentina 91C3
Frías Spain 40E1
Fribourg Switzerland 33C2
Fribourg canton Switzerland 33B2
Frick Switzerland 33D1
Fridtjof Nansen,Mt Antarctica 15L1
Friedland E Germany 36E2
Friedrichshafen W Germany 36C5
Friend Nebr. USA 83K2
Friesland prov. Netherlands 32D1
Frimley England UK 27N6
Friuli-Venezia Giulia region Italy 44D2
Frobisher B NW Terr. Canada 77S4
Frobisher L Sask. Canada 76K5
Frohavet,B Norway 34C5
Frome England UK 26K6
Frome,L S Aus. Australia 97A2
Frome,R England UK 27K7
Fronteira Portugal 40C3
Frontera Mexico 88F4
Fronteras Mexico 88C1
Front Ra Col. USA 82F2
Front Royal Va USA 84B3
Frosinone Italy 45D5
Frostburg Md USA 84B3
Frøya,I Norway 34C5
Frozen Str. NW Terr. Canada 77P3
Frunze Kirgiz. USSR 50J5
Frutigen Switzerland 33C2
Fruto Calif. USA 80B6
Frydek Czech. 37H4
Fthiótis dist. Greece 47D5
Fu'an China 55K9
Fucheng China 54J4
Fuchuan China 55F10
Fuchun Jiang river China 55K8
Fuding China 55L9
Fuente-Alamo de Murcia Spain 41F4
Fuente del Arco Spain 40D3
Fuentes de Oñoro Spain 40C2
Fuerte,R Mexico 88C2
Fuerteventura,I Canary Is 68C3
Fugu China 54F3
Fu He river China 55J9
Fujian province China 55K9
Fu Jiang China 54C7
Fujin China 52K1
Fuji-san mt Japan 56F7
Fujiyama = Fuji-san
Fukuei Chiao cape Taiwan 55L10
Fukui Japan 56E6
Fukui prefecture Japan 56E7
Fukuoka Japan 56B8
Fukuoka prefecture Japan 56B8
Fukushima Japan 56G6
Fukushima prefecture Japan 56G6
Fukuyama Japan 56C7
Fulda,R W Germany 36C3
Fuling China 55D8
Fullerton Nebr. USA 83K2
Fulton Ky USA 85C2
Fulton Miss. USA 85C3
Fulton Mo USA 83N3
Fulton NY USA 84C1
Fulton Chain Ls NY USA 84D1
Funchal Madeira I 68B2
Fundão Portugal 40C2
Fundy,B of New Br./No. Sc. Canada 78E4
Fünen = Fyn
Funing = Xiapu
Funing Hebei China 54K3
Funing Jiangsu China 54K6
Funing Wan bay China 55L9
Funiu Shan mts China 54G6
Funk I Newf. Canada 78M2
Fuping Hebei China 54H3
Fuping Shaanxi China 54E5
Fuqing China 55K10
Fürg Iran 63H4
Furka P Switzerland 33D2
Furneaux Grp. islands Tas. Australia 97F4
Furness region England UK 25B4
Furqlus Syria 64F3
Fürstenwalde E Germany 36F2
Fürth W Germany 36D4
Fusagasuga Colombia 92C3
Fushan China 54L4
Fushun Guizhou China 55C8
Fushun Liaoning China 54M2
Fusio Switzerland 33D2
Füssen W Germany 36D5
Fusui China 55D11
Fu Xian Liadong China 54M3
Fu Xian Shaanxi China 54E4
Fuxin China 54L1
Fuyang Anhui China 54H6
Fuyang Zhejiang China 55K7
Fuying Dao island China 55L9
Fuyi Shui river China 55F9
Fuyu China 52H1
Fuzhou Fujian China 55K9
Fuzhou Jiangxi China 55J8
Fyne,Loch Scotland UK 29F7
Fyn,I Denmark 35D9
Fyresdals Vatn lake Norway 35C7

G

Gaalkacyo Somalia 71K3
Gabarus No. Sc. Canada 78H4
Gabela Angola 70C7
Gabès Tunisia 69H2
Gabes,G of Tunisia 69H2
Gąbin Poland 37H2
Gabo I NSW Australia 97D3
Gabon country Africa 70C5
Gaborone Botswana 72D4
Gabrovo Bulgaria 46E3
Gach Saran Iran 63G3
Gadag India 58E5
Gadmen Switzerland 33D2
Gadsden Ala. USA 85E3
Gael Hamkes B Greenland 14M2
Gaerwen Wales UK 26F2
Găeşti Romania 46E2
Gaeta Italy 45D5
Gaeta,G di Italy 45D5
Gaffney S Car. USA 85G3
Gafsa Tunisia 69G2
Gagetown New Br. Canada 78E4
Gagil island Yap Is 94A19
Gagnoa Ivory Coast 68D7
Gagnon Que. Canada 77S6
Gaiah Pakistan 60C3
Gaibanda Bangladesh 61G3
Gai Bau,I Vietnam 57D2
Gaillac France 43D5
Gaillimh = Galway
Gaimán Argentina 91C6
Gainesboro Tenn. USA 85E2
Gainesville Ala. USA 85C4
Gainesville Fla USA 85F6
Gainesville Ga USA 85F3
Gainesville Mo USA 83M4
Gainesville Texas USA 83K6
Gainsborough England UK 25G6
Gairdner,L S Aus. Australia 99H6
Gairloch Scotland UK 28E4
Gairlochy Scotland UK 28F6
Gais Switzerland 33E1
Gaixian China 54M2
Gakuch Kashmir India 60C2
Galana,R Kenya 71H5
Galangue Angola 70D7
Galapagos,Is Pacific Ocean 95S8
Gala,R Scotland UK 29L8
Galashiels Scotland UK 29L8
Galathea,B Nicobar Is India 59H7
Galati Romania 46F2
Galatz = Galati
Galax Va USA 85G2
Galdhøpiggen,Mt Norway 35C6
Galeana Mexico 88C1
Galeana Mexico 88D3
Galeh Dār Iran 63G4
Galena Ill. USA 83N1
Galenstock mt Switzerland 33D2
Galesburg Ill. USA 83N2
Galeton Pa USA 84C2
Galgate England UK 25C5
Galich USSR 49F1
Galicia region Spain 40C1
Galilee,L Queens. Australia 99K4
Galilee,Sea of = Tiberias,L
Galiuro Mts. Ariz. USA 82C6
Gallarate Italy 44B3
Gallatin Tenn. USA 85D2
Galle Sri Lanka 58F7
Gallegos,R Argentina 91B8
Galley Hd Ireland, Rep. of 31F10
Gallipoli = Gelibolu
Gallipoli Italy 45F5
Gällivare Sweden 34J3
Gallo Mts New Mex. USA 82D5
Galloway,Mull of Scotland UK 29G10
Gallup New Mex. USA 82D5
Galong NSW Australia 97C2
Galston Scotland UK 29H8
Galtymore mt Ireland, Rep. of 31G9
Galty Mts Ireland, Rep. of 31G9
Galva Ill. USA 83N2
Galveston Texas USA 83L8
Galveston B Texas USA 83L8
Gálvez Argentina 91D4
Galway Ireland, Rep. of 31E7
Galway county Ireland,Rep. of 31E7
Galway B Ireland, Rep. of 31E7
Gama Hanu Kashmir India 60E3
Gambaga Ghana 68E6
Gambia,R Africa 68B6
Gambia, The country Africa 68B6
Gambo Newf. Canada 78L2
Gamboma Congo 70D5
Gamlakarfeby = Kokkola
Gams Switzerland 33E1
Gananoque Ont. Canada 79H3
Gancheng China 55E13
Gand = Gent
Gandak,R India 61E2
Gandak,R India 61E2
Gandava Pakistan 58C3
Gander airport Newf. Canada 78L2
Gander B Newf. Canada 78M2
Gander L Newf. Canada 78L2
Gandesa Spain 41G2
Gandhinagar India 58D4
Gandhi Sagar India 58E4
Gandia Spain 41F3
Ganga,Mouths of Bangladesh/ India 59G4
Ganganagar India 60C6
Ganga,R India 61E3
Gangaw Burma 59H4
Gangbei Gang point China 55E13
Gangdisê Shan mts Tibet China 58F2
Ganges,R = Ganga,R
Gangoh India 60E6
Gangtok India 61G2
Ganjam India 59G5
Gan Jiang river China 55H9
Ganmam NSW Australia 97C2
Gannat France 42E3
Gannett Pk Wyo. USA 81C4
Ganquan China 54E4
Gansu province China 54C5
Gantheaume B W Aus. Australia 98C5
Gantheaume,C S Aus. Australia 97A3
Ganton England UK 25G4
Ganyu China 54K5
Ganza CAR 69K7
Ganzhou China 55H10
Gao Mali 68E5
Gao'an China 55H8
Gaochun China 54K7
Gaomi China 54K4
Gaoping China 54G5
Gaoqing China 54K4
Gaotang China 54J4
Gaoua Upper Volta 68E6
Gaoual Guinea 68C6
Gaoyou China 54K6
Gaoyou Hu lake China 54K6
Gaoyt China 54H4
Gap France 43G4
Gar Tibet China 58E2
Garachine Panama 89D5
Gara Gorfu mt Ethiopia 71H3
Garah NSW Australia 97C1
Gara,L Ireland, Rep. of 30F6
Garanhuns Brazil 93K5
Garba Tula Kenya 71H4
Gard dep. France 43F4
Garda,L di Italy 44C3
Garden Mich. USA 79C3
Garden City Kans. USA 82H4
Garden Grove Calif. USA 80E9
Gardiner Maine USA 78D4
Gardiner Mont. USA 81B3
Gardiner Oreg. USA 80A4
Gardiners B NY USA 84E2
Gardiners I NY USA 84E2
Gardner,I Hawaii USA 94K5
Gardner I Phoenix Is 94J8
Gardnerville Nev. USA 80D6
Garelochhead Scotland UK 29G7
Garforth England UK 25F5
Garhakota India 61B4
Garhi India 61B4
Garhmuktesar India 60F6
Garhshankar India 60E5
Garhwa India 61D3
Garibaldi Brazil 91F3
Garibaldi Park BC Canada 76G6
Garies South Africa 72B6
Garissa Kenya 71H5
Garland Mont. USA 81D3
Garlugubi Ethiopia 71J3
Garm Tadzhik. USSR 50J6
Garmisch W Germany 36D5
Garmsar Iran 63G2
Garnpung,L NSW Australia 97B2
Garo Hills India 59H3
Garola India 61B3
Garonne,R France 43D5
Garoua Cameroun 69H7
Garrauli India 61B3
Garraway Liberia 68D8
Garrison Mont. USA 80G2
Garrison N Dak. USA 81G2
Garron Point N Ireland 30L3
Garrovillas Spain 40C3
Garry,L NW Terr. Canada 76L3
Garsen Kenya 71J5
Garstang England UK 25C5
Garvagh N Ireland 30K4
Garve Scotland UK 28G4
Gary Ind. USA 79C5
Garyarsa Tibet China 58F2
Garza Argentina 91D3
Garzon Colombia 92B3
Gasan Kuli Turkmen. USSR 50G6
Gascogne prov. France 43D5
Gascogne,G de France/Spain 43B5
Gasconade,R Misssouri 83N3
Gascoyne,R W Aus. Australia 98D5
Gashaka Nigeria 69H7
Gasharbrum,Mt Kashmir India 60E3
Gasht Iran 63J4
Gaspé Que. Canada 78F2
Gaspé B Que. Canada 78F2
Gaspé,C Que. Canada 78F2
Gaspé Pen. Que. Canada 78F2
Gaspésian Park Que. Canada 78E2
Gasselte Netherlands 32E2
Gastonia N Car. USA 85G3
Gastre Argentina 91C6
Gata Spain 40C2
Gata,C Cyprus 64B3
Gata,C de Spain 41E4
Gate City Va USA 85F2
Gatehouse of Fleet Scotland UK 29H10
Gateshead England UK 25E3
Gatineau,R Que. Canada 79J2
Gatun L Panama 89D5
Gaud-i-Zirreh region Afghanistan 63J4
Gauhati India 59H3
Gauja,R Latviy USSR 35L8
Gaula,R Norway 34D5
Gaurihar India 61C3
Gavarnie France 43C5
Gavāter Iran 63J4
Gāvbandī Iran 63G4
Gávdhos island Kríti Greece 47D7
Gavião Portugal 40C3
Gaviota Calif. USA 80C8
Gävle Sweden 35G6
Gävleborg county Sweden 35F6
Gävlebukten bay Sweden 35G6
Gavur Dagh Turkey 62D2
Gawler S Aus. Australia 97A2
Gawler Ra. mts S Aus. Australia 99H6
Gaya India 61E3
Gaya Niger 68F6
Gayaza Uganda 71G5
Gaylord Mich. USA 79D3
Gaza CAR 69J8
Gaza Egypt 64C6
Gaziantep Turkey 62D2
G. Chama mt Malaysia 57C5
Gdańsk Poland 37H1
Gdansk voivodship Poland 37H1
Gdynia Poland 37H1
Gebeit Sudan 69N5
Gebel Katherina mt Egypt 69M3
Gebel Maghara hill Egypt 64B7
Gedaref Sudan 69N6
Gedinne Belgium 32C5
Geel Belgium 32C3
Geelong Vic. Australia 97B3
Geeveston Tas. Australia 97F5
Geidam Nigeria 69H6
Geikie,R Sask. Canada 76L5
Geislingen W Germany 36C4
Gela Sicily Italy 45E7
Gelderland prov. Netherlands 32D2
Geldrop Netherlands 32D3
Geleen Belgium 32D4
Gelibolu Turkey 62B1
Gelidonya Burun cape Turkey 62C2
Gelinden Belgium 32D4
Gel,R Sudan 69M7
Gelsenkirchen W Germany 36B3
Gemas Malaysia 57C6
Gembloux Belgium 32C4
Gemena Zaire 70D4
Gemert Netherlands 32D3
Gemmenich Belgium 32D4
Gemmi Pass Switzerland 33C2
Gemsbok Nat. Pk Botswana 72C5
Genappe Belgium 32C4
Gendari Mt Pakistan 60A6
Gendringen Netherlands 32E3
Geneina Sudan 69K6
Genemuiden Netherlands 32E2
General Acha Argentina 91D5
General Alvarado Argentina 91E5
General Alvear Argentina 91C4
General Alvear Argentina 91D5
General Arenales Argentina 91D4
General Belgrano Argentina 91E5
General Capdevila Argentina 91D3
General Grant Grove Sect. Nat. Pk Calif. USA 80D7
General Guido Argentina 91E5
General La Madrid Argentina 91D5
General Lavalle Argentina 91E5
General Pico Argentina 91D5
General Pinto Argentina 91D4
General Roca Argentina 91C5
General Viamonte Argentina 91D5
General Villegas Argentina 91D4
Genesee Idaho USA 80E2
Geneseo NY USA 84C1
Geneva = Genève
Geneva Nebr. USA 83K2
Geneva NY USA 84C1
Geneva,L of = Lac Leman
Genève Switzerland 33B2
Genk Belgium 32D4
Genkai nada bay Japan 56A8
Gennargentu,Monti del mts Sardinia Italy 45B5
Gennep Netherlands 32D3
Genoa = Genova
Genoa Vic. Australia 97C3

Genoa,R Gramsbergen

Genoa,R Argentina 91B6
Genova Italy 44B3
Genova,G di Italy 44B3
Gent Belgium 33B3
Geographe B W Aus. Australia 98D6
Geographe Chan. W Aus. Australia 98C4
George,L NSW Australia 97C3
George,L NY USA 84E1
George,R Que. Canada 77S5
George Sd New Zealand 100B7
Georgetown Del. USA 79J6
Georgetown Ga USA 85E5
George Town Gr. Cayman West Indies 89C3
Georgetown Guyana 92F2
Georgetown Ky USA 85E1
George Town Pinang Malay. 57C5
Georgetown Pr. Ed. I. Canada 78G3
Georgetown Queens. Australia 99J3
Georgetown S Car. USA 85H4
George Town Tas. Australia 97F5
Georgetown Va USA 84C3
George VI Sd Antarctica 15S3
George V Land Antarctica 15K3
Georgheni Romania 46E1
Georgia state USA 87K5
Georgian B Ont. Canada 79F3
Georgian B Is Nat. Pk Ont. Canada 79F3
Georgina,R Queens. Australia 99H4
Georgiu-Dezh USSR 48L6
Georgiyevka Kazakh. USSR 50K5
Georgiyevsk USSR 50F5
Gera E Germany 36E3
Geraardsbergen Belgium 32B4
Geral de Goias,Serra mts Brazil 93H6
Geraldine New Zealand 100D7
Geraldton W Aus. Australia 98C5
Gerlach Nev. USA 80D5
Germania Argentina 91D4
Germania Land Greenland 14M2
Germiston South Africa 72D5
Gérone = Girona
Gers dep. France 43D5
Gerze Turkey 62D1
Getafe Spain 40E2
Gethsemani Que. Canada 78H1
Gettysburg Pa USA 84C3
Gettysburg S Dak. USA 81G3
Getz Ice Shelf Antarctica 15Q2
Gevgelija Yugoslavia 46D4
Geysir Iceland 34U12
Ghabaghib Syria 64E4
Ghadai Pakistan 60B3
Ghaggar,Dry Bed of Pakistan 60C6
Ghāghara,R India 61D2
Ghaida South Yemen 62F7
Ghana country Africa 68E7
Ghantur Syria 64F3
Gharandal Jordan 64D7
Ghardaïa Algeria 68F2
Gharyan Libya 69H2
Ghat Libya 69H4
Ghatal India 61F4
Ghatampur India 61C2
Ghatghat Saudi Arabia 62F5
Ghatoraba,R India 58D5
Ghats,Eastern,Mts India 58F5
Ghats,Western,Mts India 58D5
Ghayl Saudi Arabia 62F5
Ghazaouet Algeria 68E1
Ghaziabad India 60E6
Ghazipur India 61D3
Ghazir Lebanon 64D3
Ghazni Afghanistan 63K3
Ghent = Gent
Ghislenghien Belgium 32B4
Ghizao Afghanistan 63K3
Ghorak Afghanistan 63K3
Ghotki Pakistan 58C3
Ghudámis Lybia 69G2
Ghurian Afghanistan 63J3
Giant's Causeway N Ireland 30K3
Giarre Sicily Italy 45E7
Gibara Cuba 89D2
Gibbonsville Idaho USA 80F3
Gibeon Namibia 72B5
Gibraltar Spain 40D4
Gibraltar, Str. of Morocco/Spain 40D5
Gibson Desert W Aus. Australia 98E4
Giddings Texas USA 83K7
Gide,R Sweden 34G4
Gidole Ethiopia 71H3
Gien France 42E3
Giessen W Germany 36C3
Gifford Scotland UK 29L8
Gifhorn W Germany 36D2
Gifu Japan 56E7
Gifu prefecture Japan 56E7
Giganta, La mt Mexico 88B2
Gigha island Scotland UK 29E8
Gijón Spain 40D1
Gila Des. Ariz. USA 86D5
Gila,R Ariz. USA 82C6
Gila,R Sudan 69M7
Gilau Romania 46D1
Gilbert Is = Kiribati
Gilberton Queens. Australia 99J3
Gilbert,R Queens. Australia 99J3
Gilbués Brazil 93J5
Gilead region Jordan 64D5
Gilgandra NSW Australia 97C2
Gilgit Kashmir India 60D3
Gilgit district Kashmir India 60D2
Gilgit,R Kashmir India 60C2
Gilgunnia NSW Australia 97C2
Gilles Nev. USA 80D6
Gillett Ark. USA 83N5
Gillette Wyo. USA 81E3
Gillingham Dorset,England UK 27K6
Gillingham Kent,England UK 27R6
Gill,L Ireland, Rep. of 30G5
Gilmore Idaho USA 80G3
Gilroy Calif. USA 80C7
Gimel Switzerland 33B2
Ginglan Gang point China 55E13
Ginir Ethiopia 71J3
Gio island Vietnam 57D3
Giogo dello Stelvio pass Italy/Switz. 33F2
Gioia,G di Italy 45E6
Giornico Switzerland 33D2
Gippsland region Vic. Australia 97C3
Girardot Colombia 92C3
Girdle Ness cape Scotland UK 28M5
Giresun Turkey 62D1
Girga Egypt 69M3
Giridih India 61F3
Girilambone NSW Australia 97C2
Girishk Afghanistan 63J3
Girnat Hills India 58D4
Girona Spain 41H1
Girona prov. Spain 41H1
Gironde dep. France 43C4
Gironde,R France 42C4
Girvan Scotland UK 29G9
Girvan,R Scotland UK 29G9
Gisborne New Zealand 100H4
Gisors France 42D2
Giswil Switzerland 33D2
Gitch,Mt Ethiopia 71H2
Giuletti,L Ethiopia 71J2
Giurgiu Romania 46E3
Givors France 42F4
Givry Belgium 32C4
Givry island Truk Is 94A16
Gizhiga USSR 51T3
Gizycko Poland 37J1
Gjerstad Norway 35C7
Gjirokastër Albania 47C4
Gjoa Haven NW Terr. Canada 76M3
Gjøvik Norway 35D6
Glabbeak Belgium 32C4
Glace Bay No. Sc. Canada 78H3
Glacier BC Canada 76H6
Glacier Cook Kerguelen 65S12
Glacier Nat. Pk Mont. USA 76J7
Gladstone Mich. USA 79C3
Gladstone NSW Australia 97D2
Gladstone Queens. Australia 99L4
Gladstone S Aus. Australia 97A2
Gladstone Tas. Australia 97F5
Gladwin Mich. USA 79D3
Glamis Scotland UK 29K6
Glamoc Yugoslavia 44F3
Glanaruddery Mts Ireland, Rep. of 31D9
Glärnisch mt Switzerland 33D2
Glarus Switzerland 33E1
Glarus canton Switzerland 33D2
Glasgow Ky USA 85E2
Glasgow Mont. USA 81D1
Glasgow Scotland UK 29H8
Glas Maol mt Scotland UK 29K6
Glassboro New J USA 84D3
Glass,L Scotland UK 28H4
Glastonbury England UK 26J6
Glatt,R Switzerland 33D1
Glauchau E Germany 36E3
Glazov USSR 49L1
Glen Mont. USA 80G3
Glen New H USA 79L3
Glen Affric Scotland UK 28F5
Glen Afton New Zealand 100F3
Glénan,Is de France 42A2
Glenarm N Ireland 30L4
Glenbrook Nev. USA 80D6
Glenburnie S Aus. Australia 97B3
Glen Cannich Scotland UK 28G5
Glen Carron valley Scotland UK 28F4
Glen Clova valley Scotland UK 29K6
Glencoe Minn. USA 81K3
Glencoe S Aus. Australia 97B3
Glen Coe valley Scotland UK 29G6
Glendale Ariz. USA 82B6
Glendale Calif. USA 80D8
Glen Davis NSW Australia 97D2
Glendive Mont. USA 81E2
Glendowan Mts Ireland, Rep. of 30G4
Gleneagles Scotland UK 29J7
Glenelg S Aus. Australia 97A2
Glenelg Scotland UK 28E5
Glenelg,R Vic. Australia 97B3
Glen Ellen Calif. USA 80B6
Glenfinnan Scotland UK 29F6
Glengad Hd N Ireland 30J3
Glengariff Ireland, Rep. of 31D10
Glen Garry Scotland UK 28F5
Glen Garry valley Scotland UK 29H6
Glen Innes NSW Australia 97D1
Glenluce Scotland UK 29G10
Glen Lyon Scotland UK 29H6
Glen More valley Scotland UK 28G5
Glennamaddy Ireland, Rep. of 30F6
Glenner,R Switzerland 33E2
Glenns Ferry Idaho USA 80F4
Glenreagh NSW Australia 97D2
Glenrothes Scotland UK 29K7
Glens Falls NY USA 84E1
Glen Shee valley Scotland UK 29K6
Glen Spean valley Scotland UK 29G6
Glenties Ireland, Rep of 30G4
Glenville W Va USA 79F6
Glenwood Iowa USA 83L2
Glenwood Minn. USA 81K3
Glenwood Springs Col. USA 82E3
Gletsch Switzerland 33D2
Glin Ireland,Rep. of 31E8
Glittertind,Mt Norway 35C6
Gliwice Poland 37H3
Globe Ariz. USA 82C6
Glogau = Głogów
Głogów Poland 37G3
Glomma,R Norway 35D6
Glommerträsk Sweden 34H4
Gloppen Norway 34B6
Glossop England UK 25E6
Gloucester England UK 27K5
Gloucester Mass. USA 84F1
Gloucester NSW Australia 97D2
Gloucester Va USA 85J2
Gloucester City New J USA 84D3
Gloucestershire county England UK 27K5
Glovelier Switzerland 33C1
Gloversville NY USA 84D1
Glukhov Ukrain. USSR 48H6
Glyndebourne England UK 27Q7
G Massif Galliéni per. Kerguelen 65S12
Gmünd Austria 36E5
Gmünd W Germany 36C4
Gmunden Austria 36E5
Gniezno Poland 37G2
Goa India 58D5
Goa, Daman & Diu prov. India 58D5
Goalpara India 59H3
Goalundt Ghat Bangladesh 61G4
Gobabis Namibia 72B4
Gobi desert Mongolia 51M5
Gobindpur India 61F4
Godalming England UK 27N6
Godavari,Mouths of India 59F5
Godavari,R India 58E5
Godda India 61F3
Godech Bulgaria 46D3
Goderich Ont. Canada 79F4
Godhra India 58D4
Godmanchester England UK 27P4
Gödöllö Hungary 37H5
Gods L Man. Canada 76M6
Gods,R Man. Canada 77N5
Godthåb = Nûûk
Goes Netherlands 32B3
Gogama Ont. Canada 79F2
Gogebic Ra upland Mich. USA 79B2
Gog Magog Hills England UK 27Q4
Gogra,R = Ghagara,R
Gogrial Sudan 69L7
Gohana India 60E6
Goharganj India 61A4
Goiânia Brazil 93H7
Goiás Brazil 93G7
Goil,L Scotland UK 29G7
Goirle Netherlands 32D3
Gökçeada island Turkey 47E4
Goksun Turkey 62D2
Golaghat India 59H3
Golchikha USSR 50K2
Golconda Ill. USA 83P4
Golconda India 58E5
Golconda Nev. USA 80E5
Goldap Poland 37K1
Goldau Switzerland 33D1
Gold Beach Oreg. USA 80A4
Gold Coast = Ghana
Golden B New Zealand 100E5
Goldendale Wash. USA 80C3
Golden Gate Ra. Nev. USA 80F6
Golden Lake Ont. Canada 79H3
Golden Throne mt Kashmir India 60E3
Golden Vale valley Ireland, Rep. of 31G8
Goldfield Nev. USA 80E7
Goldsboro N Car. USA 85J3
Goleniow Poland 36F2
Golfito Costa Rica 89C5
Golfo de Cadiz Spain 40C4
Gol Gol NSW Australia 97B2
Golmo China 52B3
Golpāyegān Iran 63G3
Golspie Scotland UK 28J4
Goltva Ukrain. USSR 48H7
Gomal,P Pakistan 60B4
Gomati,R India 61C2
Gombe Nigeria 69H6
Gomel Belorus. USSR 48G5
Gomera,I Canary Is 68B3
Gómez Farias Mexico 88D3
Gómez Palacio Mexico 88D2
Gonaïves Haiti 89E3
Gonâve,I de la Haiti 89E3
Gonbad-e Kāvūs Iran 63H2
Gonda India 61D2
Gondal India 58D4
Gondar Ethiopia 71H2
Gondiądz Poland 37K2
Gondo Switzerland 33D2
Gongcheng China 55F10
Gonggan Shan mts China 52D5
Gonggar Tibet China 59H3
Gongga Shan mt China 52D5
Gongola,R Nigeria 69H6
Gongolgon NSW Australia 97C2
Gong Shui river China 55H10
Gong Xian China 54G5
Gonzales Calif. USA 80C7
Gonzales Texas USA 83K8
Goodenough I Papua New Guinea 99L1
Gooderham Ont. Canada 79G3
Good Hope,C of South Africa 72B6
Goodland Kans. USA 82H3
Goodooga NSW Australia 97C1
Goodrich Wis. USA 79A3
Goodwin Sands England UK 27T6
Goole England UK 25G5
Goolgowie NSW Australia 97C2
Goolwa S Aus. Australia 97A3
Goomalling W Aus. Australia 98D6
Goombalie NSW Australia 97C1
Goondiwindi Queens. Australia 99L5
Goor Netherlands 32E2
Goose Bay Newf. Canada 77T6
Goose Creek Ra. Nev./Utah USA 80F5
Goose,L Calif./Oreg. USA 80C5
Gopalpur India 59F5
Göppingen W Germany 36C4
Gor Spain 40E4
Gorakhpur India 61D2
Gorbachovo USSR 48K5
Gordola Switzerland 33D2
Gordon Nebr. USA 82G1
Gordon S Aus. Australia 97A2
Gordon,R Tas. Australia 97C5
Gordon's Bay South Africa 72J10
Gordonsville Va USA 85H1
Goré Chad 69J7
Gore Ethiopia 71H3
Gore New Zealand 100C8
Gore Bay Ont. Canada 79E3
Gorebridge Scotland UK 29K8
Gorey Channel Is UK 27W11
Gorey Ireland, Rep. of 31L8
Gorgān Iran 63G2
Gorgona island Columbia 92B3
Gorgona island Italy 44B4
Gorinchem Netherlands 32C3
Gorizia Italy 44D3
Gor'kiy USSR 49F2
Gor'kovskoye Vdkhr res. USSR 49F2
Gorlice Poland 37J4
Görlitz E Germany 36F3
Gorlovka Ukrain. USSR 48K7
Gormanstown Tas. Australia 97F5
Gornergratt Switzerland 33C3
Gorno Altaysk USSR 50K4
Gorodets USSR 49F2
Gorodishche USSR 49G4
Gorodnitsa Ukrain. USSR 48E6
Goroke Vic. Australia 97B3
Gorongoza Nat. Pk Mozambique 72E3
Gorontalo Celebes Indon. 53H10
Gorrahei Ethiopia 71J3
Gorsel Netherlands 32E2
Gort Ireland, Rep. of 31F7
Gorumna I Ireland, Rep. of 31D7
Gory Byrranga mts USSR 51L2
Gory Putorana region USSR 51L3
Gory Sikhote Alin mts USSR 51Q5
Gorzów Wielkopolski Poland 36F2
Gosainthan = Xixabangma Fehg
Gosainthan,Mt China/Nepal 59G3
Göschenen Switzerland 33D2
Gosford NSW Australia 97D2
Gosforth England UK 25B4
Gosforth England UK 25E2
Goshanak Pakistan 58B3
Goshen Calif. USA 80D7
Goshen NY USA 84D2
Gospić Yugoslavia 44E3
Gosport England UK 27M7
Gossa,I Norway 34B5
Gossau Switzerland 33E1
Gosselies Belgium 32C4
Gostivar Yugoslavia 46C4
Gostynin Poland 37H2
Göta Älv river Sweden 35E7
Göteborg Sweden 35D8
Götesborgs och Bohus county Sweden 35D7
Gotha E Germany 36D3
Gothenburg = Göteborg
Gothenburg Nebr. USA 82H2
Gotland,I Sweden 35H8
Gotō Retto islands Japan 56A8
Gotska Sandon Nat. Pk,I Sweden 35H7
Göttingen W Germany 36C3
Gottwaldov Czech. 37G4
Gouda Netherlands 32C2
Goudswaard Netherlands 32C3
Gough,I Atlantic Ocean 73M13
Gouin Res. Que. Canada 78A2
Goulburn NSW Australia 97C2
Goulburn,R Vic. Australia 97C3
Goundam Mali 68E5
Gourdon France 43D4
Gouré Niger 69H6
Gourma Rarous Mali 68E5
Gournay France 42D2
Gouro Chad 69J5
Gourock Scotland UK 29G8
Gourock Ra NSW Australia 97C3
Gouverneur NY USA 79J3
Governador Valadares Brazil 93J7
Gowanda NY USA 84B1
Gower pen. Wales UK 26F5
Gowna,L Ireland, Rep. of 30H6
Goya Argentina 91E3
Gozo island Medit. Sea 45E7
Graaff Reinet South Africa 72C6
Grabo Ivory Coast 68D8
Grabouw South Africa 72K10
Grabów Poland 37H3
Gračac Yugoslavia 44E3
Gracefield Que. Canada 79H2
Gracias Honduras 89B4
Graciosa island Açores 68Q9
Gradaus,Serra dos mts Brazil 93G5
Gradets Bulgaria 46F3
Grado Spain 40C1
Grafton N Dak. USA 81J1
Grafton NSW Australia 97D1
Grafton W Va USA 79F6
Grafton,Is Chile 91B8
Grafton Pk Nev. USA 80F6
Graham Texas USA 83J6
Graham Land Antarctica 15S3
Grahamstown South Africa 72D6
Graiguenamanagh Ireland,Rep. of 31K8
Grain England UK 27R6
Grajau Brazil 93J5
Grajewo Poland 37K2
Grammont = Geraardsbergen
Grampian region Scotland UK 28L5
Grampian Mts Scotland UK 29G7
Grampians mts Vic. Australia 97B3
Gramsbergen Netherlands 32E2

Granada, Gullane

Granada Nicaragua 89B4
Granada Spain 40E4
Granada prov. Spain 40D4
Granard Ireland, Rep. of 30J6
Gran Baja,R Argentina 91C7
Granby Que. Canada 79K3
Gran Canaria,I Canary Is 68B3
Gran Chaco region Argentina 91D3
Grand Bahama I The Bahamas 89D1
Grand Bank Newf. Canada 78L3
Grand Bassam Ivory Coast 68E7
Grand Calumet,I du Que. Canada 79H3
Grand Canyon Ariz. USA 80G8
Grand Canyon Nat. Pk Ariz. USA 82B4
Grand Cayman island West Indies 89C3
Grand Combin mt Switzerland 33C3
Grand Coulee mts Wash. USA 80D2
Grand Coulee Dam Wash. USA 86C2
Grande-Anse New Br. Canada 78F3
Grande,B Argentina 91C8
Grande Comore,I Comoros 71J7
Grande de Santiago,R Mexico 88D3
Grande,I Brazil 93J8
Grande Prairie Alta Canada 76H5
Grande Prairie Texas USA 83K6
Grande, Rio river Brazil 93G7
Grande Rivière Que. Canada 78F2
Grande Ronde,R Oreg. USA 80E3
Grand Falls New Br. Canada 78E3
Grand Falls Newf. Canada 78L2
Grand Forks BC Canada 76H7
Grand Forks N Dak. USA 81J2
Grand Haven Mich. USA 79C4
Grand I Mich. USA 79C2
Grand I NY USA 84B1
Grandin,L NW Terr. Canada 76H4
Grand Island Nebr. USA 83J2
Grand Junction Col. USA 82D3
Grand Junction Tenn. USA 85C3
Grand L Canada/USA 78E4
Grand L La USA 83M8
Grand L New Br. Canada 78F4
Grand L Newf. Canada 78K2
Grand Lac Victoria Res. Que. Canada 79H2
Grand Lahou Ivory Coast 68D7
Grand Lahou Ivory Coast 68E7
Grand Ledge Mich. USA 79D4
Grand Manan island New Br. Canada 78E4
Grand Marais Minn. USA 79A2
Grandmenil Belgium 32D4
Grand-Mère Que. Canada 79K2
Grand Mesa Col. USA 82D3
Grand Muveran mt Switzerland 33C2
Grandola Portugal 40B3
Grand,R Mich. USA 79D4
Grand,R S Dak. USA 81G3
Grand Rapids Mich. USA 79D4
Grand Rapids Minn. USA 81L2
Grandrieu Belgium 32C4
Grand River = Grande Rivière
Grand St Bernard Pass Italy/Switz. 44A3
Grandson Switzerland 33B2
Grand Teton mt Wyo. USA 81B4
Grand Teton Nat. Pk Wyo. USA 81B4
Grand Tower Ill. USA 83P4
Grane Norway 34E4
Graney,L Ireland, Rep. of 31F8
Grangemouth Scotland UK 29J7
Granger Wyo. USA 81B5
Granges Switzerland 33B2
Grangeville Idaho USA 80E3
Granite City Ill. USA 83N3
Granite Falls Minn. USA 81K3
Granite Ra. Nev. USA 80D5
Granja Brazil 93J4
Grankulla Finland 35L6
Granokoro Nauru 94A22
Granollers Spain 41H2
Granön Sweden 34H4
Grant Ont. Canada 77O6
Grant City Mo USA 83L2
Grantham England UK 25G7
Grant,Mt Nev. USA 80E6
Granton Scotland UK 29K8
Grantown on Spey Scotland UK 28J5
Grant Ra. Nev. USA 80F6
Grants New Mex. USA 82E5
Grants Pass Oreg. USA 80B4
Grantsville Utah USA 82B2
Granville France 42C2
Granville N Dak. USA 81G1
Granville NY USA 84E1
Granville L Man. Canada 76L5
Grapevine Mts Nev. USA 80E7
Gr. Armagosa Des. Nev. USA 80E7
Grasett Ont. Canada 79D1
Graskop South Africa 72E4
Gras,L de NW Terr. Canada 76J4
Grasmere England UK 25B4
Gräsö,I Sweden 35H6
Grassano Italy 45F5
Grasse France 43G5
Graubünden canton Switzerland 33E2
Graus Spain 41G1
Gr. Australian Bight bay Australia Australia 98F6
Gravarne Sweden 35D7
Grave Netherlands 32D3
Gravelbourg Sask. Canada 76K7
Gravenhurst Ont. Canada 79G3
Gravesend England UK 27Q6
Gravesend NSW Australia 97D1
Gray France 42F3
Grayling Mich. USA 79D3
Grays England UK 27Q6
Grays Harb. Wash. USA 80A2
Grayville Ill. USA 83P3
Graz Austria 37F5
Gr. Bahama Bank West Indies 89D1
Gr. Barrier I New Zealand 100F3
Gr. Barrier Reef Australia 99K3
Gr. Bernera island Scotland UK 28C3
Gr. Catwick Is Vietnam 57D4
Gr. Coco Ih4 Bay of Bengal 59H6
Gr. Dividing Ra mts Australia 99K4
Gr. Drakenstein Mts South Africa 72J9
Great Abaco I The Bahamas 89D1
Great Barrington Mass. USA 84E1
Great Basin Nev. USA 86C3
Great Bear L NW Terr. Canada 76G3
Great Bend Kans. USA 83J3
Great Blasket I Ireland, Rep. of 31B9
Great Britain British Isles UK 22F4
Great Colorado V Ariz./Calif. USA 80F9
Great Driffield England UK 25H4
Greater Manchester county England UK 25D5
Great Fall Guyana 92E2
Great Falls Mont. USA 81B2
Great Inagua island The Bahamas 89E2
Great L Tas. Australia 97F5
Great Lake = Tonle Sap
Great Malvern England UK 26K4
Great Mecatina I Que. Canada 78J1
Great North Mts Va/W Va USA 84B3
Great Point Mass. USA 84F2
Great Rapids Man. Canada 76M6
Great Rowsley England UK 25E7
Great Sacandaga L NY USA 84D1
Great Salt L Utah USA 82B2
Great Salt Lake Des. Utah USA 82B2
Great Sand Dunes Nat. Mon. Col. USA 82F4
Great Sandy Des. W Aus. Australia 98E4
Great Slave L NW Terr. Canada 76H4
Great Smoky Mts Tenn. USA 85F3
Great Smoky Mts Nat. Park Tenn. USA 85F3
Great South B NY USA 84E2
Great Torrington England UK 26F7
Great Wass I Maine USA 78E4
Great Whernside England UK 25E4
Great Yarmouth England UK 27T3
Grebbestad Sweden 35D7
Greco,C Cyprus 64C3
Greece country Europe 39L6
Greeley Col. USA 82F2
Green B Wis. USA 79C3
Green Bay Wis. USA 79B3
Greencastle Ind. USA 79C6
Greenfield Ind. USA 79D6
Greenfield Iowa USA 83L2
Greenfield Mass. USA 84E1
Greenland country Europe 14P2
Greenland Sea Arctic Ocean 14M2
Green Mts Vt USA 79K4
Green Mts Wyo. USA 81D4
Greenock Scotland UK 29G8
Greenore Ireland,Rep. of 30L5
Greenore Point Ireland, Rep. of 31L9
Green Point South Africa 72H9
Greenport NY USA 84E2
Green,R Ky USA 85D2
Green R Utah USA 82C3
Green River Utah USA 82C3
Green River Wyo. USA 81C5
Greensboro Ga USA 85F4
Greensboro N Car. USA 85H2
Greensburg Kans. USA 83J4
Greensburg Ky USA 85E2
Greensburg Pa USA 84B2
Greenstone Point Scotland UK 28D4
Greenville Ala. USA 85D5
Greenville Calif. USA 80C5
Greenville Ill. USA 83P3
Greenville Ky USA 85D2
Greenville Liberia 68D7
Greenville Maine USA 78D4
Greenville Mich. USA 79D4
Greenville Miss. USA 85B4
Greenville Mo USA 83N4
Greenville N Car. USA 85J3
Greenville S Car. USA 85F3
Greenville Tenn. USA 85F2
Greenville Texas USA 83K6
Greenwich Conn. USA 84E2
Greenwich England UK 27P6
Greenwich RI USA 84F2
Greenwood Miss. USA 85B4
Greenwood S Car. USA 85F3
Greenwood Wis. USA 79A3
Greenwood L New J/NY USA 84D2
Gregório,R Brazil 92C5
Gregory S Dak. USA 81H4
Gregory,L S Aus. Australia 97A1
Gregory Ra mts Queens. Australia 99J3
Greifen See lake Switzerland 33D1
Greifswald E Germany 36E1
Grein Austria 36F4
Greina P Switzerland 33D2
Greiz E Germany 36E3
Grellingen Switzerland 33C1
Grenå Denmark 35D8
Grenada Miss. USA 85C4
Grenada country Windward Is 89G4
Grenadines islands Windward Is 89G4
Grenchen Switzerland 33C1
Grenfell NSW Australia 97C2
Grenoble France 43F4
Grenora N Dak. USA 81F1
Grenville,C Queens. Australia 99J2
Gresham Oreg. USA 80B3
Gressåmoen Nat. Pk Norway 34E4
Gretna La USA 83N8
Gretna Va USA 85H2
Gretna Green Scotland UK 29K10
Grevelingen inlet Netherlands 32B3
Grevená Greece 47C4
Grevena dist. Greece 47C4
Greybull Wyo. USA 81C3
Greycliff Mont. USA 81C3
Greylock,Mt Mass. USA 84E1
Greymouth New Zealand 100D6
Grey,R New Zealand 100D6
Grey Ra mts NSW/Queens. Australia 99J5
Grey Res. Newf. Canada 78K2
Greystones Ireland, Rep. of 31L7
Greytown = San Juan del Norte
Greytown New Zealand 100F5
Gr. Fisher Bank North Sea 22J4
Gr. Hanish I Ethiopia 71J2
Gridlev Calif. USA 80C6
Griesalp Switzerland 33C2
Gries P Italy/Switz. 33D2
Griesta Sweden 35G7
Griffin Ga USA 85E4
Griffith NSW Australia 97C2
Grimari CAR 69K7
Grim,C Tas. Australia 97E5
Grimmialp Switzerland 33C2
Grimsby England UK 25H5
Grimsel P Switzerland 33D2
Grimsstadhir Iceland 34X12
Grimstad Norway 35C7
Grindelwald Switzerland 33D2
Grind Stone City Mich. USA 79E3
Grinnell Iowa USA 83L2
Grinnell Pen. NW Terr. Canada 76N1
Griquatown South Africa 72C5
Gris Nez,C France 42D1
Griva Latvia USSR 35M9
Gr. Nicobar island Nicobar Is India 59H7
Grobina Latvia USSR 35J8
Gröbming Austria 36E5
Grodno Belorus. USSR 48C5
Grodzisk Poland 37G2
Groenlo Netherlands 32E2
Groet Netherlands 32C2
Groix,I de France 42B3
Groningen Netherlands 32E1
Groningen prov. Netherlands 32E1
Grono Switzerland 33E2
Grootebroek Netherlands 32D2
Groote Eylandt island N Terr. Australia 99H2
Grootfontein Namibia 72B3
Grosser Aletsch Gl. Switzerland 33C2
Grosseto Italy 44C4
Grossevichi USSR 51Q5
Gross Glockner mt Austria 36E5
Groton NY USA 84C1
Groton S Dak. USA 81H3
Grouw Netherlands 32D1
Grover City Calif. USA 80C8
Groznyy USSR 50F5
Grudziadz Poland 37H2
Grues,I aux Que. Canada 79L2
Gruinard B Scotland UK 28E4
Grüsch Switzerland 33E2
Gruyères Switzerland 33C2
Gruž Yugoslavia 46B3
Gruzinskaya SSR rep. USSR 50F5
Gr. Victoria Des. W Aus. Australia 98F5
Gr. Western Tiers mts Tas. Australia 97F5
Grybów Poland 37J4
Grytviken S Georgia Antarctica 15A4
Gstaad Switzerland 33C2
Gsteig Switzerland 33C2
Guabito Panama 89C5
Guacanayabo,G de Cuba 89D2
Guachipas Argentina 91C3
Guachiria,R Columbia 92C2
Guadalaja Spain 40E2
Guadalajara Mexico 88D3
Guadalajara prov. Spain 41E2
Guadalaviar,R Spain 41F3
Guadalcanal Spain 40D3
Guadalcanal,I Solomon Is 94F9
Guadalcazar Mexico 88D3
Guadalquivir,R Spain 40C4
Guadalupe Calif. USA 80C8
Guadalupe Mexico 88D3
Guadalupe I Mexico 88A2
Guadalupe Mts Nat. Pk Texas USA 82F7
Guadalupe,R Texas USA 83K8
Guadalupe y Calvo Mexico 88C2
Guadarrama Spain 40D2
Guadarrama,Sa de mts Spain 40D2
Guadeloupe country Leeward Is 89G3
Guadiana,R Port./Spain 40C3
Guadix Spain 40E4
Guafo,I Chile 91B6
Guainia,R Columbia 92D3
Guairá Brazil 93G8
Guaitecas,Is Chile 91B6
Guajará Mirim Brazil 92D6
Guajaratuba Brazil 92E5
Guajira,Pen. de Columbia 92C1
Gualala Calif. USA 80B6
Gualeguaychu Argentina 91E4
Guamá Brazil 93H4
Guam,I Pacific Ocean 94E6
Guamini Argentina 91D5
Guamo Colombia 92B3
Guanabacoa Cuba 89C2
Guanabara state Brazil 93J8
Guanacevi Mexico 88C2
Guanaja,I Honduras 89B3
Guanajuato Mexico 88D3
Guanare Venezuela 92D2
Guanare,R Venezuela 92D2
Guanarito Venezuela 92D2
Guandacol Argentina 91C3
Guane Cuba 89C2
Guang'an China 55D7
Guangchang China 55J9
Guangde China 54K7
Guangdong province China 55G11
Guangfeng China 55K8
Guanghai China 55G12
Guanghua China 54F6
Guangnan China 55C10
Guangning China 55G11
Guangshan China 54H6
Guangxi province China 55D11
Guangyuan China 54C6
Guangze China 55J9
Guangzhou China 55G11
Guangzong China 54H4
Guánica Puerto Rico 89F3
Guanling China 55C10
Guanping China 54H4
Guantánamo Cuba 89D2
Guan Xian China 54B7
Guanyang China 55F10
Guanyun China 54K5
Guapi Colombia 92B3
Guapiles Costa Rica 89C4
Guaporé Brazil 91F3
Guapore Brazil 92D6
Guapore,R Bolivia/Brazil 92E6
Guaqui Bolivia 92D7
Guarapuava Brazil 91F3
Guarda Portugal 40C2
Guariba,R Brazil 92F5
Guarico,R Venezuela 92D2
Guasdualito Venezuela 92C2
Guasipati Venezuela 92E2
Guasuba,R India 61G5
Guatemala Guatemala 88F5
Guatemala country Central America 88F5
Guatrache Argentina 91D5
Guaviare,R Colombia 92D3
Guaxupé Brazil 93H8
Guayabal Venezuela 92D2
Guayama Puerto Rico 89F3
Guayaneco,Arch. Chile 91A7
Guayaquil Ecuador 92B4
Guayaquil,G of Ecuador 92A4
Guaymas Mexico 88B2
Guba Buorkhaya bay USSR 51Q2
Gubal Str. Red Sea 69M3
Guben E Germany 36F3
Gubin = Guben
Gucheng Hubei China 54F6
Gucheng Shandong China 54J4
Gudbrands Dalen valley Norway 35C6
Gudiyatam India 58E6
Gudri,R Pakistan 58B3
Guékédou Guinea 68C7
Guelma Algeria 68G1
Guelph Ont. Canada 79F4
Guemes Argentina 91C2
Guera,Mt Chad 69J6
Guéret France 42D3
Guernsey,I Channel Is UK 42B2
Guernsey Res. Wyo. USA 81E4
Guerrero Mexico 88C2
Guerrero Mexico 88E2
Guerrero state Mexico 88D4
Guev Lith. USSR 35K9
Güferhorn mt Switzerland 33E2
Gugera Pakistan 60C5
Guiana Highlands S America 92F3
Guichi China 54J7
Guide China 52D3
Guidong China 55G9
Guier,L de Sénégal 68B5
Guiglo Ivory Coast 68D7
Guija Mozambique 72E4
Gui Jiang river China 55F11
Guildford England UK 27N6
Guilford Maine USA 78D4
Guilin China 55F10
Guillaumes France 43G4
Guimarães Brazil 93J4
Guimarães Portugal 40B2
Guinda Calif. USA 80B6
Guinea country Africa 68C6
Guinea-Bissau country Africa 68B6
Guinea,G of Africa 70A4
Guines Cuba 89C2
Guingamp France 42B2
Guiping China 55F11
Guipúzcoa prov. Spain 41E1
Guira de Melena Cuba 89C2
Guiria Venezuela 92E1
Guisborough England UK 25F3
Guise France 42E2
Guisisil vol. Nicaragua 89B4
Guixi China 55J8
Gui Xian China 55E11
Guiyang Guizhou China 55D9
Guiyang Hunan China 55G10
Guizhou province China 55C9
Gujarat state India 58D4
Gujar Khan Pakistan 60C4
Gujranwala Pakistan 60D4
Gujrat Pakistan 60D4
Gulang China 54B4
Gulargambone NSW Australia 97C2
Gulbarga India 58E5
Gulbene Latvia USSR 35M8
Gulfport Miss. USA 85C5
Gulgong NSW Australia 97C2
Gulin China 55C8
Gulistan Pakistan 58C2
Gul Koh mt Afghanistan 63K3
Gullane Scotland UK 29L7

Gulpen, Hay River

Gulpen Netherlands 32D4
Gulran Afghanistan 63J2
Gulu Uganda 71G4
Gummersbach W Germany 36B3
Gummi Nigeria 68G6
Gümüsane Turkey 62D1
Guna India 61A3
Gunbar NSW Australia 97C2
Gundagai NSW Australia 97C3
Gungu Zaire 70D6
Gunial Kashmir India 60D3
Gunisao R Man. Canada 76M6
Gunma prefecture Japan 56F6
Gunnedah NSW Australia 97D2
Gunning NSW Australia 97C2
Gunnislake England UK 26F7
Gunnison Col. USA 82E3
Gunnison Utah USA 82C3
Gunnison,R Col. USA 82E3
Guntakal India 58E5
Gunten Switzerland 33C2
Guntersville Ala. USA 85D3
Guntersville L Ala. USA 85D3
Guntur India 58F5
Guo He river China 54J6
Guoyang China 54J6
Gurais Kashmir India 60D3
Gurdaspur India 60D4
Gurdon Ark. USA 83M6
Gurer,I Kwajalein,Is 94A17
Gurgaon India 60E6
Gurgl Austria 36D5
Gurha India 58D3
Gurkha Nepal 61E2
Gurla Mandhata,Mt Tibet China 58F2
Gurnigel Switzerland 33C2
Gursköy,I Norway 34A5
Gurué Mozambique 71H8
Gurupá Brazil 93G4
Gurupá,I Brazil 93G4
Gurupi,B de Brazil 93H4
Gurupi,R Brazil 93H4
Gurupi,Serra do mts Brazil 93H4
Guru Sikha Mt India 58D4
Guruve Zimbabwe 72E3
Gur'yev Kazakh. USSR 50G5
Gushi China 54H6
Guspini Sardinia Italy 45B6
Güstrow E Germany 36E2
Gütersloh W Germany 36C3
Guthrie Ky USA 85D2
Guthrie Okla. USA 83K5
Guthrie Center Iowa USA 83L2
Gutian China 55K9
Guttanen Switzerland 33D2
Guyana country S America 92F3
Guyang China 54E2
Guyenne prov. France 43D4
Guymon Okla. USA 82H4
Guyra NSW Australia 97D2
Guyuan Ninxia China 54D5
Guyuan Shansi China 54H2
Guzhang China 55E8
Guzhou = Rongjiang
Gwa Burma 59H5
Gwabegar NSW Australia 97C2
Gwadar Pakistan 58B3
Gwalior India 61B2
Gwanda Zimbabwe 72D4
Gweebarra B Ireland, Rep. of 30F4
Gwent county Wales UK 26H5
Gweru Zimbabwe 72D3
Gwydir,R NSW Australia 97D2
Gwynedd county Wales UK 26G3
Gyangzê Tibet China 59G3
Gyaring Hu lake China 52C4
Gydanski Polstrov peninsula USSR 50J2
Gympie Queens. Australia 99L5
Györ Hungary 37G5
Gypsumville Man. Canada 76M6
Gyula Hungary 37J5
Gzhatsk,R USSR 48J4

H

Haacht Belgium 32C4
Haafeva island Tonga 95V30
Haag Switzerland 33E1
Haaksbergen Netherlands 32E2
Haano island Tonga 95V30
Ha'apai Group islands Tonga 95V30
Haapajänä Finland 34L5
Haapsalu Eston. USSR 35K7
Haarlem Netherlands 32C2
Haastrecht Netherlands 32C2
Habana Cuba 89C2
Habban South Yemen 62F7
Habbaniyah Iraq 62E3
Habigang Bangladesh 59H4
Habkern Switzerland 33C2
Haboro Japan 56G2
Hab,R Pakistan 58C3
Habsburg Switzerland 33D1
Hachinohe Japan 56G4
Hackberry Ariz. USA 80G8
Hack,Mt S Aus. Australia 97A2
Hadasan Mongolia 52D1
Hadda Saudi Arabia 62D5
Haddington Scotland UK 29L8
Hadejia Nigeria 69G6
Hadera Israel 64C5
Haderslev Denmark 35C9
Hadibu Socotra South Yemen 71L2
Hadleigh England UK 27R4
Hadra Maut region South Yemen 62F6
Haeju N Korea 52J3
Hafar Saudi Arabia 62F4
Haffe = Babenna
Hafnarfjordhur Iceland 34U12
Hafursfjordhur bay Iceland 34T12
Hagen W Germany 36B3
Hagerstown Md USA 84C3
Hagi Japan 56B7
Hahnville La USA 83N8
Hai'an China 54L6
Haicheng China 54M2
Haifa Israel 64C5
Haifa,B of Israel 64C5
Haifeng China 55H11
Haig W Aus. Australia 98F6
Hai He river China 54J3
Haikou China 55F12
Hail Saudi Arabia 62E4
Hailar China 52G1
Hailey Idaho USA 80F4
Haileybury Ont. Canada 79G2
Hailing Dao island China 55F12
Hailsham England UK 27Q7
Hailun China 52J1
Hailuoto Finland 34L4
Haimen China 54L7
Hainan Dao island China 55E13
Hainaut prov. Belgium 32B4
Haines Alaska USA 76D5
Haining China 55L7
Haiphong Vietnam 57D2
Hair Saudi Arabia 62F5
Haiti country West Indies 89E3
Haitou China 55E13
Haiyan China 54L7
Haiyang China 54L4
Haiyang Dao island China 54M3
Haiyuan China 54C4
Hajduböszörmény Hungary 37J5
Hajipur India 61E3
Hajjar China 52B3
Haka Burma 59H4
Hakansson,Mts Zaire 70F6
Hakau Fusi island Tonga 95V30
Hakkâri Turkey 62E2
Hakodate Japan 56G4
Hal = Halle
Hala Pakistan 58C3
Halab Syria 64F1
Halacho Mexico 88F3
Halba Lebanon 64E3
Halberstadt E Germany 36D3
Halden Norway 35D7
Haleb = Halab
Halen Belgium 32D4
Halesworth England UK 27S4
Half Moon Bay Calif. USA 80B7
Hali Saudi Arabia 62E6
Halia India 61D3
Haliburton Ont. Canada 79G3
Halifax England UK 25E5
Halifax N Car. USA 85J2
Halifax No. Sc. Canada 78G4
Halifax B Queens. Australia 99K3
Halifax Harb. No. Sc. Canada 78G4
Halkett,C Alaska USA 87X11
Halland county Sweden 35E8
Halle Belgium 32C4
Halle E Germany 36D3
Hallein Austria 36E5
Hallen Sweden 34F5
Halley B Antarctica 15A2
Hällinäs Sweden 34H4
Hallingdal valley Norway 35C6
Hallingskarvet,R Norway 35B6
Hall,Is Caroline Is 94F7
Halliste Eston. USSR 35L7
Hall Land Greenland 14P1
Hallock Minn. USA 81J1
Hallowell Maine USA 78D4
Halls Creek W Aus. Australia 98F3
Hallstavik Sweden 35H6
Hallum Netherlands 32D1
Hallweg Netherlands 32C2
Hallwil Switzerland 33D1
Hallwiller See lake Switzerland 33D1
Halmahera island Indonesia 53J10
Halmstad Sweden 35E8
Halsa Norway 34C5
Halstead England UK 27R5
Haltwhistle England UK 25D3
Halul island Qatar 63G4
Hamada Japan 56C7
Hamadān Iran 62F3
Hamāh Syria 64E2
Hamam Saudi Arabia 62F5
Hamamatsu Japan 56E7
Hamar Norway 35D6
Hamar Saudi Arabia 62F5
Hambantota Sri Lanka 58F7
Hamburg Iowa USA 83L2
Hamburg NY USA 84B1
Hamburg Pa USA 84D2
Hamburg W Germany 36D2
Hamdāniya Syria 64E2
Hämeenlinna Finland 35L6
Hameln W Germany 36C2
Hamhung North Korea 52J3
Hami Xinjiang China 52B2
Hamidiya Syria 64D3
Hamilton Ala. USA 85C3
Hamilton Mont. USA 80F2
Hamilton N Car. USA 85J3
Hamilton New Zealand 100F3
Hamilton NY USA 84D1
Hamilton Ohio USA 79D6
Hamilton Ont. Canada 79G4
Hamilton Scotland UK 29H8
Hamilton Tas. Australia 97F5
Hamilton Vic. Australia 97B3
Hamilton Wash. USA 76G7
Hamilton Inl. Newf. Canada 77U6
Hamilton,L Ark. USA 83M5
Hamilton,R = Churchill,R
Hamina Finland 35M6
Hamirpur India 60E5
Hamirpur India 61C3
Hamlet N Car. USA 85H3
Hamley Bridge S Aus. Australia 97A2
Hamm W Germany 36B3
Hamme Belgium 32C3
Hammerdal Sweden 34F5
Hammerfest Norway 34K1
Hammersley Ra mts W Aus. Australia 98D4
Hammond Ind. USA 79C5
Hammond La USA 83N7
Hammond S Aus. Australia 97A2
Hammonton New J USA 84D3
Hamont Belgium 32D3
Hampden N Dak. USA 81H1
Hampden Newf. Canada 78K2
Hampden New Zealand 100D7
Hampshire county England UK 27M6
Hampton Ark. USA 83M6
Hampton Iowa USA 83M1
Hampton New Br. Canada 78F4
Hampton New H USA 84F1
Hampton Oreg. USA 80C4
Hampton S Car. USA 85G4
Hamun-i Helmand salt flat Iran 63J3
Hamun-i-Lora Pakistan 58B3
Hamun-i-Mashkel Pakistan 58B3
Hamun-i-Puzak salt flat Afghanistan 63J3
Han Belgium 32D4
Hanau W Germany 36C3
Hancheng China 54F5
Hanchuan China 55G7
Hancock Mich. USA 79B2
Hancock NY USA 84D2
Handan China 54H4
Handegg Switzerland 33D2
Handeni Tanzania 71H6
Hanford Calif. USA 80D7
Hanford Wash. USA 80D2
Hanga Roa Easter I 95V32
Hango = Hanko
Hangu Pakistan 60B4
Hangzhou China 55L7
Hangzou Wan bay China 54L7
Han Jiang river China 55J10
Hankinson N Dak. USA 81J2
Hanko Finland 35K7
Hanko Fj. Finland 35K7
Hanle Kashmir India 58E2
Hanley England UK 25D6
Hanmer Springs New Zealand 100E6
Hanna Alta Canada 76J6
Hanna Wyo. USA 81D5
Hannibal Mo USA 83N3
Hannover W Germany 36C2
Hannut Belgium 32D4
Hanobukten bay Sweden 35F9
Hanoi Vietnam 57D2
Hanover Ont. Canada 79F3
Hanover Pa USA 84C3
Hanover Va USA 85J2
Hanover,I Chile 91B8
Hanshou China 55F8
Han Shui river China 54G7
Hansi India 60E6
Hansweert Netherlands 32C3
Hanumangarh India 60D6
Hanyang China 55H7
Hanyin China 54E6
Hanzhong China 54D6
Hao,I Tuamotu Arch. 95M9
Haparanda Sweden 34L4
Hapur India 60E6
Haql Saudi Arabia 62C4
Haraiya India 61D2
Harak Saudi Arabia 62D4
Haramukh mt Kashmir India 60D3
Harardera Somalia 71K4
Harare Zimbabwe 72E3
Harazé Chad 69J6
Harbin China 52J1
Harbor Beach Mich. USA 79E4
Harbor Springs Mich. USA 79D3
Harburg W Germany 36C2
Harda India 58E4
Hardanger Fj. Norway 35A6
Hardangerfjell region Norway 35B6
Hardanger Nat. Pk Norway 35B6
Hardanger vidda region Norway 35B6
Hardenberg Netherlands 32E2
Harderwijk Netherlands 32D2
Hardin Mont. USA 81D3
Harding South Africa 72D6
Hardoi India 61C2
Hardwicke B S Aus. Australia 97A2
Hardy, Pen. Chile 91C9
Hare B Newf. Canada 78L1
Hare I = Lièvres,I aux
Hareidland,I Norway 34A5
Hare Indian,R NW Terr. Canada 76F3
Harelbeke Belgium 32B4
Hargeysa Somalia 71J3
Harib Saudi Arabia 62F6
Haridwar India 60F6
Harihar India 58E6
Harim Syria 64E1
Haripur Pakistan 60C4
Hariq Saudi Arabia 62F5
Hari,R Sumatra Indon. 53D11
Harishpur India 59G4
Harjavalta Finland 35K6
Harlan Iowa USA 83L2
Harlan Ky USA 87K4
Harlech Wales UK 26F3
Harlem Mont. USA 81C1
Harleston England UK 27S4
Harlingen Netherlands 32D1
Harlingen Texas USA 82T10
Harlow England UK 27Q5
Harlowton Mont. USA 81C2
Harmanli = Kharmanli
Harmerhill England UK 25C7
Harney Basin Oreg. USA 86B3
Harney,L Oreg. USA 80D4
Harney Pk S Dak. USA 81F4
Härnösand Sweden 34G5
Har Nuur lake, Mongolia 51L5
Harold Calif. USA 80D8
Harper Liberia 68D8
Harrai India 61B4
Harran Turkey 62D2
Harrat al'Uwayrid upland Saudi Arabia 62D4
Harray,L of Orkney Scotland 28K1
Harrington Harbour Que. Canada 78J1
Harrisburg Ark. USA 83N5
Harrisburg Ill. USA 83P4
Harrisburg Oreg. USA 80B3
Harrisburg Pa USA 84C2
Harris,I Scotland UK 28C4
Harrison Ark. USA 83M4
Harrison Mich. USA 79D3
Harrison Mont. USA 80H3
Harrisonburg La USA 83N7
Harrisonburg Va USA 85H1
Harrison,C Newf. Canada 77U6
Harrison L BC Canada 76G7
Harrisonville Mo USA 83L3
Harris,Sd of Scotland UK 28B4
Harrisville Mich. USA 79E3
Harrodsburg Ky USA 85E2
Harrogate England UK 25E5
Harrow England UK 27P5
Harsprånget,R Sweden 34J3
Harstad Norway 34G2
Hart Mich. USA 79C4
Hartford Conn. USA 84E2
Hartland New Br. Canada 78E3
Hartland Point England UK 26E6
Hartlepool England UK 25F3
Hartsville Tenn. USA 85D2
Hartville Mo USA 83M4
Har Us Nuur lake Mongolia 52B1
Harvard Ill. USA 83P1
Harvard,Mt Col. USA 82E3
Harvey N Dak. USA 81H2
Harvey New Br. Canada 78E4
Harwell England UK 27M5
Harwich England UK 27S5
Haryana state India 60D6
Harz mts Germany 36D3
Hasan Dagh mt Turkey 62C2
Hasanpur India 61B1
Hāsbaiya Lebanon 64D4
Haseva Israel 64D7
Haslemere England UK 27N6
Hasli Tal valley Switzerland 33D2
Hassan India 58E6
Hasselt Belgium 32D4
Hasselt Netherlands 32E2
Hassi Inifel Algeria 68F3
Hassi Messaoud Algeria 68G2
Hassi Rmel Algeria 68F2
Hassleholm Sweden 35E8
Hastiere Belgium 32C4
Hastings England UK 27R7
Hastings Mich. USA 79D4
Hastings Minn. USA 81L3
Hastings Nebr. USA 83J2
Hastings New Zealand 100G4
Hastings,R NSW Australia 97D2
Hateg Romania 46D2
Hatfield Herts.,England UK 27P5
Hatfield NSW Australia 97B2
Hatfield Sth. Yorks.,England UK 25F5
Hatha Saudi Arabia 62E5
Hatham,Mt Vic. Australia 97C3
Hathersage England UK 25E6
Hathras India 61B2
Ha Tinh Vietnam 57D3
Hatta India 61B3
Hattah Vic. Australia 97B2
Hatteras,C N Car. USA 85K3
Hattiesburg Miss. USA 85C5
Hatton Headland NW Terr. Canada 77S4
Hatvan Hungary 37H5
Hat Yai Thailand 53D9
Haugesund Norway 35A7
Haukipudas Finland 34L4
Haukivesi,L Finland 34N5
Haura South Yemen 62F7
Hauraki G New Zealand 100F3
Hauroko,L New Zealand 100B7
Hauser Idaho USA 80E2
Hausstock mt Switzerland 33D2
Hauta Saudi Arabia 62F5
Haut Atlas,Mts Morocco 68D2
Haute-Garonne dep. France 43D5
Haute-Loire dep. France 43E4
Haute-Marne dep. France 42F2
Hautes-Alpes dep. France 43G4
Haute-Saône dep. France 42G3
Haute Savoie dep. France 42G3
Hautes-Pyrénées dep. France 43D5
Haute Vienne dep. France 42D4
Haute Volta = Upper Volta
Haut,I au Maine USA 78D4
Haut Rhin dep. France 42G3
Hauts Plateaux plat. Algeria 68F2
Havana = Habana
Havant England UK 27N7
Havasu L Ariz./Calif. USA 80F8
Havelange Belgium 32D4
Havelland region E Germany 36E2
Havelock New Br. Canada 78F3
Havelock,I Andaman Is India 59H6
Havelock North New Zealand 100G4
Haverfordwest Wales UK 26E5
Haverhill England UK 27Q4
Haverhill Mass. USA 84F1
Haverstraw NY USA 84D2
Havre Belgium 32C4
Havre Mont. USA 81C1
Havre de Grace Md USA 84C3
Hawaii state USA 94K5
Hawaii,I Hawaii USA 95L6
Hawarden Iowa USA 83K1
Hawea Flat New Zealand 100C7
Hawera New Zealand 100F4
Hawesville Ky USA 85D2
Hawick Scotland UK 29L9
Hawke B New Zealand 100G4
Hawke,C NSW Australia 97D2
Hawker S Aus. Australia 97A2
Hawke's Bay stat. area New Zealand 100G4
Hawkesbury Ont. Canada 79J3
Hawkhurst England UK 27R6
Hawkshead England UK 25B4
Hawley Calif. USA 80C6
Hawr al Hammar Iraq 62F3
Hawras Saniyah lake Iraq 62F3
Hawthorne Nev. USA 80D6
Hay NSW Australia 97B2
Hayantpur India 61F3
Hayes Halvø region Greenland 14Q2
Hayfork Calif. USA 80B5
Hayling,I England UK 27N7
Hayneville Ala. USA 85D4
Hay on Wye Wales UK 26H4
Hay,R Alta Canada 76H5
Hay River NW Terr. Canada 76H4

Hays, Houma

Hays Kans. USA 83J3
Hayward Calif. USA 80B7
Hayward Wis. USA 81M2
Haywards Heath England UK 27P6
Hazarajat mts Afghanistan 63J3
Hazard Ky USA 85F2
Hazaribagh India 61E4
Hazaribagh,Ra mts India 61D4
Hazelton BC Canada 76F5
Hazerswoude Netherlands 32C2
Hazlehurst Ga USA 85F5
Hazleton Pa USA 84D2
Hazro Pakistan 60C4
Headford Ireland, Rep. of 31E7
Healdsburg Calif. USA 80B6
Healesville Vic. Australia 97C3
Heard I Indian Ocean 65F10
Hearst Ont. Canada 77P7
Heathcote Vic. Australia 97B3
Hebbronville Texas USA 82S10
Hebei province China 54H3
Heber City Utah USA 82C2
Heber Springs Ark. USA 83M5
Hebi China 54H5
Hebron Jordan 64D6
Hebron N Dak. USA 81F2
Hebron Nebr. USA 83K2
Hebron Newf. Canada 77T5
Hecate Str. BC Canada 76E6
Hecelchakan Mexico 88F3
Hechi China 55E10
Hechingen W.Germany 36C4
Hechtel Belgium 32D3
Hector,Mt New Zealand 100F5
Hede Sweden 34E5
Hedemora Sweden 35F6
Hedensäset Sweden 34K3
Hedmark county Norway 35D6
Heemskerk Netherlands 32C2
Heemstede Netherlands 32C2
Heer Netherlands 32D4
Heerenveen Netherlands 32D2
Heerhugewaard Netherlands 32C2
Heerlen Netherlands 32D4
Hefei China 54J7
Heide W Germany 36C1
Heidelberg W Germany 36C4
Heidelburg South Africa 72D5
Heiden Switzerland 33E1
Heijen Netherlands 32D3
Heilbronn W Germany 36C4
Heiligenstadt E Germany 36D3
Heilongjiang prov. China 52J1
Heinola Finland 35M6
Heinze B Burma 59J6
Heinze Is Burma 59J6
Heisan China 54M2
Heist Belgium 32B3
Hejaz region Saudi Arabia 62D4
Hejiang China 55C8
He Jiang river China 55F10
Hejin China 54F5
Hekla,Mt Iceland 34V13
Hekou China 55B11
Helan Shan mts China 54C3
Helchteren Belgium 32D3
Helena Ark. USA 83N5
Helena Mont. USA 80G2
Helensburgh Scotland UK 29G7
Helensville New Zealand 100F3
Helgoland island W Germany 36B1
Helgoländer Bucht bay W Germany 36B1
Heligoland = Helgoland
Hella Iceland 34U13
Hellevoetsluis Netherlands 32C3
Hell Gate BC Canada 76F5
Hellin Spain 41F3
Hell's Canyon = Snake R Canyon
Helmand,R Afghanistan 63J3
Helme Eston. USSR 35L8
Helmond Netherlands 32D3
Helmsdale Scotland UK 28J3
Helmsley England UK 25F4
Helsenhorn mt Italy/Switz. 33D2
Helsingborg Sweden 35E8
Helsingfors = Helsinki
Helsingør Denmark 35E8
Helsinki Finland 35L6
Helston England UK 26D8
Helvellyn mt England UK 25B3
Helvick Hd Ireland, Rep. of 31H9
Helwan Egypt 69M3
Hemel Hempstead England UK 27P5
Hemelum Netherlands 32D2
Hemnes Norway 34E3
Hemse Sweden 35H8
Henan province China 54G5
Hen & Chickens Is New Zealand 100F2
Hendaye France 43C5
Henderson Ky USA 85D2
Henderson Minn. USA 81K3
Henderson N Car. USA 85H2
Henderson NY USA 79H4
Henderson Tenn. USA 85C3
Henderson,I Pacific Ocean 95P10
Hendersonville N Car. USA 85F3
Henegouwen = Hainaut
Hengchow = Hengyang
Heng-chun Taiwan 55L11
Hengelo Netherlands 32E2
Hengelo Netherlands 32E2
Hengshan Hunan China 55G9
Hengshan Shaanxi China 54E4
Heng Shan mts China 55G9
Heng Xian China 55E11
Hengyang China 55G9
Henley on Thames England UK 27N5
Henlopen,C New J USA 84D3
Hennebont France 42B3
Henqam island Iran 63H4
Henrietta Texas USA 83J6
Henrietta Maria,C Ont. Canada 77P6
Henryetta Okla. USA 83K5
Henry Mts Utah USA 82C3
Henty NSW Australia 97C3
Henzada Burma 59J5
Heping China 55H10
Heppner Oreg. USA 80D3
Hepu China 55E12
Hequ China 54F3
Heran Yemen 62E6
Herat Afghanistan 63J3
Hérault dep. France 43E5
Herbertville New Zealand 100G5
Herbertville Station Que. Canada 78C2
Herbesthal Belgium 32D4
Herceg Novi Yugoslavia 46B3
Heredia Costa Rica 89C4
Hereford England UK 26J4
Hereford Texas USA 82G5
Heref. & Worcs. county England UK 26K4
Hereheretue,I Pacific Ocean 95M9
Herford W Germany 36C2
Herington Kans. USA 83K3
Heriot New Zealand 100C7
Herisau Switzerland 33E1
Herkimer NY USA 84D1
Hermance Switzerland 33B2
Herma Ness Shetland Scotland 28R7
Hermann Mo USA 83N3
Hermel Lebanon 64E3
Hermidale NSW Australia 97C2
Hermitage B Newf. Canada 78K3
Hermite,Is Chile 91C9
Hermon,Mt = Jebel esh Sheikh
Hermosillo Mexico 88B2
Herne Belgium 32C4
Herne Bay England UK 27R6
Herning Denmark 35C8
Héron Belgium 32D4
Herowābād Iran 62F2
Herräng Sweden 35H6
Herrera Argentina 91D3
Herrera di Pisuerga Spain 40D1
Herrick Tas. Australia 97F5
Herselt Belgium 32C3
Hersey Mich. USA 79D4
Hersfeld W Germany 36C3
Herstal Belgium 32D4
Herstmonceux England UK 27Q7
Hertford England UK 27P5
Hertford N Car. USA 85J2
Hertfordshire county England UK 27P5
Hervas Spain 40D2
Hervé Belgium 32D4
Hervey B Queens. Australia 99L4
Hervey,Is Cook Is 95L9
Herzberg E Germany 36E3
Herzliyya Israel 64C5
Herzogenbuchsee Switzerland 33C1
Hesdin France 42D1
Heshui China 54D5
Heshun China 54G4
Hesperia Calif. USA 80E8
Hessen state W Germany 36C3
Het Zoute Belgium 32B3
Heught,Mt N Terr. Australia 98G4
Heusden Netherlands 32D3
Hève,C de la France 42D2
Hexham England UK 25D3
He Xian Anhui China 54K7
He Xian Guangxi China 55F10
Heyang China 54E5
Heytesbury England UK 27K6
Heyuan China 55H11
Heywood Vic. Australia 97B3
Heze China 54H5
Hiawatha Kans. USA 83L3
Hibbing Minn. USA 81L2
Hicks Bay New Zealand 100H3
Hidalgo Mexico 88E2
Hidalgo state Mexico 88E3
Hidalgo del Parral Mexico 88C2
Hieflau Austria 36F5
Hierādhsvoln,R Iceland 34V12
Hierro,I Canary Is 68B3
High Des. Oreg. USA 80C4
Highland region Scotland UK 28E5
Highland Park Ill. USA 83Q1
Highmore S Dak. USA 81H3
High Point N Car. USA 85G2
Highwood Mts Mont. USA 81B2
High Wycombe England UK 27N5
Hiiumaa,I Eston. USSR 35K7
Hijar Spain 41F2
Hijaz = Hejaz
Hiko Nev. USA 80F7
Hikone Japan 56E7
Hikurangi New Zealand 100F2
Hildesheim W Germany 36C2
Hill City Idaho USA 80F4
Hill City Kans. USA 83H3
Hill City Minn. USA 81L2
Hillman Mich. USA 79E3
Hillsboro Ill. USA 83P3
Hillsboro N Car. USA 85H2
Hillsboro Oreg. USA 80B3
Hillsboro Texas USA 83K6
Hillsdale Mich. USA 79D5
Hillston NSW Australia 97C2
Hillsville Va USA 85G2
Hilo Hawaii USA 95V27
Hilversum Netherlands 32D2
Himachal Pradesh state India 60E5
Himachuli mt Nepal 61E1
Himalaya mts China/Nepal 61D1
Himalaya Mts Central Asia 18J6
Himanka Finland 34K4
Himare Albania 47B4
Himeji Japan 56D7
Ḥimṣ Syria 64E3
Hinckley England UK 25F7
Hinckley Minn. USA 81L2
Hindelbank Switzerland 33C1
Hindeloopen Netherlands 32D2
Hindley England UK 25C5
Hindman Ky USA 85F2
Hindmarsh,L Vic. Australia 97B3
Hindubagh Pakistan 58C2
Hindu Kush mts Afghan./Pakistan 60A3
Hindupur India 58E6
Hingan = Ankang
Hinganghat India 58E4
Hingham England UK 27R3
Hingham Mont. USA 81B1
Hinglaj Pakistan 58C3
Hingoli India 58E5
Hingol,R Pakistan 58C3
Hinis Turkey 62E2
Hinnoy,I Norway 34F2
Hinsdale Mont. USA 81D1
Hinsdale New H USA 84E1
Hinterrhein Switzerland 33E2
Hinter Rhein,R Switzerland 33E2
Hinton W Va USA 85G2
Hinwil Switzerland 33D1
Hiroo Japan 56H3
Hirosaki Japan 56G4
Hiroshima Japan 56C7
Hiroshima prefecture Japan 56C7
Hîrşova Romania 46F2
Hisar India 60D6
Hisarönü Turkey 62C1
Hisban Jordan 64D6
Hispaniola island West Indies 89E3
Hisua India 61E3
Hisya Syria 64E3
Hit Iraq 62E3
Hitchin England UK 27P5
Hitiaa Tahiti 95V32
Hitra,I Norway 34C5
Hiva Oa,I Marquesas Is 95N8
Hiwasa Japan 56D8
Hjälmaren,L Sweden 35F7
Hjelte Fj. Norway 35A6
Hjørring Denmark 35C8
Hkamti Burma 59J3
Ho Ghana 68F7
Hobart Okla. USA 83J5
Hobart Tas. Australia 97F5
Hobbs New Mex. USA 82G6
Hoboken Belgium 32C3
Hobro Denmark 35C8
Hobyo Somalia 71K3
Hochdorf Switzerland 33D1
Hoch Ducan mt Switzerland 33E2
Ho Chi Minh City Vietnam 57D4
Höchstetten Switzerland 33C2
Hochuan China 55D7
Hodal India 60E7
Hodder,R England UK 25D5
Hoddesdon England UK 27Q5
Hodeida = Al Ḥudaydah
Hodgson Man. Canada 76M6
Hódmezövásárhely Hungary 37J5
Hodonin Czech. 37G4
Hoek van Holland Netherlands 32C2
Hof W Germany 36D3
Höfs jökull glacier Iceland 34V12
Hofsos Iceland 34V12
Hofūf = Al Hufūf
Höganäs Sweden 35E8
Hohe Tauern mts Austria 36E5
Hohgant mt Switzerland 33C2
Hoh Xil Shan mts Tibet China 59F1
Hoi An Vietnam 57D3
Hokianga Harb. New Zealand 100E2
Hokitika New Zealand 100D6
Hokkaidō island Japan 56F3
Hokksund Norway 35C7
Holbaek Denmark 35D9
Holbeach England UK 27Q3
Holbeach Marsh England UK 27Q3
Holberg BC Canada 76F6
Holbrook Ariz. USA 82C5
Holbrook NSW Australia 97C3
Holdenville Okla. USA 83K5
Holdredge Nebr. USA 83J2
Holguin Cuba 89D2
Holland Mich. USA 79C4
Holland NY USA 84B1
Holland Mts South Africa 72J10
Hollange Belgium 32D5
Hollick-Kenyon Plat. Antarctica 15Q2
Hollidaysburg Pa. USA 84B2
Hollis Okla. USA 83J5
Hollogne Belgium 32D4
Holly Col. USA 82G3
Holly Mich. USA 79E4
Holly Springs Miss. USA 85C3
Hollywood Calif. USA 80D8
Holm Norway 34E4
Holmestrand Norway 35D7
Holmhead Scotland UK 29H9
Holmön Sweden 34J5
Holmsund Sweden 34J5
Holsteinsborg = Sisimiut
Holsterbro Denmark 35C8
Holsworthy England UK 26F7
Holt England UK 27S3
Holten Netherlands 32E2
Holton Kans. USA 83L3
Holwerd Netherlands 32D1
Holy Cross Alaska USA 87W12
Holy Cross,Mt of the Col. USA 86E4
Holyhead Wales UK 26E2
Holy I England UK 25E1
Holy,I Wales UK 26E2
Holy L Scotland UK 29G7
Holyoke Col. USA 82G2
Holyoke Mass. USA 84E1
Holyrood Newf. Canada 78M3
Holywell Wales UK 26H2
Holywood N Ireland 30M4
Hombori Mali 68E5
Home B NW Terr. Canada 77S3
Homer Alaska USA 87X13
Homer La USA 83M6
Homer NY USA 84C1
Homer Tun. New Zealand 100C7
Homestead Pa USA 79G5
Homfray,Str. Andaman Is India 59H6
Hommelvik Norway 34D5
Hommerts Netherlands 32D2
Homs = Ḥimṣ
Honan = Luoyang
Honan = Henan
Honda Colombia 92C2
Honda,B Cuba 89C2
Hondo Mexico 88D2
Honduras country Central America 89B4
Honduras,C Honduras 89B3
Honduras,G of Central America 89B3
Hønefoss Norway 35D6
Honesdale Pa USA 84D2
Honey L Calif. USA 80C5
Honfleur France 42D2
Hong'an China 54H7
Honghai Wan bay China 55H11
Hong He river China 54H6
Hong Kong SE Asia 55H11
Hongshui He river China 55C10
Hongtong China 54F4
Honguedo Pass. Que. Canada 78F2
Hongze Hu lake China 54K6
Honiara,I Solomon Is 94G8
Honiton England UK 26H7
Honolulu Hawaii USA 95V26
Honomu Hawaii USA 95V27
Honor Mich. USA 79C3
Honshū island Japan 56C7
Hoodfdplaat Netherlands 32B3
Hood,Mt Oreg. USA 80C3
Hoofddorp Netherlands 32C2
Hooger Smilde Netherlands 32E2
Hoogeveen Netherlands 32E2
Hoogezand-Sappemeer Netherlands 32E1
Hooghalen Netherlands 32E2
Hooghly India 61G4
Hooghly,R India 61F5
Hoogstraten Belgium 32C3
Hoogvliet Netherlands 32C3
Hooker Calif. USA 80B5
Hooker,C Prince Edward Is Indian Ocean 65P12
Hook Hd Ireland, Rep. of 31K9
Hook of Holland = Hoek van Holland
Hoona Mts Algeria 68F1
Hoopeston Ill. USA 83Q2
Hoosick Falls NY USA 84E1
Hoover Dam Ariz. USA 80F8
Hope Ark. USA 83M6
Hope BC Canada 76G7
Hopedale Newf. Canada 77T5
Hopeh = Hebei
Hopen,I Barents Sea 50D2
Hopes Advance,C Que. Canada 77S4
Hopetoun Vic. Australia 97B3
Hope Town Andaman Is India 59H6
Hopetown South Africa 72C5
Hopewell Va USA 85J2
Hopi Ind. Resn Ariz. USA 82C4
Hopkinsville Ky USA 85D2
Hoquiam Wash. USA 80B2
Horaždovice Czech. 36E4
Horcasitas Mexico 88B2
Hordaland county Norway 35B6
Horgen Switzerland 33D1
Horinger China 54F2
Horka E Germany 36F3
Horley England UK 27P6
Hormoz Iran 63G4
Hormoz island Iran 63H4
Hormuz,Str. of Iran/Oman 63H4
Horn Austria 37F4
Horn Iceland 34T11
Horn Netherlands 32D3
Hornavan,L Sweden 34G3
Hornby New Zealand 100E6
Horn,C = Hornos,C de
Horncastle England UK 25H6
Hörnefors Sweden 34H5
Hornell NY USA 84C1
Hörnli mt Switzerland 33D1
Horn Mts NW Terr. Canada 76H4
Hornopiren,Mt Chile 91B6
Hornos,C de Chile 91C9
Hornsby NSW Australia 97D2
Hornsea England UK 25H5
Horonobe Japan 56G2
Horqueta Paraguay 91E2
Horseheads NY USA 84C1
Horsens Denmark 35C9
Horse Shoe W Aus. Australia 98D5
Horseshoe L Ariz. USA 82C5
Horsham England UK 27P6
Horsham Vic. Australia 97B3
Horšovsky Tyn Czech. 36E4
Horst Netherlands 32E3
Horten Norway 35D7
Hortlax Sweden 34J4
Horton Kans. USA 83L3
Horton Mont. USA 81D2
Horton R NW Terr. Canada 76G3
Horwich England UK 25C5
Hose Ra mts Sarawak Malay. 53F10
Hoshangabad India 61A4
Hoshiarpur India 60D5
Hospel India 58E5
Hospenthal Switzerland 33D2
Hospice Switzerland 33C3
Hospital Ireland,Rep. of 31G9
Hossegor France 43B5
Hoste,I Chile 91C9
Hosur India 58E6
Hotagen Sweden 34F5
Hotan Xinjiang China 50J6
Hoting Sweden 34G4
Hot Springs N Car. USA 85F3
Hot Springs S Dak. USA 81F4
Hot Springs Nat. Pk Ark. USA 83M5
Hotton Belgium 32D4
Houdelaincourt France 42F2
Houffalize Belgium 32D4
Houghton L Mich. USA 79D3
Houghton-le-Spring England UK 25F3
Houlton Maine USA 78E3
Houma China 54F5
Houma La USA 83N8

Hounslow Íos

Hounslow *England* UK 27P6
Hourn,L *Scotland* UK 28E5
Housatonic,R *Conn.* USA 84E2
House Ra *Utah* USA 82B3
Houston *Miss.* USA 85C4
Houston *Mo* USA 83N4
Houston *Texas* USA 83L8
Hout B South Africa 72H10
Houtman Abrolhos *islands W Aus.* Australia 98C5
Hovd Mongolia 51L5
Hove *England* UK 27P7
Hövsgöl Nuur *lake* Mongolia 51M4
Howard *Pa* USA 84C2
Howard *S Dak.* USA 81J3
Howard City *Mich.* USA 79D4
Howden *England* UK 25G5
Howden Res. *England* UK 25E6
Howe *Idaho* USA 80G4
Howe,C *NSW* Australia 97D3
Howe,I Kerguelen 65S12
Howell *Mich.* USA 79E4
Howick South Africa 72E5
Howland,I Pacific Ocean 94J7
Howley *Newf.* Canada 78K2
Howrah India 61G4
Howth Ireland, Rep. of 31L7
Howth,Mt *Vic.* Australia 97C3
Hoyes Spain 40C2
Hoy, I *Orkney* Scotland 28K2
Hoyt *New Br.* Canada 78E4
Hozat Turkey 62D2
Hradec Králové Czech. 37F3
Hrubieszów Poland 37K3
Hsawnghsup = Thaungdut
Hsenwi Burma 59J4
Hsinchu Taiwan 55L10
Hsinking = Changchun
Hsipaw Burma 59J4
Hua'an China 55J10
Huacho Peru 92B6
Huacrachuco Peru 92B5
Huading Shan *mt* China 55L8
Huai'an China 54K6
Huaibei China 54J5
Huai He *river* China 54H6
Huailai China 54H2
Huainan China 54J6
Huairen China 54G3
Huaiyang China 54H6
Huaiyuan China 54J6
Hualapai Ind. Resn *Ariz.* USA 80G8
Hualgayoc Peru 92B5
Huallaga,R Peru 92B5
Hualong China 54B4
Hualtien Taiwan 55L11
Huambo Angola 70D7
Huanay Bolivia 92D7
Huancabamba Peru 92B5
Huancane Peru 92D7
Huancavelica Peru 92B6
Huancayo Peru 92B6
Huanchaca Bolivia 92D8
Huanchaco Peru 92B5
Huangchuan China 54H6
Huanggang China 54H7
Huanggang Shan *mt* China 55J9
Huang Hai *sea* China 54L5
Huang He *river* China 54F3
Huanghe Kou China 54K3
Huangmei China 55J7
Huangshi China 55H7
Huang Shui *river* China 54B4
Huang Xian China 54L4
Huangyan China 55L8
Huaniao Shan China 54M7
Huan Jiang *river* China 54D4
Huanta Peru 92C6
Huanuco Peru 92B5
Huan Xian China 54D4
Huaonta Nicaragua 89C4
Huara Chile 91C1
Huaráz Peru 92B5
Huards,L aux *Que.* Canada 78C2
Huariaca Peru 92B6
Huarmey Peru 92B6
Huascarán *mt* Peru 92B5
Huasco Chile 91B3
Hua Xian China 55G11
Huaylas Peru 92B5
Hubei *province* China 54G7
Hubli India 58E5
Hucknall *England* UK 25F6
Huddersfield *England* UK 25E5
Hudiksvall Sweden 35G6
Hudson *Maine* USA 78D4
Hudson *NY* USA 84E1
Hudson *Wis.* USA 81L3
Hudson B Canada 77O5
Hudson Falls *NY* USA 84E1
Hudson,R *NY* USA 84E1
Hudson Str. Canada 77R4
Hue Vietnam 57D3
Hueco Mts *New Mex./Texas* USA 82F6
Huedin Romania 46D1
Huehuetenango Guatemala 88F4
Huejutla Mexico 88E3
Huelva Spain 40C4
Huelva *prov.* Spain 40C4
Huequi,Pen. Chile 91B6
Huereal Overa Spain 41F4
Huesca *prov.* Spain 41F1
Huete Spain 41E2
Hughenden *Queens.* Australia 99J4
Hugh Town *England* UK 26B9
Hugo *Okla.* USA 83L5
Huguan China 54G5
Hui'an China 55K10
Huiarau Ra *mts* New Zealand 100G4
Huichang China 55H10
Huicheng = She Xian
Hŭichŏn N Korea 52J2
Huilai China 55J11
Huimin China 54J4
Huinan China 52J2
Huitong China 55E9
Hui Xian China 54D6
Huiyang = Huizhou
Huizen Netherlands 32D2
Huizhou China 55H11
Hukawng Valley Burma 59J3
Hukou China 55J8
Hulin China 52K1
Hull *England* UK 25H5
Hull *Que.* Canada 79J3
Hull I Phoenix Is 94J8
Hull,R *England* UK 25H5
Hulst Netherlands 32C3
Huludao China 54L2
Hulun = Hailar
Hulun Nur *lake* Mongolia 52G1
Huluo He *river* China 54G3
Huma *Heilong.* China 51P4
Humacao Puerto Rico 89F3
Humaita Brazil 92E5
Humaita Paraguay 91E3
Humansdorp South Africa 72C6
Humber,R *England* UK 25H5
Humberside *county England* UK 25G5
Humboldt *Iowa* USA 83L1
Humboldt *Nev.* USA 80D5
Humboldt *Sask.* Canada 76K6
Humboldt *Tenn.* USA 85C3
Humboldt B *Calif.* USA 86A3
Humboldt Gletscher *glacier* Greenland 14Q2
Humboldt,L *Nev.* USA 80D5
Humboldt,R *Nev.* USA 80D5
Humenne Czech. 37J4
Hume Res. *NSW* Australia 97C3
Humphrey *Idaho* USA 80G3
Humphreys,Mt *Calif.* USA 80D7
Humphreys Pk *Ariz.* USA 82C5
Hun Libya 69J3
Húnaflói,B Iceland 34U12
Hunan *province* China 55F9
Hunga Fofoa *islands* Tonga 95V30
Hungary *country* Europe 39K4
Hungerford *England* UK 27M6
Hungerford *Queens.* Australia 97B1
Hun He *river* China 54F2
Hun He *river* China 54M2
Hunjiang China 52J2
Hunmanby *England* UK 25H4
Hunsrück *region* W Germany 36B4
Hunstanton *England* UK 27R3
Hunter Is *Tas.* Australia 97F5
Hunter,R *NSW* Australia 97D2
Hunterstone *Scotland* UK 29G8
Huntersville *W Va* USA 85G1
Huntingburg *Ind.* USA 85D1
Huntingdon *England* UK 27P4
Huntingdon *Pa* USA 84B2
Huntington *NY* USA 84E2
Huntington *Oreg.* USA 80E3
Huntington *Utah* USA 82C3
Huntington *W Va* USA 85F1
Huntington Beach *Calif.* USA 80D9
Huntley *Mont.* USA 81C3
Huntly New Zealand 100F3
Huntly *Scotland* UK 28L5
Huntsville *Ala.* USA 85D3
Huntsville *Ont.* Canada 79G3
Huntsville *Tenn.* USA 85E2
Huntsville *Texas* USA 83L7
Hunucma Mexico 88G3
Hunyuan China 54G3
Hunza,R *Kashmir* India 60D2
Huolu China 54H3
Huon,Is Pacific Ocean 94G9
Huon Pen. Papua New Guinea 99K1
Huon,R *Tas.* Australia 97F5
Huoqiu China 54J6
Huoshan China 54J7
Huo Xian China 54F4
Hupeh = Hubei
Hurd,C *Ont.* Canada 79F3
Hurghada Egypt 69M3
Hurliness *Orkney* Scotland 28K2
Huron *Calif.* USA 80C7
Huron *S Dak.* USA 81H3
Huron,L Canada/USA 79E3
Hurtsboro *Ala* USA 85E4
Hurunui,R New Zealand 100E6
Husavik Iceland 34W11
Husevig Faeroerne 34Z15
Huskisson *NSW* Australia 97D3
Huskvarna Sweden 35F8
Husn Jordan 64D5
Husn el Akrad Syria 64E3
Husum W Germany 36C1
Hutchinson *Kans* USA 83J3
Hutchinson *Minn.* USA 81K3
Hüttenberg Austria 36F5
Hutton Rudby *England* UK 25F4
Huttwil Switzerland 33C1
Hu Xian China 54E5
Huy Belgium 32D4
Hvar *island* Yugoslavia 44F4
Hwaiyan Shan *mts* China 54H7
Hyde *England* UK 25D6
Hyden *Ky* USA 85F2
Hyde Park *Vt* USA 79K3
Hyderabad India 58E5
Hyderabad Pakistan 58C3
Hyères France 43G5
Hyères,Is d' France 43G5
Hyland,R *Yukon* Canada 76F4
Hyndman Pk *Idaho* USA 86D3
Hyogo *prefecture* Japan 56D7
Hyöto *prefecture* Japan 56D7
Hyrum *Utah* USA 82B2
Hyrynsalmi Finland 34N4
Hythe *Hamps.,England* UK 27M7
Hythe *Kent,England* UK 27S6
Hyvinkää Finland 35L6

I

Iaat Lebanon 64E3
Ialomita,R Romania 46F2
Iaşi Romania 48E8
Ibadan Nigeria 68F7
Ibague Colombia 92B3
Ibaraki *prefecture* Japan 56G6
Ibar,R Yugoslavia 46C3
Ibarra Ecuador 92B3
Ibb Yemen 62E7
Ibba or Toni,R Sudan 69L7
Ibembo Zaire 70E4
Ibera,L Argentina 91E3
Ibi Nigeria 69G7
Ibiapaba,Serra da *mts* Brazil 93J4
Ibicui Brazil 91E3
Ibicuí,R Uruguay 91E3
Ibiza,I *Balearic Is* Spain 41G3
Ibresi USSR 49H3
Ibri Oman 63H5
Ica Peru 92B6
Icana,R Brazil 92D3
Icá,R Brazil 92D4
Içel = Mersin
Iceland *country* Europe 22C2
Ichak India 61E3
Ichwaro India 61A3
Icoraci Brazil 93H4
Idabel *Okla.* USA 83L6
Ida Grove *Iowa* USA 83L1
Idah Nigeria 68G7
Idaho *state* USA 86C3
Idaho Falls *Idaho* USA 80G4
Idanga,R India 58D5
Idanha *Oreg* USA 80B3
Idanha South Africa 72B6
Ideles Algeria 68G4
Ideriyn *river* China 52C1
Idfu Egypt 69M4
Idhi Óros *mt Kríti* Greece 47E7
Idhra *island* Greece 47D6
Idlib Syria 64E2
Idutywa South Africa 72D6
Ieper Belgium 32A4
Ierissós,G of Greece 47D4
Ifakara Tanzania 71H6
Ife Nigeria 68F7
Iférouane Niger 68G5
Igan *Sarawak* Malay. 53F10
Igarapé Miri Brazil 93H4
Igarka USSR 50K3
Iglesias *Sardinia* Italy 45B6
Igli Algeria 68E2
Igoma Tanzania 71G6
Igoumenitsa Greece 47C5
Igra USSR 49L2
Iguacú,R Brazil 91F3
Iguala Mexico 88E4
Iguapé Brazil 91G2
Iguatu Brazil 93K5
Igumira Tanzania 71G6
Ihosy Madagascar 71N11
Iisalmi Finland 34M5
Ijebu-Ode Nigeria 68F7
IJmuiden Netherlands 32C2
Ijsselmeer *sea* Netherlands 32D2
Ijsselmonde *region* Netherlands 32C3
Ijsselmuiden Netherlands 32D2
Ijssel,R Netherlands 32E2
Ijsselstein Netherlands 32D2
Ijui Brazil 91F3
Ijuw Nauru 94A22
Ijzendijke Netherlands 32B3
Ikaalinen Finland 35K6
Ikaría *island* Greece 47F6
Ikhtiman Bulgaria 46D3
Ikisu Tanzania 71G5
Ikla *Eston.* USSR 35L8
Ikonde Tanzania 71G6
Ilagan Philippines 53H7
Ilam Iran 62F3
Ilam Nepal 61F2
Ilanz Switzerland 33E2
Iława Poland 37H2
Ilchester *England* UK 26J7
Ile-à-la Crosse,L *Sask.* Canada 76K5
Ile-de-France *prov.* France 42E2
Ile d'Orléans *Que.* Canada 79L2
Ilford *England* UK 27Q5
Ilfracombe *England* UK 26F6
Ilha do Bananal Brazil 93G6
Ilhas do Cabo Verde = Cape Verde Is
Ilhavo Portugal 40B2
Ilhéus Brazil 93K6
Ilia *dist.* Greece 47C6
Iliamna,L *Alaska* USA 87X13
Ilic Turkey 62D2
Ilich *Kazakh.* USSR 50H5
Iligan Philippines 53H9
Ilimsk USSR 51M4
Iliodhrómia *island* Greece 47D5
Ilion *NY* USA 84D1
Ili,R *Kazakh.* USSR 50J5
Ilkeston *England* UK 25F7
Ilkley *England* UK 25E5
Illapel Chile 91B4
Ille et Vilaine *dep.* France 42C2
Illescas Spain 40E2
Illimani *mt* Bolivia 92D7
Illinois *state* USA 87H4
Illinois,R *Ill.* USA 83N3
Illizi Algeria 68G3
Illora Spain 40E4
Ilmen Ozero *lake* USSR 48G2
Ilminster *England* UK 26J7
Ilo Peru 92C7
Iloilo Philippines 53H8
Ilorin Nigeria 68F7
Ilwaco *Wash.* USA 80A2
Imabari Japan 56C7
Imataca,Serra de *mts* Venezuela 92E2
Imathia *dist.* Greece 47D4
Imatra Finland 35N6
Imerimandroso Madagascar 71N10
Imi Ethiopia 71J3
Immendingen W.Germany 36C5
Immingham *England* UK 25H5
Imnaha,R *Oreg.* USA 80E3
Imola Italy 44C3
Imperatriz Brazil 92D5
Imperatriz Brazil 93H5
Imperia Italy 44B4
Imperial Dam *Ariz.* USA 86D5
Imphal India 59H4
Imroz = Gökçeada
Imtan Syria 64E5
Inaccessible I Tristan da Cunha Is 72G8
Inambari,R Peru 92C6
Inari Finland 34M2
Inarijärvi,L Finland 34M2
In Belbel Algeria 68F3
Incahusai *mt* Argentina 91C3
Inch Ireland, Rep. of 31L8
Inchkeith,I *Scotland* UK 29K7
Inchŏn S Korea 52J3
Incourt Belgium 32C4
Indaal,L *Scotland* UK 29D8
Indalsalven *river* Sweden 34G5
Indalsälven,R Sweden 34F5
Indaw Burma 59J4
Indawgyi,L Burma 59J3
Independence *Calif.* USA 80D7
Independence *Idaho* USA 80G3
Independence *Iowa* USA 83N1
Independence *Kans.* USA 83L4
Independence *Mo* USA 83L3
Independence *Oreg.* USA 80B3
Independence Fj. Greenland 14N1
Independence Mts *Nev.* USA 80E5
Independencia Argentina 91C4
India *country* S Asia 58E4
Indiana *Pa* USA 84B2
Indiana *state* USA 87J3
Indianapolis *Ind.* USA 79C6
Indian Des = Thar Des
Indian Head *Sask.* Canada 76L6
Indian House L *Que.* Canada 77S5
Indian L *NY* USA 84D1
Indianola *Iowa* USA 83M2
Indian Springs V *Nev.* USA 80E7
Indiga USSR 50F3
Indigirka,R USSR 51R3
Indigirka,R USSR 51R3
Indochina *region* SE Asia 57D4
Indonesia *country* SE Asia 19M10
Indore India 58E4
Indravati,R India 58F5
Indre *dep.* France 42D3
Indre-et-Loire *dep.* France 42D3
Indre,R France 42C3
Indur = Nizamabad
Indur = Nizamabad
Indus,Mouths of India 58C4
Indus,R Pakistan 60C3
İnebolu Turkey 62C1
Inez *Ky* USA 85F2
In Gall Niger 68G5
Ingelmunster Belgium 32B4
Ingeniero Luiggi Argentina 91D5
Ingersoll *Ont.* Canada 79F4
Ingham *Queens.* Australia 99K3
Ingleborough *mt England* UK 25D4
Inglefield Inlet Greenland 14Q2
Inglefield Land Greenland 14Q2
Inglenook *Calif.* USA 80B6
Inglewood *Calif.* USA 80D8
Inglewood New Zealand 100F4
Inglewood *Vic.* Australia 97B3
Ingolfshöfdhi *islands* Iceland 34W13
Ingolstadt W Germany 36D4
Ingrid Christensen Coast Antarctica 15F3
Inhambane Mozambique 72F4
Inharrime Mozambique 72F4
Inishark,I Ireland, Rep. of 30C6
Inishbofin *island* Ireland,Rep. of 30G3
Inishbofin,I Ireland, Rep. of 30C6
Inishcrone Ireland, Rep. of 30E5
Inisheer,I Ireland, Rep. of 31D7
Inishkea,I Ireland, Rep. of 30C5
Inishmaan,I Ireland, Rep. of 31D7
Inishmore,I Ireland, Rep. of 31D7
Inishmurray,I Ireland, Rep. of 30F5
Inishowen Pen. Ireland, Rep. of 30J3
Inishtrahull,I Ireland, Rep. of 30J3
Inishtrahull Sd Ireland, Rep. of 30J3
Inishturk,I Ireland, Rep. of 30C6
Injune *Queens.* Australia 99K5
Inklin,R *BC* Canada 76E5
Inkom *Idaho* USA 80G4
Inland Sea = Seto Naikai
Innerleithen *Scotland* UK 29K8
Inner Mongolia *auton. region* China 54F2
Inner Sd *Scotland* UK 28E5
Innerthal Switzerland 33D1
Innertkirchen Switzerland 33D2
Inniscarra Res. Ireland,Rep. of 31F10
Innisfail *Queens.* Australia 99K3
Inn,R Austria 36D5
Innsbruck Austria 36D5
Inowrocław Poland 37H2
Inquisivi Bolivia 92D7
Inrida,R Columbia 92D3
Ins Switzerland 33C1
In Salah Algeria 68F3
Insar USSR 49G4
Insch *Scotland* UK 28L5
Insein Burma 59J5
Insterburg = Chernyakhovsk
Intendente Alvear Argentina 91D5
Interlaken Switzerland 33C2
International Falls *Minn.* USA 81L1
Interview,I *Andaman Is* India 59H6
Intragna Switzerland 33D2
Inutil,B Chile 91C8
Inveraray *Scotland* UK 29F7
Inverbervie *Scotland* UK 29M6
Invercargill New Zealand 100C8
Inverell *NSW* Australia 97D1
Invergordon *Scotland* UK 28H4
Inverkeithing *Scotland* UK 29K7
Inverness *No. Sc.* Canada 78H3
Inverness *Scotland* UK 28H5
Invershin *Scotland* UK 28H4
Inverurie *Scotland* UK 28M5
Investigator Str. *S Aus.* Australia 99H7
Inyati Zimbabwe 72D3
Inyo Ra. *Calif.* USA 80D7
Inza USSR 49H4
Inzer USSR 49N3
Ioánnina Greece 47C5
Iola *Kans.* USA 83L4
Iona *No. Sc.* Canada 78H4
Iona,I *Scotland* UK 29D7
Ionia *Mich.* USA 79D4
Ionian Is Greece 47C5
Ionian Sea Medit. Sea 39K6
Ionishkis *Lith.* USSR 35K8
Ionnina *dist.* Greece 47C5
Íos *island* Greece 47E6

Iouicoui,Mt Brazil 93G3
Iowa state USA 87H3
Iowa City Iowa USA 83N2
Iowa Falls Iowa USA 83M1
Ipala Mexico 88C3
Ipameri Brazil 93H7
Ipiales Colombia 92B3
Ípiros region Greece 47C5
Ipixuna,R Brazil 92C5
Ipoh Malaysia 57C6
Ippy CAR 69K7
Ipswich England UK 27S4
Ipswich Queens. Australia 99L5
Ipswich S Dak. USA 81H3
Ipu Brazil 93J4
Iquique Chile 91B2
Iquitos Peru 92C4
Iracoubo Fr. Guiana 93G2
Iráklia island Greece 47E6
Iráklion Kríti Greece 47E7
Iráklion dist. Greece 47E7
Iran country SW Asia 18G6
Iran country SW Asia 63G3
Iränshar Iran 63J4
Irapa Venezuela 92E1
Irapuato Mexico 88D3
Iraq country SW Asia 62E3
Irazu vol. Costa Rica 89C4
Irbid Jordan 64D5
Irbit USSR 49R2
Ireland, Rep of country NW
Europe 22F5
Irene South Africa 72M12
Irgah South Yemen 62F7
Irgiz Kazakh. USSR 50H5
Irian Jaya New Guinea Indon.
53L12
Iricoume,Serra mts Brazil 92F3
Iringa Tanzania 71H6
Iriomote Jima island Japan
56K14
Iriri,R Brazil 93G4
Irish Sea British Isles 22G5
Irkutsk USSR 51M4
Irkutskaya Oblast region USSR
51M4
Ironbridge England UK 25D7
Iron City Tenn. USA 85D3
Irondale Ont. Canada 79G3
Iron Knob S Aus. Australia 99H6
Iron Mountain Mich. USA 79B3
Iron Mt Mo USA 83N4
Iron River Mich. USA 79B2
Iron River Wis. USA 81M2
Ironton Mo USA 83N4
Ironton Ohio USA 85F1
Ironwood Mich. USA 79A2
Iroquois Ont. Canada 79J3
Irrawaddy,Mouths of Burma
59J5
Irrawaddy,R Burma 59J4
Irthing,R England UK 25C3
Irtysh,R USSR 50H4
Irumu Zaire 71F4
Irvine Scotland UK 29G8
Irvine,R Scotland UK 29G8
Irvinestown N Ireland 30H4
Irymple Vic. Australia 97B2
Isabela,I Galapagos Is 95S8
Isabella Calif. USA 80D8
Isaccea Romania 46G2
Ísafjördhur Iceland 34T11
Isai Kalat Pakistan 58B3
Isa Khel Pakistan 60B4
Isangi Zaire 70E4
Ísari Greece 47C6
Ischia island Italy 45D5
Iseghem = Izegem
Iselin Pa USA 84B2
Iseltwald Switzerland 33C2
Isère dep. France 43F4
Isère,R France 43F4
Isernia Italy 45E5
Ise wan bay Japan 56E7
Isfahan = Esfahän
Ishigaki jima island Japan
56L14
Ishikari,R Japan 56H3
Ishikari wan bay Japan 56G3
Ishikawa prefecture Japan 56E6
Ishim USSR 50H4
Ishimbay USSR 49N4
Ishinomaki wan bay Japan
56G5
Ishkamish Afghanistan 63K2
Ishkashim Afghanistan 63L2
Ishpeming Mich. USA 79C2
Isil Kul USSR 50J4
Isiolo Kenya 71H4
Isisford Queens. Australia 99J4
Iskenderun Turkey 62D2
Iskilip Turkey 62C1
Iskitim USSR 50K4
Iskut,R BC Canada 76E5
Islamabad Pakistan 60C4
Islampur India 61E3
Island L Man. Canada 76N6
Island Pond Vt USA 79L3
Islands,B of Newf. Canada 78J2
Islands,B of New Zealand
100F2
Islas Malvinas = Falkland Is
Islay island Scotland UK 29D8

Isle,R France 43D4
Isleton Calif. USA 80C6
Ismâ'iliya Egypt 69M2
Isna Egypt 69M3
Isojoki Finland 35J5
Isoka Zambia 72E2
Isparta Turkey 62C2
Israel country SW Asia 64C5
Issoire France 42E4
Issoudun France 42D3
İstanbul Turkey 62B1
Istiaia Greece 47D5
Istmina Colombia 92B2
Istra pen. Yugoslavia 44D3
Istranca Daǧlari mts Turkey
46F4
Istro Zaire 71F4
Itabaiana Brazil 93K5
Itabuna Brazil 93K6
Itacaré Brazil 93K6
Itacoatiara Brazil 92F4
Itaeté Brazil 93J6
Itaituba Brazil 93F4
Itajai Brazil 91G3
Italy country Europe 38H5
Itapecurum Mirim Brazil 93J4
Itaperuna Brazil 93J8
Itapetininga Brazil 93H8
Itaqui Brazil 91E3
Itarsi India 58E4
Itasca,L Minn. USA 81K2
Itchen,R England UK 27M7
Itéa Greece 47D5
Ithaca Mich. USA 79D4
Ithaca NY USA 84C1
Itháci = Ithaka
Ithaka Greece 47C5
Itiés Greece 47C4
Itimbiri,R Zaire 70E4
Itkhari India 61E3
Itperuna Brazil 93J8
Ittoggortoomiit Greenland 14N2
Itula Congo 71F5
Itultaba Brazil 93H7
Iturbe Argentina 91C2
Itzehoe W Germany 36C2
Iuruá,R Brazil 92C5
Ivailovgrad Bulgaria 46F4
Ivalo Finland 34M2
Ivalo Joki river Finland 34M2
Ivanhoe NSW Australia 97B2
Ivanic Grad Yugoslavia 44F3
Ivano-Frankovsk Ukrain. USSR
48D7
Ivanovka USSR 49K4
Ivanovka USSR 49L4
Ivanovo USSR 48M3
Ivdel USSR 50H3
Ivittüüt Greenland 14P3
Iviza,I = Ibiza,I
Ivory Coast country Africa
68D7
Ivrea Italy 44A3
Ivujivik Que. Canada 77Q4
Ivybridge England UK 26G8
Iwaki Japan 56G6
Iwakuni Japan 56C7
Iwaniska Poland 37J3
Iwate prefecture Japan 56G5
Iwee Rivieten Botswana 72C5
Ixiamas Bolivia 92D6
Ixtla Mexico 88E4
Ixtlan de Juarez Mexico 88E4
Iyo nada bay Japan 56B8
Izabal,L de Guatemala 88G4
Izamal Mexico 88G3
Izegem Belgium 32B4
Izgal Pakistan 60C3
Izhevsk USSR 49L2
Izhma,R USSR 50G3
Izki Oman 63H5
Izmail Ukrain. USSR 48F9
İzmir Turkey 62B2
İzmit Turkey 62B1
Izra Syria 64E5
Iztapa Guatemala 88F5
Izu Hantö peninsula Japan 56F7
Izu Shotö islands Japan 56F7
Izyum Ukrain. USSR 48K7

J

Jaakkima USSR 35O6
Jabal al Akhdar mts Oman
63H5
Jabäl-Bärez mts Iran 63H4
Jabal el Akhdar plat. Libya
69K2
Jabalpur India 61C4
Jabal Qara mts Oman 63H6
Jabal Shammar region Saudi
Arabia 62E4
Jabal Tuwayq mts Saudi Arabia
62F5
Jabbeke Belgium 32B3
Jabbul Syria 64F1
Jablonec Czech. 37F3
Jabrin Oasis Saudi Arabia 62F5
Jaburú Brazil 92D4
Jaca Spain 41F1
Jacarezinho Brazil 93H8
Jachal Argentina 91C4
Jacksboro Tenn. USA 85E2

Jackson Calif. USA 80C6
Jackson Ky USA 85F2
Jackson La USA 83N7
Jackson Mich. USA 79D4
Jackson Minn. USA 81K4
Jackson Miss. USA 85B4
Jackson Mo USA 83P4
Jackson N Car. USA 85J2
Jackson Ohio USA 79E6
Jackson Tenn. USA 85C3
Jackson Wyo. USA 81B4
Jackson,C New Zealand 100F5
Jackson Mts Nev. USA 80D5
Jacksonville Ark. USA 83M5
Jacksonville Fla USA 85J3
Jacksonville Ill. USA 83N3
Jacksonville N Car. USA 85J3
Jacksonville Oreg. USA 80B6
Jacksonville Texas USA 83L6
Jacmel Haiti 89E3
Jacobabad Pakistan 58C3
Jacobina Brazil 93J6
Jacques Cartier,Mt Que.
Canada 78E2
Jacques Cartier Pass. Que.
Canada 78F1
Jacquet River New Br. Canada
78E3
Jacui,R Uruguay 91F3
Jacundá,R Brazil 93G4
Jade Mines Burma 59J3
Jädib South Yemen 63G6
Jadu Libya 69H2
Jaén Spain 40E4
Jaén prov. Spain 40D4
Jafarabad India 58D4
Jaffa,C S Aus. Australia 97A3
Jaffna Sri Lanka 58E7
Jagadhri India 60E5
Jagdispur India 61E3
Jagraon India 60D5
Jaguarão Brazil 91F4
Jaguari Brazil 91F3
Jaguariaiva Brazil 93H8
Jaguaruna Brazil 91G3
Jahanabad India 61E3
Jahangirabad India 60F6
Jahrom Iran 63G4
Jaicos Brazil 93J5
Jaipur India 58G4
Jaipur India 59C4
Jaipure India 59H3
Jais India 61C2
Jaisalmer India 58D3
Jäjarm Iran 63H2
Jakarta Java Indon. 53E12
Jäkkvik Sweden 34G3
Jakobstad = Pietarsaari
Jalalabad Afghanistan 60B3
Jalalabad India 60D5
Jalalpur India 61D2
Jalalpur Pakistan 60B6
Jalalpur Pakistan 60D4
Jalapa Enriquez Mexico 88E4
Jalasjärvi Finland 34K5
Jalaun India 61B2
Jaldak Afghanistan 63K3
Jaleswar Nepal 61E2
Jalgaon India 58E4
Jalisco state Mexico 88D3
Jalna India 58E5
Jalor India 58D3
Jalpaiguri India 61G2
Jaluit,I Marshall Is 94G7
Jamaica country West Indies
89D3
Jamaja Eston. USSR 35K7
Jamalabad Iran 62F2
Jamalpur Bangladesh 61H3
Jamalpur India 61F3
Jamberoo NSW Australia 97D2
James B Ont./Que. Canada
77P6
Jamesburg Calif. USA 80C7
James,R S Dak. USA 81J4
James,R Va USA 85H2
James Ra mts N Terr. Australia
98G4
James Ross I Antarctica 15T3
Jamestown N Dak. USA 81H2
Jamestown NY USA 84B1
Jamestown S Aus. Australia
97A2
Jamestown Res. N Dak. USA
81H2
Jamiltepec Mexico 88E4
Jammer Bugt bay Denmark
35C8
Jammu Pakistan 60D4
Jammu & Kashmir state India
60D3
Jamnagar India 58D4
Jampur Pakistan 60B6
Jamrad Afghanistan 63K3
Jamrao Pakistan 58C3
Jämsä Finland 35L6
Jamshedpur India 61H4
Jamtara India 61F4
Jämtland county Sweden 34E5
Jamui India 61F3
Jamuna,R Bangladesh 61G3
Jandaq Iran 63G3
Jandiala India 60D5

Jandiala India 60E4
Jandiatuba,R Brazil 92D4
Janesville Wis. USA 79B4
Janeville New Br. Canada 78F3
Jangipur India 61G3
Jani Khel Pakistan 60B4
Janjira India 58D5
Jan Mayen,I Arctic Ocean 50A2
Janos Mexico 88C1
Jansath India 60E6
Jansenville South Africa 72C6
Jan Smuts Pk Pr. Edward Is
Indian Ocean 65P12
Januária Brazil 93J7
Janzé France 42C2
Jaora India 58E4
Japan country E. Asia 52L3
Japan,Sea of E Asia 52L2
Japurá Brazil 92D4
Japurá,R Brazil 92D4
Japvo,Mt India 59H3
Jaráguá Brazil 93H7
Jaraguá do Sul Brazil 91G3
Jarales New Mex. USA 82E5
Jaramillo Argentina 91C7
Jarandilla Spain 40D2
Jarash Jordan 64D5
Jardim do Serido Brazil 93K5
Jardines de la Reina islands
Cuba 89D2
Jargalant = Hovd
Jarji Nigeria 68G6
Jarocin Poland 37G2
Jaromer Czech. 37F3
Jaroslaw Poland 37K3
Järpen Sweden 34E5
Jarrow England UK 25F3
Jartai China 54C3
Jartai Yanchi lake China 54C3
Jarvis,I Pacific Ocean 94K8
Järvsö Sweden 35G6
Jashpurnagar India 61E4
Jåsk Iran 63H4
Jaslo Poland 37J4
Jaso India 61C3
Jason,I Falkland Is 91D8
Jasper Alta Canada 76H6
Jasper Fla USA 85F5
Jasper Ga USA 85E3
Jasper Texas USA 83M7
Jasper Nat. Pk Alta Canada
76H6
Jassy = Iaşi
Jastrowie Poland 37G2
Jaswantnagar India 61B2
Jaszberény Hungary 37H5
Jatai Brazil 93G7
Jatobá Brazil 93H4
Jaú Brazil 93H8
Jauaperi,R Brazil 92E3
Jauche Belgium 32C4
Jauharabad Pakistan 60C4
Jauja Peru 92B6
Jaumave Mexico 88E3
Jaunjelgava Latvia USSR 35L8
Jaunpur India 61D3
Java island Indonesia 53E12
Javadi Hills India 58E6
Java,I = Jawa,I
Javari,R Brazil-Peru 92C5
Javhlant = Uliastay
Javier,I Chile 91B7
Jawa Nigeria 69H6
Jawai,R India 58D3
Jawalamukhi India 60E5
Jawarah Oman 63H6
Jayapura Indonesia 53M11
Jayrüd Syria 64E4
Jebba Nigeria 68F7
Jebel Abdul Aziz Syria 62D2
Jebel ash Shaykh = Jebel esh
Sheikh
Jebel Dibbagh Saudi Arabia
62D4
Jebel ed Druz mt Syria 64E5
Jebel el Ansariye Syria 64E2
Jebel el Bishri Syria 62D2
Jebel el Sharr mt Saudi Arabia
62D4
Jebel esh Sharqi mts Leb./Syria
64E4
Jebel esh Sheikh mt Syria
64D4
Jebel Hajima mt Saudi Arabia
62D5
Jebel Jildiah mt Saudi Arabia
62E4
Jebel Radhwa mt Saudi Arabia
62D5
Jebel Sa'diya mt Saudi Arabia
62E5
Jebel Sanam Iraq 62F3
Jebel Sinjar mt Iraq 62E2
Jebel Subh mt Saudi Arabia
62E6
Jebel Terban Saudi Arabia 62D5
Jebel Unaysah Iraq 62D3
Jeble Syria 64D2
Jech Doab region Pakistan
60C4

Jedda = Jiddah
Jedede Saudi Arabia 62E5
Jedrzejów Poland 37J3
Jefferson Ga USA 85F3
Jefferson Wis. USA 79B4
Jefferson City Mo USA 83M3
Jefferson,Mt Nev. USA 80E6
Jefferson,Mt Oreg. USA 80C3
Jeffersonville Ind. USA 85E1
Jega Nigeria 68F6
Jékabpils Latvia USSR 35L8
Jelenia Góra Poland 37F3
Jelgava Latvia USSR 35K8
Jelšava Czech. 37J4
Jemeppe Belgium 32C4
Jena E Germany 36D3
Jenin Jordan 64D5
Jenipapo Brazil 92F5
Jennings La USA 83M7
Jenolan Caves NSW Australia
97C2
Jeparit Vic. Australia 97B3
Jeppo = Jepua
Jepua Finland 34K5
Jerablus Syria 64F1
Jérémie Haiti 89E3
Jeremoabo Brazil 93K6
Jerez de la Frontera Spain
40C4
Jericho Jordan 64D6
Jericho Queens. Australia 99K4
Jerilderie NSW Australia 97C3
Jerome Ariz. USA 82B5
Jerome Idaho USA 80F4
Jerruck Pakistan 58C3
Jersey City New J USA 84D2
Jersey,I Channel Is UK 42B2
Jersey Shore Pa USA 84C2
Jerseyville Ill. USA 83N3
Jerusalem Israel/Jordan 64D6
Jervis B NSW Australia 97D3
Jervis,C S Aus. Australia 97A3
Jervois Ra mts N Terr. Australia
99H4
Jesenik region Czech. 37G3
Jesi Italy 44D4
Jesselton = Kota Kinabalu
Jessore Bangladesh 61G4
Jesup Ga USA 85G5
Jésus,I Que. Canada 79K3
Jesus María Argentina 91D4
Jetalsar India 58D4
Jeypore India 59F5
Jez Mamry lake Poland 37J1
Jezzine Lebanon 64D4
J. Gurgei mt Sudan 69K6
Jhal Pakistan 58C3
Jhalawar India 58E4
Jhang Maghiana Pakistan 60C5
Jhansi India 61B3
Jhau Pakistan 58C3
Jhelum Pakistan 60C4
Jhelum,R India 60C3
Jhelum,R. Pakistan 60C4
Jhunjhunu India 60D6
Jialing Jiang river China 54C6
Jiamusi China 52K1
Ji'an China 55H9
Jiande China 55C8
Jiangbei China 55D8
Jiangdu China 54K6
Jiang'an China 55C8
Jianghua China 55F10
Jiangkou China 55E9
Jiangle China 55J9
Jiangling China 55G7
Jiangmen China 55G5
Jiangpu China 54K6
Jiangshan China 55K8
Jiangsu province China 55H9
Jiangxi China 55H9
Jiangyin China 54L7
Jiangyong China 55F10
Jianhe China 55E9
Jianli China 55G8
Jianning China 55J8
Jian'ou China 55K9
Jianping China 54L2
Jianpur India 61D2
Jianshui China 52D6
Jianyang China 55C7
Jianyang China 55K9
Jiao Xian China 54K4
Jiaozhou Wan bay China 54L4
Jiaozuo China 54G5
Jiashan China 54K6
Jiashan China 54L7
Jia Xian China 54F3
Jiaxiang China 54J5
Jiaxing China 54L7
Jiayu China 55G8
Jicaro Nicaragua 89B4
Jičin Czech. 37F3
Jiddah Saudi Arabia 62D5
Jieshi China 55H11
Jieshi Wan bay China 55H11
Jieyang China 55J11
Jigni India 61B3
Jihlava Czech. 37F4
Jilin China 52J2

Jimena de la Frontera, Kap Desolation

Jimena de la Frontera Spain **40D4**
Jiménez Mexico **88D2**
Jiménez Mexico **88E3**
Jimma Ethiopia **71H3**
Jimo China **54L4**
Jim Thorpe *Pa* USA **84D2**
Jinan China **54J4**
Jincheng China **54G5**
Jind India **60E6**
Jing'an China **55H8**
Jingchuan China **54D5**
Jingde China **55K7**
Jingdezhen China **55J8**
Jingdong China **52D6**
Jinggu China **52D6**
Jinghai China **54J3**
Jing He *river* China **54E5**
Jingjiang China **54L6**
Jingmen China **54G7**
Jingning China **54C5**
Jing Shan *mts* China **54F7**
Jingxi China **55D11**
Jing Xian China **54K7**
Jing Xian China **55E9**
Jingyuan China **54C4**
Jingyuan China **54C5**
Jingzhou = Jiangling
Jingziguan P China **54F6**
Jinhua China **55K8**
Jining China **54G2**
Jining China **54J5**
Jinja Uganda **71G4**
Jinjiang China **55K10**
Jin Jiang *river* China **55H8**
Jinotega Nicaragua **89B4**
Jinping China **55E9**
Jinsha China **55D9**
Jinsha Jiang *river* China **52C4**
Jinxi China **54L2**
Jin Xian China **54L3**
Jinxiang China **54J5**
Jinzhou China **54L2**
Jiparaná,R Brazil **92E5**
Jipe,L Tanzania **71H5**
Jipijapa Ecuador **92A4**
Jishah Saudi Arabia **62F4**
Jishan China **54F5**
Jishui China **55H9**
Jisrash Shughur Syria **64E2**
Jiujiang China **55J8**
Jiulian Shan *mts* China **55H10**
Jiuling Shan *mts* China **55H8**
Jiulong Jiang *river* China **55J10**
Jiul,R Romania **46D2**
Jiushan Liedao *island* China **55M8**
Jiuxiangcheng China **54H6**
Jixi China **55K7**
Ji Xian China **54F4**
Ji Xian China **54H4**
Ji Xian China **54H5**
Ji Xian China **54J2**
Jiyang China **54J4**
Jiyun He *river* China **54J3**
Jiza Jordan **64D6**
Jizan Saudi Arabia **62E6**
João Pessoa Brazil **93L5**
Joch P Switzerland **33D2**
Jodhpur India **58D3**
Joensuu Finland **34N5**
Jōetsu Japan **56F6**
Jofane Mozambique **72E4**
Johannesburg South Africa **72D5**
Johila,R India **61C4**
John Day Fossil Beds Nat. Mon. *Oreg.* USA **80C3**
John Day,R *Oreg.* USA **80C3**
John O'Groates House *Scotland* UK **28K2**
Johnsonburg *Pa* USA **84B2**
Johnson,C *Wash.* USA **80A2**
Johnson City *Tenn.* USA **85F2**
Johnstone *Scotland* UK **29G8**
Johnston,I Pacific Ocean **94K6**
Johnstown Ireland, Rep. of **31K7**
Johnstown *NY* USA **84D1**
Johnstown *Pa* USA **84B2**
Johor *state* Malaysia **57C6**
Johor Baharus Malaysia **57C6**
Jõhvi *Eston.* USSR **35M7**
Joigny France **42E3**
Joinville Brazil **91G3**
Joinville France **42F2**
Joinville I Antarctica **15T3**
Jokkmokk Sweden **34H3**
Joliet *Ill.* USA **83P2**
Joliette *Que.* Canada **79K2**
Jolo *island* Philippines **53H9**
Jōl Plat. Saudi Arabia **62F6**
Joma *mt* China **52B4**
Jonava *Lith.* USSR **35L9**
Jonesboro *Ark.* USA **83N5**
Jonesboro *Ga* USA **85E4**
Jonesboro *Ill.* USA **83P4**
Jonesboro *La* USA **83M6**
Jonglei *region* Sudan **69M7**
Jonkershoek Mts South Africa **72J9**
Jönköping Sweden **35F8**
Jönköping *county* Sweden **35F8**
Jonquière *Que.* Canada **78C2**
Jonuta Mexico **88F4**
Jonzac France **42C4**
Joplin *Mo* USA **83L4**
Jordan *Minn.* USA **81L3**
Jordan *Mont.* USA **81D2**
Jordan *country* SW Asia **62D3**
Jordan,R Israel **64D5**
Jorhat India **59H3**
Jorje Montt,I Chile **91B8**
Jörn Sweden **34J4**
Jornada del Muerto *region New Mex.* USA **82E6**
Joseph *Oreg.* USA **80E3**
Joseph Bonaparte G. *W Aus.* Australia **98F2**
Joshipur India **61F5**
Joshua Tree Nat. Mon. *Calif.* USA **80F9**
Josselin France **42B3**
Jostedals Bre *glacier* Norway **35B6**
Jotunheimen Norway **35C6**
Jotunheimen *region* Norway **35C6**
Jounié Lebanon **64D4**
Jowai India **59H3**
Juan de Fuca,Str. of Canada/USA **86B2**
Juan Fernandez,Is Chile **95U11**
Juan Stuven,I Chile **91A7**
Juárez Argentina **91E5**
Juazeire do Norte Brazil **93K5**
Juba India **61D4**
Juba Sudan **69M8**
Jubail Lebanon **64D3**
Jubbah Saudi Arabia **62E4**
Jubbulpore = Jabalpur
Juby,C Western Sahara **68C3**
Júcaro Cuba **89D2**
Júcar,R Spain **41F3**
Juchipila Mexico **88D3**
Juchitan Mexico **88E4**
Judeidat el Wadi Syria **64E4**
Judenburg Austria **36F5**
Judique *No. Sc.* Canada **78H4**
Juist *island* W Germany **36B2**
Juiz de Fora Brazil **93J8**
Jujuy *prov.* Argentina **91C2**
Jukkasjarvi Sweden **34J3**
Julaca Bolivia **92D8**
Julesburg *Col.* USA **82G2**
Juli Peru **92D7**
Juliaca Peru **92C7**
Julia Creek *Queens.* Australia **99J4**
Julianehåb = Qaqortoq
Julianstown Ireland, Rep. of **30L6**
Julier P Switzerland **33E2**
Julio de Castilhos Brazil **91F3**
Jullundur India **60D5**
Jumaymah Iraq **62E4**
Jumentos,Is The Bahamas **89D2**
Jumet Belgium **32C4**
Jumilla Spain **41F3**
Jumla Nepal **61D1**
Junagadh India **58D4**
Junction City *Kans.* USA **83K3**
Junction City *Oreg.* USA **80B3**
Jundiaí Brazil **93H8**
Juneau *Alaska* USA **87Z13**
Junee *NSW* Australia **97C2**
Jun el'Akkar *bay* Lebanon **64D3**
Jungfrau *mt* Switzerland **33C2**
Jungfraujoch Switzerland **33C2**
Junilian China **55C8**
Junin Argentina **91B5**
Junín Argentina **91D4**
Junin Peru **92B6**
Juning = Junan
Junin,L de Peru **92B6**
Juniper *New Br.* Canada **78E3**
Juniper Mt *Oreg.* USA **80D4**
Juniper Mts *Ariz.* USA **80G8**
Juniya = Jounié
Junsele Sweden **34G5**
Jun Xian China **54F6**
Juo Jarvi *lake* Finland **34N5**
Jupia Brazil **93G8**
Juquila Mexico **88E4**
Jura *canton* Switzerland **33C1**
Jura *dep.* France **42F3**
Jura *mts* France/Switz. **42G3**
Jurado Colombia **92B2**
Jura,I *Scotland* UK **29E7**
Jura,Sd of *Scotland* UK **29E7**
Jurbarkas *Lith.* USSR **35K9**
Jurf ed Darawish Jordan **64D7**
Jüri *Eston.* USSR **35L7**
Jurm Afghanistan **63L2**
Juruá,R Brazil **92D4**
Juruena Brazil **92F6**
Jurutí Brazil **93F4**
Jusiye Syria **64E3**
Jussy Switzerland **33B2**
Justlahuaco Mexico **88E4**
Justo Daract Argentina **91C4**
Jutai,R Brazil **92D4**
Juticalpa Honduras **89B4**
Jutland = Jylland
Juuka Finland **34N5**
Juwain Afghanistan **63J3**
Ju Xian China **54K5**
Jūymand Iran **63H3**
Jylland,Pen. Denmark **35C8**
Jylland, South *region* Denmark **35C9**
Jyväskylä Finland **34L5**

K

K2 *mt* *Kashmir* India **60E3**
Kaala *mt* *Hawaii* USA **95V26**
Kabadak,R Bangladesh **61G4**
Kabaena,I Indonesia **53H12**
Kabala Sierra Leone **68C7**
Kabale Uganda **71G5**
Kabalega Falls Uganda **71G4**
Kabambare Zaire **71F5**
Kabara Mali **68E5**
Kabba Nigeria **68G7**
Kabbani,R India **58F6**
Kabel Surinam **93F3**
Kabinda Zaire **70E6**
Kabir Kūh *mts* Iran **62F3**
Kabirwala Pakistan **60C5**
Kabongo Zaire **70F6**
Kabosa,I Burma **59J6**
Kabul Afghanistan **63K3**
Kabul,R Afghanistan **63K3**
Kabunda Zaire **71F7**
Kabwe Zambia **72D2**
Kačanik Yugoslavia **46C3**
Kachchh,G of India **58C4**
Kachin *state* Burma **59J3**
Kachiry *Kazakh.* USSR **50J4**
Kachuga USSR **51M4**
Kadan Kyun *island* Burma **59J6**
Kadaura India **61B2**
Kade Guinea **68C6**
Kadina *S Aus.* Australia **97A2**
Kadiri India **58E6**
Kadiyevka *Ukrain.* USSR **48L7**
Kadmat *island* *Amindivi Is* India **58D6**
Kadoka *S Dak.* USA **81G4**
Kadom USSR **49F3**
Kadoma Zimbabwe **72D3**
Kadugli Sudan **69L6**
Kaduna Nigeria **68G6**
Kadur India **58E6**
Kadyy USSR **49F2**
Kaedi Mauritania **68C5**
Kaesong N Korea **52J3**
Kaf Saudi Arabia **62D3**
Kafakumba Congo **70E6**
Kafanchan Nigeria **68G7**
Kafirévs Str. Greece **47E6**
Kafr Behum Syria **64E2**
Kafrun Syria **64E3**
Kafue Dam Zambia **72D3**
Kafue Nat. Pk Zambia **72D3**
Kafue,R Zambia **72D3**
Kagan Pakistan **60C3**
Kagan *Uzbek.* USSR **50H6**
Kagawa *prefecture* Japan **56D7**
Kagi = Chiai
Kagoshima Japan **56B9**
Kagoshima *prefecture* Japan **56B9**
Kagoshima wan *bay* Japan **56B9**
Kagul *Moldav.* USSR **48F9**
Kahafa Saudi Arabia **62E4**
Kahama Tanzania **71G5**
Kahemba Zaire **70D6**
Kahoka *Mo* USA **83N2**
Kahoolawe *island* *Hawaii* USA **95V26**
Kahperusvaarat *mt* Sweden **34J2**
Kahror Pakistan **60B6**
Kahuta Pakistan **60C4**
Kaiama Nigeria **68F7**
Kaiapoi New Zealand **100E6**
Kaieteur Falls Guyana **92F2**
Kaifeng China **54H5**
Kaihua China **55K8**
Kaihwa = Wenshan
Kai Kep *archipelago* Indonesia **53K12**
Kaikoura New Zealand **100E6**
Kaikoura Ra *mts* New Zealand **100E6**
Kailua *Hawaii* USA **95V26**
Kaimanawa Mts New Zealand **100F4**
Kaimganj India **61B2**
Kaimur Ra *mts* India **61C3**
Kaipara Harb. New Zealand **100F3**
Kaiping China **55G11**
Kairana India **60E6**
Kairouan Tunisia **69G1**
Kairovo USSR **49N3**
Kaisarie = Kayseri
Kaiserslautern W Germany **36B4**
Kaiserstuhl Switzerland **33D1**
Kaisetjåkkå,Mt Sweden **34G3**
Kaišiadorys *Lith.* USSR **35L9**
Kaitangata New Zealand **100C8**
Kaithal India **60E6**
Kaiwi Chan. *Hawaii* USA **95V26**
Kai Xian China **54E7**
Kaiyang China **55D9**
Kaiyuan China **54M1**
Kajaani Finland **34M4**
Kaja,R Sudan **69K6**
Kajiado Kenya **71H5**
Kajiki Japan **56B9**
Kakamega Kenya **71G4**
Kakhk Iran **63H3**
Kakhovskoye Vdkhr. *Ukrain.* USSR **48J8**
Kakinada India **59F5**
Kakisa,L *NW Terr.* Canada **76H4**
Kakori India **61C2**
Kaksha USSR **49H1**
Kala Pakistan **60B5**
Kalaalit Nunaat = Greenland
Kalabagh Pakistan **60B4**
Kalabáka Greece **47C5**
Kalabo Zambia **72C3**
Kalach USSR **49E5**
Kalahari Des. Botswana **72C4**
Kalajoki Finland **34K4**
Kala Joki *river* Finland **34L4**
Kalak Iran **63H4**
Kalakan USSR **51N4**
Kalakepen *Sumatra* Indon. **53C10**
Kalámai Greece **47D6**
Kalamáta = Kalámai
Kalamazoo *Mich.* USA **79D4**
Kalamboa Sudan **69L6**
Kalambo Falls Tanzania **71G6**
Kalanaur India **60E6**
Kalangali Tanzania **71G6**
Kalannie *W Aus.* Australia **98D6**
Kala Oya,R Sri Lanka **58E7**
Kalat Pakistan **58C3**
Kalat-i-Ghilzai Afghanistan **63K3**
Kalaw Burma **59J4**
Kale Burma **59H4**
Kalediran Turkey **62C2**
Kalémié Zaire **71F6**
Kalewa Burma **59H4**
Kalgoorlie *W Aus.* Australia **98E6**
Kalikino USSR **49M4**
Kalimantan = Borneo
Kálimnos *island* Greece **47F6**
Kalingapatnam India **59F5**
Kalinin USSR **48J3**
Kaliningrad *Lith.* USSR **35J9**
Kalininsk USSR **49G5**
Kali,R Nepal **61C1**
Kali Sindh,R India **58E4**
Kalispell *Mont.* USA **86D2**
Kalisz Poland **37H3**
Kaliua Tanzania **71G5**
Kalix Sweden **34K4**
Kalix Al *river* Sweden **34K3**
Kalix Älv *river* Sweden **34J3**
Kalixfors Sweden **34J3**
Kalka India **60E5**
Kalkaska *Mich.* USA **79D3**
Kalkfeld Namibia **72B4**
Kalkfontein Botswana **72C4**
Kallaste *Eston.* USSR **35M7**
Kallavesi,L Finland **34M5**
Kalloni *Lésvos* Greece **47F5**
Kallsijön,L Sweden **34E5**
Kallur Kot Pakistan **60B4**
Kalmar Sweden **35G8**
Kalmar *county* Sweden **35F8**
Kalmar Sund *sound* Sweden **35G8**
Kalmthout Belgium **32C3**
Kalmykovo *Kazakh.* USSR **50G5**
Kalna India **61G4**
Kalocsa Hungary **37H5**
Kalokhorio Cyprus **64A2**
Kalpeni *island* *Laccadive Is* India **58D6**
Kalpi India **61B2**
Kaltag *Alaska* USA **87X12**
Kaluga USSR **48K4**
Kalule N. Zaire **70F6**
Kalundborg Denmark **35D9**
Kalundu Zambia **72D2**
Kalutara Sri Lanka **58E7**
Kalvarija *Lith.* USSR **35K9**
Kalyan India **58D5**
Kalyazin USSR **48K3**
Kamah *Newf.* Canada **77T5**
Kamaishi Japan **56G5**
Kamalampaka Tanzania **71G6**
Kamalia Pakistan **60C5**
Kaman India **60E7**
Kama,R USSR **50G3**
Kamaran *island* Red Sea **62E6**
Kamasin India **61C3**
Kamchatka,Pen. USSR **51S4**
Kamchatskaya Oblast *region* USSR **51T4**
Kamen USSR **50K4**
Kamenets Podolskiy *Ukrain.* USSR **48E7**
Kamenskoye USSR **51T3**
Kamensk Shakhinsky USSR **49E6**
Kamensk Ural'skiy USSR **49Q2**
Kamet,Mt India **58E2**
Kamiah *Idaho* USA **80E2**
Kamina Zaire **70E6**
Kamla,R India **61E2**
Kamloops *BC* Canada **76G6**
Kamnik Yugoslavia **44E2**
Kamoa Mts Brazil/Guyana **92F3**
Kamoenai Japan **56G3**
Kampala Uganda **71G4**
Kampen Netherlands **32D2**
Kampenhout Belgium **32C4**
Kampot Cambodia **57C4**
Kamptee India **58E4**
Kampuchea = Cambodia
Kamsack *Sask.* Canada **76L6**
Kamyshin USSR **49G5**
Kamyshlov USSR **49R2**
Kanab *Utah* USA **82B4**
Kanab Cr. *Ariz./Utah* USA **82B4**
Kanagawa *prefecture* Japan **56F7**
Kana Karnafuli Res. Bangladesh **59H4**
Kananga Zaire **70E6**
Kanastraion,C Greece **47D5**
Kanawha,R *W Va* USA **85G1**
Kanazawa Japan **56E6**
Kanchanaburi Thailand **57B4**
Kancheepuram India **58E6**
Kandahar Afghanistan **63K3**
Kandahar *region* Afghanistan **63K3**
Kanda Kanda Zaire **70E6**
Kandalaksha USSR **50E3**
Kandava *Latvia* USSR **35K8**
Kandavu,I Fiji **94H9**
Kandersteg Switzerland **33C2**
Kandhla India **60E6**
Kandhura Pakistan **60B3**
Kandi Benin **68F6**
Kandi India **61G4**
Kandla India **58D4**
Kandos *NSW* Australia **97C2**
Kandri India **61D4**
Kandy Sri Lanka **58F7**
Kane *Pa* USA **84B2**
Kane Basin Greenland **14Q2**
Kaneohe *Hawaii* USA **95V26**
Kanev *Ukrain.* USSR **48G7**
Kangan Iran **63G4**
Kangaroo I *S Aus.* Australia **99H7**
Kangasala Finland **35L6**
Kangāvar Iran **62F3**
Kangbao China **54H2**
Kangchenjunga,Mt Nepal **61G2**
Kangerdlugssuaq Greenland **14N3**
Kangertittivaq Greenland **14N2**
Kangiqsualujjuaq *Que.* Canada **77S5**
Kangiqsujuaq *Que.* Canada **77R4**
Kangmar India **58E2**
Kango Gabon **70C4**
Kangping China **54M1**
Kangra India **60E4**
Kangra *district* India **60E4**
Kangsa,R Bangladesh **59H3**
Kang Xian China **54C6**
Kanhar,R India **61D3**
Kani Burma **59H4**
Kaniama Zaire **70E6**
Kaniva *Vic.* Australia **97B3**
Kankai,R India/Nepal **61F2**
Kankakee *Ill.* USA **83Q2**
Kankan Guinea **68D6**
Kanker India **58F4**
Kankesanturai Sri Lanka **58E7**
Kanmaw Kyun *island* Burma **59J6**
Kannauj India **61B2**
Kannonkoski Finland **34L5**
Kannus Finland **34K5**
Kano Nigeria **68G6**
Kanpur India **61C2**
Kansas *state* USA **86F4**
Kansas City *Kans.* USA **83L3**
Kansas City *Mo* USA **83L3**
Kansas,R *Kans.* USA **83K3**
Kansk USSR **51L4**
Kansu = Gansu
Kantai India **61E2**
Kantaralak Thailand **57C4**
Kantchari Upper Volta **68F6**
Kanturk Ireland, Rep. of **31F9**
Kanuku Mts Guyana **92F3**
Kanuma Japan **56F6**
Kaohsiung Taiwan **55L11**
Kaolack Senegal **68B6**
Kapaa *Hawaii* USA **95V28**
Kapanga Zaire **70E6**
Kapaus,R *Borneo* Indon. **53F10**
Kap Bismark *cape* Greenland **14M2**
Kap Bridgman *cape* Greenland **14N1**
Kapchagay USSR **50J5**
Kap Cort Adelaer *cape* Greenland **14P3**
Kap Desolation *cape* Greenland **14P3**

Kapenguria Khrebet Cherskogo

Kapenguria Kenya 71H4
Kap Farvel = Uummarnarsuaq
Kapfenberg Austria 37F5
Kap Gustav Holm *cape* Greenland 14N3
Kapiri Mposhi Tanzania 71F7
Kapiskau,R *Ont.* Canada 77P6
Kapiti I New Zealand 100F5
Kaplice Czech. 36F4
Kap Morris Jesup *cape* Greenland 14N1
Kapoeta Sudan 69M8
Kaposvár Hungary 46A1
Kappeln W Germany 36C1
Kapp Norvegia *cape* Antarctica 15B2
Kapsabet Kenya 71H4
Kapsukas *Lith.* USSR 35K9
Kapunda *S Aus.* Australia 97A2
Kapurthala India 60D5
Kapuskasing *Ont.* Canada 77P7
Kaputar,Mt *NSW* Australia 97D2
Kap York *cape* Greenland 14Q2
Kara USSR 50H3
Karabuk Turkey 62C1
Karacabey Turkey 62B1
Karaca Dagh *mt* Turkey 62C2
Karachev USSR 48J5
Karachi Pakistan 58C4
Karaganda *Kazakh.* USSR 50J4
Karaikal India 58E6
Karaj Iran 63G2
Karak Jordan 64D6
Karak *Tibet* China 58E2
Kara Kalpakskaya ASSR *Uzbek.* USSR 50G5
Karakelong *island* Indonesia 53J10
Karakoram Ra *mts* *Kashmir* India 60D2
Karakorum P China/India 60E3
Kara Kum *region* *Turkmen.* USSR 50G6
Kara Kum Can. *Turkmen.* USSR 63J2
Karaman Turkey 62C2
Karamea New Zealand 100E5
Karamea Bight *bay* New Zealand 100D5
Karamsar,P Pakistan 60C2
Karand Iran 62F3
Karasa USSR 49K3
Karasburg Namibia 72B5
Kara Sea USSR 50J2
Karasjok Norway 34L2
Karatsu Japan 56A8
Karaul USSR 50K2
Karauli India 61A2
Karaurgan Turkey 62E1
Karbala Iraq 62E3
Kardhitsa Greece 47C5
Karditsa *dist.* Greece 47C5
Karelskaya ASSR *rep.* USSR 50E3
Karesuando Sweden 34K2
Karganrud Iran 62F2
Kargil *Kashmir* India 60E3
Kargopol' USSR 48L1
Karhal India 61B2
Kariba Zimbabwe 72D3
Kariba,L Zambia/Zimb. 72D3
Karibib Namibia 72B4
Karima Sudan 69M5
Karimata *island* Indonesia 53E11
Karin Somalia 71K2
Karisimbi,Mt Zaire 71F5
Kariz Iran 63J3
Karjaa Finland 35K6
Karkaralinsk USSR 50J5
Karkheh,R Iran 62F3
Karkkila Finland 35L6
Karla Marksa,Pik *mt* *Tadzhik.* USSR 63L2
Karlidi India 61D4
Karlidi India 61D4
Karlik Shan *mt* *Xinjiang* China 52B2
Karl-Marx Stadt E Germany 36E3
Karlovac Yugoslavia 44E3
Karlovy Vary Czech. 36E3
Karlsbad = Karlovy Vary
Karlsborg Sweden 34K4
Karlsborg Sweden 35F7
Karlshamn Sweden 35F8
Karlskoga Sweden 35F7
Karlskrona Sweden 35F8
Karlsruhe W Germany 36C4
Karlstad Sweden 35E7
Karmøy,I Norway 35A7
Karnal India 60E6
Karnataka *state* India 58E6
Karnes City *Texas* USA 82T9
Karnten *state* Austria 36E5
Karona Fall Guyana 92F3
Karoonda *S Aus.* Australia 97A3
Karora Ethiopia 71H1
Karpáthos *island* Greece 47F7
Karpáthos Str. Greece 47F7
Karperón Greece 47C5
Kärpf *mt* Switzerland 33E2
Karroo Great *plat.* South Africa 72C6
Kars Turkey 62E1
Karsakpay *Kazakh.* USSR 50H5
Kärsämäki Finland 34L5
Kārsava *Latvia* USSR 35M8
Karshi *Uzbek.* USSR 50H6
Karstula Finland 34L5
Karsun USSR 49H3
Kartaly USSR 49Q4
Kartarpur India 60D5
Kartse *Kashmir* India 60E3
Karungi Sweden 34K3
Karungu Kenya 71G5
Karunki Finland 34L3
Karun,R Iran 63G3
Karur,R India 58E6
Karvia Finland 35K5
Karvina Czech. 37H4
Karwar India 58D6
Karymskoye USSR 51N4
Kasai,R Zaire 70D5
Kasama Zambia 72E2
Kasanga Tanzania 71G6
Kasauli India 60E5
Kasba L *NW Terr.* Canada 76L4
Kasempa Zambia 72D2
Kasenga Zaire 71F7
Kasenga Zambia 72D3
Kasganj India 61B2
Kashan Iran 63G3
Kashi *Xinjiang* China 50J6
Kashira USSR 48L4
Kashiwazaki Japan 56F6
Kāshmar Iran 63H2
Kashmir = Jammu and Kashmir
Kashmor Pakistan 58C3
Kasimov USSR 49E3
Kaskinen Finland 34J5
Kasko = Kaskinen
Kas Kong,I Cambodia 57C4
Kasonga Lunda Zaire 70D6
Kasongo Zaire 70F5
Kásos *island* Greece 47F7
Kásós Str. *Kríti* Greece 47F7
Kaspichan Bulgaria 46F3
Kas Rong,I Cambodia 57C4
Kassala Sudan 71H1
Kassala *region* Sudan 69M5
Kassandra *pen.* Greece 47D4
Kassel W Germany 36C3
Kastamonu Turkey 62C1
Kastélli *Kríti* Greece 47D7
Kasterlee Belgium 32C3
Kastoria Greece 47C4
Kastornaya USSR 48L6
Kastrosikiá Greece 47C5
Kasulu Tanzania 71G5
Kasumpti India 60E5
Kasungu Malawi 71G7
Kasur Pakistan 60D5
Katahdin Iron Works *Maine* USA 78D4
Katahdin,Mt *Maine* USA 78D4
Katákolon Greece 47C6
Katang = Shaba
Katanning *W Aus.* Australia 98D6
Katav Ivanovsk USSR 49P3
Katchall *island* *Nicobar Is* India 59H7
Katerini Greece 47D4
Katha Burma 59J4
Kathawachaga L *NW Terr.* Canada 76J3
Katherine *N Terr.* Australia 98G2
Kathmandu Nepal 61E2
Kathua *Kashmir* India 60D4
Kathua *district* India 60D4
Katihar India 61F3
Katima Mulilo Zambia 72C3
Katmai Vol. *Alaska* USA 87X13
Kato China 54N3
Kato Akhaia Greece 47C5
Káto Nevrokópion Greece 46D4
Katoomba *NSW* Australia 97D2
Katowice Poland 37H3
Katowice *voivodship* Poland 37H3
Katrineholm Sweden 35G7
Katrine,L *Scotland* UK 29G7
Katsina Nigeria 68G6
Kattegat,Str. Denmark/Sweden 35D8
Katwa India 61G4
Katwijk-aann-Zee Netherlands 32C2
Kauai,I *Hawaii* USA 95L5
Kaufbeuren W Germany 36D5
Kauhava Finland 34K5
Kaukauna *Wis.* USA 79B3
Kauliranta Sweden 34K3
Kauntan Malaysia 57C6
Kaunus *Lith.* USSR 35K9
Kauriya India 59F4
Kautokeino Norway 34K2
Kavak Turkey 62D1
Kavali India 58E6
Kaválla Greece 47E4
Kaválla *dist.* Greece 46E4
Kavaratti *island* *Laccadive Is* India 58D6
Kaw Fr. Guiana 93G3
Kawakawa New Zealand 100F2
Kawakini,Mt *Hawaii* USA 95V28
Kawambwa Zambia 72D1
Kawanoe Japan 56C7
Kawardha India 61C4
Kawasaki Japan 56F7
Kawerau New Zealand 100G4
Kawhia New Zealand 100F4
Kawich Ra *Nev.* USA 80E7
Kawkareik Burma 59J5
Kayah Burma 59J5
Kayes Mali 68C6
Kayseri Turkey 62D2
Kaysville *Utah* USA 82C2
Kazach'ye USSR 51Q2
Kazakhskaya SSR *rep.* USSR 50H5
Kazalinsk *Kazakh.* USSR 50H5
Kazan' USSR 49J3
Kazanlük Bulgaria 46E3
Kāzērūn Iran 63G4
Kdyne Czech. 36E4
Kéa *island* Greece 47E6
Keady *N Ireland* UK 30K5
Kealaikahiki Chan. *Hawaii* USA 95V26
Kearney *Nebr.* USA 83J2
Keban Turkey 62D2
Kebbi,R Nigeria 68F6
Kebnekaise *mt* Sweden 34H3
Kech Pakistan 58B3
Kechika,R *BC* Canada 76F5
Kecskemét Hungary 37H5
Kedah *state* Malaysia 57C5
Kedainiai *Lith.* USSR 35K9
Kedgeree India 61G4
Kedgwick *New Br.* Canada 78E3
Kediri *Java* Indon. 53F12
Kedougou Sénégal 68C6
Keele Pk *NW Terr.* Canada 76F4
Keeler *Calif.* USA 80E7
Keele,R *NW Terr.* Canada 76F4
Keeling Is = Cocos Is
Keelung = Chilung
Keene *New H* USA 84E1
Keeper Hill *mt* Ireland, Rep. of 31G8
Keeseville *NY* USA 79K3
Keetmanshoop Namibia 72B5
Kefallinía Greece 47C5
Keflavik Iceland 34T12
Kegashka *Que* Canada 77U6
Kegueur Terbi *mt* Chad 69J4
Kehsi Mansam Burma 59J4
Keighley *England* UK 25E5
Keila *Eston.* USSR 35L7
Keitele Finland 34M5
Keith *S Aus.* Australia 97B3
Keith *Scotland* UK 28L4
Keith Arm *bay* *NW Terr.* Canada 76G3
Keklau Palau Is 94A20
Kelan China 54F3
Kelang Malaysia 57C6
Kelantan *state* Malaysia 57C5
Kelcyre Albania 47C4
Kelibia Tunisia 69H1
Kelkit,R Turkey 62D1
Kellet,C *NW Terr.* Canada 76F2
Kelloselka Finland 34N3
Kells Ireland, Rep. Of 30K6
Kelme *Lith.* USSR 35K9
Kelo Chad 69J7
Kelowna *BC* Canada 76H7
Kelseyville *Calif.* USA 80B6
Kelso *Scotland* UK 29M8
Kelso *Wash.* USA 80B2
Kem *Karel.* USSR 50E3
Ké Macina Mali 68D6
Kemerovo USSR 50K4
Kemi Finland 34L4
Kemi Jarvi *lake* Finland 34M3
Kemi Joki,R Finland 34L3
Kemmerer *Wyo.* USA 81B5
Kempele Finland 34L4
Kemp,L *Texas* USA 83J6
Kemp Land Antarctica 15E3
Kempsey *NSW* Australia 97D2
Kempten W Germany 36D5
Kempt,L *Que.* Canada 79J2
Kempton *Tas.* Australia 97F5
Kempton Park South Africa 72N12
Kenai Pen. *Alaska* USA 87X12
Kenamuke Swamp Sudan 69M7
Kenda India 61D4
Kendal *England* UK 25C4
Kendall *NY* USA 84B1
Kendall,C *NW Terr.* Canada 77O4
Kendari *Celebes* Indon. 53H11
Kendawangan *Borneo* Indon. 53F11
Kenema Sierra Leone 68C7
Kenge Zaire 70D5
Keng-tung Burma 59J4
Kenhardt South Africa 72C5
Kenilworth *England* UK 27L4
Kenilworth South Africa 72H9
Kenitra Morocco 68D2
Kenmare Ireland, Rep. of 31D10
Kenmare *N Dak.* USA 81F1
Kenmare,R Ireland,Rep. of 31C10
Kenmore *Scotland* UK 29J6
Kennebec *S Dak.* USA 81H4
Kennebec,R *Maine* USA 78D4
Kennebunk *Maine* USA 84F1
Kennet,R *England* UK 27L6
Kennett *Mo* USA 83N4
Kennet,Vale of *England* UK 27M6
Kennewick *Wash.* USA 80D2
Kenogami *Que.* Canada 78C2
Kenogami,L *Que.* Canada 78C2
Keno Hill *Yukon* Canada 76D4
Kenora *Ont.* Canada 76N7
Kenosha *Wis.* USA 79C4
Kensington *Pr. Ed. I.* Canada 78G3
Kent *New Br.* Canada 78F3
Kent *Wash.* USA 80B1
Kent *county* *England* UK 27R6
Kentford *England* UK 27Q4
Kent I *Md* USA 84C3
Kent Pen. *NW Terr.* Canada 76K3
Kentucky *state* USA 87J4
Kentucky L *Ky/Tenn.* USA 85C2
Kent,Vale of *England* UK 27Q6
Kentville *No. Sc.* Canada 78F4
Kenya *country* Africa 71H4
Kenya,Mt Kenya 71H5
Keokuk *Iowa* USA 83N2
Keonjhar India 59G4
Kéos (Tziá),I = Kéa,I
Kepler Mts New Zealand 100B7
Kepno Poland 37G3
Keppel,I Falkland Is 91D8
Kerala *state* India 58E6
Kerama Retto *islands* Japan 56M13
Kerang *Vic.* Australia 97B3
Kerava Finland 35L6
Kerch' USSR 48K9
Kerchoual Mali 68F5
Kerema Papua New Guinea 99K1
Keren Ethiopia 71H1
Kerguelen,Is Indian Ocean 65E9
Kericho Kenya 71H5
Kerinci *mt* *Sumatra* Indon. 53D11
Kerio,R Kenya 71H4
Kerkenbosch = Zuidwolde
Kerkenna,Is Tunisia 69H2
Kerki *Turkmen.* USSR 50H6
Kérkira Greece 47B5
Kérkira *island* Greece 47B5
Kerkrade Netherlands 32E4
Kermadec,Is Pacific Ocean 94H10
Kerman *Calif.* USA 80C7
Kermān Iran 63H3
Kerman Des. Iran 63H4
Kermanshah Iran 62F3
Kern Pk *Calif.* USA 80D7
Kerrville *Texas* USA 83J7
Kerry *county* Ireland, Rep. of 31D9
Kerry Hd Ireland, Rep. of 31D9
Kerulen,R Mongolia 52F1
Kerzaz Algeria 68E3
Kerzers Switzerland 33C2
Kesagami L *Ont.* Canada 77P6
Kesariya India 61E2
Keski Suomen *prov* Finland 34L5
Kesteren Netherlands 32D3
Kestilä Finland 34M4
Keswick *England* UK 25B3
Keszthely Hungary 37G5
Keta Ghana 68F7
Ketapang *Borneo* Indon. 53E11
Ketchikan *Alaska* USA 87Z13
Ketchum *Idaho* USA 80F4
Ketrzyn Poland 37J1
Ketsok-aw Kyun *island* Burma 59J6
Kettering *England* UK 27N4
Ketumbaine *mt* Tanzania 71H5
Keuka L *NY* USA 84C1
Keuruu Finland 34L5
Kewanee *Ill.* USA 83P2
Kewaunee *Wis.* USA 79C3
Keweenaw B *Mich.* USA 79B2
Keweenaw Pen. *Wis.* USA 87J2
Key Harbour *Ont.* Canada 79F3
Key,L Ireland, Rep. of 30G5
Key Largo *island* *Fla* USA 85M9
Keynsham *England* UK 26J6
Keyser *W Va* USA 84B3
Keysville *Va* USA 85H2
Key West *island* *Fla* USA 85M9
Kéž Czech. 37J4
Kezhma USSR 51M4
Khabab Syria 64E4
Khabarovsk USSR 51Q5
Khabarovsky Kray *region* USSR 51Q4
Khābūrah Oman 63H5
Khadro Pakistan 58C3
Khafs Maqran Saudi Arabia 62F5
Khagaul India 61E3
Khairabad India 61C2
Khairpur Pakistan 60C6
Khaiwan Yemen 62E6
Khajuri Kach Pakistan 60A4
Khakhea Botswana 72C4
Khalamba La *mt* *Tibet* China 59G2
Khalasa *hist. site* Israel 64C6
Khálki *island* Greece 47F6
Khalkidhikí *dist.* Greece 47D4
Khalkis Greece 47D5
Khalturin USSR 49J1
Khaluf Oman 63H5
Khambhat India 58D4
Khamhāt,G of India 58D4
Khamiab Afghanistan 63K2
Khamis Mushayt Saudi Arabia 62E6
Kham Keut Laos 57C3
Khamr Yemen 62E6
Khanabad Afghanistan 63K2
Khān al Baghdādi Iraq 62E3
Khānaqin Iraq 62F3
Khancoban *NSW* Australia 97C3
Khandela India 60D7
Khandesh India 58D4
Khandwa India 58E4
Khan ez Zabib Jordan 64E6
Khanfar South Yemen 62F7
Khangarh Pakistan 60B6
Khanh Hoa Vietnam 57D4
Khaniá *Kríti* Greece 47D7
Khaniá *dist.* Greece 47D7
Khaniadhana India 61B3
Khanpur Pakistan 60B6
Khan Sheikhun Syria 64E2
Khanty Mansiysk USSR 50H3
Khanūj Iran 63H4
Khan Yunis Egypt 64C6
Khao Chamao *mt* Thailand 57C4
Khao Sai Dao Tai *mt* Thailand 57C4
Khapalu *Kashmir* India 60E3
Kharaghoda India 58D4
Kharagpur India 61F3
Kharagpur India 61F4
Kharan Pakistan 58C3
Khārān,R Iran 63H4
Kharar India 61F4
Khar'kov *Ukrain.* USSR 48K6
Kharmanli Bulgaria 46E4
Kharna India 60E4
Kharovsk USSR 48M2
Kharsawan India 61E4
Khartaksho *Kashmir* India 60E3
Khartoum Sudan 69M5
Khasfah *well* Saudi Arabia 63G6
Khash Rud *river* Afghanistan 63J3
Khasi Hills India 59H3
Khaskovo Bulgaria 46E4
Khasmel Girba Sudan 69N5
Khatanga USSR 51M2
Khatangskiy Guba *bay* USSR 51N2
Khatpa Thanbo India 60F4
Khawr Ḩamīdan *well* Saudi Arabia 63G5
Khaybar Saudi Arabia 62D4
Kheda India 58D4
Khemmarat Thailand 57D3
Kheni Karan India 60D5
Kheralu India 58D4
Kheri India 61C2
Kherson *Ukrain.* USSR 48H8
Khetri India 60D7
Khilok USSR 51N4
Khinjan Afghanistan 63K2
Khios *Khiós* Greece 47E5
Khirgi Pakistan 60B4
Khiri Khan Thailand 57B4
Khisfin Syria 64D5
Khiva *Uzbek.* USSR 50H5
Kh Khiaw,Mt Thailand 57C4
Kh. Luang,Mt Thailand 57B5
Khmel'nitskiy *Ukrain.* USSR 48E7
Khmer = Cambodia
Kholm USSR 48G3
Kholmsk USSR 51R5
Khomeyn Iran 63G3
Khone Cambodia 57D4
Khong Laos 57D4
Khor USSR 51Q5
Khóra Sfakion *Kríti* Greece 47E7
Khorramabad Iran 62F3
Khorramshahr Iran 62F3
Khosf Iran 63H3
Khouribga Morocco 68D2
Khrebet Cherskogo *mts* USSR 51R3

Khrebet Dzhagdy Koroit

Khrebet Dzhagdy *mts* USSR 51P4
Khrebet Dzhugdzhur *mts* USSR 51Q4
Khrebet Kolymskiy USSR 51S3
Khrebet Orulgan *mts* USSR 51P3
Khrebet Pay-Khoy *region* USSR 50H3
Khrebet Tarbagatay *mts* *Kazakh.* USSR 50K5
Khrisoúpolis Greece 46E4
Khrojna Bulgaria 46E4
Khros *island* Greece 47E5
Khuis Botswana 72C5
Khulna Bangladesh 61G4
Khunjerab P *Kashmir* India 60D2
Khunsar Iran 63G3
Khūr Iran 63H3
Khurai India 61B3
Khurja India 60E6
Khushab Pakistan 60C4
Khushalgarh Pakistan 60B4
Khushniya Syria 64D4
Khvāf Iran 63J3
Khvalynsk USSR 49H4
Khvor Iran 63H3
Khvoy Iran 62E2
Khyber P Pakistan 60B3
Kiama *NSW* Australia 97D2
Kiambi Zaire 71F6
Kiangsi = Jiangsi
Kiangsu = Jiangsu
Kianta Järvi *lake* Finland 34N4
Kibangula Zaire 70F5
Kibombo Zaire 70F5
Kibondo Tanzania 71G5
Kičevo Yugoslavia 46C4
Kicking Horse P *Alta* Canada 76H6
Kidal Mali 68F5
Kidderminster *England* UK 27K4
Kidete Tanzania 71H6
Kidnappers,C New Zealand 100G4
Kiel W Germany 36D1
Kielce Poland 37J3
Kielce *voivodship* Poland 37J3
Kieldrecht Belgium 32C3
Kieler Bucht *bay* W Germany 36D1
Kiel Kanal *canal* W Germany 36C1
Kienchang = Nancheng
Kiev = Kiyev
Kiffa Mauritania 68C5
Kigali Rwanda 71G5
Kigoma Tanzania 71F5
Kiimingin,R Finland 34L4
Kiiminki Finland 34L4
Kii suidō *strait* Japan 56D8
Kijabe Kenya 71H5
Kikinda Yugoslavia 46C2
Kikládhes *islands* Greece 47E6
Kikori Papua New Guinea 99J1
Kikori,R Papua New Guinea 99J1
Kikwit Zaire 70D6
Kila Drosh Pakistan 60B3
Kilbeggan Ireland, Rep. of 31J7
Kilbrennan Sd *Scotland* UK 29F8
Kilchu N Korea 52J2
Kilcormac Ireland, Rep. of 31H7
Kilcullen Ireland, Rep. of 31K7
Kildare Ireland, Rep. of 31K7
Kildare *county* Ireland,Rep. of 31K7
Kilfenora Ireland,Rep. of 31E8
Kilfinnane Ireland, Rep. of 31G9
Kilgarvan Ireland, Rep. of 31E10
Kilifi Kenya 71H5
Kilimanjaro,Mt Tanzamia 71H5
Kilindini Kenya 71H5
Kilkee Ireland, Rep. of 31D8
Kilkeel N Ireland 30M5
Kilkenny Ireland, Rep. of 31J8
Kilkenny *county* Ireland,Rep. of 31J8
Kilkieran B Ireland, Rep. of 31D7
Kilkis Greece 47D4
Kilkis *region* Greece 46D4
Kill Ireland, Rep. of 31K7
Killala Ireland,Rep. of 30E5
Killala,B Ireland, Rep. of 30E5
Killaloe Ireland, Rep. of 31G8
Killarney Ireland, Rep. of 31D9
Killarney *Ont.* Canada 79F2
Killary Harb. Ireland, Rep. of 30C6
Killashandra Ireland, Rep. of 30H5
Killiecrankie,P of *Scotland* UK 29J6
Killimor Ireland, Rep. of 31G7
Killin *Scotland* UK 29H7
Killíni Greece 47C6
Killorglin Ireland, Rep. of 31D9
Killybegs Ireland, Rep. of 30G4
Killyleagh N Ireland 30M5
Kilmacthomas Ireland, Rep. of 31J9
Kilmallock Ireland, Rep. of 31F9
Kilmarnock *Scotland* UK 29H8
Kil'mez USSR 49J5
Kilmore *Vic.* Australia 97B3
Kilosa Tanzania 71H6
Kilrea N Ireland 30K4
Kilrush Ireland, Rep. of 31E8
Kilsyth *Scotland* UK 29H8
Kiltimagh Ireland, Rep. of 30E6
Kilwa Kivinje Tanzania 71H6
Kilwinning *Scotland* UK 29G8
Kima Zaire 70F5
Kimball *S Dak.* USA 81H4
Kimberley South Africa 72C5
Kimberley Plat. *W Aus.* Australia 98F3
Kimbolton *England* UK 27P4
Kimi Greece 47E5
Kimito,I Finland 35K6
Kimolos *island* Greece 47E6
Kimvula Zaire 70D6
Kinabalu *mt Sabah* Malay. 53G9
Kinbrace *Scotland* UK 28J3
Kincardine *Ont.* Canada 79F3
Kincardine on Forth *Scotland* UK 29J7
Kincraig *Scotland* UK 28J5
Kindat Burma 59H4
Kindersley *Sask.* Canada 76K6
Kindia Guinea 68C6
Kindu Zaire 70F5
Kinel USSR 49K4
Kinel Cherkkassy USSR 49L4
Kineo *Maine* USA 78D4
Kineshma USSR 49F2
Kineton *England* UK 27M4
King and Queen *Va* USA 85J2
Kingaroy *Queens.* Australia 99L5
King City *Calif.* USA 80C7
Kingfisher *Okla.* USA 83K5
King George I *S Shetland Is* Antarctica 15T3
King George,Is Pacific Ocean 95M9
King George,Mt *BC* Canada 76H6
King George Sd *W Aus.* Australia 98D7
King George VI Falls Guyana 92E2
King I *Tas.* Australia 99J7
Kingisepp *Eston.* USSR 35K7
King Leopold Ra *mts* *W Aus.* Australia 98E3
Kingman *Ariz.* USA 80F8
Kingman *Kans.* USA 83J4
Kingsbridge *England* UK 26G8
King's Canyon Nat. Pk *Calif.* USA 80D7
Kingsclere *England* UK 27M6
Kingscote *S Aus.* Australia 97A3
Kingscourt Ireland, Rep. of 30K6
King Sd *W Aus.* Australia 98E3
Kings Lynn *England* UK 27Q3
Kings Pk *Utah* USA 82C2
Kingsport *Tenn.* USA 85F2
Kingston Jamaica 89D3
Kingston New Zealand 100C7
Kingston *NY* USA 84D2
Kingston *Ont.* Canada 79H3
Kingston *S Aus.* Australia 97A3
Kingston on Thames *England* UK 27P6
Kingston-upon-Hull *England* UK 25G5
Kingstown St Vincent 89G4
Kingstree *S Car.* USA 85H4
Kingswear *England* UK 26G8
Kington *England* UK 26H4
Kingussie *Scotland* UK 28H5
King William I *NW Terr.* Canada 76M3
King Williams Town South Africa 72D6
Kingwood *W Va* USA 79G6
Kingyüan = Yishan
Kinlochewe *Scotland* UK 28F4
Kinlochleven *Scotland* UK 29G6
Kinloch Rannoch *Scotland* UK 29H6
Kino Mexico 88B2
Kinross *Scotland* UK 29K7
Kinsale Ireland, Rep. of 31F10
Kinsale,Old Hd of Ireland, Rep. of 31F10
Kinshasa Zaire 70D5
Kintampo Ghana 68E7
Kintap *Borneo* Indon. 53G11
Kintyre *Scotland* UK 29E8
Kintyre, Mull of *Scotland* UK 29E9
Kinvarra Ireland, Rep. of 31F7
Kinyangiri Tanzania 71G5
Kiowa *Kans.* USA 83J4
Kiparissía Greece 47C6
Kiparissía,G of Greece 47C6
Kipawa *Que.* Canada 79G2
Kipawa,L *Que.* Canada 79G2
Kipini Kenya 71J5
Kirá Panayiá,I = Pélagos,I
Kirchberg Switzerland 33C1
Kirensk USSR 51M4
Kirgizskaya SSR *rep.* USSR 50J5
Kiribati,Is Pacific Ocean 94H8
Kirit Somalia 71K3
Kiritimati,I Pacific Ocean 95L7
Kiriwina *island* Papua New Guinea 99L1
Kiriwina Is = Trobriand Is
Kirkağaç Turkey 62B2
Kirkby Lonsdale *England* UK 25C4
Kirkby Stephen *England* UK 25D4
Kirkcaldy *Scotland* UK 29K7
Kirkconnel *Scotland* UK 29H9
Kirkcudbright *Scotland* UK 29H10
Kirkee India 58D5
Kirkenes Norway 34O2
Kirkesdal Norway 34H2
Kirkham *England* UK 25C5
Kirkintilloch *Scotland* UK 29H8
Kirkland Lake *Ont.* Canada 79G1
Kirkoswald *England* UK 25C3
Kirksville *Mo* USA 83M2
Kirkūk Iraq 62E2
Kirkwall *Orkney* Scotland 28L2
Kirov USSR 48J4
Kirov USSR 49J1
Kirovograd *Ukrain.* USSR 48H7
Kirovsk USSR 50E3
Kirriemuir *Scotland* UK 29K6
Kirsanov USSR 49F4
Kirsehir Turkey 62C2
Kirstenbosch South Africa 72H9
Kirthar Ra *mts* Pakistan 58C3
Kiruna Sweden 34J3
Kirundu Zaire 70F5
Kisanga Tanzania 71G6
Kisangani Zaire 70F4
Kisbér Hungary 37G5
Kisengwa Zaire 70F6
Kishanganj India 61G2
Kishangarh India 58D3
Kishi Nigeria 68F7
Kishinev *Moldav.* USSR 48F8
Kishtwar *Kashmir* India 60D4
Kisii Kenya 71G5
Kisiju Tanzania 71H6
Kiska *island* *Aleutian Is* USA 87U13
Kiskisink *Que.* Canada 78B3
Kiskunfélégyháza Hungary 37H5
Kismaayo Somalia 71J5
Kismayu = Chisimaio
Kispest Hungary 37H5
Kissidougou Guinea 68C7
Kisujszallás Hungary 37J5
Kisumu Kenya 71G5
Kisvárda Hungary 37K4
Kiswe Syria 64E4
Kita Mali 68D6
Kitab *Uzbek.* USSR 50H6
Kita-Kyūshū Japan 56B8
Kitale Kenya 71H4
Kitchener *Ont.* Canada 79F4
Kitgum Uganda 71G4
Kithiarai Chan. Greece 47D7
Kithira *island* Greece 47D6
Kithnos *island* Greece 47E6
Kittanning *Pa* USA 84B2
Kittatinny Mts *New J* USA 84D2
Kittilä Finland 34L3
Kitui Kenya 71H5
Kitunda Tanzania 71G6
Kitzingen W Germany 36D4
Kiumbi Zaire 70F6
Kiuruvesi Finland 34M5
Kivi Jarvi *lake* Finland 34L5
Kivu,L Zaire/Rwanda 71F5
Kiwai I Papua New Guinea 99J1
Kiyev *Ukrain.* USSR 48G6
Kiyevskoye Vdkhr *res.* USSR 48G6
Kiyma *Kazakh.* USSR 50H4
Kizel USSR 50G4
Kizil Irmak,R Turkey 62C1
Kizil Jilga *Kashmir* India 58E1
Kizil'skoye USSR 49P4
Kizyl Arvat *Turkmen.* USSR 50G6
Kjerringøy Norway 34F3
Kladanj Yugoslavia 46B2
Kladno Czech. 36E3
Klagenfurt Austria 36F5
Klaipėda *Lith.* USSR 35J9
Klaksvig Faerøerne 34Z14
Klamath *Calif.* USA 80B5
Klamath Falls *Oreg.* USA 80C4
Klamath R *Calif.* USA 80B5
Klar Alv. *river* Sweden 35E6
Klausen P Switzerland 33D2
Kleine Emme,R Switzerland 33D2
Kleinlützel Switzerland 33C1
Klerksdorp South Africa 72D5
Kleszczele Poland 37K2
Klickitat,R *Wash.* USA 80C3
Klimpfjall Sweden 34F4
Klintsy USSR 48H5
Klisura Bulgaria 46E3
Ključ Yugoslavia 44F3
Kłodawa Poland 37H2
Kłodzko Poland 37G3
Klofta Norway 35D6
Kłomnice Poland 37H3
Klondike,R *Yukon* Canada 76D4
Kloosterzande Netherlands 32C3
Klosters Switzerland 33E2
Kloten Switzerland 33D1
Kluane,L *Yukon* Canada 76D4
Kluczbork Poland 37H3
Kluichi USSR 49G4
Klundert Netherlands 32C3
Klyuchevskaya Sopka *mt* USSR 51T4
Knaresborough *England* UK 25F4
Knarsdale *England* UK 25C3
Knighton *Wales* UK 26H4
Knights Ferry *Calif.* USA 80C7
Knin Yugoslavia 44F3
Knob,C *W Aus.* Australia 98D6
Knobel *Ark.* USA 83N4
Knockboy *mt* Ireland, Rep. of 31E10
Knocklayd *mt* *N Ireland* UK 30L3
Knockmealdown Mts Ireland, Rep. of 31G9
Knockowen *mt* Ireland, Rep. of 31D10
Knokke Belgium 32B3
Knoppieslaagie South Africa 72N11
Knottingley *England* UK 25F5
Knox *Pa* USA 84B2
Knox Coast Antarctica 15H3
Knoxville *Iowa* USA 83M2
Knoxville *Tenn.* USA 85F3
Knutsford *England* UK 25D6
Knysna South Africa 72C6
Knyszyn Poland 37K2
Kobarid Yugoslavia 44D2
Kōbe Japan 56D7
København Denmark 35E9
Koblenz Switzerland 33D1
Koblenz W Germany 36B3
Kobrin *Belorus.* USSR 48D5
Kobroör *island* Indonesia 53K12
Kocaeli = İzmit
Kočani Yugoslavia 46D4
Kočevje Yugoslavia 44E3
Ko Chang,I Thailand 57C4
Kōchi Japan 56C8
Kōchi *prefecture* Japan 56C8
Kochkar USSR 49Q3
Kochow = Moaming
Kodiak *Alaska* USA 87X13
Kodiak I *Alaska* USA 87X13
Koehn,L *Calif.* USA 80E8
Koel,R India 61D3
Koes Namibia 72B5
Koffiefontein South Africa 72D5
Koforidua Ghana 68E7
Kofu Japan 56F7
Kogaluk,R *Que.* Canada 77Q5
Køge Denmark 35E9
Køge B Denmark 35E9
Køge B Greenland 14N3
Kohala,Mt *Hawaii* USA 95V27
Kohat Pakistan 60B4
Koh-i-Baba *mts* Afghanistan 63K3
Kohima India 59H3
Kohtla-Järve *Eston.* USSR 35M7
Koil = Aligarh
Kojonup *W Aus.* Australia 98D6
Kokand *Uzbek.* USSR 63L1
Kokchetav *Kazakh.* USSR 50H4
Koki Sénégal 68B5
Kokkola Finland 34K5
Kokoda Papua New Guinea 99K1
Kokomo *Ind.* USA 79C5
Kokpekty *Kazakh.* USSR 50K5
Kokstad South Africa 72D6
Ko Kut,I Thailand 57C4
Kolahoi *Kashmir* India 60D3
Kolai Pakistan 60C3
Ko Lanta *island* Thailand 57B5
Kolar India 58E6
Kolari Finland 34K3
Kolarovgrad = Shumen
Kolberg = Kołobrzeg
Kolda Senegal 68C6
Kolding Denmark 35C9
Kole Zaire 70F4
Kolekole *mt Hawaii* USA 95V26
Kolhapur India 58D5
Kolin Czech. 36F3
Kolkas Rags,C *Latvia* USSR 35K8
Kollam = Quilon
Köln W Germany 36B3
Kolno Poland 37J2
Koło Poland 37H2
Kolo Tanzania 71H5
Kołobrzeg Poland 37F1
Kologriv USSR 49G1
Kolokani Mali 68D6
Kolomna USSR 48L4
Kolomyya *Ukrain.* USSR 48D7
Kolosia Kenya 71H4
Kolozsvár = Cluj
Kolpashevo USSR 50K4
Kolwezi Zaire 70F7
Kolyma,R USSR 51S3
Kolymskaya USSR 51S3
Komadugu Gana,R Nigeria 69H6
Komandorskiye Ostrova *island* USSR 51T4
Komariya Sri Lanka 58F7
Komárno Czech. 37H5
Komatsu Japan 56E6
Komi ASSR *rep.* USSR 50G3
Koming China 55G11
Kommunarsk *Ukrain.* USSR 48L7
Kom Ombo Egypt 69M4
Komotini Greece 46E4
Kompong Chnang Cambodia 57C4
Kompong Kleang Cambodia 57C4
Kompong Speu Cambodia 57C4
Kompong Thom Cambodia 57C4
Komsomol'ska-na-Amur USSR 51Q4
Konar Res. India 61E4
Kondinskoe USSR 50H3
Kondoa Tanzania 71H5
Kong Ivory Coast 68E7
Kong Christian IX Land *region* Greenland 14N3
Kong Frederik VIII Land *region* Greenland 14N1
Kong Frederik VI Kyst *region* Greenland 14P3
Kong Karl's Land Arctic Ocean 50D2
Kongor Sudan 69M7
Kongsberg Norway 35C7
Kongsmoen Norway 34E4
Kongsvinger Norway 35E6
Kongur Shan *mt* China 60D1
Kongwa Tanzania 71H6
Kong Wilhelms Land *region* Greenland 14N2
Königsberg = Kaliningrad
Königsee W Germany 36E5
Konin Poland 37H2
Konispol Albania 47C5
Konjic Yugoslavia 46A3
Könkämä Alv *river* Sweden 34J2
Konotop *Ukrain.* USSR 48H6
Kon Plong Vietnam 57D4
Konstantinovka *Ukrain.* USSR 48K7
Konstantinovsk USSR 49E7
Konstanz Switzerland 36C5
Kontiomaki Finland 34N4
Konya Turkey 62C2
Konza Kenya 71H5
Koondrook *Vic.* Australia 97B3
Koorawatha *NSW* Australia 97C2
Kootwijk Netherlands 32D2
Kopervik Norway 35A7
Kopeysk USSR 49Q3
Ko Phuket *island* Thailand 57B5
Köping Sweden 35F7
Kopmanholmen Sweden 34H5
Kopparberg Sweden 35F7
Kopparberg *county* Sweden 35F6
Koppigen Switzerland 33C1
Koprivnica Yugoslavia 44F2
Kora India 61C2
Korarou,L Mali 68E5
Korbel *Calif.* USA 80B5
Korcë Albania 47C4
Korcula *island* Yugoslavia 44F4
Kordorfan,Northern *region* Sudan 69L5
Kordorfan,Southern *region* Sudan 69L6
Korea Bay China/Korea 54M3
Korea Str. = Tsushima Kaikyō
Korhogo Ivory Coast 68D7
Korinthía & Argolís *dist.* Greece 47D6
Kórinthos Greece 47D6
Kórinthos,G of Greece 47D5
Koritza = Korcë
Kormakiti,C Cyprus 64A2
Kornat *island* Yugoslavia 44E4
Korneuburg Austria 37G4
Korogwe Tanzania 71H6
Koroit *Vic.* Australia 97B3

Koromba,Mt Lais Alv

Koromba,Mt *Viti Levu* Fiji **94A25**
Korong Vale *Vic.* Australia **97B3**
Körös,R Hungary **46C1**
Korosten *Ukrain.* USSR **48F6**
Koro Toro Chad **69J5**
Korpo Finland **35J6**
Korsakov USSR **51R5**
Korsnas Finland **34J5**
Korsnes Norway **34G2**
Kortemark Belgium **32B3**
Kortessem Belgium **32D4**
Kortgem Netherlands **32B3**
Korti Sudan **69M5**
Kortrijk Belgium **32B4**
Korumburra *Vic.* Australia **97C3**
Korwai India **61B3**
Koryakskiy Khrebet *mts* USSR **51T3**
Kos *island* Greece **47F6**
Ko Samui,I Thailand **57C5**
Kościerzyna Poland **37H1**
Kosciusko Nat. Pk *NSW* Australia **97C3**
Koscuisko *Miss.* USA **85C4**
Koscuisko,Mt *NSW* Australia **97C3**
Kosha Sudan **69M4**
Koshchagyl *Kazakh.* USSR **50G5**
Koshikijima Retto *islands* Japan **56A9**
Koshki USSR **49K3**
Kosi India **60E7**
Košice Czech. **37J4**
Kosi,L South Africa **72E5**
Kosi,R India **61F2**
Koskullskulle Sweden **34J3**
Koslan USSR **50F3**
Köslin = Koszalin
Kosovo Metohija Yugoslavia **46C3**
Kosovo-Mitrovica Yugoslavia **46C3**
Kostajnica Yugoslavia **44F3**
Kosti Sudan **69M6**
Kostroma USSR **48M3**
Kostrzyn Poland **36F2**
Koszalin Poland **37G1**
Koszalin *voivodship* Poland **37G2**
Kota India **58E3**
Kota Baharu Malaysia **57C5**
Kot Adda Pakistan **60B5**
Kota Kinabalu *Sabah* Malay. **53G9**
Kotalpur India **61F4**
Ko Tao *island* Thailand **57B4**
Kotcha L *BC* Canada **76G5**
Kotchandpur Bangladesh **61G4**
Kotel Bulgaria **46F3**
Kotelnich USSR **49J1**
Köthen E Germany **36D3**
Kothi India **61C3**
Kotido Uganda **71G4**
Kotka Finland **35M6**
Kot Kapura India **60D5**
Kot Kasim India **60E6**
Kotkhai India **60E5**
Kotlas USSR **50F3**
Kotli *Kashmir* India **60C4**
Kotn Group *islands* Tonga **95V30**
Kotonkoro Nigeria **68G6**
Kotri Pakistan **58C3**
Kotturu India **58E6**
Kotuy,R USSR **51M2**
Kotwar Pk India **61D4**
Kotzebue Sd *Alaska* USA **87W12**
Kouango CAR **69K7**
Koudougou Upper Volta **68E6**
Kouilou,R Congo **70C5**
Koula Moutou Gabon **70C5**
Koulikoro Mali **68D6**
Koumra Chad **69J7**
Koup Atoll Truk Is **94A16**
Kourou Fr. Guiana **93G2**
Kouroussa Guinea **68D6**
Koutiala Mali **68D6**
Kovel *Ukrain.* USSR **48D6**
Kovno = Kaunas
Kovrov USSR **49E2**
Kowloon China **55H11**
Koyukuk,R *Alaska* USA **87X12**
Kozan Turkey **62D2**
Kozáni Greece **47C4**
Kozani *dist.* Greece **47C4**
Kozhikode = Calicut
Kra *island* Thailand **57C5**
Kraaifontein South Africa **72J9**
Kragerø Norway **35C7**
Kragujevac Yugoslavia **46C2**
Kra,Isthmus of Thailand **57B5**
Krakow Poland **37H3**
Krakow *voivodship* Poland **37H3**
Kraljevo Yugoslavia **46C3**
Kramatorsk *Ukrain.* USSR **48K7**
Kramsfors Sweden **34G5**
Kranj Yugoslavia **44E2**
Kranystaw Poland **37K3**
Krapina Yugoslavia **44E2**
Krasino USSR **50G2**
Kraśnik Poland **37K3**
Krasnoarmeysk USSR **49G5**
Krasnobród Poland **37K3**
Krasnodar USSR **50E5**
Krasnograd *Ukrain.* USSR **48J7**
Krasnoufimsk USSR **49N2**
Krasnovishersk USSR **50G3**
Krasnovodsk *Turkmen.* USSR **50G5**
Krasnoyarsk USSR **51L4**
Krasnoyarskiy Kray *region* USSR **51L3**
Krasnyi Kholm USSR **48K2**
Krasny Kut USSR **49H5**
Krasnyy Yar USSR **49G5**
Kratie Cambodia **57D4**
Krefeld W Germany **36B3**
Kremenchug *Ukrain.* USSR **48H7**
Kremensk USSR **49F6**
Krems Austria **37F4**
Kretinga *Lith.* USSR **35J9**
Kreuzlingen Switzerland **33E1**
Kribi Cameroun **69G8**
Krichev USSR **48G5**
Kriens Switzerland **33D1**
Krimml Austria **36E5**
Krimpen Netherlands **32C3**
Krishna,Mouths of India **58F5**
Krishnanagar India **61G4**
Krishna,R India **58E5**
Krishnaraja Res. India **58E6**
Kristiansand Norway **35B7**
Kristianstad Sweden **35F8**
Kristianstad *county* Sweden **35E8**
Kristiansund Norway **34B5**
Kristiinankaupunki Finland **34J5**
Kristinehamn Sweden **35F7**
Kristinestad = Kristiinankaupunki
Kríti *island* Greece **47E7**
Kriva Palanka Yugoslavia **46D3**
Krivoy Rog *Ukrain.* USSR **48H8**
Križevci Yugoslavia **44F2**
Krk *island* Yugoslavia **44E3**
Krnov Czech. **37G3**
Kroken Norway **34F4**
Krokom Sweden **34F5**
Kroměříz Czech. **37G4**
Kromy USSR **48J5**
Krong,R Cambodia/Vietnam **57D4**
Kronoberg *county* Sweden **35E8**
Kronoby Finland **34K5**
Kronprinsesse Martha Kyst Antarctica **15B2**
Kronshtadt USSR **48F1**
Kronsprins Olav Kyst Antarctica **15E3**
Kroonstad South Africa **72D5**
Kropotkin USSR **50F5**
Krosno Poland **37J4**
Krotoszyn Poland **37G3**
Krško Yugoslavia **44E3**
Krugersdorp South Africa **72D5**
Krugersdorp South Africa **72M12**
Krug Thep = Bangkok
Kruishoutem Belgium **32B4**
Krujë Albania **46B4**
Krumbach W Germany **36D4**
Krupnik Bulgaria **46D4**
Kruševac Yugoslavia **46C3**
Krustpils *Latvia* USSR **35L8**
Krylbo Sweden **35G6**
Krym *pen.* USSR **48H9**
Krzyz Poland **37G2**
Ksar el Boukhari Algeria **68F1**
Ksar-el-Kebir Morocco **68D2**
Ksours,Mts de Algeria **68F2**
Ktima Cyprus **64A3**
Kuai He *river* China **54J6**
Kuaize He *river* China **55C10**
Kuala *Sumatra* Indon. **53C10**
Kuala Kangsar Malaysia **57C6**
Kuala Kelawang Malaysia **57C6**
Kuala Kerai Malaysia **53D9**
Kuala Lipis Malaysia **57C6**
Kuala Lumpur Malaysia **57C6**
Kuandang *Celebes* Indon. **53H10**
Kuantan Malaysia **53D10**
Kuching *Sarawak* Malay. **53F10**
Kudat *Sabah* Malay. **53G9**
Kudymkar USSR **50G4**
Kueishan Tao *island* Taiwan **55L10**
Küfstein Austria **36E5**
Kuhak Iran **63J4**
Kühbonan Iran **63H3**
Kühe Bazmān *mt* Iran **63H4**
Küh-e-Bül *mt* Iran **63G3**
Kuh-e-Dinar Iran **63G3**
Kuh-e-Furgān *mt* Iran **63H4**
Küh-e-Taftān *mt* Iran **63J4**
Kuhmo Finland **34N4**
Kühpayeh Iran **63G3**
Kuhsan Afghanistan **63J3**
Kuibis Namibia **72B5**
Kuinre Netherlands **32D2**
Kuivaniema Finland **34L4**
Kukatush *Ont.* Canada **79E1**
Kukawa Nigeria **69H6**
Kukës Albania **46C3**
Kulal,Mt Kenya **71H4**
Kuldiga *Latvia* USSR **35K8**
Kulhakangri,Mt *Tibet* China **59H3**
Kullaa Finland **35K6**
Kulmbach W Germany **36D3**
Kulu India **60E5**
Kulunda USSR **50J4**
Ku-lu Shan *mts* China **54G2**
Kulwin *Vic.* Australia **97B2**
Kumai *Borneo* Indon. **53F11**
Kumamoto Japan **56B8**
Kumamoto *prefecture* Japan **56B8**
Kumara New Zealand **100D6**
Kumara USSR **51P4**
Kumasi Ghana **68E7**
Kumbakonam India **58E6**
Kumher India **61A2**
Kumora USSR **51N4**
Kumta India **58D6**
Kumukahi,C *Hawaii* USA **95V27**
Kunch India **61B3**
Kunda *Eston.* USSR **35M7**
Kundi,L Sudan **69L6**
Kunduz Afghanistan **63K2**
Kungchang = Longxi
Kung-kang Pass China **54B6**
Kungnang India **59H4**
Kungrad *Uzbek.* USSR **50G5**
Kungsbacka Sweden **35E8**
Kungur USSR **49N2**
Kunlong Burma **59J4**
Kunlun Shan *mts* *Tibet* China **59F1**
Kunming China **52D5**
Kunsan S Korea **52J3**
Kuocang Shan *mts* China **55L8**
Kuopio Finland **34M5**
Kuopio *prov* Finland **34M5**
Kuovola Finland **35M6**
Kupang *Timor* Indon. **53H13**
Kupa,R Yugoslavia **44E3**
Kupiškis *Lith.* USSR **35L9**
Kupyansk *Ukrain.* USSR **48K7**
Kuqa *Xinjiang* China **50K5**
Kurdistan *region* Iran **62E2**
Kure Japan **56C7**
Kure,I *Hawaii* USA **94J5**
Kureika USSR **50K3**
Kurgan USSR **50H4**
Kuria Muria Is Oman **63H6**
Kurigram Bangladesh **61G3**
Kurikka Finland **34K5**
Kuril Is = Kuril'skiye Ostrova
Kuril'skiye Ostrova *islands* USSR **51R5**
Kurlachi Pakistan **60B4**
Kurnool India **58E5**
Kurnub *hist. site* Israel **64D6**
Kurow New Zealand **100D7**
Kurram Pakistan **60B4**
Kurram,R Pakistan **60B4**
Kurri Kurri *NSW* Australia **97D2**
Kursk USSR **48K6**
Kurskiy Zaliv *lagoon* *Lith.* USSR **35J9**
Kurtalan Turkey **62E2**
Kuru Finland **35K6**
Kuruman South Africa **72C5**
Kuruman,R South Africa **72C5**
Kurume Japan **56B8**
Kurunegala Sri Lanka **58F7**
Kusa USSR **49P3**
Kusaie,I Caroline Is **94G7**
Kushersk USSR **49M1**
Kushiro Japan **56J3**
Kushk Afghanistan **63J3**
Kushka *Turkmen.* USSR **50H6**
Kushtia Bangladesh **61G4**
Kushva USSR **49P1**
Kuskokwim B *Alaska* USA **87W13**
Kusma Nepal **61D1**
Küsnacht Switzerland **33D1**
Küssnacht Switzerland **33D1**
Kustanay *Kazakh.* USSR **50H4**
Kütahya Turkey **62B2**
Kutai,R *Borneo* Indon. **53G10**
Kutchan Japan **56G3**
Kutina Yugoslavia **44F3**
Kutno Poland **37H2**
Kutu Zaire **71D5**
Kutum Sudan **69K6**
Kuusamo Finland **34N4**
Kuusjärvi Finland **34N5**
Kuwait Kuwait **62F4**
Kuwait *country* SW Asia **62F4**
Kuybyshev USSR **49K4**
Kuybyshev USSR **50J4**
Kuybyshevskoye Vdkhr. *res.* USSR **49J3**
Kuytan USSR **51M4**
Kuyuwini,R Guyana **92F3**
Kuzhbal USSR **49G1**
Kuzino USSR **49P2**
Kuzmin Yugoslavia **46B2**
Kuznetsk USSR **49H4**
Kuzovatovo USSR **49H4**
Kvaløy,North,I Norway **34H1**
Kvaløy,South,I Norway **34H2**
Kvarken, Ostra Sweden **34J5**
Kvarner *gulf* Yugoslavia **44E3**
Kvarnerić *gulf* Yugoslavia **44E3**
Kvesmenes Norway **34J2**
Kwajalein,I Kwajalein,Is **94A17**
Kwajalein,Is Marshall Is **94G7**
Kwakoegron Surinam **93F2**
Kwamouth Zaire **70D5**
Kwangchow = Guangzhou
Kwango,R Zaire **70D6**
Kwangsi = Gwangxi
Kwangsin = Shangrao
Kwangtung = Guangdong
Kwania,L Uganda **71G4**
Kweichow = Guizhou
Kweiteh = Shangqiu
Kweiteh = Shangqiu
Kwidzyń Poland **37H2**
Kwilu,R Zaire **70D6**
Kwitao Burma **59J3**
Kwoka *mt* *New Guinea* Indon. **53K11**
Kyabram *Vic.* Australia **97C3**
Kyaikkama Burma **59J5**
Kyaikto Burma **59J5**
Kyakhta USSR **51M4**
Kyalite *NSW* Australia **97B2**
Kyaukpyu Burma **59H5**
Kyaukse Burma **59J4**
Kyauktaw Burma **59H4**
Kybybolite *S Aus.* Australia **97B3**
Kyelang India **60E4**
Kyle of Lochalsh *Scotland* UK **28E5**
Kymi Finland **35M6**
Kymi Joki *river* Finland **35M6**
Kyneton *Vic.* Australia **97B3**
Kynuna *Queens.* Australia **99J4**
Kyoga,L Uganda **71G4**
Kyōto Japan **56D7**
Kyrenia Cyprus **64B2**
Kyrön Joki *river* Finland **34K5**
Kyshtym USSR **49Q3**
Kythrea Cyprus **64B2**
Kyūshū *island* Japan **56B8**
Kyustendil Bulgaria **46D3**
Kyusyur USSR **51P2**
Kywong *NSW* Australia **97C2**
Kyzyl USSR **51L4**
Kyzyl Kum *Kazakh./Uzbek.* USSR **50H5**
Kzyl Orda *Kazakh.* USSR **50H5**

L

la Almunia de Doña Godina Spain **41F2**
Laanila Finland **34M2**
La Araucania *prov.* Chile **91B5**
La Ascención Mexico **88C1**
La Asunción Venezuela **92E1**
Laban Jordan **64D7**
La Banda Argentina **91D3**
La Bañeza Spain **40D1**
Labang *Sarawak* Malay. **53F10**
Labe Guinea **68C6**
Labelle *Que.* Canada **79J2**
Laberge,L *Yukon* Canada **76D4**
Laboué Lebanon **64E3**
Labouheyre France **43C4**
Laboulaye Argentina **91D4**
Labrador *region* *Newf.* Canada **77T6**
Labrador Sea Can./Greenl'd **77U4**
La Brea Trinidad **92E1**
Labuan *island* *Sabah* Malay. **53G9**
Labuk B *Sabah* Malay. **53G9**
Lac Allard *Que.* Canada **78G1**
La Canoa Venezuela **92E2**
la Capelle France **42E2**
La Carlota Argentina **91D4**
La Carolina Spain **40E3**
Lac au Goeland *lake* *Que.* Canada **77Q7**
Laccadive,Is *Lakshadweep* India **58D6**
Lac Cratere *lake* St Paul I **65T12**
Lac d'Annecy *lake* France **42G4**
Lac de Gruyère Switzerland **33C2**
Lac de Joux *lake* Switzerland **33B2**
Lac de Neuchâtel *lake* Switzerland **33B2**
Lac Édouard *Que.* Canada **79K2**
La Ceiba Honduras **89B3**
La Ceiba Venezuela **92C2**
Lacepede B *S Aus.* Australia **97A3**
Lac Frontière *Que.* Canada **78C3**
la Charité France **42E3**
la Châtre France **42D3**
La Chaux de Fonds Switzerland **33B1**
Lachen Switzerland **33D1**
Lachlan,R *NSW* Australia **97C2**
Lachmangarh India **60D7**
La Chorrera Panama **89D5**
Lachute *Que.* Canada **79J3**
la Ciotat France **43F5**
Lackawanna *NY* USA **84B1**
Lackawaxen *Pa* USA **84D2**
Lac la Plonge *lake* *Sask.* Canada **76K5**
Lac la Ronge *lake* *Sask.* Canada **76L5**
Lac Léman *lake* Switzerland **33B2**
Lac Mégantic *lake* *Que.* Canada **78C4**
La Cocha Argentina **91C3**
Lacombe *Alta* Canada **76J6**
Laconia *New H* USA **84F1**
La Copelina Argentina **91C5**
La Coruña *prov.* Spain **40B1**
La Coruña *region* Spain **40B1**
La Côte *region* Switzerland **33B2**
Lac-Rémi *Que.* Canada **79J2**
La Crosse *Wis.* USA **81M4**
La Cruz Colombia **92B3**
Lac Seul *lake* *Ont.* Canada **77N6**
Ladakh *district* India **60E3**
Ladakh Ra *mts* *Tibet* China **58E2**
Ladamaqua,Massif de *mt* Cameroun **69H7**
Lādīz Iran **63J4**
Ladoga,L = Ladozhskoye Ozero
La Dôle *mt* Switzerland **33B2**
La Dorada Colombia **92C2**
Ladozhskoye Ozero *lake* USSR **48G1**
Ladwa India **60E6**
Lady Newnes Ice Shelf Antarctica **15L2**
Ladysmith *BC* Canada **76G7**
Ladysmith South Africa **72D5**
Ladysmith *Wis.* USA **81M3**
Lae Papua New Guinea **99K1**
Laeken Belgium **32C4**
Laes,I Denmark **35D8**
La Esperanza Honduras **89B4**
La Estrada Spain **40B1**
Lafayette *Ga* USA **85E3**
Lafayette *Ind.* USA **79C5**
Lafayette *La* USA **83N7**
La Flèche France **42C3**
Lafontaine *Que.* Canada **78D3**
La Fouly Switzerland **33C3**
Lagan,R N Ireland **30L4**
Lages Brazil **93K5**
Laggan *Scotland* UK **28H5**
Laggan,L *Scotland* UK **28H6**
Laghouat Algeria **68F2**
Lagkor Co *lake* *Tibet* China **59F2**
Lago Dilolo Angola **70E7**
Lago di Lugano *lake* Italy/Switz. **33E3**
Lagonegro Italy **45E5**
Lagos Nigeria **68F7**
Lagos Portugal **40B4**
Lagos de Moreno Mexico **88D3**
La Grande *Oreg.* USA **80D3**
La Grande,R *Que.* Canada **77Q6**
La Grange *Ga* USA **85E4**
Lagrange *Ind.* USA **79D5**
La Grange *Ky* USA **85E1**
La Grange *W Aus.* Australia **98E3**
La Granja Spain **40D2**
La Gran Sabana *mts* Venezuela **92E2**
La Guaira Venezuela **92D1**
La Guardia Argentina **91C3**
La Guardia Spain **40B2**
la Guerche France **42C3**
Laguna Brazil **91G3**
Laguna de las Perlas *lagoon* Nicaragua **89C4**
Laguna de Tamiahua *lagoon* Mexico **88E3**
Laguna de Terminos *lagoon* Mexico **88F4**
Laguna Madre *lagoon* Mexico **88E3**
Laguna Madre *lagoon* *Texas* USA **82T10**
Lagunas Peru **92B5**
Lagunillas Bolivia **92E7**
Laharpur India **61C2**
La Have I *No. Sc.* Canada **78F4**
Lahej South Yemen **62E7**
Lahījān Iran **63G2**
Laholm Sweden **35E8**
Lahore Pakistan **60D5**
Lahti Finland **35L6**
Lai Chad **69J7**
Lai'an China **54K6**
Laibach = Ljubljana
Laibin China **55E11**
Lai Chau Vietnam **57C2**
Laifeng China **55E8**
L'Aigle France **42D2**
Laingsburg South Africa **72C6**
Lainio Alv *river* Sweden **34K3**
Lairg *Scotland* UK **28H3**
Lais Alv *river* Sweden **34F3**

Laisamis Lemberg

Laisamis Kenya 71H4
Laishev USSR 49J3
Laiwu China 54J4
Laiyuan China 54H3
Laizhou Wan *bay* China 54K4
Laja,L Chile 91B5
La Japonesa Argentina 91C5
Lajes Brazil 91F3
La Jolla *Calif.* USA 80E9
La Jonquera Spain 41H1
La Junta *Col.* USA 82G4
Lakaträsk Sweden 34J3
Lake Andes *S Dak.* USA 81H4
Lake Boga *Vic.* Australia 97B3
Lake Butler *Fla* USA 85F5
Lake Charles *La* USA 83M7
Lake City *Calif.* USA 80C5
Lake City *Fla* USA 85F5
Lake City *Mich.* USA 79D3
Lake District *region* England UK 25B3
Lake Edward (Can.) = Lac Édouard
Lake Elsinore *Calif.* USA 80E9
Lakefield *Ont.* Canada 79G3
Lake Geneva *Wis.* USA 79B4
Lake George *NY* USA 84E1
Lake Harbour *NW Terr.* Canada 77S4
Lake Havasu City *Ariz.* USA 80F8
Lakeland *Fla* USA 85L7
Lake Mead Nat. Rec. Area *Ariz./Nev.* USA 80F7
Lake Nash *N Terr.* Australia 99H4
Lake Pleasant *NY* USA 84D1
Lakeport *Calif.* USA 80B6
Lake Providence *La* USA 83N6
Lake Pukaki New Zealand 100D7
Lakes Entrance *Vic.* Australia 97C3
Lakeside *Utah* USA 82B2
Lakeview *Oreg.* USA 80C4
Lakewood *New J* USA 84D2
Lakewood *NY* USA 84B1
Lakewood *Ohio* USA 79F5
Lake Worth *Fla* USA 85M8
Lakhimpur India 59H3
Lakhimpur India 61C2
Lakhnadon India 61B4
Lakhpat India 58C4
Lakki Pakistan 60B4
Lakonia *dist.* Greece 47D6
Lakonia,G of Greece 47D6
Lakota Ivory Coast 68D7
Lakota *N Dak.* USA 81H1
Lakse,Fj. Norway 34M1
Lakshadweep,Is Indian Ocean 58D6
Lakshandau,R India 61E2
Lala Musa Pakistan 60D4
Lalbagh India 61G3
Lalganj India 61E3
La Libertad Ecuador 92A4
La Libertad El Salvador 89B4
La Libertad Guatemala 88F4
La Libertad Nicaragua 89B4
La Ligua Chile 91B4
Lalin Spain 40B1
Lalitpur India 61B3
La Maddalena *island* *Sardinia* Italy 45B5
La Malbaie *Que.* Canada 79L2
La Mancha *region* Spain 40E3
Lamar *Col.* USA 82G3
Lamar *Mo* USA 83L4
Lamastre France 43F4
Lambach Austria 36E4
Lamballe France 42B2
Lambayeque Peru 92A5
Lambay I = Liuchiu Hsu
Lambay I Ireland, Rep. of 31L6
Lambert Land Greenland 14M2
Lamberts Bay South Africa 72B6
Lambertville *New J* USA 84D2
Lámbia Greece 47C6
Lamb's Hd Ireland, Rep. of 31C10
Lamé Chad 69H7
Lamego Portugal 40C2
Lameroo *S Aus.* Australia 97B3
La Mesa *Calif.* USA 80E9
Lamesa *Texas* USA 82H6
Lamia Greece 47D5
Lamington *Scotland* UK 29J8
l'Amiral,Pen. de Kerguelen 65S12
Lamlash *Scotland* UK 29F8
Lammermuir Hills *upland* *Scotland* UK 29L8
Lamoil *island* Truk Is 94A16
La Montana *plat.* Peru 92C5
Lamotrek,Is Caroline Is 94E7
La Motte Switzerland 33C1
La Moure *N Dak.* USA 81H2
Lampa Peru 92C7
Lampang Thailand 57B3
Lampazos Mexico 88D2
Lampedusa,I Medit. Sea 69H1
Lampeter *Wales* UK 26F4
Lamphun Thailand 57B3
Lampton,C *NW Terr.* Canada 76G2
Lamu Kenya 71J5
Lamud Peru 92B5
Lanaas,R Sweden 34H3
Lanai *island* *Hawaii* USA 95V26
Lanark *Scotland* UK 29J8
Lanbi Kyun,I Burma 59J6
Lancang Jiang *river* China 52C5
Lancashire *county* *England* UK 25C5
Lancaster *Calif.* USA 80D8
Lancaster *England* UK 25C4
Lancaster *Mo* USA 83M2
Lancaster *New H* USA 79L3
Lancaster *NY* USA 84B1
Lancaster *Pa* USA 84C2
Lancaster *S Car.* USA 85G3
Lancaster *Wis.* USA 79A4
Lancaster Sd *NW Terr.* Canada 77O2
Lanciano Italy 44E4
Landeck Austria 36D5
Landen Belgium 32D4
Lander *Wyo.* USA 81C4
Landerneau France 42A2
Landeron Switzerland 33C1
Landes *dep.* France 43C4
Landfall,I Chile 91B8
Landi Kotal Pakistan 60B3
Landon Sweden 34F5
Landquart Switzerland 33E2
Landsberg = Gorzów Wielkopolski
Landsberg W Germany 36D4
Land's End *point* *England* UK 26C8
Landshut W Germany 36E4
Landskrona Sweden 35E9
Langaa Denmark 35C8
Langadhas Greece 47D4
Langana,L Ethiopia 71H3
Langar Pakistan 60C4
Langeac France 43E4
Langeland *island* Denmark 35D9
Langenthal Switzerland 33C1
Langeoog *island* W Germany 36B2
Langesund Norway 35C7
Langholm *Scotland* UK 29L9
Lang Jökull *glacier* Iceland 34U12
Langkawi,I Malaysia 57B5
Langnau Switzerland 33C2
Langogne France 43E4
Langon France 43C4
Langøy,I Norway 34F2
Langport *England* UK 26J6
Langres France 42F3
Langsa *Sumatra* Indon. 53C10
Långsele Sweden 34G5
Lang Son Vietnam 57D2
Lang Suan Thailand 57B4
Långträsk Sweden 34J4
Languedoc *prov.* France 43E5
Languuya,R India 59F5
Långvattnet Sweden 34G4
Langzhong China 54D7
Lanin *mt* Chile 91B5
Lankao China 54H5
Lankor Tso *lake* *Tibet* China 59F2
Lannion France 42B2
Lansdale *Pa* USA 84D2
Lanshan China 55F10
Lansing *Mich.* USA 79D4
Lanxi China 55K8
Lan Xian China 54F3
Lan Yu *island* Taiwan 55L11
Lanzarote,I Canary Is 68C3
Lanzhou China 54B4
Laoag Philippines 53H7
Lao Bao Vietnam 57D3
Lao Cai Vietnam 57C2
Laois *county* Ireland, Rep. Of 31H8
Laon France 42E2
La Oroya Peru 92B6
Laos *country* SE Asia 57C3
Laoshan China 54L4
Laotie Shan *cape* China 54L3
Lapalisse France 42E3
La Palma,I Canary Is 68B3
La Pampa *prov.* Argentina 91C5
La Paragua Venezuela 92E2
La Paz Argentina 91C4
La Paz Argentina 91E4
La Paz Bolivia 92D7
La Paz Honduras 89B4
La Paz Mexico 88B3
Lapchung,L *Tibet* China 59G2
Lapeer *Mich.* USA 79E4
La Pelada Argentina 91D4
La Pérade *Que.* Canada 79K2
Lapford *England* UK 26G7
La Piedad Mexico 88D3
La Pine *Oreg.* USA 80C4
Lapinlahti Finland 34M5
Lapithos Cyprus 64B2
La Plata Argentina 91E4
La Plata,Rio de *river* Argentina 91E5
La Porte *Ind.* USA 79C5
Laporte *Pa* USA 84C2
La Porte City *Iowa* USA 83M1
Lapovo Yugoslavia 46C2
Lappa Järvi,L Finland 34K5
Lappeenranta Finland 35N6
Lappia *prov.* Finland 34L3
Lappland *territory* Europe 34J2
Lappträsk Sweden 34K3
Laprida Argentina 91D5
Laptev Sea USSR 51P2
Lapuana Joki *river* Finland 34K5
La Punt Switzerland 33E2
La Purísima Mexico 88B2
La Push *Wash.* USA 80A2
Lapwai *Idaho* USA 80E2
Łapy Poland 37K2
La Quiaca Argentina 91C2
L'Aquila Italy 44D4
La Quille St Paul I 65T12
Lar Iran 63G4
Larache Morocco 68D1
Laragne France 43F4
Laramate Peru 92C6
Laramie *Wyo.* USA 81E5
Laramie Mts *Wyo.* USA 81D4
Laramie Pk *Wyo.* USA 81E4
Laranjeiras Brazil 93K6
La Rasse Switzerland 33B1
Larbert *Scotland* UK 29J7
Lårdal Norway 35C7
Laredo Spain 40E1
Laredo *Texas* USA 82S10
La Réole France 43C4
Largeau Chad 69J5
Largo *Scotland* UK 29L7
Largs *Scotland* UK 29G8
Larino Italy 45E5
La Rioja Argentina 91C3
La Rioja *prov.* Argentina 91C3
La Rioja *region* Spain 41E1
Lárisa Greece 47D5
Larisa *dist.* Greece 47D5
Larkana Pakistan 58C3
Larnaca Cyprus 64B3
Larnaka B Cyprus 64B3
Larne N Ireland 30M4
Larned *Kans.* USA 83J3
La Robla Spain 40D1
La Roca Spain 40C3
La Roche Switzerland 33C2
La Rochelle France 42C3
la Roche-sur-Yon France 42C3
La Roda Spain 41E3
La Romano Dom. Rep. 89F3
La Rosa Switzerland 33F2
Lars Christensen Coast Antarctica 15F2
Laruns France 43C5
Larvik Norway 35D7
Laryak USSR 50J3
La Salle *Ill.* USA 83P2
Las Animas *Col.* USA 82G3
La Sarraz Switzerland 33B2
Las Caanood Somalia 71K3
Las Cejas Argentina 91D3
Lascelles *Vic.* Australia 97B3
Las Coloradas Argentina 91B5
Las Cruces *New Mex.* USA 82E6
La Serena Chile 91B3
Las Flores Argentina 91E5
Lashio Burma 59J4
Lashkar India 61B2
La Sila *mts* Italy 45F6
Lasíthi *dist.* *Kríti* Greece 47E7
Lasjerd Iran 63G2
Las Lajas Argentina 91B5
Las Lomitas Argentina 91D2
Las Marismas *marshland* Spain 40C4
la Souterraine France 42D3
Las Palmas Canary Is 68B3
Las Perlas Nicaragua 89C4
La Spezia Italy 44B3
Las Pipinas Argentina 91E5
Las Plumas Argentina 91C6
Las Qoray Somalia 71K2
Lassen Pk *Calif.* USA 80C5
Lassen Volcanic Nat. Pk *Calif.* USA 80C5
Las Tablas Panama 89C5
Lastarria *mt* Arg./Chile 91C3
Last Mountain L *Sask.* Canada 76K6
Lastovo *island* Yugoslavia 44F4
Las Tres Virgenes *mt* Mexico 88B2
Las Varas Mexico 88C3
Las Vegas *Nev.* USA 80F7
Las Vegas *New Mex.* USA 82F5
Latacunga Ecuador 92B4
Lataseno,R Finland 34K2
Late *island* Tonga 95V30
Lat Hane Laos 57C2
Latheron *Scotland* UK 28K3
Lathrop *Calif.* USA 80C7
Latina Italy 45D5
La Tortuga *island* Venezuela 92D1
la Tour du Pin France 42F4
Latrobe *Pa* USA 84B2
Latrobe *Tas.* Australia 97F5
Latrun Jordan 64C6
La Tuque *Que.* Canada 79K2
Latvia *rep.* USSR 35K8
Latviyskaya SSR *rep.* USSR 50D4
Lauder *Scotland* UK 29L8
Lauenen Switzerland 33C2
Laufen Switzerland 33C1
Laufen Switzerland 33D1
Laufenburg Switzerland 33D1
Launceston *England* UK 26F7
Launceston *Tas.* Australia 97F5
Laune,R Ireland, Rep. of 31D9
Launggyaung Burma 59J3
Launglon Bok Is Burma 59J6
La Unión Chile 91B6
La Union El Salvador 89B4
La Unión Mexico 88D4
La Union Spain 41F4
Laupen Switzerland 33C2
Laura *Queens.* Australia 99J3
Laura *S Aus.* Australia 97A2
La Urbana Venezuela 92D2
Laurel *Md* USA 84C3
Laurel *Miss.* USA 85C5
Laurel *Mont.* USA 81C3
Laurel Hill *upland* *Pa* USA 84B2
Laurencekirk *Scotland* UK 29M6
Laurens *S Car.* USA 85F3
Laurens Pen. Heard I 65R12
Laurent *Que.* Canada 79K2
Laurentide Mts *Que.* Canada 78B3
Laurentides Park = Parc prov. des Laurentes
Lauria Italy 45E5
Lauricocha,L Peru 92B6
Laurie I *S Orkneys* Antarctica 15T3
Laurinburg *N Car.* USA 85H3
Lausanne Switzerland 33B2
Laut *island* *Borneo* Indon. 53G11
Lautaro Chile 91B5
Lauterbrunnen Switzerland 33C2
Lauzon *Que.* Canada 79L2
Lava Beds Nat. Mon. *Calif.* USA 80C5
Lavacherie Belgium 32D4
Laval France 42C2
Laval,B *Que.* Canada 78D2
Lavalleja = Minas
Lavamund Austria 36F5
Lavardac France 43D4
La Vega Dom. Rep 89E3
La Vela Venezuela 92D1
Laverton *W Aus.* Australia 98E5
Lavey Switzerland 33C2
Lavina *Mont.* USA 81C2
Lavras Brazil 91F4
Lavras Brazil 93H8
Lavrentiya USSR 51V3
Lávrion Greece 47D6
Lawgi *Queens.* Australia 99L4
Lawksawk Burma 59J4
Lawra Ghana 68E6
Lawrence *Kans.* USA 83L3
Lawrence *Mass.* USA 84F1
Lawrence New Zealand 100C7
Lawrenceburg *Tenn.* USA 85D3
Lawrenceville *Ill.* USA 83Q3
Lawton *Okla.* USA 83J5
Laxey *Isle of Man* UK 25L9
Laxford, Loch *Scotland* UK 28F3
Layla Saudi Arabia 62F5
La'youn Morocco 68C3
Lay,R France 42C3
Laysan,I *Hawaii* USA 94J5
Lazarevac Yugoslavia 46C2
Lázaro Cárdenas Mexico 88D4
L'azawak,Vallée de *valley* Mali/Niger 68F5
Lazio *region* Italy 45D4
Lead *S Dak.* USA 81F3
Leadhills *Scotland* UK 29J9
Leadville *Col.* USA 82E3
Leahy,C Antarctica 15Q2
Leakesville *Miss.* USA 85C5
Leaksville *N Car.* USA 85H2
Leamington *Ont.* Canada 79E4
Leamington *Utah* USA 82B3
Le'an China 55H9
Leane,L Ireland, Rep. of 31D9
Le'an Jiang China 55J8
Lea,R *England* UK 27P5
Leatherhead *England* UK 27P6
Leavenworth *Ind.* USA 85D1
Leavenworth *Kans.* USA 83L3
Leavitt Pk *Calif.* USA 80D6
Łeba Poland 37G1
Lebanon *Ky* USA 85E2
Lebanon *Mo* USA 83M4
Lebanon *New H* USA 84E1
Lebanon *Oreg.* USA 80B3
Lebanon *Pa* USA 84C2
Lebanon *country* W Asia 62D3
Lebesby Norway 34M1
le Blanc France 42D3
Lebombo,Mts South Africa 72E4
Lebork Poland 37G1
Le Brassus Switzerland 33B2
Lebu Chile 91B5
Le Carroz Switzerland 33B2
le Cateau France 42E1
Lecce Italy 45G5
Lecco Italy 44B3
Le Châble Switzerland 33C2
Le Chasseron *mt* Switzerland 33B2
Lechlade *England* UK 27L5
Lech,R Austria/W Ger. 36D4
Lech Tal *valley* Austria 36D5
le Conquet France 42A2
le Creusot France 42F3
le Croisic France 42B3
Lectourre France 43D5
Ledbury *England* UK 26K4
Ledesma Argentina 91D2
Ledesma Spain 40C2
Ledo India 59J3
le Dorat France 42D3
Ledu China 54B4
Lee *Nev.* USA 80F5
Leech L *Minn.* USA 81K2
Leeds *England* UK 25F5
Leek *England* UK 25D6
Leek Netherlands 32E1
Leende Netherlands 32D3
Lee,R Ireland, Rep. of 31F10
Leer W Germany 36B2
Leerbeek Belgium 32C4
Leerdam Netherlands 32D3
Leesburg *Va* USA 84C3
Leesville *La* USA 83M7
Leeton *NSW* Australia 97C2
Leeuwarden Netherlands 32D1
Leeuwin,C *W Aus.* Australia 98D6
Leeward Is West Indies 89G3
Leffinge Belgium 32A3
Lefini,R Congo 70D5
Lefka Cyprus 64A2
Lefkara Cyprus 64B3
Lefkoniko Cyprus 64B2
Lefroy,L *W Aus.* Australia 98E6
Legan,I Kwajalein,Is 94A17
Legaspi Philippines 53H8
Legges Tor *mt* *Tas.* Australia 97F5
Leghorn = Livorno
Le Gibloux *mt* Switzerland 33C2
Legnago Italy 44C3
Legnica Poland 37G3
Leh *Kashmir* India 60E3
Le Havre France 42D2
Lehi *Utah* USA 82C2
Lehman Caves Nat. Mon. *Nev.* USA 80F6
Lehua,I *Hawaii* USA 95V29
Leiah Pakistan 60B5
Leibo China 55B8
Leicester *England* UK 25F7
Leicestershire *county* *England* UK 25F7
Leichhardt,R *Queens.* Australia 99H3
Leiden Netherlands 32C2
Leidschendam Netherlands 32C2
Leie,R Belgium 32B4
Leigh *England* UK 25C5
Leigh Creek *S Aus.* Australia 97A2
Leighlinbridge Ireland, Rep. of 31K8
Leighton Buzzard *England* UK 27N5
Leignon Belgium 32D4
Leimuiden Netherlands 32C2
Leinster *prov.* Ireland, Rep. of 31J6
Leinster,Mt Ireland, Rep. of 31K8
Leipzig E Germany 36E3
Leisele Belgium 32A4
Lei Shui *river* China 55G9
Leissigen Switzerland 33C2
Leitchfield *Ky* USA 85D2
Leith *Scotland* UK 29K7
Leitrim *county* Ireland, Rep. of 30G5
Leixlip Ireland, Rep. of 31L7
Leiyang China 55G9
Leizhou Bamdao *peninsula* China 55E12
Leizhou Wan *bay* China 55F12
Leka Norway 34D4
Lekeleka Tonga 95V30
Leksands Noret Sweden 35F6
Leksvik Norway 34D5
Leland *Mich.* USA 79D3
Leland *Miss.* USA 85B4
Leleque Argentina 91B6
Le Locle Switzerland 33B1
le Luc France 43G5
Lelystad Netherlands 32D2
Le Mans France 42D2
Le Mars *Iowa* USA 83K1
Lemberg = L'vov

Lemhi P **Llanos de Guarayos**

Lemhi P *Mont.* USA **80G3**
Lemhi Ra *mts Idaho* USA **80G3**
Lemnos,I = Limnos,I
Le Môle St Nicolas Haiti **89E3**
Lemoncove *Calif.* USA **80D7**
Le Mont Dore France **42E4**
Lemoore *Calif.* USA **80D7**
le Muy France **43G5**
Lemyethna Burma **59J5**
Lena,R USSR **51P3**
Lengshuijiang China **55F9**
Leninabad *Uzbek.* USSR **50H5**
Leninakan *Armyan.* USSR **50F5**
Leningrad USSR **48G2**
Leninogorsk *Kazakh.* USSR **50K4**
Leninogorsk USSR **49L3**
Leninsk Kuznetskiy USSR **50K4**
Lenk Switzerland **33C2**
Lennox,I Argentina/Chile **91C9**
Lenoir *N Car.* USA **85G3**
Le Noirmont *mt* Switzerland **33B2**
Lens France **42E1**
Lent Netherlands **32D3**
Lentiira Finland **34N4**
Lenvik Norway **34H2**
Lenya Burma **59J6**
Lènz Switzerland **33E2**
Lenzburg Switzerland **33D1**
Lenzerheide Switzerland **33E2**
Léo Upper Volta **68E6**
Leoben Austria **36F5**
Leola *S Dak.* USA **81H3**
Leominster *England* UK **26J4**
Leominster *Mass.* USA **84F1**
León France **43C5**
León Mexico **88D3**
León Nicaragua **89B4**
León Spain **40D1**
León *prov.* Spain **40C1**
Leongatha *Vic.* Australia **97C3**
Leonidhion Greece **47D6**
Leonora *W Aus.* Australia **98E5**
Leontevo USSR **48K2**
Leopold & Astrid Coast Antarctica **15G3**
Leopold II,L = Mai-Ndombe,L
Leopoldsburg Belgium **32D3**
Léopoldville = Kinshasa
le Palais France **42B3**
Leping China **55J8**
Le Pont Switzerland **33B2**
Lepreau *New Br.* Canada **78E4**
le Puy France **43E4**
Lercara Friddi *Sicily* Italy **45D7**
Lerdo Mexico **88D2**
Lérida = Lleida
Lerma Spain **40E1**
Lermoos Austria **36D5**
Le Roeulx Belgium **32C4**
Léros *island* Greece **47F6**
Le Roy *NY* USA **84B1**
Le Rozier France **43E4**
Lerwick *Shetland* Scotland **28Q8**
les Abrets France **42F4**
Les Avants Switzerland **33B2**
Les Borges Blanques Spain **41G2**
Lesbos,I = Lesvos,I
Les Brenets Switzerland **33B1**
L'Escala Spain **41H1**
Les Diablerets Switzerland **33C2**
Le Sépey Switzerland **33C2**
Les Escoumains *Que.* Canada **78D2**
les Eyzies France **43D4**
Leshan China **55B8**
Les Haudères Switzerland **33C2**
Leskovac Yugoslavia **46C3**
Les Landes *region* France **43C4**
Les Monts Notre Dame = Notre Dame Mts
Lesneven France **42A2**
Lesotho *country* Africa **72D5**
Lesozavodsk USSR **51Q5**
Lesparre France **43C4**
Les Ponts de Martel Switzerland **33B2**
les Sables d'Olonne France **42C3**
Lesser Slave L *Alta* Canada **76H5**
Lessines Belgium **32B4**
l'Est,I de Crozet Is **65U12**
Lestijärvi Finland **34L5**
Les Verrières Switzerland **33B2**
Lésvos *island* Greece **47F5**
Leszno Poland **37G3**
Letcher *S Dak.* USA **81H4**
Letchworth *England* UK **27P5**
Letea I Romania **46G2**
Lethbridge *Alta* Canada **76J7**
Le Thuy Vietnam **57D3**
Leticia Colombia **92D4**
Leti Kep. Indonesia **53J12**
Leting China **54K3**
L'Etivaz Switzerland **33C2**
le Touquet-Paris-Plage France **42D1**
Letpadan Burma **59J5**
le Tréport France **42D1**
Lette *NSW* Australia **97B2**
Letterfrack Ireland, Rep. of **31D6**
Letterkenny Ireland, Rep. of **30H3**
Letur Spain **41E3**
Leucate France **43E5**
Leuchars *Scotland* UK **29L7**
Leucite Hills *Wyo.* USA **81C5**
Leuk Switzerland **33C2**
Leukerbad Switzerland **33C2**
Leuser *mt* *Sumatra* Indon. **53C10**
Leuven Belgium **32C4**
Leuze Belgium **32B4**
Leuzigen Switzerland **33C1**
Levádhia Greece **47D5**
Levanger Norway **34D5**
Leven *Scotland* UK **29K7**
Leven,L *Scotland* UK **29K7**
L'Evêque *mt* Switzerland **33C3**
Levêque,C *W Aus.* Australia **98E3**
Leverburgh *Scotland* UK **28C4**
le Verdon France **42C4**
Levice Czech. **37H4**
le Vigan France **43E5**
Levin New Zealand **100F5**
Lévis *Que.* Canada **79L2**
Levitha *island* Greece **47F6**
Lévka Óri *mt Kríti* Greece **47D7**
Levkás *island* Greece **47C5**
Levoča Czech. **37J4**
Levrier,B du Mauritania **68B4**
Lewes *England* UK **27P7**
Lewes,R *Yukon* Canada **76D4**
Lewisburg *Pa* USA **84C2**
Lewisburg *Tenn.* USA **85D3**
Lewisburg *W Va* USA **85G2**
Lewis, Butt of *point* Scotland UK **28D2**
Lewis,I *Scotland* UK **28C3**
Lewis P New Zealand **100E6**
Lewis Ra *mts Mont.* USA **86D2**
Lewis Smith L *Ala.* USA **85D3**
Lewiston *Idaho* USA **80E2**
Lewiston *Maine* USA **78C4**
Lewiston *Mich.* USA **79D3**
Lewiston *N Car.* USA **85J2**
Lewistown *Ill.* USA **83N2**
Lewistown *Mont.* USA **81C2**
Lewistown *Pa* USA **84C2**
Lexington *Ga* USA **85F4**
Lexington *Ky* USA **85E1**
Lexington *Mo* USA **83M3**
Lexington *N Car.* USA **85G3**
Lexington *Nebr.* USA **83J2**
Lexington *Tenn.* USA **85C3**
Lexington *Va* USA **85H2**
Leyburn *England* UK **25E4**
Leydsdorp South Africa **72E4**
Leyland *England* UK **25C5**
Leyre,R France **43C4**
Leysin Switzerland **33C2**
Leyte *island* Philippines **53H8**
Lezajsk Poland **37K3**
Lhasa *Tibet* China **59H3**
Lhasa He *river* *Tibet* China **59H3**
Lhazê *Tibet* China **59G3**
Lhünzê *Tibet* China **59H3**
Liadong *peninsula* China **54M2**
Liadong Wan *bay* China **54L2**
Liancheng China **55J10**
Lianchow = Wuwei
Liangping China **54D7**
Lianhua Shan *mt* China **55H11**
Lianjiang China **55F12**
Lianjiang China **55K9**
Lian Jiang *river* China **55H10**
Lianping China **55H10**
Lianshan China **55G10**
Lianshui China **54K6**
Liant,C Thailand **57C4**
Lian Xian China **55G10**
Lianyungang China **54K5**
Lianzhou = Hepu
Liaocheng China **54J4**
Liaoning *province* China **54L2**
Liaoyang China **54M2**
Liaqatabad Pakistan **60B4**
Liard,R *NW Terr.* Canada **76G4**
Liari Pakistan **58C3**
Libenga Zaire **70D4**
Liberal *Kans.* USA **82H4**
Liberec Czech. **36F3**
Liberia Costa Rica **89B4**
Liberia *country* Africa **68C7**
Liberty *Mo* USA **83L3**
Libo China **55D10**
Libourne France **43C4**
Libreville Gabon **70B4**
Libya *country* Africa **69J3**
Libyan Des. Libya **69K3**
Libyan Plat. Egypt **69L2**
Licata *Sicily* Italy **45D7**
Lichfield *England* UK **25E7**
Lichtensteig Switzerland **33E1**
Lichuan China **55E7**
Licking R *Ky* USA **85E1**
Lida *Belorus.* USSR **48D5**
Lida *Nev.* USA **80E7**
Lida di Roma = Lido di Ostia
Liddel,R *Eng./Scot.* UK **29L9**
Liddes Switzerland **33C3**
Liddon G *NW Terr.* Canada **76J1**
Lidjombo Cameroun **70D4**
Lidköping Sweden **35E7**
Lido Italy **44D3**
Lido di Ostia Italy **45D5**
Lidzbark Poland **37J1**
Liechtenstein *country* Europe **33E1**
Liège Belgium **32D4**
Liège *prov.* Belgium **32D4**
Liegnitz = Legnica
Lieksa Finland **34O5**
Lienz Austria **36E5**
Liepāja *Latvia* USSR **35J8**
Lier Belgium **32C3**
Lierneux Belgium **32D4**
Liers Belgium **32D4**
Liestal Switzerland **33C1**
Lièvre,R du *Que.* Canada **79J2**
Lièvres,I aux *Que.* Canada **78D3**
Liezen Austria **36F5**
Liffey,R Ireland,Rep. of **31K7**
Lifford Ireland, Rep. of **30J4**
Lifton *England* UK **26F7**
Lifu,I Îs Loyauté **94G10**
Lifuka *island* Tonga **95V30**
Lightning Ridge *NSW* Australia **97C1**
Ligny Belgium **32C4**
Liguria *region* Italy **44B3**
Ligurian Sea Italy **44B4**
Lihue *Hawaii* USA **95V28**
Lijiang China **52D5**
Likasa Zaire **70F7**
Likati Zaire **70E4**
Likhoslavl USSR **48J3**
Likimi Zaire **70E4**
Liljedal Sweden **35E7**
Lilla Edet Sweden **35E7**
Lille Belgium **32C3**
Lille France **42E1**
Lille Belt,Str. Denmark **35C9**
Lillehammer Norway **35D6**
Lillesand Norway **35C7**
Lillestrøm Norway **35D7**
Lillhärdal Sweden **35D6**
Lillo Belgium **32C3**
Lillo Spain **40E3**
Lillooet *BC* Canada **76G6**
Lilongwe Malawi **71G7**
Lima *Mont.* USA **80G3**
Lima *Ohio* USA **79D5**
Lima Peru **92B6**
Limache Chile **91B4**
Limassol Cyprus **64B3**
Limavady N Ireland **30K3**
Limay Mahuida Argentina **91C5**
Limay,R Argentina **91C5**
Limbaži *Latvia* USSR **35L8**
Limbe Malawi **71H8**
Limburg *prov.* Belgium **32D4**
Limburg W Germany **36C3**
Limburg *prov.* Belgium **32D4**
Limburg *prov.* Netherlands **32D4**
Limeira Brazil **93H8**
Limerick Ireland, Rep. of **31F8**
Limerick *county* Ireland,Rep. of **31E9**
Limes Belgium **32D5**
Limestone *Maine* USA **78E3**
Lim Fj. Denmark **35C8**
Limigka Finland **34L4**
Limmat,R Switzerland **33D1**
Limmen Netherlands **32C2**
Limmen Bight *bay* *N Terr.* Australia **99H2**
Límni Greece **47D5**
Límnos *island* Greece **47E4**
Limoges France **42D4**
Limon *Col.* USA **82G3**
Limón Costa Rica **89C4**
Limousin *prov.* France **42D4**
Limoux France **43E5**
Limpopo,R Mozambique **72E4**
Limu *island* Tonga **95V30**
Lin'an China **55K7**
Linares Chile **91B5**
Linares Mexico **88E3**
Linares Spain **40E3**
Lincheng China **54H4**
Linchwan = Fuzhou
Lincoln Argentina **91D4**
Lincoln *Calif.* USA **80C6**
Lincoln *England* UK **25G6**
Lincoln *Ill.* USA **83P2**
Lincoln *Maine* USA **78D4**
Lincoln *Mich.* USA **79E3**
Lincoln *Nebr.* USA **83K2**
Lincoln New Zealand **100E6**
Lincoln Edge *hills* *England* UK **25H6**
Lincoln I *Paracel Is* China **57E3**
Lincoln Sea Arctic Ocean **14Q1**
Lincolnshire *county* *England* UK **25H6**
Lincolnton *N Car.* USA **85G3**
Lincoln Wolds *upland* *England* UK **25H6**
Lindau W Germany **36C5**
Linden Berg *mts* Switzerland **33D1**
Lindesay,Mt *Queens.* Australia **99L5**
Lindesnes Norway **35B7**
Lindi Tanzania **71H6**
Lindley South Africa **72D5**
Lindos *Ródhos* Greece **47G6**
Lindsay *Ont.* Canada **79G3**
Line,Is Pacific Ocean **95L7**
Linfen China **54F4**
Lingao China **55E13**
Lingayen Philippines **53H7**
Lingbao China **54F5**
Lingbi China **54J6**
Lingbo Sweden **35G6**
Lingchuan China **54G5**
Lingchuan China **55F10**
Lingen W Germany **36B2**
Lingga *island* Indonesia **53D11**
Lingling China **55F9**
Lingshan China **55E11**
Lingshi China **54F4**
Lingshut China **55F13**
Lingtai China **54D5**
Linguère Senegal **68B5**
Lingwu China **54D3**
Ling Xian China **55G9**
Lingyun China **55D10**
Linhai China **55L8**
Linhares Brazil **93J7**
Linhe China **54D2**
Linköping Sweden **35F7**
Linkuva *Lith.* USSR **35K8**
Linli China **55F8**
Linlithgow *Scotland* UK **29J8**
Linn *Mo* USA **83N3**
Linnhe,Loch *Scotland* UK **29E6**
Linosa *island* Medit. Sea **45D8**
L'Inoudine,Mt *Corsica* France **43K7**
Linqing China **54H4**
Linru China **54G5**
Linshui China **55D7**
Linslade *England* UK **27N5**
Lintan China **54B5**
Lintao China **54B5**
Linthal Switzerland **33D2**
Linth,R Switzerland **33E2**
Linton *Que.* Canada **79K2**
Linwu China **55G10**
Linxi China **52G2**
Linxia China **54B5**
Lin Xian China **54F4**
Lin Xian China **54H4**
Linxiang China **55G8**
Linyi China **54F5**
Linyi China **54K5**
Linying China **54G6**
Linz Austria **36F4**
Lion,G du France **43E5**
Lion Point *NW Terr.* Canada **76G2**
Lio Porgyul,Mt *Tibet* China **58E2**
Liouesso Congo **70D4**
Lipa Yugoslavia **44F3**
Lipari Italy **45E6**
Lipari Is Italy **45E6**
Lipetsk USSR **48L5**
Liping China **55E9**
Lipovets *Ukrain.* USSR **48F7**
Lippstadt W Germany **36C3**
Lipsói *island* Greece **47F6**
Liptrap,C *Vic.* Australia **97C3**
Lipu China **55F10**
Lira Uganda **71G4**
Lircay Peru **92C6**
Lisala Zaire **70E4**
Lisboa Portugal **40B3**
Lisbon = Lisboa
Lisburn N Ireland **30L4**
Lisburne,C *Alaska* USA **87W12**
liscannor B Ireland, Rep. of **31E8**
Lisdoonvarna Ireland, Rep. of **31E7**
Lishi China **54F4**
Lishui China **54K7**
Li Shui *river* China **55F8**
Lishun China **55K8**
Lisianski,I *Hawaii* USA **94J5**
Lisichonsk USSR **48L7**
Lisieux France **42D2**
Liskeard *England* UK **26F8**
L'Isle Switzerland **33B2**
L'Islet *Que.* Canada **79L2**
Lismore Ireland, Rep. of **31H9**
Lismore *NSW* Australia **99L5**
Lismore,I *Scotland* UK **29E6**
Lisnaskea N Ireland **30J5**
Listowel Ireland, Rep. of **31E9**
Listowel *Ont.* Canada **79F4**
Lit. Barrier I New Zealand **100F3**
Litchfield *Ill.* USA **83P3**
Litchfield *Minn.* USA **81K3**
Lit. Colorado,R *Ariz.* USA **82C5**
Lithgow *NSW* Australia **97D2**
Lithinon,C *Kríti* Greece **47E7**
Lithuania *rep.* USSR **35K9**
Litoměrice Czech. **36F3**
Litovskaya SSR *rep.* USSR **50D4**
Little Abaco I The Bahamas **89D1**
Little Andaman *Andaman Is* India **59H6**
Little Belt Mts *Mont.* USA **81B2**
Little Cayman *island* West Indies **89C3**
Little Coco I Bay of Bengal **59H6**
Little Current *Ont.* Canada **79E3**
Little Desert *Vic.* Australia **97B3**
Little Falls *Minn.* USA **81K2**
Little Falls *NY* USA **84D1**
Little Gandak,R India **61E2**
Littlehampton *England* UK **27N7**
Little Horn Mts *Ariz.* USA **80G9**
Little Inagua *island* The Bahamas **89E2**
Little Mecatina I *Que.* Canada **78J1**
Little Minch *Scotland* UK **28C4**
Little Nicobar *island* *Nicobar Is* India **59H7**
Little Ouse,R *England* UK **27Q4**
Little,R *Mo* USA **83P4**
Little Rock *Ark.* USA **83M5**
Little Rocky Mts *Mont.* USA **81C2**
Little Smoky,R *Alta* Canada **76H6**
Littleton *Col.* USA **82F3**
Littleton *New H* USA **79L3**
Little Valley *NY* USA **84B1**
Litunde Mozambique **71H7**
Liuba China **54D6**
Liucheng China **55E10**
Liuchiu Hsu *island* Taiwan **55L11**
Liuchong He *river* China **55C9**
Liuheng Dao *island* China **55M8**
Liupan Shan *mts* China **54C5**
Liusvaara *Karel.* USSR **34P5**
Liuzhou China **55E10**
Live Oak *Fla* USA **85F5**
Livermore *Calif.* USA **80C7**
Liverpool *England* UK **25C6**
Liverpool *No. Sc.* Canada **78F4**
Liverpool *NSW* Australia **97D2**
Liverpool, B *England* UK **25B5**
Liverpool Coast Greenland **14N2**
Liverpool Ra *mts NSW* Australia **97D2**
Livingston *Ala.* USA **85C4**
Livingston Guatemala **88G4**
Livingston *Mont.* USA **81B3**
Livingston *Scotland* UK **29J8**
Livingston *Tenn.* USA **85E2**
Livingston *Texas* USA **83L7**
Livingstone = Maramba
Livingstone Zambia **72D3**
Livingston I Antarctica **15S3**
Livingstonia Malawi **71G7**
Livno Yugoslavia **44F4**
Livny USSR **48K5**
Livo Joki,R Finland **34M4**
Livorno Italy **44C4**
Livramento Brazil **91E4**
Liwale Tanzania **71H6**
Li Xian China **54B7**
Li Xian China **54C5**
Li Xian China **55F8**
Liyang China **54K7**
Lizard *England* UK **26D9**
Lizard Point *England* UK **26D9**
Ljubljana Yugoslavia **44E2**
Ljubuški Yugoslavia **44F4**
Ljungan,R Sweden **34G5**
Ljungdalen Sweden **34E5**
Ljusdal Sweden **35G6**
Ljusnan,R Sweden **34E5**
Llanadog *Wales* UK **26G5**
Llandaff *Wales* UK **26H6**
Llandeilo *Wales* UK **26G5**
Llandovery *Wales* UK **26G5**
Llandrindod Wells *Wales* UK **26H4**
Llandudno South Africa **72H10**
Llandudno *Wales* UK **26G2**
Llanelli *Wales* UK **26F5**
Llanerchymedd *Wales* UK **26F2**
Llanes Spain **40D1**
Llanfairfechan *Wales* UK **26G2**
Llanfyllin *Wales* UK **26H3**
Llangernyw *Wales* UK **26G2**
Llangollen *Wales* UK **26H3**
Llanguihue,L Chile **91B6**
Llanllyfni *Wales* UK **26F2**
Llano Estacado *plat. New Mex.* USA **82G5**
Llanos de Chiquitos *lowland* Bolivia **92E7**
Llanos de Guarayos *lowland* Bolivia **92E7**

Llanos de Mojas Lymington

Llanos de Mojas *lowland* Bolivia 92E6
Llanrhaiadr *Wales* UK 26H3
Llanrwst *Wales* UK 26G2
Llanwrtyd Wells *Wales* UK 26G4
Llanymynech *Wales* UK 26H3
Lleida Spain 41G2
Lleida *prov.* Spain 41G1
Llerena Spain 40C3
Lleyn Pen. *Wales* UK 26E3
Llico Chile 91B4
Lliria Spain 41F3
Lloydminster *Sask.* Canada 76J6
Lluchmayor *Balearic Is* Spain 41H3
Llullaillaco *mt* Chile 91C2
Llungan,R Sweden 34E5
Lluta,R Chile 91C1
Llwyngwril *Wales* UK 26F3
Llyn Brenig *res. Wales* UK 26G2
Loange,R Zaire 70D6
Loango Congo 70C5
Lobbes Belgium 32C4
Loberia Argentina 91E5
Lobito Angola 70C7
Lobonas Sweden 35F6
Lobos Argentina 91E5
Lobos,I de Mexico 88E3
Locarno Switzerland 33D2
Lochaber *Scotland* UK 29F6
Lochalsh *Ont.* Canada 79D1
Lochboisdale *Scotland* UK 28B5
Lochbuie *Scotland* UK 29E7
Lochcarron *Scotland* UK 28E5
Lochearnhead *Scotland* UK 29H7
Lochem Netherlands 32E2
Lochgelly *Scotland* UK 29K7
Lochgilphead *Scotland* UK 29F7
Lochgoilhead *Scotland* UK 29G7
Lochinver *Scotland* UK 28F3
Loch Lomond *Scotland* UK 29G7
Lochmaben *Scotland* UK 29K9
Lochmaddy *Scotland* UK 28B4
Lochnagar *mt Scotland* UK 28K6
Loch Ness *Scotland* UK 28G5
Lochristie Belgium 32B3
Lochy,L *Scotland* UK 28G6
Lockeport *No. Sc.* Canada 78F5
Lockerbie *Scotland* UK 29K9
Lockhart *NSW* Australia 97C3
Lock Haven *Pa* USA 84C2
Lockport *NY* USA 84B1
Loc Ninh Vietnam 53E8
Locri Italy 45F6
Lod Israel 64C6
Loddon,R *Vic.* Australia 97B3
Lodeynoye Pole USSR 48H1
Lodhran Pakistan 60B6
Lodi *Calif.* USA 80C6
Lodi Italy 44B3
Lodi *Wis.* USA 79B4
Lødingen Norway 34F2
Lodwar Kenya 71H4
Łódź Poland 37H3
Łódź *Voivodship* Poland 37H3
Loenen Netherlands 32D2
Lofer Austria 36E5
Lofoten,Is Norway 34E2
Loftus *England* UK 25G3
Logan *Utah* USA 82C2
Logandale *Nev.* USA 80F7
Logan,Mt *Que.* Canada 78E2
Logan,Mt *Yukon* Canada 76C4
Logansport *Ind.* USA 79C5
Lögde Alv *river* Sweden 34H4
Loge,R Angola 70C6
Logone,R Cameroun/Chad 69H6
Logroño Spain 41E1
Lohardaga India 61E4
Loharu India 60D6
Lohja Finland 35L6
Loikaw Burma 59J5
Loimaa Finland 35K6
Loire *dep.* France 42E4
Loire Atlantique *dep.* France 42C3
Loire,R France 42C3
Loiret *dep.* France 42E3
Loir-et-Cher *dep.* France 42D3
Loir,R France 42C3
Loja Ecuador 92B4
Loja Spain 40D4
Lokandu Zaire 70F5
Lokeren Belgium 32B3
Lokka Finland 34M3
Løkken Denmark 35C8
Løkken Norway 34C5
Lokoja Nigeria 68G7
Lokoro,R Zaire 70D5
Loks I *NW Terr.* Canada 77T4
Lola Angola 70C7
Lolland,I Denmark 35D9
Lolo *Mont.* USA 80F2
Lom Bulgaria 46D3
Loman *Minn.* USA 81L1
Lomani,R Zaire 70F5
Lomas Colorados *region* Argentina 91C6
Lomas de Zamora Argentina 91E4
Lombard *Mont.* USA 81B2
Lombardia *region* Italy 44B3
Lomblen,I Indonesia 53H12
Lombok *island* Indon. 53G12
Lome Togo 68F7
Lomela Zaire 70E5
Lomie Cameroun 69H8
Lommel Belgium 32D3
Lomond Hills *upland* Scotland UK 29K7
Lompoc *Calif.* USA 80C8
Łomża Poland 37J2
Lonaken Belgium 32D4
Loncoché Chile 91B5
Loncopué Argentina 91B5
Londiani Kenya 71H5
London *England* UK 27P5
London *Ont.* Canada 79F4
Londonderry *N Ireland* UK 30J3
Londonderry *county* N Ireland UK 30J4
Londonderry,C *W Aus.* Australia 98F2
Londonderry,I Chile 91B9
Lone Pine *Calif.* USA 80D7
Long'an China 55D11
Longa,R Angola 72B3
Long B *S Car.* USA 85H4
Long Beach *Calif.* USA 80D9
Long Beach *New J* USA 84D3
Long Branch *New J* USA 84D2
Longchamps Belgium 32D4
Longchang China 55C8
Longchuan China 55H10
Long Eaton *England* UK 25F7
Longford Ireland, Rep. of 30H6
Longford *Tas.* Australia 97F5
Longford *county* Ireland,Rep. of 30H6
Longhua China 54J2
Long I *No. Sc.* Canada 78E4
Long I *NY* USA 84E2
Long I The Bahamas 89D2
Long Island City *NY* USA 84E2
Long Island Sd *Conn./NY* USA 84E2
Long Jiang China 55E10
Longkou China 54L4
Long L *Maine* USA 78D3
Long L *Ont.* Canada 77O7
Long,L *Scotland* UK 29G7
Longli China 55D9
Longlin China 55C10
Long Melford *England* UK 27R4
Longmen China 55H11
Longming China 55D11
Longmont *Col.* USA 82F2
Longnan China 55H10
Long Point *Ont.* Canada 79F4
Long Prairie *Minn.* USA 81K2
Longquan China 55K8
Longquan Xi *river* China 55K8
Long Ra *mts* Newf. Canada 78K2
Long Range Mts *Newf.* Canada 78J2
Longreach *Queens.* Australia 99J4
Longshan China 55E8
Longsheng China 55E10
Longsheng China 55G11
Longs Pk *Col.* USA 82F2
Long Stratton England UK 27S4
Long Sutton *England* UK 27Q3
Longton *England* UK 25D7
Longtown *England* UK 25C2
Longué France 42C3
Longueuil *Que.* Canada 79K3
Longuyon France 42F2
Longview *Texas* USA 83L6
Longview *Wash.* USA 80B2
Longwy France 42F2
Longxi China 54C5
Long Xian China 54D5
Long Xuyen Vietnam 57D4
Longyan China 55J10
Longzhou China 55D11
Lonneker Netherlands 32E2
Lons le Saunier France 42F3
Looc Philippines 53H8
Looe,East *England* UK 26F8
Lookout,C *N Car.* USA 85J3
Lookout,C *Oreg.* USA 80A3
Loolmalasin,Mt Tanzania 71H5
Loop Hd Ireland, Rep. of 31D8
Lopez,C Gabon 70B5
Lopik Netherlands 32C3
Lop Nur *lake Xinjiang* China 52B2
Lopphavet *bay* Norway 34J1
Lorain *Ohio* USA 79E5
Loralai Pakistan 58C2
Loranchet Pen. Kerguelen 65S12
Lorca Spain 41F4
Lord Howe,I Pacific Ocean 94F11
Lord Loughborough,I Burma 59J6
Lordsburg *New Mex.* USA 82D6
Lorena Brazil 93J8
Loreto Brazil 93H5
Loreto Italy 44D4
Loreto Mexico 88B2
Lorient France 42B3
Lorne *Vic.* Australia 97B3
Lorn, Firth of *bay* Scotland UK 29E7
Lorrach W Germany 36B5
Lorraine *prov.* France 42G2
Los Alamos *New Mex.* USA 82E5
Los Andes Chile 91B4
Los Angeles *Calif.* USA 80D8
Los Angeles Chile 91B5
Los Blancos Argentina 91D2
Los Gatos *Calif.* USA 80B7
Los Hermanos *islands* Venezuela 92E1
Lošinj *island* Yugoslavia 44E3
Los Lagos *prov.* Chile 91B6
Los Menucos Argentina 91C6
Los Mochis Mexico 88C2
Los Pozos Chile 91B3
Los Roques *islands* Venezuela 92D1
Los Santos Panama 89C5
Los Santos de Maimona Spain 40C3
Lossiemouth *Scotland* UK 28K4
Lossie,R *Scotland* UK 28K4
Los Teques Venezuela 92D1
Los Testigos *islands* Venezuela 92E1
Los Tigres Argentina 91D3
Lost River Mts *Idaho* USA 80G3
Lost Trail P *Mont.* USA 80G3
Lostwithiel *England* UK 26E8
Los Vilos Chile 91B4
Lot *dep.* France 43D4
Lota Chile 91B5
Lotbinière *Que.* Canada 79L2
Lot-et-Garonne *dep.* France 43D4
Lothian *region* Scotland UK 29K8
Lot,R France 43D4
Lötschberg Tun. Switzerland 33C2
Lötschen Tal *valley* Switzerland 33C2
Lottigna Switzerland 33D2
Loubet Coast Antarctica 15S3
Loudeac France 42B2
Loudima Congo 70C5
Loudon Malawi 71G7
Loudon *Tenn.* USA 85E3
Loudun France 42D3
Louga Senegal 68B5
Loughborough *England* UK 25F7
Lough Foyle N Ireland 30J3
Lough Neagh N Ireland 30L4
Loughor *Wales* UK 26F5
Loughrea Ireland, Rep. of 31F7
Louhans France 42F3
Louisa *Ky* USA 85F1
Louisburg *N Car.* USA 85H2
Louiseville *Que.* Canada 79K2
Louisiade Arch. Papua New Guinea 99L2
Louisiana *state* USA 87H5
Louis Trichardt South Africa 72D4
Louisville *Ky* USA 85E1
Louisville *Miss.* USA 85C4
Loule Portugal 40B4
Loup City *Nebr.* USA 83J2
Lourdes France 43C5
Lourenço Marques = Maputo
Lourinhã Portugal 40B3
Louth *England* UK 25H6
Louth Ireland, Rep. of 30K6
Louth *NSW* Australia 97C2
Louth *county* Ireland,Rep. of 30K6
Louvain = Leuven
Louveigne Belgium 32D4
Louviers France 42D2
Lövanger Sweden 34J4
Lövberga Sweden 34G5
Loveland *Col.* USA 82F2
Lovell *Wyo.* USA 81C3
Lovelock *Nev.* USA 80D5
Loviisa Finland 35M6
Lovington *New Mex.* USA 82G6
Lövlid Sweden 34G4
Lowa Zaire 70F5
Lowarai P Pakistan 60B3
Low,C *NW Terr.* Canada 77O4
Lowell *Mass.* USA 84F1
Lowell *Mich.* USA 79D4
Lowell *Oreg.* USA 80B4
Lower Brule *S Dak.* USA 81H3
Lower Hutt New Zealand 100F5
Lowestoft *England* UK 27T4
Lowick *England* UK 25E1
Łowicz Poland 37H2
Lowland *N Car.* USA 85J3
Lowville *NY* USA 79J4
Loxton *S Aus.* Australia 97B2
Loyaute,Is Pacific Ocean 94G10
Loyne,L *Scotland* UK 28F5
Lozère *dep.* France 43E4
Lozin *island* Malaysia 57C5
Loznica Yugoslavia 46B2
Luachima Angola 70E6
Lualaba,R Zaire 70F5
Luampa Zambia 72C3
Lu'an China 54J7
Luanda Angola 70C6
Luanda *region* Angola 70D6
Luang Prabang Laos 57C3
Luan He *river* China 54J2
Luanping China 54J2
Luan Xian China 54K3
Luarca Spain 40C1
Luashi Zaire 70E7
Lubaczow Poland 37K3
Lubāna *Latvia* USSR 35M8
Lubānas Ezers *lake* Latvia USSR 35M8
Lubango Angola 70C7
Lubartow Poland 37K3
Lubben E Germany 36E3
Lubbock *Texas* USA 82H6
Lubeck *Vic.* Australia 97B3
Lübeck W Germany 36D2
Lübecker B Germany 36D1
Lubefu Zaire 70E5
Lubin Poland 37G3
Lublin Poland 37K3
Lublin *voivodship* Poland 37K3
Lubliniec Poland 37H3
Lubnaig,L *Scotland* UK 29H7
Lubumbashi Zaire 71F7
Lubutu Zaire 70F5
Lucala Angola 70D6
Lucan Ireland, Rep. of 31L7
Lucania = Basilicata
Lucca Italy 44C4
Lucea Jamaica 89D3
Luce B *Scotland* UK 29G10
Lucena Spain 40D4
Lučenec Czech. 37H4
Lucens Switzerland 33B2
Lucera Italy 45E5
Lucerne = Luzern
Luch USSR 49F2
Luchiang Taiwan 55L10
Luchuan China 55F11
Lucia *Calif.* USA 80C7
Lucile *Idaho* USA 80E3
Lucinda *Pa* USA 84B2
Lucindale *S Aus.* Australia 97B3
Lucira Angola 70C7
Luckau E Germany 36E3
Luckenwalde E Germany 36E2
Lucknow India 61C2
Lucknow *Ont.* Canada 79F4
Lucon France 42C3
Lüda China 54L3
Luderitz Namibia 72B5
Luderitz B South Africa 72B5
Ludgershall *England* UK 27L6
Ludhiana India 60D5
Ludington *Mich.* USA 79C4
Ludlow *England* UK 26J4
Ludogorie *region* Bulgaria 46F3
Ludvika Sweden 35F6
Ludwigsburg W Germany 36C4
Ludwigshafen W Germany 36C4
Ludwigslust E Germany 36D2
Ludza *Latvia* USSR 35M8
Luebo Zaire 70E6
Luena,R Angola 70E7
Lueno Angola 70D7
Lueyang China 54D6
Lufeng China 55H11
Luga USSR 48F2
Lugano Switzerland 33D2
Lugasi India 61B3
Lugenda,R Mozambique 71H7
Lugnezer Tal *valley* Switzerland 33E2
Lugo Italy 44C3
Lugo Spain 40C1
Lugo *prov.* Spain 40C1
Lugoj Romania 46C2
Lugovay *Kazakh.* USSR 50J5
Luhit,R India 59J3
Luichow Pen. = Leizhou Bandao
Luik = Liège
Luimneach = Limerick
Luinana Angola 72C3
Luinana,R Angola 72C3
Luing *Scotland* UK 29E7
Luitpold Coast Antarctica 15A2
Luiyang China 54L4
Luján Argentina 91C4
Lujan Argentina 91E4
Lujiang China 54J7
Lujin China 54K4
Lukenie,R Zaire 70D5
Lukmanier P Switzerland 33D2
Lukolela Zaire 70D5
Lukovit Bulgaria 46E3
Łuków Poland 37K3
Lukoyanov USSR 49G3
Lukuga,R Zaire 71F6
Lukula Zaire 70C6
Lulea Sweden 34K4
Lule Älv *river* Sweden 34J3
Lüleburgaz Turkey 46F4
Luliang China 55B10
Luliang Shan *mts* China 54F4
Lulong China 54K3
Lulonga,R Zaire 70E4
Lulu,R Zaire 70E4
Lumbala Angola 70E7
Lumberton *N Car.* USA 85H3
Lumbres France 42D1
Lummen Belgium 32D4
Lumsden New Zealand 100C7
Lumsden *Scotland* UK 28L5
Luna,L Argentina 91E3
Lunan China 55B10
Lunan B *Scotland* UK 29M6
Lund Sweden 35E9
Lund *Utah* USA 80G6
Lundy,I *England* UK 26E6
Lüneburg W Germany 36D2
Lüneburger Heide *region* W Germany 36D2
Lunel France 43E5
Lune,R *England* UK 25C4
Lunéville France 42G2
Luni India 58D3
Luning *Nev.* USA 80D6
Lunino USSR 49G4
Luni,R India 58D3
Lunkha India 60C6
Lunz Austria 36F5
Luocheng China 55E10
Luochuan China 54E5
Luodian China 55D10
Luoding China 55F11
Luoding Jiang *river* China 55F11
Luohe China 54H6
Luo He *river* China 54E4
Luo He *river* China 54F5
Luolo Kivu Zaire 71F5
Luoning China 54F5
Luoping China 55C10
Luoqing Jiang *river* China 55E10
Luoshan China 54H6
Luotian China 54H7
Luoyang China 54G5
Lupiro Tanzania 71H6
Lupkow Poland 37K4
Luputa Zaire 70E6
Luray *Va* USA 85H1
Lure France 42G3
Lurgan N Ireland 30L5
Luribay Bolivia 92D7
Lurøy Norway 34E3
Lusaka Zambia 72D3
Lusambo Zaire 70E5
Lushi China 54F5
Lushnjë Albania 47B4
Lushun China 54L3
Lusk *Wyo.* USA 81E4
Luss *Scotland* UK 29G7
Lussac France 42C3
Lu Tao *island* Taiwan 55L11
Lut Des. = Dasht-e Lut
Luther *Mich.* USA 79D3
Luthernbad Switzerland 33C1
Luton *England* UK 27P5
Lutry Switzerland 33B2
Lutsen *Minn.* USA 79A2
Lutsk *Ukrain.* USSR 48D6
Luttre Belgium 32C4
Luvia Finland 35J6
Luvua,R Zaire 71F6
Luwuk *Celebes* Indon. 53H11
Luxembourg Luxembourg 36A4
Luxembourg *country* Europe 32D5
Luxembourg *prov.* Belgium 32D5
Luxemburg = Luxembourg
Luxeuil France 42G3
Luxi China 55B10
Luxi China 55F8
Luxor Egypt 69M3
Luyi China 54H6
Luzern Switzerland 33D1
Luzern *canton* Switzerland 33C1
Luzhou China 55C8
Luziana Brazil 93H7
Luzon *island* Philippines 53H7
Luzon Str. Philippines 52H6
Luzy France 42E3
L'vov *Ukrain.* USSR 48D7
Lybster *Scotland* UK 28K3
Lycksele Sweden 34H4
Lydda = Lod
Lydenburg South Africa 72E5
Lydford *England* UK 26F7
Lydney *England* UK 26J5
Lyduenai *Lith.* USSR 35K9
Lye *England* UK 27K4
Lyell,Mt *BC* Canada 76H6
Lyell,Mt *Calif.* USA 80D7
Lyell Ra *mts* New Zealand 100E5
Lykens *Pa* USA 84C2
Lyme B *England* UK 26H7
Lyme Regis *England* UK 26J7
Lymington *England* UK 27L7

Lynchburg, Mammoth Cave

Lynchburg Va USA 85H2
Lyndhurst S Aus. Australia 97A2
Lyngdal Norway 35B7
Lyngen Norway 34J2
Lynn Mass. USA 84F1
Lynton England UK 26G6
Lyon France 42F4
Lyonnais prov. France 42F4
Lyons Ga USA 85F4
Lyons Kans. USA 83J3
Lyons NY USA 84C1
Lyons,R W Aus. Australia 98D4
Łyse Poland 37J2
Lysekil Sweden 35D7
Lys,R = Leie,R
Lyss Switzerland 33C1
Lyster Que. Canada 79L2
Lys'va USSR 49N1
Lytham St Annes England UK 25B5
Lyttelton New Zealand 100E6
Lytton BC Canada 76G6

M

Maaia Mozambique 71J7
Ma'an Jordan 64D7
Maarheeze Netherlands 32D3
Maarianhamina = Mariehamn
Ma'arret en Numan Syria 64E2
Maarssen Netherlands 32D2
Maasbree Netherlands 32E3
Maaseik Belgium 32D3
Maasmechelen Belgium 32D4
Maas,R Netherlands 32D3
Maassluis Netherlands 32C3
Maastricht Belgium 32D4
Maatsuyker Is Tas. Australia 97F5
Mabian China 55B8
Mablethorpe England UK 25J6
Mabote Mozambique 72E4
Mabton Wash. USA 80C2
Mabuki Tanzania 71G5
McAdam New Br. Canada 78E4
Macaé Brazil 93J8
Macaiba Brazil 93K5
McAlester Okla. USA 83L5
Macalister Mt NSW Australia 97C2
Macalister,R Vic. Australia 97C3
Macao SE Asia 55G11
Macapá Brazil 93G3
Macás Ecuador 92B4
Macau Brazil 93K5
Macauba Brazil 93G6
Macau I China 55G11
Macaulay I Kermadec Is 94J10
M'Banza Congo Angola 70C6
McCammon Idaho USA 80G4
McCann Calif. USA 80B5
Macclesfield England UK 25D6
McClintock Chan. NW Terr. Canada 76L2
McCloud Calif. USA 80B5
McClure,C NW Terr. Canada 76G2
McClure Str. NW Terr. Canada 76H2
McComb Miss. USA 85B5
McConnellsburg Pa USA 84B3
McCook Nebr. USA 82H2
McDermitt Nev. USA 80E5
Macdonald,L W Aus. Australia 98F4
Macdonnell Ra mts N Terr. Australia 98G4
McDouall Ra mts N Terr. Australia 99G3
Macduff Scotland UK 28M4
Macedon mt Vic. Australia 97B3
Macedonia = Makedonija
Maceió Brazil 93K5
Macenta Guinea 68D7
Macerata Italy 44D4
McGill Nev. USA 80F6
Macgillycuddy's Reeks mts Ireland, Rep. of 31D10
McGregor Texas USA 83K7
McGregor Ra mts Queens. Australia 99J5
Mach Pakistan 58C3
Machakos Kenya 71H5
Machala Ecuador 92B4
Machareti Bolivia 92E8
Macheng China 54H7
Machghara Lebanon 64D4
Machhlishahr India 61D3
Machias Maine USA 78E4
Machias B Maine USA 78E4
Machiasport Maine USA 78E4
Machilipatnam India 58F5
Machiques Venezuela 92C1
Machiwara India 60E5
Machu Picchu Peru 92C6
Machynlleth Wales UK 26G3
Măcin Romania 46G2
McIntosh S Dak. USA 81G3
Mackay Idaho USA 80G4
Mackay Queens. Australia 99K4
Mackay L NW Terr. Canada 76J4
Mackay,L W Aus. Australia 98F4
McKean I Phoenix Is 94J8
McKeesport Pa USA 84B2
McKenzie Tenn. USA 85C2
Mackenzie B Antarctica 15F3
Mackenzie B NW Terr./Yukon Canada 76D3
McKenzie Fork,R Oreg. USA 80B3
Mackenzie King I NW Terr. Canada 76J1
Mackenzie Mts NW Terr. Canada 76E4
Mackenzie,R NW Terr. Canada 76F3
Mackinac I Mich. USA 79D3
Mackinac,Str. of Mich. USA 79D3
Mackinaw City Mich. USA 79D3
McKinley,Mt Alaska USA 87X12
Mackintosh,L Tas. Australia 97F5
Mackintosh,Mt Antarctica 15L2
McKittrick Calif. USA 80D8
Macksville NSW Australia 97D2
Maclean NSW Australia 97D1
McLeansboro Ill. USA 83P3
Macleay,R NSW Australia 97D2
McLeod B NW Terr. Canada 76J4
McLoughlin,Mt Oreg. USA 80B4
MacMahon Algeria 68F3
McMillan,L New Mex. USA 82F6
Macmillan,R Yukon Canada 76E4
Macmillan Ra mts Yukon Canada 76D4
McMinnville Oreg. USA 80B3
McMinnville Tenn. USA 85E3
McMurdo Sd Antarctica 15L2
McNary Ariz. USA 82D5
Macomb Ill. USA 83N2
Macomer Sardinia Italy 45B5
Macon Belgium 32C4
Mâcon France 42F3
Macon Ga USA 85F4
Macon Miss. USA 85C4
Macon Mo USA 83M3
McPherson Kans. USA 83K3
Macpherson Ra mts Queensland 99L5
Macquarie NSW Australia 97C2
Macquarie Harb. Tas. Australia 97F5
Macquarie,I Pacific Ocean 94F13
Macquarie,L NSW Australia 97D2
Macquarie Marshes NSW Australia 97C2
Macquarie Mt NSW Australia 97C2
Macquarie,R Tas. Australia 97F5
McRae Ga USA 85F4
MacRobertson Land region Antarctica 15F2
Macroom Ireland, Rep. of 31F10
Macuata,I Vanua Levu Fiji 94A24
Macuje Colombia 92C3
Macusani Peru 92C6
McVicar Arm bay NW Terr. Canada 76H3
Madaba Jordan 64D6
Madagascar,I Indian Ocean 71N9
Madahy Brazil 93H5
Madain Salih Saudi Arabia 62D4
Madan Iran 63H2
Madaoua Niger 68G6
Madaripur Bangladesh 59H4
Madawaska Ont. Canada 79G3
Maddaloni Italy 45E5
Madeira Is Atlantic Ocean 68B2
Madeira,R Brazil 92E5
Madeleine,C de la Que. Canada 78F2
Madeleine,Is de la Que. Canada 78G3
Madeline Calif. USA 80C5
Madera Calif. USA 80C7
Madhepur India 61F2
Madhipura India 61F3
Madhopur India 60D4
Madhubani India 61F2
Madhupur India 61F3
Madhya Pradesh state India 58E4
Madinat ash Sh'ab South Yemen 62E7
Madi,R 61E1
Madison Ga USA 85F4
Madison Kans. USA 83K3
Madison N Car. USA 85H2
Madison Nebr. USA 83K2
Madison New J USA 84D2
Madison S Dak. USA 81J3
Madison Wis. USA 79B4
Madison Ra mts Mont. USA 80H3
Madisonville Ky USA 85D2
Madoc Ont. Canada 79H3
Madona Latvia USSR 35M8
Madras India 58F6
Madre de Dios,R Bolivia/Peru 92D6
Madre de Dois,I Chile 91A8
Madre del Sur,Sa mts Mexico 88D4
Madre Occidental,Sa mts Mexico 88C2
Madre Oriental,Sa mts Mexico 88D2
Madre,Sa mts Wyo. USA 81D5
Madrid New Mex. USA 82E5
Madrid Spain 40E2
Madrid region Spain 40E2
Madridejos Spain 40E3
Madura island Indonesia 53F12
Madurai India 58E7
Maebashi Japan 56F6
Maeseyck = Maaseik
Maestra,Sa Cuba 89D2
Mafeking South Africa 72D5
Mafia,I Tanzania 71H6
Mafra Portugal 40B3
Mafraq Jordan 64E5
Magadan USSR 51S4
Magadanskaya region USSR 51T3
Magadi Kenya 71H5
Magadino Switzerland 33D2
Magad Plat. = Jöl Plat.
Magaliesburg South Africa 72M11
Magallanes = Punta Arenas
Magallanes Antartica Chilena arch. Chile 91A8
Magallanes,Estrecho de Chile 91B8
Magangue Colombia 92C2
Magaz Spain 40D2
Magbar India 61D2
Magburaka Sierra Leone 68C7
Magdala Ethiopia 71H2
Magdalena Bolivia 92E6
Magdalena Mexico 88B1
Magdalena New Mex. USA 82E5
Magdalena,B Mexico 88B3
Magdalena,I Chile 91B6
Magdalena,R Colombia 92C2
Magdalena,R Mexico 88B1
Magdalen Is = Madeleine,Is de la
Magdeburg E Germany 36D2
Magee,I N Ireland 30M4
Magellan, Str. of = Magallanes,Estrecho de
Magerøya,I Norway 34L1
Magerrain mt Switzerland 33E1
Maggia Switzerland 33D2
Maggiore,L Italy 44B2
Magharee Is Ireland, Rep. Of 31C9
Maghera N Ireland UK 30K4
Magherafelt N Ireland UK 30K4
Maglaj Yugoslavia 46B2
Maglie Italy 45G5
Magnessia dist. Greece 47D5
Magnitogorsk USSR 49P4
Magnolia Ala. USA 85D4
Magnolia Ark. USA 83M6
Magnolia Miss. USA 85B5
Magnolia N Car. USA 85H3
Magog Que. Canada 79K3
Magpie Que. Canada 78F1
Magpie L Que. Canada 78F1
Maguan China 55C11
Maguarinho,C Brazil 93H4
Magwe Burma 59J4
Magwe prov. Burma 59H4
Mahabad Iran 62F2
Mahabaleshwar India 58D5
Mahaban India 60E7
Mahaban India 61A2
Mahabharat Ra mts Nepal 61E2
Mahadday Weyn Somalia 71K4
Mahadeo Hills India 61A4
Mahagi Uganda 71G4
Mahail Saudi Arabia 62E6
Mahajamba,B de Madagascar 71N10
Mahajan India 60C6
Mahajanga Madagascar 71N10
Mahalapye Botswana 72D4
Mahallat Iran 63G3
Maham India 60E6
Mahanadi,Mouths of India 59G4
Mahanadi,R India 58F4
Mahanoro Madagascar 71N10
Mahanoy City Pa USA 84C2
Maharashtra state India 58D5
Maha Sarakham Thailand 57C3
Mahbubnagar India 58E5
Mahdia Tunisia 69H1
Mahé India 58E6
Mahé island Seychelles 71K1
Mahebourg Mauritius 65N12
Mahendragiri,Mt India 59F5
Mahenge Tanzania 71H6
Mahia Pen. New Zealand 100G4
Mahi,R India 58D4
Mahmudabad India 61C2
Mahmūdābād Iran 63G2
Mahón Menorca Spain 41J3
Mahone B No. Sc. Canada 78F4
Mahuva India 58D4
Maichen China 55E12
Maida Yemen 62E6
Maidan Afghanistan 63K3
Maidenhead England UK 27N5
Maidstone England UK 27R6
Maiduguri Nigeria 69H6
Maienfeld Switzerland 33E1
Maigualida,Serra mts Venezuela 92D2
Maigue,R Ireland, Rep. of 31F8
Maihar India 61C3
Maikal Ra mts India 58F4
Maimana Afghanistan 63J2
Main Barrier Ra mts NSW Australia 97B2
Mainburg W Germany 36D4
Mai-Ndombe,L Zaire 70D5
Maine prov. France 42C2
Maine state USA 87M2
Maine,G of USA 78D5
Main et Loire dep. France 42C3
Maing Kaing Burma 59J4
Maingkwan Burma 59J3
Mainland island Orkney Scotland 28K1
Mainland island Shetland Scotland 28Q8
Mainpuri India 61B2
Main,R N Ireland 30L4
Main,R W Germany 36C4
Mainstream Maine USA 78D4
Mainz W Germany 36C4
Maio Cape Verde 68T10
Maipo,Mt Argentina 91C4
Maipú Argentina 91E5
Maiquetía Venezuela 92D1
Maire,Estrecho de le strait Argentina 91C8
Maissin Belgium 32D5
Maithon Res. India 61F4
Mait,I Somalia 71K2
Maitland NSW Australia 97D2
Maitland S Aus. Australia 97A2
Maitland,L W Aus. Australia 98E5
Maitlands South Africa 72H9
Maiz Mexico 88E3
Maiz,Is del Nicaragua 89C4
Maizura Japan 56D7
Majagual Colombia 92C2
Majia He river China 54J4
Majiang China 55D9
Majie China 55C11
Majitha India 60D5
Majmaa Saudi Arabia 62F4
Majorca = Mallorca
Majuro,Is Marshall Is 94H7
Maka Sénégal 68C6
Makale Ethiopia 71H2
Makalu,Mt Nepal 61F2
Makanya Tanzania 71H5
Makariev USSR 49F2
Makarjev USSR 49G2
Makarwal Pakistan 60B4
Makassar = Ujung Pandang
Makassar Str. Indonesia 53G11
Makatea,I Tuamotu Arch. 95M9
Makedhonia region Greece 47C4
Makedonija rep. Yugoslavia 46C4
Makemo,I Tuamotu Arch. 95M9
Makeyevka Ukrain. USSR 48K7
Makhachkala USSR 50F5
Makindu Kenya 71H5
Makkah = Mecca
Makkinga Netherlands 32E2
Mako Hungary 46C1
Makokou Gabon 70C4
Makongai,I Viti Levu Fiji 94A25
Makongolosi Tanzania 71G6
Makorako,Mt New Zealand 100G4
Makoua Congo 70D4
Makram Saudi Arabia 62D5
Makri India 58F5
Maksamaa Finland 34K5
Maku Iran 62E2
Makum India 59J3
Makumbi Zaire 70E6
Makung Taiwan 55K11
Makurdi Nigeria 68G7
Makwa Nauru 94A22
Makwiro Zimbabwe 72E3
Mala Peru 92B6
Malå Sweden 34H4
Malabang Philippines 53H9
Malabar Coast India 58D6
Malabo Eq. Guinea 68G8
Malacca Str. Malaysia/Sumatra 57C6
Malacca, Str. of Malay/Indon 53D10
Malacoota Inlet Vic. Australia 97C3
Malad City Idaho USA 80G4
Maladeta = Montes Maldiditos
Málaga Spain 40D4
Málaga prov. Spain 40D4
Malagasy Republic = Madagascar
Malahide Ireland,Rep. of 31L7
Malaita,I Solomon Is 94G8
Malakal Sudan 69M7
Malakand Pakistan 60B3
Malakand P Pakistan 60B3
Malancha,R Bangladesh 61G5
Malang Java Indon. 53F12
Malanje Angola 70D6
Malaren,L Sweden 35G7
Malargue Argentina 91C5
Malatya Turkey 62D2
Malawi country Africa 71G7
Malayir Iran 62F3
Malaysia country SE Asia 57C5
Malazgirt Turkey 62E2
Mal B Ireland, Rep. of 31E8
Mal B Que. Canada 78F2
Malbork Poland 37H1
Malchin E Germany 36E2
Malchow E Germany 36E2
Malda India 61G3
Maldegem Belgium 32B3
Malden Mass. USA 84F1
Malden Mo USA 83N4
Malden,I Pacific Ocean 95L8
Maldive Is = Maldives
Maldives country Indian Ocean 18J9
Maldon England UK 27R5
Maldonado Uruguay 91F4
Maléa,C Greece 47D6
Maleit,L Sudan 69L7
Malé Karpaty Czech. 37G4
Malekula,I Vanuatu 94G9
Máleme Kríti Greece 47D7
Maler Kotla India 60D5
Malesherbes France 42E2
Malgomaj,R Sweden 34G4
Malheur,L Oreg. USA 80D4
Malheur,R Oreg. USA 80E4
Mali country Africa 68E5
Malihabad India 61C2
Mali Kyun island Burma 59J6
Malimba,Mts Zaire 71F6
Malinau Borneo Indon. 53G10
Malindi Kenya 71J5
Malines = Mechelen
Malin Hd Ireland, Rep. of 30J3
Malin More Ireland,Rep. of 30F4
Malkangiri India 59F5
Malkara Turkey 46F4
Malko Tŭrnovo Bulgaria 46F4
Mallacoota Vic. Australia 97C3
Mallaig Scotland UK 28E5
Mallawi Egypt 69M3
Mállia,G Kríti Greece 47E7
Malloggia = Maloja
Mallorca,I Balearic Is Spain 41H3
Mallow Ireland, Rep. of 31F9
Malmberget Sweden 34J3
Malmédy Belgium 32E4
Malmesbury England UK 27K5
Malmö Sweden 35E9
Malmohus county Sweden 35E9
Malmyzh USSR 49K2
Maloja Switzerland 33E2
Malombe,L Malawi 71H7
Malone NY USA 79J3
Malong China 55B10
Malonga Zaire 70E7
Malo Yaroslavets USSR 48K4
Malpeque Pr. Ed. I. Canada 78G3
Malpeque B Pr. Ed. I. Canada 78G3
Målselv Norway 34H2
Malta Mont. USA 81D1
Malta island Mediterranean Sea 45E8
Malta Chan. Medit. Sea 45E7
Maltahöhe Namibia 72B5
Maltby England UK 25F6
Malters Switzerland 33D1
Malton England UK 25G4
Malung Sweden 35E6
Malvaglia Switzerland 33D2
Malvan India 58D5
Malvern Ark. USA 83M5
Malvern Hills England UK 26K4
Malvina Que. Canada 79L3
Malyykavkaz mts USSR 50F5
Mama USSR 51N4
Mamantel Mexico 88F4
Mambasa Zaire 71F4
Mambone Mozambique 72F4
Mammoth Cave Ky USA 85D2

Mammoth Cave Nat. Pk Mau

Mammoth Cave Nat. Pk *Ky* USA **85D2**
Mamonovo *Lith.* USSR **35H9**
Mamou Guinea **68C6**
Mampoko Zaire **70D4**
Mam Soul *mt* Scotland UK **28F5**
Mamuju *Celebes* Indon. **53G11**
Man India **61D3**
Man Ivory Coast **68D7**
Manacapuru Brazil **92E4**
Manacor *Balearic Is* Spain **41H3**
Manado *Celebes* Indon. **53H10**
Managua Nicaragua **89B4**
Managua L Nicaragua **89B4**
Manakhah Yemen **62E6**
Manamah Bahrain **63G4**
Mananjary Madagascar **71N11**
Manantenina Madagascar **71N11**
Manapouri L New Zealand **100B7**
Manasquan *New J* USA **84D2**
Manassas *Va* USA **85J1**
Manaus Brazil **92E4**
Man Banipur India **61B3**
Manbij Syria **64F1**
Manbij Turkey **62D2**
Mancelona *Mich.* USA **79D3**
Manche *dep.* France **42C2**
Manchester *England* UK **25D5**
Manchester *Iowa* USA **83N1**
Manchester *New H* USA **84F1**
Manchester *Tenn.* USA **85D3**
Manchuria = **Heilongjiang**
Manchuria *region* China **54M2**
Manda Tanzania **71G7**
Mandal Norway **35B7**
Mandalay Burma **59J4**
Mandalgovi Mongolia **52E1**
Mandan *N Dak.* USA **81G2**
Mandargiri Hill India **61F3**
Mandera Kenya **71J4**
Mandeville Jamaica **89D3**
Mandeville *La* USA **83N7**
Mandi India **60E5**
Mandinga Panama **89D5**
Manding Mt Mali **68D6**
Mandla India **61C4**
Mandritsara Madagascar **71N10**
Manduria Italy **45F5**
Mandvi India **58C4**
Manfalut Egypt **69M3**
Manfredonia Italy **45E5**
Manfredonia,G di Italy **45E5**
Manfuha Saudi Arabia **62F5**
Mangaia,I Cook Is **95L10**
Mangakino New Zealand **100F4**
Mangaldai India **59H3**
Mangalme Chad **69J6**
Mangalore India **58D6**
Mangareva,I Tuamotu Arch. **95N10**
Mangerton *mt* Ireland,Rep. of **31E10**
Mangfall Gebirge *mts* W Germany **36D5**
Mangla India **60C4**
Manglar Alto Ecuador **92A4**
Mango Tonga **95V30**
Mangoche Malawi **71H7**
Mangoky,R Madagascar **71M11**
Mangoni New Zealand **100E2**
Mangrol India **58D4**
Mangualde Portugal **40C2**
Mangueira,L da Brazil **91F4**
Manhatten *Kans.* USA **83K3**
Manhuaça Brazil **93J8**
Manicoré Brazil **92E5**
Manicouagan Res. *Que.* Canada **78D1**
Manifold,C *Queens.* Australia **99L4**
Manihari India **61F3**
Manihi India **61E3**
Manihiki,I Pacific Ocean **94K9**
Manikarchar India **61G3**
Manikganj = **Dasara**
Manikpur Bangladesh **59H4**
Manikuagan,R *Que.* Canada **78D1**
Manila Philippines **53H8**
Manilla *NSW* Australia **97D2**
Man,I of Irish Sea **25K9**
Manipur *state* India **59H3**
Manisa Turkey **62B2**
Manistee *Mich.* USA **79C3**
Manistee,R *Mich.* USA **79D3**
Manistique *Mich.* USA **79C3**
Manitoba *prov.* Canada **76L6**
Manitoba,L *Man.* Canada **76M6**
Manitou Gorge *Que.* Canada **77S5**
Manitou Is *Mich.* USA **79C3**
Manitou,L *Que.* Canada **78F1**
Manitoulin I *Ont.* Canada **79E3**
Manitowaning *Ont.* Canada **79F3**
Manitowoc *Wis.* USA **79C3**
Maniwaki *Que.* Canada **79H2**
Maniyah Saudi Arabia **62E3**
Manizales Colombia **92B2**
Manja Madagascar **71M11**
Manjimup *W Aus.* Australia **98D6**
Manjra,R India **58E5**
Mankato *Minn.* USA **81K3**
Mankheri India **61E4**
Mankono Ivory Coast **68D7**
Manlleu Spain **41H1**
Manly *NSW* Australia **97D2**
Manmad India **58D4**
Mannahill *S Aus.* Australia **97A2**
Mannar Sri Lanka **58E7**
Mannar,G of India **58E7**
Mannargudi India **58E6**
Mannheim W Germany **36C4**
Männifluh *mt* Switzerland **33C2**
Mannin B Ireland,Rep. of **31C7**
Manning *S Car.* USA **85G4**
Manningtree *England* UK **27S5**
Mannum *S Aus.* Australia **97A2**
Manoa Bolivia **92D5**
Manokwari *New Guinea* Indon. **53K11**
Manonga Tanzania **71G5**
Manono Zaire **70F6**
Manorhamilton Ireland, Rep. of **30G5**
Manosque France **43F5**
Manouane,L *Que.* Canada **78C1**
Manresa Spain **41G2**
Mansa Zambia **72D2**
Mansehra Pakistan **60C3**
Mansel I *NW Terr.* Canada **77P4**
Mansfield *England* UK **25F6**
Mansfield *La* USA **83M6**
Mansfield *Mass.* USA **84F1**
Mansfield *Ohio* USA **79E5**
Mansfield *Pa* USA **84C2**
Mansfield *Vic.* Australia **97C3**
Mansfield,Mt *Vt* USA **79K3**
Mansi Burma **59J4**
Mansilla de Las Mulas Spain **40D1**
Manta Ecuador **92A4**
Mantaro,R Peru **92B6**
Mantes France **42D2**
Manti *Utah* USA **82C3**
Mantova Italy **44C3**
Mantta Finland **35L5**
Mantua = **Mantova**
Mantyharju Finland **35M6**
Mäntyluoto Finland **35J6**
Manu Peru **92C6**
Manua,I Samoa **94K9**
Manuel Rodriguez,I Chile **91B8**
Manūjān Iran **63H4**
Manukau New Zealand **100F3**
Manus,I Admiralty Is **94E8**
Many *La* USA **83M7**
Manyara,L Tanzania **71H5**
Manyoni Tanzania **71G6**
Manzai Pakistan **60B4**
Manzala,L Egypt **69M2**
Manzanares Spain **40E3**
Manzanillo Cuba **89D2**
Manzanillo Mexico **88D4**
Manzanillo Bay Haiti **89E3**
Manzhouli China **52G1**
Mao Chad **69J6**
Maoming China **55F12**
Maowen China **54B7**
Map *island* Yap Is **94A19**
Mapai Mozambique **72D4**
Mapia,Is Pacific Ocean **94D7**
Mapimi Mexico **88D2**
Maping = **Liuzhou**
Mapire Venezuela **92E2**
Maple Creek *Sask.* Canada **76K7**
Mapuera,R Brazil **92F4**
Maputo Mozambique **72E5**
Maqainama Saudi Arabia **62F5**
Maqna Saudi Arabia **62C4**
Maquela do Zombo Angola **70D6**
Maquinchao Argentina **91C6**
Maquoketa *Iowa* USA **83N1**
Maraã Brazil **92D4**
Maraba Brazil **93H5**
Maracaçumé Brazil **93H4**
Maracaibo Venezuela **92C1**
Maracá,I de Brazil **93G3**
Maracanã Brazil **93H4**
Maracay Venezuela **92D1**
Maraciabo,L de Venezuela **92C2**
Maradah Libya **69J3**
Maradi Niger **68G6**
Maradi,R Niger **68G6**
Maragheh Iran **62F2**
Maragoji Brazil **93K5**
Maraisburg South Africa **72M12**
Marajo *island* Brazil **93G4**
Marakei,I Kiribati **94H7**
Marali CAR **69J7**
Maralinga *S Aus.* Australia **98G6**
Marand Iran **62F2**
Marang Buru India **61E4**
Maranguape Brazil **93K4**
Marañón,R Peru **92B4**
Maras Turkey **62D2**
Maraú Brazil **93K6**
Maravilha Brazil **92D5**
Marazion *England* UK **26D8**
Marbella Spain **40D4**
Marble Bar *W Aus.* Australia **98D4**
Marble Canyon *Ariz.* USA **82C4**
Marblehead *Mass.* USA **84F1**
Marbul P India **60D4**
Marburg W Germany **36C3**
Marca Somalia **71J4**
March *England* UK **27Q3**
Marche *prov.* France **42D3**
Marche *region* Italy **44D4**
Marche-en-Famenne Belgium **32D4**
Marchena Spain **40D4**
Marchin Belgium **32D4**
Mar Chiquita *lake* Argentina **91D4**
Marcy,Mt *NY* USA **79J3**
Mardan Pakistan **60C3**
Mar del Plata Argentina **91E5**
Marden *England* UK **26J4**
Mardin Turkey **62E2**
Mareb,R Ethiopia **71H2**
Marechal Deodoro Brazil **93K5**
Mareeba *Queens.* Australia **99K3**
Maree, Loch *Scotland* UK **28E4**
Mare,I *Îs Loyauté* **94G10**
Marengo *Wis.* USA **79A2**
Margam *Wales* UK **26G5**
Margarita,I Venezuela **92E1**
Margarites *Kríti* Greece **47E7**
Margate *England* UK **27S6**
Maria I *Tas.* Australia **97F5**
Marianao Cuba **89C2**
Marianas,Is Pacific Ocean **94E6**
Marianna *Ark.* USA **83N5**
Marianna *Fla* USA **85E5**
Marianske Lázně Czech. **36E4**
Maria,R Brazil **92D4**
Marias,R *Mont.* USA **86D2**
Maria-Theresiopel = **Subotica**
Maria van Diemen,C New Zealand **100E2**
Marib Yemen **62E6**
Maribor Yugoslavia **44E2**
Maricourt = **Kangiqsujuaq**
Maridi Sudan **69L8**
Maridi,R Sudan **69L7**
Marie Byrd Land *region* Antarctica **15P2**
Mariefred Sweden **35G7**
Marie Galante *island* Leeward Is **89G3**
Mariehamn Finland **35H6**
Marienbad = **Marianske Lázně**
Marienberg Netherlands **32E2**
Marienbourg Belgium **32C4**
Marienburg = **Malbork**
Mariental Namibia **72B4**
Marienville *Pa* USA **84B2**
Mariestad Sweden **35E7**
Marietta *Ga* USA **85E4**
Marietta *Ohio* USA **79F6**
Mari Indus Pakistan **60B4**
Marilia Brazil **93G8**
Marine City *Mich.* USA **79E4**
Marinette *Wis.* USA **79C3**
Marinha Grande Portugal **40B3**
Marion *Ark.* USA **83N5**
Marion *Ill.* USA **83P4**
Marion *Ind.* USA **79D5**
Marion *Iowa* USA **83N1**
Marion *Ky* USA **85C2**
Marion *N Car.* USA **85F3**
Marion *N Dak.* USA **81H2**
Marion *Ohio* USA **79E5**
Marion *Va* USA **85G2**
Marion B *Tas.* Australia **97F5**
Marion I *Pr. Edward Is* Indian Ocean **65P12**
Mariposa *Calif.* USA **80D6**
Mariscal Estigarribia Paraguay **91D2**
Maritsa,R Bulgaria/Turkey **46E4**
Mariyskaya ASSR *rep.* USSR **50F4**
Märjamaa *Eston.* USSR **35L7**
Marjaoun Lebanon **64D4**
Marjata,R Bangladesh **61G4**
Markapur India **58E5**
Markaryd Sweden **35E8**
Markelo Netherlands **32E2**
Marken *region* Netherlands **32D2**
Market Deeping *England* UK **25H7**
Market Drayton *England* UK **25D7**
Market Harborough *England* UK **27N4**
Markethill N Ireland **30K5**
Market Rasen *England* UK **25H6**
Markham,L *Tibet* China **59F1**
Markham,Mt Antarctica **15K1**
Marknesse Netherlands **32D2**
Markovo USSR **51U3**
Marks USSR **49H5**
Markstay *Ont.* Canada **79F2**
Marlborough *England* UK **27L6**
Marlborough Guyana **92F2**
Marlborough *Mass.* USA **84F1**
Marlborough *Queens.* Australia **99K4**
Marlborough *stat. area* New Zealand **100E5**
Marlette *Mich.* USA **79E4**
Marlo *Vic.* Australia **97C3**
Marlow *England* UK **27N5**
Marmande France **43D4**
Marmara, Sea of Turkey **62B1**
Marmaris Turkey **62B2**
Marne *dep.* France **42F2**
Marnoo *Vic.* Australia **97B3**
Marondera Nat. Pk Zimbabwe **72E3**
Maros,R = **Muresul,R**
Maroua Cameroun **69H6**
Marouini,R French Guiana **93G3**
Marquerite B Antarctica **15S3**
Marquesas,Is Pacific Ocean **95N8**
Marquette *Mich.* USA **79C2**
Marquina Spain **41E1**
Marrakech Morocco **68D2**
Marra,R *NSW* Australia **97C2**
Marrawah *Tas.* Australia **97F5**
Marree *S Aus.* Australia **97A1**
Marris Pakistan **58C3**
Marsabit Kenya **71H4**
Mar,Sa do *mts* Brazil **91G3**
Marsa Fatma Ethiopia **71J2**
Marsala *Sicily* Italy **45D7**
Marsan India **61A2**
Marsa Susah Libya **69K2**
Marsden *NSW* Australia **97C2**
Marseille France **43F5**
Marshall *Ill.* USA **83Q3**
Marshall *Mich.* USA **79D4**
Marshall *Minn.* USA **81K3**
Marshall *Mo* USA **83M3**
Marshall *Texas* USA **83L6**
Marshall,Is Pacific Ocean **94G7**
Marshalltown *Iowa* USA **83M1**
Marshfield *Mo* USA **83M4**
Marshfield *Wis.* USA **79A3**
Marsh Harbour The Bahamas **89D1**
Marsh I *La* USA **83M8**
Mars Hill *Maine* USA **78E3**
Marstrand Sweden **35D8**
Martaban Burma **59J5**
Martaban,G of Burma **59J5**
Martelange Belgium **32D5**
Marthas Vineyard *island Mass.* USA **84F2**
Martigny-Ville Switzerland **33C2**
Martigues France **43F5**
Martin *S Dak.* USA **81G4**
Martina Switzerland **33F2**
Martina Franca Italy **45F5**
Martinborough New Zealand **100F5**
Martinez *Calif.* USA **80B6**
Martinique *island* Windward Is **89G4**
Martin L *Ala.* USA **85D4**
Martinsburg *W Va* USA **84C3**
Martinsville *Va* USA **85H2**
Marton New Zealand **100F5**
Martos Spain **40E4**
Martre, Lac la *lake NW Terr.* Canada **76H4**
Maruf Afghanistan **63K3**
Marugame Japan **56C7**
Marulan *NSW* Australia **97D2**
Marum Netherlands **32E1**
Marunga,Mts Zaire **71F6**
Marutea,I Tuamotu Arch. **95M9**
Marvejols France **43E4**
Marvine,Mt *Utah* USA **82C3**
Mary *Turkmen.* USSR **50H6**
Maryborough Queensland **99L5**
Maryborough *Vic.* Australia **97B3**
Marydale South Africa **72C5**
Maryland *state* USA **87L4**
Maryport *England* UK **25B3**
Mary's Pk *S Aus.* Australia **97A2**
Marystown *Newf.* Canada **78L3**
Marysvale *Utah* USA **82B3**
Marysville *Calif.* USA **80C6**
Marysville *Kans.* USA **83K3**
Marysville *New Br.* Canada **78E3**
Marysville *Wash.* USA **80B1**
Maryville *Mo* USA **83L2**
Marzuq Libya **69H3**
Masada *hist. site* Israel **64D6**
Masaka Uganda **71G5**
Masasi Tanzania **71H7**
Masaya Nicaragua **89B4**
Masbate *island* Philippines **53H8**
Mascara Algeria **68F1**
Maseru Lesotho **72D5**
Mashaki Afghanistan **63K3**
Masham *England* UK **25E4**
Masharbrum,Mt *Kashmir* India **60E3**
Mashhad Iran **63H2**
Mashiz Iran **63H4**
Mashkel,R Pakistan **58B3**
Masi-Manimba Zaire **70D5**
Masindi Uganda **71G4**
Maşirah *island* Oman **63H5**
Maşirah Chan. Oman **63H5**
Maşirah,G of Oman **63H6**
Masjed Soleymān Iran **62F3**
Mask,L Ireland, Rep. of **30E6**
Masoala,C Madagascar **71P10**
Mason *Mich.* USA **79D4**
Mason City *Iowa* USA **83M1**
Masøy Norway **34L1**
Masqat = **Muskat**
Massa Italy **44C3**
Massachusetts *state* USA **87M3**
Massachusetts B *Mass.* USA **84F1**
Massacre Ls *Nev.* USA **80D5**
Massafra Italy **45F5**
Massakori Chad **69J6**
Massangena Mozambique **72E4**
Massapé Brazil **93J4**
Massawa Ethiopia **71H1**
Massawa Chan. Ethiopia **71J1**
Massena *NY* USA **79J3**
Massénya Chad **69J6**
Masseube France **43D5**
Massey *Ont.* Canada **79E2**
Massif Central *region* France **43E4**
Massif de la Hotte *region* Haiti **89E3**
Massif des Bongos *mt* CAR **69K7**
Massillon *Ohio* USA **79F5**
Massinga Mozambique **72F4**
Masterton New Zealand **100F5**
Mastuj Pakistan **60C2**
Mastung Pakistan **58C3**
Mastura Saudi Arabia **62D5**
Masvingo Zimbabwe **72E4**
Masyaf Syria **64E2**
Mat India **61A2**
Mata Amarilla Argentina **91B7**
Matagalpa Nicaragua **89B4**
Matagorda B *Texas* USA **82T9**
Matagorda I *Texas* USA **82T9**
Matagorda Pen. *Texas* USA **82T9**
Matakana I New Zealand **100G3**
Matale Sri Lanka **58F7**
Matam Senegal **68C5**
Matamoros Mexico **88D2**
Matamoros Mexico **88E2**
Matane *Que.* Canada **78E2**
Matanzas Cuba **89C2**
Matão,Sa do *mts* Brazil **93G5**
Matapan,C = **Tainaron,C**
Matapedia *Que.* Canada **78E2**
Matapedia,L *Que.* Canada **78E2**
Matapozuelos Spain **40D2**
Matara Sri Lanka **58F7**
Mataram *Lombok* Indon. **53G12**
Mataro Spain **41H2**
Matatiele South Africa **72D6**
Mataule Brazil **93G3**
Mataura New Zealand **100C8**
Matautu Western Samoa **95V31**
Matautu Harb. Western Samoa **95V31**
Mataveri Easter I **95V32**
Matehuala Mexico **88D3**
Matera Italy **45F5**
Mátészalka Hungary **37K5**
Mateur Tunisia **69G1**
Matfors Sweden **34G5**
Mathew Town The Bahamas **89E2**
Mathry *Wales* UK **26D5**
Mathuna India **60E7**
Mathura India **61A2**
Matiara India **59G3**
Matin India **61D4**
Matla,R India **61G5**
Matlock *England* UK **25E6**
Matna Sudan **69N6**
Mato Grosso Brazil **92F6**
Mato Grosso,Planalto de *plat.* Brazil **93G7**
Matra *mt* Hungary **37H5**
Matrah Oman **63H5**
Matruh Egypt **69L2**
Matsue Japan **56C7**
Matsumoto Japan **56F6**
Matsu Shan *island* China **55L9**
Matsuyama Japan **56C8**
Mattawa *Ont.* Canada **79G2**
Matterhorn *mt* Italy/Switz. **33C3**
Matter Vispa,R Switzerland **33C2**
Mattoon *Ill.* USA **83P3**
Matucana Peru **92B6**
Matun Afghanistan **63K3**
Matura Brazil **92D4**
Maturín Venezuela **92E2**
Matvaieva USSR **49N2**
Mau India **61C3**
Mau India **61C4**

Mau Aimma, Mill Is

Mau Aimma India 61C3
Maual Nepal 61C1
Maubeuge France 42E1
Maubin Burma 59J5
Maubourguet France 43C5
Mauchline Scotland UK 29H8
Maudaha India 61C3
Maude NSW Australia 97B2
Maudheim Antarctica 15B2
Maués Brazil 93F4
Mauganj India 61C3
Maugerville New Br. Canada 78E4
Maui,I Hawaii USA 95L5
Maule prov. Chile 91B5
Mauleon Licharre France 43C5
Maumakeogh mt Ireland,Rep. of 30E5
Maumturk Mts Ireland, Rep. of 31D6
Mauna Kea mt Hawaii USA 95V27
Mauna Loa mt Hawaii USA 95V27
Maungmagan Is Burma 59J6
Maurawan India 61C2
Mauriac France 43E4
Maurice,L S Aus. Australia 98G5
Mauritania country Africa 68C4
Mauritius,I Indian Ocean 65D6
Maurs France 43E4
Maur,Wadi Yemen 62E6
Mauston Wis. USA 79A4
Mavinga Angola 72C3
Mawk Mai Burma 59J4
Mawson Pk Heard I 65R12
Maxan Argentina 91C3
Maxcanu Mexico 88F3
Maxixe Mozambique 72F4
Maxton N Car. USA 85H3
Maxwelltown Scotland UK 29J9
Maya island Indonesia 53E11
Mayādīn Syria 62E2
Mayaguana island The Bahamas 89E2
Mayagüez Puerto Rico 89F3
Maya Mts Belize 89B3
Mayang China 55E9
Mayari Cuba 89D2
Maybole Scotland UK 29G9
May,C USA 84D3
Maydena Tas. Australia 97F5
Mayen W Germany 36B3
Mayenne France 42C2
Mayenne dep. France 42C2
Mayersville Miss. USA 85B4
Mayfield Ky USA 85C2
May,I of Scotland UK 29L7
Maykop USSR 50F5
Maymyo Burma 59J4
Maynooth Ireland, Rep. of 31K7
Maynooth Ont. Canada 79G3
Mayo county Ireland, Rep. of 30E6
Mayotte,I Indian Ocean 71K7
Mays Landing New J USA 84D3
Maysville Ky USA 85F1
Mayurakshi,R India 61F3
Mayūrdm India 58E6
Mayville N Dak. USA 81J2
Mayville NY USA 84B1
Maza Argentina 91D5
Mazabuka Zambia 72D3
Mazagão Brazil 93G4
Mazamet France 43E5
Mazán Peru 92C4
Mazan,R Peru 92C4
Mazapil Mexico 88D3
Mazara del Vallo Sicily Italy 45D7
Mazar-i-Sharif Afghanistan 63K2
Mazarredo Argentina 91C7
Mazarrón Spain 41F4
Mazatenango Guatemala 88F5
Mazatlán Mexico 88C3
Mazeikiai Lith. USSR 35K8
Mazirbe Latviy USSR 35K8
Mazurdni,R Guyana 92E2
Mbabane Swaziland 72E5
Mbale Uganda 71G4
Mbandaka Zaire 70D4
Mbarara Uganda 71G5
Mbengga,R Viti Levu Fiji 94A25
Mbeya Tanzania 71G6
Mbini Eq. Guinea 70C4
M Bour Sénégal 68B6
Mbout Mauritania 68C5
Mbozi Tanzania 71G6
Mbuji-Mayi Zaire 70E6
Mead L Ariz/Nev USA 80F7
Meadows Idaho USA 80E3
Meadville Pa USA 79F5
Meaford Ont. Canada 79F3
Measach Falls Scotland UK 28F4
Meath county Ireland, Rep. of 30K6
Meaux France 42E2
Mebridege,R Angola 70C6
Mecca Saudi Arabia 62D5
Mechanicville NY USA 84E1
Mechelen Belgium 32C3
Mecheria Algeria 68E2
Mechol Yap Is 94A19
Mecur Utah USA 82B2
Medak India 58E5
Medak Yugoslavia 44E3
Medan Sumatra Indon. 53C10
Medanos Argentina 91D5
Medellín Colombia 92B2
Medemblik Netherlands 32D2
Medenine Tunisia 69H2
Meder Ethiopia 71J2
Méderdra Mauritania 68B5
Medford Oreg. USA 80B4
Medford Wis. USA 79A2
Medgidia Romania 46G2
Media Pa USA 84D3
Medias Romania 46E1
Medical Lake Wash. USA 80E2
Medicine Bow Wyo. USA 81D5
Medicine Bow Ra mts Col./Wyo. USA 81D5
Medicine Hat Alta Canada 76J6
Medina N Dak. USA 81H2
Medina NY USA 84B1
Medina Ohio USA 79F5
Medina Saudi Arabia 62D5
Medinaceli Spain 41E2
Medina del Campo Spain 40D2
Medina de Rioseco Spain 40D2
Medina Sidonia Spain 40D4
Médine Mali 68C6
Mediterranean Sea Europe 38G6
Mednogorsk USSR 49N5
Medoc region France 43C4
Medog China 52C5
Medora N Dak. USA 81F2
Medvezhegorsk Karel. USSR 50E3
Medvezhiy Yar USSR 51L2
Medway,R England UK 27Q6
Meekatharra W Aus. Australia 98D5
Meerle Belgium 32C3
Meerlo Netherlands 32E3
Meersburg W Germany 36C5
Meerssen Netherlands 32D4
Meerut India 60E6
Meeuwen Belgium 32D3
Mega Ethiopia 71H4
Megalópolis Greece 47D6
Mégantic,L Que. Canada 78C4
Mégara Greece 47D6
Meghalaya state India 59H3
Megiddo hist. site Israel 64D5
Megiskan Que. Canada 79H1
Mehandragarh India 61D4
Mehar Pakistan 58C3
Meherpur Bangladesh 61G4
Mehndawal India 61D2
Meiganga Cameroun 69H7
Mei Jiang river China 55H11
Meiktila Burma 59J4
Meilen Switzerland 33D1
Meiningen E Germany 36D3
Meinisberg Switzerland 33C1
Meiringen Switzerland 33D2
Meishan China 55B7
Meissen E Germany 36E3
Meisterschwanden Switzerland 33D1
Meitan China 55D9
Meitene Latvia USSR 35K8
Mei Xian China 55J10
Mejillones Chile 91B2
Mekatina Ont. Canada 79D2
Meknes Morocco 68D2
Mekong,Mouths of Vietnam 57D5
Mekong,R S E Asia 57C3
Melaka Malaysia 57C6
Melaka state Malaysia 57C6
Melanesia,Arch. Pacific Ocean 94E7
Melbourne Fla USA 85M7
Melbourne Vic. Australia 97B3
Melchnau Switzerland 33C1
Melekeiok Palau Is 94A20
Meleuz USSR 49M4
Melfi Italy 45E5
Melfort Sask. Canada 76L6
Melide Switzerland 33D3
Meligalá Greece 47C6
Melilla Morocco 68E1
Melipilla Chile 91B4
Melitopol Ukrain. USSR 48J8
Melk Austria 36F4
Melksham England UK 27K6
Melle France 42C3
Mellier Belgium 32D5
Mellingen Switzerland 33D1
Mellu I Kwajalein Is 94A17
Mělnik Czech. 36F3
Melo Uruguay 91F4
Melreux Belgium 32D4
Melrose Minn. USA 81K3
Melrose Scotland UK 29L8
Melton Mowbray England UK 25G7
Melun France 42E2
Melut Sudan 69M6
Melvich Scotland UK 28J2
Melville Sask. Canada 76L6
Melville B Greenland 14Q2
Melville,C Queens. Australia 99J2
Melville I N Terr. Australia 98G2
Melville I NW Terr. Canada 76J1
Melville,L Newf. Canada 77U6
Melville Pen. NW Terr. Canada 77P3
Melvin,L Ireland 30G5
Memba Mozambique 71J7
Memel = Klaipeda
Memphis Tenn. USA 85B3
Memphremagog,L Que. Canada 79K3
Memramcook New Br. Canada 78F3
Mena Ark. USA 83L5
Menai Bridge Wales UK 26F2
Menai Str. Wales UK 26F2
Ménaka Mali 68F5
Menan Idaho USA 80G3
Menasha Wis. USA 79B3
Mendak Saudi Arabia 62E5
Mendawai,R Borneo Indon. 53F11
Mende France 43E4
Mendebo,Mts Ethiopia 71H3
Menderez,R Turkey 62B2
Mendip Hills England UK 26J6
Mendocino Calif. USA 80B6
Mendocino,C Calif. USA 80A5
Mendota Calif. USA 80C7
Mendota Ill. USA 83P2
Mendota,L Wis. USA 79B4
Mendoza Argentina 91C4
Mendoza prov. Argentina 91C4
Mendrisio Switzerland 33D3
Menen Belgium 32B4
Menfi Sicily Italy 45D7
Meng Chainat Thailand 57C3
Mengcheng china 54J6
Meng Kemmarat Thailand 57D3
Mengshan China 55F10
Mengyin China 54K5
Menin = Menen
Menindee NSW Australia 97B2
Menindee L NSW Australia 97B2
Meningie S Aus. Australia 97A3
Menominee Mich. USA 79C3
Menominee,R Mich. USA 79C3
Menomonie Wis. USA 81L3
Menorca,I Balearic Is Spain 41J2
Mentawai Is = Mentawai Kep
Mentawai Kep islands Indon. 53C11
Mentawi Kep islands Indonesia 53L9
Mentok Bangka Indon. 53E11
Menton France 43G5
Menyapa mt Borneo Indon. 53G10
Menzelinsk USSR 49L3
Menzies W Aus. Australia 98E5
Menzingen Switzerland 33D1
Meona Israel 64D4
Meoqui Mexico 88C2
Meppel Netherlands 32E2
Meppen W Germany 36B2
Merabéllou G Kríti Greece 47E7
Merano Italy 44C2
Merari,Sa mts Brazil 92E3
Merasheen I Newf. Canada 78L3
Meratus Peg mts Borneo Indon. 53G11
Merauke New Guinea Indon. 53M12
Merbem Vic. Australia 97B2
Mercara India 58E6
Merced Calif. USA 80C7
Mercedario,Mt Argentina 91B4
Mercedes Argentina 91E3
Mercedes Argentina 91E4
Mercedes Bolivia 92D6
Mercedes Uruguay 91E4
Merced Pk Calif. USA 80D6
Mercer Pa USA 79F5
Merchtem Belgium 32C4
Mercury B New Zealand 100F3
Mercury Is New Zealand 100F3
Mercy,C NW Terr. Canada 77T3
Meredith Mich. USA 79D3
Meredith,C Falkland Is 91D8
Meregh Somalia 71K4
Mergui Burma 59J6
Mergui,Arch. Burma 59J6
Meribah S Aus. Australia 97B2
Merida Mexico 88G3
Mérida Spain 40C3
Mérida Venezuela 92C2
Merida,Cord. do mts Venezuela 92C2
Meriden Conn. USA 84E2
Meridian Idaho USA 80E4
Meridian Miss. USA 85C4
Merimbula NSW Australia 97C3
Meringur Vic. Australia 97B2
Merishausen Switzerland 33D1
Merksplas Belgium 32C3
Merowe Sudan 69M5
Merredin W Aus. Australia 98D6
Merrick mt Scotland UK 29H9
Merrill Wis. USA 79B3
Merrimack,R Mass./New H USA 84F1
Merriwa NSW Australia 97D2
Merrygoen NSW Australia 97C2
Mersey,R England UK 25C6
Merseyside county England UK 25B6
Mersin Turkey 62C2
Mersing Malaysia 53D10
Mērsrags Latvia USSR 35K8
Merta India 58D3
Merthyr Tydfil Wales UK 26H5
Mértola Portugal 40C4
Merton England UK 26F7
Meru Kenya 71H4
Merzig W Germany 36B4
Mesa Ariz. USA 82C6
Mesa de Yambi plat. Columbia 92C3
Mesagne Italy 45F5
Mesará B Kríti Greece 47E7
Mesa Verde Nat. Pk Col. USA 82D4
Mesegon island Truk Is 94A16
Mesen Belgium 32A4
Meseta de Montemayor region Argentina 91C6
Meshed = Mashhad
Mesken Syria 64G1
Mesmiye Syria 64E4
Mesocco Switzerland 33E2
Mesolóngion Greece 47C5
Mesötúr Hungary 37J5
Mesquite Nev. USA 80F7
Messancy Belgium 32D5
Messina Sicily Italy 45E6
Messina South Africa 72D4
Messina, Str. di Italy 45E6
Messini Greece 47C6
Messinía dist. Greece 47C6
Messinía,G of Greece 47C6
Mestre Italy 44D3
Mesudiye Turkey 62D1
Metán Argentina 91D3
Metaponto Italy 45F5
Meta,R Columb./Venez. 92D2
Méthana Pen. Greece 47D6
Methven New Zealand 100D6
Metis sur Mer Que. Canada 78D2
Metkovic Yugloslavia 46A3
Metlakatla Alaska USA 87Z13
Metlika Yugoslavia 44E3
Metropolis Ill. USA 83P4
Metropolitan Mich. USA 79C2
Métsovon Greece 47C5
Mettet Belgium 32C4
Mettlen Switzerland 33C2
Mettur Dam India 58E6
Metz France 42G2
Meulebeke Belgium 32B4
Meurthe-et-Moselle dep. France 42G2
Meuse dep. France 42F2
Meuse,R France 42F2
Mevagissey England UK 26E8
Mevis,L Scotland UK 28E5
Mexcala Mexico 88E4
Mexiana do Sul,I Brazil 93H3
Mexicali Mexico 88A1
Mexico Mexico 88E4
Mexico NY USA 84C1
Mexico country Central America 88D3
Mexico B NY USA 84C1
Mexico,G of 88F2
Meybod Iran 63G3
Meyersdale Pa USA 84B3
Meymac France 42E4
Meyrin Switzerland 33B2
Mèze France 43E5
Mezen USSR 50F3
Mezieres France 42F2
Mezöbereny Békés Hungary 37J5
Mezökövesd Hungary 37J5
Mezquitic Mexico 88D3
Mgori Tanzania 71G5
Mhow India 58E4
Miadao Qundao islands China 54L3
Miahuatlán Mexico 88E4
Miajadas Spain 40D3
Miami Ariz. USA 82C6
Miami Fla USA 85M9
Miami Okla. USA 83L4
Miandowab Iran 62F2
Miandrivazo Madagascar 71N10
Mianeh Iran 62F2
Miani India 60D5
Miani Pakistan 60C4
Mian Kalai Pakistan 60B3
Mianwali Pakistan 60B4
Mianyang China 54C7
Mianyang China 55G7
Miass USSR 49Q3
Miastko Poland 37G1
Micang Shan mts China 54D6
Micay Colombia 92B3
Michailovsk USSR 49Q4
Michalovce Czech. 37J4
Michigan state USA 87J2
Michigan City Ind. USA 79C5
Michigan,L USA 79C4
Michipicoten B Ont. Canada 79D2
Michipicoten I Ont. Canada 77O7
Michoacan state Mexico 88D4
Michurin Bulgaria 46F3
Michurinsk USSR 49E4
Micronesia,Is Pacific Ocean 94E6
Middelburg Netherlands 32B3
Middelburg South Africa 72D5
Middelharnis Netherlands 32C3
Middelkerke Belgium 32A3
Middenmeer Netherlands 32D2
Middleboro Mass. USA 84F2
Middleburg Pa USA 84C2
Middleburgh NY USA 84D1
Middlebury Vt USA 79K3
Middleham England UK 25E4
Middleport NY USA 84B1
Middlesboro Ky USA 85F2
Middlesbrough England UK 25F3
Middleton England UK 25C4
Middleton No. Sc. Canada 78F4
Middleton in Teesdale England UK 25D3
Middletown Conn. USA 84E2
Middletown Del. USA 84D3
Middletown NY USA 84D2
Middletown Ohio USA 79D6
Middletown Pa USA 84C2
Middlewich England UK 25D6
Mid Glamorgan county Wales UK 26H5
Midland Mich. USA 79D4
Midland Ont. Canada 79G3
Midland Texas USA 82G7
Midland Gap England UK 25C7
Midleton Ireland, Rep. of 31G10
Midnapur India 61F4
Midway,Is Hawaii USA 94J5
Midwest Wyo. USA 81D4
Midwest City Okla. USA 83K5
Midye Turkey 62B1
Mie prefecture Japan 56E7
Miécourt Switzerland 33C1
Miedzyrzec Poland 37K2
Mielic Poland 37J3
Mier Mexico 88E2
Mieres Spain 40D1
Mifflintown Pa USA 84C2
Mijdrecht Netherlands 32C2
Mikhaylovgrad Bulgaria 46D3
Mikhrot Timna Israel 64C8
Mikhyalovka USSR 49F5
Mikindani Tanzania 71J7
Mikkeli Finland 35M6
Mikonos island Greece 47E6
Milaca Minn. USA 81L3
Milan = Milano
Milan Mo USA 83M2
Milan New H USA 79L3
Milan Tenn. USA 85C3
Milang S Aus. Australia 97A3
Milano Italy 44B3
Milas Turkey 62B2
Milazzo Sicily Italy 45E6
Milbank S Dak. USA 81J3
Mildenhall England UK 27R4
Mildura Vic. Australia 97B2
Mile China 55B10
Miléai Greece 47D5
Miles Queens. Australia 99K5
Milesburg Pa USA 84C2
Miles City Mont. USA 81E2
Milevsko Czech. 36F4
Milford Del. USA 84D3
Milford Mass. USA 84F1
Milford Pa USA 84D2
Milford Utah USA 82B3
Milford Haven Wales UK 26D5
Milford Haven bay Wales UK 26D5
Milford Sd New Zealand 100B7
Miliana Algeria 68F1
Mili,Is Marshall Is 94H7
Milkovo USSR 51S4
Milk,R Mont. USA 81D1
Mill Netherlands 32D3
Millau France 43E4
Millbridge Ont. Canada 79H3
Mill City Nev. USA 80D5
Mille Lacs,L Minn. USA 81L2
Miller S Dak. USA 81H3
Millerovo USSR 49E6
Millersburg Ohio USA 79F5
Millertown Newf. Canada 78K2
Millford Ireland, Rep. of 30H3
Mill I Antarctica 15H3
Millicent S Aus. Australia 97B3
Millinocket Maine USA 78D4
Mill Is NW Terr. Canada 77Q4

Mora Cameroun 69H6
Mora Ethiopia 71H2
Mora Minn. USA 81L3
Mora Portugal 40B3
Mora Spain 40E3
Mora Sweden 35F6
Moradabad India 61B1
Mora de Rubielos Spain 41F2
Moramanga Madagascar 71N10
Morano Calabro Italy 45F6
Morar India 61B2
Morar,L Scotland UK 28E6
Morat = Murten
Moratalla Spain 41F3
Morava,R Czech. 37G4
Morava,R Yugoslavia 46C2
Moravia region Czech. 37G4
Moravska Třebová Czech. 37G4
Morawhanna Guyana 92F2
Moray Firth bay Scotland UK 28J4
Morbi India 58D4
Morbihan dep. France 42B3
Morbihan,B de Kerguelen 65S12
Morden Man. Canada 76M7
Mordialloc Vic. Australia 97C3
Mordova USSR 49E4
Mordovskava ASSR rep. USSR 50F4
More county Norway 34B5
Moreau,R S Dak. USA 81G3
Morecambe England UK 25C4
Morecambe B England UK 25B4
Moreda Spain 40E4
Moree NSW Australia 97C1
Morehead City N Car. USA 85J3
Moreira Brazil 92E4
More,L Scotland UK 28G3
Mörel Switzerland 33D2
Morelia Mexico 88D4
Morella Spain 41F2
Morelos Mexico 88C2
Morelos Mexico 88D2
Morelos state Mexico 88E4
Morena India 61B2
Morena,Sa mts Brazil 92F5
Morena,Sa mts Spain 40D3
Morenci Ariz. USA 82D6
Morere New Zealand 100G4
Moreton B Queensland 99L5
Moretonhampstead England UK 26G7
Morez France 42F3
Morgan S Aus. Australia 97A2
Morgan City La USA 83N8
Morganton N Car. USA 85G3
Morgat France 42A2
Morges Switzerland 33B2
Morgins Switzerland 33B2
Morhar,R India 61E3
Moriah,Mt Nev. USA 80F6
Moriani India 59H3
Morice L BC Canada 76F6
Morinville Alta Canada 76J6
Morioka Japan 56G5
Morisset NSW Australia 97D2
Morjärv Sweden 34K3
Morkalla Vic. Australia 97B2
Morlaix France 42B2
Mormagão India 58D5
Mormon Ra mtsNev. USA 80F7
Mornington Vic. Australia 97C3
Mornington,I Chile 91A7
Mornington,I Queens. Australia 99H3
Moro Oreg. USA 80C3
Morobe Papua New Guinea 99K1
Morocco country Africa 68D2
Moro G Philippines 53H9
Morogoro Tanzania 71H6
Morokweng South Africa 72C5
Moron Cuba 89D2
Morón Venezuela 92D1
Moron mt Switzerland 33C1
Morona Ecuador 92B4
Morona,R Peru 92B4
Morondava Madagascar 71M11
Morón de la Frontera Spain 40D4
Moron Us He river Tibet China 59H2
Morotai island Indonesia 53J10
Moroto Uganda 71G4
Morpeth England UK 25E2
Morpeth NSW Australia 97D2
Morphou Cyprus 64A2
Morphou B Cyprus 64A2
Morrilton Ark. USA 83M5
Morrinhos Brazil 93H7
Morrinsville New Zealand 100F3
Morris Ill. USA 83P2
Morris Man. Canada 76M7
Morris Minn. USA 81K3
Morrisburg Ont. Canada 79J3
Morrison Ill. USA 83P2
Morriston Wales UK 26G5

Morristown New J USA 84D2
Morrisville NY USA 84D1
Morro Bay Calif. USA 80C8
Morrosquillo,G de Colombia 92B2
Morrumbene Mozambique 72F4
Morshansk USSR 49E4
Mors,I Denmark 35C8
Mortagne France 42D2
Mortagua Portugal 40B2
Mortain France 42C2
Morte Point England UK 26F6
Mortlake Vic. Australia 97B3
Morton Nat. Pk NSW Australia 97D2
Morundah NSW Australia 97C2
Moruya NSW Australia 97D3
Morven New Zealand 100D7
Morven Queens. Australia 99K5
Morwell Vic. Australia 97C3
Moscos Is Burma 59J6
Moscow = Moskva
Moscow Idaho USA 80E2
Moselle dep. France 42G2
Moselle,R France 42G2
Mosgiel New Zealand 100D7
Moshi Tanzania 71H5
Mosjøen Norway 34E4
Moskenesøy,I Norway 34E3
Moskenstraumen island Norway 34E3
Moskva USSR 48K4
Mosquera Colombia 92B3
Moss Norway 35D7
Mossaka Congo 70D5
Mossburn New Zealand 100C7
Mossel,B South Africa 72C6
Mossendjo Congo 70C5
Mossgiel NSW Australia 97B2
Mossoró Brazil 93K5
Moss Vale NSW Australia 97D2
Most Czech. 36E3
Mostaganem Algeria 68E1
Mostar Yugoslavia 46A3
Mostardas Brazil 91F4
Mosul Iraq 62E2
Mota del Marques Spain 40D2
Motala Sweden 35F7
Motatan Venezuela 92C2
Motherwell Scotland UK 29J8
Môtier Switzerland 33C2
Môtiers Switzerland 33B2
Motihari India 61E2
Motôt Switzerland 33C2
Motril Spain 40E4
Mott N Dak. USA 81F2
Motueka New Zealand 100E5
Motu Iti island Society Is 95L9
Motul Mexico 88G3
Moudhros Greece 47E5
Moudjéria Mauritania 68C5
Moudon Switzerland 33B2
Mouila Gabon 70C5
Moulamein NSW Australia 97B3
Moulamein,R NSW Australia 97B3
Moulapamok Laos 57D4
Moulins France 42E3
Moulmein Burma 59J5
Moulouya,R Morocco 68E2
Moulton Ala. USA 85D3
Mound City Ill. USA 83P4
Moundou Chad 69J7
Mounga One island Tonga 95V30
Mountain Ash Wales UK 26H5
Mountain City Nev. USA 80F5
Mountain Grove Mo USA 83M4
Mountain Home Ark. USA 83M4
Mountain Home Idaho USA 80F4
Mountain Sheep Bluffs Mont. USA 81E2
Mountain ViewArk. USA 83M5
Mount Ayr Iowa USA 83L2
Mount Barker S Aus. Australia 97A3
Mount Bellew Bridge Ireland, Rep. of 31G7
Mount Carmel Ill. USA 83Q3
Mount Carmel Pa USA 84C2
Mount Carroll Ill. USA 83P1
Mount Clemens Mich. USA 79E4
Mount Darwin Zimbabwe 72E3
Mount Desert I Maine USA 78D4
Mount Drysdale NSW Australia 97C2
Mount Dutton S Aus. Australia 99H5
Mount Forest Ont. Canada 79F3
Mount Gambier S Aus. Australia 97B3
Mount Hebron Calif. USA 80C5
Mount Holly New J USA 84D3
Mount Hope NSW Australia 97C2

Mount Isa Queens. Australia 99H4
Mount Jewett Pa USA 84B2
Mount Lofty Ra mts S Aus. Australia 97A3
Mount Magnet W Aus. Australia 98D5
Mount Manara NSW Australia 97B2
Mountmellick Ireland, Rep. of 31J7
Mount Morgan Queens. Australia 99K4
Mount Morris NY USA 84C1
Mount Olive Miss. USA 85C5
Mount Olive N Car. USA 85H3
Mount Pleasant Iowa USA 83N2
Mount Pleasant Mich. USA 79D4
Mount Pleasant Pa USA 84B2
Mount PleasantS Aus. Australia 97A2
Mount Pleasant Tenn. USA 85D3
Mount Pleasant Texas USA 83L6
Mount Pleasant Utah USA 82C3
Mountrath Ireland, Rep. of 31J7
Mount Robson Park BC Canada 76G6
Mounts B England UK 26D8
Mount Shasta Calif. USA 80B5
Mount Sterling Ky USA 85F1
Mount Stewart Pr. Ed. I. Canada 78G3
Mount Union Pa USA 84B2
Mount Vernon Ill. USA 83P3
Mount Vernon Ind. USA 85D1
Mount Vernon Ky USA 85E2
Mount Vernon Va USA 79H6
Moura Brazil 92E4
Moura Portugal 40C3
Mourão Portugal 40C3
Mourne Mts N Ireland 30L5
Mourne,R N Ireland 30J4
Mousa island Shetland Scotland 28Q8
Moussoro Chad 69J6
Moutier Switzerland 33C1
Moville Ireland,Rep. of 30J3
Mowlaik Burma 59H4
Moyale Kenya 71H4
Moyamba Sierra Leone 68C7
Moyen Atlas mts Morocco 68D2
Moyobamba Peru 92B5
Moy,R Ireland, Rep. of 30E6
Mozambique Mozambique 71J8
Mozambique country Africa 72E4
Mozhga USSR 49L2
Mozyr Belorus. USSR 48F5
Mpanda Tanzania 71G6
Mpélé,Mt Gabon 70C5
Mporokoso Zambia 72E1
Mstislavl' Belorus. USSR 48G4
Mtakuja Tanzania 71G6
Mt Idaho Idaho USA 80E3
Mtito Andei Kenya 71H5
Mt Rushmore Nat. Mem. S Dak. USA 81F4
Mtsensk USSR 48K5
Muang Chaiya Thailand 57B5
Muang Khon Kaen Thailand 57C3
Muang Nan Thailand 57C3
Muang Phitsanulok Thailand 57C3
Muaungmya Burma 59H5
Mubende Uganda 71G4
Mubi Nigeria 69H6
Muchalls Scotland UK 28M5
Muchinga,Mts Zambia 72E2
Much Wenlock England UK 25C7
Muck island Scotland UK 29D6
Muckish mt Ireland, Rep. of 30H3
Muckros Hd Ireland, Rep. of 30F4
Muconda Angola 70E7
Mudanjiang China 52J2
Mudanya Turkey 62B1
Mudawwara Jordan 64D8
Mudgee NSW Australia 97C2
Mudros = Moudhros
Mufu Shan mts China 55H8
Mugdisho Somalia 71K4
Mugford,C Newf. Canada 77T5
Muggendorf W Germany 36D4
Mugia Spain 40B1
Mugla Turkey 62B2
Muglad Sudan 69L6
Mugne Laos 57C2
Mugu Karnali Nepal 61D1
Muhamdi India 61C2
Muhammadgarh India 61B4
Muharraq Bahrain 63D4
Mühldorf W Germany 36E4
Mühlehorn Switzerland 33E1

Mühlhausen E Germany 36D3
Muhos Finland 34L4
Muhu Eston. USSR 35K7
Muhu Väin sound Eston. USSR 35K7
Mui Bai Bung Vietnam 57C5
Muine Bheag Ireland, Rep. of 31K8
Muizenberg South Africa 72H10
Mukdahan Thailand 57C3
Mukden = Shenyang
Mukhtuya USSR 51N3
Muktinath Nepal 61D1
Muktsar India 60D5
Mula Spain 41F3
Mulanje,Mt Malawi 71H8
Mulbekh Kashmir India 60E3
Mulchén Chile 91B5
Muldersdrif South Africa 72M12
Mulege Mexico 88B2
Mulgrave No. Sc. Canada 78H4
Mülheim W Germany 36B3
Mulhouse France 42G3
Mulki India 58D6
Mullaghareirk Mts Ireland, Rep. of 31E9
Mullaittivu Sri Lanka 58F7
Mullaley NSW Australia 97C2
Muller Geb. mts Borneo Indon. 53F10
Mullet L Mich. USA 79D3
Mullewa W Aus. Australia 98D5
Mull Hd Orkney Scotland 28L1
Müllheim Switzerland 33D1
Mull,I Scotland UK 29E7
Mullingar Ireland, Rep. of 31J6
Mullion Creek NSW Australia 97C2
Mull,Sd of Scotland UK 29E6
Muloorina S Aus. Australia 97A1
Mulroy B Ireland, Rep. of 30H3
Multan Pakistan 60B5
Multan territory Pakistan 60C5
Multia Finland 34L5
Mumbles Wales UK 26F5
Mumbondo Angola 70C7
Mumbwa Zambia 72D2
Muna Indonesia 53H9
München W Germany 36D4
Münchenbuchsee Switzerland 33C1
Munchinabad Pakistan 60C5
Muncie Ind. USA 79D5
Münden W Germany 36C3
Mundo Novo Brazil 93J6
Munfordville Ky USA 85E2
Mungari Mozambique 72E3
Mungeli India 61C4
Mungindi Queens. Australia 97C1
Munich = München
Muniesa Spain 41F2
Munising Mich. USA 79C2
Munkflohögen Sweden 34F5
Munkfors Sweden 35E7
Munnerstadt W Germany 36D3
Munoz Gamero,Pen. Chile 91B8
Münsingen Switzerland 33C2
Münster Switzerland 33D2
Munster Switzerland 33F2
Münster W Germany 36B3
Munster prov. Ireland, Rep. of 31E9
Munyeru,R India 58E5
Munzur Silsilesi mts Turkey 62D2
Muodoslompolo Sweden 34K3
Muong Hai Laos 57C2
Muong Phichit Thailand 57C3
Muong Sing Laos 57C2
Muonio Sweden 34K3
Muonio,R Fin./Swed. 34K3
Muota Tal valley Switzerland 33D2
Muotathal Switzerland 33D1
Muping China 54L4
Mu,R Burma 59J4
Murakami Japan 56F5
Murat Dagh mt Turkey 62B2
Murat,R Turkey 62E2
Murça Portugal 40C2
Murcheh Khvort Iran 63G3
Murchison New Zealand 100E5
Murchison,C NW Terr. Canada 77T4
Murchison Falls = Kabalega Falls
Murchison Mts New Zealand 100B7
Murchison,R W Aus. Australia 98D5
Murcia Spain 41F4
Murcia prov. Spain 41F4
Murcia region Spain 41E3
Murdo S Dak. USA 81G4
Muresul,R Romania 46C1
Muret France 43D5
Murfreesboro Tenn. USA 85D3
Murgon Queens. Australia 99L5

Muri India 61D4
Muri Switzerland 33D1
Muriaé Brazil 93J8
Murias de Paredes Spain 40C1
Müritz See lake E Germany 36E2
Murjek Sweden 34J3
Murmansk USSR 50E3
Murom USSR 49E3
Muroran Japan 56G3
Muros Spain 40B1
Murphy Idaho USA 80E4
Murphy N Car. USA 85E3
Murphysboro Ill. USA 83P4
Murray Idaho USA 80E2
Murray Ky USA 85C2
Murray Utah USA 82C2
Murray Bridge S Aus. Australia 97A3
Murray Harbour Pr. Ed. I. Canada 78G3
Murray,R Australia 97B3
Murray River Pr. Ed. I. Canada 78G3
Murrayville Vic. Australia 97B3
Murree Pakistan 60C4
Mürren Switzerland 33C2
Murrumbidgee,R NSW Australia 97B2
Murrumbidgee,R NSW Australia 97C2
Murrumburrah & Harden NSW Australia 97C2
Murrurundi NSW Australia 97D2
Mursan India 60E7
Murshidabad India 61G3
Murten Switzerland 33C2
Murten See lake Switzerland 33C2
Murtoa Vic. Australia 97B3
Murupara New Zealand 100G4
Mururoa,I Tuamotu Arch. 95N12
Murwara India 61C4
Muryo mt Java Indon. 53F12
Mus Turkey 62E2
Musa Khel Bazar Pakistan 60A5
Musa Qala Afghanistan 63J3
Muscat Oman 63H5
Muscatine Iowa USA 83N2
Muscat & Oman = Oman
Muscongus B Maine USA 78D5
Musemur South Yemen 62E7
Musgrave Queens. Australia 99J2
Musgrave Ra mts S Aus. Australia 98G5
Musgravetown Newf. Canada 78M2
Musheramore mt Ireland, Rep. of 31F9
Mushie Zaire 70D5
Muskeget Chan. Mass. USA 84F2
Muskegon Mich. USA 79C4
Muskegon,R Mich. USA 79D4
Muskogee Okla. USA 83L5
Muskwaro,L Que. Canada 78H1
Musmar Sudan 69N5
Musoma Tanzania 71G5
Mussau,I Pacific Ocean 94E8
Musselburgh Scotland UK 29K8
Mussidan France 43D4
Mussuma Angola 70E7
Mustahil Ethiopia 71J3
Mustajidda Saudi Arabia 62E4
Mustang Nepal 61D1
Mustang I Texas USA 82T10
Musters,L Argentina 91C7
Mustvee Eston. USSR 35M7
Muswellbrook NSW Australia 97D2
Mut Egypt 69L3
Mut Turkey 62C2
Mutanda Zambia 72D2
Mutare Zimbabwe 72E3
Muth India 60F5
Mutoko Zimbabwe 72E3
Mutoray USSR 51M3
Mutshatsha Zaire 70E7
Mutsu wan bay Japan 56G4
Muttler mt Switzerland 33F2
Mutton I Ireland, Rep. of 31D8
Mutumbo Angola 70D7
Mutupet India 58E6
Mutusjarvi Finland 34M2
Muwale Tanzania 71G6
Muxima Angola 70C6
Muya USSR 51N4
Muy Muy Nicaragua 89B4
Muynak Uzbek. USSR 50G5
Muzaffarabad Kashmir India 60C3
Muzaffargarh Pakistan 60B5
Muzaffarnagar India 60E6
Muzaffarpur India 61E2
Muzhi USSR 50H3
Múzquiz Mexico 88D2
Muztag mt Tibet China 59G1
Muztagta,Mt China 60D1
Mvolo Sudan 69L7

Mvuma, Newark

Mvuma Zimbabwe 72E3
Mwanza Tanzania 71G5
Mweelrea mt Ireland, Rep. of 30D6
Mwenezi Zimbabwe 72E4
Mweru,L Zaire/Zambia 71F6
Mwinilunga Zambia 72C2
Myall L NSW Australia 97D2
Myanaung Burma 59F5
Myebon Burma 59H4
Myenmoletkhat,Mt Burma 59J6
Myggbukta Greenland 14N2
Myingyan Burma 59J4
Myitkyina Burma 59J3
Myjava Czech. 37G4
Mymensingh Bangladesh 59H4
Mynydd Bach upland Wales UK 26F4
Mynydd Eppynt upland Wales UK 26G4
Myohaung Burma 59H4
Myrdal Norway 35B6
Myrdals Jokull glacier Iceland 34V13
Myrtle Beach S Car. USA 85H4
Myrtle Creek Oreg. USA 80B4
Myrtleford Vic. Australia 97C3
Myrtle Point Oreg. USA 80A4
Myrtle Springs S Aus. Australia 97A2
Myślenice Poland 37H4
Myslowice Poland 37H3
Mysore India 58E6
My Tho Vietnam 57D4
Myvatn glacier Iceland 34W12
Mziha Tanzania 71H6
Mzimba Malawi 71G7

N

Naam,R Sudan 69L7
Naarden Netherlands 32D2
Naas Ireland, Rep. of 31K7
Näätämojoki,R Finland 34N2
Nabadwip India 61G4
Nabatiyet et Tahta Lebanon 64D4
Nabberu,L W Aus. Australia 98E5
Nabha India 60E5
Nablus Jordan 64D5
Nacaome Honduras 89B4
Nachvak Fj Newf. Canada 77T5
Nacimiento Mexico 88D2
Nackara S Aus. Australia 97A2
Nackten lake Sweden 34F5
Naco Ariz. USA 82D7
Nacogdoches Texas USA 83L7
Nacozari de Garcia Mexico 88C1
Nadia = Nabadwip
Nadiad India 58D4
Naerøy Norway 34D4
Naestved Denmark 35D9
Nafels Switzerland 33E1
Naga Philippines 53H8
Naga Yemen,DR 62F7
Naga Hills India 59H3
Nagaland state India 59H3
Nagambie Vic. Australia 97C3
Nagano Japan 56F6
Nagano prefecture Japan 56F6
Nagaoka Japan 56F6
Nagapattinam India 58E6
Nagar India 58F5
Nagar India 60E4
Nagar Karnul India 58E5
Nagar Parkar India 58D4
Nagasaki Japan 56A8
Nagasaki prefecture Japan 56A8
Nagaur India 58D3
Nagda India 58E4
Nagercoil India 58E7
Nagha Kalat Pakistan 58C3
Nagina India 61B1
Nagir Kashmir India 60D2
Nagod India 61C3
Nagoya Japan 56E7
Nagpur India 58E4
Nagu Finland 35J6
Nagykanizsa Hungary 37G5
Naha Japan 56M13
Nahan India 60E5
Nahanni,R NW Terr. Canada 76F4
Nahariya Israel 64D4
Nahcotta Wash. USA 80A2
Nahuel,L Argentina 91B6
Nahuel Niyeu Argentina 91C6
Naifar Iraq 62F3
Naigaon India 61A3
Naihati India 61G4
Nā'īn Iran 63G3
Nain Newf. Canada 77T5
Nai Ngani,I Viti Levu Fiji 94A25
Naini Tal India 61B1
Nairn Scotland UK 28J4
Nairn,R Scotland UK 28H5
Nairobi Kenya 71H5
Naivasha Kenya 71H5
Naivasha,L Kenya 71H5
Najafabad Iran 63G3
Najera Spain 41E1
Najibabad India 61B1
Najran Saudi Arabia 62E6
Nakajō Japan 56F5
Nak'amef Ethiopia 71H3
Nakatsu Japan 56B8
Nakawn Pathom Thailand 57C4
Nakfa Ethiopia 71H1
Nakhaun Phanom Thailand 57C3
Nakhichevan USSR 50F6
Nakhon Ratchasima Thailand 57C4
Nakhon Sawan Thailand 57C3
Nakhon Si Thammarat Thailand 57B5
Nakina Ont. Canada 77O6
Nakl Mubarak Saudi Arabia 62D5
Nakodar India 60D5
Nakskov Denmark 35D9
Nakuru Kenya 71H5
Nalagarh India 60E5
Nalgonda India 58E5
Nallamalai Hills India 58E5
Nalut Libya 69H2
Namakzar-e-Shadad Iran 63H3
Namangan Uzbek. USSR 50J5
Namaqualand region Namibia/S Africa 72B5
Namasagali Uganda 71G4
Namatail Mozambique 71H8
Namatinna,R Sudan 69L7
Nambala Zambia 72D3
Nambucca Heads NSW Australia 97D2
Namcha Barwa mt Tibet China 59J3
Nam Co lake Tibet China 59G2
Nam Dinh Vietnam 57D2
Namen = Namur
Namhoi = Nanhai
Namib Des. Namibia 72A4
Namibia country Africa 72B4
Namlea Buru Indon. 53J11
Namling Tibet China 59G3
Nammada,R India 58D4
Namoi,R NSW Australia 97D2
Namonuito,Is Caroline Is 94E7
Namorona Madagascar 71N11
Nampa Idaho USA 80E4
Nampula Mozambique 71H8
Namsen,R Norway 34E4
Nams Fj. Norway 34D4
Namsos Norway 34D4
Namsvatnet,L Norway 34E4
Namtsy USSR 51P3
Namtu Burma 59J4
Namur Belgium 32C4
Namur prov. Belgium 32C4
Namutoni Namibia 72B3
Namwala Zambia 72D3
Nanaimo BC Canada 76F7
Nana Kru Liberia 68D8
Nanan = Dayu
Nan'an China 55K10
Nan'ao China 55J11
Nanao Japan 56E6
Nanchang China 55H8
Nancheng China 55J9
Nanchong China 54D7
Nanchuan China 55D8
Nancowry island Nicobar Is India 59H7
Nancy France 42G2
Nanda Devi,Mt India 58E2
Nandan China 55D10
Nandewar Ra mts NSW Australia 97D2
Nandrau Plat Viti Levu Fiji 94A25
Nandu Jiang river China 55E13
Nandval India 58E5
Nanfeng China 55J9
Nanga Parbat,Mt Kashmir India 60D3
Nangchangshan Dao island China 54L4
Nangong China 54H4
Nanhai China 55G11
Nanhui China 54L7
Nanjangud India 58E6
Nanjiang China 54D6
Nanjing province China 54K7
Nankang China 55H10
Nannine W Aus. Australia 98D5
Nanning China 55E11
Nanortakik Greenland 14P3
Nanpara India 61C2
Nanpi China 54J3
Nanping China 55K9
Nan,R Thailand 57C3
Nanri Dao island China 55K10
Nanripo Mozambique 71H7
Nantes France 42C3
Nanticoke Pa USA 84C2
Nanto Taiwan 55L11
Nantong China 54L6
Nantucket Mass. USA 84F2
Nantucket I Mass. USA 84F2
Nantucket Sd Mass. USA 84F2
Nantwich England UK 25C6
Nanuque Brazil 93J7
Nanxiong China 55H10
Nanyang China 54G6
Nanyuki Kenya 71H4
Nanzhang China 54F7
Nao,C de Spain 41G3
Naoetsu Japan 56F6
Naoshera Pakistan 60D4
Naozhou Dao island China 55F12
Napa Calif. USA 80B6
Napanee Ont. Canada 79H3
Napas USSR 50K4
Nape Laos 57D3
Napf mt Switzerland 33C2
Napier New Zealand 100G4
Naples = Napoli
Naples Fla USA 85M8
Napoleon N Dak. USA 81H2
Napoli Italy 45E5
Napo,R Ecuador 92B4
Naqb Ishtar Jordan 64D7
Naqoura Lebanon 64D4
Nara Mali 68D5
Nara prefecture Japan 56D7
Naracoorte S Aus. Australia 97B3
Naradhan NSW Australia 97C2
Narathiwat Thailand 57C5
Narayanganj Bangladesh 59H4
Narberth Wales UK 26E5
Narbonne France 43E5
Nares Land region Greenland 14P1
Nares Str. Can./Greenland 14Q2
Nari,R Pakistan 58C3
Narken Sweden 34K3
Narmada,R India 61B4
Narnaul India 60E6
Narok Kenya 71H5
Narooma NSW Australia 97D3
Narovchat USSR 49F4
Narowal Pakistan 60D4
Narrabri NSW Australia 97C2
Narrabri West NSW Australia 97C2
Narragansett B RI USA 84F2
Narranderra NSW Australia 97C2
Narran L NSW Australia 97C1
Narran,R NSW Australia 97C1
Narresundby Denmark 35C8
Narrogin W Aus. Australia 98D6
Narromine NSW Australia 97C2
Narsarsuaq Greenland 14P3
Narsimhapur India 61B4
Narsinghgarh India 61B4
Naruto Japan 56D7
Narva Eston. USSR 35N7
Narva Laht,B Eston. USSR 35M7
Narva,R Eston USSR 35M7
Narvik Norway 34G2
Narwar India 61A3
Naryan Mar USSR 50G3
Narykary USSR 50H3
Narym USSR 50K4
Naryn Kirgiz. USSR 50J5
Naseby New Zealand 100D7
Nash Point Wales UK 26G6
Nashua New H USA 84F1
Nashua,R Mass./New J USA 84F1
Nashville Ark. USA 83M6
Nashville Ill. USA 83P3
Nashville N Car. USA 85H2
Nashville Tenn. USA 85D2
Nasian Ivory Coast 68E7
Nasi Jarvi lake Finland 35K6
Nasik India 58D4
Nasir Sudan 69M7
Nasirabad India 58D3
Naskaupi,R Newf Canada 77T6
Nasriganj India 61E3
Nassau The Bahamas 89D1
Nassau,B de Chile 91C9
Nassau,I Pacific Ocean 94K9
Nasser City Egypt 69M4
Nasser,L Egypt 69M4
Nässjö Sweden 35F8
Nassob,R Botswana/S Africa 72C5
Nata Panama 89C5
Natal Brazil 92E5
Natal Brazil 93K5
Natal Sumatra Indon. 53C10
Natal province South Africa 72E5
Natanes Plat. Ariz. USA 82D6
Natanya Israel 64C5
Natashquan Que. Canada 78H1
Natashquan,R Que. Canada 78H1
Natchez Miss. USA 85B5
Natchitoches La USA 83M7
Nathana India 60D5
Natimuk Vic. Australia 97B3
National City Calif. USA 80E9
Natitingou Benin 68F6
Natividade Brazil 93H6
Natron,L Tanzania 71H5
Nattavaara Sweden 34J3
Naturaliste,C W Aus. Australia 98C6
Naturawit L NW Terr. Canada 76M4
Naumburg E Germany 36D3
Náuplia = Návplion
Naur Jordan 64D6
Nauru,I Pacific Ocean 94G8
Naushahra = Nowshera
Naushahro Pakistan 58C3
Naushki USSR 51M4
Nauta Peru 92C4
Nava del Rey Spain 40D2
Navajo Ind. Resn Ariz. USA 82C4
Navajo,Mt Utah USA 82C4
Navalcarnero Spain 40D2
Navalmoral de la Mata Spain 40D3
Navara region Spain 41F1
Navarino,I Chile 91C9
Navarra region Spain 41F1
Navarre Vic. Australia 97B3
Navarre prov. France 43C5
Navplion Greece 47D6
Navrongo Ghana 68E6
Navsari India 58D4
Nawa Syria 64E5
Nawab Basoda India 61B4
Nawabganj India 61B1
Nawabganj India 61C2
Nawabganj India 61D2
Nawada India 61E3
Nawagai Pakistan 60B3
Nawai India 58E3
Nawalgarh India 60D7
Naxi China 55C8
Náxos island Greece 47E6
Nayakhan USSR 51S3
Nayarit state Mexico 88C3
Nay Band Iran 63G4
Nay Band Iran 63H3
Nayfah well Saudi Arabia 63G6
Nayoro Japan 56H2
Nazaré Brazil 93K6
Nazaré da Mata Brazil 93K5
Nazareth Israel 64D5
Nazca Peru 92C6
Naze,The = Lindesnes
Nazilli Turkey 62B2
Nazimovo USSR 51L4
Ncheu Malawi 71G7
Ndala Tanzania 71G5
N'Dalatando Angola 70C6
Ndele CAR 69K7
Ndeni,I Santa Cruz Is 94G9
N'Djamena Chad 69J6
Ndjolé Gabon 70C5
Ndola Zambia 72D2
Néapolis Kríti Greece 47E7
Near Is Aleutian Is USA 87U13
Neath Wales UK 26G5
Nebikon Switzerland 33C1
Nebit-Dag Turkmen. USSR 50G6
Nebolch USSR 48H2
Nebo,Mt Utah USA 82B3
Nebraska state USA 86F3
Nebraska City Nebr. USA 83L2
Necedah Wis. USA 79A3
Nechl,R Columbia 92B2
Neckar,R W Germany 36C4
Necochea Argentina 91E5
Nederweert Netherlands 32D3
Nêdong Tibet China 59H3
Neede Netherlands 32E2
Needham Market England UK 27S4
Needle Ra mts Utah USA 80G6
Needles Calif. USA 80F8
Needles, The mts Ariz. USA 80F8
Neemuch India 58D4
Neenah Wis. USA 79B3
Neerpelt Belgium 32D3
Nefa island Tonga 95V30
Nefud Des. = An Nafud
Negaunee Mich. USA 79C2
Negev des. Israel 64C6
Negombo Sri Lanka 58E7
Negrais,C Burma 59H5
Negro,R Argentina 91D6
Negro,R Brazil 92E4
Negro,R Uruguay 91E4
Negros island Philippines 53H9
Nehalem Oreg. USA 80B3
Nehavand Iran 62F3
Nehbandān Iran 63H3
Neijiang China 55C8
Neillsville Wis. USA 79A3
Neisse = Nysa
Neiva Colombia 92B3
Neixiang China 54F6
Neksø Bornholm I Denmark 35F9
Nelia Gaari NSW Australia 97B2
Nelkan USSR 51Q4
Nell,I Kwajalein,Is 94A17
Nelligen NSW Australia 97D3
Nellore India 58F6
Nelma USSR 51Q5
Nelson Ariz. USA 80G8
Nelson BC Canada 76H7
Nelson Calif. USA 80C6
Nelson England UK 25D5
Nelson New Zealand 100E5
Nelson Vic. Australia 97B3
Nelson stat. area New Zealand 100D5
Nelson,C Vic. Australia 97B3
Nelson Hd NW Terr. Canada 76G2
Nelson,Mt BC Canada 76H6
Nelson,R Man. Canada 76N5
Néma Mauritania 68D5
Neman Litov USSR 35K9
Nemikiachi,L = Némiscachingue,L
Némiscachingue,L Que. Canada 79J2
Nemours France 42E2
Nemunas,R Lith. USSR 35K9
Nemuro Japan 56J3
Nemuro wan bay Japan 56J3
Nenagh Ireland, Rep. of 31G8
Nendeln Liechtenstein 33E1
Nene,R England UK 27P4
Nenjiang China 52J1
Nen Jiang river China 52H1
Neodesha Kans. USA 83L4
Neosho Mo USA 83L4
Nepa USSR 51M4
Nepal country Asia 58K7
Nepalganj Nepal 61C1
Nephi Utah USA 82C3
Nephin mt Ireland, Rep. of 30E5
Nephin Beg mt Ireland, Rep. of 30D5
Nérac France 43D4
Nerchinsk USSR 51N4
Nereta Latviy USSR 35L8
Neringa Litov USSR 35J9
Neris,R Litov USSR 35L9
Nerpio Spain 41E3
Nerriga NSW Australia 97D3
Nes USSR 50F3
Neskowin Oreg. USA 80B3
Nesna Norway 34E3
Nesøy island Norway 34E3
Nespawa Man. Canada 76M6
Ness City Kans. USA 83H3
Nesset Norway 34C5
Nesslau Switzerland 33E1
Nesthorn mt Switzerland 33C2
Nesttun Norway 35A6
Netherlands country Europe 22K5
Nettilling L NW Terr. Canada 77R3
Nettuno Italy 45D5
Neubrandenburg E Germany 36E2
Neuburg W Germany 36D4
Neuchâtel Switzerland 33B1
Neuchâtel canton Switzerland 33B1
Neufchâteau Belgium 32D5
Neufchâteau France 42F2
Neufchâtel France 42D2
Neufelden Austria 36E4
Neuhausen Switzerland 33D1
Neumünster W Germany 36C1
Neunkirch Switzerland 33D1
Neuquén Argentina 91C5
Neuruppin E Germany 36E2
Neuse,R N Car. USA 85J3
Neusiedler See lake Austria 37G5
Neuss W Germany 36B3
Neustadt W Germany 36D1
Neustadt an der Aisch W Germany 36D4
Neustettin = Szczecinek
Neustrelitz E Germany 36E2
Neu Ulm W Germany 36D4
Neuva,I Argentina/Chile 91C9
Neuva Lubeca Argentina 91B6
Neuveville Switzerland 33C1
Neuvitas Cuba 89D2
Nevada Iowa USA 83M1
Nevada Mo USA 83L4
Nevada state USA 86C4
Nevada,Sa mts Argentina 91C5
Nevada,Sa mts Calif. USA 80C5
Nevada,Sa mts Spain 40E4
Nev. de Toluca mt Mexico 88E4
Nevel USSR 48F3
Nevel'sk USSR 51R5
Nevers France 42E3
Nevertire NSW Australia 97C2
Nevesinje Yugoslavia 46B3
Neveyezhkino USSR 49G5
Nevis island Leeward Is 89G3
Nevsehir Turkey 62C2
Nevs Ojos del Salado,Mts Arg./Chile 91C3
Nevyansk USSR 49Q2
New Albany Ind. USA 85E1
New Albany Miss. USA 85C3
New Almaden Calif. USA 80C7
New Amsterdam Guyana 93F2
New Angledool NSW Australia 97C1
Newark Del. USA 84D3
Newark New J USA 84D2

Newark, **North Powder**

Newark *Ohio* USA **79E5**
Newark-on-Trent *England* UK **25G6**
Newaygo *Mich.* USA **79D4**
New Bedford *Mass.* USA **84F2**
Newberg *Oreg.* USA **80B3**
New Bern *N Car.* USA **85J3**
Newbern *Tenn.* USA **85C2**
Newberry *Mich.* USA **79D2**
Newberry *S Car.* USA **85G3**
New Bloomfield *Pa* USA **84C2**
New Braunfels *Texas* USA **83J8**
Newbridge on Wye *Wales* UK **26H4**
New Britain *Conn.* USA **84E2**
New Britain,I Bismarck Arch. **94E8**
New Brunswick *New J* USA **84D2**
New Brunswick *prov.* Canada **77S7**
Newburg *New Br.* Canada **78E3**
Newburgh *NY* USA **84D2**
Newburgh *Scotland* UK **28M5**
Newburgh *Scotland* UK **29K7**
Newbury *England* UK **27M6**
Newburyport *Mass.* USA **84F1**
Newby Bridge *England* UK **25C4**
New Carlisle *Que.* Canada **78F2**
Newcastle *Del.* USA **84D3**
New Castle *Del.* USA **84D3**
Newcastle Ireland,Rep. of **31L7**
Newcastle *New Br.* Canada **78F3**
Newcastle N Ireland **30M5**
Newcastle *NSW* Australia **97D2**
New Castle *Pa* USA **79F5**
Newcastle South Africa **72D5**
Newcastle *Wyo.* USA **81E4**
Newcastle Emlyn *Wales* UK **26F4**
Newcastle-under-Lyme *England* UK **25D6**
Newcastle-upon-Tyne *England* UK **25E3**
Newcastle Waters *N Terr.* Australia **99G3**
Newcastle West Ireland,Rep. of **31E9**
Newchwang = Yingkou
New City *NY* USA **84D2**
New England Ra *mts* *NSW* Australia **97D2**
Newent *England* UK **26K5**
Newfane *Vt* USA **84E1**
New Forest *England* UK **27L7**
Newfoundland *prov.* Canada **77T5**
New Galloway *Scotland* UK **29H9**
New Georgia,I Solomon Is **94F8**
New Germany *No. Sc.* Canada **78F4**
New Glasgow *No. Sc.* Canada **78G4**
New Guinea *island* Pacific Ocean **19Q10**
New Hampshire *state* USA **87M3**
New Hampton *Iowa* USA **83M1**
New Harmony *Utah* USA **80G7**
New Haven *Conn.* USA **84E2**
Newhaven *England* UK **27Q7**
New Haven *Mo* USA **83N3**
New Hebrides,Is = Vanuatu
New Holland *England* UK **25H5**
New Iberia *La* USA **83N7**
New Ireland,I Bismarck Arch. **94F8**
New Jersey *state* USA **87M3**
New Liskeard *Ont.* Canada **79G2**
New London *Conn.* USA **84E2**
New London *Wis.* USA **79B3**
New Luce *Scotland* UK **29G10**
New Madrid *Mo* USA **83P4**
Newman *Calif.* USA **80C7**
Newman *W Aus.* Australia **98D4**
Newmarket *England* UK **27Q4**
Newmarket Ireland, Rep. of **31E9**
Newmarket *Ont.* Canada **79G3**
New Mexico *state* USA **86E5**
Newnham *England* UK **26K5**
New Norfolk *Tas.* Australia **97F5**
New Ord River *W Aus.* Australia **98F3**
New Orleans *La* USA **83N7**
New Pitsligo *Scotland* UK **28M4**
New Plymouth New Zealand **100F4**
Newport *Ark.* USA **83N5**
Newport *England* UK **25D7**
Newport *England* UK **27Q5**
Newport *I of Wight* England **27M7**
Newport Ireland, Rep. of **30D6**
Newport *Ky* USA **79D6**
Newport *New H* USA **84E1**
Newport *Oreg.* USA **80A3**
Newport *Que.* Canada **78F2**
Newport *RI* USA **84F2**
Newport *Vt* USA **79K3**
Newport *Wales* UK **26E4**
Newport *Wales* UK **26H5**
Newport Beach *Calif.* USA **80E9**
Newport News *Va* USA **85J2**
Newport-on-Tay *Scotland* UK **29L7**
Newport Pagnell *England* UK **27N4**
New Providence *island* The Bahamas **89D2**
Newquay *England* UK **26D8**
New Quay *Wales* UK **26F4**
New Radnor *Wales* UK **26H4**
New Richmond *Que.* Canada **78F2**
New Richmond *Wis.* USA **81L3**
New Rochelle *NY* USA **84E2**
New Rockford *N Dak.* USA **81H2**
New Romney *England* UK **27R7**
New Ross Ireland, Rep. of **31K9**
Newry N Ireland **30L5**
New Salem *N Dak.* USA **81G2**
New Siberian Is = Novosibirskiye Ostrova
New South Wales *state* Australia **99J6**
Newton *Iowa* USA **83M2**
Newton *Kans.* USA **83K3**
Newton *Mass.* USA **84F1**
Newton *New J* USA **84D2**
Newton Abbot *England* UK **26G7**
Newton Aycliffe *England* UK **25E3**
Newtonmore *Scotland* UK **28H5**
Newton Stewart *Scotland* UK **29H10**
Newtown *Wales* UK **26H3**
Newtownabbey *N Ireland* UK **30M4**
Newtownards N Ireland **30M4**
Newtown Butler N Ireland **30J5**
Newtownhamilton N Ireland **30K5**
Newtown Mount Kennedy Ireland, Rep. of **31L7**
Newtownstewart N Ireland **30J4**
New Ulm *Minn.* USA **81K3**
New Waterford *No. Sc.* Canada **78H3**
New Westminster *BC* Canada **76G7**
New World I *Newf.* Canada **78L2**
New York *NY* USA **84E2**
New York *state* USA **87L3**
New Zealand *country* Australasia **94H12**
Neya USSR **49F1**
Neyriz Iran **63G4**
Neyshābūr Iran **63H2**
Nezhin *Ukrain.* USSR **48G6**
Nez Perce *Idaho* USA **80E2**
Nez Perce P *Idaho* USA **80F3**
Ngami,L Botswana **72C4**
Ngangezê Co *lake* *Tibet* China **59G2**
Ngangla Ringco *lake* *Tibet* China **59F2**
N'Gaoundéré Cameroun **69H7**
Ngardmau Palau Is **94A20**
Ngaruawehia New Zealand **100F3**
Ngatik,I Caroline Is **94F7**
Ngauruhoe,Mt New Zealand **100F4**
N'Giva Angola **72B3**
Ngong Kenya **71H5**
Ngoring Hu *lake* China **52C4**
Nguigmi Niger **69H6**
Ngulu,I Pacific Ocean **94D7**
Ngwasi Tanzania **71H6**
Nhamunda,R Brazil **92F4**
Nha Trang Vietnam **57D4**
Nhavarre,L Mozambique **72E4**
Nhill *Vic.* Australia **97B3**
Niafounke Mali **68E5**
Niagara Falls *NY* USA **79G4**
Niagara Falls *Ont.* Canada **79G4**
Niagara-on-the-Lake *Ont.* Canada **79G4**
Niah *Sarawak* Malay. **53F10**
Niamey Niger **68F6**
Nian Zaire **70F4**
Nia Nia Zaire **71F4**
Niapa *mt* *Borneo* Indon. **53G10**
Nias *island* Indonesia **53C10**
Nicaragua *country* Central America **89B4**
Nicaragua L Nicaragua **89B4**
Nicastro Italy **45F6**
Nice France **43G5**
Nicobar,Is Indian Ocean **59H7**
Nicolet *Que.* Canada **79K2**
Nicosia Cyprus **64B2**
Nicoya Costa Rica **89B4**
Nicoya,G de Costa Rica **89C5**
Nicoya Pen. Costa Rica **89B4**
Nidau Switzerland **33C1**
Nidd,R *England* UK **25E4**
Nidwalden *canton* Switzerland **33D2**
Nidzica Poland **37J2**
Niedere Tauern *mts* Austria **36E5**
Nieder Lausitz *region* E Germany **36F3**
Nieder Osterreich *state* Austria **37F4**
Niedersachsen *state* W Germany **36B2**
Nieder Simmental *valley* Switzerland **33C2**
Niederweningen Switzerland **33D1**
Nied Urnen Switzerland **33E1**
Nielle Ivory Coast **68D6**
Nienberg W Germany **36C2**
Niesen *mt* Switzerland **33C2**
Niete,Mt Liberia **68D7**
Nieuw Amsterdam Surinam **93F2**
Nieuwendijk Netherlands **32C3**
Nieuwersluis Netherlands **32C2**
Nieuwkerke Belgium **32A4**
Nieuwkoop Netherlands **32C2**
Nieuw Nickerie Surinam **93F2**
Nieuwpoort Belgium **32A3**
Nieuwpoort Netherlands **32C3**
Nieves Mexico **88D3**
Niévre *dep.* France **42E3**
Niewwegein Netherlands **32D2**
Nif Yap Is **94A19**
Nigde Turkey **62D2**
Niger *country* Africa **68G5**
Nigeria *country* Africa **68G7**
Niger,R Africa **68E5**
Nighasan India **61C1**
Nightingale I Tristan da Cunha Is **72G8**
Nigula *Eston.* USSR **35K7**
Niigata Japan **56F6**
Niigata *Prefecture* Japan **56F6**
Niihau,I *Hawaii* USA **94K5**
Nijil Jordan **64D7**
Nijkerk Netherlands **32D2**
Nijmegen Netherlands **32D3**
Nikaría,I = Ikaría,I
Nikiforos Greece **46E4**
Nikki Benin **68F7**
Nikko Nat. Pk Japan **56F6**
Nikolayev *Ukrain.* USSR **48G8**
Nikolayevskiy USSR **49G5**
Nikolayevsk-na-Amure USSR **51R4**
Nikolo Berezovka USSR **49M2**
Nikolo Kozelsk *Ukrain.* USSR **48H8**
Nikolskaya Pestrovka USSR **49G4**
Nikonga,R Tanzania **71G5**
Nikopol *Ukrain.* USSR **48J8**
Niksar Turkey **62D1**
Nikshahr Iran **63J4**
Nikšić Yugoslavia **46B3**
Nila *island* Indonesia **53J12**
Nile,R Africa **69M3**
Niles *Mich.* USA **79C5**
Nilgiri India **59G4**
Nilgiri Hills India **58E6**
Nilphamari Bangladesh **61G3**
Nimach = Neemuch
Nimba,Mt Ivory Coast **68D7**
Nîmes France **43F5**
Nimgiri,Mt India **59F5**
Nimmitabel *NSW* Australia **97C3**
Nimrod Bay = Xiangshan Gang
Nimule Uganda **71G4**
Nimu,R *Kashmir* India **60E3**
Nine Degree Chan. Arabian Sea **58D7**
Nine de Julio Argentina **91D5**
Ninety Mile Beach New Zealand **100E2**
Ninety Mile Beach *Vic.* Australia **97C3**
Nineveh Iraq **62E2**
Ning'an China **52J2**
Ningbo China **55L8**
Ningde China **55K9**
Ningdu China **55H9**
Ninggang China **55H9**
Ningguo China **54K7**
Ninghai China **55L8**
Ninghe China **54K3**
Ninghsien = Ningbo
Ninghua China **55J9**
Ningi I Kwajalein Is **94A17**
Ningjin China **54J4**
Ningkwo = Xuancheng
Ningming China **55D11**
Ningqiang China **54D6**
Ningshan China **54E6**
Ning-sia (China) = Yinchuan
Ningsia (China) = Ningxia
Ningwu China **54G3**
Ningxia *province* China **54C4**
Ning Xian China **54D5**
Ningxiang China **55G8**
Ningyang China **54J5**
Ningyuan China **55F10**
Ninh Binh Vietnam **57D2**
Ninove Belgium **32C4**
Niobrara,R *Nebr.* USA **82G1**
Nioro Mali **68D5**
Niort France **42C3**
Níos,I = Íos,I
Nipe,B de Cuba **89D2**
Nipigon *Ont.* Canada **77O7**
Nipigon,L *Ont.* Canada **77O7**
Nipissing,L *Ont.* Canada **79G2**
Nira,R India **58D5**
Nirmal India **58E5**
Nis Yugoslavia **46C3**
Nish = Nis
Nishapur = Neyshābūr
Nísiros *island* Greece **47F6**
Nissan Solomon Is **94F8**
Nisser Vatn *lake* Norway **35C7**
Nissi *Eston.* USSR **35L7**
Niterói Brazil **93J8**
Nith,R *Scotland* UK **29J9**
Nithsdale *Scotland* UK **29J9**
Nitra Czech. **37H4**
Nitrianske Pravno Czech. **37H4**
Niue,I Cook Is **94K9**
Niulan Jiang *river* China **55B9**
Niut *mt* *Borneo* Indon. **53E10**
Nivala Finland **34L5**
Nivelles Belgium **32C4**
Nivernais *prov.* France **42E3**
Nizamabad India **58E5**
Nizampatnam India **58F5**
Nizhne Udinsk USSR **51L4**
Nizhni Lomov USSR **49G4**
Nizhniye Serogozy *Ukrain.* USSR **48J8**
Nizhniy Tagil USSR **49P2**
Nizh' Pesha USSR **50F3**
Nizke Tatry *mts* Czech. **37H4**
Nizzana *hist. site* Israel **64C7**
Njombe Tanzania **71G6**
Nkhota-Kota Malawi **71G7**
N'Kongsamba Cameroun **69G8**
Nmai,R Burma **59J3**
Noagarh India **59F4**
Noakhali Bangladesh **59H4**
Noanama Colombia **92B3**
Noatak,R *Alaska* USA **87W12**
Nobber Ireland, Rep. of **30K6**
Nocera Italy **45E5**
Nochixtlán Mexico **88E4**
Nodales,B de los Argentina **91C7**
Noerbø Norway **35A7**
Nogales *Ariz.* USA **82C7**
Nogales *Sonora* Mexico **88B1**
Nogaro France **43C5**
Nogent-le-Rotrou France **42D2**
Nogent-sur-Seine France **42E2**
Noginsk USSR **48L4**
Nohar India **60D6**
Noirmoutier France **42B3**
Noirmoutier,I de France **42B3**
Nokhtuysk USSR **51N4**
Nola CAR **70D4**
Nola Italy **45E5**
Nome *Alaska* USA **87W12**
Nominingve,L *Que.* Canada **79J2**
Nom Mhai *mt* Vietnam **57D4**
Nomoi,Is Caroline Is **94F7**
Nomuka Group *islands* Tonga **95V30**
Nonacho L *NW Terr.* Canada **76K4**
Nonancourt France **42D2**
Nong Han Thailand **57C3**
Nong Khai Thailand **57C3**
Nongoma South Africa **72E5**
Nonno Ethiopia **71H3**
Nonoava Mexico **88C2**
Nonouti,I Kiribati **94H8**
Nõo *Eston.* USSR **35M7**
Noojee *Vic.* Australia **97C3**
Noonthurungee *NSW* Australia **97B2**
Noord Brabant *prov.* Netherlands **32C3**
Noordeloos Netherlands **32C3**
Noord-Holland Netherlands **32C2**
Noordwolde Netherlands **32E2**
Nootka I *BC* Canada **76F7**
Nora Sweden **35F7**
Nora I Ethiopia **71J1**
Noranda *Que.* Canada **79G1**
Norbotten *county* Sweden **34G3**
Norcia Italy **44D4**
Nord *dep.* France **42E1**
Nord Cap = Horn
Norddal Norway **34B5**
Norderney *island* W Germany **36B2**
Norderøer *islands* Faerøerne **34Z14**
Nord Fj. Norway **34A6**
Nord Friesische,Is W. Germany **35C9**
Nordhausen E Germany **36D3**
Nordkapp,I Norway **34L1**
Nordkinn Halvøya,Pen. Norway **34M1**
Nordland *county* Norway **34F3**
Nördlingen W Germany **36D4**
Nordostrundingen *cape* Greenland **14M1**
Nordreisa Norway **34J2**
Nordrhein-Westfalen *state* W Germany **36B3**
Nord Slesvig = South Jylland
Nordstrand *island* W Germany **36C1**
Nordvik USSR **51N2**
Nore Norway **35C6**
Nore,R Ireland, Rep. of **31J8**
Norfolk *Nebr.* USA **83K1**
Norfolk *Va* USA **85J2**
Norfolk *county* England UK **27R3**
Norfolk Broads *region* England UK **27S3**
Norfolk Edge *England* UK **27R3**
Norfolk,I Pacific Ocean **94G10**
Norfolk L *Ark.* USA **83M4**
Norgama Pakistan **58C3**
Norham *England* UK **25D1**
Norheimsund Norway **35B6**
Norily USSR **50K3**
Norman *Calif.* USA **80B6**
Norman *Okla.* USA **83K5**
Normanby I Papua New Guinea **99L1**
Normandie *prov.* France **42C2**
Normanton *Queens.* Australia **99J3**
Norman Wells *NW Terr.* Canada **76F3**
Norquin Argentina **91B5**
Norquinco Argentina **91B6**
Norra Dellen Södra *lake* Sweden **35G6**
Norrälje Sweden **35H7**
Norris *Mont.* USA **80H3**
Norris Arm *Newf.* Canada **78L2**
Norris,L *Tenn.* USA **85E2**
Norris Point *Newf.* Canada **78K2**
Norristown *Pa* USA **84D2**
Norrköping Sweden **35G7**
Norrsundet Sweden **35G6**
Norseman *W Aus.* Australia **98E6**
Norsholm Sweden **35F7**
Norte,Sa do *mts* Brazil **92F6**
North Adams *Mass.* USA **84E1**
Northallerton *England* UK **25F4**
Northam *England* UK **26F6**
Northam *W Aus.* Australia **98D6**
Northampton *England* UK **27N4**
Northampton *Mass.* USA **84E1**
Northampton *W Aus.* Australia **98C5**
Northamptonshire *county* England UK **27N4**
North Battleford *Sask.* Canada **76K6**
North Bay *Ont.* Canada **79G2**
North Bend *Oreg.* USA **80A3**
North Berwick *Scotland* UK **29L7**
North Bloomfield *Calif.* USA **80C6**
North Bourke *NSW* Australia **97C1**
Northbridge *Mass.* USA **84F1**
North,C Antarctica **15L2**
North C New Zealand **100E2**
North,C *No. Sc.* Canada **78H3**
North C *Pr. Ed. I.* Canada **78G3**
North Carolina *state* USA **87K4**
North Chan. N Ire./Scot. **30M3**
North Chan. *Ont.* Canada **79E2**
North Creek *NY* USA **79J4**
North Dakota *state* USA **86F2**
North Downs *upland* England UK **27Q6**
Northern Bight *Newf.* Canada **78L2**
Northern Circars,Mts India **58F5**
Northern Ireland *country* Great Britain **22G5**
Northern Territory *state* Australia **98G3**
Northfield *Minn.* USA **81L3**
North I New Zealand **100E3**
North Koel,R India **61E4**
North Korea *country* Asia **52J2**
North Land = Severnaya Zemlya
Northland *stat. area* New Zealand **100E2**
North Lisbon *Wis.* USA **79A4**
North Little Rock *Ark.* USA **83M5**
North Minch *Scotland* UK **28D3**
North Platte *Nebr.* USA **82H2**
North Portal *Sask.* Canada **76L7**
North Powder *Oreg.* USA **80E3**

Penobscot B, Plymouth

Penobscot B *Maine* USA 78D4
Penobscot,R *Maine* USA 78D4
Penola *S Aus.* Australia 97B3
Penong *S Aus.* Australia 98G6
Penonome Panama 89C5
Penrhyn,I Pacific Ocean 95L8
Penrith *England* UK 25C3
Penrith *NSW* Australia 97D2
Penryn *England* UK 26D8
Pensacola *Fla* USA 85D5
Penshurst *Vic.* Australia 97B3
Pentland Firth *Scotland* UK 28K2
Pentland Hills *upland* *Scotland* UK 29K8
Pentland Skerries *islands* *Orkney* Scotland 28L2
Pentwater *Mich.* USA 79C4
Penza USSR 49G4
Penzance *England* UK 26C8
Penzhino USSR 51T3
Penzhinskaya Guba *bay* USSR 51T3
Peoria *Ill.* USA 83P2
Peperga Netherlands 32E2
Pepinster Belgium 32D4
Peqin Albania 46B4
Pequop *Nev.* USA 80F5
Peradeniya Sri Lanka 58F7
Perak *state* Malaysia 57C6
Peralta Spain 41E1
Perce *Que.* Canada 78F2
Perdido,Mt Spain 41G1
Perdido,R Argentina 91C6
Pereira Colombia 92B3
Perello Spain 41G2
Perez Chile 91C3
Pergamno Argentina 91D4
Perhentian Besar *island* Malaysia 57C5
Perho Finland 34L5
Peribonca,R *Que.* Canada 78C1
Perico Argentina 91C2
Périgeux France 43D4
Perigord *region* France 43D4
Perija,Sa de *mts* Columb./Venez. 92C2
Peri L *NSW* Australia 97B2
Perim I South Yemen 62E7
Peristéra *island* Greece 47D5
Perlas, Arch. de las Panama 89D5
Perlis *state* Malaysia 57B5
Perly Switzerland 33B2
Perm USSR 49N1
Pernambuco = Recife
Pernik Bulgaria 46D3
Peronne France 42E2
Péronnes Belgium 32C4
Perote,Cerro de *mt* Mexico 88E4
Perpetua,C *Oreg.* USA 80A3
Perpignan France 43E5
Perranporth *England* UK 26D8
Perrot I *Que.* Canada 79J3
Perry *Iowa* USA 83L2
Perry *NY* USA 84B1
Perry *Okla.* USA 83K4
Perry,R *NW Terr.* Canada 76L3
Perryville *Mo* USA 83P4
Persepolis Iran 63G3
Pershore *England* UK 27K4
Persia = Iran
Persian Gulf = The Gulf
Perth *New Br.* Canada 78E3
Perth *Ont.* Canada 79H3
Perth *Scotland* UK 29K7
Perth *W Aus.* Australia 98D6
Perth Amboy *New J* USA 84D2
Peru *Ind.* USA 79C5
Peru *country* S America 92C6
Perugia Italy 44D4
Peruibe Brazil 93H8
Peruwelz Belgium 32B4
Pervijze Belgium 32A3
Pervomaysk *Ukrain.* USSR 48G7
Perwez Belgium 32C4
Pesaro Italy 44D4
Pescadores = Penghu
Pescadores Chan Taiwan 55K11
Pescadores Is = Penghu Is
Pescara Italy 44E4
Peschici Italy 45F5
Peshawar Pakistan 60B3
Peshtigo,R *Wis.* USA 79B3
Peso de Regua Portugal 40C2
Pesqueira Brazil 93K5
Pestravka USSR 49J4
Petacalco B Mexico 88D4
Petah Tiqwa Israel 64C5
Petalioí *island* Greece 47E5
Petalioi,G of Greece 47E6
Peterborough *England* UK 25H7
Peterborough *Ont.* Canada 79G3
Peterborough *S Aus.* Australia 97A2
Peterhead *Scotland* UK 28N4
Peter I Øy *island* Antarctica 15R3
Peterlee *England* UK 25F3
Petermann Fj. Greenland 14P1
Petermann Pk Greenland 14P2
Petermann Ra *mts* *W Aus.* Australia 98F4
Peter Pond L *Sask.* Canada 76K5
Petersburg *Alaska* USA 87Z13
Petersburg *Va* USA 85J2
Petersfield *England* UK 27N6
Petit Bois I *Ala.* USA 85C5
Petitot R *BC* Canada 76G5
Peto Mexico 88G3
Petone New Zealand 100F5
Petoroa Chile 91B4
Petoskey *Mich.* USA 79D3
Petra *hist-site* Jordan 64D7
Petrich Bulgaria 46D4
Petrified Forest Nat. Pk *Ariz.* USA 82D5
Petrinja Yugoslavia 44F3
Petrodvorets USSR 48F2
Petrolia *Calif.* USA 80A5
Petrolia *Ont.* Canada 79E4
Petrolina Brazil 93J5
Petropavlovsk *Kazakh.* USSR 50H4
Petropavlovsk Kamchatskiy USSR 51S4
Petropolis Brazil 93J8
Petrovac Yugoslavia 46C2
Petrovsk USSR 49G4
Petrovsk USSR 49N4
Petrovsk Zabaykalskiy USSR 51M4
Petrozavodsk USSR 50E3
Petsamo = Pechenga
Petten Netherlands 32C2
Pettigoe Ireland, Rep. of 30H4
Pevant Ra *mts* *Utah* USA 82B3
Pevek USSR 51U3
Pewsey *England* UK 27L6
Pewsey,Vale of *England* UK 27L6
Pézenas France 43E5
Pfäfers Switzerland 33E1
Pfäffikon *Schwyz* Switzerland 33D1
Pfäffikon *Zürich* Switzerland 33D1
Pforzheim W Germany 36C4
Phagwara India 60D5
Phalodi India 58D3
Phanom Dang Raek,Mt Thailand 57C4
Phan Rang Vietnam 57D4
Phan Thiet Vietnam 57D4
Phaphund India 61B2
Phenix City *Ala.* USA 85E4
Phet Thailand 57C3
Phet-Buri Thailand 57B4
Phetchabun Thailand 57C3
Philadelphia *Pa* USA 84D2
Philip *S Dak.* USA 81G3
Philippeville Belgium 32C4
Philippeville,G of Algeria 68G1
Philippi *W Va* USA 79F6
Philippi,L *Queens.* Australia 99H4
Philippines *country* Pacific Ocean 53H8
Philippopolis = Plovdiv
Philipsburg *Mont.* USA 80G2
Phillaur India 60D5
Phillip Edward I *Ont.* Canada 79F3
Phillip I *Vic.* Australia 97C3
Phillips *Maine* USA 78C4
Phillips *Wis.* USA 79A3
Phillipsburg *Kans.* USA 83J3
Phillipsburg *New J* USA 84D2
Phillipsville *Calif.* USA 80B5
Philomena *Alta* Canada 76J5
Phimai Thailand 57C3
Phnom-Penh Cambodia 57C4
Phoenix *Ariz.* USA 82B6
Phoenix,I Phoenix Is 94J8
Phoenix,Is Pacific Ocean 94J8
Phoenixville *Pa* USA 84D2
Phou Lai Leng *mt* Laos 57C3
Phou Loi *mt* Laos 57C2
Phou San *mt* Laos 57C3
Phrae Thailand 57C3
Phu Cuong Vietnam 57D4
Phu Dieh Vietnam 57D3
Phuket Thailand 57B5
Phulji Pakistan 58C3
Phulpur India 61D3
Phu My Vietnam 57D4
Phu Qui Vietnam 57D3
Phu-Quoc,I Cambodia 57C4
Piacenza Italy 44B3
Pian Chih *lake* China 52D6
Piangil *Vic.* Australia 97B3
Pianguan China 54F3
Pian,R *NSW* Australia 97C2
Piatra Neamt Romania 46F1
Piazza Armerina *Sicily* Italy 45E7
Piazzi,I Chile 91B8
Pibor Post Sudan 69M7
Picardie *prov.* France 42D1
Pic de Tanoicaro *mt* Mexico 88D4
Pichanal Argentina 91D2
Picher *Okla.* USA 83L4
Pichilemu Chile 91B4
Pickens *Miss.* USA 85C4
Pickering *England* UK 25G4
Pickwick L *Ala/Tenn.* USA 85C3
Pico *island* Açores 68Q9
Pico Blanco *mt* Costa Rica 89C5
Pico de Turquino *mt* Cuba 89D2
Picola *Vic.* Australia 97C3
Pico Mulhacen *mt* Spain 40E4
Pico Ojo del Toro Cuba 89D3
Picton New Zealand 100E5
Picton *NSW* Australia 97D2
Picton *Ont.* Canada 79H3
Picton,Mt *Tas.* Australia 97F5
Pictou *No. Sc.* Canada 78G4
Pictou I *No. Sc.* Canada 78G4
Pic Tousside *mt* Chad 69J4
Picún Leufú Argentina 91C5
Pidark Pakistan 58B3
Pidurutallagala,Mt Sri Lanka 58F7
Piedmont *Que.* Canada 79J3
Piedmont *S Car.* USA 85F3
Piedmont *S Dak.* USA 81F3
Piedrahita Spain 40D2
Piedras Negras Mexico 88D2
Piedra Sola Uruguay 91E4
Piedras,R de la Peru 92C6
Pieksämäki Finland 34M5
Pielinen,L Finland 34N5
Pieman,R *Tas.* Australia 97E5
Piemonte *region* Italy 44A3
Pieria *dist.* Greece 47D4
Pierre *S Dak.* USA 81G3
Pierreville *Que.* Canada 79K2
Pieske Jaure *lake* Sweden 34G3
Pietarsaari Finland 34K5
Pieter Both Mauritius 65N12
Pietermaritzburg South Africa 72E5
Pietersburg South Africa 72D4
Piggott *Ark.* USA 83N4
Pigüé Argentina 91D5
Pihtipudas Finland 34L5
Pikes Pk *Col.* USA 82F3
Pikeville *Ky* USA 85F2
Pik Kommunisma *mt* *Tadzhik.* USSR 50J6
Pik Lenina *mt* *Kirgiz.* USSR 50J6
Pik Pobedy *mt* China/USSR 50K5
Pila Argentina 91E5
Piła Poland 37G2
Pilão Arcado Brazil 93J6
Pilar Argentina 91D4
Pilar Paraguay 91E3
Pilar,C Chile 91B8
Pilatus *mt* Switzerland 33D2
Pilcaniyeu Argentina 91B6
Pilibhit India 61B1
Pilliga *NSW* Australia 97C2
Pilos Greece 47C6
Pilot Knob *Mo* USA 83N4
Pilot Pk *Wyo.* USA 81B3
Pilot Rock *Oreg.* USA 80D3
Pilot, The *mt* *NSW* Australia 97C3
Pilsen = Plzeň
Piltene *Latvia* USSR 35J8
Pimentel Peru 92B5
Pina Spain 41F2
Pinaki,I Tuamotu Arch. 95N9
Pinaleno Ra *Ariz.* USA 82C6
Pinang,I Malaysia 57C5
Pinarbaşi Turkey 62D2
Pinar del Rio Cuba 89C2
Pinckneyville *Ill.* USA 83P3
Pind Dadan Khan Pakistan 60C4
Pindhos *mts.* Greece 47C5
Pindi Gheb Pakistan 60C4
Pindus Mts = Pindhos
Pine Bluff *Ark.* USA 83M5
Pine City *Minn.* USA 81L3
Pine Creek *N Terr.* Australia 98G2
Pinedale *Wyo.* USA 81C4
Pine Forest Mts *Nev.* USA 80D5
Pinehurst *N Car.* USA 85H3
Pine I *Fla* USA 85L8
Pine Island B Antarctica 15Q2
Pine Mts *Ky* USA 85F2
Pineola *N Car.* USA 85G2
Pine Ridge Ind. Resn *S Dak.* USA 81F4
Pine River *Minn.* USA 81K2
Pinerolo Italy 44A3
Pinetown South Africa 72E5
Pineville *Ky* USA 85F2
Pineville *Mo* USA 83L4
Pineville *W Va* USA 85G2
Piney Buttes *Mont.* USA 81D2
Pingal *Kashmir* India 60C2
Pingchang China 54D7
Pingdingshan China 54G6
Pingdu China 54K4
Pingelap,I Caroline Is 94G7
Pingelly *W Aus.* Australia 98D6
Pinghai China 55K10
Pinghe China 55J10
Pingjiang China 55G8
Pingle China 55F10
Pingliang China 54D5
Pinglu China 54F5
Pinglu China 54G3
Pingluo China 54D3
Pingnam China 55K9
Pingnan China 55F11
Pingouins,I des Crozet Is 65U12
Pingquan China 54K2
Ping,R Thailand 57B3
Pingrup *W Aus.* Australia 98D6
Pingshan China 54H3
Pingtan China 55K10
Pingtan Dao *island* China 55K10
Pingtang China 55D10
Pingtung Taiwan 55L11
Pingwu China 54C6
Pingxiang China 54H4
Pingxiang China 55D11
Pingxiang China 55G9
Pingyang = Linfen
Pingyang China 55L9
Pingyao China 54G4
Pingyin China 54J4
Pingyüan China 54J4
Pingyuan China 55H10
Pingyüanchow = Zhijin
Pinhel Portugal 40C2
Pini *island* Indonesia 53C10
Pinjarra *W Aus.* Australia 98D6
Pinnacles Nat. Mon. *Calif.* USA 80C7
Pinnaroo *S Aus.* Australia 97B3
Pinos Mexico 88D3
Pinos,I de Cuba 89C2
Pinos,Mt *Calif.* USA 80D8
Pinrang *Celebes* Indon. 53G11
Pinsk *Belorus.* USSR 48E5
Pintados Chile 91C2
Pinto Argentina 91D3
Pioche *Nev.* USA 80F7
Piombino Italy 44C4
Piora Switzerland 33D2
Piorini,L Brazil 92E4
Piotrków Trybunalski Poland 37H3
Pipar India 58D3
Piper Pk *Nev.* USA 80E7
Pipestone *Minn.* USA 81J4
Pipestone Nat. Mon. *Minn.* USA 81J3
Pipli India 60D6
Pipmuacan,Res. *Que.* Canada 78C2
Pippli India 59G4
Piqua *Ohio* USA 79D5
Piracuruca Brazil 93J4
Piraeus = Piraievs
Piraievs Greece 47D6
Piramide,Mt Chile 91B7
Piranhas Brazil 93K5
Pirapora Brazil 93H7
Piratini Brazil 91F4
Piray Argentina 91F3
Pires do Rio Brazil 93H7
Pirgos Greece 47C6
Pirgos Greece 47D6
Pírgos *Kríti* Greece 47E7
Pirin Planina *mts* Bulgaria/Greece 46D4
Piripiri Brazil 93J4
Piritu Venezuela 92E1
Pirmasens W Germany 36B4
Pirna E Germany 36E3
Pirot Yugoslavia 46D3
Pir Panjal P India 60D4
Pir Panjal Ra *mts* *Kashmir* India 60D3
Pirwala Pakistan 60B6
Pisa Italy 44C4
Pisagua Chile 91B1
Pisa,R Poland 37J2
Pisco Peru 92B6
Písek Czech. 36F4
Pishin Iran 63J4
Pishin Pakistan 58C2
Pisticci Italy 45F5
Pistoia Italy 44C4
Pita Guinea 68C6
Pitangui Brazil 93J7
Pitarpunga L *NSW* Australia 97B2
Pitcairn,I Pacific Ocean 95N10
Piteå Sweden 34J4
Pite Älv *river* Sweden 34G3
Piterka USSR 49H5
Piteşti Romania 46E2
Pithiviers France 42E2
Pithoragarh India 61C1
Pithoria India 61B3
Pitihra India 61B4
Pitlochry *Scotland* UK 29J6
Piton de la Fournaise *mt* Réunion 65O12
Piton des Neiges *mt* Réunion 65O12
Pit R *Calif.* USA 80C5
Pitti *island* *Amindivi Is* India 58D6
Pittsboro *N Car.* USA 85H3
Pittsburg *Kans.* USA 83L4
Pittsburgh *Pa* USA 79G5
Pittsfield *Ill.* USA 83N3
Pittsfield *Maine* USA 78D4
Pittsfield *Mass.* USA 84E1
Pittston *Pa* USA 84D2
Piuă-Petri Romania 46F2
Piura Peru 92A5
Piute Pk *Calif.* USA 80D8
Piza *Latvia* USSR 35J8
Piz Bernina *mt* Switzerland 33E2
Piz Beverin *mt* Switzerland 33E2
Piz Buin *mt* Austria/Switz. 33F2
Piz d'Err *mt* Switzerland 33E2
Piz Ela *mt* Switzerland 33E2
Piz Kesch *mt* Switzerland 33E2
Piz Languard *mt* Switzerland 33E2
Piz Linard *mt* Switzerland 33F2
Piz Medel *mt* Switzerland 33D2
Piz Nuna *mt* Switzerland 33F2
Pizol *mt* Switzerland 33E2
Piz Platta *mt* Switzerland 33E2
Piz Quattervals *mt* Switzerland 33F2
Piz Sardona *mt* Switzerland 33E2
Piz Sesvenna *mt* Italy/Switz. 33F2
Piz Umbrail *mt* Italy/Switz. 33F2
Piz Vadret *mt* Switzerland 33E2
Pizzo Ouadro *mt* Italy/Switz. 33E2
Pizzo Rotondo *mt* Switzerland 33D2
Pjema CAR 69L7
Placentia *Newf.* Canada 78M3
Placentia B *Newf.* Canada 78L3
Placer Guadalupe Mexico 88C2
Placerville *Calif.* USA 80C6
Placerville *Idaho* USA 80F4
Placetas Cuba 89D2
Plaffeien Switzerland 33C2
Plainfield *New J* USA 84D2
Plains *Mont.* USA 80F2
Plainview *Nebr.* USA 83K1
Plainview *Texas* USA 82H5
Plainwell *Mich.* USA 79D4
Pláka B *Kríti* Greece 47E7
Plakoti,C Cyprus 64C2
Plana Czech. 36E4
Planaltina Brazil 93H7
Planina Yugoslavia 44E3
Plant City *Fla* USA 85L7
Plascenia Spain 40C2
Plaški Yugoslavia 44E3
Plassen Norway 35E6
Plaster Rock *New Br.* Canada 78E3
Plastun USSR 51Q5
Platamón Greece 47D4
Plata,R de la Argentina 91E4
Plat. de Langres France 42F3
Plati Greece 47D4
Plato Ust Yurt *region* USSR 50G5
Platres Cyprus 64A3
Platte,R *Nebr.* USA 82H2
Platteville *Wis.* USA 83N1
Plattsburg *Mo* USA 83L3
Plattsburgh *NY* USA 79K3
Plattsmouth *Nebr.* USA 83L2
Plauen E Germany 36E3
Plav Yugoslavia 46B3
Plavnica Yugoslavia 46B3
Playas *New Mex.* USA 82D7
Plaza Huincul Argentina 91C5
Pleasant B *Maine* USA 78E4
Pleasant Grove *Utah* USA 82C2
Pleasant V *Nev.* USA 80E5
Pleasantville *New J* USA 84D3
Pleiku Vietnam 53E8
Plenty,B of New Zealand 100G3
Plentywood *Mont.* USA 81E1
Plessisville *Que.* Canada 79L2
Pleszew Poland 37G3
Plettenberg,B South Africa 72C6
Pleureur *mt* Switzerland 33C2
Pleven Bulgaria 46E3
Pljevlja Yugoslavia 46B3
Płock Poland 37H2
Ploieşti Romania 46F2
Plomarion *Lésvos* Greece 47F5
Plomb du Cantal *mt* France 43E4
Plomosa Mts *Ariz.* USA 80G9
Plön W Germany 36D1
Płonsk Poland 37J2
Plouaret France 42B2
Plovdiv Bulgaria 46E3
Plumtree Zimbabwe 72D4
Plymouth *England* UK 26F8
Plymouth *Ind.* USA 79C5
Plymouth *Mass.* USA 84F2

Prichernomorskaya Nizmennost' Quillabamba

Prichernomorskaya Nizmennost' plain USSR 48H8
Priego de Córdoba Spain 40D4
Prienai Lith. USSR 35K9
Prieska South Africa 72C5
Prignitz region E Germany 36D2
Prijedor Yugoslavia 44F3
Prijepolje Yugoslavia 46B3
Prilep Yugoslavia 46C4
Priluki Ukrain. USSR 48H6
Prim,Point Pr. Ed. I. Canada 78G3
Primrose L Sask. Canada 76K6
Prince Albert Sask. Canada 76K6
Prince Albert South Africa 72C6
Prince Albert Mts Antarctica 15L2
Prince Albert Nat. Pk Sask. Canada 76K6
Prince Albert Pen. NW Terr. Canada 76H2
Prince Albert Sd NW Terr. Canada 76J2
Prince Alfred,C Canada 76G2
Prince Charles I NW Terr. Canada 77Q3
Prince Edward I Canada 77T7
Prince Edward I Pr. Edward Is Indian Ocean 65P12
Prince Edward,Is Indian Ocean 65B9
Prince George BC Canada 76G6
Prince of Wales,C Alaska USA 87W12
Prince of Wales I Alaska USA 87Z13
Prince of Wales I NW Terr. Canada 76L2
Prince of Wales I Queens. Australia 99J2
Prince of Wales Str. NW Terr. Canada 76H2
Prince Patrick I NW Terr. Canada 76G1
Prince Regent Inl. NW Terr. Canada 77N2
Prince Rupert BC Canada 76E6
Princes Lake Ont. Canada 79G3
Princess Charlotte B Queens. Australia 99J2
Princess Elizabeth Land region Antarctica 15F2
Princess Royal I BC Canada 76F6
Princeton Ill. USA 83P2
Princeton Ind. USA 85D1
Princeton Ky USA 85D2
Princeton Maine USA 78E4
Princeton Wis. USA 79B4
Princetown England UK 26G7
Prince William Sd Alaska USA 87Y12
Principe da Beira Brazil 92E6
Principe,I G. of Guinea 70B4
Prineville Oreg. USA 80C3
Pringle B South Africa 72J10
Pringles Argentina 91D6
Prinses Margrietkanaal canal Netherlands 32D1
Prinsesse Astrid Kyst Antarctica 15C2
Prinsesse Ragnhild Kyst Antarctica 15D2
Prins Harald Kyst Antarctica 15D2
Prins Karl's Forland,I Arctic Ocean 50C2
Prinzapolca Nicaragua 89C4
Pripyat,R Belorus. USSR 48F6
Priština Yugoslavia 46C3
Pritzwalk E Germany 36E2
Privolnoye USSR 49H5
Prizren Yugoslavia 46C3
Prizzi Sicily Italy 45D7
Progreso Mexico 88G3
Prokop'yevsk USSR 50K4
Prokuplie Yugoslavia 46C3
Proliv Dmitriya Lapteva strait USSR 51R2
Proliv Dmitriya Lapteva strait USSR 51R2
Proliv Karskiye Vorota strait USSR 50G2
Prome Burma 59J5
Propriá Brazil 93K6
Proserpine Queens. Australia 99K4
Prosna,R Poland 37G3
Prosser Wash. USA 80D2
Prostějov Czech. 37G4
Provence prov. France 43F5
Providence Ky USA 85C2
Providence RI USA 84F2
Providence,C NW Terr. Canada 76J2
Providence,I Indian Ocean 65D5
Providence Mts Calif. USA 80F8
Providencia,I de Colombia 89C4
Provins France 42E2
Provo Utah USA 82C2
Prozor Yugoslavia 44F4
Prudentópolis Brazil 91F3
Prudhoe Land Greenland 14Q2
Prüm W Germany 36B3
Prut,R USSR 48F9
Prydz B Antarctica 15F3
Przasnysz Poland 37J2
Przemyśl Poland 37K4
Przhevalsk Kirgiz. USSR 50J5
Psará island Greece 47E5
Pskov USSR 48F3
Pskovskoye Ozero lake USSR 48F2
Pta Alice point Italy 45F6
Pta da Marca point Angola 72A3
Pta de la Estaca de Bares cape Spain 40C1
Pta Delgada point Argentina 91D6
Pta de Mono Nicaragua 89C4
Pta do Dande point Angola 70C6
Pta Gallinas point Columbia 92C1
Pta Marroqui cape Spain 40D4
Pta Medanosa point Argentina 91C7
Pta Padrão point Angola 70C6
Pta Rasa point Argentina 91D6
Pta San Blas Panama 89D5
Pte de Barfleur cape France 42C2
Pte de la Novara Amsterdam I 65Q12
Pte de la Recherche point Amsterdam I 65Q12
Pte de St Mathieu point France 42A2
Pte des Gaiets point Réunion 65O12
Pte Kouango Gabon 70C5
Pte Noire Congo 70C5
Pte Ste Catharine point Gabon 70B5
Pte Tshibobo Gabon 70C5
Pte Vlaming point Amsterdam I 65Q12
Pt Louis Mauritius 65N12
Ptuj Yugoslavia 44E2
Puán Argentina 91D5
Pu'an China 55C10
Pu'apu'a Western Samoa 95V31
Pucacuro Peru 92B4
Pucallpa Peru 92C5
Pucheng China 55K9
Puchezh USSR 49F2
Puck Poland 37H1
Pudasjärvi Finland 34M4
Pudukkottai India 58E6
Puebla Mexico 88E4
Puebla state Mexico 88E4
Puebla de Alcocer Spain 40D3
Puebla de Sanabria Spain 40C1
Puebla de Trives Spain 40C1
Pueblo Col. USA 82F3
Pueblo Hundido Chile 91B3
Puelches Argentina 91C5
Puerco,R Ariz. USA 82D5
Puerto Armuelles Panama 89C5
Puerto Asis Colombia 92B3
Puerto Ayacucho Venezuela 92D2
Puerto Aysen Chile 91B7
Puerto Barrios Guatemala 88G4
Puerto Bermudez Peru 92C6
Puerto Berrío Colombia 92C2
Puerto Cabello Venezuela 92D1
Puerto Cabezas Nicaragua 89C4
Puerto Carreño Colombia 92D2
Puerto Casado Paraguay 91E2
Puerto Chicama Peru 92B5
Puerto Chirambirá Columbia 92B3
Puerto Coig Argentina 91C8
Puerto Colombia Colombia 92C1
Puerto Córdoba Colombia 92D4
Puerto Cortés Honduras 89B3
Puerto Cumarebo Venezuela 92D1
Puerto Eten Peru 92B5
Puerto Gracias a Dios Nicaragua 89C4
Puerto Grether Bolivia 92E7
Puerto Harberton Argentina 91C8
Puerto Heath Bolivia 92D6
Puerto la Cruz Venezuela 92E1
Puerto Leguisamo Colombia 92C4
Puerto Libertad Mexico 88B2
Puertollano Spain 40D3
Puerto Lobos Argentina 91C6
Puerto Lomas Peru 92C7
Puerto Madryn Argentina 91C6
Puerto Maldonado Peru 92D6
Puerto Montt Chile 91B6
Puerto Morelos Mexico 88G3
Puerto Natales Chile 91B8
Puerto Pinasco Paraguay 91E2
Puerto Pirámides Argentina 91D6
Puerto Plata Dom. Rep. 89E3
Puerto Princesa Philippines 53G9
Puerto Principe Colombia 92C3
Puerto Quellen Chile 91B6
Puerto Quijarro Bolivia 92F7
Puerto Rico island West Indies 89F3
Puerto Saavedra Chile 91B5
Puerto San Julián Argentina 91C7
Puerto Sastre Paraguay 91E2
Puerto Suarez Bolivia 92F7
Puerto Sucre Bolivia 92D6
Puerto Varas Chile 91B6
Puerto Victoria Peru 92C5
Puerto Villamizar Colombia 92C2
Puerto Visser Argentina 91C7
Puerto Wilches Colombia 92C2
Pueyrredón,L Argentina 91B7
Pugachev USSR 49J4
Pugal India 60C6
Puget France 43G4
Puget Sd Wash. USA 86B2
Puglia region Italy 45F5
Pugwash No. Sc. Canada 78G4
Pühalepa Eston. USSR 35K7
Puimro Brazil 93G3
Pujiang China 55K8
Pukaki,L New Zealand 100D7
Pukapuka,I Pacific Ocean 94K9
Pukapuka,I Tuamotu Arch. 95N9
Pukchong N Korea 52J2
Pukekohe New Zealand 100F3
Puketaraki Ra mts New Zealand 100E6
Pula Yugoslavia 44D3
Pulacayo Bolivia 92D8
Pula,C di Sardinia Italy 45B6
Pulap,I Caroline Is 94E7
Pulaski NY USA 84C1
Pulaski Tenn. USA 85D3
Pulaski Va USA 85G2
Pulau Tioman,I Malaysia 57C6
Puławy Poland 37J3
Pulicat,I India 58F6
Pulkkila Finland 34L4
Pullen Ont. Canada 77P7
Pullman Wash. USA 80E2
Pultneyville NY USA 84C1
Pułtusk Poland 37J2
Pulundian Wan bay China 54L3
Puma Tanzania 71G5
Puma Yumco lake Tibet China 59H3
Pumerend Netherlands 32C2
Pumsaint Wales UK 26G4
Punaania Tahiti 95V32
Puna de Atacama plat. Argentina 91C3
Puna,I Ecuador 92A4
Punakha Bhutan 61G2
Punch Kashmir India 60D4
Pundri India 60E6
Pune India 58D5
Pungpa Tso lake Tibet China 59G2
Puning China 55J11
Punjab region India 60D5
Puno Peru 92C7
Punta Alta Argentina 91D5
Punta Arenas Chile 91B8
Punta Colorado Chile 91B3
Punta del Faro point Sicily Italy 45E6
Punta de Pedras Brazil 93H4
Punta Gorda Belize 89B3
Punta Manzanillo point Panama 89D5
Puntarenas Costa Rica 89C4
Punte Licosa point Italy 45E5
Punto de Pajares Spain 40D1
Punto Fijo Venezuela 92C1
Punxsutawney Pa USA 84B2
Puolanka Finland 34M4
Puqi China 55G8
Puquios Chile 91C3
Puràng Chaka,L Tibet China 59F2
Purbeck Downs England UK 26J7
Purénées Atlantique dep. France 43C5
Purgatoire R Col. USA 82G4
Puri India 59G5
Purificación Colombia 92C3
Purley England UK 27P6
Purna India 58E5
Purnea India 61F3
Pursat Cambodia 57C4
Purulia India 61F4
Purus,R Brazil 92D5
Purvé,R Brazil 92D4
Purvis Miss. USA 85C5
Purwa India 61C2
Pusan S Korea 52J3
Pushchino USSR 51M4
Pusht-i-kūh region Iran 62F3
Putao Burma 59J3
Putaruru New Zealand 100F4
Putbus E Germany 36E1
Putian China 55K10
Putignano Italy 45F5
Putnam Conn. USA 84F2
Putnok Hungary 37J4
Puttalam Sri Lanka 58E7
Putte Netherlands 32C3
Putten Netherlands 32D2
Puttgarden W Germany 36D1
Putumayo,R Colombia 92C4
Putussibau Borneo Indon. 53F10
Puu Hualalei mt Hawaii USA 95V27
Puulavesi,L Finland 35M6
Puurs Belgium 32C3
Pu Xian China 54F4
Puyallup Wash. USA 80B2
Puy de Dôme dep. France 42E4
Puy de Dôme mt France 42E4
Puy de Sancy mt France 42E4
Puysegur Point New Zealand 100B8
Pwllheli Wales UK 26E3
Pyapon Burma 59J5
Pyatistennoye USSR 51T3
Pyhä Järvi lake Finland 34L5
Pyhä Jarvi lake Finland 35K6
Pyhajoki Finland 34L4
Pyha Joki river Finland 34L4
Pyhäntä Finland 34M4
Pyinmana Burma 59J5
Pyŏngyang N Korea 52J3
Pyramid Hill Vic. Australia 97B3
Pyramid I Paracel Is China 57E3
Pyramid L Nev. USA 80D5
Pyramid Pk Calif. USA 80C6
Pyrénées mts France/Spain 41F1
Pyrénées Orientales mts France 43E5
Pyrzyce Poland 36F2
Pyu Burma 59J5
Pyzdry Poland 37G2

Q

Qabatiya Israel 64D5
Qafar Saudi Arabia 62E4
Qaidam Pendi region China 52B3
Qaiya Saudi Arabia 62F5
Qala Nau Afghanistan 63J3
Qala Panja Afghanistan 63L2
Qala Sarkari Afghanistan 63K2
Qal'at al Akhdhar Saudi Arabia 62D4
Qal'at Bīshah Saudi Arabia 62E5
Qal'at el Marqab Syria 64D2
Qalat es Sālihiya Syria 62E3
Qal'at Uneiza Jordan 64D7
Qal el Mu'azzan Saudi Arabia 62D4
Qalqiliya Jordan 64C5
Qamar B South Yemen 63G6
Qamdo China 52C4
Qamea,I Vanua Levu,I Vanua Levu 94A24
Qaqortoq Greenland 14P4
Qara Egypt 69L3
Qardaha Syria 64D2
Qartaba Lebanon 64D3
Qasim region Saudi Arabia 62E4
Qasr Amij Iraq 62E3
Qasr el Azraq Jordan 64E6
Qaṣr-e Qand Iran 63J4
Qasr-e-Shirin Iran 62F3
Qasr ibn Aliya Saudi Arabia 62E4
Qa taba Yemen 62E7
Qatana Syria 64E4
Qatar country Middle East 63G4
Qattara Depression Egypt 69L3
Qāyen Iran 63H3
Qazvin Iran 62F2
Qemoy China 55K10
Qena Egypt 69M3
Qeshm island Iran 63H4
Qeys island Iran 63G4
Qianjiang China 55E8
Qianjiang China 55G7
Qianshan China 54J7
Qianwei China 55B8
Qianxi China 55D9
Qian Xian China 54E5
Qichun China 55H7
Qidong China 54L7
Qijiang China 55D8
Qilian Shan mts China 52B3
Qimen China 55J8
Qin'an China 54C5
Qingdao China 54L4
Qingfeng China 54H5
Qinghai Hu lake China 52D3
Qingjiang China 54K6
Qingjiang China 55H8
Qingliang Jiang river China 54J4
Qingliu China 55J9
Qingshen China 55B8
Qingshuihe China 54F3
Qingshui He river China 54C4
Qingtian China 55L8
Qing Xian China 54J3
Qingyang China 54D4
Qingyuan China 55G11
Qingyuan China 55K9
Qin He river China 54G5
Qinhuangdao China 54K3
Qin Ling mts China 54E6
Qin Xian China 54G4
Qinyanq China 54G5
Qinzhou China 55E12
Qionghai China 55E13
Qionglai China 54B7
Qiongshan China 55E13
Qiongzhou = Qiongshan
Qiongzhou Haixia strait China 55E12
Qiqihar China 52H1
Qiryat Gat Israel 64C6
Qishan China 54D5
Qishn South Yemen 63G6
Qishran island Saudi Arabia 62D5
Qiubei China 55C10
Qixai China 54L4
Qi Xian China 54H5
Qiyan China 55F9
Qi yat Shemona Israel 64D4
Qom Iran 63G3
Qomisheh Iran 63G3
Qornet es Saouda mt Lebanon 64D3
Qotur Iran 62E2
Qoubaiyat Lebanon 64E3
Qoz Bal 'Air Saudi Arabia 62E6
Quabbin Res. Mass. USA 84E1
Quaidabad Pakistan 60B4
Quakenbrück W Germany 36B2
Quambatook Vic. Australia 97B3
Quambone NSW Australia 97C2
Quang Ngai Vietnam 57D3
Quang Tri Vietnam 57D3
Quanjiao China 54K6
Quantock Hills England UK 26H6
Quanzhou China 55F9
Quanzhou China 55K10
Quarai Brazil 91E4
Quatre Bras Belgium 32C4
Qūchān Iran 63H2
Queanbeyan NSW Australia 97C3
Québec Que. Canada 78C3
Quebec prov. Canada 77R6
Queen Alexandra Ra mts Antarctica 15K1
Queen Anne Md USA 84D3
Queen Charlotte,B Falkland Is 91D8
Queen Charlotte Is BC Canada 76E6
Queen Charlotte Sd BC Canada 76F6
Queen Charlotte Str. BC Canada 76F6
Queen Elizabeth Is NW Terr. Canada 76J1
Queen Mary Land Antarctica 15G3
Queen Maud G NW Terr. Canada 76L3
Queen Maud Ra mts Antarctica 15N1
Queen's Chan. N Terr. Australia 98F2
Queenscliff Vic. Australia 97B3
Queensland state Australia 99J4
Queenstown New Zealand 100C7
Queenstown South Africa 72D6
Queenstown Tas. Australia 97F5
Queenstown (Ireland) = Cóbh
Queets,R Wash. USA 80A2
Queimadas Brazil 93K6
Quela Angola 70D6
Quelimane Mozambique 72F3
Quemu Quemú Argentina 91D5
Quequen Argentina 91E5
Queretaro Mexico 88D3
Queshan China 54H6
Quesnel BC Canada 76G6
Quesnel L BC Canada 76G6
Quetta Pakistan 58C2
Quezaltenango Guatemala 88F5
Quezon City Philippines 53H8
Quibdo Colombia 92B2
Quiberon France 42B3
Quiberon B de France 42B3
Quievrain Belgium 32B4
Quila Mexico 88C3
Quilán,C Chile 91B6
Quilca Peru 92C7
Quilcene Wash. USA 80B1
Quilino Argentina 91D4
Quillabamba Peru 92C6

Quillan, Riaza

Quillan France 43E5
Quillota Chile 91B4
Quilon India 58E7
Quilpie Queens. Australia 99J5
Quimper France 42A2
Quimperlé France 42B3
Quinault Ind. Resn Wash. USA 80A2
Quinault,R Wash. USA 80A2
Quincy Calif. USA 80C6
Quincy Ill. USA 83N3
Quincy Mass. USA 84F1
Quincy Mich. USA 79D4
Quincy Wash. USA 80D2
Quines Argentina 91C4
Qui Nhon Vietnam 57D4
Quinnimont W Va USA 85G2
Quinn River Ra mts Nev. USA 80D5
Quintana de la Serena Spain 40D3
Quintanar de la Orden Spain 40E3
Quintana Roo state Mexico 88G4
Quinto,R Argentina 91D4
Quipapa Brazil 93K5
Quirindi NSW Australia 97D2
Quiriquire Venezuela 92E1
Quiroga Spain 40C1
Quissanga Mozambique 71J7
Quissico Mozambique 72E4
Quitapa Angola 70D7
Quito Ecuador 92B4
Quixadá Brazil 93K4
Quixeramobim Brazil 93K5
Qu Jiang China 55D7
Qujing China 55B10
Qumar He river Tibet China 59H1
Qunsuliye Saudi Arabia 62E5
Quoich,L Scotland UK 28F5
Quorn S Aus. Australia 97A2
Quryyāt Oman 63H5
Qus Egypt 69M3
Quşay'ir South Yemen 63G6
Quseir Egypt 69M3
Qusuriya Saudi Arabia 62E5
Qutan Xia China 54E7
Quteife Syria 64E4
Qu Xian China 54D7
Qu Xian China 55K8
Quyang China 54H3
Quyon Que. Canada 79H3
Quzhou China 54H4

R

Raahe Finland 34L4
Raak Plain Vic. Australia 97B2
Raasay Scotland UK 28D5
Raasay,Sd of Scotland UK 28D5
Raas Caseyr,C Somalia 71L2
Rab island Yugoslavia 44E3
Raba Sumbawa Indon. 53G12
Raba,R Hungary 37G5
Rabat Morocco 68D2
Rabat Karim Iran 63G2
Rabigh Saudi Arabia 62D5
Rabi,I Vanua Levu Fiji 94A24
Rabkob = Dharmjaygarh
Race,C Newf. Canada 78M3
Rach Gia Vietnam 57D4
Raciborz Poland 37H3
Racine Wis. USA 79C4
Rada Yemen 62E7
Radak Chain,Is Marshall Is 94H6
Rădăuti Romania 48D8
Radford Va USA 85G2
Radhanpur India 58D4
Radnevo Bulgaria 46E3
Radnor Forest Wales UK 26H4
Radom Poland 37J3
Radomir Bulgaria 46D3
Radomsko Poland 37H3
Radøy island Norway 35A6
Radstadt Austria 36E5
Radstock England UK 26K6
Radviliškis Lith. USSR 35K9
Radzanow Poland 37H2
Radzyń Podlaski Poland 37K3
Rae NW Terr. Canada 76H4
Rae Bareli India 61C2
Rae Isthmus NW Terr. Canada 77O3
Rae,R NW Terr. Canada 76H3
Raeside,L W Aus. Australia 98E5
Raetihi New Zealand 100F4
Rafaela Argentina 91D4
Rafah Egypt 64C6
Rafsanjan Iran 63H3
Rafz Switzerland 33D1
Raga Sudan 69L7
Raghugarh India 61A3
Raghunathpur India 61F4
Raglan New Zealand 100F3
Raglan Ra mts New Zealand 100E6
Rago Nat. Pk Norway 34F3
Ragunda Sweden 34G5
Ragusa Sicily Italy 45E7
Ragusa (Yugosl.) = Dubrovnik
Rahaeng = Tak
Råhjerd Iran 63G3
Raiatea,I Society Is 95L9
Raichur India 58E5
Raida South Yemen 62F7
Raiganj India 61G3
Raikot India 60D5
Raimangal,R Bangla./India 61G5
Rainbow Vic. Australia 97B3
Raingarh India 60E5
Rainier Oreg. USA 80B2
Rainier,Mt Wash. USA 80C2
Rainy L Ont. Canada 77N7
Raipur India 58F4
Raisen India 61A4
Raivavae,I Tubuai Is 95M10
Raiwind Pakistan 60D5
Rajahmundry India 58F5
Rajakhera India 61B2
Rajang,R Sarawak Malay. 53F10
Rajanpur Pakistan 60B6
Rajapalaiyam India 58E7
Rajapur India 61C2
Rajasthan state India 58D3
Rajgarh India 60D6
Rajhara India 61E3
Rajkot India 58D4
Rajmahal India 61F3
Rajmahal Hills India 61F3
Rajshahi district Bangladesh 61G3
Rajura India 58E5
Rakahanga,I Pacific Ocean 94K8
Rakaposhi,Mt Kashmir India 60D2
Raka Zangbo,R Tibet China 59G3
Rakni,R Pakistan 60A6
Rakshan,R Pakistan 58B3
Rakvere Eston. USSR 35M7
Raleigh N Car. USA 85H3
Raleigh NSW Australia 97D2
Ralik Chain,Is Marshall Is 94G7
Ram Jordan 64D8
Rama Ethiopia 71J2
Rama Israel 64D5
Ramallah Jordan 64D6
Ramallo Argentina 91D4
Ramanthapuran India 58E7
Rambouillet France 42D2
Rame Hd Vic. Australia 97C3
Rameswaram India 58E7
Ramgarh India 60D6
Ramgarh India 61C4
Ramgarh India 61E4
Ramhormoz Iran 62F3
Ramillies Belgium 32C4
Ramkola India 61D4
Ramla Israel 64C6
Ramnagar India 61C3
Ramnagar India 61C4
Ramnagar Kashmir India 60D4
Ramore Ont. Canada 79F1
Ramotswa Botswana 72D4
Rampart House Yukon Canada 76C3
Rampur India 59F4
Rampur India 60E5
Rampur India 61B1
Rampur Boalia India 61G3
Ramree Burma 59H5
Ramsay Ont. Canada 79E2
Ramsbottom England UK 25D5
Ramsei Switzerland 33C1
Ramsele Sweden 34G5
Ramsey England UK 27P4
Ramsey Isle of Man UK 25L9
Ramsey I Wales UK 26D5
Ramsgate England UK 27S6
Ramsgate Tas. Australia 97F5
Ramsjö Sweden 35F5
Ramskapelle Belgium 32A3
Rams Pk Oreg. USA 80C4
Ramtha Jordan 64D5
Ramtok India 58E4
Ranaghas India 61G4
Rancagua Chile 91B4
Rance Belgium 32C4
Ranchi India 61E4
Rancho Mirage Calif. USA 80E9
Ranco,L Chile 91B6
Rand NSW Australia 97C3
Randalstown N Ireland 30L4
Randazzo Sicily Italy 45E7
Randburg South Africa 72M12
Randers Denmark 35D8
Randfontein South Africa 72M12
Randjiesfontein South Africa 72N11
Randolph Vt USA 79K4
Random I Newf. Canada 78M2
Randsburg Calif. USA 80E8
Randsfjord Norway 35D6
Råne Alv river Sweden 34J3
Ranenburg USSR 49E4
Ran,Fj. Norway 34E3
Ranfurly New Zealand 100D7
Rangamati Bangladesh 59H4
Rangeley Maine USA 78C4
Rangeley L Maine USA 78C4
Ranger Texas USA 83J6
Rangiora New Zealand 100E6
Rangitaiki,R New Zealand 100G4
Rangitikei,R New Zealand 100F5
Rangitoto Ra mts New Zealand 100F4
Rangoon Burma 59J5
Rangoon,R Burma 59J5
Rangpur Bangladesh 61G3
Rania India 60D6
Ranibennur India 58E6
Raniganj India 61F3
Raniganj India 61F4
Ranijula Pk India 61D4
Ranikhet India 61B1
Rankin Inl. NW Terr. Canada 77N4
Rankins Springs NSW Australia 97C2
Rannoch,L Scotland UK 29H6
Rannoch Moor upland Scotland UK 29G6
Ranong Thailand 53C9
Rantauparapap Sumatra Indon. 53C10
Rantekombola mt Celebes Indon. 53G11
Rantsila Finland 34L4
Ranua Finland 34M4
Raoul I Kermadec Is 94J10
Rapadama Upper Volta 68E6
Rapa,I Tubuai Is 95M10
Rapallo Italy 44B3
Raphoe Ireland, Rep. of 30H4
Rapid City S Dak USA 81F3
Rapla Eston. USSR 35L7
Rappahannock,R Va USA 85J1
Rapperswil Switzerland 33D1
Raron Switzerland 33C2
Rarotonga,I Cook. Is 94K10
Ras Abu-mad cape Saudi Arabia 62D5
Ra's al Hadd cape Oman 63H5
Ras al Khaimah UAE 63H4
Ra's al Madrakah cape Oman 63H6
Ra's ash Sharbatāt cape Oman 63H6
Ras Fartak cape South Yemen 63G6
Rashad Sudan 69M6
Rashadiya Jordan 64D7
Rashaïya Lebanon 64D4
Rashid Egypt 69M2
Rashm Iran 63G2
Rasht Iran 62F2
Raška Yugoslavia 46C3
Ras Kasar Ethiopia 71H1
Ras Lanuf Libya 69J2
Ras Musandam cape Oman 63H4
Rason,L W Aus. Australia 98E5
Raşova Romania 46F2
Rasskazovo USSR 49E4
Rasu Inagar India 60C4
Ratangarh India 60D6
Ratchaburi Thailand 57B4
Ratchathani Thailand 57C3
Rathangan Ireland,Rep. of 31J7
Rathdrum Ireland, Rep. of 31L8
Rathenow E Germany 36E2
Rathfriland N Ireland 30L5
Rathkeale Ireland, Rep. of 31F8
Rathlin,I N Ireland 30L3
Rathmelton Ireland, Rep. of 30H3
Rathnew Ireland, Rep. of 31L8
Ratibor = Raciborz
Rätikon mts Austria/Switz. 33E1
Ratnagiri India 58D5
Raton New Mex. USA 82F4
Rattlesnake Ra Wyo. USA 81D4
Rattray Hd Scotland UK 28N4
Rättvik Sweden 35F6
Rauch Argentina 91E5
Raukumara Ra mts New Zealand 100G3
Raukumara Ra mts New Zealand 100G4
Rauma Finland 35J6
Rauma,R Norway 34C5
Raurkela India 61E4
Rautas Sweden 34H2
Rautavaara Finland 34N5
Rautio Finland 34L4
Ravenglass England UK 25B4
Ravenna Italy 44D3
Ravensburg W Germany 36C5
Raver Iran 63H3
Ravestein Netherlands 32D3
Ravi,R India/Pakistan 60D5
Rawaidha Saudi Arabia 62E5
Rawalpindi Pakistan 60C4
Rawandiz Iraq 62E2
Rawatsar India 60D6
Rawd,R India 61B3
Rawene New Zealand 100E2
Rawenstall England UK 25D5
Rawicz Poland 37G3
Rawlinna W Aus. Australia 98F6
Rawlins Wyo. USA 81D5
Rawson Argentina 91C6
Raya mt Borneo Indon. 53F11
Rayadrug India 58E6
Rayak Lebanon 64E4
Ray,C Newf. Canada 78J3
Rayleigh England UK 27R5
Raymond Alta Canada 76J7
Raymond Wash. USA 80B2
Raymondville Texas USA 82T10
Rayon Mexico 88B2
Rays Hill upland Pa USA 84B3
Razelm,L Romania 46G2
Razgrad Bulgaria 46F3
Razmak Pakistan 60A4
Reading England UK 27N6
Reading Pa USA 84D2
Real Castillo Mexico 88A1
Real, Cord. mts Bolivia 92D7
Real,Cord. mts Ecuador 92B4
Realico Argentina 91D5
Realp Switzerland 33D2
Reata Mexico 88D2
Rebun island Japan 56G2
Recalde Argentina 91D5
Recherche,Arch. of the W Aus. Australia 98E6
Rechna Doab region Pakistan 60C5
Recht Belgium 32E4
Recife Brazil 93K5
Réclère Switzerland 33C1
Reconquista Argentina 91E3
Recreio Brazil 92F5
Redang island Malaysia 57C5
Red Bank New J USA 84D2
Red Bluff Calif. USA 80B5
Red Bluff L New Mex./Texas USA 82G7
Redby Minn. USA 81K2
Redcar England UK 25F3
Red Cliffs Vic. Australia 97B2
Red Cloud Nebr. USA 83J2
Red Deer Alta Canada 76J6
Red Deer R Alta Canada 76J6
Red Des. Wyo. USA 81C4
Redding Calif. USA 80B5
Redditch England UK 27L4
Redfield Ark. USA 85A3
Redfield S Dak. USA 81H3
Redhill England UK 27P6
Red Hill S Aus. Australia 97A2
Red Hill Vic. Australia 97B3
Red Indian L Newf. Canada 78K2
Red L Minn. USA 81K1
Redlands Calif. USA 80E8
Red Lodge Mont. USA 81C3
Red Oak Iowa USA 83L2
Redon France 42B3
Redondela Spain 40B1
Redondo Beach Calif. USA 80D9
Red Pine New Br. Canada 78F3
Red,R = Hong,R
Red R Canada/USA 76M7
Red,R La USA 83M7
Red River,Mouths of the Vietnam 57D2
Redruth England UK 26D8
Red Sea Africa/Arabian Pen. 62D4
Red Wing Minn. USA 81L3
Redwood City Calif. USA 80B7
Redwood Falls Minn. USA 81K3
Redwood Nat. Pk Calif. USA 80A5
Reed City Mich. USA 79D4
Reedsburg Wis. USA 79A4
Reefton New Zealand 100D6
Ree,L Ireland, Rep. of 31G6
Reelfoot L Tenn. USA 85C2
Reese,R Nev. USA 80E6
Refresco Chile 91C3
Regensburg W Germany 36E4
Reggan Algeria 68F3
Reggio di Calabria Italy 45E6
Reggio nell'Emilia Italy 44C3
Reghin Romania 46E1
Regina Sask. Canada 76L6
Registan region Afghanistan 63J3
Registro do Araguaia Brazil 93G7
Rehar,R India 61D4
Rehli India 61B4
Rehoboth Namibia 72B4
Rehovot Israel 64C6
Reichenau Switzerland 33E2
Reichenbach E Germany 36E3
Ré,I de France 42C3
Reidsville N Car. USA 85H2
Reigate England UK 27P6
Reigi Eston. USSR 35K7
Reims France 42E2
Reina Adelaide, Arch. de la Chile 91A8
Reinach Switzerland 33D1
Reindeer L Sask. Canada 76L5
Reinosa Spain 40D1
Reisen Elv river Norway 34J2
Reitan Norway 34D5
Reitz South Africa 72D5
Rekinniki USSR 51T3
Relizane Algeria 68F1
Remanso Brazil 93J5
Remarkable,Mt S Aus. Australia 97A2
Rembang Java Indon. 53F12
Remedios Cuba 89D2
Remedios Panama 89C5
Remeshk Iran 63H4
Remiremont France 42G2
Remoulins France 43F5
Remscheid W Germany 36B3
Remüs Switzerland 33F2
Rena Norway 35D6
Renaix = Ronse
Renca Argentina 91C4
Rendsburg W Germany 36C1
Renfrew Ont. Canada 79H3
Renfrew Scotland UK 29H8
Rengat Sumatra Indon. 53D11
Renhua China 55G10
Renhuai China 55D9
Renigunta India 58E6
Renk Sudan 69M6
Renkum Netherlands 32D3
Renmark S Aus. Australia 97B2
Rennell,I Solomon Is 94G9
Rennes France 42C2
Reno Nev. USA 80D6
Renovo Mont. USA 80G3
Renovo Pa USA 84C2
Rensselaer NY USA 84E1
Renswoude Netherlands 32D2
Renton Wash. USA 80B1
Renville Minn. USA 81K3
Reo Flores Indon. 53H12
Republican,R Nebr. USA 83J2
Repulse B NW Terr. Canada 77O3
Repulse B Queens. Australia 99K4
Requa Calif. USA 80A5
Requena Peru 92C4
Requena Spain 41F3
Rer,R India 61D3
Resistencia Argentina 91E3
Resita Romania 46C2
Resolution I New Zealand 100B7
Resolution I NW Terr. Canada 77T4
Restigouche Que. Canada 78E2
Rethel France 42F2
Rethímni dist. Greece 47E7
Réthimnon Kríti Greece 47E7
Retie Belgium 32D3
Réunion,I Indian Ocean 65D7
Reusel Netherlands 32D3
Reuss,R Switzerland 33D1
Reutlingen W Germany 36C4
Reutte Austria 36D5
Revda USSR 49P2
Revel = Tallinn
Revelstoke BC Canada 76H6
Revilla Gigedo Is Mexico 88B4
Revivim Israel 64C6
Rewa India 61C3
Rewa,R Viti Levu Fiji 94A25
Rewari India 60E6
Reydarfjordur,Fj. Iceland 34Y12
Reyes Mexico 88D4
Rey,I del Panama 89D5
Reykir Iceland 34U12
Reykjavik Iceland 34U12
Reynosa Mexico 88E2
Rēzekne Latvia USSR 35M8
Rhayader Wales UK 26H4
Rheden Netherlands 32E2
Rheine,R W Germany 36B2
Rheinfall Switzerland 33D1
Rheinland-Pfalz W Germany 36B3
Rhein,R Europe 36B3
Rheinwaldhorn Italy/Switz. 33E2
Rhenen Netherlands 32D3
Rheydt W Germany 36B3
Rhine = Rhein
Rhinelander Wis. USA 79B3
Rhode I RI USA 84F2
Rhode Island state USA 87M3
Rhodes,I = Rodhos,I
Rhodesia = Zimbabwe
Rhodesia,N = Zambia
Rhondda Wales UK 26H5
Rhondda V Wales UK 26G5
Rhône dep. France 42F4
Rhône,R France/Switz. 43F4
Rhön Gebirge mts W Germany 36C3
Rhosllanerchrugog Wales UK 26H2
Rhyl Wales UK 26H2
Ria de Vigo river Spain 40B1
Riaño Spain 40D1
Riau, Kep. archipelago Indonesia 53D10
Riaza Spain 40E2

Ribadeo, Rukumkot

Ribadeo Spain 40C1
Ribadesella Spain 40D1
Ribas do Rio Pardo Brazil 93G8
Ribatejo *region* Portugal 40B3
Ribble,R *England* UK 25D5
Ribe Denmark 35C9
Ribeirão Preto Brazil 93H8
Ribera *Sicily* Italy 45D7
Riberalta Bolivia 92D6
Riccall *England* UK 25F5
Rice Lake *Wis.* USA 81M3
Richards Bay South Africa 72E5
Richards I *NW Terr.* Canada 76E3
Richardson Mts New Zealand 100C7
Richardton *N Dak.* USA 81F2
Richey *Mont.* USA 81E2
Richfield *Utah* USA 82B3
Richibucto *New Br.* Canada 78F3
Richland *Mo* USA 83M4
Richland *Wash.* USA 80D2
Richland Center *Wis.* USA 79A4
Richmond *Calif.* USA 80B7
Richmond *England* UK 25E4
Richmond *England* UK 27P6
Richmond *Ind.* USA 79D6
Richmond *Ky* USA 85E2
Richmond *Maine* USA 78D4
Richmond New Zealand 100E5
Richmond *NSW* Australia 97D2
Richmond *NY* USA 79J5
Richmond *Que.* Canada 79K3
Richmond *Queens.* Australia 99J4
Richmond South Africa 72C6
Richmond *Utah* USA 82C2
Richmond *Va* USA 85J2
Richmond,R *NSW* Australia 97D1
Richmond Ra *mts* New Zealand 100E5
Richterswil Switzerland 33D1
Richwood *Minn.* USA 81K2
Richwood *W Va* USA 85G1
Rickleån,R Sweden 34J4
Rickmansworth *England* UK 27P5
Ricla Spain 41F2
Ridderkerk Netherlands 32C3
Riddes Switzerland 33C2
Ridgetown *Ont.* Canada 79F4
Ridgway *Pa* USA 84B2
Ridi Nepal 61D2
Riding Mount Nat. Pk *Man.* Canada 76L6
Ridout *Ont.* Canada 79E2
Riesa E Germany 36E3
Riesco,Pen. Chile 91B8
Rietavas *Lith.* USSR 35J9
Rieti Italy 44D4
Rifle *Col.* USA 82E3
Riga *Latvia* USSR 35L8
Riga,G of *Latvia* USSR 35K8
Rigân Iran 63H4
Rigas Jūrmala *Latviy* USSR 35K8
Rigby *Idaho* USA 80G3
Rigi *mts* Switzerland 33D1
Rig Mati Iran 63H4
Rigolet *Newf.* Canada 77U6
Rig Rig Chad 69H6
Rihand Dam India 61D3
Riihimäki Finland 35L6
Rijeka Yugoslavia 44E3
Rijssen Netherlands 32E2
Rijswijk Netherlands 32C2
Rimatara,I Tubuai Is 95L10
Rimbo Sweden 35H7
Rimini Italy 44D3
Rimini *Mont.* USA 80G2
Rîmnicu Sărat Romania 46F2
Rîmnicu Vîlcea Romania 46E2
Rimouski *Que.* Canada 78D2
Rimpfischhorn *mt* Switzerland 33C2
Rimrock,L *Wash.* USA 80C2
Rim Sobota Czech. 37J4
Rincon *New Mex.* USA 82E6
Rinconada Argentina 91C2
Rindal Norway 34C5
Ringarooma B *Tas.* Australia 97F5
Ringelspitz *mt* Switzerland 33E2
Ringkøbing Denmark 35C8
Ringvassøy,I Norway 34H2
Ringwood *England* UK 27L7
Riñihue Chile 91B5
Rinjani *mt* *Lombok* Indon. 53G12
Riobamba Ecuador 92B4
Rio Branco Brazil 91G3
Rio Branco Brazil 92D5
Rio Branco Uruguay 91F4
Rio Bravo *Calif.* USA 80D8
Rio Bravo del Norte Mexico/USA 88C1
Rio Bueno Chile 91B6
Río Chico Argentina 91C7
Rio Chico Venezuela 92D1
Rio Colorado Argentina 91D5
Rio Cuarto Argentina 91D4
Rio de Janeiro Brazil 93J8
Rio do Sul Brazil 91G3
Rio Gallegos Argentina 91C8
Rio Grande Argentina 91C8
Rio Grande Brazil 91F4
Rio Grande *river* Mexico/USA 86F6
Rio Grande City *Texas* USA 82S10
Rio Grande do Sul *state* Brazil 91F3
Riohacha Colombia 92C1
Rio Hondo Argentina 91D3
Rio Muerto Argentina 91D3
Rio Mulato Bolivia 92D7
Rio Negro Brazil 91G3
Rio Negro *prov.* Argentina 91C6
Rio Negro *prov.* Uruguay 91E4
Rionero in Vulture Italy 45E5
Rio Verde Brazil 93G7
Rio Verde Ecuador 92B3
Rioverde Mexico 88E3
Rio Vista *Calif.* USA 80C6
Rioz France 42G3
Riozinho Brazil 92D5
Ripats Sweden 34J3
Ripley *Calif.* USA 80F9
Ripley *England* UK 25E4
Ripley *England* UK 25F6
Ripley *Miss.* USA 85C3
Ripley *NY* USA 84B1
Ripley *Tenn.* USA 85C3
Ripley *W Va* USA 79F6
Ripon *England* UK 25E4
Ripon *Que.* Canada 79J3
Ripon *Wis.* USA 79B4
Risafe Syria 62D2
Risalpur Pakistan 60C3
Risbäck Sweden 34J3
Risca *Wales* UK 26H5
Rishiri *island* Japan 56G2
Rishon-le-Zion Israel 64C5
Risør Norway 35C7
Ristijärvi Finland 34N4
Ritchie's Arch. *Andaman Is* India 59H6
Ritter,Mt *Calif.* USA 80D6
Ritzville *Wash.* USA 80D2
Rivadavia Argentina 91D2
Rivas Nicaragua 89B4
Rivera Argentina 91D5
Rivera Uruguay 91E4
Riverhead *NY* USA 84E2
Riverina *region* *NSW* Australia 97B2
Rivero,I Chile 91B7
Riversdale New Zealand 100C7
Riverside *Calif.* USA 80E9
Riverside *Oreg.* USA 80D4
Riverton New Zealand 100C8
Riverton *S Aus.* Australia 97A2
Riverton *Wyo.* USA 81C4
Riviera *Ariz.* USA 80F8
Riviera di Levante Italy 44B3
Riviera di Ponente Italy 44A4
Rivière-à-Pierre *Que.* Canada 79K2
Rivière au Renard *Que.* Canada 78F2
Rivière du Loup *Que.* Canada 78D3
Rivoli Italy 44A3
Rivulet *Mont.* USA 80F2
Riyadh Saudi Arabia 62F5
Rize Turkey 62E1
Rizhao China 54K5
Rizokarpaso Cyprus 64C2
Rizzuto,C Italy 45F6
Rjukan Norway 35C7
Rkiz,L Mauritania 68B5
Roa Spain 40E2
Roanne France 42F3
Roanoke *Ala.* USA 85E4
Roanoke *Va* USA 85H2
Roanoke,R *N Car./Va* USA 85H2
Roan Plat. *Col.* USA 82D3
Roaringwater B Ireland, Rep. of 31E10
Roatán,I Honduras 89B3
Robbins I *Tas.* Australia 97F5
Robe *S Aus.* Australia 97A3
Robe,Mt *NSW* Australia 97B2
Robe,R Ireland, Rep. of 30E6
Roberts *Idaho* USA 80G4
Roberts *Mont.* USA 81C3
Robertsfors Sweden 34J4
Robertsganj India 61D3
Robertsport Liberia 68C7
Robertstown Ireland, Rep. of 31K7
Robertstown *S Aus.* Australia 97A2
Roberval *Que.* Canada 78B2
Robeson Chan. Can./Greenland 14Q1
Robin Hood's Bay *England* UK 25G3
Robinson *Ill.* USA 83Q3
Robinson Bar *Idaho* USA 80F3
Robinson Crusoe,I Juan Fernandez Is 95U11
Robinson's *Newf.* Canada 78J2
Robinvale *Vic.* Australia 97B2
Robore Bolivia 92F7
Robson,Mt *BC* Canada 76H6
Robstown *Texas* USA 82T10
Rocha Uruguay 91F4
Rochdale *England* UK 25D5
Rochefort Belgium 32D4
Rochefort France 42C4
Rochers de Naye Switzerland 33B2
Rochester *England* UK 27R6
Rochester *Mich.* USA 79E4
Rochester *Minn.* USA 81L3
Rochester *New H* USA 84F1
Rochester *NY* USA 84C1
Rochester *Vic.* Australia 97B3
Rochford *England* UK 27R5
Rockall *island* Atlantic Ocean 22E4
Rock Creek *Idaho* USA 80F4
Rockefeller Plat. Antarctica 15P2
Rockford *Ill.* USA 83P1
Rockhampton *Queens.* Australia 99L4
Rock Hill *S Car.* USA 85G3
Rockingham *England* UK 25G7
Rockingham *N Car.* USA 85H3
Rock Island *Ill.* USA 83N2
Rockland *Maine* USA 78D4
Rockland *Mass.* USA 84F1
Rockland *Ont.* Canada 79J3
Rocklands Res. *Vic.* Australia 97B3
Rock Point New Zealand 100E5
Rockport *Ind.* USA 85D2
Rock Port *Mo* USA 83L2
Rock,R *Ill.* USA 83P1
Rock Sound The Bahamas 89D2
Rock Springs *Wyo.* USA 81C5
Rockstone Guyana 92F2
Rockville *Md* USA 84C3
Rockwell City *Iowa* USA 83L1
Rockwood *Tenn.* USA 85E3
Rocky Bar *Idaho* USA 80F4
Rocky Ford *Col.* USA 82G3
Rocky Mount *N Car.* USA 85J2
Rocky Mount *Va* USA 85H2
Rocky Mt Nat. Pk *Col.* USA 82F2
Rocky Mts N America 76G6
Rocroi France 42F2
Rødby Denmark 35D9
Rodel *Scotland* UK 28B4
Roden Netherlands 32E1
Rodersdorf Switzerland 33C1
Rodez France 43E4
Rodhopi *dist.* Greece 46E4
Ródhos *Ródhos* Greece 47F6
Ródhos *island* Greece 47F6
Rodkhan Pakistan 58B3
Rodney *Miss.* USA 85B5
Rodopi Planina *mts* Bulg./Greece 46D4
Rodosto = Tekirdağ
Rodrigues,I Indian Ocean 65E6
Roebourne *W Aus.* Australia 98D4
Roe,R N Ireland 30K3
Roermond Netherlands 32D3
Roesbrugge Belgium 32A4
Roeselare Belgium 32B4
Roes Welcome Sd *NW Terr.* Canada 77O4
Rogachev *Belorus.* USSR 48G5
Rogagua,L Bolivia 92D6
Rogaland *county* Norway 35A7
Rogers *Ark.* USA 83L4
Rogers City *Mich.* USA 79E3
Rogers,L *Calif.* USA 80E8
Rogersville *New Br.* Canada 78F3
Rogersville *Tenn.* USA 85F2
Rogliano *Corsica* France 43K8
Rogoaguado,L Bolivia 92D6
Rogue,R *Oreg.* USA 80B4
Rogue River *Oreg.* USA 80B4
Rohri Pakistan 58C3
Rohtak India 60E6
Rohtas India 61D3
Roi Et Thailand 57C3
Roi I Kwajalein Is 94A17
Roisin Belgium 32B4
Roja *Latviy* USSR 35K8
Rojas Argentina 91D4
Rojo,C Mexico 88E3
Rokiškis *Lith.* USSR 35L9
Rolde Netherlands 32E2
Rolla *Mo* USA 83N4
Rolle Switzerland 33B2
Rolvsøy,I Norway 34K1
Roma Italy 45D5
Roma *Queens.* Australia 99K5
Roma Sweden 35H8
Romaine,R *Que.* Canada 78G1
Roman Romania 46F1
Romang I Indonesia 53J12
Romania *country* Europe 39M4
Romans France 43F4
Romanshorn Switzerland 33E1
Romanzof,C *Alaska* USA 87W12
Rome = Roma
Rome *Ga* USA 85E3
Rome *NY* USA 84D1
Rome *Oreg.* USA 80E4
Romerée Belgium 32C4
Romford *England* UK 27Q5
Romilly France 42E2
Romney *W Va* USA 79G6
Romney Marsh *England* UK 27R6
Romny *Ukrain.* USSR 48H6
Romodanovo USSR 49G3
Rømø,I Denmark 35C9
Romont Switzerland 33B2
Romorantin France 42C3
Rompin,R Malaysia 57C6
Romsdalshorn Norway 34B5
Romsey *England* UK 27L7
Ron Vietnam 57D3
Ronald *Wash.* USA 80C2
Ronan *Mont.* USA 80F2
Roncador,Sa do *mts* Brazil 93G6
Ronda *Kashmir* India 60D3
Ronda Spain 40D4
Rondane Norway 35D6
Rondane Nat. Pk Norway 35D6
Rondonia *state* Brazil 92E6
Rongjiang China 55D10
Rong Jiang *river* China 55E10
Rongshui China 55E10
Rong Xian China 55F11
Rønne *Bornholm I* Denmark 35F9
Ronneby Sweden 35F8
Ronne Entrance Antarctica 15S2
Ronne Ice Shelf Antarctica 15S2
Ronse Belgium 32B4
Roodepoort South Africa 72M12
Roosendaal Netherlands 32C3
Roosevelt I Antarctica 15M1
Rooseveltown *NY* USA 79J3
Roosevelt,R Brazil 92E5
Roosky Ireland, Rep. of 30H6
Roper,R *N Terr.* Australia 99G2
Roquefort France 43C4
Roque,R *Oreg.* USA 80A4
Rora Hd *Scotland* UK 28K2
Roraima *mt* Guyana/Venez. 92E2
Rori India 60D6
Røros Norway 34D5
Rorschach Switzerland 33E1
Rosablanche *mt* Switzerland 33C2
Rosamond *Calif.* USA 80D8
Rosario Argentina 91D4
Rosário Brazil 93J4
Rosario Chile 91B2
Rosario Mexico 88A1
Rosario Mexico 88C2
Rosario Mexico 88C3
Rosario Paraguay 91E2
Rosario de la Frontera Argentina 91D3
Rosario de Lerma Argentina 91C2
Rosario del Tala Argentina 91E4
Rosário do Sull Brazil 91E4
Rosário Oeste Brazil 93F6
Roscommon Ireland, Rep. of 30G6
Roscommon *Mich.* USA 79D3
Roscommon *county* Ireland,Rep. of 30G6
Roscrea Ireland, Rep. of 31H8
Roseau Dominica 89G3
Roseau *Minn.* USA 81K1
Rosebery *Tas.* Australia 97F5
Rosebud *S Dak.* USA 81G4
Roseburg *Oreg.* USA 80B4
Rosedale *Miss.* USA 85B4
Rosehearty *Scotland* UK 28M4
Rose Hill Mauritius 65N12
Rose,I Samoa 94K9
Rosenheim W Germany 36E5
Roses Spain 41H1
Roses,G de Spain 41H1
Rosetown *Sask.* Canada 76K6
Roseville *Calif.* USA 80C6
Roseworth *Idaho* USA 80F4
Rosiers,C *Que.* Canada 78F2
Rosignano Marittimo Italy 44C4
Rosignol Guyana 92F2
Roslavl' USSR 48H5
Rosport Luxembourg 32E5
Ross *England* UK 26J5
Ross New Zealand 100D6
Ross *Tas.* Australia 97F5
Rossa Switzerland 33E2
Rossano Italy 45F6
Rosscarberry Ireland, Rep. of 31E10
Ross Carbery Ireland,Rep. of 31E10
Ross Dependency Antarctica 15M2
Rosseau L *Ont.* Canada 79G3
Rossel I Papua New Guinea 99L2
Ross I Antarctica 15L2
Ross Ice Shelf Antarctica 15M1
Rossignol Belgium 32D5
Rossignol Res. *No. Sc.* Canada 78F4
Rossland *BC* Canada 76H7
Rosslare Ireland, Rep. of 31L9
Rosslea *N Ireland* UK 30J5
Rosslyn *Va* USA 84C3
Ross,Mt Kerguelen 65S12
Rosso Mauritania 68B5
Ross,R *Yukon* Canada 76E4
Ross Sea Antarctica 15M2
Røssvatnet,L Norway 34F4
Rosta Norway 34H2
Rosthern *Sask.* Canada 76K6
Rostock E Germany 36E1
Rostov USSR 48L3
Rostov-na-Donu USSR 49D7
Rostrenen France 42B2
Roswell *New Mex.* USA 82F6
Rosyth *Scotland* UK 29K7
Rota,I Mariana Is 94E6
Rotbühl Spitze *mt* Austria/Switz. 33E2
Rothbury *England* UK 25E2
Rothenburg W Germany 36D4
Rotherham *England* UK 25F6
Rother,R *England* UK 27R6
Rothesay *Scotland* UK 29F8
Rothkreuz Switzerland 33D1
Rothorn *mt* Switzerland 33D2
Roti *island* Indonesia 53H13
Roto *NSW* Australia 97C2
Rotorua New Zealand 100G4
Rotorua,L New Zealand 100G4
Rotterdam Netherlands 32C3
Rotuma,I Fiji 94H9
Roubaix France 42E1
Rouen France 42D2
Rõuge *Eston.* USSR 35M8
Roulers = Roeselare
Round Mt *NSW* Australia 97D2
Roundup *Mont.* USA 81C2
Roura Fr. Guiana 93G3
Rousay I *Orkney* Scotland 28K1
Rouse's Point *NY* USA 79K3
Rous, Pen. Chile 91C9
Roussillon *prov.* France 43E5
Rouveen Netherlands 32E2
Rouyn *Que.* Canada 79G1
Rovaniemi Finland 34L3
Roveredo Switzerland 33E2
Rovereto Italy 44C3
Rovigo Italy 44C3
Rovinari Romania 46D2
Rovno *Ukrain.* USSR 48E6
Rovuma,R Mozambique 71H7
Rowena *NSW* Australia 97C1
Roxburgh New Zealand 100C7
Roxburgh *Scotland* UK 29M8
Roxbury *NY* USA 84D1
Royal Ca. Ireland, Rep. of 31K7
Royale,I *Mich.* USA 79B1
Royal Leamington Spa *England* UK 27L4
Royan France 42C4
Royston *England* UK 27P4
Rozet *Wyo.* USA 81E3
Rožňava Czech. 37J4
Rozwadow Poland 37K3
Rth Luirc Ireland, Rep. of 31F9
Rtishchevo USSR 49F4
Ruabon *Wales* UK 26H3
Ruac *island* Truk Is 94A16
Ruahine Ra *mts* New Zealand 100G5
Ruapehu,Mt New Zealand 100F4
Rub' al Khāli *des.* Saudi Arabia 62F6
Rubi,R Zaire 70F4
Rubtsovsk USSR 50K4
Ruby *Alaska* USA 87X12
Ruby Valley *Nev.* USA 80F5
Rucheng China 55G10
Rudauli India 61C2
Rudbar Afghanistan 63J3
Ruddervoorde Belgium 32B3
Ruddington *England* UK 25F7
Rudkøbing Denmark 35D9
Rudnaya Pristan' USSR 51Q5
Rudolf,L Kenya 71H4
Rudong China 54L6
Rudyard Res. *England* UK 25D6
Ruel *Ont.* Canada 79F2
Ruffec France 42D3
Rufino Argentina 91D4
Rugao China 54L6
Rugby *England* UK 27M4
Rugby *N Dak.* USA 81H1
Rugeley *England* UK 25E7
Rügen *island* E Germany 36E1
Ruhnu Saar *island* *Latviy* USSR 35K8
Rui'an China 55L9
Ruichang China 55H8
Ruijin China 55H10
Rūjiena *Latvia* USSR 35L8
Ruk Pakistan 58C3
Rukumkot Nepal 61D1

Rukwa,L, St Regis

Rukwa,L Tanzania **71G6**
Rumania = Romania
Rumbek Sudan **69L7**
Rumburk Czech. **36F3**
Rum Cay *island* The Bahamas **89E2**
Rumegies France **32B4**
Rumford Falls *Maine* USA **78C4**
Rum,I *Scotland* UK **28D5**
Rumigny France **32C5**
Rumillies Belgium **32B4**
Rum Jungle *N Terr.* Australia **98G2**
Rümlang Switzerland **33D1**
Rumoi Japan **56G3**
Rumsey *Calif.* USA **80B6**
Rumung *island* Yap Is **94A19**
Rumuruti Kenya **71H4**
Runan China **54H6**
Runanga New Zealand **100D6**
Runaway,C New Zealand **100G3**
Runcorn *England* UK **25C6**
Rundvik Sweden **34H5**
Rungwa Tanzania **71G6**
Rungwa Tanzania **71G6**
Rungwe,Mt Tanzania **71G6**
Runswick *England* UK **25G3**
Runu Yap Is **94A19**
Ruoqiang *Xinjiang* China **50K6**
Rupanco,L Chile **91B6**
Rupar India **60E5**
Rupbas India **61A2**
Rupert *Idaho* USA **82B1**
Rupperswil Switzerland **33D1**
Rupshu *district* India **60D4**
Rupununi,R Guyana **92F3**
Rurrenabaque Bolivia **92D6**
Rurutu,I Tubuai Is **95L10**
Rusape Zimbabwe **72E3**
Ruschuk = Ruse
Ruse Bulgaria **46E3**
Ruseifa Jordan **64E5**
Rusele Sweden **34H4**
Rush Ireland,Rep. of **31L6**
Rushan China **54L4**
Rushden *England* UK **27N4**
Rushville *Ill.* USA **83N2**
Rushworth *Vic.* Australia **97B3**
Russas Brazil **93K4**
Russelkonda India **59F5**
Russell *Kans.* USA **83J3**
Russell New Zealand **100F2**
Russell,C *NW Terr.* Canada **76H1**
Russell Point *NW Terr.* Canada **76H2**
Russellville *Ala.* USA **85D3**
Russellville *Ky* USA **85D2**
Russkoye Ustye USSR **51R2**
Russo Switzerland **33D2**
Rustak Afghanistan **63K2**
Rustburg *Va* USA **85H2**
Ruston *La* USA **83M6**
Ruth *Nev.* USA **80F6**
Rutherfordton *N Car.* USA **85G3**
Rutherglen *Scotland* UK **29H8**
Rüthi Switzerland **33E1**
Ruthin *Wales* UK **26H2**
Rüti Switzerland **33D1**
Rutland *Vt* USA **84E1**
Rutland,I *Andaman Is* India **59H6**
Rutog *Tibet* China **58E2**
Ruurlo Netherlands **32E2**
Ruweiba Sudan **69L5**
Ruwenzori,Mts Uganda **71F4**
Ružomberok Czech. **37H4**
Rwanda *country* Africa **71F5**
Ryan *Calif.* USA **80E7**
Ryan,L *Scotland* UK **29F10**
Ryazan USSR **48L4**
Ryazhsk USSR **48M5**
Rybinsk USSR **48L2**
Rybinskoye Vodok *res.* USSR **48L2**
Rybnoye USSR **51M2**
Ryde *I of Wight* England **27M7**
Rye *England* UK **27R7**
Rye Patch Res. *Nev.* USA **80D5**
Rylstone *NSW* Australia **97C2**
Rýmarov Czech. **37G4**
Rypin Poland **37H2**
Rzeszów Poland **37J3**
Rzeszow *voivodship* Poland **37K3**
Rzkev USSR **48J3**

S

Saalfeld E Germany **36D3**
Saana *mt* Sweden **34J2**
Saane Switzerland **33C2**
Saanen Switzerland **33C2**
Saarbrücken W Germany **36B4**
Saarburg W Germany **36B4**
Saaremaa,I *Eston.* USSR **35K7**
Saarland *state* W Germany **36B4**
Saarlouis W Germany **36B4**
Saar Selkä *region* Finland/USSR **34N2**
Saas Grund Switzerland **33C2**
Saas Tal *valley* Switzerland **33C2**
Saaui B *Nicobar Is* India **59H7**
Saavedra Argentina **91D5**
Saba *island* Leeward Is **89G3**
Sabac Yugoslavia **46B2**
Sabadell Spain **41H2**
Sabah *state* *Borneo* Malaysia **53G9**
Sabalan *mt* Iran **62F2**
Sabalgarh India **58E3**
Sabana, Arch. de Cuba **89C2**
Sabanalarga Colombia **92C1**
Sabancuy Mexico **88F4**
Sabari,R India **58F5**
Sabarmati,R India **58D4**
Sab' Bi'ār Syria **64F4**
Sabhah Libya **69H3**
Sabile *Latvia* USSR **35K8**
Sabiñánigo Spain **41F1**
Sabinas Mexico **88D2**
Sabine *Texas* USA **83M8**
Sabine L *La/Texas* USA **83M8**
Sabine,Mt Antarctica **15L2**
Sabine,R *La/Texas* USA **83M7**
Sablé France **42C3**
Sable,C *Fla* USA **85M9**
Sable,C *No. Sc.* Canada **78F5**
Sable I *No. Sc.* Canada **78H5**
Sabrina Coast Antarctica **15H3**
Sabya Yemen **62E6**
Sabzawar = Shindand
Sabzevar Iran **63H2**
Sacandaga,R *NY* USA **84D1**
Sac City *Iowa* USA **83L1**
Sacedon Spain **41E2**
Sachigo,R *Ont.* Canada **77N6**
Sackets Harbor *NY* USA **79H4**
Sackville *New Br.* Canada **78F4**
Saco *Maine* USA **78C5**
Saco *Mont.* USA **81D1**
Sacramanto,R *Calif.* USA **80B6**
Sacramento Brazil **93H7**
Sacramento *Calif.* USA **80C6**
Sacramento Mts *New Mex.* USA **82F6**
Sádaba Spain **41F1**
Sadabad India **61B2**
Sá da Bandeira = Lubango
Sadad Syria **64E3**
Sadda Pakistan **60B4**
Sadhaura India **60E5**
Sadiya India **59J3**
Sado *island* Japan **56F5**
Saeki Japan **56B8**
Safad = Zefat
Safata B Western Samoa **95V31**
Safed Koh Ra *mts* Afghan./Pakistan **60B3**
Safford *Ariz.* USA **82D6**
Saffron Walden *England* UK **27Q4**
Safi Jordan **64D6**
Safi Morocco **68D2**
Sāfidabeth Iran **63J3**
Safien Tal *valley* Switzerland **33E2**
Safita Syria **64E3**
Safotulafai Western Samoa **95V31**
Safranbolu Turkey **62C1**
Saga Japan **56B8**
Saga *Tibet* China **59G3**
Saga *prefecture* Japan **56B8**
Sagaing Burma **59J4**
Sagaing *state* Burma **59H4**
Sagami wan *bay* Japan **56F7**
Sagar India **61B4**
Sagar,I India **61G5**
Sagauli India **61E2**
Sag Fj. Norway **34F3**
Saginaw *Mich.* USA **79D4**
Saginaw B *Mich.* USA **79E4**
Sagone,G de *Corsica* France **43J6**
Sagua la Grande Cuba **89C2**
Saguenay,R *Que.* Canada **78C2**
Sagunto Spain **41F3**
Sahand *mt* Iran **62F2**
Sahara India **58D3**
Sahara Des. Africa **68D4**
Saharanpur India **60E6**
Saharien Atlas,Mts Algeria **68F2**
Sahaswan India **61B1**
Sahiadriparvat Ra *mts* India **58E4**
Sahibganj India **61F3**
Sahiwal Pakistan **60C5**
Sahm Oman **63H5**
Sahora India **61C4**
Sahuaripa Mexico **88C2**
Sahuayo Mexico **88D3**
Sahugún Spain **40D1**
Sahy Czech. **37H4**
Sahyadri,Mts = Ghats, Western
Saibai *island* Papua New Guinea **99J1**
Saïda Lebanon **64D4**
Saida Yemen **62E6**
Sa'īdābād Iran **63H4**
Saidapet India **58F6**
Said Bundas Sudan **69K7**
Saidpur India **61D3**
Saidpur India **61G3**
Saidu Pakistan **58D2**
Saignelégier Switzerland **33B1**
Saigon = Ho Chi Minh City
Sailana India **58D4**
Saillon Switzerland **33C2**
Saimaa Kanal *canal* Finland/USSR **35N6**
Saimaa,L Finland **35M6**
St Abb's Hd *Scotland* UK **29M8**
St Affrique France **43E5**
St Agatha *Maine* USA **78D3**
St Agnes *island* *Is of Scilly* England **26B9**
St Agrève France **43F4**
St Albans *England* UK **27P5**
St Albans *Vt* USA **79K3**
St Albans Hd *England* UK **27K7**
St Amand Mont Rond France **42E3**
St Amour France **42F3**
St André *Que.* Canada **78D3**
St André Réunion **65O12**
St André C Madagascar **71M10**
St Andrews *New Br.* Canada **78E4**
St Andrews *Scotland* UK **29L7**
St Anne *Channel Is* UK **27W10**
Ste Anne de Beaupré *Que.* Canada **78C3**
Ste Anne de la Pérade = La Pérade
Ste Anne de la Pocatière *Que.* Canada **78C3**
Ste Anne des Monts *Que.* Canada **78E2**
St Anns Bay Jamaica **89D3**
St Anthonis = St Antonis
St Anthony *Idaho* USA **80H4**
St Antönien Switzerland **33E2**
St Antonis Netherlands **32D3**
St Arnaud *Vic.* Australia **97B3**
St Asaph *Wales* UK **26H2**
St Aubin *Channel Is* UK **27W11**
St Augustin,B Madagascar **71M11**
St Augustine *Fla* USA **85G6**
St Austell *England* UK **26E8**
St Austell B *England* UK **26E8**
St Barthélemy *island* Leeward Is **89G3**
St Béat France **43D5**
St Bees *England* UK **25A4**
St Bees Hd *England* UK **25A3**
St Benoit Réunion **65O12**
St Blaize,C South Africa **72C6**
St Blazey *England* UK **26E8**
St Boniface *Man.* Canada **76M6**
St Bride's B *Wales* UK **26D5**
St Brieuc France **42B2**
St Calais France **42D3**
St Catherines *Ont.* Canada **79G4**
St Catherine's Point *I of Wight* England **27M7**
Ste Cécile-de-Whitton *Que.* Canada **79L3**
St Cergue Switzerland **33B2**
St Chamond France **42F4**
St Charles *Mich.* USA **79D4**
St Charles *Mo* USA **83N3**
St Charles,C *Newf.* Canada **77U6**
St Chély d'Apcher France **43E4**
St Christopher = St Kitts
St Clair *Mich.* USA **79E4**
St Clair,L Canada/USA **79E4**
St Clair,L *Tas.* Australia **97F5**
St Claude France **42F3**
St Cloud *Minn.* USA **81K3**
Ste Croix Switzerland **33B2**
St Croix *island* West Indies **89G3**
St Croix,R *Wis.* USA **81L3**
St Davids *Wales* UK **26D5**
St Davids Hd *Wales* UK **26D5**
St Denis France **42E2**
St Denis Réunion **65O12**
St Dié France **42F2**
St di Nova Siri Italy **45F5**
St Dizier France **42F2**
St Elias,Mt *Alaska* USA **87Y12**
St Elias Mts *Yukon* Canada **76C4**
Saintes France **42C4**
St Étienne France **42F4**
St Eustatius *island* Leeward Is **89G3**
St Fabien *Que.* Canada **78D2**
St Fargeau France **42E3**
St Felicien *Que.* Canada **78B2**
Saintfield N Ireland **30M4**
St Fillans *Scotland* UK **29J7**
St Finans B Ireland, Rep. of **31C10**
St Florent *Corsica* France **43K6**
St Florent,G de *Corsica* France **43K6**
St Florentin France **42E2**
St Flour France **43E4**
St Francis *Maine* USA **78D3**
St Francis B South Africa **72D6**
St Francis,C South Africa **72C6**
St Francis,L *Que.* Canada **79J3**
St Francis,L (Can.) = St François,L
St Francis,R *Ark.* USA **83N5**
St Francis,R *Que.* Canada **79K3**
St François,L *Que.* Canada **78C4**
St Fulgent France **42C3**
St Gabriel *Que.* Canada **79K2**
St Gabriel de Brandon = St Gabriel
St Gallen Switzerland **33E1**
St Gallen *canton* Switzerland **33E1**
St Gaudens France **43D5**
St Gédéon *Que.* Canada **78C2**
Ste Genevieve *Mo* USA **83N3**
St George *New Br.* Canada **78E4**
St George *Queens.* Australia **99K5**
St George *Utah* USA **80G7**
St George Hd *NSW* Australia **97D3**
St George I Bering Sea **87W13**
St Georges Fr. Guiana **93G3**
St George's Grenada **89G4**
St Georges *Que.* Canada **78C3**
St George's B *Newf.* Canada **78J2**
St Georges B *No. Sc.* Canada **78H4**
St George's Chan. UK **26B5**
St Gérard Belgium **32C4**
St Germain France **42E2**
St Gheorghe I Romania **46G2**
St Ghislain Belgium **32B4**
St Gilgen Austria **36E5**
St Gilles France **43F5**
St Gillis Belgium **32C3**
St Gillis-Waas Belgium **32C3**
St Gingolph Switzerland **33B2**
St Girons France **43D5**
St Gotthard *mt* Switzerland **33D2**
St Gotthard Tun. Switzerland **33D2**
St Gowans Hd *Wales* UK **26E5**
St Guenolé France **42A3**
St Helena *Calif.* USA **80B6**
St Helena,B South Africa **72B6**
St Helena,I Atlantic Ocean **73M10**
St Helens *England* UK **25C6**
St Helens *Oreg.* USA **80B3**
St Helens,Mt *Wash.* USA **80B2**
St Helier *Channel Is* UK **42B2**
St Hubert Belgium **32D4**
St Hyacinthe *Que.* Canada **79K3**
St Ignace *Mich.* USA **79D3**
St Imier Switzerland **33B1**
St Irénée *Que.* Canada **78C3**
St Ives *England* UK **26D8**
St Ives B *England* UK **26D8**
St Jacques *New Br.* Canada **78D3**
St James *Minn.* USA **81K3**
St James,C *BC* Canada **76E6**
St Jan Belgium **32A4**
St Jean France **42G4**
St Jean d'Angély France **42C4**
St Jean de Luz France **43C5**
St Jean,L *Que.* Canada **78B2**
St Jérôme *Que.* Canada **79J3**
St Joachim *Que.* Canada **78C3**
St John *New Br.* Canada **78E4**
St John B *Newf.* Canada **78K1**
St John,L = St Jean,L
St Johns *Ariz.* USA **82D5**
St John's *Mich.* USA **79D4**
St Johns *Newf.* Canada **78M3**
St Johnsbury *Vt* USA **79K3**
St Johns Chapel *England* UK **25D3**
St John's Point Ireland, Rep. of **30F4**
St John's Point *N Ireland* UK **30M5**
St Johns,R *Fla* USA **85G5**
St Joseph *La* USA **83N7**
St Joseph *Mich.* USA **79C4**
St Joseph *Mo* USA **83L3**
St Joseph *Que.* Canada **78C3**
St Joseph Réunion **65O12**
St Joseph I *Ont.* Canada **79E2**
St Joseph L *Ont.* Canada **77N6**
St Junien France **42C4**
Ste Justine *Que.* Canada **78C3**
St Kilda,I *Scotland* UK **28A1**
St Kitts *island* Leeward Is **89G3**
St Laurent French Guiana **93G2**
St Lawrence *Queens.* Australia **99K4**
St Lawrence,G of Canada **78G2**
St Lawrence I *Alaska* USA **87V12**
St Lawrence,R *Que.* Canada **78C3**
St Lawrence Seaway Canada/USA **79J3**
St Léger Belgium **32D5**
St Léonard France **42D4**
St Leonard *New Br.* Canada **78E3**
St Leonards *England* UK **27R7**
St Leu Réunion **65O12**
St Lewis,C *Newf.* Canada **77U6**
St Lô France **42C2**
St Louis Mauritania **68B5**
St Louis *Mich.* USA **79D4**
St Louis *Mo* USA **83N3**
St Louis Réunion **65O12**
St Louis de Kent *New Br.* Canada **78F3**
St Louis,L *Que.* Canada **79K3**
St Lucia *country* Windward Is **89G4**
St Lucia,C South Africa **72E5**
St Lucia,L South Africa **72E5**
St Maartensdijk Netherlands **32C3**
St Magnus B *Shetland* Scotland **28P8**
St Maixent France **42C3**
St Malo France **42B2**
St Malo,G de France **42C2**
St Marc Haiti **89E3**
St Mard Belgium **32D5**
St Margaret's B *No. Sc.* Canada **78G4**
St Margrethen Switzerland **33E1**
Ste Marie,C Madagascar **71N12**
St Maries *Idaho* USA **80E2**
St Marks *Fla* USA **85E5**
St Martin *island* Leeward Is **89G3**
St Martins *New Br.* Canada **78F4**
St Martins *island* *Is of Scilly* England **26B9**
St Mary,Is India **58D6**
St Mary Is *Que.* Canada **78J1**
St Marys *Ont.* Canada **79F4**
St Marys *Pa* USA **84B2**
St Marys *Tas.* Australia **97F5**
St Marys *island* *Is of Scilly* England **26B9**
St Mary's B *Newf.* Canada **78M3**
St Mary's B *No. Sc.* Canada **78E4**
St Mary's L *Scotland* UK **29K9**
St Matthew I *Alaska* USA **87V12**
St Maurice Switzerland **33C2**
St Maurice de Labrieville *Que.* Canada **78D2**
St Maurice,R *Que.* Canada **79K2**
St Maximin France **43F5**
St Meen France **42B2**
Ste Menehould France **42F2**
St Michael *Alaska* USA **87W12**
St Michaels *Md* USA **84C3**
St Moritz Switzerland **33E2**
St Nazaire France **42B3**
St Neots *England* UK **24P4**
St Nicolaasga Netherlands **32D2**
St Nicolas = St Niklaas
St Niklaas Belgium **32C3**
St Niklaus Switzerland **33C2**
St Odilienberg Netherlands **32E3**
St Omer France **42E1**
Saintonge *prov.* France **42C4**
St Paul *Minn.* USA **81L3**
St Paul Réunion,I **65O12**
St Paul de Fenouillet France **43E5**
St Paul I Bering Sea **87V13**
St Paul,I Indian Ocean **65F8**
St Peter *Minn.* USA **81L3**
St Peter,L *Que.* **= St Pierre,L**
St Peter Port *Channel Is* UK **42B2**
St Peters *Pr. Ed. I.* Canada **78G3**
St Petersburg *Fla* USA **85L8**
St Petersburg *Pa* USA **84B2**
St Philipsland Netherlands **32C3**
St Pierre Martinique **89G4**
St Pierre,L *Que.* Canada **79K2**
St Pierre & Miquelon Is Atlantic Ocean **78K3**
St Pol France **42E1**
St Pölten Austria **37F4**
St Pons France **43E5**
St Pourçain France **42E3**
St Quentin France **42E2**
St Quentin *New Br.* Canada **78E3**
Ste Raphaël France **43G5**
St Raymond *Que.* Canada **78C3**
St Regis *Mont.* USA **80F2**

St Rémi d'Amherst Sanmenxia

St Rémi d'Amherst = Lac-Rémi
St Rémy France 43F5
St Sampson Channel Is UK 27V11
St Sébastien,C Madagascar 71N9
St Sernin-sur-Rance France 43E5
St Servan France 42B2
St Sever France 43C5
St Siméon Que. Canada 78D3
St Simon Que. Canada 78D2
St Stephen New Br. Canada 78E4
St Sulpice Switzerland 33B2
Ste Suzanne Réunion 65O12
Ste Thècle Que. Canada 79K2
Ste Thérèse,L NW Terr. Canada 76G4
St Thomas Ont. Canada 79F4
St Thomas island Virgin Is 89F3
St Trond = St Truiden
St Tropez France 43G5
St Truiden Belgium 32D4
St Ursanne Switzerland 33C1
St Valery France 42D1
St Valéry-en-Caux France 42D2
St Veit Austria 36F5
St Vincent country Windward Is 89G4
St Vincent,C Madagascar 71M11
St Vincent,G S Aus. Australia 97A2
St Vith Belgium 32E4
St Xavier Mont. USA 81D3
Saipal mt Nepal 61C1
Saipan,I Mariana Is 94E6
Sai,R India 61C2
Saitama prefecture Japan 56F7
Saivomuotka Sweden 34K2
Saiyidwala Pakistan 60C5
Sakai Japan 56D7
Sakakah Saudi Arabia 62E4
Sakakawea,L N Dak. USA 81F2
Sakania Zaire 71F7
Sakarya,R Turkey 62C1
Sakata Japan 56F5
Sakesar Pakistan 60C4
Sakha Nepal 61D1
Sakha Saudi Arabia 62E5
Sakhalin island USSR 51R4
Sakhalinskaya Oblast region USSR 51R4
Sakhalinskiy Zaliv bay USSR 51R4
Saki USSR 48H9
Šakiai Lith. USSR 35K9
Sakisgarh India 61D3
Sakishima Shot islands Japan 56K14
Sakmara,R USSR 49M5
Sakti India 61D4
Sakylä Finland 35K6
Sal island Cape Verde 68T10
Šala Czech. 37G4
Sala Sweden 35G7
Salaca,R Latviy USSR 35L8
Salacgriva Latvia USSR 35L8
Sala Consilina Italy 45E5
Salada,Grande lake Argentina 91C6
Salada,L Mexico 88A1
Salado,R Argentina 91C5
Salado,R Argentina 91C6
Salado,R Argentina 91D3
Salado,R Mexico 88E2
Salado,R Texas USA 82S10
Salaga Ghana 68E7
Sala'ilua Western Samoa 95V31
Sala'ilua,R Western Samoa 95V31
Salala Oman 63G6
Salama Guatemala 88F4
Salamanca Mexico 88D3
Salamanca NY USA 84B1
Salamanca Spain 40D2
Salamanca prov. Spain 40C2
Salamaua Papua New Guinea 99K1
Salamina Colombia 92B2
Salamis Greece 47D6
Salangen Norway 34G2
Salar de Atacama lake Argentina 91C2
Salas Spain 40C1
Salas de los Infantes Spain 40E1
Salavat USSR 49M4
Salaverry Peru 92B5
Salayar island Indonesia 53H12
Sala-y-Gomez,I Pacific Ocean 95R10
Salbris France 42E3
Salcombe England UK 26G8
Saldana Spain 40D1
Saldanha B South Africa 72B6
Saldus Latvia USSR 35K8
Sale England UK 25D6
Salé Morocco 68D2
Sale Vic. Australia 97C3
Salekhard USSR 50H3
Salem Ill. USA 83P3
Salem India 58E6
Salem Mass. USA 84F1
Salem Mo USA 83N4
Salem New J USA 84D3
Salem Oreg. USA 80B3
Salem Va USA 85G2
Salemi Sicily Italy 45D7
Sälen Sweden 35E6
Salerno Italy 45E5
Salerno,G di Italy 45E5
Salford England UK 25D6
Salgueiro Brazil 93K5
Salida Col. USA 82E3
Salima Malawi 71G7
Salina Kans. USA 83K3
Salina Utah USA 82C3
Salina island Italy 45E6
Salina Cruz Mexico 88E4
Salinas Calif. USA 80C7
Salinas Ecuador 92A4
Salinas Mexico 88D2
Salinas Mexico 88D3
Salinas,B de Nicaragua 89B4
Salinas Grandes region Argentina 91D3
Salinas Pk New Mex. USA 82E6
Salinas R Calif. USA 80C7
Saline,R Kans. USA 83J3
Salinitas Chile 91C3
Salinópolis Brazil 93H4
Salins France 42F3
Salisbury England UK 27L6
Salisbury Md USA 85K1
Salisbury N Car. USA 85G3
Salisbury New Br. Canada 78F3
Salisbury S Aus. Australia 97A2
Salisbury I NW Terr. Canada 77Q4
Salisbury Plain England UK 27L6
Salkhad Syria 64E5
Sallaberry-de-Valleyfield Que. Canada 79J3
Salmas Iran 62E2
Salmon Idaho USA 80G3
Salmon Mts Calif. USA 80B5
Salmon,R Idaho USA 80F3
Salmon River Mts Idaho USA 80F3
Salo Finland 35K6
Salon France 43F5
Salon India 61C2
Salonica = Thessaloniki
Salonta Romania 46C1
Salqin Syria 64E1
Salsette,I India 58D5
Salt Jordan 64D5
Salta Argentina 91B2
Salta prov. Argentina 91D2
Saltarmukhi,R India 61G5
Saltash England UK 26F8
Saltburn England UK 25G3
Saltcoats Scotland UK 29G8
Saltdal Norway 34F3
Saltee,Is Ireland, Rep. of 31K9
Salt E,R Norway 34F3
Salt,Fj. Norway 34E3
Saltillo Mexico 88D2
Salt Lake City Utah USA 82C2
Salt Ls W Aus. Australia 98F5
Salto Argentina 91D4
Salto Uruguay 91E4
Salto dep. Uruguay 91E4
Salto da Divisa Brazil 93K7
Salton Sea lake Calif. USA 80F9
Salt Plains L Okla. USA 83J4
Salt R Ariz. USA 82C6
Salt Ra mts Pakistan 58D2
Saltrou Haiti 89E3
Salt Sulphur Springs W Va USA 85G2
Saltville Va USA 85G2
Saluda Va USA 85J2
Salûm Egypt 69L2
Salûm Egypt 69L2
Salûm,G of Egypt 69L2
Salur India 59F5
Salut,Is du French Guiana 93G2
Saluzzo Italy 44A3
Salvador Brazil 93K6
Salvador,L La USA 83N8
Salvaterra de Magos Portugal 40B3
Salvatierra Mexico 88D3
Salwah Qatar 63G5
Salween,R Burma 59J4
Salyana Nepal 61D1
Salzburg Austria 36E5
Salzburg state Austria 36E5
Salzwedel E Germany 36D2
Samalut Egypt 69M3
Samaná Dom. Rep. 89F3
Samaná,B de Dom. Rep. 89F3
Samar island Philippines 53J8
Samarai Papua New Guinea 99L2
Samaria Idaho USA 80G4
Samariapo Venezuela 92D2
Samarinda Borneo Indon. 53G11
Samarkand Uzbek. USSR 50H6
Samarra Balad Iraq 62E3
Samastipur India 61E3
Sambalpur India 59F4
Sambava Madagascar 71P9
Sambeek Netherlands 32D3
Sambhal India 61B1
Sambhar L India 58D3
Sambo Angola 70D7
Sambor Ukrain. USSR 48C7
Samborombón,B Argentina 91E5
Sambre,R Belgium 32C4
Samedan Switzerland 33E2
Sami Pakistan 58B3
Samira Saudi Arabia 62E4
Samiria,R Peru 92C5
Samka Burma 59J4
Samnaun Switzerland 33F2
Sam Neuu Laos 57C2
Samoa Calif. USA 80A5
Samoa,Is Pacific Ocean 94J9
Samokov Bulgaria 46D3
Samorogouan Upper Volta 68E6
Samos island Greece 47F7
Samothrace,I = Samothráki,I
Samothráki Greece 47E4
Sampacho Argentina 91D4
Sampit Borneo Indon. 53F11
Samrée Belgium 32D4
Samsat Turkey 62D2
Samsø,R Denmark 35D9
Samsu N Korea 52J2
Samsun Turkey 62D1
Samthar India 61B3
Samundri Pakistan 60C5
San Mali 68E6
San'ā' Yemen 62E6
San Ambrosio,I Pacific Ocean 95U10
Sanandaj Iran 62F2
San Andreas Calif. USA 80C6
San Andres,I de Colombia 89C4
San Andres Mts New Mex. USA 82E6
San Andres Tuxtla Mexico 88E4
San Angelo Texas USA 82H5
San Antioco island Sardinia Italy 45B6
San Antonio Chile 91B4
San Antonio Chile 91C2
San Antonio Mexico 88B3
San Antonio Texas USA 83J8
San Antonio Abad Ibiza Spain 41G3
San Antonio B Texas USA 82T9
San Antonio,C Argentina 91E5
San Antonio,C Cuba 89C2
San Antonio Pk New Mex. USA 82E4
San Antonio,R Texas USA 82T9
San Antonio Ra mts Nev. USA 80E7
San Ardo Calif. USA 80C7
San Bartolomeo in Galdo Italy 45E5
San Benedetto del Tronto Italy 44D4
San Benito Texas USA 82T10
San Benito Is Mexico 88A2
San Bernardino Calif. USA 80E8
San Bernardino P Switzerland 33E2
San Bernardino Ra mts Calif. USA 80E8
San Bernardo Chile 91B4
San Bernardo Is Columbia 92B2
San Blas Argentina 91D6
San Blas Mexico 88C2
San Blas Mexico 88C3
San Blas,C Fla USA 85E6
San Blas G de Panama 89D5
San Borja Mexico 88B2
Sanborn N Dak. USA 81H2
San Braz,C de Angola 70C6
San Carlos Argentina 91C3
San Carlos Argentina 91C4
San Carlos Chile 91B5
San Carlos Mexico 88E3
San Carlos Nicaragua 89C4
San Carlos Venezuela 92D2
San Carlos Venezuela 92D3
San Carlos de Bariloche Argentina 91B6
San Carlos del Zulia Venezuela 92C2
San Carlos Res. Ariz. USA 82C6
Sancerre France 42E3
Sanchez Dom. Rep. 89F3
San Clementa Calif. USA 80E9
San Clemente Spain 41E3
San Cosme Paraguay 91E3
San Cristóbal Argentina 91D4
San Cristobal Mexico 88E4
San Cristobal Venezuela 92C2
San Cristóbal,B de Mexico 88A2
San Cristóbal de las Casas Mexico 88F4
San Cristobal,I Galapagos Is 95T8
San Cristobal,I Solomon Is 94G9
Sancti Spiritus Cuba 89D2
Sand Norway 35B7
Sanda island Scotland UK 29E9
Sandakan Sabah Malay. 53G9
Sanday island Orkney Scotland 28M1
Sanday Sd Orkney Scotland 28L1
Sandbach England UK 25D6
Sandefjord Norway 35D7
Sanders Ariz. USA 82D5
Sandgate England UK 27S6
Sandgate Queens. Australia 99L5
Sandhornøy,I Norway 34E3
Sandi India 61C2
Sandia Peru 92D6
San Diego Calif. USA 80E9
San Diego Texas USA 82S10
San Diego,C Argentina 91C8
San Diego de Cabrutica Venezuela 92E2
Sandikli Turkey 62C2
Sandila India 61C2
San Dimas Mexico 88C3
Sandnes Norway 35A7
Sandø island Faerøerne 34Z15
Sandoa Zaire 70E6
Sandomierski Poland 37K3
Sandomierz Poland 37J3
Sandoway Burma 59H5
Sandown I of Wight England 27M7
Sandpoint Idaho USA 86C2
Sandringham England UK 27R3
Sandstone Minn. USA 81L2
Sandstone W Aus. Australia 98D5
Sandträsk Sweden 34J3
Sandu China 55D10
Sandusky Mich. USA 79E4
Sandusky Ohio USA 79E5
Sandvig Bornholm I Denmark 35F9
Sandwich England UK 27S6
Sandy C Queens. Australia 99L4
Sandy L Newf. Canada 78K2
Sandy L Ont. Canada 77N6
San Esteban de Gormaz Spain 40E2
San Felipe Brazil 92D3
San Felipe Chile 91B4
San Felipe Guatemala 88F5
San Felipe Mexico 88B1
San Felipe Mexico 88F4
San Felipe Venezuela 92D1
San Feliu de Guixols Spain 41H2
San Feliu de Llobregat Spain 41G2
San Felix,I Pacific Ocean 95T10
San Fernando Calif. USA 80D8
San Fernando Chile 91B4
San Fernando Mexico 88A1
San Fernando Mexico 88E3
San Fernando Philippines 53H7
San Fernando Trinidad 92E1
San Fernando de Apure Venezuela 92D2
San Fernando de Atabapo Venezuela 92D3
Sanford Fla USA 85M7
Sanford Maine USA 78C5
Sanford N Car. USA 85H3
Sanford,Mt Alaska USA 87Y12
San Francisco Argentina 91C4
San Francisco Argentina 91D4
San Francisco Calif. USA 80B7
San Francisco B Calif. USA 80B7
San Francisco Mts Ariz. USA 82B5
San Franciso Dom. Rep. 89E3
San Gabriel Mts Calif. USA 80D8
Sanganj India 61F3
Sangareddipet India 58E5
Sangar,R Pakistan 60B5
Sanger Calif. USA 80D7
Sanger N Dak. USA 81G2
San German Puerto Rico 89F3
Sanggan He river China 54G3
Sanggau Borneo Indon. 53F10
Sanggou Wan bay China 54M4
Sangihe island Indonesia 53J10
Sangihe Kep. archipelago Indonesia 53J10
San Giovanni in Fiore Italy 45F6
Sangkulirang Borneo Indon. 53G10
Sangla Pakistan 60C5
Sangli India 58D5
Sangre de Cristo Mts Col./New Mex. USA 82F3
Sangre Grande Trinidad 92E1
Sangrur India 60D5
Sangwin Liberia 68D7
Sanhe China 54J2
Sanhe (China) = Sandu
San Ignacio Bolivia 92D6
San Ignacio Bolivia 92E7
San Ignacio Mexico 88B2
San Ignacio Mexico 88C3
San Ignacio Paraguay 91E3
San Javier Argentina 91D4
San Javier Chile 91B5
San João de Pesqueira Portugal 40C2
San Joaquin Bolivia 92E6
San Joaquin,R Calif. USA 80C7
San Jorge,G Argentina 91C7
San Jose Calif. USA 80C7
San José Costa Rica 89C5
San José Guatemala 88F5
San José Uruguay 91E4
San José Carpizo Mexico 88F4
San José da Ocune Colombia 92C3
San José de Amacuro Venezuela 92E2
San José de Chiquitos Bolivia 92E7
San José de Feliciano Argentina 91E4
San José del Cabo Mexico 88C3
San José del Guaviare Colombia 92C3
San José,G Argentina 91D6
San José I Mexico 88B2
San Jose I Texas USA 82T10
San Juan Argentina 91C4
San Juan Bolivia 92F7
San Juan Puerto Rico 89F3
San Juan Venezuela 92D2
San Juan prov. Argentina 91C4
San Juan,C Argentina 91D8
San Juan de Camarones Mexico 88C2
San Juan de Guadalupe Mexico 88D3
San Juan del Norte Nicaragua 89C4
San Juan de los Cayos Venezuela 92D1
San Juan de los Lagos Mexico 88D3
San Juan del Río Mexico 88D3
San Juan del Rio Mexico 88E3
San Juan del Sur Nicaragua 89B4
San Juan Mts Col. USA 82E4
San Juan,R Columbia 92B3
San Juan,R Mexico 88E4
San Juan,R Nicaragua 89C4
San Juan R Utah USA 82C4
San Julián Argentina 91C7
San Justo Argentina 91D4
Sankarani,R Guinea 68D6
Sankh,R India 61E4
San Lázaro,C Mexico 88B3
San Leandro Calif. USA 80B7
San Lorenzo Argentina 91D4
San Lorenzo Ecuador 92B3
San Lorenzo Honduras 89B4
San Lorenzo Mexico 88B1
San Lorenzo Peru 92D6
San Lorenzo de El Escorial Spain 40D2
San Lorenzo Is Mexico 88B2
Sanlucar la Mayor Spain 40C4
San Lucas Bolivia 92E8
San Lucas,C Mexico 88C3
San Luis Argentina 91C4
San Luis Argentina 91E3
San Luis Cuba 89D2
San Luis prov. Argentina 91C4
San Luis de la Paz Mexico 88D3
San Luis,L Bolivia 92E6
San Luis Obispo Calif. USA 80C8
San Luis Potosi Mexico 88D3
San Luis Potosi state Mexico 88D3
San Luis,Sa de mts Argentina 91C4
Sanluri Sardinia Italy 45B6
San Marcos Colombia 92B2
San Marino country Europe 44D4
San Martin Argentina 91B6
San Martín Colombia 92C3
San Martín de los Andes Argentina 91B6
San Martin de Valdeiglesais Spain 40D2
San Martin,L Argentina/Chile 91B7
San Mateo Calif. USA 80B7
San Mateo Fla USA 85G6
San Mateo Spain 41G2
San Mateo Pk New Mex. USA 82E6
San Matias Bolivia 92F7
San Matias,G Argentina 91D6
San Maura,I = Levkás,I
Sanmen Wan bay China 55L8
Sanmenxia China 54F5

San Miguel, Scone

San Miguel Bolivia 92E7
San Miguel Calif. USA 80C8
San Miguel El Salvador 89B4
San Miguel Peru 92C6
San Miguel Allende Mexico 88D3
San Miguel,B de Panama 89D5
San Miguel de Huachi Bolivia 92D7
San Miguel de Tucuman Argentina 91C3
San Miguel,I = Isla del Rey
San Miguel I Calif. USA 80C8
San Miguel,R Bolivia 92E7
Sanming China 55J9
San Nicolás Argentina 91D4
San Nicolau island Cape Verde 68T10
Sanok Poland 37K4
San Pablo Bolivia 92D8
San Pablo,C Argentina 91C8
San Pedro Argentina 91E4
San Pedro Belize 89B3
San Pedro Calif. USA 80D9
San Pedro Ivory Coast 68D8
San Pedro Mexico 88D2
San Pedro Paraguay 91E2
San Pedro Chan. Calif. USA 80D9
San Pedro de Arimena Colombia 92C3
San Pedro del Gallo Mexico 88D2
San Pedro de Lloc Peru 92B5
San Pedro de Macorís Dom. Rep. 89F3
San Pedro do Sul Portugal 40B2
San Pedro R Ariz. USA 82C6
San Pedro Sula Honduras 89B3
San Pietro I Sardinia Italy 45B6
San Quintin Mexico 88A1
San Quintin,B Mexico 88A1
San Rafael Argentina 91C4
San Rafael Calif. USA 80B7
San Ramón Peru 92B6
San Remo Italy 44A4
San Roque Argentina 91E3
San Salvador El Salvador 89B4
San Salvador island The Bahamas 89E2
San Salvador de Jujuy Argentina 91C2
Sansanne Mango Togo 68F6
San Sebastián Argentina 91C8
San Sebastián Spain 41E1
San Severo Italy 45E5
Sanshui China 55G11
San Simeon Calif. USA 80C8
San Simeon B Calif. USA 80C8
Sans Souci Ont. Canada 79F3
Sansui China 55E9
Santa Peru 92B5
Santa Ana Bolivia 92D6
Santa Ana Bolivia 92E7
Santa Ana Calif. USA 80E9
Santa Ana Ecuador 92A4
Santa Ana El Salvador 89B4
Santa Ana Mexico 88B1
Santa Barbara Calif. USA 80D8
Santa Barbara Honduras 89B4
Santa Barbara Mexico 88C2
Santa Bárbara Venezuela 92E2
Santa Barbara Chan. Calif. USA 80C8
Santa Catalina Argentina 91C2
Santa Catalina Chile 91C3
Santa Catalina I Calif. USA 80D9
Santa Catalina I Mexico 88B2
Santa Catarina Mexico 88C3
Santa Catarina,I Brazil 91G3
Santa Clara Brazil 92D4
Santa Clara Calif. USA 80C7
Santa Clara Cuba 89C2
Santa Colma de Farners Spain 41H2
Santa Cruz Argentina 91C7
Santa Cruz Bolivia 92E7
Santa Cruz Calif. USA 80B7
Santa Cruz Chile 91B4
Santa Cruz Mexico 88B1
Santa Cruz Peru 92B5
Santa Cruz Philippines 53H8
Santa Cruz prov. Argentina 91B7
Santa Cruz Chan. Calif. USA 80D8
Santa Cruz de la Zarza Spain 40E2
Santa Cruz del Sur Cuba 89D2
Santa Cruz de Tenerife Canary Is 68B3
Santa Cruz Is Pacific Ocean 94G9
Santa Cruz,R Argentina 91B8
Santa de Chipchiahue Argentina 91C6
Santa Elena Ecuador 92A4
Santa Eufemia,G di Italy 45E6
Santa Fé Argentina 91D4
Santa Fé Cuba 89C2
Santa Fé New Mex. USA 82F5
Santa Fé prov. Argentina 91D4
Santa Filomena Brazil 93H5
Santa Helena Brazil 91F2
Santa Helena Brazil 93H4
Santai China 54C7
Santa Inés,I Chile 91B8
Santa Innes,B Mexico 88B2
Santa Isabel Argentina 91C5
Santa Isabel (Eq Guin.) = Malabo
Santa Isabel,I Solomon Is 94F8
Santa Lucia Cuba 89D2
Santa Margarita,I Mexico 88B3
Santa María Argentina 91C3
Santa Maria Brazil 91F3
Santa Maria Calif. USA 80C8
Santa Maria Switzerland 33F2
Santa Maria del Rio Mexico 88D3
Santa Maria di Leuca,C Italy 45G6
Santa Maria,I Açores Is 68Q9
Santa Maria,I Chile 91B5
Santa Maria la Real de Nieva Spain 40D2
Santa Maria,Mt Argentina 91C5
Santa Marta Colombia 92C1
Santa Monica Calif. USA 80D8
Santa Monica B Calif. USA 80D9
Santander Colombia 92B3
Santander Spain 40E1
Santañy Mallorca Spain 41H3
Santa Paula Calif. USA 80D8
Santa Quiteria Brazil 93J4
Santarem Portugal 40B3
Santa Rosa Argentina 91C4
Santa Rosa Bolivia 92E7
Santa Rosa Brazil 91F3
Santa Rosa Calif. USA 80B6
Santa Rosa Honduras 89B4
Santa Rosa New Mex. USA 82F5
Santa Rosa Uruguay 91C4
Santa Rosa de Toay Argentina 91D5
Santa Rosa I Calif. USA 80C9
Santa Rosalia Mexico 88B2
Santa Rosa Mts Calif. USA 80E9
Santa Rosa Ra mts Nev. USA 80E5
Santa Vitoria do Palmar Brazil 91F4
Santa Ynez,R Calif. USA 80C8
Santerem Brazil 93G4
Santiago Baja Calif. Mexico 88C3
Santiago Brazil 91F3
Santiago Chile 91B4
Santiago Dom. Rep. 89E3
Santiago Nyarit Mexico 88C3
Santiago Panama 89C5
San Tiago island Cape Verde 68T10
Santiago prov. Chile 91B4
Santiago de Compostela Spain 40B1
Santiago de Cuba Cuba 89D2
Santiago del Estero Argentina 91D3
Santiago del Estero prov. Argentina 91C3
Santiago Mts Texas USA 82G7
Santiago Papasquiaro Mexico 88C3
Santiago,R Peru 92B4
Santiago,Sa de mts Bolivia 92E7
Santiam,R Oreg. USA 80B3
Santiao Chiao cape Taiwan 55L10
Santillana Spain 40D1
Santipur India 61G4
Säntis mt Switzerland 33E1
Santo Angelo Brazil 91F3
Santo Antonio Brazil 92E5
Santo Antônio Brazil 92E6
Santo Antonio Brazil 93G4
Santo Corazón Bolivia 92F7
Santo Domingo Cuba 89C2
Santo Domingo Dom. Rep. 89F3
Santo Domingo Mexico 88A1
San Tomé Venezuela 92E2
Santoríni,I = Thíra,I
Santos Brazil 93H8
Santos Dumont Brazil 93J8
Santo Tomas Mexico 88A1
Santo Tomás Peru 92C6
Santo Tomé Argentina 91E3
Santvliet = Zantvliet
Sanup Plat. Ariz. USA 80G7
San Urbano Argentina 91D4
San Valentin,Mt Chile 91B7
San Vicente island Cape Verde 68S10
San Vicente C de Portugal 40B4
San Vicente de la Barquera Spain 40D1
San Vincente El Salvador 89B4
San Vito,C Italy 45F5
São Antonio do Içá Brazil 92D4
São Bento do Norte Brazil 93K5
São Borja Brazil 91E3
São Carlos Brazil 93H8
São Christovão Brazil 93K6
São Domingos Brazil 93H6
São Domingos do Capin Brazil 93H4
São Félix Brazil 93G5
São Francisco Brazil 93J5
São Francisco Brazil 93J7
São Francisco do Sul Brazil 91G3
São Francisco,R Brazil 93J6
Sao Hill Tanzania 71H6
São Jeronimo Brazil 93G8
Sao Jeronymo,Sa de mts Brazil 93G7
São João da Barra Brazil 93J8
São Joao da Bôa Vista Brazil 93H8
São João del Rei Brazil 93J8
São João do Araguaia Brazil 93H5
São João do Piaui Brazil 93J5
São Joaquim Brazil 92D3
São Jorge island Açores 68Q9
São José Brazil 91G3
São José Brazil 92D4
São José do Mipibú Brazil 93K5
São José do Norte Brazil 91F4
São José do Rio Prêto Brazil 93H8
São Leopoldu Brazil 91F3
São Lourenço Brazil 91F4
São Lourenço Brazil 93F7
São Luis Brazil 93J4
São Luis,I de Brazil 93J4
São Luiz Gonzaga Brazil 91F3
São Manuel,R Brazil 93F5
São Marcelino Brazil 92D3
São Marcos,B Brazil 93H8
São Martinho Brazil 93F5
São Mateus Brazil 93K7
São Mateus do Sul Brazil 91F3
São Miguel,I Açores Is 68Q9
Saona island Dom. Rep. 89F3
Saône et Loire dep. France 42F3
Saône,R France 42F3
São Paulo Brazil 93H8
Sao Paulo de Olivenca Brazil 92D4
São Raimundo Nonato Brazil 93J5
São Romão Brazil 92D5
São Roque,C de Brazil 93K5
São Salvador = M'Banzo Congo
São Sebastião Brazil 93H8
São Sebastiao,I de Brazil 93H8
São Simão Brazil 93H8
São Tomé,I G. of Guinea 70B4
Saoura Algeria 68E3
São Vicente Brazil 93H5
São Vicente Brazil 93H8
Sapiéntza island Greece 47C6
Saposoa Peru 92B5
Sapporo Japan 56G3
Sapri Italy 45E5
Sapulpa Okla. USA 83K5
Saqqez Iran 62F2
Saragossa = Zaragoza
Saraikela India 61E4
Sarajevo Yugoslavia 46B3
Sarala USSR 50K4
Saranac Lake NY USA 79J3
Sarandi del Yi Uruguay 91E4
Sarangarh India 59F4
Saransk USSR 49G3
Sarapul USSR 49L2
Sarasota Fla USA 85L8
Saratoga Wyo. USA 81D5
Saratoga L NY USA 84E1
Saratoga Springs NY USA 84E1
Saratov USSR 49G5
Saravane Laos 57D3
Sarawak state Malay. 53F10
Sarayköy Turkey 62B2
Sarbāz Iran 63J4
Sárbogárd Hungary 37H5
Sarco Chile 91B3
Sardalas Libya 69H3
Sardarshahr India 60D6
Sardegna,I Italy 45B5
Sardhana India 60E6
Sardinia,I = Sardegna,I
Sardis Miss. USA 85C3
Sardis L Miss. USA 85C3
Sardoal Portugal 40B3
Sareks Nat. Pk Sweden 34G3
Sargans Switzerland 33E1
Sargodha Pakistan 60C4
Sarh Chad 69J7
Sari Iran 63G2
Sarikamis Turkey 62E1
Sarina Queens. Australia 99K4
Sariñena Spain 41F2
Sar-i-Pul Afghanistan 63K2
Sarir Libya 69K3
Sarkad Hungary 37J5
Sark,I Channel Is UK 42B2
Sarlat France 43D4
Sarles N Dak. USA 81H1
Sarmi New Guinea Indon. 53L11
Sarmiento Argentina 91C7
Sarmiento,Mt Chile 91B8
Sarna Sweden 35E6
Sarnen Switzerland 33D2
Sarner See lake Switzerland 33D2
Sarnia Ont. Canada 79E4
Sarno Italy 45E5
Saronic G Greece 47D6
Saronno Italy 44B3
Sarpsborg Norway 35D7
Sarrebourg France 42G2
Sarreguemines France 42G2
Sarre Union France 42G2
Sarria Spain 40C1
Sart Belgium 32D4
Sartène Corsica France 43J7
Sarthe dep. France 42D3
Sarthe,R France 42D3
Sarufutso Japan 56H2
Saru Pk India 61E4
Sarvar Hungary 37G5
Sarzeau France 42B3
Sasa Baneh Ethiopia 71J3
Sasaram India 61E3
Sasebo Japan 56A8
Sashi Botswana 72D4
Saskatchewan prov. Canada 76K6
Saskatoon Sask. Canada 76K6
Saskylakh USSR 51N2
Sasovo USSR 49E3
Sassandra Ivory Coast 68D8
Sassandra,R Ivory Coast 68D7
Sassari Sardinia Italy 45B5
Sassenheim Netherlands 32C2
Sassnitz E Germany 36E1
Sassuolo Italy 44C3
Sastre Argentina 91D4
Sas-van-Gent Netherlands 32B3
Satadougou Mali 68C6
Satara India 58D5
Säter Sweden 35F6
Satevo Mexico 88C2
Satka USSR 49P3
Satkhira Bangladesh 61G4
Satna India 61C3
Sátoraljaujhely Hungary 37J4
Satpura Ra mts India 58D4
Sattel Switzerland 33D1
Satu Mare Romania 37K5
Satun Thailand 57C5
Sauda Norway 35B7
Saudhárkrókur Iceland 34V12
Saudi Arabia country SW Asia 62
Sauerland region W Germany 36C3
Saugerties NY USA 84E1
Saugus Calif. USA 80D8
Sauk Center Minn. USA 81K3
Sauk Rapids Minn. USA 81K3
Saulieu France 42F3
Sault Ste Marie Mich. USA 79D2
Sault Ste Marie Ont. Canada 79D2
Saumur France 42C3
Saunders I S Sandwich Is Antarctica 15A4
Sausalito Calif. USA 80B7
Savaii island Western Samoa 95V31
Savai'i,I Samoa 94J9
Savanna Ill. USA 83P1
Savannah Ga USA 85G4
Savannah Mo USA 83L3
Savannah,R Ga/S Car. USA 85G4
Savannakhet Laos 57C3
Savanna la Mar Jamaica 89D3
Savantvadi India 58D5
Savanur India 58E6
Sava,R Yugoslavia 46B2
Sävarån,R Sweden 34J4
Savé Benin 68F7
Savēh Iran 63G2
Savenay France 42C3
Save,R Mozambique 72E4
Savigny Switzerland 33B2
Savoie dep. France 42G4
Savoie prov. France 42G4
Savona Italy 44B3
Savonlinna Finland 34N6
Savukoski Finland 34N3
Savu Sea Indonesia 53H12
Sawankhalok Thailand 57B3
Sawatch Mts Col. USA 82E3
Sawel mt N Ireland UK 30J4
Sawknah Libya 69J3
Sawqirah B Oman 63H6
Sawston England UK 27Q4
Sawu island Indonesia 53H13
Saxmundham England UK 27S4
Saxnäs Sweden 34F4
Saxon Switzerland 33C2
Saxton Pa USA 84B2
Say Niger 68F6
Saya Syria 64D2
Sayaboury Laos 57C3
Sayan Peru 92B6
Sayhūt South Yemen 63G6
Saynshand Mongolia 52F1
Sayre Okla. USA 83J5
Sayre Pa USA 84C2
Sayula Mexico 88D4
Saywūn South Yemen 62F6
Sazin Pakistan 60C3
Scafell Pikes mt England UK 25B4
Scalby England UK 25H4
Scalea Italy 45E6
Scânteia Romania 46F1
Scanzano Italy 45F5
Scapa Flow Orkney Scotland 28K2
Scarba,I Scotland UK 29E7
Scarborough England UK 25H4
Scarborough Maine USA 78C5
Scarborough Tobago 92E1
Scariff,I Ireland, Rep. of 31C10
Scărisoara Romania 46D1
Scarp island Scotland UK 28B3
Scatarie I No. Sc. Canada 78J3
Scavaig,L Scotland UK 28D5
Scenic Wash. USA 80C2
Schaffhausen Switzerland 33D1
Schaffhausen canton Switzerland 33D1
Schagen Netherlands 32C2
Schams valley Switzerland 33E2
Schangnau Switzerland 33C2
S Chay,R Vietnam 57C2
Scheidegg mt Switzerland 33D2
Schelde,R Belgium 32C3
Schenectady NY USA 84E1
Scherhorn mt Switzerland 33D2
Scherzligen Switzerland 33C2
Scheveningen Netherlands 32C2
Schiedam Netherlands 32C3
Schiehallion mt Scotland UK 29H6
Schiermonnikoog island Netherlands 32E1
Schindel Netherlands 32D3
Schio Italy 44C3
Schiphol Netherlands 32C2
Schleins Switzerland 33F2
Schleitheim Switzerland 33D1
Schleswig W Germany 36C1
Schleswig-Holstein state W Germany 36C1
Schneidemühl = Piła
Schöftland Switzerland 33D1
Schoharie NY USA 84D1
Schönbühl Switzerland 33C1
Schönebeck E Germany 36D2
Schongau W Germany 36D5
Schoonhoven Netherlands 32C3
Schötz Switzerland 33C1
Schouten I Tas. Australia 97F5
Schouwen island Netherlands 32B3
Schreckhorn mt Switzerland 33D2
Schuchinsk Kazakh. USSR 50J4
Schull Ireland, Rep. of 31D10
Schuls = Scuol
Schüpfheim Switzerland 33D2
Schurz Nev. USA 80D6
Schuyler Nebr. USA 83K2
Schwabach W Germany 36D4
Schwabisch Hall W Germany 36C4
Schwägalp Switzerland 33E1
Schwanden Switzerland 33E2
Schwandorf W Germany 36E4
Schwaner Geb. mts Borneo Indon. 53F11
Schwarzenburg Switzerland 33C2
Schwarzhorn mt Switzerland 33C2
Schwarzhorn mt Switzerland 33D2
Schwarzhorn mt Switzerland 33E2
Schwarz See lake Switzerland 33C2
Schwarzwald region W Germany 36C4
Schwedt E Germany 36F2
Schwefelberg Switzerland 33C2
Schweidnitz = Swidnica
Schweinfurt W Germany 36D3
Schwerin E Germany 36D2
Schwyz Switzerland 33D1
Schwyz canton Switzerland 33D1
Sciacca Sicily Italy 45D7
Scilly,Is of England UK 26B9
Scio Oreg. USA 80B3
Scipio Utah USA 82B3
Scituate Mass. USA 84F1
Scobey Mont. USA 81E1
Scone NSW Australia 97D2
Scone Scotland UK 29K7

Scoresby,C Shrewsbury

Scoresby,C NW Terr. Canada 77N2
Scoresby Sd = Ittoqqortoomiit
Scotia Calif. USA 80A5
Scotia Ont. Canada 79G3
Scotia Sea Atlantic Ocean 15T4
Scotland S Dak. USA 81J4
Scotland country Great Britain 22G4
Scott,C BC Canada 76F6
Scott City Kans. USA 82H3
Scott Inl. NW Terr. Canada 77R2
Scott,Mt Oreg. USA 80C4
Scottsbluff Nebr. USA 82G2
Scottsdale Ariz. USA 82B6
Scottsdale Tas. Australia 97F5
Scourie Scotland UK 28F3
Scrabster Scotland UK 28J2
Scranton Pa USA 84D2
Scridain,L Scotland UK 29D7
Scugog,L Ont. Canada 79G3
Scunthorpe England UK 25G5
Scuol Switzerland 33F2
Scutari (Albania) = Shkodër
Scutari (Turkey) = Üsküdar
Seaford Del. USA 79J6
Seaford England UK 27Q7
Seaham England UK 25F3
Seahorse Point NW Terr. Canada 77Q4
Sea Isle City New J USA 84D3
Sea Lake Vic. Australia 97B3
Sea Lion,Is Falkland Is 91E8
Seal R Man. Canada 76M5
Searcy Ark. USA 83N5
Searles,L Calif. USA 80E8
Seaside Oreg. USA 80B3
Seaton England UK 26H7
Seattle Wash. USA 80B2
Sebago L Maine USA 78C5
Sebastián Vizcaino,B de Mexico 88B2
Sebastopol Calif. USA 80B6
Sebenico = Sibenik
Sebewaing Mich. USA 79E4
Sebinkarahisar Turkey 62D1
Sebree Ky USA 85D2
Sechura,B de Peru 92A5
Sečovce Czech. 37J4
Secretary I New Zealand 100B7
Secunderabad India 58E5
Seda Lith. USSR 35K8
Sedalia Mo USA 83M3
Sedan France 42F2
Sedan S Aus. Australia 97A2
Sedano Spain 40E1
Sedbergh England UK 25C4
Seddonville New Zealand 100D5
Sederot Israel 64C6
Sedgefield England UK 25F3
Sedgemoor England UK 26J6
Sedhiou Senegal 68B6
Sedom Israel 64D6
Sedrun Switzerland 33D2
Seeheim Namibia 72B5
Seeland region Switzerland 33C1
Seelisberg Switzerland 33D2
Seerücken upland Switzerland 33D1
Sées France 42D2
Seewis Switzerland 33E2
Seez,R Switzerland 33E1
Sefrou Morocco 68E2
Sefton,Mt New Zealand 100D6
Segnes P Switzerland 33E2
Segorbe Spain 41F3
Ségou Mali 68D6
Segovia Spain 40D2
Segovia prov. Spain 40D2
Segovia,R = Coco
Segré France 42C3
Séguela Ivory Coast 68D7
Segura,R Spain 41F3
Sehwan Pakistan 58C3
Seibo Dom. Rep. 89F3
Seiland,I Norway 34K1
Seinajoki Finland 34K5
Seine et Marne dep. France 42E2
Seine-Maritime dep. France 42D2
Seine,R France 42D2
Seitovsk USSR 49M5
Sekenke Tanzania 71G5
Seki Japan 56E7
Sekondi Ghana 68E7
Sektyakh USSR 51P2
Sekuheh Iran 63J3
Selangor state Malaysia 57C6
Selat Lombok strait Indonesia 53G12
Selat Sunda strait Indonesia 53D12
Selby England UK 25F5
Selby S Dak. USA 81G3
Selemiya Syria 64F2
Selenga,R Mong./USSR 51M4
Sélibaby Mauritania 68C5
Seliger Oz. lake USSR 48H3
Selima Oasis Sudan 69L4
Selinsgrove Pa USA 84C2
Seljord Norway 35C7
Selkirk Man. Canada 76M6
Selkirk Scotland UK 29L8
Selkirk Mts BC Canada 76H6
Selles France 42D3
Selle,Sa de la mts Haiti 89E3
Selma Ala. USA 85D4
Selma Calif. USA 80D7
Selma N Car. USA 85H3
Selous,Mt Yukon Canada 76E4
Selsey Bill point England UK 27N7
Selva Argentina 91D3
Selwyn Queens. Australia 99J4
Selwyn Mts Yukon Canada 76E4
Selwyn Ra mts Queens. Australia 99H4
Selzach Switzerland 33C1
Sem Norway 35D7
Semarang Java Indon. 53F12
Sembrancher Switzerland 33C2
Seminoe Res. Wyo. USA 81D4
Semipalatinsk Kazakh. USSR 50K4
Semnān Iran 63G2
Sempach Switzerland 33D1
Sempacher See lake Switzerland 33D1
Senador Pompeu Brazil 93K5
Sena Madureira Brazil 92D5
Senatobia Miss. USA 85C3
Sendai Japan 56G5
Seneca Falls NY USA 84C1
Seneca L NY USA 84C1
Sénégal country Africa 68B6
Sénégal,R Africa 68C5
Senev Mich. USA 79D2
Senga Hill Zambia 72E1
Senghar,R India 61B2
Sengilei USSR 49J4
Seng,R Laos 57C2
Senhor de Bonfim Brazil 93J6
Senigallia Italy 44D4
Senise Italy 45F5
Senj Yugoslavia 44E3
Senja,I Norway 34G2
Senneterre Que. Canada 79H1
Sens France 42E2
Sense,R Switzerland 33C2
Senta Yugoslavia 46C2
Sentinel Ra mts Antarctica 15R2
Seondha India 61B2
Seoni India 61B4
Seoni-Malwa India 61A4
Seoul = Sŏul
Separation Point New Zealand 100E5
Sępólno Poland 37G2
Sept-Iles Que. Canada 78E1
Septimer P Switzerland 33E2
Sepulveda Spain 40E2
Sequeros Spain 40C2
Sequoia Nat. Pk Calif. USA 80D7
Serafimovich USSR 49F6
Serai Syria 64D2
Serakhs Turkmen. USSR 50H6
Seram island Indonesia 53J11
Serampur India 61G4
Serbia = Srbija
Serdobsk USSR 49G4
Serengeti Nat. Pk Tanzania 71G5
Sergach USSR 49G3
Sergiyevsk USSR 49K3
Sérifos island Greece 47E6
Seringa,Serra da mts Brazil 93F6
Sermata island Indonesia 53J12
Serov USSR 50H4
Serowe Botswana 72D4
Serpa Portugal 40C4
Serpukhov USSR 48K4
Sérrai Greece 46D4
Serra San Bruno Italy 45F6
Serrezuela Argentina 91C4
Sertã Portugal 40B3
Sertânia Brazil 93K5
Sertig Switzerland 33E2
Serule Botswana 72D4
Sérvia Greece 47D4
Serviceton Vic. Australia 97B3
Sesheke Zambia 72C3
Sestri Levante Italy 44B3
Sète France 43E5
Sete Lagoas Brazil 93J7
Setesdal valley Norway 35B7
Sétif Algeria 68G1
Seto Naikai sea Japan 56C7
Settat Morocco 68D2
Settle England UK 25D4
Setúbal Portugal 40B3
Sevastopol' USSR 48H9
Sevelen Switzerland 33E1
Seven Devils Mts Idaho USA 80E3
Seven Islands = Sept Iles
Sevenoaks England UK 27Q6
Sévérac-Le-Château France 43E4
Severnaya Dvina river USSR 50F3
Severnaya Zemlya USSR 51L1
Severn,R England UK 26J5
Severn,R Ont. Canada 77O6
Severn,R Wales UK 26G4
Severo Baykal'skoye Nagorye region USSR 51N4
Sevier L Utah USA 80G6
Sevier R Utah USA 82B3
Sevilla Spain 40D4
Sevilla prov. Spain 40D4
Seville = Sevilla
Sèvre,R France 42C3
Seward Alaska USA 87Y12
Seward Pen. Alaska USA 87W12
Seybaplaya Mexico 88F4
Seychelles,Is Indian Ocean 65D5
Seydhisfjördhur Iceland 34Y12
Seyhan Turkey 62D2
Seylac Somalia 71J2
Seymchan USSR 51S3
Seymour Ind. USA 79D6
Seymour Vic. Australia 97C3
Seyne France 43G5
Sézanne France 42E2
Sfakiá = Khóra Sfakion
Sfax Tunisia 69H2
Sfîntu Gheorghe Romania 46E2
Sfira Syria 64F1
's Gravenhage Netherlands 32C2
's Gravenzande Netherlands 32C2
Sgurr Mor mt Scotland UK 28F4
Shaanxi province China 54E5
Shabua India 58D4
Shache China 60E1
Shackleton Antarctica 15A2
Shadegan Iran 62F3
Shadheri Pakistan 60C4
Shadrinsk USSR 49R2
Shadwan,I Egypt 69M3
Shafter Nev. USA 80F5
Shaftesbury England UK 27K6
Shahabad India 60E5
Shahabad India 61C2
Shahba Syria 64E5
Shahbandar Pakistan 58C4
Shahdād Iran 63H3
Shahdadkot Pakistan 58C3
Shahdadpur Pakistan 58C3
Shahdara India 60E6
Shahdol India 61C4
Shahe China 54H4
Shahganj India 61D2
Shahin Dezh Iran 62F2
Shahjahanpur India 61B2
Shahjui Afghanistan 63K3
Shāhpūr = Salmas
Shahpur India 61A4
Shahpur Pakistan 60C4
Shahpura India 58D3
Shahpura India 61C4
Shāhrakht Iran 63H3
Shahr-e-Babak Iran 63H3
Shahresa = Qomisheh
Shahr Kord Iran 63G3
Shahrūd = Emamrūd
Shakhty USSR 49E7
Shaki Nigeria 68F7
Shakopee Minn. USA 81L3
Shala,L Ethiopia 71H3
Shamil Iran 63H4
Shamokin Pa USA 84C2
Shandian He river China 54H1
Shandong province China 54J4
Shangcai China 54H6
Shangcheng China 54H7
Shangchuan Dao island China 55G12
Shangdu China 54G2
Shanggao China 55H8
Shanghai China 54L7
Shanghang China 55J10
Shanghe China 54J4
Shanglin China 55E11
Shangrao China 55J8
Shangshui China 54H6
Shangsi China 55E11
Shanguan China 54F6
Shang Xian China 54E6
Shangyi China 54H2
Shangyou China 55H9
Shangzhi China 52J1
Shaniko Oreg. USA 80C3
Shanklin I of Wight England 27M7
Shan-mo mts Taiwan 55L11
Shannon New Zealand 100F5
Shannon I Greenland 14M2
Shannon,R Ireland, Rep. of 31F8
Shan P China 55J9
Shan Pass China 55J9
Shanqiu China 54H5
Shansi = Shanxi
Shan State Burma 59J4
Shantarskiye Ostrova island USSR 51Q4
Shantou China 55J11
Shantung = Shandong
Shanxi province China 54G3
Shan Xian China 54J5
Shanyang China 54E6
Shaoguan China 55G10
Shaowu China 55J9
Shaoxing China 55L7
Shaoyang China 55F9
Shap England UK 25C3
Shapinsay,I Orkney Scotland 28L1
Shaqa Saudi Arabia 62E6
Shaqra Saudi Arabia 62F4
Shaqrā South Yemen 62F7
Sharakpur Pakistan 60D5
Sharjah UAE 63H4
Shark B W Aus. Australia 98C5
Sharon Pa USA 79F5
Sharon,Plain of Israel 64C5
Sharya USSR 49G1
Shashi China 55G7
Shasta Calif. USA 80B5
Shasta,L Calif. USA 80B5
Shasta,Mt Calif. USA 80B5
Shatt-al-Arab river Iraq 62F3
Shaubak Jordan 64D7
Shawano Wis. USA 79B3
Shawinigan Que. Canada 79K2
Shawnee Okla. USA 83K5
Shawneetown Ill. USA 83P4
Sha Xian China 55J9
Shaykh Uthman South Yemen 62E7
Shchors Ukrain. USSR 48G6
Sheboygan Wis. USA 79C4
Shediac New Br. Canada 78F3
Sheelin,L Ireland, Rep. of 30J6
Sheep Haven bay Ireland, Rep. of 30G3
Sheep's Hd Ireland, Rep. of 31D10
Sheerness England UK 27R6
Sheffield Ala. USA 85D3
Sheffield England UK 25E6
Sheffield New Zealand 100E6
Sheffield Tas. Australia 97F5
Shefford England UK 27P4
Sheikh Miskin Syria 64E5
Sheik Seraq Syria 64F4
Shekatika Bay Que. Canada 78J1
Shekha South Yemen 62F6
Shekhupura Pakistan 60D5
Shelburne No. Sc. Canada 78F5
Shelburne Ont. Canada 79F3
Shelby Mich. USA 79C4
Shelby Mont. USA 81B1
Shelby N Car. USA 85G3
Shelbyville Ill. USA 83P3
Shelbyville Ky USA 85E1
Shelbyville Tenn. USA 85D3
Sheldon Iowa USA 83L1
Sheldrake Que. Canada 78F1
Shelford England UK 27Q4
Shellharbour NSW Australia 97D2
Shelter Cove Calif. USA 80A5
Shelter I NY USA 84E2
Shelter Point Stewart I New Zealand 100C8
Shelton Wash. USA 80B2
Shenandoah Iowa USA 83L2
Shenandoah Pa USA 84C2
Shenandoah Nat. Pk Va USA 85H1
Shenandoah,R Va USA 84B3
Shenchow = Yüanling
Shendam Nigeria 69G7
Shendi Sudan 69M5
Shëngjin Albania 46B4
Shengsi Liedao China 54M7
Sheng Xian China 55L8
Shenkursk USSR 50F3
Shenmu China 54F3
Shenqiu China 54H6
Shenyang China 54M2
Sheopur India 58E3
Shepetovka Ukrain. USSR 48E6
Shepparton Vic. Australia 97C3
Sheppey,I of England UK 27R6
Shepton Mallet England UK 26J6
Sherada Ethiopia 71H3
Sherard Osborn Fj. Greenland 14P1
Sherborne England UK 26J7
Sherbro,I Sierra Leone 68C7
Sherbrooke No. Sc. Canada 78H4
Sherbrooke Que. Canada 79L3
Sheridan Oreg. USA 80B3
Sheridan Wyo. USA 81D3
Sheridan,Mt Wyo. USA 81B3
Sherman Texas USA 83K6
Sherpur Bangladesh 61G3
Sherridon Man. Canada 76L5
s'Hertogenbosch Netherlands 32D3
Shetland islands Scotland UK 22H3
Shevaroy Hills India 58E6
She Xian Shaanxi China 54G4
She Xian Zhejiang China 55K8
Sheyenne N Dak. USA 81H2
Sheykh Sho'eyb island Iran 63G4
Shiant,Is Scotland UK 28D4
Shiant,Sd of Scotland UK 28D4
Shibam South Yemen 62F6
Shibarghan Afghanistan 63K2
Shibata Japan 56F6
Shibetsu Japan 56J3
Shibin el Kom Egypt 69M2
Shicheng China 55J9
Shicheng Dao island China 54M3
Shichiyo Is Truk Is 94A16
Shickshock Mts Que. Canada 78E2
Shidao China 54M4
Shieldaig Scotland UK 28E4
Shiel,Loch Scotland UK 29E6
Shigak prefecture Japan 56E7
Shigar Kashmir India 60D3
Shijiazhuang China 54H3
Shijiu Hu lake China 54K7
Shikarpur Pakistan 58C3
Shiki Is Truk Is 94A16
Shikohabad India 61B2
Shikoku island Japan 56C8
Shildon England UK 25E3
Shilka USSR 51N4
Shilka,R USSR 51N4
Shillelagh Ireland, Rep. of 31K8
Shillong India 59H3
Shiloh Tenn. USA 85C3
Shilong China 55G11
Shilou China 54F4
Shimane prefecture Japan 56C7
Shimen China 55F8
Shimoga India 58E6
Shimo Jima island Japan 56A8
Shimoni Kenya 71H5
Shimonoseki Japan 56B7
Shinās Oman 63H5
Shindand Afghanistan 63J3
Shinghar Pakistan 60A5
Shingo P India 60E4
Shingshal Kashmir India 60D2
Shingshal mt Kashmir India 60D2
Shingū Japan 56D8
Shinjo Japan 56G5
Shin, Loch Scotland UK 28G3
Shinshar Syria 64E3
Shinyanga Tanzania 71G5
Shipley England UK 25E5
Shippegan New Br. Canada 78F3
Shippegan I New Br. Canada 78F3
Shiqian China 55E9
Shiquan China 54E6
Shirāz Iran 63G4
Shireza Pakistan 58C3
Shir Kuh mt Iran 63G3
Shirley Mont. USA 81E2
Shirley Mts Wyo. USA 81D4
Shiroishi Japan 56G6
Shishou China 55G8
Shisur well Saudi Arabia 63G6
Shitai China 55J7
Shiuhing = Zhaoqing
Shiuhing China 55G11
Shivpuri India 61A3
Shixing China 55H10
Shiyan China 54F6
Shiyang He river China 54B3
Shizhu China 55E7
Shizong China 55C10
Shizugawa Japan 56G5
Shizuishan China 54D3
Shizuoka Japan 56F7
Shizuoka prefecture Japan 56F7
Shklov USSR 48G4
Shkodër Albania 46B3
Shoalhaven,R NSW Australia 97D2
Shoeburyness England UK 27R5
Shonai = Tsuruoka
Shoreham by Sea England UK 27P7
Shorkot Pakistan 60C5
Short Mo USA 85B2
Short Mts W Va USA 84B3
Short Pine Hills S Dak. USA 81F3
Shoshone Calif. USA 80E8
Shoshone Idaho USA 80F4
Shoshone Falls Idaho USA 80F4
Shoshone Mts Nev. USA 80E6
Shoshone Mts Wyo. USA 81C3
Shoshone Res. Wyo. USA 86E3
Shouning China 55K9
Shou Xian China 54J6
Shouyang China 54G4
Shovo Tso lake Tibet China 59F2
Shpola USSR 48G7
Shreveport La USA 83M6
Shrewsbury England UK 25C7

Shropshire Soheb

Shropshire county England UK 25C7
Shubenacadie No. Sc. Canada 78G4
Shubuta Miss. USA 85C5
Shucheng China 54J7
Shu He river China 54K5
Shuicheng China 55C9
Shuikou China 55G11
Shujaabad Pakistan 60B6
Shumagin Is Alaska USA 87X13
Shumen Bulgaria 46F3
Shumerlya USSR 49H3
Shuo Xian China 54G3
Shūrab Iran 63H3
Shurchang China 55J9
Shurma Saudi Arabia 62E5
Shurugwi Zimbabwe 72D3
Shuru Tso lake Tibet China 59G2
Shusf Iran 63J3
Shushal Kashmir India 58E2
Shūshtar Iran 62F3
Shuttleton NSW Australia 97C2
Shuya USSR 49E2
Shuyang China 54K5
Shvok,R Kashmir India 60E3
Shwedaung Burma 59J5
Shwegyin Burma 59J5
Shweli,R Burma 59J4
Sialkot Pakistan 60D4
Siam = Thailand
Siargao island Philippines 53J9
Siaton Philippines 53H9
Šiauliai Lith. USSR 35K9
Sib Oman 63H5
Sibenik Yugoslavia 44E4
Siberut island Indonesia 53C11
Sibi Pakistan 58C3
Sibiti Congo 70C5
Sibiu Romania 46E2
Sibolga Sumatra Indon. 53C10
Sibsagar India 59H3
Sibu Sarawak Malay. 53F10
Sibu island Malaysia 57C6
Sicasica Bolivia 92D7
Sichuan province China 54C7
Sicie,C France 43F5
Sicilia,I Italy 45D6
Sicilian Chan. Medit. Sea 45C7
Sicily,I = Sicilia,I
Sico,R Honduras 89B3
Sicuani Peru 92C6
Sid Yugoslavia 46B2
Sideby Finland 35J5
Siderno Italy 45F6
Sidheros,C Kríti Greece 47F7
Sidhout India 58E6
Sidi Barrani Egypt 69L2
Sidi-bel-Abbes Algeria 68E1
Sidi Ifni Morocco 68C3
Sidlaw Hills upland Scotland UK 29K6
Sidmouth England UK 26H7
Sidnaw Mich. USA 79B2
Sidney Mont. USA 81E2
Sidney Nebr. USA 82G2
Sidney NY USA 84D1
Sidon = Saida
Siedlce Poland 37K2
Siegen W Germany 36C3
Siem Reap Cambodia 57C4
Siena Italy 44C4
Sieradz Poland 37H3
Sierpc Poland 37H2
Sierra City Calif. USA 80C6
Sierra Colorado Argentina 91C6
Sierra de Famatina mts Argentina 91C3
Sierra Grande Argentina 91C6
Sierra Leone country Africa 68C7
Sierra Madre Mts Calif. USA 80C8
Sierra Mojada Mexico 88D2
Sierra Nevada de Santa Marta mts Columbia 92C1
Sierra Rosada Argentina 91C6
Sierre Switzerland 33C2
Sífnos island Greece 47E6
Sigean France 43E5
Sighet Romania 37K5
Sighisoara Romania 46E1
Siglufjördhur Iceland 34V11
Sigmaringen W Germany 36C4
Signal Ariz. USA 80G8
Sigourney Iowa USA 83M2
Sigsig Ecuador 92B4
Sigtuna Sweden 35G7
Sigüenza Spain 41E2
Siguiri Guinea 68D6
Sigulda Latvia USSR 35L8
Sihl Switzerland 33D1
Sihl See lake Switzerland 33D1
Siikainen Finland 35J6
Siikajoki Finland 34L4
Siika Joki river Finland 34L4
Siilinjärvi Finland 34M5
Siirt Turkey 62E2
Sijiao Shan China 54M7
Sikandarabad India 60E6
Sikandra Rao India 61B2
Sikar India 60D7
Sikasso Mali 68D6
Sikhothai Thailand 57B3
Sikinos island Greece 47E6
Sikkim state India 61G2
Silairsk USSR 49N4
Silao Mexico 88D3
Silchar India 59H4
Silenen Switzerland 33D2
Silenrieux Belgium 32C4
Silesia Mont. USA 81C3
Sil Gharhi Nepal 61C1
Silifke Turkey 62C2
Siling Co lake Tibet China 59G2
Silistra Bulgaria 46F2
Siljan,L Sweden 35F6
Silkeborg Denmark 35C8
Sillajhuay mt Chile 91C1
Silloth England UK 25B3
Sils Switzerland 33E2
Silvaplana Switzerland 33E2
Silva Porto = Bie
Silver City Idaho USA 80E4
Silver City New Mex. USA 82D6
Silver Cr. Oreg. USA 80D4
Silver,L Oreg. USA 80C4
Silver Lake Oreg. USA 80C4
Silverpeak Nev. USA 80E7
Silver Peak Ra. Nev. USA 80E7
Silverton Col. USA 82E4
Silverton NSW Australia 97B2
Silverton Oreg. USA 80B3
Silves Brazil 92F4
Silves Portugal 40B4
Silvies,R Oreg. USA 80D4
Silvretta mts Austria/Switz. 36C5
Silvretta Gruppe mts Austria/ Switz. 33F2
Silvrettahorn mt Austria/Switz. 33F2
Sima Joki river Finland 34L4
Simao China 52D6
Simard,L Que. Canada 79G2
Simcoe Ont. Canada 79F4
Simcoe,L Ont. Canada 79G3
Simdega India 61E4
Simeulue island Indonesia 53C10
Simferopol' USSR 48J9
Sími island Greece 47F6
Simla India 60E5
Simleu Silvaniei Romania 37K5
Simme,R Switzerland 33C2
Simo Finland 34L4
Simö Järvi lake Finland 34M3
Simola Finland 35N6
Simon,L Que. Canada 79J2
Simonstown South Africa 72H10
Simpelveld Netherlands 32D4
Simplon Switzerland 33D2
Simplon P Switzerland 33C2
Simplon Tun. Switzerland 33D2
Simpson C Alaska USA 76A2
Simpson Des. Australia 99H5
Simpson,I Chile 91B7
Simrishamn Sweden 35F9
Simuna Eston. USSR 35M7
Sinai,Pen. Egypt 69M3
Sinaloa Mexico 88C2
Sinaloa state Mexico 88C2
Sinaloa,R Mexico 88C2
Sinamaica Venezuela 92C1
Sinan China 55E9
Sinbo Burma 59J4
Sinceljo Columbia 92B2
Sinclair's B Scotland UK 28K2
Sind prov. Pakistan 58C3
Sindel Bulgaria 46F3
Sindhara India 61A4
Sindh,R India 61A3
Sindhuli Garhi Nepal 61E2
Sindi Sudan 69L6
S Indian L Man. Canada 76M5
Sind Sagar Doab region Pakistan 60B5
Sines Portugal 40B4
Singa Sudan 69M6
Singapore country SE Asia 57C6
Singapore Str Indon./Singapore 57C6
Singaraja Bali Indon. 53G12
Singatoka,R Viti Levu Fiji 94A25
Singen W Germany 36C5
Singida Tanzania 71G5
Singitic G Greece 47D4
Singkawang Borneo Indon. 53E10
Singkep island Indonesia 53D11
Singleton NSW Australia 97D2
Singora = Songkhla
Siniscola Sardinia Italy 45B5
Sinj Yugoslavia 44F4
Sinjar Iraq 62E2
Sinjil Israel 64D5
Sinkiang = Xinjiang
Sinnamary French Guiana 93G2
Sinoe,L Romania 46G2
Sinop Turkey 62D1
Sinton Texas USA 82T9
Sintra Portugal 40B3
Sinuiju N Korea 52H2
Sinu,R Columbia 92B2
Sion Switzerland 33C2
Sioux City Iowa USA 83K1
Sioux Falls S Dak. USA 81J4
Sioux Lookout Ont. Canada 77N6
Siparia Trinidad 92E1
Sipora island Indonesia 53C11
Siquisique Venezuela 92D1
Sira = Siros I
Sira India 58E6
Siracusa Sicily Italy 45E7
Sira,I = Síros,I
Sirajganj Bangladesh 61G3
Sir Douglas,Mt Alta Canada 76H6
Sir Edward Pellew Grp. islands N Terr. Australia 99H3
Siretul,R Romania 46F1
Sirhind India 60E5
Siri Ethiopia 71H3
Sirjan Iran 63H4
Sirmur India 60E5
Sirna island Greece 47F6
Sironcha India 58F5
Sironj India 61A3
Siros island Greece 47E6
Sirsa India 60D6
Sirsi India 58D6
Sirsi India 61B1
Sirte,G of Libya 69J2
Sisak Yugoslavia 44F3
Sisaket Thailand 57C3
Sisal Mexico 88F3
Sishui China 54J5
Sisimiut Greenland 14P3
Sisophon Cambodia 57C4
Sissach Switzerland 33C1
Sister I,E Tas. Australia 97F4
Sister I,W Tas. Australia 97F4
Sisteron France 43F4
Sitamárhi India 61E2
Sitamau India 58E4
Sitapur India 61C2
Sithonia pen. Greece 47D4
Sitia Kríti Greece 47F7
Sitka Alaska USA 87Z13
Sitpur Pakistan 60B6
Sittang,R Burma 59J5
Sittard Netherlands 32D4
Sitter,R Switzerland 33E1
Sittingbourne England UK 27R6
Siuruan Joki river Finland 34M4
Sivand Iran 63G3
Sivas Turkey 62D2
Siverek Turkey 62D2
Sivrihisar Turkey 62C2
Sivry Belgium 32C4
Siwa Egypt 69L3
Siwalik Hills India 58E2
Siwan India 61E2
Si Xian China 54J6
Sixmilebridge Ireland, Rep. of 31F8
Six Mile Spruit,R South Africa 72N11
Sixteen Mont. USA 81B2
Siyang China 54K6
Sjælland,I Denmark 35D9
Sjötorp Sweden 35E7
Skadarsko Jezero lake Alb./ Yugosl. 46B3
Skaftet Sweden 35G8
Skagafjord Iceland 34V11
Skagen Denmark 35D8
Skagerrak,Str. Denmark/Norway 35B8
Skagway Alaska USA 87Z13
Skamokawa Wash. USA 80B2
Skaneateles L NY USA 84C1
Skara Sweden 35E7
Skaraborg county Sweden 35E7
Skardu Kashmir India 60D3
Skarnes Norway 35D6
Skarzysko-Kamienna Poland 37J3
Skaw,The cape Denmark 35D8
Skeena R BC Canada 76F6
Skegness England UK 25J6
Skellefteå Sweden 34J4
Skellefte Alv river Sweden 34H4
Skelton Coast Namibia 72A3
Skerries Ireland,Rep. of 30L6
Skiathos island Greece 47D5
Skibbereen Ireland, Rep. of 31E10
Skiddaw mt England UK 25B3
Skien Norway 35C7
Skierniewice Poland 37J3
Skiftet Kihti,Arch. Finland 35J6
Skikda Algeria 68G1
Skipton England UK 25D5
Skiros island Greece 47E5
Skive Denmark 35C8
Skjalfandi bay Iceland 34W11
Skjern Denmark 35C9
Skodje Norway 34B5
Skofia Loka Yugoslavia 44E2
Skomer I Wales UK 26D5
Skópelos island Greece 47D5
Skopin USSR 48L5
Skopje Yugoslavia 46C3
Skövde Sweden 35E7
Skovorodino USSR 51P4
Skowhegan Maine USA 78D4
Skradin Yugoslavia 44E4
Skrunda Latvia USSR 35K8
Skudeneshavn Norway 35A7
Skull Valley Ind. Resn Utah USA 82B2
Skuodas Lith. USSR 35J8
Skwierzyna Poland 37F2
Skye, I Scotland UK 28D5
Slagelse Denmark 35D9
Slaithwaite England UK 25E5
Slamet mt Java Indon. 53E12
Slane Ireland, Rep. of 30K6
Slaney,R Ireland, Rep. of 31K9
Slapin, L Scotland UK 28D5
Slatina Romania 46E2
Slatina Yugoslavia 46A2
Slatington Pa USA 84D2
Slăveni Romania 46E2
Slave,R NW Terr. Canada 76J4
Slavgorod USSR 50J4
Slavkov Czech. 37G4
Slavonia rep. Yugoslavia 46A2
Slavonski Brod Yugoslavia 44F3
Slavyansk Ukrain. USSR 48K7
Sleaford England UK 25H7
Slea Hd Ireland, Rep. of 31C9
Sleat,Sd of Scotland UK 28E5
Sleeper Is NW Terr. Canada 77P5
Sleidinge Belgium 32B3
Slide Mt NY USA 84D2
Sliedrecht Netherlands 32C3
Slievanea mt Ireland, Rep. of 31C9
Slieve Anierin mt Ireland, Rep. of 30H5
Slieve Aughty Mts Ireland, Rep. of 31F7
Slieve Beagh mt N Ireland UK 30J5
Slieve Bernagh mts Ireland, Rep. of 31F8
Slieve Bloom Mts Ireland, Rep. of 31H7
Slieve Car mt Ireland, Rep. of 30D5
Slieve Donard mt N Ireland 30M5
Slieve Elva mt Ireland,Rep. of 31E7
Slievefelim Mts Ireland, Rep. of 31G8
Slieve Gamph Mts Ireland, Rep. of 30E5
Slieve Gullion mt N Ireland UK 30L5
Slieve League mt Ireland, Rep. of 30F4
Slieve Mish mts Ireland, Rep. of 31D9
Slieve Miskish mts Ireland, Rep. of 31C10
Slievemore mt Ireland, Rep. of 30C6
Slievenakilla mt Ireland, Rep. of 30H5
Slievenamon mt Ireland, Rep. of 31H9
Slieve Snaght mt Ireland, Rep. of 30J3
Slieve Tooey mt Ireland, Rep. of 30F4
Sligo Ireland, Rep. of 30F5
Sligo county Ireland,Rep. of 30F5
Sligo B Ireland, Rep. of 30F5
Slioch mt Scotland UK 28F4
Slite Sweden 35H8
Sliven Bulgaria 46F3
Sliwobo Burma 59J4
Slobodskoy USSR 49K1
Slobozia Romania 46F2
Slonim Belorus. USSR 48D5
Sloten Netherlands 32D2
Slough England UK 27N5
Slovakia region Czech. 37H4
Slovenia = Slovonia
Slovenija Yugoslavia 44E3
Slovensko region Czech. 37H4
Sluis Netherlands 32B3
Sluiskil Netherlands 32B3
Slunj Yugoslavia 44E3
Słupsk Poland 37G1
Slussfors Sweden 34G4
Slutsk Belorus. USSR 48E5
Slyne Hd Ireland, Rep. of 31C7
Slyudyanka USSR 51M4
Sma Glen Scotland UK 29J7
Smallwood Res. Que. Canada 77T6
Smara Morocco 6C3
Smederevo Yugoslavia 46C2
Smela USSR 48G7
Smerwick Harb. Ireland, Rep. of 31C9
Smethport Pa USA 84B2
Smethwick England UK 25D7
Smilde Netherlands 32E2
Smiltene Latvia USSR 35L8
Smith Alta Canada 76J5
Smith Arm bay NW Terr. Canada 76G3
Smith B NW Terr. Canada 77Q1
Smithers BC Canada 76F6
Smithfield N Car. USA 85H3
Smithfield Utah USA 82C2
Smithfield Va USA 85J2
Smith I Antarctica 15S3
Smith I Que. Canada 77Q4
Smithland Ky USA 85C2
Smith River Calif. USA 80A5
Smiths Falls Ont. Canada 79H3
Smiths Farm South Africa 72H10
Smithton Tas. Australia 97F5
Smithtown NSW Australia 97D2
Smoke Creek Des. Nev. USA 80D5
Smoky C NSW Australia 97D2
Smoky Hill,R Kans. USA 83J3
Smoky,R Alta Canada 76H5
Smøla,I Norway 34B5
Smolensk USSR 48G4
Smolyan Bulgaria 46E4
Smoothstone L Sask. Canada 76K6
Smyrna = İzmir
Snaefell mt Isle of Man UK 25L9
Snaith England UK 25F5
Snake,R Idaho USA 80D2
Snake R Yukon Canada 76E3
Snake R Canyon Idaho/Oreg. USA 80E3
Snake R Plain Idaho USA 80G4
Snåsa Norway 34E4
Snåsa Vatn,L Norway 34D4
Sneek Netherlands 32D1
Sneem Ireland, Rep. of 31D10
Sneeuw Gebergte = Pegunungan Maoke
Snizort, Loch Scotland UK 28C4
Snøhetta,Mt Norway 34C5
Snohomish Wash. USA 80B1
Snow Crest Ra. Mont. USA 80G3
Snowdon mt Wales UK 26F2
Snowflake Ariz. USA 82C5
Snow Lake Man. Canada 76L6
Snowtown S Aus. Australia 97A2
Snowy Mts NSW/Vic. Australia 97C3
Snowy,R Vic. Australia 97C3
Snyder Texas USA 82H6
Soay island St Kilda,Scotland UK 28A1
Soay island Scotland UK 28D5
Soazza Switzerland 33E2
Sobakin USSR 49J4
Sobat,R Sudan 69M7
Soblago USSR 48H3
Soboko CAR 69K7
Sobrado Brazil 93G5
Sobral Brazil 93J4
Sobrance Czech. 37K4
Sobraon India 60D5
Sochaczew Poland 37J2
Sochi USSR 50E5
Social Circle Ga USA 85F4
Society,Is Pacific Ocean 95L9
Socompa mt Chile 91C2
Socorro Colombia 92C2
Socorro New Mex. USA 82E5
Socorro,I Mexico 88B4
Socotra,I Indian Ocean 71L2
Sodankylä Finland 34M3
Soda Springs Idaho USA 82C1
Söderfors Sweden 35G6
Söderhamn Sweden 35G6
Söderköping Sweden 35G7
Södermanland county Sweden 35G7
Södertälje Sweden 35G7
Sodiri Sudan 69L6
Sodus NY USA 84C1
Sodus Point NY USA 84C1
Soepiori island New Guinea Indon. 53L11
Soest Netherlands 32D2
Soest W Germany 36C3
Sofala NSW Australia 97C2
Sofia = Sofiya
Sofiya Bulgaria 46D3
Sogamosa,R Columbia 92C2
Sogamoso Colombia 92C2
Sogndal Norway 35B7
Sogne Fj. Norway 35A6
Sognog county Norway 35B6
Sohâg Egypt 69M3
Sohagpur India 61B4
Sohagpur India 61C4
Sohan,R Pakistan 60C4
Sohar Oman 63H5
Sohawal India 61C3
Soheb South Yemen 62F7

Sohna, — Stirling City

Sohna India **60E6**
Soignies Belgium **32C4**
Soissons France **42E2**
Söke Turkey **62B2**
Sok Karmalinsk USSR **49L3**
Sokode Togo **68F7**
Sokol USSR **48M2**
Sokółka Poland **37K2**
Sokolo Mali **68D6**
Sokota Ethiopia **71H2**
Sokoto Nigeria **68G6**
Sokotow Podalska Poland **37K2**
Solai Kenya **71H4**
Solapur India **58E5**
Solbad Hall Austria **36D5**
Soledad Venezuela **92E2**
Soledade Brazil **92D5**
Solenzara *Corsica* France **43K7**
Solihull *England* UK **27L4**
Sol Iletsk USSR **49M5**
Solimões,R Brazil **92D4**
Solingen W Germany **36B3**
Sollefteå Sweden **34G5**
Sollum = Salûm.
Solok *Sumatra* Indon. **53D11**
Solomon,Is Pacific Ocean **94F8**
Solomon,R *Kans.* USA **83J3**
Solon India **60E5**
Solothurn Switzerland **33C1**
Solothurn *canton* Switzerland **33C1**
Solsona Spain **41G2**
Soltaniyeh Iran **62F2**
Soltau W Germany **36C2**
Solund,I Norway **35A6**
Solvesborg Sweden **35F8**
Solway *Minn.* USA **81K2**
Solway Firth *Eng./Scot.* UK **25A3**
Solwezi Zambia **72D2**
Soma Turkey **62B2**
Somalia *country* Africa **71J4**
Sombor Yugoslavia **46B2**
Sombrerete Mexico **88D3**
Sombrero *island* Leeward Is **89G3**
Sombrero,Chan. *Nicobar Is* India **59H7**
Şomcuta Mare Romania **37K5**
Someren Netherlands **32D3**
Somerset *Ky* USA **85E2**
Somerset *Pa* USA **84B2**
Somerset *Queens.* Australia **99J2**
Somerset *county* England UK **26H6**
Somerset I *NW Terr.* Canada **76N2**
Somerset Res. *Vt* USA **84E1**
Somerset West South Africa **72J10**
Somerville *New J* USA **84D2**
Somerville *Tenn.* USA **85C3**
Somme Belgium **32D4**
Somme *dep.* France **42E1**
Somme,R France **42D1**
Sommieres France **43F5**
Somoto Nicaragua **89B4**
Somuncurá,Sierra *mts* Argentina **91C6**
Somzee Belgium **32C4**
Sonamukhi India **61F4**
Sonara Pk *Calif.* USA **80D6**
Sonbarsa India **61F3**
Sonceboz Switzerland **33C1**
Sønderborg Denmark **35C9**
Sonepat India **60E6**
Song Ba,R Vietnam **57D4**
Song Cau Vietnam **57D4**
Songea Tanzania **71H7**
Songhua Hu *lake* China **52J2**
Songhua Jiang *river* China **52H1**
Songjiang China **54L7**
Songkhla Thailand **57C5**
Songpan China **54B6**
Song Shan *mts* China **54G5**
Songtao China **55E8**
Songxi China **55K9**
Song Xian China **54G5**
Songyin Xi *river* China **55K8**
Songzi China **55F7**
Son Ha Vietnam **57D3**
Sonhat India **61D4**
Sonid Youqi China **54G1**
Sonkajärvi Finland **34M5**
Sonkovo USSR **48K3**
Sonmiani Pakistan **58C3**
Sonneberg E Germany **36D3**
Sonnenhorn *mt* Italy/Switz. **33D2**
Sonogno Switzerland **33D2**
Sonoita Mexico **88B1**
Sonoma *Calif.* USA **80B6**
Sonora *Calif.* USA **80C7**
Sonora *state* Mexico **88B2**
Sonora,R Mexico **88B2**
Sonpur India **59F4**
Sonpur India **61E3**
Son,R India **61E3**
Sonsón Colombia **92B2**
Sopa,R Sudan **69L7**
Sopley *England* UK **27L7**
Sopot Poland **37H1**
Sopron Hungary **37G5**
Sopur *Kashmir* India **60D3**
Sora Italy **45D5**
Sorata Bolivia **92D7**
Sorbas Spain **41E4**
Sorell *Tas.* Australia **97C5**
Sorell L *Tas.* Australia **97F5**
Sörenberg Switzerland **33D2**
Sorfjord Norway **34E3**
Sørfold Norway **34F3**
Sorgono *Sardinia* Italy **45B5**
Soria Spain **41E2**
Soria *prov.* Spain **41E2**
Soriano Uruguay **91E4**
Sørir Norway **34E4**
Sornico Switzerland **33D2**
Sorocaba Brazil **93H8**
Soroki *Moldav.* USSR **48F7**
Sorol,I Caroline Is **94E7**
Soron India **61B2**
Sorong *New Guinea* Indon. **53K11**
Sororoca Brazil **92E3**
Soroti Uganda **71G4**
Sørøya,I Norway **34K1**
Sørøysund *sound* Norway **34K1**
Sorrento Italy **45E5**
Sorrento *Vic.* Australia **97B3**
Sorsele Sweden **34G4**
Sortavala *Karel.* USSR **34O6**
Sosnovka USSR **49E4**
Sosnovo Ozerskoye USSR **51N4**
Sosnowiec Poland **37H3**
Sosva USSR **50H4**
Soto la Marina Mexico **88E3**
Sotra,I Norway **35A6**
Sotuta Mexico **88G3**
Souanke Congo **70C4**
Soudan *N Terr.* Australia **99H4**
Souflíon Greece **46F4**
Soufrière St Lucia **89G4**
Souillac France **43D4**
Souillac Mauritius **65N12**
Sŏul S Korea **52J3**
Sour Lebanon **64D4**
Soure Brazil **93H4**
Soure Portugal **40B2**
Souris *Man.* Canada **76L7**
Souris *Pr. Ed. I.* Canada **78G3**
Sousa Brazil **93K5**
Sousse Tunisia **69H1**
South Africa *country* Africa **72B6**
Southam *England* UK **27M4**
Southampton *England* UK **27M7**
Southampton *NY* USA **84E2**
Southampton *Ont.* Canada **79F3**
Southampton,C *NW Terr.* Canada **77O4**
Southampton I *NW Terr.* Canada **77O4**
South Auckland/Bay of Plenty *stat. area* New Zealand **100F4**
South Australia *state* Australia **98G5**
South Bend *Ind.* USA **79C5**
South Bend *Wash.* USA **80B2**
South Benfleet *England* UK **27R5**
Southborough *England* UK **27Q6**
South Boston *Va* USA **85H2**
Southbridge *Mass.* USA **84E1**
South Carolina *state* USA **87K5**
South China Sea Asia **19M9**
South Dakota *state* USA **86F3**
South Downs *upland* England UK **27N7**
South East C *Tas.* Australia **97F5**
South East C *Vic.* Australia **97C3**
Southend-on-Sea *England* UK **27R5**
Southern Alps *mts* New Zealand **100C6**
Southern Cross *W Aus.* Australia **98D6**
Southern Ocean Antarctica **15C3**
Southern Uplands *mts Scotland* UK **29H9**
South Esk,R *Scotland* UK **29L6**
South Foreland *England* UK **27S6**
South Georgia *Falkland Is Dep.* Antarctica **15A4**
South Glamorgan *county Wales* UK **26H6**
South Hadley Falls *Mass.* USA **84E1**
South Haven *Mich.* USA **79C4**
South I New Zealand **100C6**
South Jacksonville *Fla* USA **85G5**
South Koel,R India **61E4**
South Korea *country* Asia **52J3**
Southland *stat. area* New Zealand **100B7**
South Milwaukee *Wis.* USA **79C4**
South Orkney Is *Falkland Is Dep.* Antarctica **15T4**
South Otterington *England* UK **25F4**
South Paris *Maine* USA **78C4**
South Pittsburg *Tenn.* USA **85E3**
South Polar Plat. Antarctica **15M1**
South Pole Antarctica **15A1**
Southport *England* UK **25B5**
Southport Queensland **99L5**
South River *New J* USA **84D2**
South Rona *island Scotland* UK **28E4**
South Ronaldsay,I *Orkney* Scotland **28L2**
South Sandwich Is *Falkland Is Dep.* Atlantic Ocean **15A4**
South Shetland Is *Falkland Is Dep* Antarctica **15T3**
South Shields *England* UK **25F3**
South Tong,R India **61C3**
South Uist, I *Scotland* UK **28B5**
South West Africa = Namibia
South West C *Tas.* Australia **97F5**
Southwold *England* UK **27T4**
South Yemen *country* SW Asia **62F7**
South Yolla Bolla Mts *Calif.* USA **80B6**
South Yorkshire *county England* UK **25F5**
Souzel Portugal **40C3**
Sovetsk *Lith.* USSR **35J9**
Sovetsk USSR **49J2**
Sovetskaya Gavan USSR **51R5**
Soweto South Africa **72M12**
Sox Alv *river* Sweden **34F4**
Sōya Japan **56G2**
Sōya Misaki *cape* Japan **56G2**
Soya wan *bay* Japan **56G2**
Soyo Angola **70C6**
Soyopa Mexico **88C2**
Söyüt Turkey **62C1**
Spa Belgium **32D4**
Spain *country* Europe **38D5**
Spalato = Split
Spalding *England* UK **25H7**
Spalding *S Aus.* Australia **97A2**
Spam I Canton I **94A23**
Spandau *Berlin* Germany **36E2**
Spandrock Netherlands **32C2**
Spanish *Ont.* Canada **79E2**
Spanish Fork *Utah* USA **82C2**
Spanish Town Jamaica **89D3**
Sparks *Nev.* USA **80D6**
Sparta = Spárti
Sparta *Ill.* USA **83P3**
Sparta *N Car.* USA **85G2**
Sparta *Wis.* USA **79A4**
Spartanburg *S Car.* USA **85G3**
Spárti Greece **47D6**
Spartivento,C Italy **45F7**
Spartivento,C *Sardinia* Italy **45B6**
Spask USSR **49F4**
Spask USSR **49J3**
Spassk USSR **51Q5**
Spátha,C *Kríti* Greece **47D7**
Spencer *Iowa* USA **83L1**
Spencer *S Dak.* USA **81J4**
Spencer G *S Aus.* Australia **99H6**
Spenser Mts New Zealand **100E6**
Sperrin Mts N Ireland **30J4**
Spétsai *island* Greece **47D6**
Speyer W Germany **36C4**
Spey, R *Scotland* UK **28K5**
Spezand Pakistan **58C2**
Spiez Switzerland **33C2**
Spijk Netherlands **32E1**
Spijkenisse Netherlands **32C3**
Spilsby *England* UK **25J6**
Spinazzola Italy **45F5**
Spinetta Italy **44B3**
Spiringen Switzerland **33D2**
Spirit Lake *Iowa* USA **83L1**
Spit B Heard I **65R12**
Spit Point Heard I **65R12**
Spitsbergen,I Arctic Ocean **50C2**
Spittal Austria **36E5**
Spittal *England* UK **25E1**
Split Yugoslavia **44F4**
Split L *Man.* Canada **76M5**
Splügen Switzerland **33E2**
Splügen Pass Italy/Switz. **33E2**
Spofford *Texas* USA **82H8**
Spokane *Wash.* USA **80E2**
Spokane,R *Wash.* USA **80E2**
Spokenburg Netherlands **32D2**
Spoleto Italy **44D4**
Spontin Belgium **32D4**
Sporádhes *islands* Aegean Sea **47F6**
Spotsylvania *Va* USA **85J1**
Spotted Ra. *Nev.* USA **80F7**
Sprague *Wash.* USA **80E2**
Sprague,R *Oreg.* USA **80C4**
Spratly I SE Asia **53F9**
Spree,R E Germany **36E2**
Spremberg E Germany **36F3**
Sprimont Belgium **32D4**
Springbok South Africa **72B5**
Spring City *Tenn.* USA **85E3**
Springdale *Ark.* USA **83L4**
Springdale *Mont.* USA **81B3**
Springer *New Mex.* USA **82F4**
Springerville *Ariz.* USA **82D5**
Springfield *Col.* USA **82G4**
Springfield *Ga* USA **85G4**
Springfield *Ill.* USA **83P3**
Springfield *Mass.* USA **84E1**
Springfield *Mo* USA **83M4**
Springfield *Ohio* USA **79E6**
Springfield *Oreg.* USA **80B3**
Springfield *Vt* USA **84E1**
Springfontein South Africa **72D6**
Springhill *No. Sc.* Canada **78F4**
Spring Hope *N Car.* USA **85H3**
Spring Mts *Nev.* USA **80F7**
Spring Place *Ga* USA **85E3**
Springs South Africa **72N12**
Springsure *Queens.* Australia **99K4**
Springville *NY* USA **84B1**
Springville *Utah* USA **82C2**
Spruce Brook *Newf.* Canada **78J2**
Spruce Knob *W Va* USA **84B3**
Spruga Switzerland **33D2**
Spurn Hd *England* UK **25J5**
Squillace,G di Italy **45F6**
Srbija *rep.* Yugoslavia **46C3**
Srebrenica Yugoslavia **46B2**
Sredinnyy Khrebet *mts* USSR **51S4**
Srednekolymsk USSR **51S3**
Sredne Sibirskoye Ploskogor'ye *region* USSR **51M**
Śrem Poland **37G2**
Srepok,R Cambodia **53E8**
Sretensk USSR **51N4**
Sri Govindpur India **60D5**
Srikakulam India **59F5**
Sri Lanka *country* S Asia **58F7**
Sri Madhopur India **60D7**
Srinagar *Kashmir* India **60D3**
Srirangapatnam India **58E6**
Srivilliputtur India **58E7**
Srnetica Yugoslavia **44F3**
Środa Poland **37G2**
S Saskatchewan,R *Sask.* Canada **76K6**
Sta Ana,B de Mexico **88F4**
Sta Barbara I *Calif.* USA **80D9**
Stackpool *Ont.* Canada **79F2**
Stack Skerry *island Scotland* UK **28G1**
Stack's Mts Ireland, Rep. of **31D9**
Sta Cruz do Sul Brazil **91F3**
Sta Cruz I *Calif.* USA **80D9**
Stadacona *Que.* Canada **79K2**
Stade W Germany **36C2**
Staden Belgium **32B4**
Sta Ellena,B de Ecuador **92A4**
Stäfa Switzerland **33D1**
Staffa,I *Scotland* UK **29D7**
Stafford *England* UK **25D7**
Stafford *Kans.* USA **83J4**
Stafford *Va* USA **85J1**
Staffordshire *county England* UK **25D7**
Staines *England* UK **27P6**
Stainmore Gap *England* UK **25D3**
Stalbridge *England* UK **26K7**
Stalden Switzerland **33C2**
Staliniri *Gruzin.* USSR **50F5**
Sta Luzia *island* Cape Verde **68T10**
Sta. Maria,C Portugal **40C4**
Sta Maria,R *Ariz.* USA **80G8**
Stambaugh *Mich.* USA **79B2**
Stamford *Conn.* USA **84E2**
Stamford *England* UK **25H7**
Stampede P *Wash.* USA **80C2**
Stanberry *Mo* USA **83L2**
Stanchik USSR **51S2**
Standerton South Africa **72D5**
Standish *Mich.* USA **79D4**
Stange Norway **35D6**
Stanislav = Ivano-Frankovsk
Stanke Dimitrov Bulgaria **46D3**
Stanley *England* UK **25E3**
Stanley Falkland Is **91E8**
Stanley *Tas.* Australia **97F5**
Stanley Falls = Boyoma Falls
Stanleyville = Kisangani
Stanlow *England* UK **25C6**
Stann Creek Belize **89B3**
Stanovoy Khrebet *mts* USSR **51P4**
Stans Switzerland **33D2**
Stansmore Ra *mts W Aus.* Australia **98F4**
Stanthorpe Queensland **99L5**
Stanton *Mich.* USA **79D4**
Stanton *N Dak.* USA **81G2**
Staphorst Netherlands **32E2**
Staples *Minn.* USA **81K2**
Starachowice Poland **37J3**
S Taranaki Bight *bay* New Zealand **100E4**
Stara Planina *mts* Bulgaria **46E3**
Staraya Russa USSR **48G3**
Stara Zagora Bulgaria **46E3**
Starbuck *Wash.* USA **80D2**
Starbuck,I Pacific Ocean **95L8**
Star City *Ark.* USA **83N6**
Stargard Poland **36F2**
Starkville *Miss.* USA **85C4**
Starkweather *N Dak.* USA **81H1**
Starnberg W Germany **36D4**
Starobel'sk *Ukrain.* USSR **48L7**
Starodub USSR **48H5**
Starogard Poland **37H2**
Starokonstantinov *Ukrain.* USSR **48E7**
Start B *England* UK **26G8**
Start Point *England* UK **26G8**
Staryy Oskol USSR **48K6**
Staten I *NY* USA **84D2**
Staten,I (Argentina) = Estados,I de los
Statesville *N Car.* USA **85G3**
Stattlandet,I Norway **34A5**
Staunton *Va* USA **85H1**
Stavanger Norway **35A7**
Stavelot Belgium **32D4**
Stavely *England* UK **25F6**
Stavenisse Netherlands **32C3**
Staveren Netherlands **32D2**
Stavern Norway **35D7**
Stavropol USSR **50F5**
Stawell *Vic.* Australia **97B3**
Stawno Poland **37G1**
Steckborn Switzerland **33D1**
Steele *N Dak.* USA **81H2**
Steelton *Pa* USA **84C2**
Steelville *Mo* USA **83N3**
Steenbergen Netherlands **32C3**
Steenbras,R South Africa **72J10**
Steenbras Res. South Africa **72J10**
Steensel Netherlands **32D3**
Steens Mts *Oreg.* USA **80D4**
Steenwijk Netherlands **32E2**
Steep I = Kueishan Tao
Stefanie,L Ethiopia **71H4**
Steffisburg Switzerland **33C2**
Steiermark *state* Austria **36F5**
Stein Switzerland **33D1**
Steinhuder Meer *lake* W Germany **36C2**
Steinkjer Norway **34D5**
Stekene Belgium **32C3**
Stellarton *No. Sc.* Canada **78G4**
Stellenbosch South Africa **72J9**
Stellenbosch Mts South Africa **72J9**
Stenay France **42F2**
Stendal E Germany **36D2**
Stenness,L of *Orkney* Scotland **28K1**
Stenträsk Sweden **34H3**
Stephens,C New Zealand **100E5**
Stephenson *Mich.* USA **79C3**
Stephenville *Newf.* Canada **78J2**
Stephenville *Texas* USA **83J6**
Stepnyak *Kazakh.* USSR **50J4**
Sterea *region* Greece **47C5**
Sterling *Col.* USA **82G2**
Sterling *Ill.* USA **83P2**
Sterlitamak USSR **49M4**
Sternberg E Germany **36D2**
Šternberk Czech. **37G4**
Sterrebeek Belgium **32C4**
Stettin = Szczecin
Stettler *Alta* Canada **76J6**
Steubenville *Ohio* USA **79F5**
Stevenage *England* UK **27P5**
Stevens Pk *Idaho/Mont.* USA **80F2**
Stevens Point *Wis.* USA **79B3**
Stevensville *Mont.* USA **80F2**
Stewart *BC* Canada **76F5**
Stewart,I Chile **91B8**
Stewart I New Zealand **100B8**
Stewart,R *Yukon* Canada **76D4**
Stewart River *Yukon* Canada **76D4**
Stewart Sd *Andaman Is* India **59H6**
Steyr Austria **36F4**
Stia Italy **44C4**
Stikine,R *BC* Canada **76E5**
Stillwater *Minn.* USA **81L3**
Stillwater *Nev.* USA **80D6**
Stillwater *Okla.* USA **83K4**
Stillwater Ra. *Nev.* USA **80D6**
Stimlje Yugoslavia **46C3**
Stip Yugoslavia **46D4**
Stirling *Scotland* UK **29J7**
Stirling City *Calif.* USA **80C6**

Stirling Ra, Tahakopa

Stirling Ra *mts W Aus.* Australia **98D6**
Stites *Idaho* USA **80E2**
Stjernøya,I Norway **34K1**
Sto Antão *island* Cape Verde **68S10**
Stöckalp Switzerland **33D2**
Stockholm Sweden **35H7**
Stockholm *county* Sweden **35G7**
Stockhorn *mt* Switzerland **33C2**
Stockinbingal *NSW* Australia **97C2**
Stockport *England* UK **25D6**
Stockton *Calif.* USA **80C7**
Stockton *Kans.* USA **83J3**
Stockton *NSW* Australia **97D2**
Stockton-on-Tees *England* UK **25F3**
Stoer,Point of *Scotland* UK **28F3**
Stoke Ferry *England* UK **27R3**
Stoke-on-Trent *England* UK **25D6**
Stokesley *England* UK **25F4**
Stokkseyri Iceland **34U13**
Stolbovaya USSR **51S3**
Stolp = Słupsk
Ston Yugoslavia **44F4**
Stone *England* UK **25D7**
Stonehaven *Scotland* UK **28M6**
Stonehenge *hist. site England* UK **27L6**
Stonehouse *Scotland* UK **29J8**
Stonington I Antarctica **15S3**
Stony Stratford *England* UK **27N4**
Stora Lulevatten,L Sweden **34H3**
Stora Sjöfallets Nat. Pk Sweden **34G3**
Storavan,R Sweden **34H4**
Stord,I Norway **35A7**
Store Belt,Str. Denmark **35D9**
Støren Norway **34D5**
Storforshei Norway **34F3**
Stor Laisan *lake* Sweden **34G3**
Storlien Sweden **34E5**
Storm B *Tas.* Australia **97F5**
Storm Lake *Iowa* USA **83L1**
Stornoway *Scotland* UK **28D3**
Storrensjön *lake* Sweden **34E5**
Stor Sjön,L Sweden **34F5**
Storsund Sweden **34J4**
Storuman Sweden **34G4**
Stor Uman *lake* Sweden **34G4**
Storvik Sweden **35G6**
Storvindeln,R Sweden **34G4**
Stosch,I Chile **91A7**
Stourbridge *England* UK **26K4**
Stourport *England* UK **27K4**
Stour,R *Dorset,England* UK **27K7**
Stour,R *Essex,England* UK **27R5**
Stour,R *Kent,England* UK **27S6**
Stowmarket *England* UK **27R4**
Stow on the Wold *England* UK **27L5**
Strabane N Ireland **30J4**
Strachan *Que.* Canada **79J1**
Strachan I Papua New Guinea **99J1**
Stradbally Ireland, Rep. of **31J7**
Strahan *Tas.* Australia **97F5**
Straiton *Scotland* UK **29G9**
Stralsund E Germany **36E1**
Stramproij Netherlands **32D3**
Strand Norway **35B7**
Strand South Africa **72J10**
Stranda Norway **34B5**
Strangford N Ireland **30M5**
Strangford,L N Ireland **30M4**
Strangways Springs *S Aus.* Australia **99H5**
Stranorlar Ireland, Rep. of **30H4**
Stranraer *Scotland* UK **29F10**
Strasbourg France **42G2**
Strasburg *Va* USA **84B3**
Stråssa Sweden **35F7**
Stratford *Conn.* USA **84E2**
Stratford New Zealand **100F4**
Stratford *Ont.* Canada **79F4**
Stratford *Vic.* Australia **97C3**
Stratford-upon-Avon *England* UK **27L4**
Strathalbyn *S Aus.* Australia **97A3**
Strathaven *Scotland* UK **29H8**
Strath Carron *valley Scotland* UK **28G4**
Strathclyde *region Scotland* UK **29E8**
Strathcona Park *BC* Canada **76F7**
Strath Dearn *valley Scotland* UK **28J5**
Strathfarrar *valley Scotland* UK **28G5**
Strathpeffer *Scotland* UK **28G4**
Strathroy *Ont.* Canada **79F4**
Strath Spey *valley Scotland* UK **28J5**
Strathy Point *Scotland* UK **28H2**
Strathyre *Scotland* UK **29H7**
Straubing W Germany **36E4**
Straumnes *peninsula* Iceland **34T11**
Strbské Ploso Czech. **37G4**
Streaky B *S Aus.* Australia **99G6**
Streator *Ill.* USA **83P2**
Street *England* UK **26J6**
Strelka USSR **51L4**
Strelka USSR **51S3**
Strelka Chunya USSR **51M3**
Strenči *Latvia* USSR **35L8**
Strensall *England* UK **25F4**
Stresa Italy **44B3**
Stribro Czech. **36E4**
Strichen *Scotland* UK **28M4**
Strijbeek Netherlands **32C3**
Strijen Netherlands **32C3**
Strimón,G of Greece **47D4**
Strokestown Ireland, Rep. of **30G6**
Stroma, I *Orkney* Scotland **28K2**
Stromboli *island/vol.* Italy **45E6**
Stromeferry *Scotland* UK **28E5**
Stromness *Orkney* Scotland **28K2**
Strømö *island* Færøerne **34Z14**
Strömsberg Sweden **35G6**
Strömsbruk Sweden **35G6**
Strömstad Sweden **35D7**
Strömsund Sweden **34F5**
Ströms Vattudäl,R Sweden **34F4**
Strömtorp Sweden **35F7**
Strongoli Italy **45F6**
Stronsay Firth *Orkney* Scotland **28L1**
Stronsay,I *Orkney* Scotland **28L1**
Stroud *England* UK **27K5**
Stroud *NSW* Australia **97D2**
Stroudsburg *Pa* USA **84D2**
Struer Denmark **35C8**
Struga Yugoslavia **46C4**
Strule,R N Ireland **30J4**
Struma,R Bulgaria/Greece **46D4**
Strumble Hd *Wales* UK **26D4**
Strumica Yugoslavia **46D4**
Stryy *Ukrain.* USSR **48C7**
Strzelin Poland **37G3**
Stuart *Fla* USA **85M8**
Stuart *Va* USA **85G2**
Stuart Highway *N Terr.* Australia **99G3**
Stuart,Mt *Wash.* USA **80C2**
Stuart Mts New Zealand **100B7**
Stuart Ra *mts S Aus.* Australia **99G5**
Stugun Sweden **34F5**
Stung Treng Cambodia **57D4**
Sturgeon Bay *Wis.* USA **79C3**
Sturgeon Falls *Ont.* Canada **79F2**
Sturgis *S Dak.* USA **81F3**
Sturt B *S Aus.* Australia **97A3**
Sturt Des. *S Aus.* Australia **99J5**
Sturt,Mt *NSW* Australia **97B1**
Stuttgart *Ark.* USA **83N5**
Stuttgart W Germany **36C4**
Suakin Sudan **69N5**
Suaqui Mexico **88C2**
Suarez,R Columbia **92C2**
Suarimo Angola **70E6**
Subansiri,R India **59H3**
Subarnakah,R India **61F4**
Subeita *hist. site* Israel **64C7**
Subiaco Italy **45D5**
Subotica Yugoslavia **46B1**
Sucha Poland **37H4**
Suck,R Ireland, Rep. of **31G7**
Sucre Bolivia **92D7**
Sucunduri,R Brazil **92F5**
Sucuriu,R Brazil **93G7**
Sudan *country* Africa **69**
Sudbury *England* UK **27R4**
Sudbury *Ont.* Canada **79F2**
Suddie Guyana **92F2**
Sudety *mts* Czech./Poland **37F3**
Suez Egypt **69M3**
Suez Ca. Egypt **69M2**
Suez,G of Egypt **69M3**
Suffolk *Va* USA **85J2**
Suffolk *county England* UK **27R4**
Suggsville *Ala.* USA **85D5**
Suheli Par *islands Laccadive Is* India **58D6**
Suhl E Germany **36D3**
Suhr Switzerland **33D1**
Suhr,R Switzerland **33D1**
Suichang China **55K8**
Suichuan China **55H9**
Suide China **54F4**
Sui He *river* China **54J6**
Suihua China **52J1**
Suijiang China **55B8**
Suining *Hunan* China **55F9**
Suining *Jiangsu* China **54J6**
Suipacha Bolivia **92D8**
Suiping China **54H6**
Suir,R Ireland, Rep. of **31J9**
Suixi China **55F12**
Sui Xian China **54G7**
Suiyang China **55D9**
Suizhong China **54K2**
Sujangarh India **60D7**
Sujanpur India **60D4**
Sujanpur India **60E5**
Sujica Yugoslavia **44F4**
Sukadana *Borneo* Indon. **53E11**
Sukhinichi USSR **48J4**
Sukhumi *Gruzin.* USSR **50F5**
Sukkur Pakistan **58C3**
Suklek B *Newf.* Canada **77T5**
Suktel,R India **59F4**
Sukumo Japan **56C8**
Sula *Mont.* USA **80G3**
Sulaiman Ra *mts* Pakistan **60A6**
Sula Kep. *archipelago* Indonesia **53J11**
Sula Sgeir *island Scotland* UK **28D1**
Sulaymānīyah Iraq **62F2**
Sulecin Poland **36F2**
Suleskar Norway **35B7**
Sule Skerry *island Scotland* UK **28H1**
Sulgen Switzerland **33E1**
Sulina Romania **46G2**
Sulitelma,Mt Norway **34G3**
Sullana Peru **92A4**
Sullivan *Ill.* USA **83P3**
Sullivan *Ind.* USA **79C6**
Sullivan *Mo* USA **83N3**
Sulmona Italy **45D5**
Sulphur Springs *Texas* USA **83L6**
Sultan Dagh *mt* Turkey **62C2**
Sultan Hamud Kenya **71H5**
Sultanpur India **60D5**
Sultanpur India **61D2**
Sulu Arch. Philippines **53H9**
Sulu Sea Malay/Philippines **53G9**
Sulva Finland **34J5**
Sumatra *island* Indonesia **53C10**
Sumba *island* Indonesia **53G12**
Sumbawa *island* Indonesia **53G12**
Sümber Mongolia **52E1**
Sumbø Faerøerne **34Z15**
Sumburgh Hd *Shetland* Scotland **28Q9**
Sümeg Hungary **37G5**
Sumesar Ra. *mts* India/Nepal **61E2**
Sumiswald Switzerland **33C1**
Summer Is *Scotland* UK **28F3**
Summer,L *Oreg.* USA **80C4**
Summerside *Pr. Ed. I.* Canada **78G3**
Summit *S Dak.* USA **81J3**
Sumner *Wash.* USA **80B1**
Sumner,L New Zealand **100D6**
Šumperk Czech. **37G4**
Sumprabum Burma **59J3**
Sumpter *Oreg.* USA **80D3**
Sumter *S Car.* USA **85G4**
Sumy *Ukrain.* USSR **48J6**
Suna Tanzania **71G6**
Sunagawa Japan **56G3**
Sunapee,L *New H* USA **84E1**
Sunart,Loch *Scotland* UK **29E6**
Sunbury *Pa* USA **84C2**
Sunbury *Vic.* Australia **97B3**
Suncho Corral Argentina **91D3**
Sunchow = Guiping
Suncook *New H* USA **84F1**
Sundance *Wyo.* USA **81E3**
Sundargarh India **61E4**
Sundarnargar India **60E5**
Sunderland *England* UK **25F3**
Sundridge *Ont.* Canada **79G3**
Sundsvall Sweden **34G5**
Sunndals E,R Norway **34C5**
Sunndalserd Norway **34C5**
Sunnyside *Utah* USA **82C3**
Suntar USSR **51N3**
Sunyani Ghana **68E7**
Suo Taiwan **55L10**
Suō nada *bay* Japan **56B8**
Suonnejoki Finland **34M5**
Supaul India **61F2**
Superior *Nebr.* USA **83J2**
Superior *Wis.* USA **81L2**
Superior,L Canada/USA **79B2**
Suphan Dağ *mt* Turkey **62E2**
Suq ash Shuyukh Iraq **62F3**
Suqian China **54K6**
Sūr Oman **63H5**
Surab Pakistan **58C3**
Surabaya *Java* Indon. **53F12**
Surakarta *Java* Indon. **53F12**
Suran Syria **64E2**
Surapur India **58E5**
Sura,R USSR **49G3**
Surat India **58D4**
Suratgarh India **60C6**
Surat Thani Thailand **57B5**
Surendranagar India **58D4**
Surettahorn *mt* Switzerland **33E2**
Surf *Calif.* USA **80C8**
Surgères France **42C3**
Surgidero de Batabano Cuba **89C2**
Surgut USSR **49K4**
Surgut USSR **50J3**
Suri India **61F4**
Surin Thailand **57C4**
Surinam *country* S America **93F3**
Suriname,R Surinam **93F3**
Suriya South Yemen **62F7**
Surkhet Nepal **61C1**
Surrey *county England* UK **27N6**
Sursee Switzerland **33D1**
Sursk *Ukrain.* USSR **48J7**
Surt Libya **69J2**
Susa Iran **62F3**
Susa Italy **44A3**
Sušak Yugoslavia **44E3**
Susania Hill India **61F4**
Susanville *Calif.* USA **80C5**
Susch Switzerland **33F2**
Susong China **55J7**
Susquehanna,R *Pa* USA **84C2**
Sussex *New Br.* Canada **78F4**
Sussex,Vale of *England* UK **27P7**
Sustenhorn *mt* Switzerland **33D2**
Susten P Switzerland **33D2**
Susteren Netherlands **32D3**
Sutherland South Africa **72C6**
Sutherland Falls New Zealand **100B7**
Sutlej,R Pakistan **60C5**
Sutton *England* UK **27P6**
Sutton *Ont.* Canada **79G3**
Sutton Coldfield *England* UK **25E7**
Suure Jaani *Eston.* USSR **35L7**
Suva *Viti Levu* Fiji **94A25**
Suvavesi,L Finland **34N5**
Suvorov,I Pacific Ocean **94K9**
Suwair Saudi Arabia **62E3**
Suwałki Poland **37K1**
Suweilih Jordan **64D5**
Su Xian China **54J6**
Suzhou China **54L7**
Svaerholt Halvöya Norway **34L1**
Svalbard,I Arctic Ocean **50C2**
Svanstein Sweden **34K3**
Svappavaara Sweden **34J3**
Svartenhuk Pen Greenland **14P2**
Svartisen,Pen. Norway **34E3**
Svartvik Sweden **34G5**
Sveg Sweden **35F5**
Švėkšna *Lith.* USSR **35J9**
Švekšna *Litov* USSR **35J9**
Svenčionys *Litov* USSR **35M9**
Svendborg Denmark **35D9**
Sverdlovsk USSR **49Q2**
Sverdrup Is *NW Terr.* Canada **76M1**
Svishtov Bulgaria **46E3**
Svitavy Czech. **37G4**
Svobodnyy USSR **51P4**
Svolvaer Norway **34F2**
Swabi Pakistan **60C3**
Swains I Tokelau **94J9**
Swakopmund Namibia **72A4**
Swaledale *valley England* UK **25D4**
Swale,R *England* UK **25E4**
Swanage *England* UK **27L7**
Swan Hill *Vic.* Australia **97B3**
Swan,R *W Aus.* Australia **98D6**
Swan Ra. *Mont.* USA **80G2**
Swan Reach *S Aus.* Australia **97A2**
Swan River *Man.* Canada **76L6**
Swansea *NSW* Australia **97D2**
Swansea *Tas.* Australia **97F5**
Swansea *Wales* UK **26G5**
Swansea B *Wales* UK **26F5**
Swans I *Maine* USA **78D4**
Swanton *Vt* USA **79K3**
Swarzewo Poland **37H1**
Swastika *Ont.* Canada **79F1**
Swatow = Shantou
Swat,R Pakistan **60C3**
Swaziland *country* Africa **72E5**
Sweden *country* Europe **22M4**
Sweet Grass Hills *Mont.* USA **81B1**
Sweetwater *Texas* USA **82H6**
Swellendam South Africa **72C6**
Świdnica Poland **37G3**
Swietochlowice Poland **37H3**
Swift Current *Sask.* Canada **76K6**
Swilly L Ireland, Rep. of **30H3**
Swinburne,C *NW Terr.* Canada **76M2**
Swindon *England* UK **27L5**
Swinemünde = Świnoujście
Swinford Ireland, Rep. of **30F6**
Swinoujście Poland **36F2**
Switzerland *country* Europe **33C2**
Swona *island Orkney* Scotland **28K2**
Swords Ireland, Rep. of **31L7**
Syasstroy USSR **48H1**
Sybil Point Ireland, Rep. of **31B9**
Sycamore *Ill.* USA **83P1**
Sychevko USSR **48J4**
Syderø *island* Faerøerne **34Z15**
Sydney *No. Sc.* Canada **78H3**
Sydney *NSW* Australia **97D2**
Sydney I Phoenix Is **94J8**
Sydney Mines *No. Sc.* Canada **78H3**
Syeti Vrach Bulgaria **46D4**
Syktyvkar USSR **50G3**
Sylhet Bangladesh **59H4**
Sylt *island* W Germany **36C1**
Sylte Norway **34B5**
Syracuse = Siracusa
Syracuse *Kans.* USA **82H4**
Syracuse *NY* USA **84C1**
Syr Dar'ya,R *Kazakh.* USSR **50H5**
Syria *country* W Asia **62D2**
Syrian Des. = Bādiyat ash Shām
Sysert USSR **49Q2**
Syston *England* UK **25F7**
Syurkum USSR **51R4**
Syzran USSR **49J4**
Szarvas Hungary **37J5**
Szecin *voivodship* Poland **36F2**
Szczecin Poland **36F2**
Szczecinek Poland **37G2**
Szczytno Poland **37J2**
Szechuan = Sichuan
Szeged Hungary **37J5**
Székesféheryar Hungary **37H5**
Szekszard Hungary **46B1**
Szentes Hungary **37J5**
Szentgotthard Hungary **37G5**
Szolnok Hungary **37J5**
Szombathely Hungary **37G5**
Szprotawa Poland **37F3**
Szreńsk Poland **37J2**

T

Tabarka Tunisia **69G1**
Tabas Iran **63H3**
Tabas Iran **63J3**
Tabasara,Sa de Panama **89C5**
Tabasco *state* Mexico **88F4**
Tabatinga Brazil **92D4**
Tabelbala Algeria **68E3**
Tabiang Banaba I **94A18**
Tablazo de Ita *plateaux* Peru **92B6**
Table B South Africa **72H9**
Table C New Zealand **100H4**
Table,Mt Cape Province **72B6**
Tábor Czech. **36F4**
Tabora Tanzania **71G5**
Tabou Ivory Coast **68D8**
Tabriz Iran **62F2**
Tabuaeran,I Pacific Ocean **95L7**
Tabuk Saudi Arabia **62D4**
Tabuleiro Brazil **92F5**
Tabunifi Yap Is **94A19**
Tabut South Yemen **63G6**
Tacámbaro Mexico **88D4**
Tachakett Mauritania **68C5**
Tacheng *Xinjiang* China **50K5**
Tach,L *NW Terr.* Canada **76H4**
Tacking Point *NSW* Australia **97D2**
Tacloban Philippines **53H8**
Tacna Peru **92C7**
Tacoma *Wash.* USA **80B2**
Taconic Mts *Mass./NY* USA **84E1**
Taco Pozo Argentina **91D3**
Tacuarembó Uruguay **91E4**
Tacutu,R Brazil/Guyana **92E3**
Tadcaster *England* UK **25F5**
Tademaït,Plat. du Algeria **68F3**
Tadjoura Djibouti **71J2**
Tadjoura,G of Djibouti **71J2**
Tadoussac *Que.* Canada **78D2**
Tadzhikskaya SSR *rep.* USSR **50H6**
Taegu S Korea **52J3**
Taejŏn S Korea **52J3**
Tafalla Spain **41F1**
Taff,R *Wales* UK **26H5**
Tafila Jordan **64D7**
Tafiré Ivory Coast **68D7**
Taf,R *Wales* UK **26E5**
Taft Iran **63G3**
Taftville *Conn.* USA **84E2**
Ta Fu Shan China **54H7**
Tagamrogskiy Zaliv *gulf* USSR **48L8**
Taganrog USSR **49D7**
Taga Zong Bhutan **59G3**
Taggafadi Niger **69G5**
Tagish *Yukon* Canada **76E4**
Tagula I Papua New Guinea **99L2**
Tagus *N Dak.* USA **81G2**
Tagus,R = Tajo,R
Tahakopa New Zealand **100C8**

Tahat,Mt Algeria 68G4
Tahiti,I Society Is 95M9
Tahlab,R Iran/Pakistan 58B3
Tahoe City Calif. USA 80C6
Tahoe,L Calif. USA 80C6
Taholah Wash. USA 80A2
Tahoua Niger 68G6
Tahta Egypt 69M3
Tahuna Indonesia 53J10
Tai Ivory Coast 68D7
Tai'an China 54J4
Tai'an China 54M2
Taïarapu Pen. Tahiti 95V32
Taibai Shan mt China 54D6
Taibus Qi China 54H2
Taicang China 54L7
Taichung China 55L10
Taieri,R New Zealand 100D7
Taigu China 54G4
Taihang Shan mts China 54H4
Taihape New Zealand 100F4
Taihe China 55H9
Taihu China 55J7
Tai Hu lake China 54K7
Taijiang China 55E9
Taikang China 54H5
Taiko Taiwan 55L10
Tailem Bend S Aus. Australia 97A3
Taimali Taiwan 55L11
Tain Scotland UK 28H4
Tainan Taiwan 55L11
Tainaron,C Greece 47C6
Taining China 55J9
Taipale Finland 34N5
Taipei Taiwan 55L10
Taiping China 55K7
Taiping Malaysia 57C6
Taipingchuan China 52H2
Taira = Iwaki
Tairadate strait Japan 56G4
Taisetsuzan Nat. Pk Japan 56H3
Taishan China 55G11
Tai Shan mts China 54J4
Taishun China 55K9
Taitao,Pen. de Chile 91B7
Taitung Taiwan 55L11
Taivalkoski Finland 34N4
Taiwan Haixia strait China/Taiwan 55K10
Taiwara Afghanistan 63J3
Taixing China 54L6
Taiyetos mts Greece 47D6
Taiyiba Jordan 64D7
Taiyuan China 54G4
Taiyue Shan mts China 54F4
Taizhou = Linhai
Taizhou = Linhai
Taizhou China 54K6
Taizhou Wan China 55L8
Ta'izz Yemen 62E7
Tajarhi Libya 69H4
Tajrish Iran 63G2
Tajumulco mt Guatemala 88F4
Tak Thailand 57B3
Takada Japan 56F6
Takahashi Japan 56C7
Takaka New Zealand 100E5
Takamatsu Japan 56D7
Takao = Kaohsiung
Takaoka Japan 56E6
Takapuna New Zealand 100F3
Takara kaikyō chan. Japan 56B9
Takasaki Japan 56F6
Takaungu Kenya 71H5
Takayama Japan 56E6
Takefu Japan 56E7
Take shima islands Japan 56B6
Takhta Bazar Turkmen. USSR 50H6
Takht-i-Sulaiman,Mt Pakistan 60B5
Takingeun Sumatra Indon. 53C10
Takkaze,R Ethiopia 71H2
Takla BC Canada 76F5
Takla Makan China = Taklimakan Shamo
Taklimakan Shamo des. Xinjiang 18K6
Takoradi Ghana 68E8
Takua Thung Thailand 57B5
Takum Nigeria 69G7
Talagang Pakistan 60C4
Talaimannar Sri Lanka 58E7
Talara Peru 92A4
Talar Ra mts Pakistan 58B3
Talasskiy Ala Tau mt Kirgiz. USSR 50J5
Talaud,Kep islands Indonesia 53J10
Talavera de la Reina Spain 40D3
Talca Chile 91B5
Talcahuano Chile 91B5
Taliabu island Indonesia 53H11
Taliwang Sumbawa Indon. 53G12
Talladega Ala. USA 85D4
Tallahassee Fla USA 85E5
Tallangatta Vic. Australia 97C3

Tallinn Eston. USSR 35L7
Tallow Ireland, Rep. of 31G9
Tallulah La USA 83N6
Tallulah Falls Ga USA 85F3
Talmenka USSR 50K4
Talodi Sudan 69M6
Talsi Latvia USSR 35K8
Taltal China 91B3
Talvik Norway 34K1
Talybbont Wales UK 26G4
Tamale Ghana 68E7
Tamanrasset Algeria 68G4
Tamaqua Pa USA 84D2
Tamarite de Litera Spain 41G2
Tamar,R England UK 26F7
Tamar,R Tas. Australia 97F5
Tamási Hungary 37H5
Tamaulipas state Mexico 88B3
Tamaulipas,Sierra de mts Mexico 88E3
Tamaya Chile 91B4
Tamaya,R Peru 92C5
Tambacounda Senegal 68C6
Tambo Queens. Australia 99K4
Tambo de Mora Peru 92B6
Tambohorano Madagascar 71M10
Tamboril Brazil 93J4
Tamboritha,Mt Vic. Australia 97C3
Tambov USSR 49E4
Tambura Sudan 69L7
Tame Colombia 92C2
Tamel Aiken Argentina 91B7
Tamgak Mts Niger 69G5
Tamiahua Mexico 88E3
Tamil Nadu state India 58E6
Tamina,R Switzerland 33E2
Tamins Switzerland 33E2
Tamlingtar Nepal 61F2
Tamluk India 61F4
Tammisaari Finland 35K7
Tampa Fla USA 85L8
Tampa B Fla USA 85L5
Tampere Finland 35K6
Tampico Mexico 88E3
Tamrah Saudi Arabia 62F5
Tamsagbulag Mongolia 52G1
Tamsalu Eston. USSR 35M7
Tamu Burma 59H4
Tamworth England UK 25E7
Tamworth NSW Australia 97D2
Tana Norway 34N1
Tanabe Japan 56D8
Tana,Fj. Norway 34N1
Tanaga island Aleutian Is USA 87V13
Tanah Merah Malaysia 57C5
Tana,I Vanuatu 94G9
Tanakpur Nepal 61C1
Tana,L Ethiopia 71H2
Tanami N Terr. Australia 98F3
Tanana Alaska USA 87X12
Tanana,R Alaska USA 87Y12
Tananarive = Antananarivo
Tana,R Kenya 71H5
Tana,R Norway 34M2
Tancheng China 54K5
Tanda India 61D2
Tanda Urmar India 60D5
Tandi India 60E4
Tandil Argentina 91E5
Tandola Pakistan 60B4
Tandou L NSW Australia 97B2
Tandragee N Ireland UK 30L5
Taneatua New Zealand 100G4
Tanega shima island Japan 56B9
Tanegashima Kaikyo strait Japan 56B9
Tanen-taung-gyi,Mts Burma/Thailand 57B3
Tanga Tanzania 71H6
Tanganyika = Tanzania
Tanganyika,L Africa 71F5
Tangen Norway 35D6
Tanger Morocco 68D1
Tangermünde E Germany 36D2
Tanggula Shan mts Tibet China 59H2
Tanghe China 54G6
Tangier = Tanger
Tangra Yumco lake Tibet China 59G2
Tangshan China 54K3
Tanguy USSR 51M4
Tangyin China 54H5
Tanimbar Kep. archipelago Indonesia 53K12
Tanjong Gelang cape Malaysia 57C6
Tanjungpandan Indon. 53E11
Tanjungpriok Java Indon. 53E12
Tanjungredeb Borneo Indon. 53G10
Tanjungselor Borneo Indon. 53G10
Tank Pakistan 60B4
Tankapirtti Finland 34M2
Tankse Kashmir India 58E2
Tankse Kashmir India 60F3
Tannadice Scotland UK 29L6

Tännäs Sweden 34E5
Tanshui Taiwan 55L10
Tanta Egypt 69M2
Tanunda S Aus. Australia 97A2
Tanzania country Africa 71G6
Tao Burma 59H4
Tao He river China 54B5
Taolañaro Madagascar 71N12
Taongi,I Pacific Ocean 94G6
Taormina Sicily Italy 45E7
Taos New Mex. USA 82F4
Taoudenni Mali 68E4
Taourirt Morocco 68E2
Taoyuan China 55F8
Taoyuan Taiwan 55L10
Tapa Eston. USSR 35L7
Tapachula Mexico 88F5
Tapaga,C Western Samoa 95V31
Tapah Malaysia 57C6
Tapajós,R Brazil 93F4
Tapalquen Argentina 91D5
Tapan Sumatra Indon. 53D11
Tapanui New Zealand 100C7
Tapauá Brazil 92E5
Tapaua,R Brazil 92D5
Tapioche,R Peru 92C5
Tapi,R India 58E4
Tapirapeco,Serra mts Venezuela 92D3
Tapiwa Banaba I 94A18
Tappahannock Va USA 85J2
Tapti,R India 58D4
Tapuaenuku mt New Zealand 100E5
Taqah Oman 63G6
Taquara Brazil 91F3
Taquaretinga do Norte Brazil 93K5
Tara USSR 50J4
Tarabulus al Gharb = Tripoli
Taradale New Zealand 100G4
Tarago NSW Australia 97C3
Tarakan Borneo Indon. 53G10
Tarakli Turkey 62C1
Taralga NSW Australia 97C2
Tarana NSW Australia 97C2
Taranaki stat. area New Zealand 100E4
Tarancón Spain 40E2
Taransay island Scotland UK 28B4
Taranto Italy 45F5
Taranto,G di Italy 45F5
Tarapoto Peru 92B5
Taraqua Brazil 92D4
Tararua Ra mts New Zealand 100F5
Tarascon Ariège France 43D5
Tarascon Provence France 43F5
Tarasp Switzerland 33F2
Tarata Peru 92C7
Tarauaca Brazil 92C5
Taravao Isthmus Tahiti 95V32
Tarawa,I Kiribati 94H7
Tarawera New Zealand 100G4
Tarazona Spain 41F2
Tarazona de la Mancha Spain 41F3
Tarbat Ness cape Scotland UK 28J4
Tarbert Harris,Scotland UK 28C4
Tarbert Ireland, Rep. of 31E8
Tarbert Strathclyde,Scotland UK 29F8
Tarbes France 43D5
Tarboro N Car. USA 85J3
Tarcoola S Aus. Australia 99G6
Tarcoon NSW Australia 97C2
Tarcutta NSW Australia 97C3
Taree NSW Australia 97D2
Tärendö Sweden 34K3
Tarfaya Western Sahara 68C3
Tarija Bolivia 92E8
Tarim South Yemen 62F6
Tarim He river Xinjiang China 50K5
Tarjannevesi lake Finland 35K5
Tarko Sale USSR 50J3
Tarkwa Ghana 68E7
Tarlac Philippines 53H7
Tarland Scotland UK 28K5
Tarleton England UK 25C5
Tarlton South Africa 72M12
Tarma Peru 92B6
Tarn dep. France 43E5
Tärna Sweden 34F4
Tarn-et-Garonne dep. France 43D4
Tarnobrzeg Poland 37J3
Tarnów Poland 37J3
Tarnowskie Gory Poland 37H3
Tarn,R France 43E5
Tarn Taran India 60D5
Tárom Iran 63H4
Taroom Queens. Australia 99K5
Taro,R Italy 44B3
Taroudannt Morocco 68E2
Tarporley England UK 25C6
Tarragona Spain 41G2
Tarragona prov. Spain 41G2

Tarran Hills NSW Australia 97C2
Tárrega Spain 41G2
Tarso Taro,Mt Chad 69J4
Tarsus Turkey 62C2
Tartagal Argentina 91D2
Tartas France 43C5
Tartu Eston. USSR 35M7
Tartus Syria 64D3
Tasawah Libya 69H3
Taseko Ls BC Canada 76G6
Taseyevo USSR 51L4
Tashkent Uzbek. USSR 50H5
Tasiilaq Greenland 14N3
Tasil Syria 64D5
Taskan USSR 51S3
Tasköprü Turkey 62C1
Tasman B New Zealand 100E5
Tasman Hd Tas. Australia 97F5
Tasmania island Australia 99K8
Tasman,Mt New Zealand 100D6
Tasman Mts New Zealand 100E5
Tasman Pen. Tas. Australia 97C5
Tata Hungary 37H5
Tatakoto,I Tuamotu Arch. 95N9
Tatarskaya ASSR rep. USSR 50G4
Tatarskiy Proliv strait USSR 51R4
Tathlina,L NW Terr. Canada 76H4
Tathlith Saudi Arabia 62E6
Tatinnai L NW Terr. Canada 76M4
Tatnam,C Man. Canada 77N5
Tatong Vic. Australia 97C3
Tatranská Lomnica Czech. 37J4
Tatry mts., Czech./Poland 37H4
Tatta Pakistan 58C4
Tattershall England UK 25H6
Tatui Brazil 93H8
Tau Tabuaeran Kiribati 94A26
Tauá Brazil 93J5
Tauapeçaçú Brazil 92E4
Taubaté Brazil 93H8
Taumarunui New Zealand 100F4
Taungdwingyi Burma 59J4
Taunggyi Burma 59J4
Taungup Burma 59H5
Taunton England UK 26H6
Taunton Mass. USA 84F2
Taunus region W Germany 36C3
Tau Pass. Thailand 57C5
Taupo New Zealand 100G4
Taupo,L New Zealand 100G4
Taurage Lith. USSR 35K9
Tauranga New Zealand 100G3
Tauroa Point New Zealand 100E2
Tauste Spain 41F2
Tauysk USSR 51R4
Tavda USSR 50H4
Taverne Switzerland 33D2
Taveuni,I Vanua Levu 94A24
Tavistock England UK 26F7
Tavolara island Sardinia Italy 45B5
Tavoy Burma 59J6
Tavoy,R Burma 59J6
Tavsanli Turkey 62B2
Tawang India 59H3
Tawas City Mich. USA 79E3
Tawau Sabah Malay. 53G10
Tawe,R Wales UK 26G5
Tawi,R India 60D4
Tawitawi island Philippines 53H9
Taw,R England UK 26G7
Taxco Mexico 88E4
Taxkorgan China 60D2
Tayan Borneo Indon. 53F11
Tay,Firth of Scotland UK 29K7
Tayga USSR 50K4
Tay,Loch Scotland UK 29H6
Taylor,Mt New Mex. USA 82E5
Taylorsville N Car. USA 85G3
Taylorville Ill. USA 83P3
Tayma' Saudi Arabia 62D4
Tayport Scotland UK 29L7
Tay,R Scotland UK 29K7
Tayshet USSR 51L4
Tayshir Mongolia 52C1
Tayside region Scotland UK 29J6
Taytay Philippines 53G8
Taza Morocco 68E2
Tazewell Va USA 85G2
Tazovskaya G USSR 50J3
Tbilisi Gruzin. USSR 50F5
Tchad = Chad
Tchad,L = Chad,L
Tchaourou Benin 68F7
Tczew Poland 37H1
Te Anau,L New Zealand 100B7
Teano Ra mts W Aus. Australia 98D4

Te Aroha New Zealand 100F3
Te Awamutu New Zealand 100F3
Tebay England UK 25C4
Tebingtinggi Malaysia 57C6
Teboursouk Tunisia 69G1
Tecamachalco Mexico 88E4
Tecka Argentina 91B6
Tecka,R Argentina 91B6
Tecolutla Mexico 88E3
Tecopa Calif. USA 80E8
Tecpan Mexico 88D4
Tecuci Romania 46F2
Tecumseh Nebr. USA 83K2
Tecuniseh Mich. USA 79D4
Tedzhen Turkmen. USSR 50H6
Teesdale valley England UK 25D3
Tees,R England UK 25E3
Tefé Brazil 92E4
Tegucigalpa Honduras 89B4
Tehachapi Calif. USA 80D8
Tehama Calif. USA 80B5
Tehrän Iran 63G2
Tehri India 58E2
Tehuacán Mexico 88E4
Tehuantepec Mexico 88E4
Tehuantepec,G of Mexico 88E4
Tehuantepec,Isthmus Mexico 88F4
Tehwato China 54N3
Teifi,R Wales UK 26F4
Teignmouth England UK 26H7
Teign,R England UK 26G7
Teith,R Scotland UK 29H7
Tejo,R Port./Spain 40C3
Tekapo,L New Zealand 100D6
Tekari India 61E3
Tekirdağ Turkey 62B1
Tekoa Wash. USA 80E2
Te Kuiti New Zealand 100F4
Tela Honduras 89B3
Tel Aviv Israel 64C5
Telegraph Creek BC Canada 76E5
Telemark county Norway 35C7
Telescope Pk Calif. USA 80E7
Telford England UK 25D7
Télimélé Guinea 68C6
Telkalakh Syria 64E3
Tell Bisa Syria 64E3
Tellicherry India 58E6
Teloloapan Mexico 88D4
Telpos-iz mt USSR 50G3
Telsen Argentina 91C6
Telsiai Lith. USSR 35K9
Telukbetung Sumatra Indon. 53E12
Teluk Bone gulf Celebes Indon. 53H11
Teluk Cendrawasih gulf New Guinea Indon. 53K11
Teluk Kintuni gulf New Guinea Indon. 53K11
Teluk Tol gulf Celebes Indon. 53H11
Teluk Tomini gulf Celebes Indon. 53H11
Teluk Weda bay Halmahera Indon. 53J10
Tema Ghana 68E7
Tembeling Malaysia 57C6
Tembisa South Africa 72N12
Temblador Venezuela 92E2
Teme,R England UK 26K4
Temesvar = Timisoara
Temir Kazakh. USSR 50G5
Temirtau USSR 50K4
Temiscouata L Que. Canada 78D3
Temma Tas. Australia 97E5
Temnikov USSR 49F3
Temora NSW Australia 97C2
Temósachic Mexico 88C2
Tempe Ariz. USA 82C6
Tempio Sardinia Italy 45B5
Temple Texas USA 83K7
Templemore Ireland, Rep. of 31H8
Temse Belgium 32C3
Temuco Chile 91B5
Temuka New Zealand 100D6
Tenancingo Mexico 88E4
Tenasique Mexico 88F4
Tenasserim Burma 59J6
Tenasserim,R Burma 59J6
Tenbury Wells England UK 26J4
Tenby Wales UK 26E5
Ten Degree,Chan. Andaman Is India 59H7
Tendre,Mt Switzerland 33B2
Tenerife,I Canary Is 68B3
Ténès Algeria 68F1
Tengréla Ivory Coast 68D6
Teng Xian Guanxi China 55F11
Teng Xian Shandong China 54J5
Teniger Bad Switzerland 33D2
Tenino Wash. USA 80B2
Tennant Creek N Terr. Australia 99G3
Tennessee state USA 87J4

Tennessee R, Tone,R

Tennessee R Col. USA 82E3
Tennessee,R Ky/Tenn. USA 85C3
Tensift,R Morocco 68D2
Tenterfield NSW Australia 97D1
Tenterton England UK 27R6
Ten Thousand Is Fla USA 85M9
Ten Thousand Smokes,V of Alaska USA 87X13
Teocaltiche Mexico 88D3
Teõfilo Otôni Brazil 93J7
Teotihuacán Mexico 88E4
Tepatitlan Mexico 88D3
Tepehuanes Mexico 88C2
Tepelene Albania 47B4
Tepic Mexico 88D3
Teplice Czech. 36E3
Te Puke New Zealand 100G3
Tera Niger 68F6
Teraina,I Pacific Ocean 94K7
Teram Kangri mt India 60E3
Teramo Italy 44D4
Terang Vic. Australia 97B3
Ter Apel Netherlands 32E2
Terborg Netherlands 32E3
Terceira island Açores 68Q9
Terenceville Newf. Canada 78L3
Terengganu state Malaysia 57C6
Teresina Brazil 93J5
Teressa,I Nicobar Is India 59H7
Terezin Czech. 36F3
Terhazza Mali 68D4
Termez Uzbek. USSR 50H6
Termini Imerese Sicily Italy 45D7
Termo Calif. USA 80C5
Termoli Italy 45E4
Termonde = Dendermonde
Ternate Halmahera Indon. 53J10
Terneuzen Netherlands 32B3
Terni Italy 44D4
Ternopol Ukrain. USSR 48D7
Terowie S Aus. Australia 97A2
Terra Bella Calif. USA 80D8
Terracina Italy 45D5
Terra Firma South Africa 72C5
Terralba Sardinia Italy 45B6
Terra Nova Newf. Canada 78L2
Terra Santa Brazil 93F4
Terre Adélie Antarctica 15K3
Terrebonne B La USA 83N8
Terre Haute Ind. USA 79C6
Terrell Texas USA 83K6
Terrigal NSW Australia 97D2
Terri,Mt Switzerland 33C1
Terror,Mt Antarctica 15L2
Terry Mont. USA 81E2
Terschelling island Netherlands 32D1
Teruel Spain 41F2
Teruel prov. Spain 41F2
Tervola Finland 34L3
Térvuren Belgium 32C4
Terwagne Belgium 32D4
Teshekpuk L L. Alaska USA 76A2
Teshio Japan 56G2
Teslin Yukon Canada 76E4
Teslin L Yukon Canada 76E4
Teslin,R Yukon Canada 76E4
Tessaoua Niger 68G6
Tessenderlo Belgium 32D3
Tesserete Switzerland 33D2
Testa,C Sardinia Italy 45B5
Test,R England UK 27M6
Tetbury England UK 27K5
Tete Mozambique 72E3
Teton Ra Wyo. USA 81B4
Tetsuzan China 54N3
Tetuan Morocco 68D1
Tetyushi USSR 49J3
Teufen Switzerland 33E1
Teulada Sardinia Italy 45B6
Teulada,C Sardinia Italy 45B6
Teutoburger Wald region W Germany 36C2
Tevere,R = Tiber,R
Teviot,R Scotland UK 29L8
Tevriz USSR 50J4
Te Waewae B New Zealand 100B8
Tewkesbury England UK 27K5
Texarkana Ark. USA 83L6
Texas state USA 86F5
Texcoco Mexico 88E4
Texel island Netherlands 32C1
Texoma,L Okla. USA 83K5
Tezpur India 59H3
Tezuitlán Mexico 88E4
Tg. Penurgok Malaysia Malasia 57C6
Thadiq Saudi Arabia 62F4
Thailand country SE Asia 57B3
Thailand,G of Thailand 57C4
Thakhek Laos 57C3
Thal Pakistan 60B4
Thale Luang,L Thailand 57C5
Thalkirch Switzerland 33E2
Thames New Zealand 100F3
Thames, Firth of New Zealand 100F3
Thames,R Conn. USA 84E2
Thames,R England UK 27N5
Thāne India 58D5
Thanesar India 60E6
Thanh Hoa Vietnam 57D3
Thanjavur India 58E6
Thann France 42G3
Thar Des. India 58D3
Thargomindah Queens. Australia 99J5
Tharoch India 60E5
Tharrawaddy Burma 59J5
Thásos island Greece 47E4
Thásos Str. Greece 47E4
Thatcher Ariz. USA 82D6
Thaton Burma 59J5
Thaungdut Burma 59H4
Thawil Switzerland 33D1
Thayawthadangyi Kyun island Burma 59J6
Thayer Mo USA 83N4
Thayetmyo Burma 59J5
Thayngen Switzerland 33D1
Thazi Burma 59J4
The Bahamas West Indies 89D1
Thebes = Thivai
The Bight The Bahamas 89D2
The Cheviot mt England UK 25D2
The Everglades Fla USA 85M9
The Fens region England UK 27Q3
The Hague = 's Gravenhage
Thelon R NW Terr. Canada 76L4
The Naze England UK 27S5
The Needles England UK 27L7
The North Sd Orkney Scotland 28L1
Theodore Queens. Australia 99L5
Theodore Roosevelt L Ariz. USA 82C6
Theodore Roosevelt Nat. Pk N Dak. USA 81F2
Theodul P Italy/Switz. 33C3
The Pas Man. Canada 76L6
The Peak mt England UK 25E6
The Race chan. Conn./NY USA 84E2
Thérmai,G of Greece 47D4
Thermal Calif. USA 80E9
Thérmiá,I = Kíthnos,I
Thermopolis Wyo. USA 81C4
The Rock NSW Australia 97C3
Therwil Switzerland 33C1
The Saddle mt Scotland UK 28F5
The Snares islands New Zealand 100B9
The Solent England UK 27M7
Thesprotia dist. Greece 47C5
Thessalia region Greece 47D5
Thessaloniki Greece 47D4
Thessaloniki dist. Greece 47D4
Thessaly = Thessalia
Thetford England UK 27R4
Thetford Mines Que. Canada 78C3
The Twins mt New Zealand 100E5
Theux Belgium 32D4
The Wash England UK 27Q3
The Weald region England UK 27Q6
Thibodaux La USA 83N8
Thief River Falls Minn. USA 81J1
Thielsen,Mt Oreg. USA 80B4
Thielt = Tielt
Thierberg mt Switzerland 33D2
Thies Senegal 68B6
Thimbu = Thimphu
Thimphu Bhutan 61G2
Thingvalla vatn lake Iceland 34U12
Thingvellir Iceland 34U12
Thio Ethiopia 71J2
Thionville France 42G2
Thíra island Greece 47E6
Thirsk England UK 25F4
Thirtyone Mile L = Trent et un Milles,L de
Thisted Denmark 35C8
Thistilfjord Iceland 34X11
Thitu Is SE Asia 53F8
Thityabin Burma 59J4
Thivai Greece 47D5
Thiviers France 42D4
Thjórsá,R Iceland 34V12
Thoen Thailand 57B3
Tholen Netherlands 32C3
Tholen region Netherlands 32C3
Thomaston Ga USA 85E4
Thomastown Ireland, Rep. of 31J8
Thomasville Ga USA 85E5
Thompson Falls Mont. USA 80F2
Thompsonville Conn. USA 84E1
Thomson,R Queens. Australia 99J4
Thondhe India 60E4
Thongwa Burma 59J5
Thorn = Toruń
Thornbury England UK 26J5
Thornhill Scotland UK 29J9
Thorshavn Faerøerne 34Z14
Thorshavn Faerøerne 34Z14
Thórshöfn Iceland 34X11
Thouars France 42C3
Thourout = Torhout
Thousand Is NY Canada/USA 79J3
Thousand Lake Mt Utah USA 82C3
Thousand Oaks Calif. USA 80D8
Thrace = Thraki
Thraki region Greece 46E4
Thrapston England UK 27N4
Three Creek Idaho USA 80F4
Three Hummock I Tas. Australia 97F5
Three Kings Is New Zealand 100E2
Three Points,C Ghana 68E8
Three Rivers = Trois Rivières
Three Rivers Mich. USA 79D5
Three Sisters mts Oreg. USA 80C3
Throssel Ra mts W Aus. Australia 98E4
Thueyts France 43F4
Thuillier,Mt Nicobar Is India 59H7
Thuin Belgium 32C4
Thule Greenland 14Q2
Thule I S Sandwich Is Antarctica 15A4
Thun Switzerland 33C2
Thunder B Mich. USA 79E3
Thunder Bay Ont. Canada 77O7
Thuner See lake Switzerland 33C2
Thuot Vietnam 57D4
Thurgau canton Switzerland 33D1
Thüringer Wald E Germany 36D3
Thurles Ireland, Rep. of 31H8
Thur,R Switzerland 33D1
Thursday I Queens. Australia 99J2
Thurso Scotland UK 28J2
Thurso,R Scotland UK 28J3
Thusis Switzerland 33E2
Tia NSW Australia 97D2
Tianchang China 54K6
Tianjin province China 54J3
Tianlin China 55D10
Tianmen China 54G7
Tianmu Shan mt China 55K7
Tian Shan mts China/USSR 50J5
Tianshui China 54C5
Tiantai China 55L8
Tianzhu China 55E9
Tiaret Algeria 68F1
Tiassale Ivory Coast 68D7
Tibati Cameroun 69H7
Tiberias Israel 64D5
Tiberias,L Israel 64D5
Tiber,R Italy 45D4
Tibesti mts Chad 69J4
Tibet aut. region China 18K6
Tibnin Lebanon 64D4
Tibooburra NSW Australia 97B1
Tibrikot Nepal 61D1
Tiburón Haiti 89E3
Tiburon I Mexico 88B2
Tichitt Mauritania 68D5
Ticino canton Switzerland 33D2
Ticino,R Italy 44B3
Ticino,R Switzerland 33D2
Ticonderoga NY USA 79K4
Ticul Mexico 88G3
Tidjikja Mauritania 68C5
Tidworth England UK 27L6
Tiebissou Ivory Coast 68D7
Tiefencastel Switzerland 33E2
Tiel Netherlands 32D3
Tieling China 54M1
Tielt Belgium 32B3
Tienen Belgium 32C4
Tiermas Spain 41F1
Tierra del Fuego Arch. Argentina/Chile 91C8
Tiffin Ohio USA 79E5
Tifton Ga USA 85F5
Tigăneşti Romania 46F2
Tiger I = Gio
Tighina = Bendery
Tighnabruaich Scotland UK 29F8
Tigil USSR 51S4
Tignish Pr. Ed. I. Canada 78F3
Tigris,R Iraq 62F3
Tijuana Mexico 88A1
Tikhvin USSR 48H2
Tikrit Iraq 62E3
Tiksi USSR 51P2
Tilamook Oreg. USA 80B3
Tilazya Res. India 61E3
Tilburg Netherlands 32D3
Tilbury England UK 27Q6
Tilcara Argentina 91C2
Tilichiki USSR 51T3
Tillaberi Niger 68F6
Tillamook B Oreg. USA 80A3
Tillamook Hd Oreg. USA 80A3
Tillanchong,I Nicobar Is India 59H7
Tillicoultry Scotland UK 29J7
Till,R England UK 25D1
Tillsonburg Ont. Canada 79F4
Tílos island Greece 47F6
Tilpa NSW Australia 97B2
Tilsit = Sovetsk
Timanski Kryazh region USSR 50G3
Timaru New Zealand 100D7
Timbalier B La USA 83N8
Timbédra Mauritania 68D5
Timber Lake S Dak. USA 81G3
Timboon Vic. Australia 97B3
Timbuktu = Tombouctou
Timfristós mt Greece 47C5
Timimoun Algeria 68F3
Timiskaming Que. Canada 79G2
Timisoara Romania 46C2
Timmins Ont. Canada 79F1
Timor island Indonesia 53H12
Timor Sea Aus./Indon. 98E2
Timote Argentina 91D5
Tinaca Point Philippines 53J9
Tinahely Ireland, Rep. of 31L8
Tindouf Algeria 68D3
Tineo Spain 40C1
Tinggi island Malaysia 57C6
Tingha NSW Australia 97D1
Tingo Maria Peru 92B5
Tingri Tibet China 59G3
Tingzhou = Changting
Tinhare,I de Brazil 93K6
Tinian,I Mariana Is 94E6
Tinkhannock Pa USA 84C2
Tinnoset Norway 35C7
Tinogasta Argentina 91C3
Tinos island Greece 47E6
Tinsukia India 59J3
Tintagel Hd England UK 26E7
Tintern Wales UK 26J5
Tintic Utah USA 82B3
Tintigny Belgium 32D5
Tintina Argentina 91D3
Tintinara S Aus. Australia 97B3
Tionesta Pa USA 84B2
Tipperary Ireland, Rep. of 31G9
Tipperary county Ireland,Rep. of 31G8
Tipton England UK 25D7
Tipton Iowa USA 83N2
Tipton,Mt Ariz. USA 80F8
Tiracambu,Sa do mts Brazil 93H4
Tiran island Saudi Arabia 62C4
Tirana = Tiranë
Tiranë Albania 46B4
Tiraspol' Moldav. USSR 48F8
Tire Turkey 62B2
Tireboli Turkey 62D1
Tiree,I Scotland UK 29C6
Tirgu Jiu Romania 46D2
Tîrgu Mureş Romania 46E1
Tîrgu Ocna Romania 46F1
Tirich Mir,Mt Pakistan 60B2
Tirlemont = Tienen
Tirlyanski USSR 49P3
Tirnavos Greece 47D5
Tirol state Austria 36D5
Tiruchchendur India 58E7
Tiruchchirappalli India 58E6
Tiru Kona Malai = Trincomalee
Tirunelveli India 58E7
Tirupati India 58E6
Tiruvannamalai India 58E6
Tisa = Tisza
Tisiya Syria 64E5
Tissa Nigeria 69H7
Tissinnt Morocco 68D3
Tista,R India 61G2
Tisza,R Hungary/Yugo. 39L4
Titalyah Bangladesh 61G2
Titicaca,L Bolivia/Peru 92D7
Titisee W Germany 36C5
Titlis Switzerland 33D2
Titograd Yugoslavia 46B3
Titovo Užice Yugoslavia 46B3
Titu Romania 46E2
Titule Zaire 70F4
Titusville Pa USA 79G5
Tivaouane Sénégal 68B6
Tiverton England UK 26H7
Tivoli Italy 45D5
Tiwi Oman 63H5
Tixkokob Mexico 88G3
Tixtla Mexico 88E4
Tizimin Mexico 88G3
Tizi Ouzou Algeria 68F1
Tjeldøy island Norway 34G2
Tjongs Fj. Norway 34E3
Tjörn,I Sweden 35D7
Tlacotalpán Mexico 88E4
Tlaltenango Mexico 88D3
Tlapa Mexico 88E4
Tlaxcala Mexico 88E4
Tlaxiaco Mexico 88E4
Tlemcen Algeria 68E2
Tîrgovişte Romania 46E2
Tmassah Libya 69J3
Toamasina Madagascar 71N10
Toano Ra. Nev. USA 80F5
Toay Argentina 91C5
Toba Japan 56E7
Tobago island Trin. & Tob. 89G4
Tobarro Spain 41F3
Tobel Switzerland 33E1
Tobelo Halmahera Indon. 53J10
Tobercurry Ireland, Rep. of 30F5
Tobermory Ont. Canada 79F3
Tobermory Scotland UK 29D6
Toboali Indonesia 53E11
Toboli Celebes Indon. 53H11
Tobol'sk USSR 50H4
Tocantinópolis Brazil 93H5
Tocantins,R Brazil 93H5
Toccoa Ga USA 85F3
Tochigi prefecture Japan 56F6
Toco Chile 91C2
Tocopilla Chile 91B2
Tocumwal NSW Australia 97C3
Todenyang Kenya 71H4
Tödi mt Switzerland 33D2
Todmorden England UK 25D5
Todos os Santos,B de Brazil 93K6
Todos Santos Mexico 88B3
Todos Santos,B Mexico 88A1
Toe Hd Ireland, Rep. of 31E11
Toggenburg upland Switzerland 33E1
Togo country Africa 68F7
Togtoh China 54F2
To Huping Tso lake Tibet China 59F2
Toiyabe Ra. Nev. USA 80E6
Tojo Japan 56C7
Tokachi dake mt Japan 56H3
Tokar Sudan 71H1
Tokara Rettō Japan 56N12
Tokat Turkey 62D1
Tokelau,Is Pacific Ocean 94J8
Tokmak Kirgiz. USSR 50J5
Tokomaru Bay New Zealand 100H4
Tokushima Japan 56D7
Tokushima prefecture Japan 56D8
Tokuyama Japan 56B7
Tōkyō Japan 56F7
Tokyo wan bay Japan 56F7
Tol island Truk Is 94A16
Tolaga Bay New Zealand 100H4
Tolbukhin Bulgaria 46F3
Toledo Chile 91B3
Toledo Ohio USA 79E5
Toledo Oreg. USA 80B3
Toledo Spain 40D3
Toledo prov. Spain 40D3
Toledo Bend Res. La USA 83M7
Toledo,Mts de Spain 40D3
Toliara Madagascar 71M11
Tolima mt Columbia 92B3
Tolmezzo Italy 44D2
Tolmin Yugoslavia 44D2
Tolsta Hd Scotland UK 28D3
Toluca Mexico 88E4
Tol'yatti USSR 49J4
Tomah Wis. USA 79A3
Tomahawk Wis. USA 79B3
Tomar Portugal 40B3
Tomari USSR 51R5
Tomaszów Lubelski Poland 37K3
Tomaszów Mazowiecki Poland 37H3
Tomatin Scotland UK 28H5
Tomatumari Guyana 92F2
Tombador,Serra do mts Brazil 93F6
Tombe Sudan 69M7
Tombigbee,R Ala./Miss. USA 85C4
Tombouctou Mali 68E5
Tome Chile 91B5
Tomiko Ont. Canada 79G2
Tomintoul Scotland UK 28K5
Tomkinson Ra mts W Aus. Australia 98F5
Tomma island Norway 34E3
Tommot USSR 51P4
Tomsk USSR 50K4
Tomskaya Oblast region USSR 50K4
Toms River New J USA 84D3
Tonalá Mexico 88F4
Tonate Fr. Guiana 93G3
Tonawanda NY USA 84B1
Tonbridge England UK 27Q6
Tønder Denmark 35C9
Tondi India 58E7
Tone,R England UK 26H6

Tonga Turin

Tonga NSW Australia 97B2
Tonga Sudan 69M7
Tonga,Is Pacific Ocean 94J10
Tongala Vic. Australia 97B3
Tongareva,I = Penrhyn,I
Tongatápu island Tonga 95V30
Tongatápu Group islands Tonga 95V30
Tongbai China 54G6
Tongbai Shan mts China 54G6
Tongcheng = Liaocheng
Tongcheng Anhui China 54J7
Tongcheng Jiangxi China 55G8
Tongchuan China 54E5
Tongdao China 55E9
Tongeren Belgium 32D4
Tonggu China 55H8
Tongguan China 54F5
Tonghua China 52J2
Tongjiang China 54D7
Tongking,G of = Beibu Wan
Tongliang China 55D8
Tongliao China 52H2
Tongling China 54J7
Tonglu China 55K8
Tongobory Madagascar 71M11
Tongoy Chile 91B4
Tongren China 55E9
Tongres = Tongeren
Tongshan China 55H8
Tongue Scotland UK 28H3
Tongue,Kyle of inlet Scotland UK 28H2
Tongue,R Mont. USA 81D3
Tongwei China 54C5
Tong Xian China 54J3
Tonhil Mongolia 52B1
Tonhil Mongolia 52B1
Tonichi Mexico 88C2
Tonk India 58E3
Tonkin region Vietnam 57C2
Tonkova USSR 50K3
Tonle Sap Cambodia 57C4
Tonneins France 43D4
Tonnerre France 42E3
Tonopah Nev. USA 80E6
Tønsberg Norway 35D7
Tonwarghar region India 61A2
Tooele Utah USA 82B2
Toowoomba Queensland 99L5
Topaz Idaho USA 80G4
Topeka Kans. USA 83L3
Topock Ariz. USA 80F8
Topolčany Czech. 37H4
Topolobampo Mexico 88C2
Toppenish Wash. USA 80C2
Topsham England UK 26H7
Toquerville Utah USA 80G7
Tor B England UK 26G8
Torbat-e-Heydariyeh Iran 63H2
Torbat-e Jam Iran 63J2
Torbay England UK 26G8
Töre Sweden 34K4
Torez Ukrain. USSR 49D6
Torfaj glacier Iceland 34V13
Torgau E Germany 36E3
Torhout Belgium 32B3
Tori India 61E4
Tori Fathpur India 61B3
Torino Italy 44A3
Torit Sudan 69M8
Torne Alv river Sweden 34K3
Torneträsk Sweden 34H2
Torneträsk,R Sweden 34H2
Tornio Finland 34L4
Tornquist Argentina 91D5
Törökszentmiklós Hungary 37J5
Toro,L del Chile 91B8
Toróni,G of Greece 47D4
Toronto NSW Australia 97D2
Toronto Ont. Canada 79G4
Toronto S Dak. USA 81J3
Tororo Uganda 71G4
Toros Dağlari mts Turkey 62C2
Torpe Alv river Finland 34K3
Torquay England UK 26G8
Torrance Calif. USA 80D9
Torre Annunziata Italy 45E5
Torreblanca Spain 41G2
Torre del Greco Italy 45E5
Torrelaguna Spain 40E2
Torrelapaja Spain 41F2
Torrelavega Spain 40D1
Torremolines Spain 40D4
Torrens,L S Aus. Australia 97A2
Torrent Spain 41F3
Torreon Mexico 88D2
Torres Mexico 88B2
Torres,Is Pacific Ocean 94G9
Torres Novas Portugal 40B3
Torres Str. Queens. Australia 99J2
Torres Vedras Portugal 40B3
Torrevieja Spain 41F4
Torridge,R England UK 26F7
Torridon,L Scotland UK 28E4
Torrijos Spain 40D2
Torrington Conn. USA 84E2
Torrington Wyo. USA 81E4
Torrön lake Sweden 34E5
Torrox Spain 40E4
Torsby Sweden 35E6
Tortola island Virgin Is 89G3
Tortona Italy 44B3
Tortorici Sicily Italy 45E6
Tortosa Spain 41G2
Tortosa,C de Spain 41G2
Tortuga I Mexico 88B2
Tortuqa island Haiti 89E2
Torud Iran 63H2
Torun Poland 37H2
Tory,I Ireland, Rep. of 30G3
Torzhok USSR 48J3
Tosa wan bay Japan 56C8
Toscana region Italy 44C4
Tosen Fj. Norway 34E4
Tossa Spain 41H2
Töss,R Switzerland 33D1
Tostado Argentina 91D3
Tosya Turkey 62C1
Totma USSR 50F3
Totnes England UK 26G8
Totonicapan Guatemala 88F4
Totskoye USSR 49L4
Tottenham NSW Australia 97C2
Tottori Japan 56D7
Tottori prefecture Japan 56C7
Touba Ivory Coast 68D7
Toubkal mt Morocco 68D2
Touggourt Algeria 68G2
Tougue Guinea 68C6
Toul France 42F2
Toulepleu Ivory Coast 68D7
Toulnustouc,R Que. Canada 78D1
Toulon France 43F5
Toulouse France 43D5
Toungoo Burma 59J5
Touraine prov. France 42D3
Tourakam Laos 57C3
Tourane = Da Nang
Tourbis,L Que. Canada 79J2
Tourcoing France 42E1
Tourin6al,C Spain 40B1
Tournai Belgium 32B4
Tournon France 43F4
Tournus France 42F3
Tours France 42D3
Tour Sallière mt Switzerland 33B2
Touws River South Africa 72C6
Towamba NSW Australia 97C3
Towanda Pa USA 84C2
Towari Celebes Indon. 53H11
Towcester England UK 27N4
Tower City N Dak. USA 81J2
Tow Law England UK 25E3
Townsend Mont. USA 81B2
Townsend,Mt NSW Australia 97C3
Townsville Queens. Australia 99K3
Towoeti Danau lake Celebes Indon. 53H11
Towson Md USA 84C3
Towy,R Wales UK 26F5
Toyah L Texas USA 82G7
Toyama Japan 56E6
Toyama prefecture Japan 56E6
Toyama wan bay Japan 56E6
Tozeur Tunisia 69G2
Trablous Lebanon 64D3
Trabzon Turkey 62D1
Tracadie New Br. Canada 78F3
Tracy Calif. USA 80C7
Tracy Minn. USA 81K3
Traer Iowa USA 83M1
Traiguen Chile 91B5
Traiguen,I Chile 91B7
Trail BC Canada 76H7
Traill Øy island Greenland 14N2
Trairi Brazil 93K4
Tralee Ireland, Rep. of 31D9
Tralee B Ireland,Rep. of 31D9
Tramelan Switzerland 33C1
Tramore Ireland, Rep. of 31J9
Tranås Sweden 35F7
Trancas Argentina 91C3
Trancoso Portugal 40C2
Tranent Scotland UK 29L8
Trang Thailand 57B5
Trangan island Indonesia 53K12
Trangie NSW Australia 97C2
Trani Italy 45F5
Tranquebar India 58E6
Trans-Amazonian Highway Brazil 92E5
Transcona Man. Canada 76M6
Transkei district South Africa 72D6
Transvaal prov. South Africa 72D4
Transylvania region Romania 46E1
Transylvanian Alps = Carpatii Meridionali
Trapani Sicily Italy 45D6
Traralgon Vic. Australia 97C3
Trasimeno,L Italy 44D4
Trasos Montes e Alto Douro region Portugal 40C2
Trasparga Spain 40C1
Traunstein W Germany 36E5
Traveller's L NSW Australia 97B2
Travers Switzerland 33B2
Traversay Is S Sandwich Is Antarctica 15A4
Traverse B Mich. USA 79D3
Traverse City Mich. USA 79D3
Travis,L Texas USA 83K7
Trawbreaga,B Ireland, Rep. of 30J3
Trebbia,R Italy 44B3
Třebíč Czech. 37F4
Trebinje Yugoslavia 46B3
Trebizond = Trabzon
Trebon Czech. 36F4
Tredegar Wales UK 26H5
Tregaron Wales UK 26G4
Trehorningsjo Sweden 34H5
Treig,L Scotland UK 29G6
Treinta y Tres Uruguay 91F4
Trelew Argentina 91C6
Trelleborg Sweden 35E9
Tremadoc B Wales UK 26F3
Tremblant,Mt Que. Canada 79J2
Tremiti Is Italy 44E4
Tremp Spain 41G1
Trencin Czech. 37H4
Trenel Argentina 91D5
Trenque Lauquén Argentina 91D5
Trent = Trento
Trent Ca. Ont. Canada 79G3
Trente et un Milles,L des Que. Canada 79J2
Trentino-Alto Adige region Italy 44C2
Trent Junction England UK 25F7
Trento Italy 44C2
Trenton Ga USA 85E3
Trenton Mich. USA 79E4
Trenton Mo USA 83M2
Trenton New J USA 84D2
Trenton Ont. Canada 79H3
Trenton Tenn. USA 85C3
Trent,R England UK 25G6
Trepassey Newf. Canada 78M3
Tres Arroyos Argentina 91D5
Tres Foroas,C Morocco 68E1
Treshnish Is Scotland UK 29D7
Tres Lagôas Brazil 93G8
Tres Lomas Argentina 91D5
Tres Marías,Is Mexico 88C3
Tres Montes,G Chile 91A7
Tres Montes,Pen. Chile 91A7
Tres Puéntes Chile 91B3
Trèves = Trier
Treviso Italy 44D3
Triabunna Tas. Australia 97F5
Triana Spain 40C4
Tricase Italy 45G6
Trichinopoly = Tiruchirapalli
Trichur India 58E6
Trida NSW Australia 97B2
Triengen Switzerland 33D1
Trier W Germany 36B4
Trieste Italy 44D3
Trikeri Str. Greece 47D5
Trikkala Greece 47C5
Trikkala dist. Greece 47C5
Trikomo Cyprus 64B2
Trim Ireland, Rep. Of 31K6
Trincomalee Sri Lanka 58F7
Tring England UK 27N5
Trinidad Bolivia 92E6
Trinidad Calif. USA 80A5
Trinidad Col. USA 82F4
Trinidad Columbia 92C2
Trinidad Cuba 89D2
Trinidad Uruguay 91E4
Trinidad island Trinidad & Tobago 92E1
Trinidad and Tobago country Caribbean Sea 92E1
Trinidade,I Atlantic Ocean 73K11
Trinidad,I Argentina 91D5
Trinidad,I West Indies 89G4
Trinidad & Tobago country Caribbean Sea 89G4
Trinity Newf. Canada 78M2
Trinity Texas USA 83L7
Trinity B Newf. Canada 78L2
Trinity,Mts Calif. USA 80B5
Trinity Pen. Antarctica 15T3
Trinity,R Calif. USA 80B5
Trinity,R Texas USA 83L7
Trinity Ra. Nev. USA 80D5
Trionto,C Italy 45F6
Tripoli = Trablous
Tripoli Libya 69H2
Tripolis Greece 47D6
Tripolitania region Libya 69H3
Tripura India 59H4
Tripura prov. India 59H4
Tristan da Cunha islands Atlantic Ocean 72G8
Tristan de Cunha,I Atlantic Ocean 73L12
Tristan,I Tristan da Cunha Is 72G8
Triton I Paracel Is China 57E3
Trivandrum India 58E7
Trn Bulgaria 46D3
Trnava Czech. 37G4
Trobriand Is Papua New Guinea 99L1
Trogen Switzerland 33E1
Trogir Yugoslavia 44F4
Trois Pistoles Que. Canada 78D2
Trois Ponts Belgium 32D4
Trois Rivières Que. Canada 78B3
Troitsk USSR 49F3
Troitsk USSR 49Q3
Troitsko Pechorsk USSR 50G3
Trollhättan Sweden 35E7
Trollheimen,Mt Norway 34C5
Tromen,Mt Argentina 91B5
Troms county Norway 34H2
Tromsø Norway 34H2
Trona Calif. USA 80E8
Trondelag,N county Norway 34D4
Trondelag,S county Norway 34D5
Trondheim Norway 34D5
Trondheims Fj. Norway 34D5
Troödos Cyprus 64A3
Troon Scotland UK 29G8
Tropea Italy 45E6
Troppau = Opava
Trosa Sweden 35G7
Trossachs mts Scotland UK 29H7
Trostan mt N Ireland UK 30L3
Trout Lake Mich. USA 79D2
Trowbridge England UK 27K6
Troy Idaho USA 80E2
Troy NY USA 84E1
Troy Turkey 62B1
Troyes France 42F2
Truckee Calif. USA 80C6
Truer Ra mts N Terr. Australia 98G4
Trujillo Honduras 89B3
Trujillo Peru 92B5
Trujillo Spain 40D3
Trujillo Venezuela 92C2
Truk Truk Is 94A16
Truk,I Caroline Is 94F7
Trumbull,Mt Ariz. USA 80G7
Trun Switzerland 33D2
Trundle NSW Australia 97C2
Truro England UK 26D8
Truro No. Sc. Canada 78G4
Truro S Aus. Australia 97A2
Truskmore mt Ireland, Rep. of 30G5
Trutnov Czech. 37F3
Tryavna Bulgaria 46E3
Trysil Elv river Norway 35D6
Trzebnica Poland 37G3
Tržič Yugoslavia 44E2
Tsangbe Bhutan 61G2
Tsavo Nat. Pk Kenya 71H5
Tschenstochau = Częstochowa
Tschiertschen Switzerland 33E2
Tselinograd Kazakh. USSR 50I4
Tses Namibia 72B5
Tshabong Botswana 72C5
Tshane Botswana 72C4
Tshikapa Zaire 70E6
Tsimlyanskoye Vdkhr. res. USSR 49F6
Tsivilsk USSR 49H3
Tsivory Madagascar 71N11
Tso Mirari,L Kashmir India 60F4
Tso-motre-tung lake Tibet China 59G3
Tsu Japan 56E7
Tsugaru Kaikyō strait Japan 56G4
Tsukao Shan mt Taiwan 55L10
Tsuruga Japan 56E7
Tsuruoka Japan 56F5
Tsushima Kaikō strait Japan/S Korea 52J4
Tsuyama Japan 56C7
Tua Portugal 40C2
Tua Zaire 70D5
Tuakau New Zealand 100F3
Tuam Ireland, Rep. of 31F6
Tuamarina New Zealand 100E5
Tuamotu,Arch. Pacific Ocean 95M9
Tuao Philippines 53H7
Tuapse USSR 50E5
Tuatapere New Zealand 100B8
Tubarão Brazil 91G3
Tubas Jordan 64D5
Tübingen W Germany 36C4
Tubize Belgium 32C4
Tubruq Libya 69K2
Tubuai,I Tubuai Is 95M10
Tubuai,Is Pacific Ocean 95M10
Tucacas Venezuela 92D1
Tuchan China 55G11
Tuckernuck I Mass. USA 84F2
Tuckerton New J USA 84D3
Tucson Ariz. USA 82C6
Tucson Mts Ariz. USA 82C6
Tucuman prov. Argentina 91C3
Tucumcari New Mex. USA 82G5
Tucuparé Brazil 93F5
Tucupido Venezuela 92D2
Tucupita Venezuela 92E2
Tucuruí Brazil 93H4
Tudela Spain 41F1
Tudmur Syria 62D3
Tufi Papua New Guinea 99K1
Tug Turkey 62E2
Tuggerah L NSW Australia 97D2
Tuguegarao Philippines 53H7
Tugur USSR 51Q4
Tuhai He river China 54J4
Tukums Latvia USSR 35K8
Tukuno jima island Japan 56N13
Tula Hidalgo Mexico 88E3
Tula Tamaulipas Mexico 88E3
Tula USSR 48K4
Tulancingo Mexico 88E3
Tulare Calif. USA 80D7
Tularosa New Mex. USA 82E6
Tularosa V New Mex. USA 82E6
Tulcán Ecuador 92B3
Tulcea Romania 46G2
Tul'chin Ukrain. USSR 48F7
Tuli Zimbabwe 72D4
Tulkarm Jordan 64C5
Tulla Ireland,Rep. of 31F8
Tullahoma Tenn. USA 85D3
Tullamore Ireland, Rep. of 31J7
Tullamore NSW Australia 97C2
Tulle France 43D4
Tullow Ireland, Rep. of 31K8
Tully Queens. Australia 99K3
Tulsa Okla. USA 83L4
Tulsk Ireland, Rep. of 30G6
Tulua Colombia 92B3
Tulun USSR 51M4
Tumaco Colombia 92B3
Tumany USSR 51S3
Tumba,L Zaire 70D5
Tumbarumba NSW Australia 97C3
Tumbes Peru 92A4
Tumd Zuoqi China 54F2
Tumkur India 58E6
Tumlong India 61G2
Tummel,R Scotland UK 29J6
Tummo Libya 69H4
Tump Pakistan 58B3
Tump,R Pakistan 58B3
Tumu Ghana 68E6
Tumucumaque,Sa mts Brazil 93G3
Tumupasa Bolivia 92D6
Tumut NSW Australia 97C3
Tumut,R NSW Australia 97C3
Tunari mt Bolivia 92D7
Tunas de Zaza Cuba 89D2
Tunbridge Wells England UK 27Q6
Tuncurry NSW Australia 97D2
Tundla India 61B2
Tundubi Sudan 69L5
Tunduru Tanzania 71H7
Tunga Bhadra,R India 58E5
Tungaru Sudan 69M6
Tungchwan = Dongchuan
Tungua island Tonga 95V30
Tunguska,R USSR 51L3
Tuni India 59F5
Tunica Miss. USA 85B3
Tunis Tunisia 69H1
Tunisia country Africa 69G2
Tunja Colombia 92C2
Tunlui China 54G4
Tunnisjøl,L Norway 34E4
Tunstall England UK 25D6
Tunuyán Argentina 91C4
Tunuyán,R Argentina 91C4
Tunuyán,Sierra mts Argentina 91C4
Tuo Jiang China 55C8
Tuoji Dao island China 54L3
Tuolluvaara Sweden 34J3
Tuolumne Calif. USA 80C7
Tupelo Miss. USA 85C3
Tupilco Mexico 88F4
Tupinambaranas,I Brazil 92F4
Tupiza Bolivia 92D8
Tupper Lake NY USA 79J3
Tupungato mt Argentina 91C4
Tuquarussu Brazil 93H6
Tuquerres Columbia 92B3
Tura India 59H3
Tura USSR 51L3
Turabah Saudi Arabia 62E4
Turabah Saudi Arabia 62E5
Turān Iran 63H2
Turbenthal Switzerland 33D1
Turbo Colombia 92B2
Turda Romania 46D1
Tureia,I Tuamotu Arch. 95N10
Turffontein South Africa 72N12
Turgay Kazakh. USSR 50H5
Turgi Switzerland 33D1
Turgutlu Turkey 62B2
Türi Eston. USSR 35L7
Turiaçu Brazil 93H4
Turiamo Venezuela 92D1
Turin = Torino

Turkana,L Van Buren

Turkana,L = Rudolf,L
Turkey *country* Europe/S W Asia 39N6
Turkmenskaya SSR *rep.* USSR 50G5
Turks Is West Indies 89E2
Turku Finland 35K6
Turkuja *prov.* Finland 35J6
Turkwell,R Kenya 71H4
Turlock *Calif.* USA 80C7
Turnagain,C New Zealand 100G5
Turnberry *Scotland* UK 29G9
Turneffe Is Belize 89B3
Turnhout Belgium 32C3
Turnu Măgurele Romania 46E3
Turnu Severin Romania 46D2
Turpan *Xinjiang* China 50K5
Turpan *Xinjiang* China 52A2
Turrialba Costa Rica 89C5
Turtkul *Uzbek.* USSR 50H5
Turtle Is Sierra Leone 68C7
Turtle Mts *N Dak.* USA 81G1
Turtmann Switzerland 33C2
Turukhansk USSR 50K3
Turzovka Czech. 37H4
Tus Iran 63H2
Tuscaloosa *Ala.* USA 85D4
Tuscarora Mts *Pa* USA 84C2
Tuscola *Ill.* USA 83P3
Tuscumbia *Ala.* USA 85D3
Tuscumbia *Mo* USA 83M3
Tuskar Rk Ireland,Rep. of 31L9
Tusket *No. Sc.* Canada 78F5
Tutayev USSR 48L3
Tutbury *England* UK 25E7
Tutia Khel Pakistan 60B4
Tuticorin India 58E7
Tuttlingen W Germany 36C5
Tutuila,I Samoa 94J9
Tuvalu,Is Pacific Ocean 94H8
Tuvinskaya Oblast *region* USSR 51L4
Tuwairifa *well* Saudi Arabia 62F5
Tuxford *England* UK 25G6
Tuxpan Mexico 88C3
Tuxpan Mexico 88E3
Tuxtepec Mexico 88E4
Tuxtla Gutiérrez Mexico 88F4
Tuy Spain 40B1
Tuyen Quang Vietnam 57D2
Tuy Hoa Vietnam 57D4
Tuz Gölu *salt lake* Turkey 62C2
Tuzla Yugoslavia 46B2
Tvaeraa Faerøerne 34Z15
Tvärålund Sweden 34H4
Tvärån Sweden 34J4
Tvurditsa Bulgaria 46E3
Twante Burma 59J5
Tweed *Ont.* Canada 79H3
Tweedmouth *England* UK 25E1
Tweed,R *Scotland* UK 29M8
Tweedsmuir Hills *upland Scotland* UK 29K9
Tweedsmuir Park *BC* Canada 76F6
Twelve Pins *mt* Ireland, Rep. of 31D6
Twenty-five de Mayo Argentina 91C5
Twin Buttes *Mont.* USA 81E1
Twin Falls *Idaho* USA 80F4
Twofold B *NSW* Australia 97C3
Two Harbors *Minn.* USA 81M2
Two Mountains,L of = Deux Montagnes,L des
Two Rivers *Wis.* USA 79C3
Tyedestrand Norway 35C7
Tygda USSR 51P4
Tyler *Texas* USA 83L6
Tyndall,Mt New Zealand 100D6
Tyndinskiy USSR 51P4
Tyne Gap *England* UK 25C3
Tynemouth *England* UK 25F2
Tyne,R *England* UK 25E3
Tyne & Wear *county England* UK 25F3
Tynset Norway 34D5
Tyre = Sour
Tyrone *Pa* USA 84B2
Tyrone *county* N Ireland 30J4
Tyrrell,L *Vic.* Australia 97B3
Tyrrhenian Sea Italy 45C5
Tysfjord Norway 34G2
Tyubelyakh USSR 51R3
Tyumen USSR 50H4
Tyumenskaya Oblast *region* USSR 50J3
Tywyn *Wales* UK 26F3

U

Uaupés Brazil 92D4
Ubá Brazil 93J8
Uberaba Brazil 93H7
Uberlândia Brazil 93H7
Überlingen W Germany 36C5
Ubundu Zaire 70F5
Ucayali,R Peru 92C5
Uch Pakistan 60B6
Uchiura wan *bay* Japan 56G3
Uchiza Peru 92B5
Uckermark *region* E Germany 36E2
Uckfield *England* UK 27Q7
Udaipur India 58D4
Udaipur India 60D7
Uddevalla Sweden 35D7
Udd Jaur,L Sweden 34G4
Uden Netherlands 32D3
Udhampur India 60D4
Udhampur *district* India 60D4
Udine Italy 44D2
Udipi India 58D6
Udmurtskaya S.R. *rep.* USSR 50G4
Udon Thani Thailand 57C3
Udot *island* Truk Is 94A16
Udskaya Guba *bay* USSR 51Q4
Udzi Mts Zimbabwe 72E3
Uelen USSR 51V3
Uele,R Zaire 70E4
Uelzen W Germany 36D2
Ueno Japan 56E7
Uetli Berg *mt* Switzerland 33D1
Ufa USSR 49M3
Ufa,R USSR 49P2
Uffculme *England* UK 26H7
Ugalla Tanzania 71G6
Uganda *country* Africa 71G4
Uherske Hradiště Czech. 37G4
Uig *Scotland* UK 28D4
Uige Angola 70D6
Uiha *island* Tonga 95V30
Uinta Mts *Utah* USA 82C2
Uitenhage South Africa 72D6
Uitgeest Netherlands 32C2
Uithuizen Netherlands 32E1
Ujhani India 61B2
Ujiji Tanzania 71F5
Ujjain India 58E4
Ujpest Hungary 37H5
Ujung Pandang *Celebes* Indon. 53G12
Ukhta *Karel.* USSR 50E3
Ukiah *Calif.* USA 80B6
Ukmergė *Lith.* USSR 35L9
Ukrainskaya SSR *rep.* USSR 50E5
Ulaanbaatar Mongolia 52E1
Ulaangom Mongolia 51L5
Ulan China 52C3
Ulan Buh Shamo *region* China 54C2
Ulan Ude USSR 51M4
Ula-shan *region* China 54E2
Ulcinj Yugoslavia 46B4
Ulefass Norway 35C7
Ulfborg Denmark 35C8
Uliastay Mongolia 51L5
Ulindi,R Zaire 70F5
Ulithi,I Pacific Ocean 94D6
Ulladulla *NSW* Australia 97D3
Ullapool *Scotland* UK 28F4
Ullared Sweden 35E8
Ulldecona Spain 41G2
Ulls Fj. Norway 34H2
Ullswater,L *England* UK 25C3
Ullung Do *island* Sea of Japan 56B6
Ulm *Mont.* USA 81B2
Ulm W Germany 36C4
Ulmarra *NSW* Australia 97D1
Ulrichen Switzerland 33D2
Ulrum Netherlands 32E1
Ulster *prov.* Ireland 30H4
Ulster Can. Ireland 30J5
Ultima *Vic.* Australia 97B3
Ulua,R Honduras 89B3
Uluingalau *mt Vanua Levu* Fiji 94A24
Ulukişla Turkey 62C2
Ulva,I *Scotland* UK 29D7
Ulverston *England* UK 25B4
Ulverstone *Tas.* Australia 97F5
Ul'yanovsk USSR 49J3
Uman' *Ukrain.* USSR 48G7
Umanaq Fj. Greenland 14Q2
Umarkot Pakistan 58C3
Umatac Guam 94A21
Umatilla *Oreg.* USA 80D3
Umbria *region* Italy 44D4
Umea Sweden 34J5
Ume Alv *river* Sweden 34H4
Ummal Qaiwain UAE 63H4
Umm el Qulban Saudi Arabia 62E4
Umm Kuteira Sudan 69L6
Umm Lej Saudi Arabia 62D4
Umm Qasr Iraq 62F3
Umm Ruwaba Sudan 69M6
Umnak I *Aleutian Is* USA 87W13
Umpqua,R *Oreg.* USA 80B4
Umtata South Africa 72D6
Una India 60E5
Unadilla *NY* USA 84D1
Unalakleet *Alaska* USA 87W12
Unalaska *Aleutian Is* USA 87W13
Unaós Iceland 34Y12
Una,R Yugoslavia 44F3
Unayzah Saudi Arabia 62E4
Uncastillo Spain 41F1
Uncia Bolivia 92D7
Uncompahgre Plat. *Col.* USA 82D3
Underbool *Vic.* Australia 97B3
Unecha USSR 48H5
Ungarie *NSW* Australia 97C2
Ungava B *Que.* Canada 77S5
União Brazil 93J4
União da Vitória Brazil 91F3
Uniejów Poland 37H3
Unimak I *Aleutian Is* USA 87W13
Uni,Mt Liberia 68D8
Unión Argentina 91C5
Union *Mo* USA 83N3
Union *Oreg.* USA 80E3
Union *S Car.* USA 85G3
Union City *Tenn.* USA 85C2
Union of Soviet Socialist Republics 50
Uniontown *Ky* USA 85D2
Uniontown *Pa* USA 84B3
Unionville *Mo* USA 83M2
Unionville *Nev.* USA 80D5
United Arab Emirates *country* SW Asia 63G5
United Kingdom *country* Europe 22F4
United States of America 86
Unnao India 61C2
Unst,I *Shetland* Scotland 28R7
Unter Ägeri Switzerland 33D1
Unter Engadin *mts* Switzerland 33F2
Unterwalden *cantons* Switzerland 33D2
Unturán,Serra de *mts* Venezuela 92D3
Uozu Japan 56E6
Upata Venezuela 92E2
Upemba,L Zaire 70F6
Upernavik Greenland 14Q2
Upington South Africa 72C5
Upminster *England* UK 27Q5
Upolu *island* Western Samoa 95V31
Upolu,I Samoa 94J9
Upper Hutt New Zealand 100F5
Upper Marlboro *Md* USA 84C3
Upper Sandusky *Ohio* USA 79E5
Upper Seal L *Que.* Canada 77R5
Upper Volta *country* Africa 68E6
Uppingham *England* UK 25G7
Uppsala Sweden 35G7
Uppsala *county* Sweden 35G6
Ür Iraq 62F3
Urabá,G de Columbia 92B2
Uracoa Venezuela 92E2
Urakawa Japan 56H3
Uralla *NSW* Australia 97D2
Ural,R USSR 50G4
Ural'sk USSR 50G4
Ural'skiye Khrebet *mts* USSR 50G4
Urana *NSW* Australia 97C3
Urandangi *Queens.* Australia 99H4
Uranium City *Sask.* Canada 76K5
Urapunga *N Terr.* Australia 99G2
Uraricuera,R Brazil 92E3
Ura Tyube *Tadzhik.* USSR 50H6
Urawa Japan 56F7
Urbakh USSR 49H5
Urbana *Ill.* USA 83P2
Urcos Peru 92C6
Urda USSR 50F5
Urdzhar USSR 50K5
Uren USSR 49G2
Ure,R *England* UK 25E4
Ures Mexico 88B2
Urfa Turkey 62D2
Urga = Ulaanbaatar
Urgench *Uzbek.* USSR 50H5
Urgun Afghanistan 63K3
Uri *canton* Switzerland 33D2
Uribante,R Venezuela 92C2
Uribe Colombia 92C3
Uribia Colombia 92C1
Uri Rostock *mt* Switzerland 33D2
Urisino *NSW* Australia 97B1
Urituyacu,R Peru 92B4
Urmia,L = Daryācheh-ue Urumīyeh
Urnäsch Switzerland 33E1
Ursviken Sweden 34J4
Urtazym USSR 49P4
Urtein Mongolia 52G1
Uruapan Mexico 88D4
Urubamba Peru 92C6
Urubamba,R Peru 92C6
Urubaxi,R Brazil 92D4
Urucará Brazil 93F4
Urucuia,R Brazil 93H7
Urugai,R Brazil 91F3
Uruguaiana Brazil 91E3
Uruguay *country* S America 91E4
Uruguay,R Uruguay 91E4
Urukthapel,I Palau Is 94A20
Urumes Sughra Syria 64E1
Ürümqi *Xinjiang* China 50K5
Uruqui Brazil 93J5
Urussanga Brazil 91G3
Uruzgan Afghanistan 63K3
Urville, Tg. d' *cape New Guinea* Indon. 53L11
Urwi Botswana 72C4
Uryupinsk USSR 49F5
Urzhum USSR 49J2
Urziceni Romania 46F2
Usak Turkey 62B2
Usakos Namibia 72B4
Usborne,Mt Falkland Is 91E8
Usedom *pen.* E Germany 36E1
Ushant,I = Isle d'Ouessant
Ushirombo Tanzania 71G5
Ush Tobe USSR 50J5
Ushuaia Argentina 91C8
Usk *Wales* UK 26J5
Uska India 61D2
Uskedal Norway 35A7
Usk,R *Wales* UK 26H5
Uskub = Skopje
Usküdar Turkey 62B1
Usole Sibirskoye USSR 51M4
Uspenskiy USSR 50J5
Usquil Peru 92B5
Ussel France 42E4
Ussuriysk USSR 51Q5
Ust Aldan USSR 51P3
Ust Amginskoye USSR 51Q3
Ust Belaya USSR 51U3
Ust' Chaun USSR 51U3
Uster Switzerland 33D1
Usti nad Labem Czech. 36F3
Ust Ishim USSR 50J4
Ustka Poland 37G1
Ust Kamenogorsk *Kazakh.* USSR 50K4
Ust Khayryuzovo USSR 51S4
Ust' Kut USSR 51M4
Ust Maya USSR 51Q3
Ust' Nera USSR 51R3
Ust' Port USSR 50K3
Ust Sopochnoye USSR 51S4
Ust Tsilma USSR 50G3
Ust Uda USSR 51M4
Ust Usa USSR 50G3
Ust Uskoye USSR 49R3
Ustyuzhna USSR 48K2
Usumacinta,R Mexico 88F4
Utah *state* USA 86D4
Utah L *Utah* USA 82C2
Utajarvi Finland 34M4
Uta Vavau *island* Tonga 95V30
Utena *Lith.* USSR 35L9
Utete Tanzania 71H6
Uthal Pakistan 58C3
Utiarity Brazil 92F6
Utica *NY* USA 84D1
Utiel Spain 41F3
Utikuma L *Alta* Canada 76H5
Utraula India 61D2
Utrecht Netherlands 32D2
Utrecht South Africa 72E5
Utrecht *prov.* Netherlands 32D2
Utrera Spain 40D4
Utsjoki Finland 34M2
Utsunomiya Japan 56F6
Uttaradit Thailand 57C3
Uttar Pradesh *state* India 58E3
Uttoxeter *England* UK 25E7
Uummarnarsuaq *cape* Greenland 14P4
Uusikaarlepyy = Nykarleby
Uusikaupunki Finland 35J6
Uusimaa *prov.* Finland 35L6
Uva USSR 49L2
Uvac Yugoslavia 46B3
Uvada *Utah* USA 80G7
Uva,R Columbia 92D3
Uvat USSR 50H4
Uvéa,I Îs Loyaute 94G10
Uvel'skiy USSR 49Q3
Uvira Zaire 71F5
Uvs Nuur *lake* Mongolia 51L4
Uwajima Japan 56C8
Uxbridge *Mass.* USA 84F1
Uxbridge *Ont.* Canada 79G3
Uxmal Mexico 88G3
Uyea *island Shetland* Scotland 28R7
Uyu Chaung,R Burma 59J3
Uyuni Bolivia 92D8
Uzbekskaya SSR *rep.* USSR 50H5
Uzdin Yugoslavia 46C2
Uzerche France 42C4
Uzgen *Kirgiz* USSR 50J5
Uzhgorod USSR 48C7
Uznach Switzerland 33D1
Uzunkopru Turkey 46F4
Uzyansk USSR 49N4

V

Vaagø *island* Faerøerne 34Z14
Vääkiö Finland 34N4
Vaal,R South Africa 72D5
Vaalwater South Africa 72D4
Vaasa Finland 34J5
Vaasa *prov.* Finland 34K5
Vac Hungary 37H5
Vache,I La Haiti 89E3
Vadodara India 58D4
Vadsø Norway 34N1
Vaduz Liechtenstein 33E1
Værøy,I Norway 34E3
Vags,Fj. Norway 34G2
Vah,R Czech. 37G4
Vahsel B Antarctica 15T2
Vaigui,R India 58E7
Vaihu Easter I 95V32
Vaila,I *Shetland* Scotland 28P8
Vaipar,R India 58E7
Vairowal India 60D5
Valais *canton* Switzerland 33C2
Val Brillant *Que.* Canada 78E2
Valburg Netherlands 32D2
Valcheta Argentina 91C6
Val d'Anniviers *valley* Switzerland 33C2
Valday Hills USSR 48H3
Val de Bagnes *valley* Switzerland 33C2
Valdemarsvik Sweden 35G7
Valdepeñas Spain 40E3
Valderredible Spain 40E1
Valderrobres Spain 41G2
Valdés,Pen. Argentina 91D6
Valdez *Alaska* USA 87Y12
Val d'Hérens *valley* Switzerland 33C2
Valdivia Chile 91B5
Val d'Oise *prov.* France 42E2
Valdosta *Ga* USA 85F5
Vale *Oreg.* USA 80E3
Valea-lui-Mihai Romania 37K5
Valença Brazil 93J5
Valenca Brazil 93K6
Valençáy France 42D3
Valence France 43F4
Valencia Spain 41F3
Valencia Venezuela 92D1
Valencia *region* Spain 41F3
Valencia de Alcantara Spain 40C3
Valencia de Don Juan Spain 40D1
Valencia,G. de Spain 41G3
Valencia I Ireland, Rep. of 31C10
Valenciennes France 42E2
Văleni de Munte Romania 46F2
Valentine *Nebr.* USA 82H1
Valera Venezuela 92C2
Valga *Latvia* USSR 35M8
Valjevo Yugoslavia 46B2
Valkeakoski Finland 35L6
Valkenburg Netherlands 32D4
Valkenswaard Netherlands 32D3
Valladolid Mexico 88G3
Valladolid Spain 40D2
Valladolid *prov.* Spain 40D2
Valldemosa *Balearic Is* Spain 41H3
Valle-D'Aosta *region* Italy 44A3
Valle de La Pascua Venezuela 92D2
Valle de Santiago Mexico 88D3
Valledupar Colombia 92C1
Vallejo *Calif.* USA 80B6
Valle Leventina *valley* Switzerland 33D2
Valle Maggia Switzerland 33D2
Valle Mesolcina *valley* Switzerland 33E2
Vallenar Chile 91B3
Valletta Malta 45E8
Valle Verzasca *valley* Switzerland 33D2
Valley City *N Dak.* USA 81H2
Valleyfield = Sallaberry-de-Valleyfield
Valley Springs *Calif.* USA 80C6
Vallgrund,I Finland 34J5
Vallorbe Switzerland 33B2
Valmaseda Spain 40E1
Valmiera *Latvia* USSR 35L8
Val Müstair *valley* Switzerland 33F2
Valognes France 42C2
Valona = Vlorë
Valona B = Vlores,G of
Valoria la Buena Spain 40D2
Valparaiso Chile 91B4
Valparaiso *Ind.* USA 79C5
Valparaiso Mexico 88D3
Vals Switzerland 33E2
Valsainte Switzerland 33C2
Val Tavetsch *valley* Switzerland 33D2
Valtimo Finland 34N5
Valverde de Jucar Spain 41E3
Valverde del Camino Spain 40C4
Vammala Finland 35K6
Van Turkey 62E2
Vana Vändra *Eston.* USSR 35L7
Vanavara USSR 51M3
Van Buren *Ark.* USA 83L5
Van Buren *Maine* USA 78D3
Van Buren *Mo* USA 85N4

Vanceboro, Voznesensk

Vanceboro Maine USA 78E4
Vancouver BC Canada 76G7
Vancouver Wash. USA 80B3
Vancouver I BC Canada 76F7
Vancouver,Mt Yukon Canada 76D4
Vandalia Ill. USA 83P3
Van Diemen,C N Terr. Australia 98G2
Van Diemen G N Terr. Australia 98G2
Vandres,R Norway 35C6
Vänern,L Sweden 35E7
Vänersborg Sweden 35E7
Vangaindrano Madasgascar 71K11
Van Gölü lake Turkey 62E2
Vang Vieng Laos 57C3
Van Horn Mts Texas USA 82F7
Vankarem USSR 51V3
Vännäs Sweden 34G4
Vanndale Ark. USA 83N5
Vannes France 42B3
Vannøy,I Norway 34H1
Vanrhynsdorp South Africa 72B6
Vansbro Sweden 35F6
Vanua Levu,I Fiji 94H9
Vanuatu,Is Pacific Ocean 94G9
Van Wyksrust South Africa 72M12
Var dep. France 43G5
Varallo Italy 44B3
Varanasi India 61D3
Varanger Fj. Norway 34N1
Varanger Halvøy,Pen. Norway 34N1
Varaždin Yugoslavia 44F2
Varberg Sweden 35E8
Vardar,R Greece/Yugosl. 46D4
Varde Denmark 35C9
Vardø Norway 34O1
Varese Italy 44B3
Varkaus Finland 34M5
Varmland county Sweden 35E7
Varna Bulgaria 46F3
Varnavino USSR 49G2
Värtsilä Finland 34O5
Vasa = Vaasa
Vascondagas regionSpain 41E1
Vasknarva Eston. USSR 35M7
Vassar Mich. USA 79E4
Vastanfors Sweden 35F7
Västerås Sweden 35G7
Västerbotten county Sweden 34G4
Väster Dal Älv river Sweden 35E6
Västernorrland county Sweden 34G5
Västervik Sweden 35G8
Västmanland county Sweden 35G7
Vasto Italy 44E4
Vasvar Hungary 37G5
Vatican City = Citta del Vaticano
Vaticano,C Italy 45E6
Vatnajökull glacier Iceland 34W12
Vatomandry Madagascar 71N10
Vättern,L Sweden 35F7
Vättis Switzerland 33E2
Vatuma,R Brazil 92F4
Vaucluse dep. France 43F4
Vaud canton Switzerland 33B2
Vaughn New Mex. USA 82F5
Vaupés,R Columbia 92C3
Vavau Group islands Tonga 95V30
Växjö Sweden 35F8
Vedia Argentina 91D4
Vedrin Belgium 32C4
Veendam Netherlands 32E1
Veenendaal Netherlands 32D2
Veenwouden Netherlands 32D1
Veere Netherlands 32B3
Vefsen Fj. Norway 34E4
Vefsna,R Norway 34E9
Vega Norway 34D4
Vega Fj. Norway 34D4
Veghel Netherlands 32D3
Vegorrítis,L Greece 47C4
Vegreville Alta Canada 76J6
Vejen Denmark 35C9
Vejle Denmark 35C9
Vela Argentina 91E5
Velaines Belgium 32B4
Veldhoven Netherlands 32D3
Velebit Planina mts Yugoslavia 44E3
Veles Yugoslavia 46C4
Velestinon Greece 47D5
Velez Rubio Spain 41E4
Vel Fj. Norway 34E4
Velikiye Luki USSR 48G3
Velikiy Ustyug USSR 50F3
Veliko Tŭrnovo Bulgaria 46E3
Velizh USSR 48G4
Velletri Italy 45D5
Vellore India 58E6
Velp Netherlands 32D2
Velsen Netherlands 32C2
Velsk USSR 48N1
Venado Mexico 88D3
Venado Tuerto Argentina 91D4
Venda districtSouth Africa 72E4
Vendée dep. France 42C3
Vendôme France 42D3
Venegas Mexico 88D3
Veneto region Italy 44C3
Venezia Italy 44D3
Venezia,G di Italy 44D3
Venezuela country S America 92D2
Venezuela,G de Venezuela 92C1
Vengurla India 58D5
Venice = Venezia
Venlo Netherlands 32E3
Vennacher,L Scotland UK 29H7
Venray Netherlands 32D3
Ventana,Sierra mts Argentina 91D5
Venta,R Latviy USSR 35J8
Ventimiglia Italy 44A3
Ventnor I of Wight England 27M7
Ventotene island Italy 45D5
Ventspils Latvia USSR 35J8
Ventuari,R Venezuela 92D2
Ventura Calif. USA 80D8
Venus B Vic. Australia 97C3
Vera Spain 41F4
Veracruz Mexico 88E4
Veracruz state Mexico 88E4
Veramin Iran 63G2
Veraval India 58D4
Verbania Italy 44B3
Vercelli Italy 44B3
Verde,C = Vert,C
Verde,R Argentina 91C6
Verde R Ariz. USA 82C6
Verde,R Mexico 88D3
Verdun France 42F2
Vereeniging South Africa 72D5
Vereshchagino USSR 49M1
Vereshchagino USSR 50K3
Vereya USSR 49C3
Verga,C Guinea 68C6
Vergara Uruguay 91F4
Vergennes Vt USA 79K3
Verin Spain 40C2
Verissimo Sarmento Angola 70E6
Verkhne Imbatskoe USSR 50K3
Verkhneural'sk USSR 49P4
Verkhnevilyuysk USSR 51P3
Verkhoturye USSR 50H4
Verkhoyansk USSR 51Q3
Verkhoyanskiy Khrebet mts USSR 51Q3
Verkhoye USSR 48K5
Vermala Switzerland 33C2
Vermelho,R Brazil 93G7
Vermilion S Dak. USA 81J4
Vermilion B La USA 83M8
Vermont state USA 87M3
Vernal Utah USA 82D2
Vernayaz Switzerland 33C2
Verneuil France 42D2
Verneuk Pan lake South Africa 72C5
Vernon BC Canada 76H6
Vernon Texas USA 83J5
Veroia Greece 47D4
Verona Italy 44C3
Versailles France 42E2
Versailles Ky USA 85E1
Versam Switzerland 33E2
Versoix Switzerland 33B2
Vert,C Senegal 68B6
Verte,I Que. Canada 78D2
Vertrijk Belgium 32C4
Veru Jaagupi Eston. USSR 35M7
Verviers Belgium 32D4
Vervins France 42E2
Vesanto Finland 34M5
Vesoul France 42G3
Vessem Netherlands 32D3
Vesterålen,Is Norway 34F2
Vest,Fj. Norway 34E3
Vestfold county Norway 35D7
Vestvågøy,I Norway 34E2
Vesuvio vol. Italy 45E5
Vesuvius = Vesuvio
Vesyegonsk USSR 48K2
Veszprem Hungary 37G5
Vetluga USSR 49G2
Vetluga,R USSR 49G2
Veurne Belgium 32A3
Vevey Switzerland 33B2
Vex Switzerland 33C2
Veynes France 43F4
Veys Iran 62F3
Viacha Bolivia 92D7
Viana Brazil 93J4
Viareggio Italy 44C4
Viborg Denmark 35C8
Vibo Valentia Italy 45F6
Vic Spain 41H2
Vicenza Italy 44C3
Vichada,R Columbia 92D3
Vichuquen Chile 91B4
Vichy France 42E3
Vicksburg Miss. USA 85B4
Viçosa Brazil 93J4
Vicosoprano Switzerland 33E2
Victor Harbour S Aus. Australia 97A3
Victoria Argentina 91D4
Victoria BC Canada 76G7
Victoria Hong Kong 55H11
Victoria N Terr. Australia 98G3
Victoria Texas USA 82T9
Victoria state Australia 99J7
Victoria Downs N Terr. Australia 98G3
Victoria Falls Zimbabwe 72D3
Victoria I NW Terr. Canada 76J2
Victoria,L NSW Australia 97B2
Victoria L Uganda 71G5
Victoria,L Vic. Australia 97C3
Victoria Land Antarctica 15L2
Victoria,Mt Burma 59H4
Victoria,Mt Papua New Guinea 99K1
Victoria Ra. mts New Zealand 100E6
Victoria Res. Newf. Canada 78K2
Victoriaville Que. Canada 79K2
Victoria West South Africa 72C6
Victorica Argentina 91C5
Vicuna Chile 91B4
Vicuña Mackenna Argentina 91D4
Videle Romania 46E2
Vidin Bulgaria 46D2
Viedma Argentina 91D6
Viedma,L Argentina 91B7
Vienna = Wien
Vienne France 42F4
Vienne dep. France 42D3
Vienne,R France 42D3
Vien Pou Kha Laos 57C2
Vientiane Laos 57C3
Vieques,I de West Indies 89F3
VierlingsbeekNetherlands 32D3
Vierwaldstatter See lake Switzerland 33D1
Vierzon Ville France 42E3
Viesite Latviy USSR 35L8
Vietnam country SE Asia 57D3
Vif France 43F4
Vigan Philippines 53H7
Vigevano Italy 44B3
Vigia Brazil 93H4
Vigia Chico Mexico 88G4
Vigo Spain 40B1
Vigrestad Norway 35A7
Vihanti Finland 34L4
Vijavadurg India 58F6
Vijayanagar India 58E5
Vijayawada India 58F5
Vijosë,R Albania 47B4
Vikaviskis Lith. USSR 35K9
Vikna,I Norway 34D4
Vilafranca del Penedés Spain 41G2
Vilaka Latviy USSR 35M8
Vila Machado Mozambique 72E3
Vila Maganja Mozambique 72F3
Vila Manica Mozambique 72E3
Vilanculos Mozambique 72F4
Viláni Latvia USSR 35M8
Vila Nova da Barquinha Portugal 40B3
Vila Nova de Famalicão Portugal 40B2
Vila Nova de Gerveira Portugal 40B2
Vilanova la Geltrú Spain 41G2
Vila Pery = Chimoio
Vila Real Portugal 40C2
Vilar Formoso Portugal 40C2
Vila Velha Brazil 93G3
Vila Velha de Rodao Portugal 40C3
Vila Viçosa Portugal 40C3
Vilhelmina Sweden 34G4
Vilhena Brazil 92E6
Viljandi Eston. USSR 35L7
Villa Bella Bolivia 92D6
Villablino Spain 40C1
Villacañas Spain 40E3
Villacarriedo Spain 40E1
Villach Austria 36E5
Villa Cisneros = Dakhla
Villa Cisneros = Dakhla
Villa Constitución Argentina 91D4
Villadama Mexico 88D2
Villa de Rosario Argentina 91D4
Villa Dolores Argentina 91C4
Villa Flores Mexico 88F4
Villafranca Spain 40C1
Villafranca del Cid Spain 41F2
Villafro,L Peru 92C7
Villaguay Argentina 91E4
Villa Guillermina Argentina 91E3
Villahermosa Mexico 88F4
Villa Hidalgo Mexico 88D2
Villa Iris Argentina 91D5
Villajoyosa Spain 41F3
Villalba Spain 40C1
Villalón de CamposSpain 40D1
Villalonga Argentina 91D5
Villalpando Spain 40D2
Villa Maria Argentina 91D4
Villa Mercedes Argentina 91C4
Villa Montes Bolivia 92E8
Villa Murtinho Brazil 92D6
Villaneuva de Cordoba Spain 40D3
Villanueva-de-la-Serena Spain 40D3
Villanueva de los Infantes Spain 40E3
Villaodrid Spain 40C1
Villaputzu Sardinia Italy 45B6
Villarcayo Spain 40E1
Villarreal Spain 41F3
Villarrica Chile 91B5
Villarrica Paraguay 91E3
Villarrica mt Chile 91B5
Villarrobledo Spain 41E3
Villars Switzerland 33C2
Villa Union Argentina 91C3
Villavicencio Columbia 92C3
Villaviciosa Spain 40D1
Villa Viejo Colombia 92B3
Villazon Bolivia 92D8
Villefort France 43E4
Villefranche France 42F3
Villefranche-de-Rouergue France 43E4
Ville Marie Que. Canada 79G2
Villena Spain 41F3
Villeneuve Switzerland 33B2
Villeneuve-sur-Lot France 43D4
Villeurbanne France 42F4
Villiers Switzerland 33B1
Villingen W Germany 36C4
Villisca Iowa USA 83L2
Villupuram India 58E6
Vilnius Lith. USSR 35L9
Vilvorde Belgium 32C4
Vilyuy,R USSR 51N3
Vilyuysk USSR 51P3
Vimioso Portugal 40C2
Vimperk Czech. 36E4
Vina Calif. USA 80B6
Viña del Mar Chile 91B4
Vinalhaven I Maine USA 78D4
Vinaròs Spain 41G2
Vincennes Ind. USA 79C6
Vinces Ecuador 92B4
Vinchiaturo Italy 45E5
Vindel Alv river Sweden 34H4
Vindeln Sweden 34H4
Vindhya Ra mts India 58E4
Vineland New J USA 84D3
Vineyard Sd Mass. USA 84F2
Vinh Vietnam 57D3
Vinh Loi Vietnam 57D5
Vinita Okla. USA 83L4
Vinkovci Yugoslavia 46B2
Vinnitsa Ukrain. USSR 48F7
Vinson Massif mts Antarctica 15R2
Vinton Iowa USA 83M1
Viranşehir Turkey 62D2
Virden Man. Canada 76L7
Vire France 42C2
Virginia Ireland, Rep. of 30J6
Virginia Minn. USA 81L2
Virginia state USA 87L4
Virginia Beach Va USA 85K2
Virginia City Mont. USA 80H3
Virginia City Nev. USA 80D6
Virginia Falls NW Terr. Canada 76F4
Virginia Mts Nev. USA 80D5
Virgin Is West Indies 89G3
Virgin Mts Ariz. USA 80G7
Viroqua Wis. USA 79A4
Virovitica Yugoslavia 46A2
Virpazar Yugoslavia 46B3
Virra Finland 34K5
Virserum Sweden 35F8
Virtasalmi Finland 34M5
Virton Belgium 32D5
Virtsu Eston. USSR 35K7
Virú Peru 92B5
Viru Nigula Eston. USSR 35M7
Vis island Yugoslavia 44F4
Visakhapatnam India 59F5
Visalia Calif. USA 80D7
Visby Sweden 35H8
Viscount Melville Sd NW Terr. Canada 76J2
Visé Belgium 32D4
Viseu Brazil 93H4
Viseu Portugal 40C2
Viški Latvia USSR 35M8
Visoko Yugoslavia 46B3
Viso,Monte mt Italy 44A3
Visp Switzerland 33C2
Vissoye Switzerland 33C2
Vista Calif. USA 80E9
Vista Alegre Brazil 92E3
Vistula,R = Wisla,R
Vitebsk Belorus. USSR 48G4
Viterbo Italy 44D4
Vitigudino Spain 40C2
Viti Levu,I Fiji 94H9
Vitim,R USSR 51N4
Vitória Brazil 93J8
Vitoria Spain 41E1
Vitoria de Conquista Brazil 93J7
Vitré France 42C2
Vitry-le-François France 42F2
Vittangi Alv river Finland/Sweden 34J3
Vitteaux France 42F3
Vittoria Sicily Italy 45E7
Vitznau Switzerland 33D1
Viver Spain 41F3
Vivero Spain 40C1
Vivi USSR 51L3
Vivonne S Aus. Australia 97A3
Vivonne B S Aus. Australia 97A2
Vivorata Argentina 91E5
Vizcaíno,Sierra mts Mexico 88B2
Vizianagram India 59F5
Vizirul Romania 46F2
Vizovice Czech. 37G4
Vizzini Sicily Italy 45E7
Vlaardingen Netherlands 32C3
Vladimir USSR 48M3
Vladivostok USSR 51Q5
Vlakdrift South Africa 72L11
Vlieland island Netherlands 32C1
Vlissingen Netherlands 32B3
Vlorë Albania 47B4
Vlorës,G of Albania 47B4
Vltava,R Czech. 36F3
Vöcklabruck Austria 36E4
Vogels-berg region W Germany 36C3
Voghera Italy 44B3
Vohémar = Vohimarina
Vohimarina Madagascar 71P9
Võhma Eston. USSR 35L7
Voi Kenya 71H5
Voiotía dist. Greece 47D5
Voiron France 42F4
Voitsberg Austria 36F5
Vojvodina Yugoslavia 46B2
Volcano B = Ichiura wan
Volćan Puraće mt Columbia 92B3
Volendam Netherlands 32D2
Volga,R USSR 50F5
Volgograd USSR 49G6
Volgogradskoye Vdkhr res. USSR 49G5
Volissos Khíos Greece 47E5
Volkhov,R USSR 48G2
Vollenhove Netherlands 32D2
Volochanka USSR 51L2
Volochisk Ukrain. USSR 48E7
Vologda USSR 48L2
Volokolamsk USSR 48J3
Vólos Greece 47D5
Volovets Ukrain. USSR 48C7
Volovo USSR 48K5
Volozhin Belorus. USSR 48E4
Volsk USSR 49H4
Volta Calif. USA 80C7
Volta Blanche,R Upper Volta 68E6
Volta,L Ghana 68F7
Volta Rouge,R Upper Volta 68E6
Vonêche Belgium 32C4
Voorburg Netherlands 32C2
Voorschoten Netherlands 32C2
Voorst Netherlands 32E2
Voorthuizen Netherlands 32D2
Vopna Fj. Iceland 34X12
Vopnafjordhür Iceland 34X12
Vorab mt Switzerland 33E2
Vorarlberg state Austria 36C5
Vorauen Switzerland 33D1
Vorden Netherlands 32E2
Vorder Rhein river Switzerland 33D2
Vorkuta USSR 50H3
Vorma,R Norway 35D6
Vormsi,I Eston. USSR 35K7
Voronezh USSR 48L6
Voroshilovgrad Ukrain. USSR 48L7
Võrts Järv,Ozero lake Eston. USSR 35M7
Võru Eston. USSR 35M8
Vosges mts France 42G2
Voss Norway 35B6
Vostochryy Sayan USSR 51L4
Vostock,I Pacific Ocean 95L9
Votkinsk USSR 49L2
Votkinskoye Vdkhr res. USSR 49M2
Voulijoki Finland 34M4
Vouvry Switzerland 33B2
Vouziers France 42F2
Voxna Sweden 35F6
Voyampolka USSR 51S4
Voznesensk USSR 48G8

Vrancv, Western Samoa,Is

Vrancv Czech. **37J4**
Vranje Yugoslavia **46C3**
Vratsa Bulgaria **46D3**
Vrchovina Ceskomoravska *region* Czech. **37F4**
Vredefort South Africa **72D5**
Vries Netherlands **32E1**
Vrin Switzerland **33E2**
Vrindavan India **61A2**
Vroomshoop Netherlands **32E2**
Vršac Yugoslavia **46C2**
Vrútky Czech. **37H4**
Vryburg South Africa **72C5**
Vuarrens Switzerland **33B2**
Vučitrn Yugoslavia **46C3**
Vukovar Yugoslavia **46B2**
Vulcano *island/vol.* Italy **45E6**
Vulpera Switzerland **33F2**
Vŭrbitsa Bulgaria **46F3**
Vyatka = Kirov
Vyatka,R USSR **50F4**
Vyazemskiy USSR **51Q5**
Vyazma USSR **48J4**
Vyazniki USSR **49F2**
Vyborg USSR **48F1**
Vyrnwy,L *Wales* UK **26H3**
Vyshniy Volochek USSR **48J3**
Vyskov Czech. **37G4**
Vytegra USSR **48K1**

W

Wa Ghana **68E6**
Waalwijk Netherlands **32D3**
Waarschoot Belgium **32B3**
Wabasca,R *Alta* Canada **76J5**
Wabash,R *Ind.* USA **79C6**
Waboose Dam *Ont.* Canada **77O6**
Wabuda *island* Papua New Guinea **99J1**
Wabu Hu *lake* China **54J6**
Wabuska *Nev.* USA **80D6**
Waco *Texas* USA **83K7**
Wad Pakistan **58C3**
Waddamana *Tas.* Australia **97F5**
Waddenzee *inlet* Netherlands **32D1**
Waddesdon *England* UK **27N5**
Waddington,Mt *BC* Canada **76F6**
Waddinxveen Netherlands **32C2**
Wadebridge *England* UK **26E7**
Wadena *Minn.* USA **81K2**
Wadesboro *N Car.* USA **85G3**
Wad Hamid Sudan **69M5**
Wadi Araba *valley* Israel **64D8**
Wadi Bishah *valley* Saudi Arabia **62E5**
Wadi-es-Sir Jordan **64D6**
Wadi Gemal,I Egypt **69N4**
Wadi Halfa Sudan **69M4**
Wadi Musa Jordan **64D7**
Wadi Sirhan *valley* Jordan/S Arabia **62D3**
Wad Medani Sudan **69M6**
Wadsworth *Nev.* USA **80D6**
Wafi Saudi Arabia **62E5**
Wafra Kuwait **62F4**
Wageningen Netherlands **32D3**
Wager B *NW Terr.* Canada **77O3**
Wagga Wagga *NSW* Australia **97C3**
Wagin *W Aus.* Australia **98D6**
Wagoner *Okla.* USA **83L4**
Wahoo *Nebr.* USA **83K2**
Wahpeton *N Dak.* USA **81J2**
Wahweah Ra. *Nev.* USA **80E6**
Waiau New Zealand **100E6**
Waigeo *island* *New Guinea* Indon. **53K11**
Waiheke I New Zealand **100F3**
Waihi New Zealand **100E2**
Waikaremoana,L New Zealand **100G4**
Waikari New Zealand **100E6**
Waikato,R New Zealand **100F4**
Waikerie *S Aus.* Australia **97A2**
Waikiki Beach *Hawaii* USA **95V26**
Waikiku *Hawaii* USA **95V26**
Waikouaiti New Zealand **100D7**
Waimakariri,R New Zealand **100E6**
Waimate New Zealand **100D7**
Waimea *Hawaii* USA **95V27**
Waimes Belgium **32E4**
Wainfleet All Saints *England* UK **25J6**
Wainganga,R India **58E4**
Waingapu *Sumba* Indon. **53H12**
Wainiba,I *Vanua Levu* Fiji **94A24**
Wainwright *Alaska* USA **87W11**
Waipara New Zealand **100E6**
Waipawa New Zealand **100G4**
Waipukurau New Zealand **100G4**
Wairarapa,L New Zealand **100F5**
Wairau,R New Zealand **100E5**
Wairio New Zealand **100C7**
Wairoa New Zealand **100G4**
Wairoa,R New Zealand **100G4**
Waitaki,R New Zealand **100D7**
Waitar Pakistan **60C3**
Waitara New Zealand **100F4**
Waitomo New Zealand **100F4**
Waitsburg *Wash.* USA **80D2**
Waiuku New Zealand **100F3**
Wajir Kenya **71J4**
Wakasa wan *bay* Japan **56D7**
Wakatipu,L NZ **100C7**
Wakayama Japan **56D7**
Wakayama *prefecture* Japan **56D8**
Wakefield *England* UK **25F5**
Wake,I Pacific Ocean **94G6**
Wakonichi L *Que.* Canada **78A1**
Wakrah Qatar **63G4**
Walachia *region* Romania **46E2**
Walbrzych Poland **37G3**
Walcha *NSW* Australia **97D2**
Walcheren *region* Netherlands **32B3**
Walcott,L *Idaho* USA **80G4**
Wald Switzerland **33D1**
Waldenburg Switzerland **33C1**
Waldia Ethiopia **71H2**
Waldoboro *Maine* USA **78D4**
Waldo L *Oreg.* USA **80B4**
Waldport *Oreg.* USA **80A3**
Walen See *lake* Switzerland **33E1**
Walenstadt Switzerland **33E1**
Wales *country* Great Britain **22H5**
Walgett *NSW* Australia **97C2**
Walgreen Coast Antarctica **15Q2**
Walhalla *S Car.* USA **85F3**
Walhalla *Vic.* Australia **97C3**
Walker *Minn.* USA **81K2**
Walker,L *Nev.* USA **80D6**
Walkerton *Ont.* Canada **79F3**
Wallace *Idaho* USA **80F2**
Wallaceburg *Ont.* Canada **79E4**
Wallal Downs *W Aus.* Australia **98E3**
Wallaroo *S Aus.* Australia **97A2**
Wallasey *England* UK **25B6**
Wallaston,Mt *N Terr.* Australia **98G3**
Walla Walla *NSW* Australia **97C3**
Walla-Walla *Wash.* USA **80D2**
Wallenpaupack,L *Pa* USA **84D2**
Wallingford *England* UK **27M5**
Wallisellen Switzerland **33D1**
Wallis L *NSW* Australia **97D2**
Wallowa Mts *Oreg.* USA **80E3**
Wallsend *NSW* Australia **97D2**
Wallula *Wash.* USA **80D2**
Walnawa *Hawaii* USA **95V26**
Walney,I *England* UK **25B4**
Walnut Cove *N Car.* USA **85G2**
Walsall *England* UK **25E7**
Walsenburg *Col.* USA **82F4**
Walsh *Queens.* Australia **99J3**
Walsoorden Netherlands **32C3**
Walterboro *S Car.* USA **85G4**
Waltham *England* UK **27Q5**
Waltham *Mass.* USA **84F1**
Waltham *Que.* Canada **79H3**
Walton *NY* USA **84D1**
Walton on the Naze *England* UK **27S5**
Walvis Bay Namibia **72A4**
Walwale Ghana **68E6**
Wamba Zaire **71F4**
Wamel Netherlands **32D3**
Wampsville *NY* USA **84D1**
Wan Taiwan **55L10**
Wana Pakistan **60A4**
Wanaaring *NSW* Australia **97B1**
Wanaka New Zealand **100C7**
Wanaka,L New Zealand **100C7**
Wan'an China **55H9**
Wanbi *S Aus.* Australia **97B2**
Wandiwash India **58E6**
Wandoan *Queens.* Australia **99K5**
Wandre Belgium **32D4**
Wandsbek W Germany **36D2**
Wanganella *NSW* Australia **97B3**
Wanganui New Zealand **100F4**
Wanganui,R New Zealand **100F4**
Wangaratta *Vic.* Australia **97C3**
Wangen Switzerland **33C1**
Wangeroog *island* W Germany **36B2**
Wankie Zimbabwe **72D3**
Wankie Nat. Pk Zimbabwe **72D3**
Wannian China **55J8**
Wanning China **55F13**
Wanquan China **54H2**
Wanrong China **54F5**
Wanshan China **55E9**
Wantage *England* UK **27M5**
Wan Xian China **54E7**
Wanyang Shan *mts* China **55G9**
Wanyuan China **54E6**
Wanzai China **55H8**
Wapello *Iowa* USA **83N2**
Wapiti,R *Alta* Canada **76H6**
Wappapello,L *Mo* USA **83N4**
Warandab Ethiopia **71J3**
Warangal India **58E5**
Waratah *Tas.* Australia **97F5**
Waratah B *Vic.* Australia **97C3**
Warburton *Vic.* Australia **97C3**
Wardair Ethiopia **71K3**
Wardha India **58E4**
Wardha,R India **58E4**
Wardner *Idaho* USA **80E2**
Ware *England* UK **27P5**
Wareham *England* UK **27K7**
Waremme Belgium **32D4**
Warffum Netherlands **32E1**
Warialda *NSW* Australia **97D1**
Warka Poland **37J3**
Warley *England* UK **27L4**
Warmbad Namibia **72B5**
Warmbad South Africa **72D4**
Warminster *England* UK **27K6**
Warm Springs *Nev.* USA **80E6**
Warm Springs *Oreg.* USA **80C3**
Warm Springs *Va* USA **85H1**
Warm Springs Res. *Oreg.* USA **80D4**
Warnemünde E Germany **36E1**
Warner Ra. *Calif.* USA **80C5**
Warner V *Oreg.* USA **80C4**
Warneton Belgium **32A4**
Warora India **58E4**
Warracknabeal *Vic.* Australia **97B3**
Warragul *Vic.* Australia **97C3**
Warrego,R *NSW* Australia **97C1**
Warren *Ark.* USA **83M6**
Warren *Ill.* USA **83P1**
Warren *Minn.* USA **81J1**
Warren *NSW* Australia **97C2**
Warren *Ohio* USA **79F5**
Warren *Pa* USA **84B2**
Warrenpoint N Ireland **30L5**
Warrensburg *Mo* USA **83M3**
Warrenton *Va* USA **84C3**
Warri Nigeria **68G7**
Warrington *England* UK **25C6**
Warrnambool *Vic.* Australia **97B3**
Warroad *Minn.* USA **81K1**
Warrumbungle Ra *mts* *NSW* Australia **97C2**
Warsaw = Warszawa
Warsaw *Ind.* USA **79D5**
Warsaw *N Car.* USA **85H3**
Warsaw *NY* USA **84B1**
Warszawa Poland **37J2**
Warszawa *voivodship* Poland **37J2**
Warta Poland **37H3**
Warta,R Poland **37H2**
Wartburg *Tenn.* USA **85E2**
Warwick *England* UK **27L4**
Warwick Queensland **99L5**
Warwick *RI* USA **84F2**
Warwickshire *county* *England* UK **27L4**
Wasatch Mts *Utah* USA **82C3**
Wasco *Calif.* USA **80D8**
Waseca *Minn.* USA **81L3**
Wasen Switzerland **33C1**
Washakie Needles *mts* *Wyo.* USA **81C4**
Washburn *Wis.* USA **81M2**
Washburn,Mt *Wyo.* USA **81B3**
Washington *Dist. of Columbia* USA **84C3**
Washington *Ind.* USA **79C6**
Washington *Iowa* USA **83N2**
Washington *Mo* USA **83N3**
Washington *N Car.* USA **85J3**
Washington *New J* USA **84D2**
Washington *Ohio* USA **79E6**
Washington *Pa* USA **79F5**
Washington *Va* USA **84B3**
Washington *state* USA **86B2**
Washington Land Greenland **14Q1**
Washington,Mt *New H* USA **79L3**
Washir Afghanistan **63J3**
Washoe City *Nev.* USA **80D6**
Washuk Pakistan **58B3**
Wasmes Belgium **32B4**
Wassen Switzerland **33D2**
Wassenaar Netherlands **32C2**
Wasserauen Switzerland **33E1**
Wassuk Ra. *Nev.* USA **80D6**
Watchet *England* UK **26H6**
Waterbury *Conn.* USA **84E2**
Waterford Ireland, Rep. of **31J9**
Waterford *county* Ireland, Rep. of **31H9**
Waterford Harb. Ireland, Rep. of **31J9**
Waterloo Belgium **32C4**
Waterloo *Ill.* USA **83N3**
Waterloo *Iowa* USA **83M1**
Waterloo *Ont.* Canada **79F4**
Waterloo *Que.* Canada **79K3**
Watertown *NY* USA **79J4**
Watertown *S Dak.* USA **81J3**
Watertown *Wis.* USA **79B4**
Waterville *Maine* USA **78D4**
Waterville *Wash.* USA **80C2**
Watervliet *NY* USA **84E1**
Waterways *Alta* Canada **76J5**
Watez Poland **37G2**
Watford *England* UK **27P5**
Watford City *N Dak.* USA **81F2**
Watkins Bjerge *mtn* Greenland **14N3**
Watkins Glen *NY* USA **84C1**
Watling I The Bahamas **89E2**
Watonga *Okla.* USA **83J5**
Watou Belgium **32A4**
Watrous *Sask.* Canada **76K6**
Watsa Zaire **71F4**
Watseka *Ill.* USA **83Q2**
Watsonville *Calif.* USA **80C7**
Wattenwil Switzerland **33C2**
Watts Bar L *Tenn.* USA **85E3**
Wattsville *Ala.* USA **85D4**
Wattwil Switzerland **33E1**
Wau Papua New Guinea **99K1**
Wau Sudan **69L7**
Wauchope *NSW* Australia **97D2**
Wauchope *N Terr.* Australia **99G4**
Wauchula *Fla* USA **85M8**
Waukaringa *S Aus.* Australia **97A2**
Waukegan *Ill.* USA **83Q1**
Waukesha *Wis.* USA **79C4**
Waupaca *Wis.* USA **79B3**
Waupun *Wis.* USA **79B4**
Waurika *Okla.* USA **83J5**
Wausau *Wis.* USA **79B3**
Wautoma *Wis.* USA **79B3**
Wauwatosa *Wis.* USA **79B4**
Wave Hill *N Terr.* Australia **98G3**
Waveney,R *England* UK **27S4**
Waverly *Iowa* USA **83M1**
Waverly *NY* USA **84C1**
Waverly *Ohio* USA **79E6**
Wavre Belgium **32C4**
Wawal Kabir Libya **69J3**
Waxahachie *Texas* USA **83K6**
Waycross *Ga* USA **85F5**
Wayne *W Va* USA **85F1**
Waynesboro *Ga* USA **85F4**
Waynesboro *Pa* USA **84C3**
Waynesville *N Car.* USA **85F3**
Waynoka *Okla.* USA **83J4**
Wazirabad Pakistan **60D4**
Weardale *valley* *England* UK **25D3**
Wear,R *England* UK **25E3**
Weatherford *Texas* USA **83K6**
Weatherly *Pa* USA **84D2**
Weaver,R *England* UK **25C6**
Weaverville *Calif.* USA **80B5**
Webb City *Mo* USA **83L4**
Webbwood *Ont.* Canada **79F2**
Webster *S Dak.* USA **81J3**
Webster City *Iowa* USA **83M1**
Webster Springs *W Va* USA **85G1**
Wechelderzande Belgium **32C3**
Weddell,I Falkland Is **91D8**
Weddell Sea Antarctica **15A2**
Wedderburn *Vic.* Australia **97B3**
Wedgeport *No. Sc.* Canada **78E5**
Wednesbury *England* UK **27D7**
Weed *Calif.* USA **80B5**
Weedon *Que.* Canada **78C4**
Weedsport *NY* USA **84C1**
Weeping Water *Nebr.* USA **83K2**
Weert Netherlands **32D3**
Weesen Switzerland **33E1**
Weesp Netherlands **32D2**
Wee Waa *NSW* Australia **97C2**
Weggis Switzerland **33D1**
Wehe-Den Hoorn Netherlands **32E1**
Weichang China **54J2**
Weiden W Germany **36E4**
Weidlisbach Switzerland **33C1**
Weifang China **54K4**
Weihai China **54M4**
Wei He *river* China **54D5**
Weilmoringle *NSW* Australia **97C1**
Weimar E Germany **36D3**
Weinan China **54E5**
Weinfelden Switzerland **33E1**
Weining China **55C9**
Weiningen Switzerland **33D1**
Weipa *Queens.* Australia **99J2**
Weiser *Idaho* USA **80E3**
Weishan Hu *lake* China **54J5**
Weishi China **54H5**
Weissenfels E Germany **36D3**
Weissenstein *mt* Switzerland **33C1**
Weisshorn *mt* Switzerland **33C2**
Weissmies *mt* Switzerland **33D2**
Weisstannen Switzerland **33E1**
Weisstannen Tal *valley* Switzerland **33E2**
Wei Xian China **54H4**
Weiyuan China **54C5**
Weizhou Dao *island* China **55E12**
Welch *W Va* USA **85G2**
Weldon *N Car.* USA **85J2**
Welford *Queens.* Queensland **99J5**
Welkom South Africa **72D5**
Welland *Ont.* Canada **79G4**
Welland,R *England* UK **25G7**
Wellesley Is *Queens.* Australia **99H3**
Wellin Belgium **32D4**
Wellingborough *England* UK **27N4**
Wellington *Kans.* USA **83K4**
Wellington *Nev.* USA **80D6**
Wellington New Zealand **100F5**
Wellington *NSW* Australia **97C2**
Wellington *S Aus.* Australia **97A3**
Wellington *Shropshire,England* UK **25C7**
Wellington *Somerset,England* UK **26H7**
Wellington *stat. area* New Zealand **100F4**
Wellington,I Chile **91B7**
Wellington,L *Vic.* Australia **97C3**
Wells *Nev.* USA **80F5**
Wells *Norfolk, Eng.* UK **27R3**
Wells *Somerset, Eng.* UK **26J6**
Wellsboro *Pa* USA **84C2**
Wellsville *Mo* USA **83N3**
Wellsville *NY* USA **84C1**
Wels Austria **36E4**
Welsford *New Br.* Canada **78E4**
Welshpool *Wales* UK **26H3**
Welwyn Garden City *England* UK **27P5**
Wem *England* UK **25C7**
Wema Zaire **70E5**
Wembo Niama Zaire **70E5**
Wemyss Bay *Scotland* UK **29G8**
Wenatchee *Wash.* USA **80C2**
Wench Ghana **68E7**
Wenchang China **55E13**
Wenchuan China **54B7**
Wendel *Calif.* USA **80C5**
Wendeng China **54M4**
Wendover *England* UK **27N5**
Wenduine Belgium **32B3**
Weng'an China **55D9**
Wengen Switzerland **33C2**
Wenling China **55L8**
Wenlock Edge *hills* *England* UK **26J4**
Wenshan China **55C11**
Wenshang China **54J5**
Wensleydale *valley* *England* UK **25D4**
Wensum,R *England* UK **27S3**
Wentworth *NSW* Australia **97B2**
Wenxi China **54F5**
Wen Xian China **54C6**
Wenzhou China **55L8**
Wenzhou Wan *bay* China **55L9**
Weobley *England* UK **26J4**
Wer India **61A2**
Wernhout Netherlands **32C3**
Werribee *Vic.* Australia **97B3**
Werris Creek *NSW* Australia **97D2**
Wervershoof Netherlands **32D2**
Wervik Belgium **32A4**
Wesel W Germany **36B3**
Wesenberg E Germany **36E2**
Weser,R W Germany **36C2**
Wessel Is *N Terr.* Australia **99H2**
Wesson *Miss.* USA **85B5**
West Allis *Wis.* USA **79B4**
West B *La* USA **83Q8**
West Bend *Wis.* USA **79B4**
West Branch *Mich.* USA **79D3**
West Bromwich *England* UK **25E7**
Westbrook *Maine* USA **78C5**
West Burra,I *Shetland* Scotland **28Q8**
Westbury *England* UK **27K6**
Westbury *Tas.* Australia **97F5**
Westby *NSW* Australia **97C3**
West Chester *Pa* USA **84D3**
Westende Belgium **32A3**
Westerly *RI* USA **84F2**
Western Australia *state* Australia **98D4**
Western Isles *region* *Scotland* UK **28B4**
Western Sahara *region* Morocco **68C3**
Western Samoa,Is *islands* Pacific Ocean **94J9**

Westerschelde, **Wushan**

Westerschelde *inlet* Netherlands **32B3**
Westfield *Mass.* USA **84E1**
Westfield *NY* USA **84B1**
Westfield *Pa* USA **84C2**
Westfield Beach *New Br.* Canada **78E4**
West Frankfort *Ill.* USA **83P4**
West Germany *country* Europe **36B3**
West Glamorgan *county Wales* UK **26G5**
West Indies,Is Caribbean Sea **89E2**
Westland *stat. area* New Zealand **100C6**
Westley *Calif.* USA **80C7**
West Linton *Scotland* UK **29K8**
West Looe *England* UK **26F8**
Westmeath *county* Ireland, Rep. of **31H7**
West Midlands *county England* UK **27L4**
Westminster *Md* USA **84C3**
West Nicholson Zimbabwe **72D4**
Weston *Idaho* USA **80G3**
Weston *Oreg.* USA **80D3**
Weston *Sabah* Malay. **53G9**
Weston *W Va* USA **79F6**
Westonaria South Africa **72M12**
Weston-super-Mare *England* UK **26J6**
Westplains *Mo* USA **83N4**
West Point *Ark.* USA **83N5**
West Point *Ga* USA **85E4**
West Point *Miss.* USA **85C4**
West Point *Nebr.* USA **83K2**
West Point *NY* USA **84D2**
West Point *Va* USA **85J2**
Westport *Calif.* USA **80B6**
Westport Ireland, Rep. of **30D6**
Westport New Zealand **100D5**
Westport *Ont.* Canada **79H3**
Westray Firth *Scotland* UK **28L1**
Westray,I *Orkney* Scotland **28K1**
West Sussex *county England* UK **27N7**
West Union *Iowa* USA **83N1**
West Virginia *state* USA **87K4**
West Vlaanderen *prov.* Belgium **32A4**
Westward Ho *England* UK **26F6**
Westwood *Calif.* USA **80C5**
Westwoud Netherlands **32D2**
West Wyalong *NSW* Australia **97C2**
West Yorkshire *county England* UK **25E5**
Wetar *island* Indonesia **53J12**
Wetaskiwin *Alta* Canada **76J6**
Wetherby *England* UK **25F5**
Wetterhorn *mt* Switzerland **33D2**
Wetumpka *Ala.* USA **85D4**
Wetwang *England* UK **25G4**
Wetzikon Switzerland **33D1**
Wewoka *Okla.* USA **83K5**
Wexford Ireland, Rep. of **31L9**
Wexford *county* Ireland,Rep. of **31K9**
Wexford B Ireland, Rep. of **31L9**
Weybridge *England* UK **27P6**
Weyburn *Sask.* Canada **76L7**
Weymont *Que.* Canada **79K2**
Weymouth *England* UK **26K7**
Weymouth *No. Sc.* Canada **78F4**
Wey,R *England* UK **27N6**
Whakataki New Zealand **100G5**
Whakatane New Zealand **100G3**
Whakatane,R New Zealand **100G4**
Whale,R = Baleine,R
Whales,B of Antarctica **15M2**
Whalley *England* UK **25D5**
Whalsay,I *Shetland* Scotland **28R8**
Whalton *England* UK **25E2**
Whangarei New Zealand **100F2**
Wharfedale *England* UK **25E5**
Wharfe,R *England* UK **25F5**
Wharton *Texas* USA **83K8**
Wheatland *Calif.* USA **80C6**
Wheatland *Wyo.* USA **81E4**
Wheatland Res. *Wyo.* USA **81E5**
Wheaton *Minn.* USA **81J3**
Wheeler Dam *Ala.* USA **85D3**
Wheeler L *Ala.* USA **85D3**
Wheeler Pk *mt Nev.* USA **80F6**
Wheeling *W Va* USA **79F5**
Whernside *mt England* UK **25D4**
Whetstone Buttes *N Dak.* USA **81F2**
Whiskeytown-Shasta-Trinity Nat.Rec. Area *Calif.* USA **80B5**
Whitbourne *Newf.* Canada **78M3**
Whitby *England* UK **25G4**
Whitby *Ont.* Canada **79G3**
Whitchurch *Hampshire,England* UK **27M6**
Whitchurch *Shropshire,England* UK **25C7**
White B *Newf.* Canada **78K1**
White Cliffs *NSW* Australia **97B2**
White Earth *N Dak.* USA **81F1**
Whitefish *Mont.* USA **86D2**
Whitefish B *Mich.* USA **79D2**
Whitehall *Mich.* USA **79C4**
Whitehall *NY* USA **84E1**
Whitehaven *England* UK **25A3**
Whitehead *N Ireland* UK **30M4**
Whitehorse *Yukon* Canada **76D4**
White Horse Hills *England* UK **27L5**
White L *La* USA **83M8**
White Mark *Tas.* Australia **97F5**
White Mts *New H* USA **79L3**
White Nile,R Sudan **69M6**
White Pass *BC* Canada **76E5**
White Pine Mts *Nev.* USA **80F6**
White Plains *NY* USA **84E2**
White,R *Ark.* USA **83M4**
White,R *Ind.* USA **85D1**
White,R *S Dak.* USA **81F4**
White R *Utah* USA **82D2**
White R *Yukon* Canada **76C4**
White River *Ont.* Canada **77O7**
White River *S Dak.* USA **81G4**
White River Junction *Vt* USA **87M3**
White Sulphur Springs *Mont.* USA **81B2**
White Volta,R Ghana **68E7**
Whitfield *Vic.* Australia **97C3**
Whithorn *Scotland* UK **29H10**
Whiting *New J* USA **84D3**
Whitley Bay *England* UK **25F2**
Whitney *Ont.* Canada **79G3**
Whitney,Mt *Calif.* USA **80D7**
Whitstable *England* UK **27S6**
Whitsunday I *Queens.* Australia **99K4**
Whittier *Calif.* USA **80D9**
Whittlesea *Vic.* Australia **97C3**
Whitton *NSW* Australia **97C2**
Wholdaia L *NW Terr.* Canada **76L4**
Whyalla *S Aus.* Australia **97A2**
Wiarton *Ont.* Canada **79F3**
Wichita *Kans.* USA **83K4**
Wichita Falls *Texas* USA **83J6**
Wichita Mts *Okla.* USA **83J5**
Wichita,R *Texas* USA **83J6**
Wick *Scotland* UK **28K3**
Wickenburg *Ariz.* USA **80G9**
Wickes *Mont.* USA **80G2**
Wickham *England* UK **27M7**
Wicklow Ireland, Rep. of **31L8**
Wicklow *county* Ireland,Rep. of **31K8**
Wicklow Hd Ireland, Rep. of **31M8**
Wicklow Mts Ireland, Rep. of **31L8**
Widnes *England* UK **25C6**
Wielbark Poland **37J2**
Wielen Poland **37G2**
Wieliczka Poland **37G4**
Wielun Poland **37H3**
Wien Austria **37G4**
Wiener Neustadt Austria **37G5**
Wieringermeer *region* Netherlands **32C2**
Wiesbaden W Germany **36C3**
Wiesen Switzerland **33E2**
Wigan *England* UK **25C5**
Wight,I of *England* UK **27M7**
Wigston *England* UK **25F7**
Wigton *England* UK **25B3**
Wigtown *Scotland* UK **29H10**
Wigtown B *Scotland* UK **29H10**
Wijhe Netherlands **32E2**
Wijk-bij-Duurstede Netherlands **32D3**
Wil Switzerland **33E1**
Wilbur *Wash.* USA **80D2**
Wilcannia *NSW* Australia **97B2**
Wildervank Netherlands **32E1**
Wildhorn *mt* Switzerland **33C2**
Wildstrubel *mt* Switzerland **33C2**
Wildwood *Fla* USA **85L7**
Wildwood *New J* USA **84D3**
Wilhelm II Land Antarctica **15G3**
Wilhelmsburg W Germany **36D2**
Wilhelmshaven W Germany **36C2**
Wilkes-Barre *Pa* USA **84D2**
Wilkesboro *N Car.* USA **85G2**
Wilkes I Wake Is **94A16**
Wilkes Land Antarctica **15H3**
Wilkins Str. Antarctica **15S3**
Wilkolaz Poland **37K3**
Willamette,R *Oreg.* USA **80B3**
Willandra Billabong,R *NSW* Australia **97B2**
Willapa B *Wash.* USA **80A2**
Willcox *Ariz.* USA **82D6**
Willemsdorp Netherlands **32C3**
Willemstad Curaçao,I **92D1**
Willemstad Netherlands **32C3**
William,Mt *Vic.* Australia **97B3**
Williams *Ariz.* USA **82B5**
Williamsburg *Ky* USA **85E2**
Williamsburg *Va* USA **85J2**
Williams Point *NW Terr.* Canada **76H3**
Williamsport *Ind.* USA **83Q2**
Williamsport *Newf.* Canada **78K1**
Williamsport *Pa* USA **84C2**
Williamston *N Car.* USA **85J3**
Williamsville *Mo* USA **83N4**
Willimantie *Conn.* USA **84E2**
Willisau Switzerland **33C1**
Williston *N Dak.* USA **81F1**
Williston South Africa **72C6**
Williton *England* UK **26H6**
Willits *Calif.* USA **80B6**
Willmar *Minn.* USA **81K3**
Willochra *S Aus.* Australia **97A2**
Willochra,R *S Aus.* Australia **97A2**
Willoughby,C *S Aus.* Australia **97A3**
Willow Creek *Mont.* USA **81B3**
Willow L *NW Terr.* Canada **76G4**
Willow Lake,R *NW Terr.* Canada **76G4**
Willowmore South Africa **72C6**
Willows *Calif.* USA **80B6**
Willow Springs *Mo* USA **83M4**
Wills Mt *Pa* USA **84B3**
Willunga *S Aus.* Australia **97A3**
Wilmette *Ill.* USA **83P1**
Wilmington *Del.* USA **84D3**
Wilmington *N Car.* USA **85J3**
Wilmington *S Aus.* Australia **97A2**
Wilmslow *England* UK **25D6**
Wilnis Netherlands **32C2**
Wilno *Ont.* Canada **79H3**
Wilson *N Car.* USA **85J3**
Wilson's Prom. *Vic.* Australia **97C3**
Wilton *England* UK **27L6**
Wiltshire *county England* UK **27L6**
Wiluna *W Aus.* Australia **98E5**
Wimmera,R *Vic.* Australia **97B3**
Wimmis Switzerland **33C2**
Winburg South Africa **72D5**
Wincanton *England* UK **26K6**
Winchcombe *England* UK **27L5**
Winchelsea *England* UK **27R7**
Winchendon *Mass.* USA **84E1**
Winchester *England* UK **27M6**
Winchester *Ky* USA **85E1**
Winchester *Ont.* Canada **79J3**
Winchester *Tenn.* USA **85D3**
Winchester *Va* USA **84B3**
Winchester B *Oreg.* USA **80A4**
Wind Cave Nat. Pk *S Dak.* USA **81F4**
Windermere *England* UK **25C4**
Windermere *lake England* UK **25C4**
Windhoek Namibia **72B4**
Windom *Minn.* USA **81K4**
Windorah *Queens.* Australia **99J5**
Wind,R *Yukon* Canada **76D3**
Wind River Pk *Wyo.* USA **81C4**
Wind River Ra. *mts Wyo.* USA **81C4**
Windsor *Col.* USA **82F2**
Windsor *Conn.* USA **84E2**
Windsor *England* UK **27N6**
Windsor *Mo* USA **83M3**
Windsor *N Car.* USA **85J2**
Windsor *No. Sc.* Canada **78F4**
Windsor *NSW* Australia **97D2**
Windsor *Ont.* Canada **79E4**
Windsor *Que.* Canada **79K3**
Windsor *Vt* USA **84E1**
Windward Is West Indies **89G4**
Windward Pass. West Indies **89E2**
Winfield *Kans.* USA **83K4**
Winfield *W Va* USA **85G1**
Wingen *NSW* Australia **97D2**
Wingene Belgium **32B3**
Wingham *NSW* Australia **97D2**
Wingham *Ont.* Canada **79F4**
Winisk,R *Ont.* Canada **77O6**
Winkel Netherlands **32C2**
Winkeln Switzerland **33E1**
Winlock *Wash.* USA **80B2**
Winneba Ghana **68E7**
Winnebago *Minn.* USA **81K4**
Winnebago,L *Wis.* USA **79B3**
Winnemucca *Nev.* USA **80E5**
Winnemucca L *Nev.* USA **80D5**
Winnett *Mont.* USA **81C2**
Winnfield *La* USA **83M7**
Winnipeg *Man.* Canada **76M7**
Winnipeg,L *Man.* Canada **76M6**
Winnipegosis *Man.* Canada **76L6**
Winnipegosis,L *Man.* Canada **76L6**
Winnipesaukee,L *New H* USA **79L4**
Winnsboro *S Car.* USA **85G3**
Winona *Minn.* USA **81M3**
Winona *Miss.* USA **85C4**
Winscale *England* UK **25A3**
Winschoten Netherlands **32E1**
Winsford *England* UK **25C6**
Winslow *Ariz.* USA **82C5**
Winsted *Conn.* USA **84E2**
Winston Salem *N Car.* USA **85G2**
Winsum Netherlands **32E1**
Winterhaven *Calif.* USA **80F9**
Winter Haven *Fla* USA **85M7**
Winterport *Maine* USA **78D4**
Winterset *Iowa* USA **83L2**
Winterswijk Netherlands **32E2**
Winterthur Switzerland **33D1**
Winterton *England* UK **25G5**
Winton New Zealand **100C8**
Winton *Queens.* Australia **99J4**
Wirdum Netherlands **32D1**
Wirksworth *England* UK **25E6**
Wirrabara *S Aus.* Australia **97A2**
Wirral Pen. *England* UK **25B6**
Wirrega *S Aus.* Australia **97B3**
Wirt *Minn.* USA **81L2**
Wisbech *England* UK **27Q3**
Wisconsin *state* USA **87H3**
Wisconsin,R *Wis.* USA **79B3**
Wisconsin Rapids *Wis.* USA **79B3**
Wise *Va* USA **85F2**
Wishaw *Scotland* UK **29J8**
Wishek *N Dak.* USA **81H2**
Wisła,R Poland **37J3**
Wismar E Germany **36D2**
Witham *England* UK **27R5**
Witham,R *England* UK **25H6**
Withern *England* UK **25J6**
Witry Belgium **32D5**
Witten W Germany **36B3**
Wittenberg E Germany **36E3**
Wittenberge E Germany **36D2**
Wittenoon *W Aus.* Australia **98D4**
Wittingen W Germany **36D2**
Wittstock E Germany **36E2**
Witwatersrand *region* South Africa **72M12**
Wiveliscombe *England* UK **26H6**
Wivenhoe *England* UK **27R5**
Włocławek Poland **37H2**
Włodawa Poland **37K3**
Wodonga *Vic.* Australia **97C3**
Woerden Netherlands **32C2**
Wognum Netherlands **32D2**
Wohlen Switzerland **33D1**
Wohlen See *lake* Switzerland **33C2**
Wokam *island* Indonesia **53K12**
Woking *England* UK **27N6**
Wokingham *England* UK **27N6**
Wolbrom Poland **37H3**
Woleai,I Caroline Is **94E7**
Wolf Creek *Oreg.* USA **80B4**
Wolfeboro *New H* USA **84F1**
Wolfe City *Texas* USA **83K6**
Wolfe I *Ont.* Canada **79H3**
Wolfenbüttel W Germany **36D2**
Wolf Point *Mont.* USA **81E1**
Wolfsberg Austria **36F5**
Wolfsburg W Germany **36D2**
Wolfville *No. Sc.* Canada **78F4**
Wolgast E Germany **36E1**
Wolhusen Switzerland **33D1**
Wollaston *England* UK **27N4**
Wollaston Foreland Greenland **14M2**
Wollaston,Is Chile **91C9**
Wollaston L *Sask.* Canada **76L5**
Wollemi Nat. Pk *NSW* Australia **97D2**
Wollongong *NSW* Australia **97D2**
Wolseley *S Aus.* Australia **97B3**
Wolsingham *England* UK **25E3**
Wolstenholme,C *Que.* Canada **77Q4**
Wolvega Netherlands **32D2**
Wolverhampton *England* UK **25D7**
Wolvertem Belgium **32C4**
Wolverton *England* UK **27N4**
Woman River *Ont.* Canada **79E2**
Wombell *England* UK **25F5**
Wongalaroo L *NSW* Australia **97B2**
Wŏnsan N Korea **52J3**
Wonthaggi *Vic.* Australia **97C3**
Woodbridge *England* UK **27S4**
Wood Buffalo Nat. Pk *Alta* Canada **76J5**
Woodburn *NSW* Australia **97D1**
Woodburn *Oreg.* USA **80B3**
Woodbury *New J* USA **84D3**
Woodford Ireland,Rep. of **31G7**
Woodland *Calif.* USA **80C6**
Woodlark I Papua New Guinea **99L1**
Wood,R *Sask.* Canada **76K7**
Woodroffe,Mt *S Aus.* Australia **98G5**
Woods Hole *Mass.* USA **84F2**
Woodside *Utah* USA **82C3**
Woodside *Vic.* Australia **97C3**
Woods,L *N Terr.* Australia **98G3**
Woods,L of the *Ont.* Canada **76M7**
Woodstock *England* UK **27M5**
Woodstock *Ill.* USA **83P1**
Woodstock *New Br.* Canada **78E3**
Woodstock *Ont.* Canada **79F4**
Woodstock *Va* USA **84B3**
Woodstock *Vt* USA **84E1**
Woodsville *New H* USA **79K3**
Woodville New Zealand **100F5**
Woodward *Okla.* USA **83J4**
Woodworth *Mont.* USA **80G2**
Woody Hd *NSW* Australia **97D1**
Woody I *Paracel Is* China **57E3**
Wooler *England* UK **25D1**
Woolgoolga *NSW* Australia **97D2**
Wooltana *S Aus.* Australia **97A2**
Woolwich *England* UK **27Q6**
Woomera *S Aus.* Australia **99H6**
Woonsocket *RI* USA **84F1**
Woonsocket *S Dak.* USA **81H3**
Wooton Bassett *England* UK **27L5**
Worb Switzerland **33C2**
Worcester *England* UK **27K4**
Worcester *Mass.* USA **84F1**
Worcester South Africa **72B6**
Workington *England* UK **25A3**
Worksop *England* UK **25F6**
Workum Netherlands **32D2**
Worland *Wyo.* USA **81C3**
Worms W Germany **36C4**
Worms Hd *Wales* UK **26F5**
Worthing *England* UK **27P7**
Worthington *Minn.* USA **81K4**
Worthington *Ont.* Canada **79F2**
Wotho,I Marshall Is **94G6**
Woudenberg Netherlands **32D2**
Woudrichem Netherlands **32C3**
Wour Chad **69J4**
Wouw Netherlands **32C3**
Wowoni *island* Indonesia **53H11**
Wragby *England* UK **25H6**
Wrangel I = Ostrov Vrangelya
Wrangell *Alaska* USA **87Z13**
Wrangell,Mt *Alaska* USA **87Y12**
Wrath,C *Scotland* UK **28F2**
Wray *Col.* USA **82G2**
Wrexham *Wales* UK **26J2**
Wright,Mt *NSW* Australia **97B2**
Wrightsville *Ga* USA **85F4**
Wrightsville Beach *N Car.* USA **85J3**
Wrigley *NW Terr.* Canada **76G4**
Wrigley Gulf Antarctica **15P2**
Wrocław Poland **37G3**
Wrocław *voivodship* Poland **37G3**
Wroxham *England* UK **27S3**
Września Poland **37G2**
Wuchang *Heilongjiang* China **52J2**
Wuchang *Hubei* China **55H7**
Wucheng China **54J4**
Wuchuan *Guizhou* China **55E8**
Wuchuan *Inner Mongolia* China **54F2**
Wuday'ah Saudi Arabia **62F6**
Wudi China **54J4**
Wuding He *river* China **54F4**
Wudu China **54C6**
Wufeng China **55F7**
Wugang China **55F9**
Wugong Shan *mts* China **55G9**
Wuhai China **54D3**
Wuhan *province* China **54G7**
Wuhe China **54J6**
Wuhu China **54K7**
Wuhua China **55H11**
Wujiang China **54L7**
Wu Jiang *river* China **55E8**
Wukari Nigeria **69G7**
Wular,L *Kashmir* India **60D3**
Wuleidao Wan *bay* China **54M4**
Wuning China **55H8**
Wuntho Burma **59J4**
Wuping China **55J10**
Wuppertal W Germany **36B3**
Wuqiang China **54H4**
Württemberg *state* W Germany **36C4**
Wurung *Queens.* Australia **99J3**
Würzburg W Germany **36C4**
Wurzen E Germany **36E3**
Wushan China **54E7**